ArtScroll Judaica Classics®

Rabbi Nosson Scherman / Rabbi Meir Zlotowitz

General Editors

The Weekly midrash

Volume I:
בראשית / שמות
Bereishis / Sh'mos

Translated from the Yiddish by
Miriam Stark Zakon

Introduction by
Meir Holder

with illustrations from the 1726 Frankfurt am Main edition

צאינה וראינה

mIDRash

TZ'ENAH UR'ENAH – THE CLASSIC ANTHOLOGY
OF TORAH LORE AND MIDRASHIC COMMENTARY

Published by

Mesorah Publications, ltd

3 VOLUME-EDITION
Four Impression: June 1983 ... December 1988

2 VOLUME EDITION
FIRST EDITION
Five Impressions: January 1994-December 1999
Sixth Impression ... March 2001
Seventh Impression... September 2003
Eighth Impression ... July 2007

Published and Distributed by
MESORAH PUBLICATIONS, Ltd.
4401 Second Avenue
Brooklyn, New York 11232

Distributed in Europe by
LEHMANNS
Unit E, Viking Business Park
Rolling Mill Road
Jarow, Tyne & Wear, NE32 3DP
England

Distributed in Australia and New Zealand
by **GOLDS WORLDS OF JUDAICA**
William Street 3-13
Balaclava, Melbourne 3183
Victoria, Australia

Distributed in Israel by
SIFRIATI / A. GITLER — BOOKS
Hayarkon Street 6
Bnei Brak 51127

Distributed in South Africa by
KOLLEL BOOKSHOP
Ivy Common
William Road 105
Norwood 2192, Johannesburg, South Africa

ARTSCROLL JUDAICA SERIES ·
"THE WEEKLY MIDRASH/TZ'ENAH UR'ENAH"
Vol. 1 BEREISHIS-SH'MOS/GENESIS-EXODUS
© Copyright 1983,1984,1986,1988,1994, 2007 by MESORAH PUBLICATIONS, Ltd.
4401 Second Avenue / Brooklyn, N.Y. 11232 / (718) 921-9000 / www.artscroll.com

2 Volume set:
ISBN: 0-89906-925-8

Typography by CompuScribe at ArtScroll Studios, Ltd.
4401 Second Avenue / Brooklyn, N.Y. 11232 / (718) 921-9000

Printed in the United States of America by Noble Book Press
Bound by Sefercraft, Quality Bookbinders, Ltd., Brooklyn N.Y. 11232

Table of Contents

◄§ Table of Contents

The Book of Sh'mos / שמות

◆§ Publisher's Foreword

No list of the most important Judaic literature in the three centuries before World War II could be complete without *Tz'enah Ur'enah*. This masterful anthology of Torah interpretation and Midrashic insight was compiled by Rabbi Yaakov ben Yitzchak Ashkenazi, who was both a profound scholar and a skillful *maggid* [itinerant preacher]. His craft was bringing people closer to God, and he knew it well. Like a virtuoso, he presented classic Torah knowledge in a way that would pluck heartstrings, stir consciences, stoke the fires of the Jewish soul.

His *Tz'enah Ur'enah* became an essential ingredient of the Jewish home. Every *shtetl* and neighborhood had its *zoger'keh* ["sayer"], the woman who held audiences enthralled as she read and declaimed from her worn, treasured *Tz'enah Ur'enah*. Men, too — even scholars — used it as a review of the weekly Torah reading in its breadth and depth. Many a world-famous rabbi and *rosh yeshivah* recalls fondly how his first inspiration in Torah study grew out of those hours on his mother's lap as she read to him from her *Tz'enah Ur'enah*.

It is a great privilege, therefore, for Mesorah Publications to present the Jewish public with this three-volume English translation of the great and influential Yiddish classic. Without a doubt, R' Yaakov Ashkenazi's masterpiece will gain countless enthusiasts in the English-speaking world of today as it did in its Yiddish-speaking predecessor of yesteryear. For this is far more than a slice of Old World nostalgia — though it is certainly that — it is a taste of authentic Torah interpretation that has survived the test of centuries, cultures, turmoils, and Holocaust.

We are honored to embark on this venture with the participation of REB MEIR HOLDER of Hillel Press, Jerusalem. Reb Meir has demonstrated many times before that his knowledge of *sefarim* and sensitivity to their contents will brook neither compromise nor shortcut. This project was produced under his supervision — a telling testimony to its quality.

We express our gratitude and admiration to the translator, MRS. MIRIAM STARK ZAKON, whose craftsmanship speaks for itself, and to REB URI KAPLOUN, whose editorial skill has earned him a place of honor in the field of English-language Judaica.

The beautiful woodcuts that illustrate this volume come from the 5486/1726 Frankfurt am Main edition that is a part of the JTS Library Collection. We are grateful to RABBI REUVEN PORCELAIN for his bibliographic assistance.

Mesorah Publications is grateful to a dear and loyal friend, MR. AARON L. HEIMOWITZ, whose guidance and encouragement are constant and invaluable. In his voluntary role of assisting any number of Torah institutions, he has always inspired us to bring classics of this sort to the attention of the public.

The staff of Mesorah Publications has given unstintingly of itself, inspired by the historic nature of the work and the incalculable benefits it offers generations for whom the original Yiddish is sealed shut. Especially we must single out REB SHEA BRANDER, the Torah community's graphic artist *par excellence*, and RABBI AVIE GOLD, whose careful reading helped assure the translation's accuracy. Our appreciation also goes to MR. STEPHEN BLITZ, who ably brings the ArtScroll Series to the attention of the widest possible public, and to MR. JOSEPH TIMINSKY, MRS. FAYGIE WEINBAUM, MRS. ESTHER FEIERSTEIN, CHANEE and LEA FREIER, and EDEL STREICHER, who carry their responsibilities with dedication to the cause of Torah dissemination.

We pray that *Hashem Yisborach* will enable us to continue bringing His Word to His people.

Nosson Scherman / Meir Zlotowitz
General Editors

◆§ Translator's Preface

The *Tz'enah Ur'enah*. Years ago, it evoked images in my mind of a wizened *bubba*, sitting and reading, the flickering *Shabbos* candles the only source of illumination in her impoverished home in the *shtetl*. A work of historical interest, perhaps, part of an era dead and gone.

The very language it had been written in, Yiddish, was fast following the *shtetl*, consigned to the dusty back shelves of historical interest. The language, the book, the *shtetl* — all part of a fading past.

Or so I thought.

Almost immediately upon opening the *sefer*, I realized that this was no antiquated work. This was Torah, living Torah, with the dynamic vitality that Torah never loses. The words of *Chumash*, of *Midrash*, of the commentaries, came alive under the skillful hand of their compiler.

And the "dead" language? As I read through the work, I felt, with growing excitement, the joyful sense of life which permeates it. It is a lively work, with the words practically stepping off the pages, begging you to see, to learn, to become a part of them. It is Yiddish, that wonderful, evocative, dynamic — and very much living — language.

It is my sincere hope that this translation awaken in the reader the desire to understand and read the *Tz'enah Ur'enah* in its original, inimitable form. It is, as I myself learned, an exciting, worthwhile trip to our Jewish past — and future.

It is impossible to list the many friends, neighbors and family members, both in *Eretz Yisrael* and in the United States, who have given me their assistance and support in the course of my efforts. To all of you, my thanks and love.

I am particularly grateful to Mr. Meir Holder, of Hillel Press, and his wife Mrs. Esther Holder, for their encouragement, their advice, and their devotion to this project. Special thanks also go to Rabbi Nosson Scherman and Rabbi Meir Zlotowitz of Mesorah Publications, and Mr. Uri Kaploun, who did so much to bring the manuscript to its final form.

This book, by tradition a "woman's" work, is dedicated to three men: to the memory of my father, Nathan Stark, ע״ה, who devoted so much of his life to the Torah education of his family; and יל״ח, to my husband, Rabbi Nachman Zakon, whose contribution to this work is so great that it seems almost an impertinence to dedicate it to him, for it is his work as well as mine; and to our child, Yisroel Moshe — may we be זוכה to raise him in our tradition of Torah learning.

Miriam Stark Zakon
Kiryat Nachliel, Migdal HaEmek, Israel
4 Cheshvan 5743

לז״נ אבי מורי ר׳ נחום ב״ר אברהם אשר ע״ה

◆§ Introduction

"Moshe Rabbeinu instituted that the House of Israel read the Torah publicly on the mornings of Sabbath, Monday and Thursday, so that three days should not pass without their hearing the Torah. Ezra [the Scribe] ordained that the Torah be read likewise on Sabbath at [the afternoon service of] *Minchah*, for the benefit of storekeepers [who may have missed the weekday readings]" *(Rambam, Sefer Ahavah, Hil. Tefillah 12:1).*

"Since the days of Ezra it has been customary for an interpreter to be there who translates to the people what is being read to them by the reader from the Torah so that they understand the meaning of the words" *(ibid., 12:10).*

The Talmud (Tractate *Megillah* 3a, *Nedarim* 37b, and elsewhere) traces this latter custom to the verses in *Nechemiah* (8:7-8): *And* [certain named elders] *and the Levites caused the people to understand the Torah. So they read in the book — in the Torah of God — distinctly, and gave the sense, and caused them to understand the reading.* The Talmud explains: *They read in the book* (וַיִּקְרְאוּ בַסֵּפֶר) refers to the reader; *distinctly* (מְפֹרָשׁ) refers to the function of the translator.

When *Hashem* in His infinite grace gave the Torah to His people it was not entrusted to an especially privileged elite, but it was opened wide for all the varied ranks of the people to see. Whilst Israel was still in Egypt we find Pharaoh addressing Moshe Rabbeinu: *Go and serve the Lord your God — but who are they that shall go? (Shmos* 10:8). It was natural for Pharaoh to assume that some chosen few were intended — for was not "religion" in the concept of his time a jealously guarded mystery, to be gingerly unshrouded to the awed gaze of an exclusive coterie of the initiated? One can well imagine his utter amazement with the reply of Moshe Rabbeinu: *With our young and with our old we shall go, with our sons and with our daughters (ibid.,* 10:9). Some 40 years later, when Moshe Rabbeinu was about to relinquish the leadership of his people, he again emphasized this cardinal truth by addressing them in these words: *You are standing this day all of you before the Lord your God — the heads of your tribes, your elders, and your officers, all the men of Israel; your little ones, your womenfolk, and the stranger who is in the midst of your camp, from the hewer of your wood to the drawer of your water (Devarim 29:9-10).*

Each of these component ranks of *Klal Yisrael*, then, whether elders of tribes or hewers of wood, all have a rightful share in the Torah. And it is the privilege and duty of each one of us both to absorb its teachings to our maximum capacity, and to hand them on to our fellow Jews. Throughout our long history, therefore, those whom *Hashem* has blessed with superior intellect and understanding have looked upon this blessing not "as a crown with which to aggrandize themselves nor as a spade with which to dig," as R' Tzadok says in *Pirkei Avos* (4:5), but rather as the sign of a cherished responsibility — to absorb and disseminate knowledge of the Torah to their utmost. For they realized that a division between the people of Israel and the Torah could have but one end result, God forbid — the assimilation of the people and its ultimate absorption by its various host nations.

At no time therefore were the simple people — those who through prolonged privation or brutal repression were unable to become Torah scholars — ignored. On the contrary: every effort was made to bring them near to the study of the Torah to the best of their abilities and possibilities, limited though they might be, and to the fulfillment of its *mitzvos*, and to inspire in them a true and pure faith, and a love for *HaShem*.

This unceasing activity for *hafatzas haTorah*, the spreading of Torah, has taken many forms in response to changing needs and opportunities. A pioneering campaign is the above-quoted series of regulations instituted by Ezra, which continued throughout the period of the Second *Beis HaMikdash*, when sooner or later almost every Jew came up to Yerushalayim, there to have his spiritual batteries, as it were, recharged. It continued during the days of the great *yeshivos* in Babylonia when twice a year, 30 days before Pesach and 30 days before Rosh HaShanah, special study sessions were held for the ordinary people (see Tractate *Bava Kama* 113a and *Rashi* s.v. בריגלא). A contracted continuation of this may be seen in our own times, in the *derashah* traditionally delivered on *Shabbos HaGadol*, the Sabbath preceding Pesach, and *Shabbos Shuvah*, the Sabbath following Rosh HaShanah. And in the course of the centuries every community had its rabbis and scholars who would teach the living words of the Torah both to the learned and the unlearned according to their needs.

Vital to this ongoing endeavor was the publication of numerous *sefarim*, and here too the beacons were beamed to as wide an audience as possible. It was thus natural that the Five Books of the *Chumash* should have been explained and translated in order to make them accessible to everyone. As early as in the time of Ezra the Scribe, at the beginning of the Second Commonwealth, a *targum* or translation was needed and available. Though the returning exiles were home at last, after a mere seventy years by the waters of Babylon they felt more at home in Aramaic than in the Holy Tongue of their fathers. A little later in the time of the Second *Beis HaMikdash*, in the first half of the third century B.C.E., a Greek translation — the Septuagint — was prepared on the orders of one of the Ptolemies. Since however Greek never became a language used by large numbers of Jews, it has remained a scholar's rather than a popular translation. Later still, after the destruction of the Second *Beis HaMikdash*, Onkelos — under the supervision of R' Eliezer and R' Yehoshua — wrote his classic translation (see Tractate *Megillah* 3a), known to this day simply as *"the Targum."* Generations later, as Aramaic gradually lost its place as the major spoken language, other translations appeared. In the tenth century R' Saadiah Gaon published the first (and classic) Arabic translation of the Torah. We know also of Persian, Spanish and other versions.

In the early Middle Ages Jews settled in considerable numbers in Germanic speaking areas, and the language that evolved and became the common heritage of Ashkenazi Jewry was Yiddish. Hence a number of translations of the Torah appeared in this language. However no Yiddish rendition of the Torah ever approached even remotely the popularity of that published by an itinerant preacher from Yanov, near Lublin — R' Yaakov ben Yitzchak Ashkenazi (1550-1624/8) — and known as *Tz'enah Ur'enah* (צְאֶינָה וּרְאֶינָה). The title means "Come out and see," and is borrowed from *Shir HaShirim* 3:11, which the Sages (in Tractate *Taanis* 4:1) apply to the Giving of the Torah at Sinai. The ungrammatical but universal pronunciation of the title among Yiddish speakers is *Tzenerene*, and its alternative familiar name became *Teitsch Chumash* ("Chumash Translation"). The unprecedented acclaim which the book aroused bears witness to the keen sensitivity to feedback which this born teacher must have cultivated in the course of his decades of inspirational instruction in the hamlets of his native East Poland — for before us stands a folk narrator of rare skill who intimately knew the needs of his flock.

Tackling his subject in a novel manner, he orchestrated a charmingly informal medley of Biblical paraphrase, Midrashic exegesis, illustrative narrative — and unabashedly moral instruction. In presenting selected passages from the *Chumash*, the *Haftoros* and the *Megillos*, he drew freely on the expositions of *Rashi*, *Ramban*, R' Bechaye and other classical commentators, often citing them (and likewise more ancient texts) in the form in which they were paraphrased by writers of later generations. What a blessing, then, for the thirsting masses who had neither the leisure nor the sophistication to seek out the original sources for themselves. This fact alone would suffice to explain the prodigious popularity of his work, for never before or since has a *sefer* appeared that secured for itself such an honored and beloved place in the heart of the Jewish masses. *Tz'enah Ur'enah* soon became a wellspring of salvation that in the course of three-and-a-half centuries has brought sanctity and spiritual sustenance into perhaps millions of Jewish homes.

Despite the feminine form of the two verbs that constitute its title, the book was not intended originally for women alone. Indeed the [Hebrew] title page of the oldest extant edition informs prospective readers explicitly that their author "gathered hither and thither among the sheaves [of the various commentators] in order to enable men and women to find a balm for their souls, and to understand the words of the Living God in simple language."

Nevertheless it quickly came to be the book *par excellence* for women, especially since the author frequently exalts the Jewish woman — in her traditional roles of supportive wife and educative mother. Snatching a tranquil half-hour from her daily chores, our pious great-grandmother in the Old Country would find her favorite cozy corner between the cradle and the fireplace, open up her well-thumbed *"Tzenerene"* with its familiar woodcuts and, straightening her lace kerchief, would settle down to follow the fortunes of the Children of Israel in ancient time by reading from its careworn pages on the weekly portion of the Torah. Mouthing its words in silent awe, she shared the anguish of Sarah over Yitzchak's near-sacrifice; humbly aspired to the selflessness of Mother Rachel; shed an innocent tear for young Yosef in the scorpions' pit; shuddered over the grim details of the Egyptian bondage; exulted with Miriam at the Crossing of the Sea; — and found solace for the daily trials of *Galus* in contemplating the spiritual rewards with which the matriarchs of the past together with the faithful Jewish mothers of all generations are blessed in the World to Come.

The most prominent Torah scholars of the age granted this book their recognition, and when its author published a subsequent work such giants as *Maharsha* (מהרש״א; R' Shmuel Edels, 1555-1631) and *Bach* (ב״ח; R' Yoel Sirkes, 1561-1640) gave it their approbation. Indeed, in commenting on the obligation that one must review the weekly Torah reading, שְׁנַיִם מִקְרָא וְאֶחָד תַּרְגוּם, *Twice from the Scripture and once in translation*, one of the major *poskim*, *Taz* (ט״ז; R' David ben Shmuel Halevi, 1586-1667), rules that a reading of *Tz'enah Ur'enah* constitutes a fulfillment of the "translation" requirement. He writes:

מִי שֶׁאֵינוֹ בַּר הָכִי וַדַּאי רָאוּי לִקְרוֹת בְּפֵירוּשׁ הַתּוֹרָה שֶׁיֵּשׁ בִּלְשׁוֹן
אַשְׁכְּנַז בִּזְמַנֵּנוּ כְּגוֹן סֵפֶר צְאֶינָה וּרְאֵינָה ...

One who is incapable [of comprehending *Onkelos* or *Rashi*] should surely read a Torah commentary that is available nowadays in German-Yiddish, such as *Tz'enah Ur'enah* ... (*Taz, Orach Chaim* 285:2).

The exact date of its first publication is a matter of dispute. The title page of the earliest copy extant gives the date as 1622 and the place as Basle, and mentions three preceding editions, one in Lublin and two in Cracow, all of which were out of print by 1622. The first edition may have been that of Prague in 1608, with a reprint in 1610. What is undisputed is that no other work in Yiddish has been so often published. Over 210 editions (not forgetting a partial translation into Latin!) are known to have appeared — in Europe, the United States and Israel. In a word, it would be safe to say that no Jewish home in Eastern Europe with a vestige of *Yiddishkeit* was without at least one copy of it. Indeed, so guaranteed was its popularity that not only was its title several times pirated for other religious works, but in 1822 its envious opponents of the Haskalah ("Enlightenment") movement, seeking to secure the admittance into traditional homes of Moses Mendelssohn's non-traditional Bible commentary, published a deluxe edition of the latter in Basle — with the title "*Tz'enah Ur'enah*" brazenly embossed on the outer cover!

❀ ❀ ❀

Why should this Yiddish classic be made available to the English reader? Firstly, this was the handbook by which our mothers and grandmothers loyally brought up their families in the spirit of authentic *Yiddishkeit* — in the ideals of Judaism as it is lived. This alone is something we dare not forget. Secondly, it is still the best work available of its kind. Without in any way detracting from the value of existing translations, commentaries, and anthologies, these typically demand an investment of time and concentration which is not always readily forthcoming. The freely-flowing passages of this unpretentious classic, however, can be relied upon — almost at one sitting — to fascinate regular readers of all ranks and backgrounds with an unsurpassed variety of information and insights on the weekly portion of the Torah.

Meir Holder
Hillel Pres'

Nissan 5743/1983
Jerusalem ת'ו

Yizkor
Lest We Forget

I remember *as a very young child sitting at my mother's knee listening spellbound as she read Tz'enah Ur'enah to the group of women who gathered around her.*

I remember *the exultation when the wicked Haman was hanged, and the anguish when the seven sons of Chanah went one by one to their martyr's death.*

I remember *as a self-assured yeshivah bochur of fully eighteen years trying to read Maimonides' Moreh Nevuchim, the abstruse Guide to the Perplexed. It was late at night, and my mother tiptoed into my room and asked me: "What is it that you are learning at such an hour? It doesn't look like any sefer I've ever seen in your hands before." Whereupon I, with the arrogance of youth, replied: "This is a work that proves the existence of HaShem." "Mein narish kindele," exclaimed my mother; "my silly child! For this you have to stay up and rob your eyes of sleep? Ask me: I know that there is a God!"*

Let us all remember the hundreds of thousands of Jewish mothers who found inspiration and simple but absolute faith in the pages of Tz'enah Ur'enah, and who were murdered and burned together with their families and their sacred books by the unspeakable monsters spawned by civilized Germany, ימח שמם וזכרם.

Let us remember. **We must not forget.**

M.H.

ספר בראשית

Bereishis / Genesis

פרשת בראשית
Parashas Bereishis
(1:1-6:8)

✦ Day One: The First Letter and the First Word

בְּרֵאשִׁית בָּרָא אֱלֹהִים את הַשָּׁמַיִם וְאֵת הָאָרֶץ — *At the original creation of heaven and earth, the land was desolate and empty, and God's holy throne was suspended over the water* (1:1). Why did the Torah commence with the letter *beis?* To show us that just as the letter *beis* (ב) is closed on three sides and open on the fourth, so God enclosed the world on three sides, while the northern side remained open.

Another reason is that the letter *beis* stands for the word *berachah* ("blessing," beginning with the letter *beis),* while the *alef* (the first letter of the alphabet) represents *arur* ("cursed," beginning with an *alef).* Not wishing to begin His Torah with the letter of a curse, the Almighty started with the *beis.*

Upset, the *alef* flew before God and complained that the Torah ought to begin with the first letter of the *alef-beis.* God appeased the offended letter, assuring it that the Ten Commandments given on Mt. Sinai would begin with the word *anochi* ("I"), which begins with an *alef.*

The Torah begins with the word *bereishis* to show us that the entire Creation took place only for the sake of the Torah, which is called *reishis darko (the beginning of His path; Mishlei* 8:22).

R' Yitzchak asks why the Torah begins with an account of the creation, rather than with the first commandment. The Torah, after all, was given primarily for the commandments which it contains. This was done in order to silence the seven nations of Canaan, who in the future might accuse the Jews of robbing them of *Eretz Yisrael* (the Land of Israel). The Jews can now answer that God created the world, and has the right to give it to whom He pleases. He had given *Eretz Yisrael* to the seven nations, and could rightfully take it away and bestow it upon the Jews.

The Sages say: God created the world for three objects: for the Torah, which is called *reishis darko;* for the sacrifices offered in the *Beis HaMikdash,* which is called *reishis* ("beginning") because it was created before the world itself; and for the tithes *(maasros)*, which are termed *reishis degancha* (the first of your produce; *Devarim* 18:4).

✒ The Light of the Mashiach

וְהָאָרֶץ הָיְתָה תֹהוּ וָבֹהוּ וְחֹשֶׁךְ עַל פְּנֵי תְהוֹם וְרוּחַ אֱלֹהִים מְרַחֶפֶת עַל פְּנֵי הַמָּיִם וַיֹּאמֶר אֱלֹהִים יְהִי אוֹר וַיְהִי אוֹר — *The earth was confused and empty, and darkness was on the face of the deep; and God's spirit hovered over the waters. God said, "Let there be light," and there was light* (1:2,3). The story of the creation refers to the *Beis HaMikdash*. The Torah prophesies the destruction of the *Beis HaMikdash* in the words, *the earth was confused and empty.* At the time of the Destruction, the Land will be barren and laid waste. The Presence of God will disappear from our midst. *God's spirit hovered over the waters* — these words assure us, however, that even after the Destruction the Torah will remain with us. Finally, the Torah tells us, *God said, "Let there be light,"* to reveal that God will ultimately illuminate Israel with the light of the *Mashiach*, of whom it is written, קוּמִי אוֹרִי כִּי בָא אוֹרֵךְ — *Arise, shine forth, for your light has come (Yeshayahu* 60:1) — the light being, of course, the *Mashiach.*

✒ Five Kinds of Light

וַיֹּאמֶר אֱלֹהִים יְהִי אוֹר וַיְהִי אוֹר. וַיַּרְא אֱלֹהִים אֶת הָאוֹר כִּי טוֹב וַיַּבְדֵּל אֱלֹהִים בֵּין הָאוֹר וּבֵין הַחֹשֶׁךְ. וַיִּקְרָא אֱלֹהִים לָאוֹר יוֹם וְלַחֹשֶׁךְ קָרָא לָיְלָה וַיְהִי עֶרֶב וַיְהִי בֹקֶר יוֹם אֶחָד — *God said, "Let there be light," and there was light. God saw the light, that it was good, and God separated the light and the darkness. God called the light, day ...* (1:3,5). God created two sources of light to illuminate the world — the sun and the moon. He also created a third, more splendid light. The world was not worthy of enjoying such a brilliant radiance, so He took this light and hid it for the righteous.

R' Shimon says that the word "light" appears in the text five times to represent each of the five books of the Torah, which is compared to light.

Let there be light refers to the Book of *Bereishis*, which discusses how God created the world with light. The second time it says, *and there was light*, representing the Book of *Shmos*, in which Israel's exodus from the darkness of the Egyptian exile and their subsequent redemption is presented. This redemption is compared with light, as it states, וּלְכָל בְּנֵי יִשְׂרָאֵל הָיָה אוֹר בְּמוֹשְׁבֹתָם — *and all Israel had light in their homes (Shmos* 10:23).

The third time the word appears is in the verse, *God saw the light, that it was good.* This symbolizes the Book of *Vayikra*, which deals with sacrifices. The first obligation of bringing a sacrifice was repentance, and if one repented and brought the sacrifice correctly, God gave him a share in His light. The fourth time the Torah says, *God separated the light and the darkness*, referring to the Book of *Bamidbar*, which tells us how Israel separated themselves from their evil ways, and were accompanied in the wilderness by the *Mishkan*, which illuminated their path. Finally, the fifth time it states, *God called the light*, day, representing the Book of *Devarim*, which contains only commandments and laws, which enlighten those who learn and abide by them.

From this we learn that there are five kinds of light. With the first the world was created; the second is the light of redemption; the third is reserved for one who repents; the fourth is the *Beis HaMikdash*; and the fifth is the Torah and its commandments.

The verse *Let there be light* teaches that God created the world through this light, for immediately after these words the creation began.

The word *yehi* (יְהִי; *let there be*) has a numerical equivalent of twenty-five, to show us that the world was created on the twenty-fifth day of the month of Elul. The *Gemara* tells us that Adam was created on Rosh HaShanah, the sixth day of Creation.

Why was man created last? Everything else was created before Adam to prevent man from becoming proud. Man must remember that even the animals and the beasts were created before him. Another explanation is that man was created after everything else so that he would find a fully prepared world awaiting him.

◄§ Second Day: The Waters Quarrel; the Fruits of Strife

וַיֹּאמֶר אֱלֹהִים יְהִי רָקִיעַ בְּתוֹךְ הַמָּיִם וִיהִי מַבְדִּיל בֵּין מַיִם לָמָיִם וַיַּעַשׂ אֱלֹהִים אֶת הָרָקִיעַ וַיַּבְדֵּל בֵּין הַמַּיִם אֲשֶׁר מִתַּחַת לָרָקִיעַ וּבֵין הַמַּיִם אֲשֶׁר מֵעַל לָרָקִיעַ וַיְהִי כֵן — *God said: Let there be a firmament in the midst of the waters, and it shall divide between water and water. God made the firmament and divided between the water under the firmament and the water above the firmament, and it was so (1:6,7).* God commanded that the heavens strengthen themselves in the midst of the water. On the first day the heavens were unsubstantial and weak. God reprimanded them, and as a result they strengthened themselves the next day, forming the heavens which we know.

God distinguished between the water which was above heaven and the water below, on earth. The distance between the upper water and the firmament is the same as the distance between the water of the earth and the firmament. The water above heaven is suspended in space by God's command.

The earthly waters quarreled with the waters which lie above heaven. They complained that they, too, wished to be above, rather than below, on earth. God assured them that the salt which they would yield would be placed on the altar together with the sacrifices, and no sacrifice would be brought without their salt — and the waters were appeased.

We see the words *and it was good* describe the creations of every day but the second. This is because the creation of the water on the second day was not completed until the third day. Something incomplete cannot be termed good. Since the water was actually completed on the third day, on that day it states *and it was good* twice: the first time referring to the creation of the water, and the second referring to the vegetation of the earth, which was also created on the third day.

Some Sages say that the second day's creation lacks the words *and it was good* because *Gehinnom* (Hell) was created on the second day. Others feel that the phrase is missing because the quarrel between the upper and lower waters took place on the second day, and no good can ever arise from quarreling and strife. Actually, the quarrel is the reason that *Gehinnom* was created on that day. One who quarrels will ultimately end up in *Gehinnom*, as did Korach and his followers.

In the *Gemara (Bava Basra)* Rabbah the son of Bar Chanah tells of his journey in the desert. A merchant approached him and offered to escort him to the place where Korach was swallowed into the earth. He followed the merchant and saw a crack in the earth spewing out smoke. He placed wool on a spear's tip and stuck it into the crack, and the heat of the fire within the earth singed the wool. Then he put his ear next to the ground and heard voices screaming, "Moshe (Moses) is true, and his Torah is the truth, and we are all liars!" Every thirty days the fire is rekindled in order to heighten their misery, and they all scream in unison, "Moshe is true and his Torah is the truth!" From this we learn that one must avoid quarreling.

Many Sages advise not to begin projects on Monday, because that is the day that the Torah omitted the words *and it was good*, and because strife began on that day.

From Monday onward, every day had some sort of dispute. On the third day God commanded that the earth bring forth trees which would actually contain the taste of their fruit within their bark, but the earth did not do so. On the fourth day, too, there was dissension. The moon jealously asked God why the sun shone as brightly as he. As a punishment the moon's light was lessened ... And on the sixth day Adam sinned and was cast out of Eden.

✑§ Third Day: The Sea and the Land

וַיֹּאמֶר אֱלֹהִים יִקָּווּ הַמַּיִם — *God said, "Let the waters gather together ..."* (1:9). On the third day God commanded all the waters to gather together in one place, in order to uncover the earth's surface. All the waters immediately gathered into the Great Sea. God also commanded that the earth produce trees which bear the taste of their fruits within them, but the earth did not heed His command. As a result the earth was cursed, together with Adam, after his sin.

✑§ Fourth Day: The Moon is Jealous;
the Beauty of Repentance

וַיֹּאמֶר אֱלֹהִים יְהִי מְאֹרֹת בִּרְקִיעַ הַשָּׁמַיִם לְהַבְדִּיל בֵּין הַיּוֹם וּבֵין הַלַּיְלָה וְהָיוּ לְאֹתֹת וּלְמוֹעֲדִים וּלְיָמִים וְשָׁנִים — *God said, "Let there be light in the firmament of heaven to divide between day and night. They will be as signs, and [indications of] festivals, days and years"* (1:14). Actually, the light was created on the first day, but was not placed in heaven until the fourth. On that day God suspended the sun, the moon, the constellations and the stars in the heavens. He placed the lights as omens: when the sun eclipses, it is an omen that those who worship it will soon be punished. When the moon is in eclipse it is a sign that God is angry with Israel for their misdeeds. The moon represents Israel because they follow the lunar calendar.

The sun and the moon are also given to us as signs of when to begin prayer. In the morning the sun gives us the sign of when to put on *tefillin* and when to recite the *Shema*. In the evening when the stars appear we know that the time for evening prayer has arrived. The sun and the moon were also given to help us calculate our holidays, and to allow us to differentiate between day and night, and between one year and the next.

R' Azariah said: God initially created only the sun to illuminate the world. But God realized that mankind would then worship the sun as a god, so He created the moon as well. The sun and the moon were both the same size and equally bright. But the moon asked, "Why should we both illuminate equally? Let me alone give light!" God replied: "Because you wanted to be greater than the sun, you will be smaller."

R' Bechaye explains that in *parashas Pinchas (Bamidbar* 28:15), when discussing the New Moon sacrifice of Rosh Chodesh, the Torah states that it is a *repentance offering to God* (חַטָּאת לַה'). This phrase is not used in connection with any other sacrifice. Why is this so? In the beginning, the sun and the moon were equally bright, but as a result of its jealousy the moon lost its brightness, and was doomed to receive its illumination as a mere reflection of the sun.

The moon itself gives off no light; it is dark. The moon complained bitterly to God: "Haven't You the power to let both the sun and the moon give off light? I am just as important to the world as the sun, and mankind may say, Heaven forbid, that God hasn't the strength to allow both the sun and the moon to give off their light." This angered God, who told the moon, "You want to teach Me what to do with My world? Because you have spoken these words, I will lessen the light which you reflect from the sun." And the moon became the small orb which we see today.

But the moon continued to complain, and said: "Because I spoke the truth, is it fair that You take my light and lessen it?" God answered that He had lessened the light of the moon for reasons known only to Himself. However, because the moon had spoken justly it would be rewarded. Each month the children of God, Israel, would bring a sacrifice at the time when the moon reveals itself anew. And this sacrifice would be called *a repentance offering to God;* the only one so honored.

The sun illuminates the day, and the moon lights up the night. If the light of the moon had been as strong as that of the sun, mankind would have had no means of telling the difference between night and day. Man would have worked as hard at night as he does by day, and would not have rested. Eventually, he would have died from excessive work. Therefore God gave mankind a means of differentiating between day and night.

God decreed that the night would be reserved for the learning of Torah, for one can learn best when the world is quiet and at rest.

From all of this we see that when a man repents, God shows him good will. For He commanded the Jews to bring a sacrifice on Rosh Chodesh, when the moon appears anew in the sky, in order to compensate the moon after diminishing it in size and brightness. Because of this the Torah calls the Rosh Chodesh offering *chatas laHashem (a repentance offering to God)*, which can be understood to mean God's repentance offering. From this we learn the importance of true repentance.

◆§ Fifth Day: The Blessing to the Fish

וַיֹּאמֶר אֱלֹהִים יִשְׁרְצוּ הַמַּיִם שֶׁרֶץ נֶפֶשׁ חַיָּה — God said, "Let the waters swarm with living creatures ..." (1:20). On the fifth day God commanded that the water give forth living creatures, including the great Leviathan and his mate. God gave a particular blessing to the fish, because man constantly preys on them and they need a special blessing for fertility in order to survive.

We may ask why God did not give an extra blessing to the beasts, when mankind preys on them as well. The snake is considered one of the beasts, and since God intended to curse the snake, He did not wish to include it in an extra blessing, and therefore did not bless the beasts at all.

◄§ Sea Monsters

וַיִּבְרָא אֱלֹהִים אֶת הַתַּנִּינִם הַגְּדֹלִים — *God created the giant sea monsters* ... (1:21). These were enormous fish that were many miles long. The *Gemara (Bava Basra)* tells us that Rabbah the son of Bar Chanah told of a fish which he saw cast out of the sea. People there collected three hundred barrels of fish oils from one eye alone. A year later he returned to the same place, and found the people sawing huge beams from the bones of that giant fish.

He speaks of another time when he saw a giant fish, with its back projecting out of the water. There was earth on the fish's back, and the people thought it was an island in the middle of the water. The passengers disembarked onto the fish's back, and lit fires in the earth. Reacting to the fire's heat the fish turned over, and if the boat had not been there Rabbah and his fellow passengers would surely have drowned.

R' Bechaye says that as a result of God's special blessing to the fish they survived the Flood, when all other creatures were drowned.

◄§ Sixth Day: Consulting the Angels

וַיֹּאמֶר אֱלֹהִים נַעֲשֶׂה אָדָם בְּצַלְמֵנוּ כִּדְמוּתֵנוּ — *God said, "Let us make man in our image and likeness"* (1:26). On the sixth day God said to the angels: *Come, let us create man.* God taught us from his actions that a man should not be overly proud, but should rather discuss matters with others, and heed their advice. Therefore God conferred with the angels, though in reality He alone created man, as it states, *and God created the man.* He alone created him.

◄§ In the Image of God

וַיִּבְרָא אֱלֹהִים אֶת הָאָדָם בְּצַלְמוֹ — *God created man in His image* (1:27). God thought to Himself: "If I do not now create on the earth a being patterned after the angels in the heavens, there will surely be jealousy among the created beings." He therefore created man with the same image as the angels, with intelligence and beauty, in order to avoid jealousy among His creations.

God allowed man sovereignty over the fish of the sea, the birds of the skies, and the animals and beasts of the earth.

◄§ The Twofold Blessing to Man

וַיֹּאמֶר לָהֶם אֱלֹהִים פְּרוּ וּרְבוּ וּמִלְאוּ אֶת הָאָרֶץ — *God said to them: "Be fruitful and multiply, and fill the earth ...''* (1:28). R' Bechaye writes that God gave man a twofold blessing with these words. The first blessing is that man should derive the proper benefits from his food and drink. A person's body must retain a certain amount of moisture. The body is constantly weakened because of the dehydration which it undergoes, both as a result of normal body heat and from the dry winds which buffet the body. Man restores the proper moisture through eating and drinking. It is a great blessing that the food and drink restore the correct balance of moisture in the body — no more and no less.

The second blessing is that man should cleave to his wife and have God-fearing children.

◄§ Vegetation and Meat

וַיֹּאמֶר אֱלֹהִים הִנֵּה נָתַתִּי לָכֶם אֶת כָּל עֵשֶׂב זֹרֵעַ זֶרַע אֲשֶׁר עַל פְּנֵי כָל הָאָרֶץ — *God said, "Behold, I have given you every seedbearing plant on the face of the earth ..."* (1:29). God permitted man to eat fruit and anything else which is planted on the earth. Animals and birds were allowed to eat only grass; and man was not given permission to eat the meat of animals, for every animal has a soul. Its soul cannot be compared with that of man, but it exists nevertheless.

After the Flood man was given permission to eat meat, because the animals had sinned and it was only Noach's (Noah's) merit which saved them.

◄§ Truth Cast to Earth; The Benefits of Mortality; Three Partners in Man

וַיַּרְא אֱלֹהִים אֶת כָּל אֲשֶׁר עָשָׂה וְהִנֵּה טוֹב מְאֹד — *God saw all that He had made, and it was very good* (1:31). In *Midrash Rabbah* we are told that R' Simon said: The angels gathered together when God was about to create man. Some advised not to create him because he would be a deceitful creature; others said that he ought to be created, because of the charity and good deeds which he would do in the future; while still others counseled against his creation because he would not be a peaceful creature, and would bring strife and dissension. In response, God took *emes* (''truth'') and hurled it from the skies to the earth.

Then God told the angels: "Man is better than you can ever be. You are intelligent beings and possess only the desire to do good. You are forced by your very nature to be good. But man has an evil inclination which constantly lures him to wickedness. When he remains virtuous he is much greater than you. As for your argument that man is deceitful and quarrelsome and will ultimately sin — I will decree that every man will eventually die, and will fear death. This fear will help him remain virtuous. If he does sin I will take his soul to *Gehinnom* and cleanse it of its sins, and then it will be restored to its original abode beneath My Holy Throne."

R' Simon refers to this when he says that God flung *emes* to the earth. *Emes* (אֱמֶת) is the acronym for *aron, mitah, tachrichim:* casket, bier, and shrouds. Man will die, be clothed in shrouds, placed in a casket, and carried to his final resting place on a bier. God decreed that man must die, in order to save him from pride and thereby preserve his virtue.

Our Sages tell us that the words *and it was very good* refer to death, as death is good for mankind. After living a righteous life the good man faces death and then joins God near His Throne. For this reason it is written, *the death of his pious ones is precious in God's eyes (Tehillim* 115:16). God would not have created even the righteous men, had He not also created their death, for even the best man must err; death purges him of sin and allows him to reap his full reward.

After this discussion the angels said to God: "Almighty, why do You degrade Your ornament and Your seal and cast it into the earth to decay?" In other words, why do You allow man, who is created in Your image, to be placed in the earth after death? Why not take the glory of Your creations with You to heaven?

God answered by saying, "Let truth rise from the earth." We have explained that the initials of the word *emes* (truth) represent casket, bier, and shrouds — death. It is through his death that man can rise to heaven.

The Talmud tells us that three beings have a stake in a person — the father, the mother, and the Almighty. When a person dies, God tells the parents: "Go take your share and I will take mine." God's share is the soul, and He takes His image with Him to heaven.

R' Huna says: At the time that the angels quarreled, with some saying that man should be created and others saying that he should not be, God went and created him. Then God turned to the angels and asked: "Why are you arguing? I see I have already caused an argument among you. Stop debating the issue [for I have already created man]."

An analogy can be drawn to a wealthy man who has a house full of riches and costly wines, but no guests to whom he can display his wealth. He asks himself, "What good is all this, if I cannot show off my fortune?" Similarly, who would see the beauty and variety of the creations, and the greatness of the Creator, if man had not been created?

◄§ Sixth Day: The Fives of Creation; Free Choice; The Wakeful Ones

יוֹם הַשִּׁשִּׁי —... *the sixth day* (1:31). The Torah adds an extra *hei* (fifth letter of the *alef-beis*) when speaking of man's creation, because the entire creation was done contingent upon man's learning the Five Books of the Torah (the numerical value of the letter *hei* being five) — and only thus will the world endure.

All of creation was done in fives, which shows us too that all of creation is contingent upon the Torah. Five lights were created on the first day, five heavens on the second. On the second day the word "water" appears five times. Five types of plants were formed on the third day, while on the fourth day five means of illumination were created: the sun, moon, constellations, stars, and daylight. On the fifth day God created the creatures, who have five different means of locomotion: some walk on two legs, some on four, others crawl on their bellies, still others fly, and water creatures swim. On the sixth day man was created. His soul has five names: *nefesh, ruach, neshamah, chayah, yechidah.*

It is clear that man is a being beset by inner turmoil and conflict. All other creatures lack this conflict, and only man fights within himself. When a man wishes to do good, his evil inclination tries to lure him away, and when he wishes to choose the path of evil, his inclination towards goodness fights to stop him. His life is one of constant discord and contention within himself.

Why did God create man in this manner? Why did He not allow him inner harmony and tranquility? He did it to elevate man over all other beings. Man is the only being with free choice. The beasts and animals are servants to their passions only, and their nature allows them to be interested in their bodily needs. The angels, however, are beings of pure intellect and goodness, and thus there is never the possibility of an angel straying from the proper path.

God did not wish to create only beings who were not masters of their own destiny, and so He created man. Man resembles God in this, for just as God chooses His own path, His own desires, so man, too, can choose which way to travel, what sort of life to lead. God allows man his free choice.

Before he ate of the forbidden fruit Adam, like God, was free to choose, was master of his own actions. Once he ate from the fruit, however, he became possessed of powerful and conflicting inner drives, some wicked, others pure. For this reason the forbidden tree was known as the Tree of Knowledge of Good and Evil, עֵץ הַדַּעַת טוֹב וָרָע. One who ate from it had the desires and the knowledge to do evil and good.

For this reason God said of no other creation, *Let us create in Our image*. Man, like his Creator, has the power of free choice.

Out of respect for this God-like creation, man, the Torah states: *God created man in His image, in the image of God He created him (Bereishis 1:27)*. The angels, awed by the news that God had created a being endowed with the power of free choice, wished to worship this marvelous being. God overpowered Adam with a sleep, and then displayed him to the angels, to teach them that although man did have the power of free will, he was also a being of many physical frailties. Man sleeps, and in his sleep he is not master of his own will; the angels are above such physical needs. For this very reason the angels are sometimes called *irin kadishin*, which means "wakeful, holy beings," for they are always awake.

Man was created on the same day as the animals to teach him that when he is virtuous he is greater than all other beasts, but when he is evil and follows his evil inclination he is infinitely lower than they, for they have no reason and cannot choose the path of virtue.

⋅§ Seventh Day: Completion and Desire

וַיְכַל אֱלֹהִים בַּיוֹם הַשְּׁבִיעִי — *And God finished by the seventh day* (2:2). The word *vaychal (and He finished)* can be understood to mean "he desired." On the seventh day God desired all of His creations, that is to say, He desired that all of the things which He had created in the first six days should remain as they had been created.

⋅§ The Extra Soul; Saving for Shabbos; The Emperor's Disappointment

וַיְבָרֶךְ אֱלֹהִים אֶת יוֹם הַשְּׁבִיעִי וַיְקַדֵּשׁ אֹתוֹ — *And God blessed the seventh day, and made it holy* (2:3). God blessed *Shabbos* by giving man an extra soul *(neshamah yeseirah)* especially for that day; when *Shabbos* ends we make a blessing on fragrant spices, because our extra soul has left us. He made the *Shabbos* holy by refraining on it from the labors of creation.

Midrash Rabbah writes that God gave *Shabbos* a special blessing, that it would be celebrated with good food. If we do this, God will grant us great riches. R' Chiya the son of R' Abba said: "I was once in a house in the town of Laodicea. A silver table carried by sixteen men was brought before me, laden with all of God's creations. In the middle of the table sat a small boy, crying aloud, 'All that is on the earth belongs to God!' He did this to ensure that the owner of the house would not become haughty.

"I asked the owner why he merited such riches. He answered, 'I was a butcher and whenever I had a fine animal I would save it for

Shabbos. From Sunday onward, I would save everything for *Shabbos.*'

"I said to him, 'I believe you. God promises success and blessings for one who celebrates *Shabbos* and *Yom-Tov* properly. God makes such a person rich in This World, and rewards him well in the World to Come.' "

R' Tanchuma says: Once a great noble sent his servant to buy fish on *erev* Yom Kippur, the day preceding the Day of Atonement. It happened that the fisherman had only one large fish left. The servant was bargaining with the owner for the fish, when a Jewish tailor walked in. He outbid the servant, paying twelve gold pieces for the fish. The servant returned home empty-handed, and told his angry master that a Jewish tailor had bought the last fish and had paid twelve gold coins for it.

The noble sent for the tailor and questioned him: "Why did you take the fish away from my servant?" The tailor replied, "How can I help but buy fish and other delicacies? Tomorrow is a day which God gave us to cleanse ourselves, and we hope for His forgiveness for all of our sins. Can I help but celebrate?" The noble answered: "You have acted properly."

Returning home the tailor opened the fish and found a valuable pearl within it. This he sold, and lived from the proceeds for the rest of his life.

R' Eliezer said in the name of R' Yosei: "God blessed the *Shabbos* by giving its meals a more beautiful aroma that that of weekday food."

Rebbe (R' Yehudah HaNasi) once made a meal for the emperor Antoninus on *Shabbos*. He served a cold meal, which smelled delicious. Later on he served him a hot meal, during the week. Turning to Rebbe, Antoninus said: "Please bring me cold foods, for those which you served me at the last meal smelled more tantalizing."

Rebbe answered: "I need a certain spice for that food."

"I have enough spices in my warehouse," replied Antoninus.

"But do you have a spice called *Shabbos*?" asked Rebbe, "For that is the day which is blessed with a beautiful fragrance."

Turnus Rufus once asked R' Akiva: "Why is *Shabbos* better than the other days of the week?"

R' Akiva answered: "What makes you more important than other men?"

Replied Turnus Rufus: "The king has made me higher than the others."

R' Akiva then said, "And God, the King, has made *Shabbos* higher than the other days of the week."

"How can you prove that *Shabbos* is higher than the other days, and that God so commanded it?" asked Turnus Rufus. R' Akiva answered, "The river Sambatyon proves it. During the week it shoots up stones, and on *Shabbos* it rests."

Turnus Rufus said to him: "One who wants to lie cites proofs from far-off places, where no one has ever been, so that no one can prove he is lying. You bring proof from the Sambatyon which no one has ever seen. You may be lying."

R' Akiva answered, "Go and see if you can raise the dead on *Shabbos* with magic." Turnus Rufus tried and could not, but during the week he succeeded.

Some Sages say that *Shabbos* was especially blessed because it had no mate. In this connection R' Shmuel bar Nachmani says: "*Shabbos* is unique. *Shabbos* alone is never postponed to another day, while holidays can be. Even Yom Kippur can be put off, [i.e., the calendar is so devised] so that it should not fall on a Friday or a Sunday, in order to avoid having a corpse remain unburied for two days. For otherwise, if a man died on Friday, he would lie unburied on Friday and *Shabbos*, and if he died on *Shabbos*, he would lie unburied on *Shabbos* and Sunday. But *Shabbos* is never put off."

Shabbos turned to God and asked: "Why have I no mate?" God answered that Israel would be its mate. When the Jews came to Mount Sinai, *Shabbos* told God, "Remember the *Shabbos*, to make it holy" — that is, "Remember what you promised me: that the Jews will rest on my day, and will thereby be my mate."

◆§ Six Days and Six Millennia

כִּי בוֹ שָׁבַת מִכָּל מְלַאכְתּוֹ אֲשֶׁר בָּרָא אֱלֹהִים לַעֲשׂוֹת — *because on it He rested from all of His work, which He had done in creating it* (2:3). The six days parallel the six millennia for which the world will exist. On the first day God created light. This stands for the first thousand years, in which Adam lived. He was the light of the world, for he recognized his Creator. The second day saw a separation made between the sky and the seas. This parallels the second thousand years of the world's existence, in which Noach was separated from the evil men of the world, who ultimately drowned in the Flood. The Torah does not say *and it was good* on the second day, because the Flood occurred in this millennium.

On the third day the earth grew fertile and all of the trees and fruits were created. This represents the third millennium, in which Avraham Avinu was born; his children accepted the Torah and its commandments, which are compared to the fruits of the earth. On the fourth day, two orbs were created — a great one, the sun, and a small one, the moon. This symbolizes the two Temples which were built in the fourth millennium; one Temple cast great light for the Jews, while the other gave forth less illumination.

Fish and birds were created on the fifth day, and this stands for the fifth millennium. Man was created on the sixth day, for within six thousand years the *Mashiach* will come. Just as Adam was created in God's image, so the *Mashiach* is anointed by God, and God's spirit will be upon him. We rest on *Shabbos* to symbolize the peace that we will have in the days of the *Mashiach*.

◆§ Adam and Mashiach; Adam after the Sin; Hei and Yud

אֵלֶּה תוֹלְדוֹת הַשָּׁמַיִם וְהָאָרֶץ בְּהִבָּרְאָם בְּיוֹם עֲשׂוֹת ה' אֱלֹהִים אֶרֶץ וְשָׁמָיִם —
These are the chronicles of the heaven and the earth, when they were created, on the day that God made earth and heaven (2:4). Why, in speaking of the birth of Peretz, does the Torah spell the word *toldos* ("generations") with two *vavim* (singular, *vav* — sixth letter of the *alef-beis*), and in discussing the creation of heaven and earth it likewise spells it with two *vavim*, but when discussing the creation of Adam and in other places, it is spelled with one *vav*? When God created the world there was no angel of death, while one of Peretz's descendants will be the *Mashiach*, in whose time the Angel of Death will be defeated, so *toldos* is spelled with two *vavim*. But as soon as Adam was created the Angel of Death, too, was created. All of Adam's descendants *(toldos)* will ultimately die, and so *toldos* is written missing one *vav*.

This also teaches us that six things were taken from Adam after he sinned (the numerical value of *vav* is six). His luster was taken away from him, his years were shortened, his great height was diminished, the fruits of the earth and of the trees were cursed, and the good light was taken away.

The light began to shine on Friday morning, when Adam was created, and two hours before nightfall, when Adam ate of the fruit of the Tree of Knowledge, God wanted to take the light away, for Adam was no longer worthy of it. In honor of *Shabbos*, however, God refrained from taking the light and it shone through *Shabbos*.

When *Shabbos* ended it became very dark. Adam was frightened that the snake would bite him in the darkness, so God sent him two flintstones. He struck them together to make a fire and illuminate the darkness. Adam then made the blessing "... *borei me'orei ha-esh*," blessing Him "Who creates the lights of fire." Because of this, we say this blessing every week, in the course of *Havdalah*, when *Shabbos* ends.

The world was created with a *hei* (fifth letter of the *alef-beis*).

This is implied in the word *behibaram*, which can be read *be-hei bra'am* — "He created them with a *hei*." *Hei* is a quiet letter which is open like a door both on its bottom and its side (ה). This teaches us that most of the people of this world will go to *Gehinnom*, but the righteous will instead go to heaven.

The World to Come was created with a *yud* (י), the smallest letter in the *alef-beis*, to show us that few people reach the World to Come.

◄§ Two Inclinations; Events of the Sixth Day; Heaven and Earth

וַיִּיצֶר ה' אֱלֹהִים אֶת הָאָדָם עָפָר מִן הָאֲדָמָה וַיִּפַּח בְּאַפָּיו נִשְׁמַת חַיִּים וַיְהִי הָאָדָם לְנֶפֶשׁ חַיָּה — *And God formed the man of dust from the ground, and he blew the breath of life into his nostrils, and the man became a living soul* (2:7). God created man from the earth. Why is *vayitzer* ("he formed") spelled with the letter *yud* doubled? To show us that man has within himself two inclinations (*yetzer* — "inclination"), an inclination for good and another for evil. Regarding the creation of animals, the Torah spells *vayitzer* with one *yud*, for animals have only an evil inclination, and no inclination to do good.

In the first hour of the sixth day, God gathered together the earth; in the second hour he kneaded it; in the third he covered the earth with skin; and in the fourth he gave it a soul. Adam stood on his own legs in the fifth hour; in the sixth, Adam gave names to all the other creations. His wife Chavah (Eve) was given to him in the seventh hour; in the eighth hour they had marital relations; in the ninth hour, God commanded them not to eat of the Tree of Knowledge; in the tenth hour they sinned by eating of the forbidden fruit; in the eleventh hour God judged them; and in the twelfth hour they were banished from Eden.

God took earth from all four corners of the earth and created man from it, so that when man would die the earth would accept him again for burial. He also took earth from under the altar of the *Beis HaMikdash*, so that he would be granted atonement for his sins.

God blew into his nostrils, and then said: "I must see that there is no strife or jealousy between my creations." Thus it was that on the first day God created heaven and earth. On the second God improved and strengthened the sky. The earth was pained that it had not been improved, so on the third day God proceeded with the creation on earth: He gathered together all of the waters, so that the earth would be visible. On the fourth day God once again improved the heavens and placed lights in it; on the fifth day God improved the earth and created fish and birds. On the sixth day God said, "I must make a compromise between heaven and earth so that there will be no jealousy between them" — and so God took soil from the earth and a soul from the angels in heaven and created a man.

Ramban writes that God gave man a soul endowing him with the power of speech in order to raise him above all the other creations. We have seen in the Gemara that Rava created a person using the holy Names and sent him to R' Zeira. R' Zeira spoke to him, and seeing that he was unable to answer, said: "You must be a creation of the Sages. Go back to the earth, and be earth once more."

We find in the Gemara that certain Sages created calves for Shabbos, but a man cannot create another man who can speak, for the power of speech comes from the soul, which is created in heaven. The soul is made with the holy spirit, Ruach HaKodesh, and therefore, in many respects, resembles its Creator. The soul is greater than the angels, and it was therefore created on the second day, before the angels. Whatever was created first was more important, and therefore our Sages say that a righteous man is greater than an angel, for he keeps his soul pure.

◄§ Two Trees in the Garden of Eden

וַיִּטַּע ה' אֱלֹהִים גַּן בְּעֵדֶן מִקֶּדֶם וַיָּשֶׂם שָׁם אֶת הָאָדָם אֲשֶׁר יָצָר — And God planted a Garden in Eden, in the east, and placed there the man whom he had created (2:8). There were two special trees in the Garden. One was called the Tree of Knowledge, and one who ate of its fruits gained great wisdom and the knowledge of good and evil, as well as a powerful inclination to evil; the other was called the Tree of Life, and its fruits gave immortality. Four rivers flowed from the Garden to irrigate it, and God placed Adam in the Garden so that he should plant for himself wheat and barley and fragrant spices and all sorts of good things, but commanded him to refrain from eating of the Tree of Knowledge.

Why did God not forbid him from eating of the Tree of Life? God had planned to let Adam live forever, and therefore did not forbid him the Tree of Life. But after he sinned and ate of the Tree of Knowledge, God forbade him to eat of the Tree of Life, for in transgressing against God's word he became deserving of death. God then exiled him from Eden, so that he would not eat of the Tree of Life.

Some of our Sages say that the Tree of Life stood in the middle of the Garden, and the Tree of Knowledge stood next to it. One could not reach the Tree of Life because the Tree of Knowledge blocked it. As soon as Adam ate of the Tree of Knowledge God exiled him, because Adam intended to eat of the Tree of Life after eating of the Tree of Knowledge.

The Tree of Knowledge caused one's evil inclination to grow more powerful. Before they ate of its fruit, Adam and Chavah were naked, and were not ashamed. As soon as they ate they felt shame and cut leaves to cover themselves.

◄§ A Gift to King David

וּמֵעֵץ הַדַּעַת טוֹב וָרָע לֹא תֹאכַל מִמֶּנּוּ כִּי בְּיוֹם אֲכָלְךָ מִמֶּנּוּ מוֹת תָּמוּת — *And from the Tree of Knowledge of good and evil, do not eat, for the day you eat of it, you shall die* (2:17). God told Adam that he would die on the day that he ate of the Tree of Knowledge. God then pitied him and allowed him to live one day of His days. God's day is a thousand years long. Adam should thus have lived a thousand years, but he saw in prophecy that King David was destined to be stillborn, and so gave him seventy of his years, and lived to nine hundred and thirty.

Some Sages say that what God meant when He said "you will die on the day that you eat of it," is that he would die on the same day of the week that he ate the fruit. Adam ate on Friday, and after many years died on a Friday.

Other Sages say that when God said he would die on that day, he meant that this would happen only if he did not repent. This is similar to what we find in the city of Nineveh. God sent Yonah to Nineveh to tell them that in forty days the city would be destroyed. But He did not destroy it, because they repented. So it was in this case: because Adam repented God postponed taking his life.

◄§ Adam's Helpmate

וַיֹּאמֶר ה' אֱלֹהִים לֹא טוֹב הֱיוֹת הָאָדָם לְבַדּוֹ אֶעֱשֶׂה לּוֹ עֵזֶר כְּנֶגְדּוֹ — *And God said, "It is not good for a man to be alone, I will make him a help-mate"* (2:18). God said that it is not good for man to be without a wife. All the creations would see that man is one on the earth, and they would worship him as a god. They would say that just as there is one God in heaven, so Adam is one on earth. Besides, God gave him a wife so that she should help him.

◄§ A Name for Each Creature

וַיָּבֵא אֶל הָאָדָם לִרְאוֹת מַה יִּקְרָא לוֹ וְכֹל אֲשֶׁר יִקְרָא לוֹ הָאָדָם נֶפֶשׁ חַיָּה הוּא שְׁמוֹ — *And [God] brought [the animals] to the man to see what he would call them. And all that the man called each living creature, that is its name* (2:19).

God brought all of the animals before Adam in order that he should give them names. Being very gifted, Adam gave them each a name which reflected their nature.

He saw that the donkey was a foolish creature and called it a *chamor*, which means he is as slow and dull as a dummy of clay (*chomer* — "clay"). He saw that the horse was always gay, and called it *sus* (*sason* — "joy"). He saw that every ten years the eagle loses its feathers and grows new ones, and so named it *nesher* (from the root meaning "to slough"). When the eagle is a hundred years old, it flies so high up in the heavens that it dies of the extreme heat there, and falls into the ocean.

God asked Adam, "What shall My name be?" Adam answered, "Your name will be *Adon-oy*, for You are the Master (*adon* — "master") over the entire creation." Because of this it is written, אֲנִי ה׳ הוּא שְׁמִי — *I am God, that is My Name.* My name has been that for many years, since Adam's time.

◄§ The Key to Marital Harmony

וַיַּפֵּל ה׳ אֱלֹהִים תַּרְדֵּמָה — *And God placed* [him] *in a deep sleep* (2:21). God made Adam sleep to teach us that a man should not constantly fight with his wife. If he sees that she does something which displeases him, he should pretend that he does not see it and "sleep" through it.

When God brought all the creations to Adam so that he could give them names, Adam saw that each animal had a mate except he. For this reason it says, *And for Adam he could not find a helpmate*, that is, Adam did not find a female who was worthy of being his wife. Therefore God placed Adam in a deep sleep and took a rib from his body and created a wife for him. Why did God make him sleep? So that he should not see that she came from his body, and find her displeasing.

When a man is worthy God gives him a wife whom he loves and who helps him, but when he is evil, He sends him a wife like himself, who causes him to lose both this world and the next. A good wife brings her husband to the World to Come.

There is a story of righteous man who had a wife who was a very good woman. They had no children, so they divorced. She then married an evil man and made him righteous, and he married an evil woman who turned him evil.

◄§ Woman Made from Man

וַיִּבֶן ה׳ אֱלֹהִים אֶת הַצֵּלָע אֲשֶׁר לָקַח מִן הָאָדָם לְאִשָּׁה וַיְבִאֶהָ אֶל הָאָדָם — *And God built the rib which he took from the man into a woman and He brought her to Adam* (2:22). R' Yehoshua said in the name of R' Levi: God wondered which part of the body to build the woman from. He said: "I do not want to create her from Adam's head, or she will be haughty and hold up her head in pride. If I create her from his eye she will have a roving eye; from the ear, she will want to hear everything; from the mouth, she will talk too much; from the heart, she will be envious; from the hand, she will grasp for everything; from the feet, she will be foot-loose. Therefore I will create her from a part of the body which is hidden — the rib, which does not show even when a man is naked."

But all of this did not help. God said: "I did not create her from the head, so that she should not be haughty, but the Prophet says, וַתֵּלַכְנָה נְטוּיוֹת גָּרוֹן — and they walked with outstretched necks (Yeshayahu 3:16); I did not create her from the eye, so she should not want to see everything, yet it is written וּמְשַׂקְּרוֹת עֵינָיִם — with wandering eyes (ibid.); I did not create her from the ear, so that she should not listen to things which she ought not hear — but it is written וְשָׂרָה שֹׁמַעַת פֶּתַח הָאֹהֶל — and Sarah heard at the door of the tent (18:10); I did not create her from the heart, so that she should not be jealous, but it states וַתְּקַנֵּא רָחֵל בַּאֲחֹתָהּ — and Rachel envied her sister (30:1); I did not create her from the hand, so they should not wish to take everything, yet it is written, וַתִּגְנֹב רָחֵל אֶת הַתְּרָפִים — and Rachel stole the idols (31:19); I did not create her from the feet, so that they should not wander, and yet it is written, וַתֵּצֵא דִינָה — and Dinah wandered out (34:1)."

R' Yehoshua asked: Why is it that when a child leaves his mother's womb, if it is a male he faces downward, and if it is a female she faces upward? He was answered: Because Adam was created from the earth, a male faces the earth, looking at the place where he was created. But Chavah was created from Adam, so a female faces upward, for she was created from man.

Women have sweet voices, because they were created from a bone. Strike one bone against another and it tinkles and echoes, but if you strike earth against earth it makes no such sound.

A woman is slow to forgive, for she was created from a bone. If one pours water on a bone, nothing will change, but if one pours water on the earth, it will dissolve immediately. Because of this we say, "as a father has mercy on a child," for a father is more merciful than a mother.

A man seeks a wife: a woman does not seek a husband. Woman was taken from man, and so he searches for her. It is as if someone has lost something and searches for it. But the woman has not lost anything and therefore need not search.

This is also the reason that a man goes with his hair uncovered, while a woman covers her hair. Chavah caused Adam to sin and so she walks in shame, her hair covered. Women customarily walk behind the dead, ahead of the men, for they brought death to the world. God gave women the commandment of *niddah* (ritual purity), for they spilled the blood of man [and can thereby rectify this wrong]; the commandment of *challah*, for they caused Adam to be separated from the world, and therefore they separate *challah* from the dough; and the commandment of candle lighting, for they extinguished the light of Adam's soul.

◄§ A Bone from His Bones

עַל כֵּן יַעֲזָב אִישׁ אֶת אָבִיו וְאֶת אִמוֹ וְדָבַק בְּאִשְׁתּוֹ וְהָיוּ לְבָשָׂר אֶחָד — *Therefore shall a man leave his father and mother and cleave to his wife and they shall be one flesh* (2:24). A man must leave his parents and take himself a wife, for woman is his flesh and blood, *a bone from his bones*. A woman is strong by nature because she was created from a bone, and a man is weak for he was created from earth, which dissolves quickly.

◄§ Adding to God's Prohibitions

וַיִּהְיוּ שְׁנֵיהֶם עֲרוּמִים — *And the two were naked* (2:25). Adam and Chavah were naked and unashamed, like animals. The evil snake hoped for Adam's death, because he desired Chavah. He asked Chavah if God had forbidden them to eat of all of the trees in the Garden. Although he knew that God had forbidden only the fruit of the Tree of Knowledge, he wanted to begin conversing with her.

Chavah answered that God had forbidden not only eating from the Tree of Knowledge but touching it as well. The Sages say that we should not add to what God has forbidden us. God had forbidden eating from the Tree; Chavah added the prohibition against touching, and ultimately sinned.

The snake pushed her hand onto the Tree and said, "Just as touching the Tree did not bring you death, so too you can eat without fearing death. God knows that when you eat from the fruit you will be like the angels and therefore He has forbidden you to eat from the Tree."

Chavah thought that the snake spoke truthfully: it would be good for them to have their eyes open like the eyes of the angels. So she ate, and gave some fruit to her husband to eat also. She thought to herself that if she would die, let her husband die too and not take another woman as a wife. She also gave all of the animals and birds and beasts to eat, so that they too should die. All of the creatures ate — with the exception of one bird which is called *chol*. The *chol* refused to eat from the Tree's fruit. R' Yudin says in the name of R' Shimon that the *chol* lives for one thousand years and then it begins to fade away; it loses all of its feathers and becomes as small as an egg. It then begins to grow again.

◆§ The First Sin

כִּי טוֹב הָעֵץ לְמַאֲכָל — *That the Tree was good for eating* (3:6). Some of our Sages say that this was a fig tree. As soon as they ate of the fruit of the Tree of Knowledge their eyes were opened and they were ashamed of their nakedness. This is why they used fig leaves to cover themselves.

Other Sages say that the Tree was a grapevine. Chavah squeezed grapes and gave Adam blood-red wine to drink. Still others say that it was an *esrog* (citron) tree. This is why it is customary for some women to take the *esrog* on the festival of Hoshana Rabbah and bite off the tip, and to give charity as well, and to ask God to spare them from the pangs of childbirth. For if Chavah had not eaten from the Tree every woman would have given birth easily, much like a hen, which lays its eggs painlessly. A woman should say this prayer (when she bites the tip off the *esrog):* "Master of the Universe: Because Chavah ate of the Tree of Knowledge must we women all give birth in deathly pain? If I had been there I would have had no enjoyment from the fruit. I did not want to make the *esrog* invalid (by biting off the tip) during the seven days of Succos, because it is part of a *mitzvah.* Today is Hoshana Rabbah (which comes at the conclusion of the festival of Succos) and the commandment of the *esrog* is no longer upon us. I have rendered the *esrog* invalid, and yet have not hastened to eat it. Just as I have derived almost no enjoyment from the tip of the *esrog,* so I would have derived no enjoyment from the Tree which You forbade."

◆§ The Most Cursed of Animals; A Fatal Misunderstanding

וַתִּפָּקַחְנָה עֵינֵי שְׁנֵיהֶם — *And the eyes of them both were opened* (3:7). God opened their eyes, and when they became aware that they were naked, they plucked off fig leaves and covered themselves with them. They then heard God's voice in the Garden. It was two hours before nightfall, and they hid themselves from Him. God came to them, pretending that He did not know what they had done, so that they should not be frightened. He asked them, "Where are you?" Adam answered, "I hid myself when I heard Your voice in the Garden, because I was naked." God asked, "How did you know that you should be ashamed of your nakedness? Have you eaten from the forbidden fruit?" Adam replied, "The woman whom You gave me gave it to me to eat." God turned to the woman and asked, "Why did you eat from the forbidden Tree?" She answered, "The snake talked me into it." So God said to the snake, "Because you have done this you will be more cursed than all of the beasts and animals."

A Roman once wanted to find out how long a snake carried her young. He captured a snake immediately after she had mated with a male, and kept her in a barrel until she had given birth.

When the Sages were in Rome, this Roman asked Rabban Gamliel, "How many months does a snake carry its young?" Rabban Gamliel did not know what to say and his face paled with humiliation. R' Yehoshua saw him and asked why he was so pale and glum. He told R' Yehoshua that the Roman had asked him the question for which he had no answer.

R' Yehoshua told him that a snake carries its young for seven years. A dog, which is an impure beast, carries for fifty-two days. A horse, an impure animal, carries for one year. When God cursed the snake he told him he was more accursed than both an animal and a beast. When he cursed him more than an animal, which carries for one year, what need was there to curse him more than a beast, which carries for only fifty-two days? The verse however tells us in addition that just as the animal carries seven times longer than the beast [52 x 7 is equal to one year], so the snake carries seven times longer than the animal — that is, for seven years.

Rabban Gamliel thereupon told the Roman that a snake carries its young for seven years. The Roman beat his own head in distress and said, "I went to so much trouble to find the answer which the Jew gives me with no difficulty!"

The author of *Toldos Yitzchak* writes: We can ask a few questions on this portion. First, why did Chavah lie to the snake? God never forbade touching the Tree, He only forbade eating its fruit. Second, the snake pushed Chavah's hand onto the Tree, and then assured her that just as she did not die from touching it, so she would be safe if she ate the fruit. Why did Chavah believe the snake and eat the fruit? How could she know that she would not die later in the day? God had promised that they would die *on the day* that they ate the fruit. Ought she not have waited for day's end, to make certain she would not die?

We can raise still another question: God asked Adam why he had eaten from the fruit, and Adam answered that his wife had given it to him. What kind of answer is that? If his wife had given it to him, did that make him guiltless? God Himself had forbidden the fruit to him.

Ramban writes that Adam said to God, "You gave me a wife to help me, so I thought that I must do whatever she asks me.

Therefore, I ate what she gave me." Was Adam so stupid that he listened to his wife after God had forbidden him to eat?

The answer is that Adam and Chavah thought that God had forbidden them to eat of the Tree of Knowledge only because the Tree stood in a very holy place, where God's spirit rested. The Tree stood in the very center of the Garden, and just as a king's palace customarily is in the center of his kingdom, so God's spirit rested in the center of the Garden. They thought that God had forbidden them to eat of the Tree because while picking its fruit they would of course touch it, and the real prohibition was *touching* the Tree which stood in this holy place. But they felt that if a fruit should fall from the Tree and roll away from the holy area, it would be permissible to eat it, because God would not withhold such a valuable gift from his creations.

This was an error in Adam's understanding of the command, *do not eat from it.* He thought he could not eat directly from the Tree but he could eat the fruit that fell down. This explains why the woman said to the snake, *from the fruits of the Tree which is in the midst of the Garden,* meaning, from the Tree which is in the center of the Garden: it is forbidden only because it is in the center of the Garden. And that is why the woman told the snake that God had forbidden them to touch the Tree. According to her understanding the woman did not lie: she simply misunderstood.

The snake told her that she was mistaken, and that God had forbidden them the fruit because He did not want to share its extraordinary properties, for it would make them like angels. The woman believed him. We see this from the words, וַתֵּרֶא הָאִשָּׁה כִּי טוֹב הָעֵץ — *and the woman saw that the Tree was good* (3:6). She saw that it was a good Tree which God would not share with man. Adam did not think this way, but continued to believe that the place was very holy, and that this was the reason that the fruit was forbidden. Therefore he told God that he had not been near the Tree at all. His wife had picked the fruit and had given it to him, so he was not guilty. Because he did not sin maliciously, God spared him and he did not die. Chavah, too, was not put to death, so that Adam would not remain alone.

Toldos Yitzchak gives another explanation. Adam complained to God: "You forbade me the fruit of the Tree before I had a wife, for it would give me desires. But now You have given me a wife, and a commandment to have children. My wife therefore gave me the fruit so that I would desire her, and that is why I ate."

Another explanation is that Adam defended himself by saying, "You gave me a wife to help me. She was to allow me the time to learn the Torah by cooking and baking, and taking care of our house. I should not always have to ask her if she is abiding by the laws of *kashrus:* I must have faith in her. She gave me the fruit, and I was not obligated to ask her what sort of fruit it was. I believed that it was a permitted fruit."

◆§ To Cause a Man to Sin

וַיֹּאמֶר ה' אֱלֹהִים לָאִשָּׁה מַה זֹּאת עָשִׂית — *And God said to the woman, "What is this that you have done?"* (3:13). Though God had not forbidden Chavah to eat the fruit He nevertheless asked her this question, for she was made from Adam's very body.

God first confronted Adam and Chavah, and afterwards cursed and punished them, but He did not even ask the snake for an explanation. He did not want to hear his excuses. From this our Sages learn that one who causes another to sin is punished more harshly than the sinner himself.

◆§ The Snake's Desire

עַל גְּחֹנְךָ תֵלֵךְ ... וְאֵיבָה אָשִׁית בֵּינְךָ וּבֵין הָאִשָּׁה וּבֵין זַרְעֲךָ וּבֵין זַרְעָהּ — *Upon your belly you shall crawl ... and I will put hatred between you and the woman, and between your children and hers ...* (3:14-15). God sent angels to chop off the snake's feet. The snake had desired Chavah and he tried to persuade her to give Adam the forbidden fruit, so that he would die. The snake thought that she would offer Adam the fruit first, and after Adam ate he would take the fruit away from her. He spoke to Chavah rather than Adam because women are more easily persuaded, and once she was convinced she would easily persuade her husband to eat.

◆§ Pains in Pregnancy and Childbirth

הַרְבָּה אַרְבֶּה עִצְּבוֹנֵךְ וְהֵרֹנֵךְ בְּעֶצֶב תֵּלְדִי בָנִים — *I will surely increase your pain and your childbearing; in pain shall you bear children ...* (3:16). Women were cursed with three things. Their pregnancy is painful; during childbirth they feel still more pain; and they are burdened with the curse of Chavah. All women, rich or poor, are so cursed, because Chavah sinned willfully. But not all men suffer from the curse of Adam.

We often find that rich women suffer more in childbirth and pregnancy, because they do not suffer from Adam's curse — that man must work hard for his daily bread. Women who are forced to work have easier pregnancies because God pities them.

Another kindness which God shows is that although woman is cursed in that she must obey her husband as a servant obeys his master, still she does not dislike him. God has made her love her husband, despite the fact that he rules over her. We see this in the words, וְאֶל אִישֵׁךְ תְּשׁוּקָתֵךְ – *Your desire will be towards your husband* (3:16).

R' Berachiah and R' Simon say in the name of R' Shimon Bar Yochai, that when a woman gives birth she vows in her heart never to have marital relations with her husband again, because of the pain of childbirth. Therefore, when she ends her confinement, she must bring a sacrifice to atone for this vow. Nowadays, when we have no *Beis HaMikdash*, it is customary to call her husband to the Torah when his wife ends her confinement, as an atonement for her vow.

⋖§ The Food is Cursed

וְאָכַלְתָּ אֶת עֵשֶׂב הַשָּׂדֶה – *And you shall eat the grass of the field* (3:18). Before they sinned they ate vegetables from the Garden. From the time they sinned they were forbidden to eat from the Garden, but could eat only that which grew in the fields.

בְּזֵעַת אַפֶּיךָ תֹּאכַל לֶחֶם – *By the sweat of your brow will you eat bread* (3:19). Had they not sinned they could have eaten wheat without grinding it and it would have been as good and healthy as bread.

⋖§ The Dangers of Talkativeness

וַיִּקְרָא הָאָדָם שֵׁם אִשְׁתּוֹ חַוָּה – *And Adam called his wife Chavah* (3:20). This is difficult to understand. He had previously named her *ishah* ("woman") because she came from *ish* ("man"). But because she had made him sin, he did not want to emphasize his relationship to her, so he renamed her Chavah, which means she was the life of the entire world (from the word *chai*, "alive"), for all of mankind comes from her. The name Chavah can also be derived from the root (חוה) meaning to speak, for women have nine measures of speech: because she talked too much with the snake she ultimately sinned.

⋖§ The First Garments

וַיַּעַשׂ ה׳ אֱלֹהִים לְאָדָם וּלְאִשְׁתּוֹ כָּתְנוֹת עוֹר וַיַּלְבִּשֵׁם – *God made for Adam and his wife garments of skin and clothed them* (3:21). God dressed them in coats of skin covered with pictures of all the various beasts and animals. Adam gave the coats to Cain and when he was killed they became Nimrod's property. Esau took them from Nimrod, and when Yaakov went to Yitzchak for the blessing he wore these garments. Even though they had sinned against God, He still felt compassion for them; He made them clothes and dressed them.

⋖§ Adam Leaves the Garden

וַיְשַׁלְּחֵהוּ ה׳ אֱלֹהִים מִגַּן עֵדֶן לַעֲבֹד אֶת הָאֲדָמָה אֲשֶׁר לֻקַּח מִשָּׁם וַיְגָרֶשׁ אֶת הָאָדָם – *And God exiled him from the Garden of Eden to work the land from which he was taken. And he drove out the man* (3:23-24). God had to trick Adam into leaving the Garden for he would not have left willingly, even if faced with all kinds of deaths. God said to Adam, "You must work the land which is outside of the Garden for from there you were taken, as well as the Garden itself." Adam left Eden to work the land, thinking he would return, but God locked its gates so that he could not come back. And וַיַּשְׁכֵּן מִקֶּדֶם לְגַן עֵדֶן אֶת הַכְּרֻבִים — *He stationed the angels at the east of the Garden of Eden* (3:24). God put punishing angels at the entrance. They held swords in their hands to make certain that no creature entered the Garden.

◄§ Children for the Torah

וְהָאָדָם יָדַע אֶת חַוָּה אִשְׁתּוֹ — *Adam knew Chavah, his wife* (4:1). When Adam was still in the Garden he had marital relations with his wife Chavah. When he saw that the Garden was locked away from him, and that the gates of Hell remained open, he left his wife, saying that he did not want to have children who were doomed to Hell. But when he saw that after twenty-six generations the Torah would be given to Israel, he returned to his wife in order to procreate. We learn from this how important it is to join with one's wife in order to have children who learn the Torah.

R' Elazar ben Azaryah says: "Three wondrous things came about on that day. On that same day Adam was created, and he cleaved to his wife, and children were born to them."

R' Yehoshua ben Karcha says: "Adam and Chavah lay down as two people, and rose as seven: Adam and Chavah, and Cain with his sister, and Hevel (Abel) with two sisters. Each was born with his mate."

◄§ Cain and Hevel

וַתֹּאמֶר קָנִיתִי אִישׁ אֶת ה' — *She said: "I have acquired a man from God"* (4:1). Chavah said, "I have created a man together with God. Before this, God alone had created, but now my husband and I also have a share in the child."

Three have a share in a child: the father and the mother, and God, who provides the soul.

They had another son, Hevel, who was a shepherd. Their eldest, Cain, worked in the fields. Cain brought fruit as a sacrifice for God, and Hevel brought the best of his sheep. God sent a fire from heaven and burned Hevel's sacrifice, but did not want to accept Cain's sacrifice. Cain's sin was that he ate the best fruits himself, and only brought the poor produce as a sacrifice.

Cain was angry because God rejected his sacrifice. God asked

him, "Why are you angry? Repent and I will forgive you. But if you do not repent you will go to the gates of Gehinnom and stay there. Your evil inclination will seduce you to do wrong, as it says, *Sin crouches at the door"* (4:7).

R' Ami says: "The evil inclination walks in the middle of the street. When he sees a person preoccupied with his appearance, he says, 'You are mine: *I* will teach you a lesson or two!' " Therefore a person should not spend too much time on his appearance and clothes.

◆§ Sibling Rivalry

וַיְהִי בִּהְיוֹתָם בַּשָּׂדֶה — *And it was when they were in the field* (4:8). The two brothers quarreled, and said, "Let us divide the world between us." One said, "The spot where you are standing is mine," and the other said the same; one said, "The Temple will be in my portion," and the other said the same; and they fought. The younger, Hevel, had been born with two sisters. Cain said that he would take the second as his wife, since he was the elder; Hevel said he would take her because he had been born with both.

Hevel threw Cain to the ground and lay on top of him. Cain cried, "We are our parents' only sons; would you kill me?" Hevel got up and let him stand, as it says, *and Cain rose up.* Cain stood up and killed his brother.

Who buried Hevel? R' Eliezer ben Padas says that the kosher birds and animals buried him. God rewarded them by commanding that we make a blessing when we slaughter them, and another blessing when we cover their blood with sand. God repays in kind: because they buried Hevel's blood, we are commanded to cover their blood.

❧ Cursed more than the Earth

דְמֵי אָחִיךְ — *Your brother's blood* (4:10). God asked Cain, "Where is your brother?" Cain answered, "Am I my brother's keeper?" God told him, "You evil one, your brother's blood calls to me from the earth." Significantly, the Hebrew word for "blood" is written here in the plural form, that is to say, "your brother's blood and the blood of those who ought to have descended from him." Others say that it is in the plural because Cain spilled much of Hevel's blood: he wounded him many times because he did not know which wound would prove fatal.

Cain thought that the world was to be built only by Hevel, since God had accepted his sacrifice alone. God said to Cain, "You are cursed more than the earth; it, too, is cursed, because it soaked up Hevel's blood. When you work the earth you will get few crops. Like a penitent, you will be a ceaseless wanderer."

❧ A Sign for Cain

גָּדוֹל עֲוֹנִי מִנְּשׂוֹא — *My sin is too great for me to bear ...* (4:13). Cain said, "Is my sin so great that I cannot be forgiven? You have driven me away from Your Presence, and whoever finds me will kill me!" R' Yehudah says: "The beasts and animals and birds and the snake as well wanted to take revenge on Cain, but God warned them sternly that vengeance would be taken only in seven generations' time, when Lemech would kill him" (see below, 4:23). וַיָּשֶׂם ה' לְקַיִן אוֹת — *And God set a sign for Cain* (4:15) to show that he should not be killed. R' Yosei says that a horn grew on his forehead. Others say that God put a letter from His name on Cain's forehead so that all would fear him and let him live.

❧ The Power of Repentance

וַיֵּצֵא קַיִן — *And Cain went out* (4:16). Satisfied with his judgment, Cain left. He met Adam, who asked him what the results of the judgment were. Cain answered, "I repented and my punishment was lightened." Distressed, Adam said, "I never realized that the power of repentance is so great." And he said *Psalm* 92 (*Mizmor Shir LeYom HaShabbos*), in which appear the words טוֹב לְהֹדוֹת לַה' — *It is good to praise God.*

❧ Land of Wandering

וַיֵּשֶׁב בְּאֶרֶץ נוֹד קִדְמַת עֵדֶן — *And he lived in the land of Nod, in the east of Eden* (4:16). Cain went to live in the land of Nod, where Adam was living. It was the eastern side of Eden, because the east receives those who repent. Some say that the name of the land of

Nod (from the root נדד — "to wander") indicates that wherever Cain would set foot, the land beneath would shake and tremble, and people would say, "Go away from here: you are the sinner who killed his brother!"

⋖§ Adam and Tzilah; Yaval, Yuval, and Tuval Cain

וַיִּקַּח לוֹ לֶמֶךְ שְׁתֵּי נָשִׁים — *Lemech took to himself two wives* (4:19). It was customary then to take two wives. One would bear children, while the other would be given a potion of herbs to keep her from having children, in order to preserve her beauty. One wife was named Adah (from the root עדה — "to set aside"), and the other Tzilah, because he would spend his time sitting in the shade *(tzeil —* "shade") of her beauty.

Adah had a son called Yaval who was the first to herd animals in the fields. His brother was called Yuval and he was the first to fashion harps and violins. Tzilah, too, gave birth, despite the potion which Lemech gave her. Her son was Tuval Cain, whose name means, "He improved Cain's work." Cain was a murderer and Tuval Cain made swords with which to kill people.

⋖§ Cain's Death

וַיֹּאמֶר לֶמֶךְ לְנָשָׁיו עָדָה וְצִלָּה שְׁמַעַן קוֹלִי — *And Lemech said to his wives: "Adah and Tzilah listen to me ..."* (4:23). Lemech asked his wives to rejoin him. They had left him because he had killed both Cain and Tuval Cain. Lemech was blind and one day Tuval Cain, who used to lead him, saw Cain in the distance and mistook him for a wild animal. He told Lemech to shoot the animal. Lemech took his bow and arrow and shot his forebear Cain. When he realized what he had done he was alarmed and clapped his hands together powerfully. He accidentally hit his son Tuval Cain with his hands, and killed him as well.

His wives left him, and he asked them, "Did I kill anyone maliciously? Cain intentionally killed his brother and yet God forgave him and allowed him to live for seven generations. I, too, ought to be allowed at least as long."

⋖§ To Heaven Alive

וַיִּתְהַלֵּךְ חֲנוֹךְ אֶת הָאֱלֹהִים וְאֵינֶנּוּ — *Chanoch walked with God, and he was no more* (5:24). God took Chanoch (Enoch) to heaven while he was still living. He did not die, because he was very righteous. God took him before his time so that he should not become corrupted by his generation. He took him while he was still alive, so that he could bear witness regarding those who lived before the Flood. God likewise took the prophet Eliyahu (Elijah) while he was still alive, so that he could be a witness for all those who lived after the Flood.

Why does the Torah use the words *and he died* (וַיָּמָת) when speaking of the men who lived from Adam's time until Noach's? This shows that these people were righteous and died in their beds, and not in the Flood. After Noach's time there was no Flood and thus no reason to say the words *and he died*. The Torah simply records that they had sons and daughters, and gives their age.

◄§ Noach: The Builder of the World

וַיּוֹלֶד בֵּן וַיִּקְרָא אֶת שְׁמוֹ נֹחַ — *He had a son and called him Noach* (5:28-29). Noach (Noah) was in the tenth generation after Adam, and the first from whom the world would be built. Only concerning Noach does the Torah state, *and he had a son* (Heb.: *ben*), for this word comes from the same root as does the word "building" *(binyan)* — for the world was built from Noach. He was called Noach, which means "rest" *(menuchah)*. Until Noach's time the earth yielded thorns and briers. Noach constructed a plow to till the earth which then rested from its curse and grew fine crops.

◄§ A Father's Blessings

וַיְהִי כִּי הֵחֵל הָאָדָם לָרֹב עַל פְּנֵי הָאֲדָמָה וּבָנוֹת יֻלְּדוּ לָהֶם — *And it was when men began to multiply on the earth, and daughters were born to them* (6:1). *Midrash Rabbah* writes: "Rabban Gamliel married off his daughter. When she was about to leave her father she came and asked him for his blessing. He said: 'May God grant that you never return to my house.' She asked her beloved father: 'Why did you curse me?' He answered: 'On the contrary! I have blessed you — that you should be so happy in your husband's home that you will not want to return.'

"When his daughter gave birth to a son she asked for his blessing. He said: 'My daughter, I hope you will always be saying the words, "Oh, no!" ' She asked, 'Why did you curse me?' He said, 'Not at all: I have blessed you. May you always care for your son, and always say, Oh, no, I have not fed him yet; Oh, no, I have not brought him to school yet ...' "

R' Shimon's wife gave birth to a daughter. R' Chiya said to him, "God has begun to bless you, as it states, *And it was when man began to multiply and daughters were born to them.* You will have many more children."

◄§ Immorality ...

וַיִּרְאוּ בְנֵי הָאֱלֹהִים אֶת בְּנוֹת הָאָדָם כִּי טֹבֹת הֵנָּה וַיִּקְחוּ לָהֶם נָשִׁים מִכֹּל אֲשֶׁר בָּחָרוּ — *And the sons of God saw that the daughters of man were*

good and they took them for wives, whomever they chose (6:2).
Certain important men saw the beautiful women and took them
away from their husbands to become their wives. Some say these are
actually angels of God, who married the beautiful women.

◄§ ... Leads to Mortality

לֹא יָדוֹן רוּחִי בָאָדָם לְעֹלָם בְּשַׁגַּם הוּא בָשָׂר וְהָיוּ יָמָיו מֵאָה וְעֶשְׂרִים שָׁנָה —
*My spirit shall not be in man forever, for he is also flesh, and his
days shall be one hundred and twenty years* (6:3). God said, ''I
created men with a soul like the angels, but I see that they are only
flesh and blood after all. Their soul does not help them, so I will not
allow them to be immortal like the angels. They will die as the
animals do. But I will let them live for one hundred and twenty years
to give them time to repent. If they do not repent, I will bring the
Flood upon them.''

◄§ Fallen Angels

הַנְּפִלִים הָיוּ בָאָרֶץ — *The giants were on the earth* (6:4). God had cast
the angels from the heavens down to the earth because they had
been evil, and women on earth had borne children from them. These
children were unusually large, and giants descended from them.

וַיִּנָּחֶם ה' — *And God regretted* (6:6). The more common meaning of
this verb is ''to console.'' This verse means that God as it were consoled Himself that He had created man on earth, for if He had
created him in the heavens He would have had to cast him down on
account of his sins; the earth was his proper place.

◄§ A Time to Rejoice and a Time to Grieve

וַיִּתְעַצֵּב אֶל לִבּוֹ — *And it grieved Him in his heart* (6:6). God grieved
that the world would be destroyed. A gentile asked R' Yehoshua ben
Karcha: ''If God knows all, why did He create men, knowing He
would be angry with them?'' R' Yehoshua answered: ''You had a
son and rejoiced when he was born, even though you knew that one
day he must die. Why did you rejoice?'' The gentile answered,
''When it is time to be joyous one should rejoice, and when the time
comes to grieve, one should grieve.'' R' Yehoshua said to him: ''God
too did this. He knew that the righteous would come from man and
for their sake created the wicked too.''

מֵאָדָם עַד בְּהֵמָה — *From man to beast* (6:7). God said when man is
destroyed the beasts, too, must be destroyed, for they were made for
man's sake.

פרשת נח
Parashas Noach
(6:9 — 11:32)

✍§ Noach's Righteousness

אֵלֶּה תּוֹלְדֹת נֹחַ — *These are the generations of Noach* (6:9). Shlomo HaMelech (King Solomon) says, מִתְהַלֵּךְ בְּתֻמּוֹ צַדִּיק אַשְׁרֵי בָנָיו אַחֲרָיו — *The righteous man walks in his integrity; blessed are his sons after him (Mishlei 20:7),* meaning that a man should abide by God's commandments for the sake of God, *leshem shamayim,* and not because of his own pride. We often find men who give charity and afterwards speak of it. They are erring in two ways: they are priding themselves, and they are embarrassing the poor man by announcing that he has accepted their charity. Therefore Shlomo said, *the righteous man walks in his integrity.* One who walks simply, without flattering himself, is righteous and merits to have children as good as he. Shlomo said: רָב אָדָם יִקְרָא אִישׁ חַסְדּוֹ וְאִישׁ אֱמוּנִים מִי יִמְצָא — *Many men will proclaim their own charity, but a faithful man who can find? (Mishlei 20:6).* There are many men who speak of their charity and the good that they have done, but a truly good man is rare.

The righteous have three qualities. When one is righteous he is called a *tzaddik.* When he is even better he is called a *tamim* ("one who is flawless"). The third category is known as walking with God (הִתְהַלְּכוּת). Noach had all three qualities, as it says, נֹחַ אִישׁ צַדִּיק תָּמִים הָיָה ... אֶת הָאֱלֹהִים הִתְהַלֶּךְ נֹחַ — *Noach was a righteous and a whole man; ... Noach walked with God* (6:9). He was a *tzaddik* in his deeds; he was a *tamim,* whole-heartedly good; and he did not question God's actions — he walked with God.

The word Noach is repeated three times because he saw the world when it was built up and populated, and then he saw the world destroyed by the Flood, and finally, he saw the world rebuilt and repopulated.

The Torah says בְּדֹרֹתָיו — *in his generations:* he was righteous *in his time,* when all others were evil; how much greater would he have been had he lived among righteous men! Others say that the opposite is true: in his generation he was considered righteous, but in Avraham's time, he would not have been at all remarkable, because Avraham was more righteous than he. The Torah states that Noach was righteous, and his good deeds saved him from the waters of the Flood.

⇨§ A Corrupt World

כִּי מָלְאָה הָאָרֶץ חָמָס — *For the world was filled with violence* (6:13). The people were all thieves and robbers. Even the animals were corrupt, mating out of their own species. The people worshiped false gods, and the land was full of crime.

It was the thievery which caused God to seal the decree of the Flood. Reason itself dictates that one refrain from theft, even without the Torah's prohibition.

The Flood was brought because men did not want to believe that God could rebuild and refashion the world, and because they did not believe that God watches over mankind, rewarding the righteous and punishing the evildoers. They claimed that God was in heaven and did not care about men's activities here on earth. God sent the Flood and spared Noach and his family to prove that He repays both the righteous and the wicked.

⇨§ Interceding for the World

עֲשֵׂה לְךָ תֵּבַת עֲצֵי גֹפֶר — *Make for yourself an ark of cypress wood* (6:14). God commanded Noach to build a large ark, like a huge ship, and coat it with tar from within and without. Although God could certainly have saved Noach without an ark, He wanted him to construct the ark for one hundred and twenty years, so that the people would ask him what he was doing. When he would tell them of the deluge which God planned, they would perhaps repent.

R' Bechaye asks: Why did Noach not pray that the world be saved from destruction, in the manner that Avraham prayed when God told him of the impending destruction of Sodom and Amorah (Gomorrah)? For Avraham prayed repeatedly for those evildoers, and all the prophets likewise prayed for their respective generations.

Once it was discerned that there were not even ten good men in Sodom, Avraham ceased praying. So too Noach saw that there were not even ten righteous men in his generation, and therefore he could not pray for them. Another reason that Noach did not pray is that God had warned them of the coming of the Flood for one hundred and twenty years, and they had ignored this warning.

The author of *Toldos Yitzchak* explains Noach's silence by saying that though he was good to man, he was lacking in his faith in God.

He did not really believe that God would bring a Flood: he thought that God was only trying to frighten the people into repentance.

⇜ The Ark

וְזֶה אֲשֶׁר תַּעֲשֶׂה אֹתָהּ — *And this is how you shall make it* (6:15). God commanded that the ark be built 300 cubits long, with a window for illumination. There were three floors: the top floor for the people; the middle floor for the animals, beasts and birds; and the bottom for the waste products.

וַהֲקִמֹתִי אֶת בְּרִיתִי אִתָּךְ — *I shall establish My covenant with you* (6:18). God assured Noach that the fruit and wheat which he brought with him into the ark would not spoil and that the evildoers would not kill him on account of the ark. Noach was obliged to bring aboard enough food and drink for all the creatures.

⇜ Temperate Praise

כִּי אֹתְךָ רָאִיתִי צַדִּיק לְפָנַי — *For I have seen you righteous before me* (7:1). God told Noach, "You alone are righteous in your generation." He did not call him *tamim* ("flawless") when speaking directly to him (though earlier the Torah describes him as both righteous and *tamim*). This teaches us that one should not praise a person fully in his presence. God told him to take seven pairs of kosher animals and birds, to sacrifice at the end of the journey.

The Torah writes *man and wife* when speaking of animals, for they bear children in the same manner as humans. In speaking of birds, however, it says *male and female*, for birds do not bear children in the way that humans do. Rather, they lay eggs which hatch.

⇜ Clean Speech: Pure Soul

וּמִן הַבְּהֵמָה אֲשֶׁר לֹא טְהֹרָה הִיא — *And of every animal which is not clean* (7:2). Our Sages ask why the Torah used extra words to describe impure animals. It ought to have called them "impure" rather than "animals which are not clean." The Torah wants to teach us that we should not speak of disgusting things if we can avoid this by speaking pleasantly. The Torah did not want to use the word *tamei* ("unclean") because it is not pure language and therefore described these animals as "not *tahor*" (*tahor* — "clean"). A man should avoid using disgusting language, for it soils the soul.

⇜ The Flood

כִּי לְיָמִים עוֹד שִׁבְעָה — *For in seven more days* (7:4). God put off the Flood for seven days so that they could properly mourn for

Mesushelach (Methuselah), a righteous man who had just died.

The *Gemara*, in Tractate *Zevachim*, says that everything created was in the ark. But how could a *re'em* (an animal of huge proportions, mentioned in the Torah and Talmud) fit into it? The Sages say that Noach tied the animal by the horns to the exterior of the ark. The *Gemara* then asks: R' Chisda said that the waters of the Flood were burning hot. How did the *re'em* survive without being burned? The *Gemara* answers: The water surrounding the ark remained cold. That was how Og, King of Bashan, survived. He, too, hung onto the exterior of the ark. (See below, 7:23.)

אָנֹכִי מַמְטִיר עַל הָאָרֶץ — *I will cause rain to fall on the earth* (7:4). The rain continued for forty days and forty nights.

מִפְּנֵי מֵי הַמַּבּוּל — *Because of the flood waters* (7:7). This means that Noach boarded the ark because of the great deluge. He still thought that God would not bring a flood and he did not go into the ark until forced to by the onrushing water.

בָּאוּ אֶל נֹחַ — *They came to Noach* (7:9). All the animals came to Noach of their own free will. Those whom the ark accepted were saved. The rain began falling gently to give the people time to repent. God saw that they did not repent, so He sent a deluge of hot water and they were burned.

בְּעֶצֶם הַיּוֹם הַזֶּה — *On that very day* (7:13). This means that Noach went into the ark in the middle of the day. The wicked folk said to themselves, "When Noach boards the ark we will attack him, so that he dies with us." God said, "I will take him in broad daylight into the ark, safely, despite their plans."

Noach

⋅§ Twelve Sunless Months

וַיִּסְגֹּר ה' בַּעֲדוֹ — *God shut him in* (7:16). God protected him from the water and from the wicked men who wanted to harm him. Some of our Sages say that God did not allow the sun, moon, and stars to shine for all twelve months that Noach was in the ark. How was Noach able to see anything? God gave him a marvelous stone which gave forth illumination.

When the evil men saw that there was no hope for them they wanted to overturn the ark. God sent lions and bears and other wild beasts to kill them.

וַיִּגְבְּרוּ הַמַּיִם — *The waters prevailed* (7:18). The waters increased for a hundred and fifty days.

חֲמֵשׁ עֶשְׂרֵה אַמָּה מִלְמַעְלָה — *Fifteen cubits upward* (7:20). The waters at first were level with the mountaintops and then they rose above the mountains for fifteen cubits.

⋅§ Death of All Living Things

כֹּל אֲשֶׁר נִשְׁמַת רוּחַ חַיִּים בְּאַפָּיו — *All that had the breath of life in its nostrils* (7:22). From here we learn that when one dies the soul leaves through the nostrils, just as God breathed life into Adam's nostrils.

God let the animals, beasts and birds perish before man. Just as he was created last, so he died last. God did this to give man more time to repent. In the *Gemara*, Tractate *Berachos*, it says the opposite: "R' Ami says that man perished first, as we see in the verse, וַיִּמַח אֶת כָּל הַיְקוּם אֲשֶׁר עַל פְּנֵי הָאֲדָמָה מֵאָדָם עַד בְּהֵמָה — *And He destroyed*

The Flood

every living thing which was on the face of the earth, from man to beast ... (7:23). Man is mentioned before the beasts.

מִכֹּל אֲשֶׁר בֶּחָרָבָה מֵתוּ — *Whatever was on the land died* (7:22). Only the fish survived. They fled to the ocean which encircles the entire world.

✥ The Only Survivors

וַיִּשָּׁאֶר אַךְ נֹחַ — *Only Noach was left* (7:23). Only Noach and his family survived. The Sages say that Og, King of Bashan, also survived by hanging onto a plank under the ark's roof. Noach carved a hole in the ark and gave Og food through it, for Og had sworn never to harm Noach's children.

Why does it say "only Noach?" The word "only" indicates a lessening. Once, when Noach was slow in feeding the lion, it attacked him and he lost blood.

וַיִּזְכֹּר אֱלֹהִים אֶת נֹחַ — *God remembered Noach* (8:1). God remembered Noach, and the beasts and animals, and the waters began to settle and recede. R' Bechaye asks why the birds are not mentioned here. The answer is that the beasts and animals were created on the sixth day together with man, so they were remembered together with man.

✥ The Rains Stop; The Waters Recede

וַתָּנַח הַתֵּבָה — *The ark came to rest* (8:4). On the 17th day of the month of Sivan the ark came to rest on top of Mount Ararat. *Ramban* writes: "At first it rained for forty days. Each day the water grew deeper, until it rose fifteen cubits higher than all of the mountains. The wellsprings and windows of Heaven all opened.

"For one hundred and fifty days the water was very strong. Afterwards God sent a wind to plug up the springs and the windows of Heaven. The ark stood in water two or three cubits deep until Rosh Chodesh Tammuz (the first day of the month of Tammuz), when they could see the mountaintops. By the tenth day of the month of Av, Noach opened the window in the ark. After three more weeks he sent the dove to see if the earth was dry, and after thirty days he opened the roof of the ark."

✥ The Raven; For the Sake of Eliyahu

וַיְשַׁלַּח אֶת הָעֹרֵב — *And he sent a raven* (8:7). Noach sent the raven to see if the water had receded. The raven refused to fly off. He said: "There are just two of us in the ark, a male and a female. My species will perish forever if I am destroyed.

Noach did not want to take the raven back into the ark, because the raven could not be eaten, for it is not kosher, and it could not be sacrificed, for it is not pure. But God told Noach to bring him in, for he had been destined for an important mission. In the days of the prophet Eliyahu (Elijah), when Eliyahu was hiding from King Achav (Ahab) in a cave, the raven brought him meat and bread from the palace of Yehoshafat, King of Yehudah.

◄§ The Dove

וַיְשַׁלַּח אֶת הַיּוֹנָה מֵאִתּוֹ — *And he sent the dove from him* (8:8). R' Bechaye asks why the words *from him* do not appear in connection with the raven, but only when discussing the dove. This shows that the kosher animals stayed with Noach in his room, but the unkosher animals were kept apart.

◄§ A Bitter Leaf from God

וְהִנֵּה עֲלֵה זַיִת טָרָף בְּפִיהָ — *And there was an olive leaf, plucked, in her mouth* (8:11). The dove flew back with an olive leaf in her mouth. It is difficult to understand where the dove could have taken the branch from, if all of the trees of the earth had been uprooted during the Flood. The answer is that no rain actually fell over *Eretz Yisrael*. The flood waters from the other lands flowed into it, but the trees were not destroyed.

Other Sages say that the dove brought a leaf from the Garden of Eden, but this is even more difficult to understand. How could Noach have known that the water had receded from the earth if the olive leaf had come from the Garden of Eden, where there had been no Flood at all? *Ramban* writes that the gates of Eden were locked during the Flood so that the waters would not flow into it, and when the waters had receded the gates were opened, so that the dove could fly in.

She could have taken a branch from a finer tree, but she purposely took an olive leaf, which is bitter to the taste, to show that it is better to eat a bitter leaf sent from the hand of God than sweet fruit given by man.

◄§ Permission to Leave

יָבְשָׁה הָאָרֶץ — *The earth was dry* (8:14). Noach and his household did not leave the ark, even when the earth was dry. He said, "God commanded that I enter the ark, so I shall not leave it without His permission." *Sefer HaYashar* writes that after Noach opened the window of the ark God told him not to go out until a full year had passed.

Chananiah, Mishael and Azariah learned a lesson from this incident. When Nebuchadnezzar commanded that they be thrown into a fiery pit, God miraculously caused the pit to become level with the ground. But they did not want to leave without Nebuchadnezzar's permission for it was he who had commanded that they enter.

צֵא מִן הַתֵּבָה אַתָּה וְאִשְׁתְּךָ וּבָנֶיךָ וּנְשֵׁי בָנֶיךָ אִתָּךְ — *Leave the ark — you and your wife, and your sons and your sons' wives* (8:16). Now God told them to go back to live with their wives. Thus the Torah mentions Noach and his wife and his sons and their wives. When they entered the ark the Torah mentioned husbands and wives separately, for in the ark they were forbidden to live together. All of the other creatures, too, were forbidden likewise. Three pairs did live together. The first was Cham, Noach's son. God cursed him and all of his children were black. The second that lived with its mate was the dog, and the third the raven, and they, too, were cursed.

◄§ Noach Fears for His Children

וַיֵּצֵא נֹחַ וּבָנָיו — *And Noach and his sons went out* (8:18). One may ask: God told Noach to go out together with his wife, that is to say, to live with her once again. Yet in this verse it mentions the women and men separately, indicating a separation of the sexes. The answer is that Noach did not want to live with his wife, for three reasons. The first was that since he feared that another Flood would destroy everything, he did not want to bring more children into the world. In answer to this God swore to him that He would never bring about another Flood.

The second was that Noach was afraid that the wild beasts would kill his children. From the time that Adam and his descendants sinned, God had permitted the beasts to prey on man. For the beast can argue, "If humans do not observe the Torah, how are they superior to me?" Therefore God told Noach that he did not have to fear, for He would put a dread of man into the beasts. Immediately before the verse *and your dread ... will be on the animals* (9:2) come the words *God blessed Noach and said, "Be fruitful and multiply"* — you can have children without the fear of animals and beasts.

The third reason was that Noach thought to himself that his children would do wrong and ultimately kill each other. Therefore God said, *Surely your blood ...* — when one murders another I will take revenge upon the murderer.

◄§ Companion of His Youth

כִּי יֵצֶר לֵב הָאָדָם רַע מִנְּעֻרָיו — *For the inclination of man's heart is evil from his youth* (8:21). God said, "I will never again destroy all of mankind at once because the evil inclination is with a man from the moment he is born, while the inclination towards goodness first develops in a man when he is thirteen years old. Man has great problems dealing with his evil inclination because of this, for he grew up with it from youth. The inclination towards goodness is just a guest, and so finds difficulty in challenging the evil inclination."

◄§ At the Mercy of the Seasons

עד כָּל יְמֵי הָאָרֶץ זֶרַע וְקָצִיר וְקֹר וָחֹם — *As long as the earth lasts, seed time and harvest, and cold and heat ...* (8:22). God said: "There will be a time for man to plant and a time to harvest; a time of cold and a time of heat; a season of summer and a season of winter. These will never cease, and I will not destroy all of mankind at once, as I did during the Flood. Nevertheless, men will be born and men will die." Hence, the verse states that there will be harvest and planting, that is, man will be born and will die. How will he die? Through heat and cold, as it says *cold and heat*. When seasons change it is a time of illness. We fast on the Monday, Thursday, and Monday following Succos and Pesach (the festivals of Tabernacles and Passover) for this is the time that summer passes into winter, and vice-versa, and the weather changes. We fast at these times and pray that the changes in the weather will not make us ill.

The author of *Toldos Yitzchak* writes that the verse means to tell us that God said, "I will not bring down another Flood, but I will curse mankind with cold and heat. The heat will burn the grain and the cold will stunt its growth."

◄§ Meat-eating Permitted

וְאַךְ אֶת דִּמְכֶם — *But your blood* (9:5). God told Noach that he would take note and avenge the blood of any of his offspring if they were killed not only by other humans but also by their prey while hunting for food — for God had allowed Noach (unlike Adam) to eat the meat of animals. And this is why the Torah says, וּמוֹרַאֲכֶם וְחִתְּכֶם יִהְיֶה עַל כָּל חַיַּת הָאָרֶץ — *The fear of you and the dread of you shall be upon all the beasts of the earth* (9:2).

◄§ God has Many Agents

מִיַּד כָּל חַיָּה אֶדְרְשֶׁנּוּ — *From the hand of every beast will I require it* (9:5). When a beast murders a man God will kill the beast. We can ask, does the beast have the intelligence that makes it deserving of punishment? This is the meaning: God says that when a man murders another I will avenge him through a beast. I will send a wild animal to kill the murderer.

◄§ Four Types of Murder

מִיַּד כָּל חַיָּה ... וּמִיַּד הָאָדָם מִיַּד אִישׁ אָחִיו — *At the hand of every beast ... and at the hand of man, from the hand of every man's brother ...* (9:5). We can ask why it says the words *beast, man,* and *man's brother.* The Torah teaches us that there are four ways a man can be murdered. The first is when he kills himself, and on this the verse says, *and surely your blood of your lives* ... — one who kills himself will be punished. The second is when a man sends a wild dog or animal to kill another, and on this the Torah says, *at the hand of every beast will I require it,* meaning, one who murders another by means of a wild beast will be punished. The third is when a man sends a servant to murder another, and on this the Torah says, *at the hand of man,* meaning, whoever murders one by sending a messenger will be punished; and the fourth is when one actually murders someone else, and on this the Torah writes: *Whoever sheds the blood of man* ... meaning, that whoever actually murders another will be murdered himself.

◄§ The Promise of the Rainbow

אֶת קַשְׁתִּי נָתַתִּי בֶּעָנָן — *I have set my bow in the cloud* (9:13). God told Noach: "I will give you a sign that I will keep my promise never to bring another Flood on the entire world. When mankind will be evil I will bring rain and place a rainbow in the sky to show them that they deserve that I should let the rain fall until they are all drowned, but I will keep My promise and spare them." The rainbow stands with its high point facing away from man to show that God made peace and does not want to harm us.

When there are great *tzaddikim,* righteous men, in a generation, then a rainbow is not seen in the sky, for *tzaddikim* protect their generation. Hence, there was no rainbow in the days of King Chizkiyahu (Hezekiah), nor in the days of R' Shimon bar Yochai, nor in the days of R' Yehoshua ben Levi.

◄§ Wine in Excess

וַיָּחֶל נֹחַ ... וַיִּטַּע כָּרֶם — *And Noach began ... and planted a vineyard* (9:20). Noach planted a vineyard with vines which he had taken with him in the ark. The Torah wrote of the planting of the vineyard immediately after the rainbow to show us that just as a rainbow shows that man is evil, so one who drinks too much wine will find that only evil can result, as King Shlomo said: לְמִי אוֹי לְמִי אֲבוֹי — *To whom, alas; to whom, alack* (Mishlei 23:29) — one who drinks wine and other alcoholic beverages will become unhealthy. Because of this, in earlier generations they added water to their wine when making a blessing over a goblet, for their wine was very strong. They wanted to show that the undiluted wine was not permitted for a blessing because only evil could result from it.

This is why in writing *And Noach began*, the Torah uses the word וַיָּחֶל (from the root חלל — "to profane"), meaning that holiness left Noach, because he had drunk too much. Despite the fact that he was such a *tzaddik* that he ensured the continuity of the entire world through his righteousness, when he was drunk he lay naked and as a result his children sinned and were cursed. The Torah uses thirteen *vavin* (sing. *vav*, sixth letter of the *alef-beis*) in connection with Noach's wine, to teach us that even a man who, because of his righteousness, deserves to be rewarded by going to the Garden of Eden, in which there are thirteen rivers of fine oil, and in which there are thirteen steps awaiting the righteous — even such a man will be exiled from these thirteen levels if he drinks too much wine.

It is written in *Midrash Rabbah* that when Noach went to plant the vineyard a demon approached him and offered to go into a partnership with him. "But," the demon warned, "make certain not to drink too much of the wine or I will harm you." Therefore when a man is very drunk the demon enters him and causes him to do all manner of evil.

R' Chiya bar R' Abba says: "On that day Noach planted the vineyard, and on that same day he drank the wine, and on that same day he did much wrong and was no longer holy."

וַיִּתְגַּל בְּתוֹךְ אָהֳלֹה — *And he was uncovered in his tent* (9:21). Because of the wine he lay naked. The word *vayisgal* is used for "was uncovered", from the root גלה, whose alternative meaning is "exile" (*galus*) — to show that because of an excess of wine his children were exiled. The Ten Tribes were exiled from *Eretz Yisrael* only because they had drunk wine too freely and as a result had done much evil, as it states, הַשֹּׁתִים בְּמִזְרְקֵי יַיִן — *They that drink wine in bowls* (Amos 6:6). And the tribes of Yehudah and Binyamin were also exiled because of wine, as it states, וְגַם אֵלֶּה בַּיַּיִן שָׁגוּ וּבַשֵּׁכָר תָּעוּ — *and these also were crazed with wine and erred with strong drink* (Yeshayahu 28:7).

◄§ Zeal is Rewarded

וַיַּרְא חָם אֲבִי כְנַעַן — *And Cham, the father of Canaan, saw* (9:22). Canaan, Cham's son, saw Noach lying naked, and told his father. Cham went to see his father and then told his brothers Shem and Yefes. They all mocked their father, but Shem immediately took a garment and covered his father, and Yefes then helped Shem cover him. Because of this, Shem's descendants were given the commandment of *tzitzis*, which are worn on clothing. Because he helped Shem cover his father, the children of Yefes will be covered in proper burial in the days of Gog and Magog. Gog and Magog will come from Yefes and will fight Israel in the days of the *Mashiach*. They will be killed by him, but will be buried.

When two people do a good deed, but one puts more effort and zeal into it, he receives a better reward. Because Shem hastened to cover his father and Yefes followed him, Shem was granted a richer reward than Yefes. And because Cham shamed his father and did not cover him, his descendants were shamed by falling into the hands of the King of Assyria, who led them naked before the eyes of the nations into captivity.

When Noach awoke from his stupor, he became aware of what Cham had done. He cursed Cham's fourth son Canaan with servitude. When they left the ark God had blessed them all, including Cham, so Noach did not curse Cham, but rather his son, Canaan.

◄§ Noach's Years and Posterity

וַיְחִי נֹחַ אַחַר הַמַּבּוּל שְׁלשׁ מֵאוֹת שָׁנָה וַחֲמִשִּׁים שָׁנָה — *And Noach lived three hundred and fifty years after the flood* (9:28). Noach lived for six hundred years before the Flood; he thus lived a total of nine hundred and fifty years.

וְאֵלֶּה תּוֹלְדֹת בְּנֵי נֹחַ — *And these are the generations of Noach's sons* (10:1). The Torah names seventy male descendants of Noach and from these came the seventy languages. They are mentioned so that we will know from whom Avraham is descended — from Shem.

Ramban writes that the Torah shows us that Avraham was a witness to the fact that God created the world. Avraham was fifty-eight years old when Noach died, and had spoken with him personally. Noach had told him of his father Lemech, who had seen and spoken with Adam, who had been created by God alone.

Avraham told this to Yitzchak (Isaac) and Yaakov (Jacob). Further, Yitzchak and Yaakov had seen Shem, who had been in the ark and who attested to the Flood. Yaakov in turn passed this on to his children. The text lists the names of Shem and his children to show this to us.

◄§ The Tower of Defiance

הוּא הָיָה גִבֹּר צַיִד — *He (Nimrod) was a mighty hunter* (10:9). Nimrod would ensnare people with his words and incite them to rebel against God in the time of the Tower of Babel. Because of this, when describing someone evil and brazen, people used to say, "as insolent as Nimrod."

Pirkei deR' Eliezer writes in the name of R' Yehudah: "Noach took the cloak, which God had made for Adam, with him into the ark. Afterwards, he gave it to Nimrod. When Nimrod put the cloak on, all of the animals and beasts and birds flocked to him and bowed down, because there were pictures of all the creatures drawn on the coat. As a result everyone thought that he was a mighty man and he was crowned king."

He said, "Let us build a gigantic tower to the sky." They built it twenty-seven miles high. There were stairs on both the eastern and western sides of the tower. Those carrying bricks up climbed up on the eastern stairway, and when they descended they used the western stairway, in order to avoid colliding with each other. When a person fell off and was killed they did not mourn, for there were many thousands to carry the bricks; but when a brick fell down they were greatly distressed and said, "Where can we find another brick to replace this one?" Avraham laughed at them. They told him, "Why should God be king in heaven and leave us on earth? We will climb up and battle him and then we, too, will be kings." They placed an idol on the top of the tower and put a sword in its hand, so all the world supposed that the idol was battling God.

Midrash Rabbah writes that the builders of the Tower became evil because they were too wealthy, and had too much of everything. R' Levi says that a woman was pregnant and gave birth within three days; the other Sages say, in one day. On the day of its birth the child walked and had enough intelligence to go wherever he was sent.

Why was the generation of the Flood destroyed while the generation of the Tower was not? Because the people at the time of the Flood were thieves and robbers, but the men who built the Tower loved each other, and were at peace among themselves.

Rebbe (R' Yehudah haNasi) says: "How great is peace! When Israel serves false gods, but are at peace among themselves, God says, 'I can do nothing against them.' "

The generation of the Tower said to themselves, "After one thousand six hundred and fifty-six years, the sky becomes weak. We must build four great pillars, one on each side, for the sky to lean upon, so that it will not collapse."

They said, "We will build a tower to heaven and climb up and cut out huge windows in the sky so that the water will drain out, and God will never be able to bring another Flood."

R' Yirmeyah says: "There were three types of people. One type said, 'We will climb to the sky and live there;' God took these and spread them over the entire world. The second group said, 'We will serve idols in the sky'; God confused their language. The third group said, 'We will battle God in heaven'; God cursed this group and changed them into monkeys, cats, and all manner of demons."

R' Yochanan says: "One third of the Tower was burned, one third sank into the earth, and one third remained standing."

לֹא יִבָּצֵר מֵהֶם — *Nothing will be withheld from them* (11:6). This means that they had succeeded in their construction — and this was why they were scattered.

◄§ A Confusion of Tongues

וְנָבְלָה שָׁם שְׂפָתָם — *And there confuse their speech* (11:7). *Pirkei deR' Eliezer* says: God told the seventy angels who surround His holy throne, "Let us go down and confuse them with seventy languages." God made a lottery, and each angel picked one nation and language. God's lot fell to Avraham and his children, as it states, כִּי חֵלֶק ה' עַמּוֹ — *God's portion is His nation* (*Devarim* 32:9).

Because they had sinned with their speech, by saying, "Let us build a tower," God confused their speech. Until this time all of them spoke the Holy Tongue (Hebrew), with which the world had been created. Now, when one would ask for a hammer, the other would bring him a different tool because he could not understand what he was saying. Therefore the construction could not go on.

וַיָּפֶץ ה' אֹתָם — *God scattered them* (11:8). R' Nechemiah says: "God brought all of the lands to Babel and each land swallowed up its nation." The Rabbis say that God overwhelmed them in the waters of the sea, and only thirty families were allowed to live.

◄§ Living on in One's Descendants

אֵלֶּה תּוֹלְדֹת שֵׁם — *These are the generations of Shem* (11:10). Why does the Torah say here how long each person lived, without mentioning that each one died, as it does when listing the generations from Adam until Noach? The answer is that the kingdom of David and the *Mashiach* come from Shem. The *Mashiach* is immortal, as it says, *Life he asked of You; You gave him eternal length of days* (*Tehillim* 21:5) — so the Torah does not state that they died. Also, it does not say that Noach and his sons died because the world is descended from them, while the generations between Adam and Noach were all destroyed in the Flood. Further, the generations between Adam and Noach lived for a very long time. It says in regard to them that they died, that is to say, they had lived long enough. But the generations after Noach did not live long, and so it does not say that they died.

◄§ The Folly of Idolatry

וַיָּמָת הָרָן עַל פְּנֵי תֶּרַח אָבִיו בְּאֶרֶץ מוֹלַדְתּוֹ בְּאוּר כַּשְׂדִּים — *Haran died, in the presence of his father Terach, in the land of his birth, Ur Casdim* (11:28). How could the Torah proceed to tell us how God spoke to Avram without first telling us what self-sacrifice made him deserving of such a privilege? For Avram allowed himself to be thrown into the fiery pit for the sake of God. His father Terach was a merchant of idols, and wanted Avram to sell them for him. A person came in to buy an idol, and Avram asked him his age. He answered that he was, say, fifty or sixty years old, whereupon Avram said, "You poor man! You are sixty years old, and yet you want to worship an idol which is less than one day old, one that was just made today!" Embarrassed, the man left.

One day a woman came with a bowl of oatmeal to leave as an offering for the idols. Avram took the bowl and placed it in front of them. He then took a large stick and broke them all, leaving just one large idol intact, and placed the stick in its hand.

Terach arrived and asked Avram who had done the damage. Avram said that a woman had brought the oatmeal as a sacrifice. The idols quarreled among themselves, for each wanted to eat it first. The largest then took a stick and broke all the others. Terach said to Avram, "Do these idols have any intelligence, or any life in them?" Avram answered, "If they do not have any intelligence, why should we worship them?"

Terach handed him over to Nimrod, who told him that if he did not worship the fire he would be thrown into a fiery pit. Avram's brother Haran was standing by and said to himself, "I will see if Avram is saved from the fire. If he is, I will serve his God, and if he is not, I will serve the gods of Nimrod."

When Avram came out safely they asked Haran whom he wished to worship. He answered, "The God of Avram." They then threw him into the fire. He was burned and died. An angel came and cast him out of the flames in front of his father. This is the meaning of the verse, *Haran died in the presence of his father.* Haran died because of his father's actions. If Terach had not complained to Nimrod about Avram, Haran would not have been thrown into the fire. We learn from this that a man should not rely on a miracle. When he must sacrifice himself for God he should not think that God will save him miraculously. If he relies on a miracle he has not really given his body for God's sake, so God will not save him.

Because Haran saw a miracle wrought for Avram he allowed Nimrod's men to throw him into the fire — so God did not save him. As our Sages have told us, אֵין סוֹמְכִין עַל הַנֵּס — "One does not rely on a miracle."

◆§ The Barren Matriarch

וַתְּהִי שָׂרַי עֲקָרָה — *Sarai was barren* (11:30). If the Torah says that Avram's wife Sarai was barren, we know that she had no children; why does it repeat that she had no child? The answer is that there are many women who cannot have children but after many years they finally give birth. The Torah tells us that Sarai could not have had children, even after many years. Avram and Sarai therefore decided to leave their land for Canaan, which is a holy land, in the hope that they would have children there.

Avram was a nobleman, and the master over his father's house. When he began to leave Canaan, they all made plans to accompany him. But Avram showed his respect for his father Terach and appointed him as master even over himself, and thus it states, *Terach took Avram his son and Lot the son of Haran* (11:31).

◆§ Father and Son

וַיָּמָת תֶּרַח בְּחָרָן — *Terach died in Charan* (11:32). Though until this point the Torah does not write of the death of Shem's children, why does it now tell us of Terach's death? The Sages answer: So that people should not say that Avram abandoned his father's and mother's land and left them, as it states, *Go away from your country, and your birthplace*. First the Torah says, *and Terach died*, and afterwards it says, *Go away from your country*, so that it should not be thought that Avram did not respect his father.

This was the first of the ten great tests of faith; the last test was the *Akedah*, the binding of Yitzchak. The two tests resembled each other; as we see that here the Torah says, *Go away from your country*, and before the *Akedah*, God likewise commands Avraham, *Go away to the land of Moriah*. This teaches us that a man would rather be killed than leave his homeland and family.

But if Terach was in fact still alive, why does the Torah say that *Terach died*? Because an evil man is considered dead even while still living. However, when God told Avraham, *and now you will join your ancestors in peace*, our Sages learn from this that Terach had a portion in the World to Come, because of the merit of his son Avraham. The fruit, Avraham, saved the tree, Terach. From this the *Midrash* learns that the wood of all trees could be burned on the altar, with the exception of the olive tree and the grapevine. Since we used olive oil and wine on the altar, so the fruits "saved" the trees from the fire, just as Avraham saved his father from the fires of *Gehinnom*.

The Sages say, בְּרָא מְזַכֶּה אַבָּא וְאֵין אַבָּא מְזַכֶּה בְּרָא — "A son brings merit to his father but a father does not bring merit to his son": a son can save a father from Hell but a father cannot save his son; as the verse says, וְאֵין מִיָּדִי מַצִּיל — *and there is no one to save him from My hands* (*Devarim* 32:39). Thus Avraham could not save his son Yishmael.

פרשת לך לך
Parashas Lech Lecha
(12:1 – 17:27)

⊷§ Walking with the Wise

לֶךְ לְךָ מֵאַרְצְךָ — *Go away from your country* (12:1). King Shlomo
(Solomon) says *(Mishlei 13:20)*, הוֹלֵךְ אֶת חֲכָמִים יֶחְכָּם וְרֹעֶה כְסִילִים
יֵרוֹעַ — *He who walks with the wise will grow wise, but a companion
of fools will suffer harm.* This verse teaches us that people should
stay close to wise and pious men and keep their distance from evil
men. A person who adheres to the wise constantly bears in mind
God's presence, while one who is close to an evil man forgets about
God and ultimately imitates the evil man's deeds, as we say, אוֹי
לָרָשָׁע אוֹי לִשְׁכֵנוֹ — "Woe to the evil man, woe to his neighbor." Avram
wanted to observe the Torah and serve God properly. The *Gemara*
tells us that Avram fulfilled the entire Torah, simply by following
the dictates of reason. That is why God told Avram, *Go away from
your country ... from your father's house* — for they are evil.

The Sages say that Avram was like a vial of fragrant perfume hidden in a foul-smelling place. People are unaware of its sweet aroma,
but when it is removed from there its fragrance becomes apparent.
Similarly, the righteous Avram lived among idol worshipers so God
told him to leave his land to allow his goodness to become known.

⊷§ Children, Wealth, Reputation

וְאֶעֶשְׂךָ לְגוֹי גָּדוֹל — *I will make you into a great nation* (12:2). The
Sages say: "Three things are lessened when a man travels about. He
cannot have children while traveling; he loses money; and he does
not have the opportunity to build a good reputation." God therefore
promised Avram that he would not lose by obeying His command.
On the contrary: *I will make you into a great nation* — this blessing
means, "In your land you do not merit having children, and there
you will have children"; *And I will make your name great* — "I will
bring you fame"; *I will bless you* — "You will be blessed with
riches."

⇜§ The Power to Bless

וְהְיֵה בְּרָכָה — *And you shall become a blessing* (12:2). God said to Avram, "Until now the blessings were in My hands: I blessed Adam, I blessed Noach. Today I give the power to bestow them to you, and you may bless whomever you wish."

⇜§ Five Things Nullify Evil Decrees; Three Things Shorten Life

וַאֲבָרְכָה מְבָרְכֶיךָ וּמְקַלֶּלְךָ אָאֹר — *I will bless those who bless you, and he who curses you I will curse* (12:3). This means: "First I will bless those who bless you, so that their blessing will be fulfilled; those that curse you will be cursed first, so that their curse will not be fulfilled."

Midrash Tanchuma writes that the words *lech lecha* hinted that Avram would have a child when he was one hundred years old, for the numerical equivalent of these words (לֶךְ לְךָ) is one hundred.

The *Gemara* writes in the first chapter of Tractate *Rosh HaShanah*: R' Yitzchak says, "Five things can nullify evil decrees against people: charity, as it says, וּצְדָקָה תַּצִּיל מִמָּוֶת — *Charity saves from death* (Mishlei 10:2); pleading with God, as it says, וַיִּצְעֲקוּ אֶל ה' בַּצַּר לָהֶם וּמִמְּצוּקוֹתֵיהֶם יוֹצִיאֵם — *They cried out to God in their distress, and He saved them from their plight* (Tehillim 107:28); changing a person's name, as the Torah says, *Do not call her Sarai; Sarah is her name* (Bereishis 17:15) — and with the name of Sarah she bore children; changing one's deeds can also change an evil decree; and, in the opinion of some of the Sages, changing one's place of living. When someone leaves a city where he had no luck to go to another city, he may be more fortunate.

The *Gemara* says that three things shorten a man's life: being called to the reading of the Torah and not going, as it is written, כִּי הוּא חַיֶּיךָ וְאֹרֶךְ יָמֶיךָ — *For it* (the Torah) *is your life and the length of your days* (Devarim 30:20); refusing to bless over a cup of wine which is offered him for the Grace after Meals, as it says וַאֲבָרְכָה מְבָרְכֶיךָ — *I will bless those that bless you;* and pride, as happened in the case of Yosef, who died before his brothers did, because he was proud.

⇜§ A New Life at Seventy-Five

וַיֵּלֶךְ אַבְרָם כַּאֲשֶׁר דִּבֶּר אֵלָיו ה' — *Avram went as God had directed him* (12:4). He was seventy-five years old when he left Charan. God said to him: "You are seventy-five years old, yet you must drag yourself around like a penitent. Because of this sacrifice one of your descendants will be a savior of the Jews." This refers to Queen Esther, who was seventy-five years old when she was taken to King Achashveirosh. For this reason she was called Hadassah (הֲדַסָה) which is numerically equivalent to seventy-five.

◈§ Converts to the Faith

וְאֶת הַנֶּפֶשׁ אֲשֶׁר עָשׂוּ בְחָרָן — *And the souls which they had made in Charan* (12:5). Avram had amassed many possessions and servants in Charan, and he took them along with him. One might have expected that he would first find a place to live and then bring all of his possessions, but Avram relied on God to give him a good place to live, and immediately brought everything along.

Another interpretation of *the souls which they had made* is that it refers to the converts whom Avram had made among the men and Sarai had made among the women. Yitzchak (Isaac), too, began early to make converts, as we see in the verse, וַיֵּשֶׁב יַעֲקֹב בְּאֶרֶץ מְגוּרֵי אָבִיו — *Yaakov lived in the land where his father dwelled* (37:1; *megurei*, Heb. — "dwelled", derives from a similar root to the word *ger*, Heb. — "convert"); in other words, Yaakov (Jacob) lived in the land where his father had converted his neighbors. Yaakov also made converts, as alluded to in the verse, וַיֹּאמֶר יַעֲקֹב אֶל בֵּיתוֹ וְאֶל כָּל אֲשֶׁר עִמּוֹ הָסִרוּ אֶת אֱלֹהֵי הַנֵּכָר — *Yaakov said to his household and to all that were with him, Remove the alien idols* (35:2). In Tractate *Sanhedrin, Perek Chelek*, Resh Lakish says: "One who teaches another's son Torah, it is as if he himself created him, as it is written, הַנֶּפֶשׁ אֲשֶׁר עָשׂוּ בְחָרָן — *And the souls which they made in Charan*." R' Abbahu says likewise that one who causes another to perform a mitzvah is considered as if he had created him.

◈§ Blessings and Curses

וַיַּעֲבֹר אַבְרָם בָּאָרֶץ עַד מְקוֹם שְׁכֶם — *Avram passed through the land until the place Shechem* (12:6). Avram prayed that his children [the sons of Yaakov] should be victorious in their battle in Shechem. Then he reached the plains of Mamre, where one day [at Mt. Gerizim and Mt. Eval] the Jews would swear to uphold God's Torah and His commandments.

The author of *Toldos Yitzchak* writes that Avram went from city to city and told people that there is a God in heaven who created heaven and earth. When one is not rich or well-known, his words are not taken seriously by people, and that is why the Torah says, וַאֲבָרֶכְךָ וַאֲגַדְּלָה שְׁמֶךָ — *I will bless you and make your name great.*

God told Avram to leave his land, and He would make him wealthy and famous. This poses a problem: can it be possible that

Avram served God for the reward?

Avram of course did not serve God for the reward. Rather, God said to him: "Because you want to tell people to serve Me, and they will not heed your words if you are poor, particularly since you are a foreigner and a stranger to them, I will bless you with wealth and fame, so you will be able to speak freely with the most prominent of people."

Another question can be raised. Why does the verse say, *I will bless those that bless you*, that is, the many people who will bless you, when in reference to the curses it says, *he who curses you will curse* — the one person who will curse you? The answer is that many people blessed Avram, because he made them worthy of enjoying a share in the World to Come, and so it speaks of those that bless, in the plural. But only *one* person cursed him — Nimrod — because he proved Nimrod was not a deity.

ᴥ§ In God's Name

וַיִּבֶן שָׁם מִזְבֵּחַ — *He built there an altar* (12:7). The verse does not say that "he called in the Name of God" because he was afraid to publicly cry out God's Name. Later, when he approached the mountain where Nimrod's rule did not extend, it says, וַיִּקְרָא שָׁם בְּשֵׁם ה' — *He called there in God's Name.*

We read further, וְהַכְּנַעֲנִי אָז בָּאָרֶץ — *The Canaanites were then in the land.* From this we understand that Avram told Lot that they should settle the argument between their respective shepherds because otherwise they could all be driven away by the powerful rulers of the land. And from the other appearance of these words we learn of Avram's fear of crying out in God's Name.

The author of *Toldos Yitzchak* asks: Why did Avram abandon the Holy Land, Canaan, when there was a famine, after God had commanded that he go and live there? The answer is that Avram feared that the Canaanites would say that the famine had struck them because he had come and stopped their idol worship. This was the first famine in the world's history, and the idol worshipers would have blamed him.

ᴥ§ Beauty and Modesty; Iniquity and Exile

הִנֵּה נָא יָדַעְתִּי כִּי אִשָּׁה יְפַת מַרְאֶה אָתְּ — *Behold, now I know that you are a beautiful woman* (12:11). Avram told Sarai: "I now know that you are a beautiful woman. As a rule a person's appearance suffers from the rigors of travel, yet you have remained beautiful." Another explanation is that Avram and Sarai were modest, and Avram had never seen Sarai's skin uncovered. But as they traveled over water,

Sarai was forced to lift the hem of her dress. Avram then said, "Now I know that you are beautiful. We are approaching Egypt, where they are all dark-skinned. They are not used to beautiful women and they will kill me and take you. Therefore, wherever we go, tell them that you are my sister, so at least they will let me live. Perhaps they will even give me presents" — for it was customary in those times to give presents to a bride's brother.

R' Bechaye writes in the name of *Ramban:* Avram sinned twice. First, he almost caused his wife to sin out of his fear of being killed: he let them take Sarai for a wife when she was already married. He should have relied on God's ability to save them. His second sin was leaving Canaan because of the famine. Because of this Israel was exiled in Egypt, the very land where he sinned.

Our Sages say that the exile in Egypt came for a different reason: it was a punishment for Avram's sin in asking God, בַּמָּה אֵדַע כִּי אִירָשֶׁנָּה — *With what shall I know that I shall inherit it* (the Land)? (15:8). Because the Egyptian exile was caused by improper words, it lasted 430 years. Our present exile is the result of three iniquities: evil thoughts, evil actions, and jealousy, and is therefore much longer. *Ramban* writes: Avram told Sarai to say that he was her brother, but Sarai did not want to deny that he was her husband. When they came to Egypt and Sarai's beauty was praised, the Egyptians wanted to bring her to the king. They did not ask her if she was married, and she for her part remained silent. Avram however said that she was his sister and therefore the king treated him well. Later Pharaoh confronted Avram and said: מַה זֹּאת עָשִׂיתָ לִּי — *What is this that you have done to me?* (12:18). It does not say that Pharaoh rebuked Sarai, because she had never claimed to be unmarried: she had simply been silent, rather than denying that Avram was her husband. This is the proper course for all righteous women to follow.

Why did Avram fear that they would murder him? Even among the idol worshipers of that time murder was forbidden, as was abduction of another man's wife. In fact Pharaoh said to Avram, "Why did you not say that she was your wife? I would not have looked at her!" What then was Avram afraid of?

Avram said to himself: "The Egyptians are steeped in lasciviousness. They will undoubtedly kill me, so that Sarai will not be a married woman. Even though murder is as grave a crime as adultery, if she is married then every time a man lives with her he commits a sin. If they kill me they will have committed but one sin. Besides, if I am alive they may be afraid to harm her."

Another question can be raised. A person is forbidden to cause another to sin. How could Avram have told them that he was Sarai's brother, when he might thereby cause others to transgress? The answer is that Avram circumvented the problem by divorcing Sarai for a short time, so that if they would take her she would not be a married woman.

⇜ Sarai is Discovered

וַיְהִי כְּבוֹא אַבְרָם מִצְרָיְמָה — *And it came to pass when Avram came to Egypt* (12:14). The verse seems to say that Avram came to Egypt alone. Where was Sarai? Avram had hidden her in a trunk. The Egyptians wanted to tax him and commanded that the trunk be opened, whereupon a great light shone forth, for her beauty illuminated the entire city.

⇜ The Ten Tests

וַתֻּקַּח הָאִשָּׁה בֵּית פַּרְעֹה — *The woman was taken to Pharaoh's house* (12:15). *Pirkei deR' Eliezer* writes that Avram underwent ten tests of faith:

1. When he was born, astrologers who foretold that he would bring a new belief to the world wanted to kill him. He was raised in a cave for thirteen years, without seeing the sun and the moon. When he left the cave he spoke the Holy Tongue (Hebrew), and spoke out against the idol worshipers.

2. He was held captive for ten years, seven in the land of Kuta and three in Barar. Afterwards he was thrown into a furnace, and God saved him.

3. God told him to leave his homeland and family and travel like a penitent to a strange land.

4. A famine in the land of Canaan forced him to leave to Egypt.

5. The fifth test was the abduction of his wife. This took place on Pesach (Passover). God struck Pharaoh and his household with a plague, hinting at another plague which God would in the future bring upon a later Pharaoh. Pharaoh gave Sarai a marriage contract which included all of his gold and silver, servants, and the land of Goshen. For this reason the Jews lived in Goshen when they came to Egypt. (Avimelech also wanted to take Sarai as a wife, but the Angel Michael appeared before him and threatened him with an unsheathed sword.)

6. Mighty warriors came to kill Avram but they first began to battle with Lot. The Angel Michael came to tell Avram of this, as the Torah says, וַיָּבֹא הַפָּלִיט וַיַּגֵּד לְאַבְרָם — *The survivor came and told Avram* (14:13). Michael is called "the survivor" because when the evil angel Samael was thrust out of heaven, he seized Michael and

tried to drag him down with him. God saved him and he was therefore called "the survivor."

When Avram saw that they had captured his brother's son Lot he pursued the captors and killed them. Avram then said, "Master of the Universe, I praise You for having aided me," and the angels answered, בָּרוּךְ אַתָּה ה' מָגֵן אַבְרָהָם — "Blessed is God, the Shield of Avraham."

[7. The Covenant Between the Parts (15:1-21) at which Avram was shown the Four Kingdoms that would subjugate his descendants. 8. The commandment of circumcision (17:10). 9. The eviction of Hagar and Ishmael (21:10). 10. The *Akedah* (22:1-19).]

⋟ Wives and Wealth

וּלְאַבְרָם הֵיטִיב בַּעֲבוּרָה — *He treated Avram well, for her sake* (12:16). Pharaoh gave him sheep and cattle and other animals. The *Gemara* says, in Tractate *Bava Metzia, Perek HaZahav*, that a man should always treat his wife with respect, for the blessings come upon a home because of her, as it says, *He treated Avram well, for her sake*. Rava used to tell people, "Respect your wives and you will be wealthy."

⋟ Pharaoh and Avram

וַיְנַגַּע ה' אֶת פַּרְעֹה נְגָעִים גְּדֹלִים — *God struck Pharaoh with plague* (12:17). When Pharaoh abducted Sarai, God struck him with leprosy so that he would be unable to have relations with her. Sarai prayed all through the night, saying: "Master of the Universe, You promised great things to Avram and because of that I agreed to leave him." An angel with an outstretched sword in his hand appeared, ready to kill Pharaoh. Sarai revealed that she was the wife of Avram. Pharaoh sent for him and asked why he had not told him her identity, but then told him to take his wife and leave.

First Pharaoh wanted to be certain that she was really his wife, but Avram was afraid to admit it. Pharaoh wanted to know the truth. He thought that Sarai might be saying that she was married to Avram simply because she was loath to marry Pharaoh. Therefore he told Avram, "I have taken her for a wife ," that is, as a queen, and not simply a concubine. Still Avram remained silent, and Pharaoh understood that she was truly his wife. It was only then that he told him to take his wife and leave.

R' Bechaye asks: Why in this case did Avram not reply to Pharaoh, while when Avimelech asked Avram why he had said that Sarai was his sister and not his wife he did answer? Why did he not answer Pharaoh as well? The explanation is that Pharaoh told

Avram to take his wife and leave. Avram was afraid to delay by answering, and left immediately. Avimelech did not order them to leave, so Avram answered.

◄§ Pharaoh's Reward

וַיְשַׁלְּחוּ אֹתוֹ וְאֶת אִשְׁתּוֹ וְאֶת כָּל אֲשֶׁר לוֹ — *They sent him away, with his wife, and all that he had* (12:20). The verse teaches us that Pharaoh did not take back the gifts which he had given to Avram, even though he was entitled to do so, since Avram had deceived him. God miraculously caused Pharaoh not to take back the gifts. In fact he even escorted Avram out. He walked four steps with him, and was rewarded for it: the Jews were in his country for four hundred years, a century for each step.

◄§ Return Journey

וַיֵּלֶךְ לְמַסָּעָיו — *He continued on his journey* (13:3). The word "his" suggests that Avram stayed in the same inns in which he had slept on his way from Canaan to Egypt. Our Sages tell us that Avram had borrowed money in the inns in which he had stayed on his way from Canaan, fearing to display his wealth because of robbers. He therefore stayed in the same places on his return journey in order to pay his debts. Our Sages also learn from this that a man should stay in the same inns where he has already lodged so as not to shame his former innkeepers.

◄§ The Shepherds' Quarrels

וְלֹא נָשָׂא אֹתָם הָאָרֶץ — *The land could not support them* (13:6). Avram and Lot had so many herds that there was not sufficient pasture for them all, and a bitter quarrel broke out between their respective shepherds.

וְהַכְּנַעֲנִי וְהַפְּרִזִּי אָז יֹשֵׁב בָּאָרֶץ — *The Canaanites and the Perizzites lived then in the land* (13:7). *Ramban* writes that all the seven nations of Canaan had a portion in the land. Since there was not enough pasture for their herds, each year different nations lived there, and at this particular time it was the Canaanites and Perizzites who lived in Canaan.

The shepherds of Avram and Lot said: "The Canaanites and Perizzites live alone in the land because there is little pasture for the animals. We are foreigners here. How can there be enough for us?"

Lot's shepherds were wicked and grazed their animals in other men's fields, so Avram's shepherds rebuked them for stealing. Lot's shepherds replied that God had promised the land to Avram. Lot, as his nearest relative, would inherit it all, so they were not really stealing. The verse therefore says *the Canaanites ... —* since they still lived in the land, it was not yet the proper time for Avram to inherit it. This is why Avram told Lot, "Let us not quarrel in a strange land. Let us separate." Lot chose an area near the Jordan River, because it was rich pasture land.

◆§ Lot Leaves Avram; Sodom's Sins

וַיִּסַּע לוֹט מִקֶּדֶם — *Lot journeyed east* (13:11). Lot journeyed away from God, who is called *kadmon shel olam* ("the First in the World," alluding to the resemblance between the words *kadmon* and *kedem* — "eastward"). He said, "I reject Avram and his God," and moved towards Sodom and Amorah. These were cities inhabited by wicked people, who committed evil with their bodies and with their possessions. These were the men whom Lot chose to be his fellows.

When the verse mentions Sodom and Amorah it immediately speaks of their evil. The Sages learn from this that when speaking of a wicked person, one should speak ill of him; in the words of the verse, וְשֵׁם רְשָׁעִים יִרְקָב — *The name of the wicked ones shall perish* (*Mishlei* 10:7).

The *Gemara* writes in Tractate *Sanhedrin, Perek Chelek,* that the people of Sodom became evil because God gave them enormous quantities of food, gold and silver. They said, "We will close our land to guests, who come only to steal away our treasure." Their judges ruled unjustly. A person traveling over a bridge had to pay a toll of four coins; a person traveling on the water near the bridge was forced to pay eight coins. If someone beat another man's wife and caused her to miscarry, the judges ruled that he must make her again pregnant. If a person beat another so badly that blood flowed out of his wounds, the judges held that the one who was beaten had to pay his tormentor, because he had let his blood (as the doctors of those times used to do).

Avram's servant Eliezer once came to Sodom. He was beaten until his blood ran and he took his attackers to court. The judge ruled that he should pay his attackers because they had done him a medical service by bleeding him. Eliezer took a stone and hurled it at the judge, who bled profusely. He then told the judge, "Pay me for your treatment, and then I will pay my attackers."

There was a wedding in Sodom which Eliezer attended, uninvited. He sat at the foot of the table. The man sitting next to him asked who had invited him to the wedding. Eliezer answered, "You invited me." The man fled, fearing that the others would hear Eliezer's reply. Eliezer moved up and sat next to another, who asked him the same question. Eliezer answered him the same way, and he too fled, fearing that he would be thought of as hospitable. In such a manner Eliezer spoke with all of the people at the table until there was no one left. He remained alone at the table, and ate the entire meal.

The Sodomites had a bed for guests. If the guest was tall they would chop off his feet until he would fit the bed; if he was short they stretched him until he was as long as the bed. They told Eliezer to lie down. He answered that from the day that his mistress Sarah died he had vowed never to lie down on a bed.

When a pauper would come to beg, the inhabitants of Sodom would give him no bread. Instead, each person gave him a coin with his own name engraved upon it. When the beggar died of hunger each would come and retrieve his coin.

A girl once secretly gave a beggar a piece of bread. When she went to draw water she hid a piece of bread in her bucket. She gave him the bread and a bit of water. When she was found out, the people smeared her with honey and put her on a roof, so that the bees would sting her to death. When her plaintive cries reached God's ears He said to his Heavenly Court, "Let us go and see what this outcry is about," as it says in the verse, זַעֲקַת סְדֹם וַעֲמֹרָה כִּי רָבָּה — *the outcry of Sodom and Amorah, which is great* (18:20). This refers to the screaming of the young girl — for the word *rabbah* (רָבָּה, "great") is similar to the word *rivah* (רִיבָה, "young girl").

◆§ God Speaks to Avram

וַה׳ אָמַר אֶל אַבְרָם אַחֲרֵי הִפָּרֶד לוֹט מֵעִמּוֹ — *And God said to Avram, after Lot had left him ...* (13:14). This verse teaches us that God did not speak to Avram the entire time that Lot was with him. After Lot left, God spoke with him.

קוּם הִתְהַלֵּךְ בָּאָרֶץ — *Arise, walk through the land* (13:17). God told Avram: "Arise and go throughout the land, through its length and breadth, to take possession (חֲזָקָה) of the land which I will give to you and to your children."

◆§ Avram Challenges Four Kings

וַיְהִי בִּימֵי אַמְרָפֶל — *It was in the days of Amrafel* (14:1). This was in the days of Nimrod, who was called Amrafel. The name means *amar 'pol'* (He said: "Fall!"): it was he who commanded that Avraham be thrown into the furnace.

Four kings battled and defeated an alliance of five kings, because they were mightier. Nevertheless Avram fought them because they had abducted Lot, even though Lot deserved his fate for having chosen the company of people of Sodom.

⇜§ Avram's Miracle Verified

וְעֵמֶק הַשִּׂדִּים בֶּאֱרֹת בֶּאֱרֹת חֵמָר — *The valley of Siddim was full of tar pits* (14:10). There were deep pits on the battlefield, and the five kings fell into them and died. Only the king of Sodom, by a miracle, was saved. There were people who did not believe that Avram had been thrown into the fire and had survived. Now that they saw God save the king of Sodom from the deep pits, they believed that Avram had survived being thrown into the furnace.

⇜§ Og, King of Bashan

וַיָּבֹא הַפָּלִיט וַיַּגֵּד לְאַבְרָם — *The survivor came and told Avram* (14:13). The survivor is Og, King of the Bashan, who survived the battle of the kings. He told Avram that the kings had abducted Lot, in order to make Avram pursue them. He hoped that Avram would be killed in battle and he would then take Sarai as a wife. Some Sages say that he was called "the survivor" because he survived the Flood. He was called Og because he came to Avram on the day before Pesach, when *matzos* are baked; "Og" is derived from the word *ugah*, meaning baked goods.

⇜§ Mamre's Advice

וְהוּא שֹׁכֵן בְּאֵלֹנֵי מַמְרֵא הָאֱמֹרִי — *He lived in the Plains of Mamre the Amorite* (14:13). Mamre was a friend and ally of Avram's. He had urged Avram to circumcise himself by God's command. He told him, 'If God asked you for your entire body, would you not have given it to Him? Why not give Him the foreskin alone? The God who saved you from the fire and from the famine and from the kings will save you, and you will live.'

The name Mamre (which is spelled *mem, mem, resh, alef*) indicates the four things of which he spoke to Avram: kings (*melachim*, beginning with a *mem*); circumcision (*milah*, beginning with a *mem*); famine (*ra'av*, beginning with a *resh*); and fire (*eish*, beginning with an *alef*).

⇜§ To Save a Relative

וַיִּשְׁמַע אַבְרָם כִּי נִשְׁבָּה אָחִיו — *Avram heard that his brother was captive* (14:14). It is difficult to understand why the Torah calls Lot his brother, when actually he was his brother's son. This shows us Avram's righteousness. Despite the fact that Lot was evil he did not abandon him, but pursued his persecutors as if he were Lot's own brother.

✦§ Eliezer Equals 318

וַיָּרֶק אֶת חֲנִיכָיו יְלִידֵי בֵיתוֹ שְׁמֹנָה עָשָׂר וּשְׁלֹשׁ מֵאוֹת — *He led his men, born of his house, three hundred and eighteen* (14:14). Avram armed three hundred and eighteen of his strong men, so that they could pursue the kings and save Lot. Our Sages say that he took with him only Eliezer whose name is numerically equivalent to three hundred and eighteen. R' Bechaye asks why the verse should say three hundred and eighteen men, if only Eliezer went. He answers that Avram did in fact take three hundred and eighteen men, but when they were ready for battle he announced that any of them who had sinned should return to their homes, as was done, too, in later years when Israel went out to war. All of them left, and only Eliezer remained.

The words for *he led his men* can be interpreted in two ways: first, he armed his men, and second, he emptied them (from the word *rek*, "empty," which is similar to the word *vayarek*, "he led"), meaning, he let them go home.

✦§ The Pursuit

וַיִּרְדֹּף עַד דָּן — *He pursued them until Dan* (14:14). He became weak in Dan because in the future Israel would worship idols there.

וַיֵּחָלֵק עֲלֵיהֶם לַיְלָה — *He divided* (his forces) *against them during the night* (14:15). He divided his servants, to chase after them in the darkness. The Sages explain this in another way: God divided the night. The first half of the night God miraculously allowed him to destroy his enemies. God set aside the second half of the night for Avraham's children, when their enemies in Egypt would be destroyed with the plague of the first-born on Pesach.

R' Bechaye writes that Avram divided the night as follows: The first half of the night he pursued his enemies and during the second half he destroyed them.

✦§ The King of Sodom

וַיֵּצֵא מֶלֶךְ סְדֹם — *The King of Sodom came out* (14:17). The King of Sodom came out to a valley to greet Avram, and all of the nations gathered there and crowned Avram king.

Even though Avram had destroyed his sons, the four kings, Malkitzedek, king of Yerushalayim (Jerusalem), brought bread and wine to Avram. The *Midrash* says that Malkitzedek was Shem, the son of Noach.

◆§ Malkitzedek

וַיֹּאמַר בָּרוּךְ אַבְרָם לְאֵל עֶלְיוֹן — *He said, Blessed be Avram to the
mighty God* (14:19). He praised God for having delivered Avram's
enemies into his hands. But because he blessed Avram before praising God, God took the priesthood away from Malkitzedek and gave
it to Avram. Nevertheless, Avram gave a tithe of his goods to
Malkitzedek because he was still a priest at that time.

The King of Sodom asked that Avram return to him the men
whom Avram had recaptured from the four kings, and keep the
booty for himself. Avram answered that he had vowed not to touch
even a shoelace or a piece of thread which had belonged to the King
of Sodom, so as not to allow him to say that it was he who had
enriched Avram.

◆§ Not Even a Shoelace

אִם מִחוּט וְעַד שְׂרוֹךְ נַעַל — *From a thread to a shoelace* (14:23). The
Sages teach us that God told Avram: By virtue of these words I will
give your children a commandment of threads, the commandment of
tzitzis (fringes); and the commandment of *tefillin* which are made of
laces; and the commandment of *chalitzah* (removal of a shoe in the
law of *yibum*, the levirate ritual), when a shoe is removed.

◆§ Who Will be My Heir?

אַל תִּירָא אַבְרָם אָנֹכִי מָגֵן לָךְ — *Do not fear, Avram, I am your shield*
(15:1). God told Avram three things. First, he was afraid that the
children of the kings whom he had killed would avenge their

fathers' deaths. God therefore told him not to be afraid.

Second, God promised him a son. He said, שְׂכָרְךָ הַרְבֵּה מְאֹד — *your reward will be very great (ibid.).* In the word for "very" (הַרְבֵּה), the letter *hei* appears twice. This showed that Sarah and Avraham would have a child when they would each have a *hei* in their names (the name Avram was changed to Avraham and Sarai was changed to Sarah — both had a *hei* added).

Rachel had no *hei* in her name. She gave her maidservant Bilhah to Yaakov, for in her name the letter *hei* appeared twice, and she hoped that one *hei* would be considered as hers, and she too would have children.

The third thing that God told Avram was that he would have a share in the World to Come.

Avram did not understand God's promises, because God had not said explicitly that he would have children and a share in the World to Come, and so he said to God: "Of what use are all these things which You will give me if I have no children? Who will be my heir?"

God answered, "Do not worry: your servant Eliezer will not be your heir. Your son will be your heir."

⊷§ Beyond Astrology

וַיּוֹצֵא אֹתוֹ הַחוּצָה — *He brought him outside* (15:5). God took Avram outside and showed him the stars, and said: "Just as the stars cannot be counted because they are so numerous, your children too will be uncountable."

Our Sages say that God took Avram to the sky and said: "You are above the destiny which is written for you in the stars. The stars foretell that you will be childless, but you can change your destiny. I have lifted you above the power of the constellations." This is the meaning of the words, *He brought him outside.*

⊷§ An Undeserved Gift

וְהֶאֱמִן בַּה' וַיַּחְשְׁבֶהָ לּוֹ צְדָקָה — *He believed in God and considered it charitable* (15:6). *Ramban* writes that Avram considered God's promise to him an act of charity, and not something which he deserved. (*Tzedakah,* "righteousness," can also be translated as "charity".)

R' Bechaye says that God considered Avram's belief in His promise as righteous behavior on Avram's part.

The author of *Toldos Yitzchak* asks: Why did Avram believe God's promise of children with no hesitation, without asking for a sign, yet when God promised to give his children the Land of Canaan he did ask for a sign? The answer is that since Avram asked for a sign that his children would inherit the land, this sign alone would imply without a doubt that he would have children.

The author of *Toldos Yitzchak* asks why Avram said, וְאָנֹכִי הוֹלֵךְ עֲרִירִי — *and I go childless* (15:2), when God had already promised that his children would inherit the land. Avram thought that God had promised him to give the land to members of his family or household, and not necessarily to a son. Avram was afraid that God was referring to Eliezer, who was the senior member of his household and beloved as a son. Therefore God assured him that Eliezer would not be his heir, and the Torah goes on to specify, unlike similar passages, כִּי אִם אֲשֶׁר יֵצֵא מִמֵּעֶיךָ — *One born from your own body will inherit whatever is yours* (15:4).

The author of *Toldos Yitzchak* asks still another question. It says here *he believed in God* (15:6), which implies that before this time, God forbid, he did not believe. The meaning however is that now Avram believed that God would actually bless him with children of his own, while earlier he had thought that God had referred to his servant Eliezer.

⋖§ God's Miracles for Avram

אֲנִי ה׳ אֲשֶׁר הוֹצֵאתִיךָ מֵאוּר כַּשְׂדִּים — *I am God who took you out of Ur Casdim* (15:7). God told Avram: "From the time that I took you out of Ur Casdim, and performed miracles for you, My intention was to give you this land." Avram thought that if his children would transgress or if the idol worshipers would repent, God would allow the idolaters to inherit the land. He therefore asked God if his children would inherit the land despite their sins or despite the possible repentance of the idol worshipers. To this God answered that they would still inherit the land.

R' Bechaye relates one of the miracles wrought for Avram: The *Midrash* tells that when Avram was born, a star rose in the east and engulfed four other stars. Nimrod's astrologers said, "Today a son has been born to Terach whose children will inherit the entire world, and the World to Come as well. Give Terach a great treasure to induce him to give you his son, whom you must kill."

Nimrod sent a message to Terach, offering him a treasure in exchange for his son. Terach answered with a parable: "A man says to a horse: 'I will give you a bushel of oats, but let me first chop off your head.' The horse answers: 'What use are the oats after you have chopped off my head?' Sir, who will inherit all of my riches if you kill my son?"

Nimrod said to him: "I understand that you have a son, born yesterday." Terach answered: "He died after birth." Nimrod said, "I want the one that is still living." Terach took one of his concubines' babies and brought it Nimrod, and hid Avram in a cave for three years.

God sent him two stones. Out of one flowed oil and out of the other came honey and meal. When he was three years old he left the cave and began to reflect upon the creation of heaven and earth, and of himself. He saw the sun and, thinking that it was a deity, prayed to it for the entire day. After sunset the sun disappeared and the moon and stars rose in the sky. He began to believe that the moon was the master and the stars its servants, and he prayed to the moon. When day came once more, the moon and the stars disappeared and he realized that they too were not gods. He continued reflecting, until he realized that the Lord is the one God, in heaven and earth.

◆§ The Covenant between the Parts

בַּמָּה אֵדַע כִּי אִירָשֶׁנָּה — With what shall I know that I shall inherit it (15:8).

Avram said: "Tell me in what merit my children will inherit the land." God answered: "By virtue of the sacrifices." For this reason it says, קְחָה לִי עֶגְלָה מְשֻׁלֶּשֶׁת וְעֵז מְשֻׁלֶּשֶׁת וְאַיִל מְשֻׁלָּשׁ וְתֹר וְגוֹזָל — Bring me three heifers, three goats, three rams, a dove and a young pigeon (15:9). God thus showed him that his descendants would bring sacrifices of animals and birds.

Avram cut the animals into two pieces, placed them opposite each other, and walked between them. With this form of oath he swore that he would forever serve God. God swore to Avram that He would give him the land, and sent the fire, His messenger, to pass between the pieces — as if His Presence had passed there.

Avram cut all of the animals in half, but not the birds. The Jews are compared to birds and this showed that like the birds, they too would survive. Birds of prey flew overhead, but Avram drove them away.

וְהִנֵּה אֵימָה חֲשֵׁכָה גְדֹלָה נֹפֶלֶת עָלָיו — A deep dark dread fell upon him (15:12). A great fear and a deep darkness fell upon Avram, because God showed him that his children would be exiled. Even though God had sworn to give his children the land, if they would be wicked they would be banished from its borders.

◆§ Fruits of Miserliness

יָדֹעַ תֵּדַע כִּי גֵר יִהְיֶה זַרְעֲךָ — You shall surely know that your descendants shall be strangers (15:13). God told Avram that his children would be foreigners and slaves for 400 years. The exile of Egypt is reckoned from the moment that Yitzchak (Isaac) was born.

Even though they were not in Egypt at the time, they had no land of their own and wandered through strange lands.

R' Bechaye asks: Why were they exiled for 400 years? Because they did not want to give charity, and so were called רַע עָיִן ("miserly"), which is numerically equivalent to 400.

Ramban asks: If God decreed that the Jews be exiled and enslaved in Egypt, why were the Egyptians held responsible? Why did God say that He would punish them? The answer: The Egyptians forced the Jews to do hard labor in order to destroy them, and not because they needed the work; besides, they threw the male infants into the Nile. This was harsher than God's decree.

◆§ A Father's Repentance

וְאַתָּה תָּבוֹא אֶל אֲבֹתֶיךָ בְּשָׁלוֹם — *You shall join your fathers in peace* (15:15). God here promised Avram that he would not experience exile. We learn from this verse that Avram's father Terach must have repented before his death. For had he died while still wicked God would not have told Avram that he would join him. Avram was righteous, and how can someone righteous join an evil man after death?

◆§ A Son's Repentance

תִּקָּבֵר בְּשֵׂיבָה טוֹבָה — *You will be buried at a ripe old age* (15:15). This shows us that Yishmael (Ishmael) repented during Avraham's lifetime, while Esav (Esau) did not yet become evil. In fact Avraham died five years before his time so that he should not see Esav worship idols. On the very day of Avraham's death, Esav worshiped idols and murdered a man. It is a heavy burden indeed to see one's children do wrong. God therefore said: "It is better for Avraham to die early than to see this."

◆§ Limits of Iniquity

וְדוֹר רְבִיעִי יָשׁוּבוּ הֵנָּה — *The fourth generation will return here* (15:16). God told Avram that for the next three generations his children would not be forced to wander away from *Eretz Yisrael*, because its inhabitants had not yet reached the point where they merited punishment. God punishes only when someone has reached his limit.

◆§ Queen or Maid

וְשָׂרַי אֵשֶׁת אַבְרָם ל׳א יָלְדָה לוֹ וְלָהּ שִׁפְחָה מִצְרִית וּשְׁמָהּ הָגָר — *Sarai, Avram's wife, did not bear him children. She had an Egyptian handmaiden whose name was Hagar* (16:1). The maid was the daughter of the King of Egypt. Pharaoh had said: "Because so many miracles have been performed for Avram, it is better for my daughter to be a servant in his home than a queen in someone else's home." Sarai took Hagar and gave her to Avram. She saw that she had already been in Canaan for ten years and had had no children, and now hoped that in the merit of this action God would give her a child.

⇜§ Ten Childless Years

וַיִּשְׁמַע אַבְרָם לְקוֹל שָׂרָי — *Avram listened to Sarai* (16:2). He did not intend that Hagar's children should be his heirs. The verse says *Sarai took ... the Egyptian Hagar* (16:3), to show that Sarai herself took Hagar to him. And it calls Sarai *the wife of Avram (ibid.)* to show that she said, "Avram is still my husband and I am still his wife; I shall not separate myself from him." This episode teaches us that when a man and woman have been married for ten years without having children they should divorce, as it says, מִקֵּץ עֶשֶׂר שָׁנִים — *at the end of ten years.*

⇜§ Hagar Sullies Sarai's Righteousness

וַיָּבֹא אֶל הָגָר וַתַּהַר — *He came to Hagar and she conceived* (16:4). Hagar said that Sarai was not righteous, for she had lived with Avram for so many years and was still childless, while Hagar had become pregnant immediately. She therefore mocked her mistress. So Sarai complained to Avram: "You hear Hagar mock me and yet remain silent? You ought to have prayed that we both have children; instead, you prayed only for yourself. You said, וְאָנֹכִי הוֹלֵךְ עֲרִירִי — *and I am childless,* and you did not have me in mind."

⇜§ Inviting Judgment

יִשְׁפֹּט ה' בֵּינִי וּבֵינֶיךָ — *Let the Lord judge between me and you* (16:5). Sarai cast an evil eye at the child which Hagar carried, and she miscarried. The Sages learn from this verse that one who invites a judgment from God between himself and another will see no blessing from it. Because of this sin Sarai died forty-eight years before her time: she ought to have lived as long as Avram (but instead died at the age of 127).

Avram told her, "Your maidservant Hagar is in your hands; do what you want with her." Because Sarai tormented her with hard work, the children of Hagar torment the children of Avraham and Sarah.

Hagar fled, and an angel found her.

◆§ Hagar and the Angels

הָגָר שִׁפְחַת שָׂרַי אֵי מִזֶּה בָאת וְאָנָה תֵלֵכִי — *Hagar, Sarai's maidservant, where have you come from?* (16:8). R' Bechaye asks: Why does the angel address her as *Hagar, Sarai's maidservant?* We already know who she was. This teaches us that the angel revealed himself to her only because she was Sarai's maidservant. The angel told her that she and her sons would forever serve Sarai and Sarai's children, and she must return to Sarai.

Another angel appeared and told Hagar that she would have a son called Yishmael because God had heard ("heard" — *shama)* her cries. He would be a wild person: he would fight with people, and people would fight with him. Ultimately she did give birth to a son, and Avram named him Yishmael. The spirit of prophecy rested upon him, and so he named him as the angel had foretold.

Ramban says that Hagar was embarrassed to give the baby a name, because she was not Avram's proper wife, so she told Avram that the angel had asked her to name the baby Yishmael. Avram was 86 years old at this time. The verse tells us his age so that we will know that Yishmael was thirteen years old when Avram circumcised him, and yet Yishmael did not protest or try to stop him.

◆§ The Commandment of Circumcision

אֲנִי אֵל שַׁדַּי — *I am God Almighty* (17:1). That is to say: "I am the God who can do anything, so do not be afraid. The circumcision will not harm you; I can make you well."

הִתְהַלֵּךְ לְפָנַי וֶהְיֵה תָמִים — *Go before Me and be whole-hearted* (17:1). "Do not let your body be divided," meaning, let what your mouth says reflect what your heart feels. Another interpretation of these words is, "When you are circumcised your entire body will be in God's service."

◆§ Avram becomes Avraham

וְלֹא יִקָּרֵא עוֹד אֶת שִׁמְךָ אַבְרָם וְהָיָה שִׁמְךָ אַבְרָהָם — *You will no longer be called Avram: your name shall be Avraham* (17:5). Through the circumcision you have gained five more organs which will serve God perfectly [for at the time of the circumcision God also gave Avraham complete control over his eyes and ears, and the added letter (ה) signifies "five"]. Moreover, the name Avraham signifies that you will be master over all the nations [as the same verse continues, כִּי אַב הֲמוֹן גּוֹיִם נְתַתִּיךָ — *For I have made you a father of a multitude of nations*].

◆§ Signs of the Covenant

וְהָיָה לְאוֹת בְּרִית — *It shall be a sign of the covenant* (17:11). There are three commandments in the Torah which are termed "signs", all symbols of God's oneness. These signs are *Shabbos, tefillin* and circumcision. A Jew must have two signs to testify to God's oneness during the week (two witnesses are necessary to bear witness in court), and so has his *tefillin* and the circumcision; on *Shabbos* he does not need the *tefillin* for he has two witnesses: the observance of *Shabbos* itself, and the circumcision. The *Midrash* writes that circumcision is a mitzvah of great stature which saves a person from the punishment of *Gehinnom.*

◆§ An Eternal Covenant

וְהָיְתָה בְרִיתִי בִּבְשַׂרְכֶם לִבְרִית עוֹלָם — *My covenant shall be in your flesh as an everlasting covenant* (17:13). The circumcision will be a symbol of your service to God, a symbol that will never be removed. The circumcision is greater than a sacrifice. A sacrifice is brought with money while the circumcision is of the body itself.

Pirkei deR' Eliezer writes that Avraham circumcised himself on Yom Kippur, the Day of Atonement. Each Yom Kippur God sees his blood and forgives our sins. *Ramban* writes that circumcision is commanded in order to weaken the lustful desires. The author of *Toldos Yitzchak* asks why the verse tells us Avraham's age at the time of the circumcision. God said to Avraham: "Even though you are 99 years old, and too old to have children, I will strengthen you, and after circumcision you will have a child. Moreover, I will give you Canaan by virtue of the circumcision."

◆§ Sarai becomes Sarah

לֹא תִקְרָא אֶת שְׁמָהּ שָׂרָי — *Do not call her name Sarai* (17:15). The name Sarah means that she would be queen over the entire world (from the root שרר, meaning "dominion").

The *Midrash* says that God took the *yud* from Sarai's name and divided it into two. (The numerical value of the letter *yud* is ten.) He gave half to Avraham (by adding the letter *hei*, with a numerical value of five, onto his name) and half remained with Sarah (in the *hei* of her new name). The *yud* complained to God: "Why did You take me away from a righteous woman?" God answered: "I will put you back with a righteous man, and the man previously known as Hoshea will be called Yehoshua" (Joshua, whose name was changed by the addition of a *yud*).

✥ Strength through Circumcision

וַיִּפֹּל אַבְרָהָם עַל פָּנָיו — *Avraham fell upon his face* (17:17). Before he was circumcised he could not stand before the Divine Presence. After the circumcision, however, it is written, וְאַבְרָהָם עוֹדֶנּוּ עֹמֵד לִפְנֵי ה׳ — *Avraham still stood before God* (18:22).

✥ Sarah Rejuvenated

וַיִּפֹּל אַבְרָהָם עַל פָּנָיו וַיִּצְחָק — *Avraham fell on his face, and laughed* (17:17). Avraham laughed at the thought that both he and Sarah, who were so old, could have children. God said to him: "I will bless Sarah and she will be like a young woman. Her breasts will be full of milk." Many people did not believe that Sarah had really given birth. When Sarah weaned Yitzchak, Avraham made a great celebration and invited many notables, together with their wives. They brought their children with them but not their wet nurses. When the children began to cry they told Sarah, "Come, give our children milk." Sarah took them and nursed them all, for God had blessed her with abundant milk. Then all the women knew that Sarah had given birth.

✥ Naming Yitzchak

הַלְּבֶן מֵאָה שָׁנָה יִוָּלֵד — *Can a man of a hundred years have a child* (17:17). This is difficult. How could Avraham wonder when God had explicitly told him that he would have a child? Further, we find even in our days that a man of ninety can father a child, and we see that forty years after this Avraham had many children with Keturah. But in fact Avraham was not doubting God's promise. He said, "When I was young and strong I had no children. Now Sarah and I are old, can we have children? This will require a miracle from God — and He can do anything!" Avraham rejoiced, and therefore God told him: וְקָרָאתָ אֶת שְׁמוֹ יִצְחָק — *You shall call him Yitzchak* (17:19). The name Yitzchak means joy (*tzachak*, "laughed") — *for you rejoiced*. Because the name Yitzchak was God-given, it remained unchanged. The name Avram, however, was changed to Avraham, and the name Yaakov was likewise changed to Yisrael.

R' Bechaye writes that the name was changed to Avraham (because as the Torah tells us) he was destined to become the father of many peoples (*av hamon goyim*, "father of many nations"). So too the name Yaakov was changed because Yaakov defeated an angel in battle. Nothing extraordinary happened to Yitzchak, so his name remained the same.

The child's name was Yitzchak also because of the letters: *yud* indicates the ten tests of faith undergone by Avraham; *tzaddi* (18th letter of the *alef-beis*, numerically equivalent to 90) shows Sarah's age when Yitzchak was born; *ches* (eighth letter of the *alef-beis*, equivalent to eight) is a reminder of the circumcision which took place on the eighth day; and *kuf* (19th letter of the *alef-beis*, equivalent to 100) shows that Avraham was one hundred years old when Yitzchak was born.

⇜§ Yishmael's Posterity

וּלְיִשְׁמָעֵאל שְׁמַעְתִּיךָ — *And regarding Yishmael I have heard you* (17:20). God said to Avraham: "I have heard your prayer for Yishmael; twelve princes will descend from him."

The word for "princes" is *nesi'im*, which also means "clouds" — for even though Yishmael's descendants will grow to be mighty kings, they will ultimately, like clouds, vanish from the world.

⇜§ Order of Circumcision

וַיָּמָל אֵת בְּשַׂר עָרְלָתָם — *He circumcised the flesh of their foreskin* (17:23). Avraham first circumcised the 318 servants of his household and then circumcised himself. Had he circumcised himself first he would have been too weak to properly circumcise his household.

פרשת וירא
Parashas Vayera
(18:1 — 22:24)

∞§ God Visits the Sick

וַיֵּרָא אֵלָיו ה' — *God appeared to him* (18:1). God appeared to Avraham after he had obeyed His command to circumcise himself. The Torah says that He appeared *to him* without specifying to whom, for this passage is connected with the previous chapter, regarding the circumcision. God came to visit him on the third day because he was ill as a result of the circumcision.

∞§ Fruit of an Old Tree

בְּאֵלֹנֵי מַמְרֵא — *In the Plains of Mamre* (18:1). Mamre was Avraham's ally, who had encouraged him to carry out the command of the circumcision. Because of this, God appeared to Avraham in his city.

To the Prophets, God appeared from within fire, water or wind, or on the ground, as we see in many writings. But in Avraham's case, He appeared within a tree, as we learn from the words *Elonei Mamre* ("the Plains of Mamre," which can also be read as meaning "the trees of Mamre"). God wanted to intimate to Avraham that just as an old tree still bears fruit, so would Avraham have children in his old age.

∞§ Of Angels and Men

וְהוּא יֹשֵׁב פֶּתַח הָאֹהֶל כְּחֹם הַיּוֹם ... וְהִנֵּה שְׁלֹשָׁה אֲנָשִׁים נִצָּבִים עָלָיו — *As he sat in the door of his tent in the heat of the day ... Behold, there were three men standing by him; he saw [them] and he ran to meet them* (18:1-2). Avraham sat in the doorway to allow the sun to heal him, and also in order to look for passers-by, so that he could invite them in. God brought a fierce heat so that no guest should drop by and bother him. But when He realized that Avraham was pained because he had no guests, He sent three angels in the guise of men.

Who were these angels? One was Michael, who was sent to tell Sarah that she would have a son; the second was Raphael, whose task was to cure Avraham after his circumcision; the third was Gavriel (Gabriel), who came to destroy Sodom.

Why could one angel not do all three tasks? One angel cannot do both good and bad. One angel is sent on a mission of kindness and mercy, while another brings strict justice.

But in that case, why was it that Michael, who had been sent to tell Sarah the good news, could not also heal Avraham? Raphael is appointed over all matters of healing, and no other angel can assume his responsibility. And after healing Avraham, he proceeded from there to save Lot.

Seeing that the angels were standing still, he understood that they hesitated to trouble him, so he ran towards them and invited them in.

The *Gemara* asks, in Tractate *Bava Metzia*: If the Torah says that they were standing next to Avraham, why does it later say that he ran to greet them? The *Gemara* explains that the angels had stood next to him, but when they saw that he was bandaging his wound they left, and he ran after them. But if he was running after them, why does it say that he ran *towards* them, to meet them? — Angels have faces on all sides of their heads, and so they were still facing him. Avraham therefore thought that they were prophets, who by uttering Divine Names could thus change their appearance.

It says that they were *standing by him* to show that Avraham did not see them approaching in the distance, as is the case with ordinary men. Rather, they suddenly appeared, as if they had fallen from the sky: *Behold, there were three men standing by him.* Avraham thought from this that they must be great *tzaddikim* or prophets, and hastened to greet them.

◄§ Hospitality

וַיֹּאמַר ... אַל נָא תַעֲבֹר מֵעַל עַבְדֶּךְ — He said, "My Lord ... do not pass from your servant" (18:3). He told the senior among the angels, "I beg you, do not leave." And if he would remain, the other two angels would not leave either.

How did Avraham recognize the eldest? — He understood that it must be the one who stood in the middle.

This can also be interpreted in another way entirely. Avraham said to God, "Please do not leave me: please wait until I bring these guests into my home." (In this interpretation, the words *My Lord* refer to God Himself.) We learn from this that hospitality to guests is more important than receiving the Divine Presence.

The author of *Toldos Yitzchak* asks why Avraham extended an invitation to only one angel. The angel who came to tell Sarah that she was to have a son would have to stay, and the angel who had come to heal Avraham would also remain. Avraham therefore spoke only with the third angel, who was to destroy Sodom, and begged him, too, to stay for a while, not because he had any task to perform at the time, but simply because the other two were staying.

Though when he extended his invitation he addressed only one angel, when he invited the angels to eat he spoke to all three, as it says, *Wash your feet ... and eat* [in the plural form of the verbs]. Despite the fact that the circumcision had weakened him, he strengthened himself and ran after them.

◄§ Deeds not Words

יֻקַּח נָא מְעַט מַיִם וְרַחֲצוּ רַגְלֵיכֶם — *Let a little water be taken, and wash your feet* (18:4). Avraham thought they might be Arabs who worshiped the dust on their feet, and he did not want them to bring their idolatry into his house.

The Sages say that because Avraham did not bring them the water himself, and instead allowed another to do it, when his descendants needed water in the desert God did not bring it Himself. He sent it through Moshe, His servant, who was forced to strike a stone to bring forth water. But Avraham said, *I will take a piece of bread*. He brought it himself, and therefore God Himself brought Avraham's descendants their food in the desert when He sent them the *man* (manna) from heaven.

The *Yalkut* writes that by virtue of the water which Avraham gave his guests his descendants merited having a well for forty years in the desert. This spring followed them, and when they transgressed it stayed behind, until the Sages would pray, and say: "Rise, O well, in the merit of our fathers Avraham, Yitzchak and Yaakov" — and the well would follow them again.

We learn from Avraham's actions that the righteous promise little and do much. Avraham said that he would bring them a piece of bread, and soon after had three calves slaughtered for them. Conversely, the wicked promise much and do nothing, as we see from Efron the Hittite, who offered to give his field away to Avraham and ultimately took an exorbitant sum of money for it (see 23:9-16).

◄§ As You have Said

וַיֹּאמְרוּ כֵּן תַּעֲשֶׂה כַּאֲשֶׁר דִּבַּרְתָּ — *They said: "Do as you have said"* (18:5). How can guests tell a host to do what he had promised? Surely this is far from polite! But this was actually a blessing to Avraham. The angels meant the following: "In the future may you always be able to entertain guests, after your wife Sarah has given birth to a son." This is the explanation of the author of *Toldos Yitzchak*.

Ramban writes that they meant: *Do as you have said*, and allow us to eat under the tree, without delay. Had they gone into the house it would have taken more time.

R' Bachya writes that they said: *Do as you have said*, and give us only a piece of bread, not a sumptuous dinner.

Another explanation: Please prepare the meal as promptly as you have spoken, for we must make haste.

≈§ All Guests are Equal

מַהֲרִי שְׁלֹשׁ סְאִים קֶמַח סֹלֶת — *Prepare quickly three measures of fine meal* (18:6). Why did he ask for three measures of meal? — So that he could give each an equal amount, and there would be no envy during the meal. *Ramban* adds that he asked Sarah to sieve it carefully so that it would be utterly clean.

≈§ Training One's Son

וְאֶל הַבָּקָר רָץ אַבְרָהָם — *Avraham ran to the cattle* (18:7). Despite the fact that he had numerous servants he fetched the cattle himself to show respect for his guests. He took three head of cattle, so that he could serve each guest a tongue. He brought the animals to Yishmael to prepare, for he wanted to train him in doing good deeds.

≈§ Chametz

וַיִּקַּח חֶמְאָה וְחָלָב — *He took butter and milk* (18:8). In the *Gemara* (Tractate *Shabbos, Perek Mefanin*), R' Yochanan says: The commandment of hospitality towards guests is greater than learning Torah.

R' Bechaye writes: Why did Avraham not bring bread to the meal? — Sarah was kneading the dough when she suddenly began to menstruate. She took her hands out of the dough, and it became *chametz* (for water and flour which is left unhandled for a certain period of time becomes *chametz*, leavened, and is forbidden for use on Pesach) — and this was the day before Pesach.

≈§ Guests and Hosts

וַיֹּאכֵלוּ — *And they ate* (18:8). That is, they acted as if they were eating. We learn from this that a person should not violate the customs of the place where he is visiting. Normally angels do not eat, yet they pretended that they did.

וַיֹּאמְרוּ אֵלָיו אַיֵּה שָׂרָה אִשְׁתֶּךָ — *They asked him, "Where is your wife Sarah?"* (18:9). They asked Avraham where his wife was, and he answered that she was in her tent. This teaches us that a guest ought to ask his host where the hostess is, and he ought to ask the hostess where her husband is. The angels knew where Sarah was, but they asked so as to endear her to Avraham, by showing that she was a modest woman who remained unseen. They also asked for her so that she could share in the "cup of blessing," the goblet of wine which is drunk after the Grace after Meals.

⊸§ The Good Tidings

וַיֹּאמֶר שׁוֹב אָשׁוּב אֵלֶיךָ כָּעֵת חַיָּה וְהִנֵּה בֵן לְשָׂרָה אִשְׁתֶּךָ — *He said, "I will surely return to you at this time next year and your wife Sarah will [g]ive a son"* (18:10). This took place on Pesach, and Yitzchak was born on the next Pesach. R' Bechaye writes that *at this time* means that she would have a normal pregnancy, which can last for no longer than a year. Not every woman is pregnant for nine months: some women are pregnant for less time, others for more, but none take longer than twelve months.

Chizkuni writes that this means, "We will return to you in a year exactly as we are now, for we are immortal."

וְשָׂרָה שֹׁמַעַת פֶּתַח הָאֹהֶל וְהוּא אַחֲרָיו — *Sarah was listening behind the door of the tent, and he was on the other side* (18:10). *Chizkuni* writes that the words *he was on the other side* refer to Yishmael. He stood behind the angel guarding Sarah so that she would not be left alone with him, because they thought that their guests were human.

⊸§ Signs of Age

וְאַבְרָהָם וְשָׂרָה זְקֵנִים בָּאִים בַּיָּמִים — *Avraham and Sarah were old, advanced in years* (18:11). From the time of Adam until the time of Avraham the word *zaken* ("old") does not appear. There was no difference between the young and the old. Avraham told God, "Master of the Universe, if a father and a son walk together, men cannot distinguish between the elder and the younger. How, then, can one show proper respect to the elderly? Is it not better for an aged man to have grey hair?" God answered, "You speak correctly, and from your time on I will do this" — and God turned Avraham's hair grey. For this reason, Avraham is here called old. He was the first man whose age was visible.

Yitzchak later said to God, "Master of the Universe, man dies with no pain. Then, in the World to Come, he is in agony. Is it not better for him to suffer somewhat in This World, so that it will be easier in the Next?" God answered, "You speak correctly, and I will begin with you." And indeed the Torah says, *his eyes became dim* (27:1).

Yaakov later said to God, "When a man dies suddenly, without illness, he can leave no will for his children." God answered, "You speak correctly, and I will begin with you." And the Torah says, *It was told to Yosef (Joseph), your father is ill* (48:1).

◈§ Sarah's Doubts

וַתִּצְחַק שָׂרָה — *Sarah laughed* (18:12). When the month of Tishrei came and she was not yet pregnant, she began to feel that the angel had not spoken the truth. She thought to herself, "I am not pregnant, and there are only six months left to Pesach." But Avraham did believe the promise, because he had heard it from God, while Sarah had heard it only from the angels.

But does the Torah not say that Avraham also laughed when God told him he would have a son? — Avraham did not laugh among other people, while concerning Sarah the Torah says, *Sarah laughed to herself* (*to herself — bekirbah*, alluding to a word with a similar root, *krovim*, "relatives"). That is to say, she laughed among her relatives, and told them what had happened.

Chizkuni tells a parable. A woman wished to speak harshly with her daughter-in-law. Instead, she spoke harshly to her own daughter, in her daughter-in-law's presence, so that her daughter-in-law would understand the criticism. Similarly, God asked Avraham why Sarah had laughed so that he should understand that he, too, had not acted properly in laughing.

וַתִּצְחַק שָׂרָה בְּקִרְבָּה — *Sarah laughed to herself* (18:12). The word translated *to herself* (בְּקִרְבָּה) is related to the word קְרָבַיִם, "inward parts." Hence the following interpretation of the Midrash.

Sarah laughed and put her hand on her stomach and said, "Can this withered and dry belly carry a child? These withered breasts, can they yield milk?"

◈§ For the Sake of Peace

וַאדֹנִי זָקֵן — *My lord is old* (18:12). In reporting Sarah's reaction to the divine promise God asked Avraham, *Why did Sarah scoff and ask, "How can I have children?"* God here changed Sarah's words so that Avraham would not be angry with her for having said that her *husband* was too old to have children. From this our Sages learn that for the sake of domestic peace a harmless lie is permitted.

◈§ Denial and Misunderstanding

וַתְּכַחֵשׁ שָׂרָה לֵאמֹר לֹא צָחַקְתִּי — *Sarah denied it, saying, "I did not laugh"* (18:15). Sarah said she had not laughed, being afraid to admit that she had. Or it could be that she did not admit that she had laughed because she now realized that she should instead have praised God for His good tidings. She did not know that God had told Avraham of her laughter; had she known she would not have denied God's words. When Avraham questioned her a second time she understood that God had told him that she had laughed, and so she remained silent.

Ramban writes that Sarah was unaware that God had promised that she would have a son. When God told Avraham of the promise he had not told Sarah of it, for he thought that God would send a separate angel to tell her the good news. When the angels came and told her she thought that they were humans, not angels — and that was why she laughed.

⇜§ Escorting a Guest

וְאַבְרָהָם הֹלֵךְ עִמָּם לְשַׁלְּחָם — *Avraham went with them, to send them on their way* (18:16). Because he escorted them, God appeared to him almost immediately. What is the proper distance to escort someone? A friend should escort another to the end of the town; a teacher should escort his student the distance which it is permissible to walk on *Shabbos*; a student should escort his teacher three miles; and a host ought to escort a guest for one mile.

⇜§ Praise that Leads to Humility

הַמְכַסֶּה אֲנִי מֵאַבְרָהָם אֲשֶׁר אֲנִי עֹשֶׂה — *Shall I hide from Avraham what I am going to do?* (18:17). God said, "How can I not tell Avraham whom I love — because he is pious, and teaches his household to practice charity and righteousness — what I plan to do to Sodom?" When Avraham heard that God praised him he became even more humble than before, and said, *I am dust and ashes* (18:27). We learn from this that when one is praised he should not be overimpressed, but should become even more humble.

כִּי יְדַעְתִּיו — *For I know him* (18:19). That is, I love him. R' Bechaye writes: This phrase means that God said: "I take especial care of Avraham; I make Myself known to him at all times in order to save him."

⇜§ The Evil in Sodom

וַיֹּאמֶר ה' זַעֲקַת סְדֹם וַעֲמֹרָה כִּי רָבָּה — *God said, "The cry of Sodom and Amorah is great"* (18:20). They were evil both in body and with their possessions, but their judgment in heaven was mainly because of their refusal to give charity.

◆§ Ten Righteous Men

אוּלַי יֵשׁ חֲמִשִּׁים צַדִּיקִם בְּתוֹךְ הָעִיר — *Perhaps there are fifty righteous men in the city* (18:24). That is to say, "Perhaps there are fifty righteous men in the five cities of Sodom, ten righteous men in each city. Would You destroy them? And if You will not save the wicked for the sake of the righteous, at the very least will You spare the most righteous ones?"

Ramban asks why Avraham used the words *in the city*. The answer is that Avraham wanted to include any righteous men who happened to be in the city, having just arrived there, such as Lot.

◆§ The Merit of the Multitude

חָלִלָה לְּךָ — *Far be it from You* (18:25). "People will say that You customarily destroy the righteous as well as the wicked. They will say that You did so during the Flood and for the generation which built the Tower."

God agreed that if He found fifty righteous men in the city He would spare it. Avraham answered, "What if You find only forty-five men? Because of a lack of five men, would You destroy an entire city?" Avraham maintained that if there were forty-five righteous men in the five cities, that meant nine in each city, and God could count Himself as the tenth in each city, so that there would be a righteous *minyan*.

Avraham continued: "What if there are forty righteous men? At least four of the cities ought to be saved." God answered, "I will not destroy them for the sake of the forty." Avraham went on: "If there are thirty men, should not three cities be saved?" God agreed that He would not destroy Sodom for the sake of the thirty. Avraham continued, "What if there are only twenty?" God promised not to destroy it because of the twenty. Avraham asked God if He would spare Sodom for the sake of ten righteous men, and God agreed, for the sake of the ten.

Avraham did not pray for fewer than ten righteous men. He knew that if there would not be ten righteous men God would destroy the entire world. In the time of the Flood there was only Noach, his wife, his three children and their wives. Since they were only eight people, they could not save the rest of their generation.

R' Bechaye asks why Avraham offered such an extended prayer. Once God had agreed to spare four cities in the merit of forty righteous men, could he not assume that He would save three cities for thirty and so on? The answer is that Avraham thought that the more righteous men that could be found, the greater their combined merit. God had agreed to save four cities for forty righteous men, but if there would be fewer than forty He might not want to save anyone. He therefore had to plead separately for the merit of thirty righteous men and so on.

We learn from this that we ought to pray in a large group, as the merit of a large group is very great. Our Sages say in the *Gemara* that "a small group heeding the Torah cannot compare to a large group heeding it." In this case, however, God was merciful and told Avraham that He would spare the cities even for a small group of righteous men.

⊷§ Angels of Mercy

וַיָּבֹאוּ שְׁנֵי הַמַּלְאָכִים סְדֹמָה — *The two angels came to Sodom* (19:1). Two of the angels went to Sodom. The third, who had told Sarah that she was to have a son, returned to heaven. One may ask, why is it that in reference to Lot the Torah calls them angels, while in reference to Avraham they are called men? The answer is that angels habitually came to Avraham's house, just as men did, and so they were called men; angels did not normally visit Lot's house, so they were called angels.

The angels reached Sodom in the evening. Why did the angels take so long to arrive from Chevron (Hebron) to Sodom? — They were angels of mercy, and delayed, in order to give Avraham time to try and save Sodom.

⊷§ Why Lot did not Run

וְלוֹט יֹשֵׁב בְּשַׁעַר סְדֹם וַיַּרְא לוֹט וַיָּקָם לִקְרָאתָם — *Lot was sitting at the gate of Sodom. Lot saw them and rose to greet them* (19:1). On that day Lot had been appointed one of their judges [who in olden time used to sit at the gates of each city]. Lot had learned from Avraham how to receive guests, and so rose up before them, thinking that they were people.

R' Bechaye and the author of *Toldos Yitzchak* ask why he did not run to meet them, as Avraham did. — When they arrived at Avraham's house it was still daylight, and he was able to see them from a distance. They arrived at Lot's in the darkness, and he saw them only when they were quite close to him.

⊷§ Furtive Hospitality

וַיֹּאמֶר הִנֶּה נָּא אֲדֹנַי סוּרוּ נָא אֶל בֵּית עַבְדְּכֶם וְלִינוּ וְרַחֲצוּ רַגְלֵיכֶם — *He said, "Now my lords, turn aside to my house; spend the night, and wash your feet"* (19:2). Lot invited them to his house, but asked them to enter through the back way, so that the townspeople should not see that he was showing hospitality. That would have endangered both Lot and his guests.

Why did Lot not follow Avraham's example, and first invite them to wash, before entering his house? *Chizkuni* says that Lot was afraid that the wicked people would come and see that his guests were washed, and they would say that they had been in his home for a long while.

לֹא כִּי בָרְחוֹב נָלִין — *"No, we will sleep in the street"* (19:2).

"We want to sleep outside so that the townspeople will see that we have come to destroy them. Perhaps they will repent."

⧏§ Standing on Ceremony

וַיִּפְצַר בָּם — *He pleaded with them* (19:3). They agreed to stay only after Lot had pleaded with them, while to Avraham's request they acceded immediately. From this we learn that we must immediately obey an important person's requests, and not stand on ceremony. However, we can make a lesser person ask for something several times.

⧏§ A Disturbed Feast

וַיַּעַשׂ לָהֶם מִשְׁתֶּה — *He made them a feast* (19:3). He baked *matzos*, since it was Pesach. The angels asked him if the townspeople were good or wicked, and he said that most were wicked. As they were speaking the entire town came, young and old — for there was not a single righteous man there to stop them — and told Lot to hand over the men who had come to him. Lot went out, locked the door behind him, and told them not to harm his guests.

⧏§ Lot's Proposition

הִנֵּה נָא לִי שְׁתֵּי בָנוֹת אֲשֶׁר לֹא יָדְעוּ אִישׁ — *"I have two daughters who have not known men"* (19:8). Lot said, "I will give you my two daughters, and do what you want with them. Leave the two men alone, for they are guests in my home."

They told him, "You are a stranger here, and you judge us?! We will treat you worse than we will treat the strangers!" They overpowered Lot and tried to break down the door. The angels thrust their hands outside and pulled Lot in, locking the door behind him. Everyone left on the other side of the door was stricken with blindness, and they could not find the door.

The angels asked Lot if he had any other children or sons-in-law within the city. They asked him, מִי לְךָ פֹה — *Whom do you have here?* (19:12), meaning, "How can you justify or defend these wicked men?" — for Lot had defended the townspeople all night.

◆§ The Pride of the Angels

כִּי מַשְׁחִתִים אֲנַחְנוּ אֶת הַמָּקוֹם הַזֶּה — *"For we will destroy this place"* (19:13). R' Bechaye writes that because the angels said that they would destroy the city, rather than attributing the destruction to God, they were exiled from their proper place for 138 years. In all that time they were entrusted with no mission, until God sent them to Yaakov, and Yaakov made them his emissaries to Esav. We learn from this that a person ought not think too highly of himself. Glory belongs to God alone, as Yeshayahu (Isaiah) said, מְלֹא כָל הָאָרֶץ כְּבוֹדוֹ — *The world is filled with His glory (Yeshayahu 6:3).*

Ultimately the angels admitted, וַיְשַׁלְחֵנוּ ה׳ לְשַׁחֲתָה — *God has sent us to destroy it* (19:13).

◆§ A Hasty Exit

וַיֵּצֵא לוֹט — *Lot went out* (19:14). Lot went to tell his sons-in-law to flee with him, for God intended to destroy the entire city, but they laughed at him.

As dawn broke the angels hurriedly told Lot to take his wife and the two daughters who remained in his home, or he too would be trapped and die for the town's sins. Lot tried to delay and save his wealth, so the angels grasped him and his family by the hand and led them out of the city. They did not let him take any of his money. For this reason the Torah states, כְּהוֹצִיאָם אֹתָם — *when they had taken them out* (19:17), using an expression which seems to double the word *them*. This usage emphasizes that the angels took out them alone, while their money was left behind.

The angels warned Lot not to look back, for he too was wicked, and it was only because of Avraham's merit that he and his family were saved. The *Midrash* says that the angels commanded him not to look back because the Divine Presence and the angels were hovering over the city, bringing brimstone and fire upon it.

Lot told the angel that he could not run quickly, and therefore feared that the calamity would overtake him. He asked to stay in the city of Tzoar, which was newly built, and could therefore not have committed as many sins as the neighboring towns. God granted his request and spared the city of Tzoar.

The angel told Lot to make haste and reach Tzoar, for he could do nothing to Sodom until Lot's arrival there. This was the angels' punishment for having said that they would destroy Sodom, when they ought to have said that God would destroy it. Now they had to tell Lot, לֹא אוּכַל לַעֲשׂוֹת דָּבָר — *I can do nothing* (19:22).

◄§ Sun and Moon

הַשֶּׁמֶשׁ יָצָא עַל הָאָרֶץ — *The sun had risen upon the earth* (19:23). The sun rose and the moon was still in the sky. It was in mid-month, on Pesach, when the sun and the moon appear together in the sky for a few hours during the day, that God sent a rain of sulphur and fire from heaven. Some of the people of Sodom had worshiped the sun, while others had deified the moon. If God would have punished them when the sun was out, the moon worshipers would have said that had the moon been out, it would not have allowed this to happen; if God had done it when the moon alone was in the sky, the sun worshipers would have said that if the sun was out it would not have allowed it to happen. So God brought the fire when both the sun and the moon were showing.

◄§ Sulphur and Fire ...

גָּפְרִית וָאֵשׁ — *Sulphur and fire* (19:24). When God punishes the wicked He sends sulphur and fire from the sky; when He rewards the righteous he sends manna from the sky.

◄§ ... and Salt

וַתַּבֵּט אִשְׁתּוֹ מֵאַחֲרָיו — *And his wife looked behind him* (19:26). Behind *him* (not her) — for Lot fled hindmost, driving his family ahead to safety.

Iris, Lot's wife, was worried over the two daughters whom they had left behind with their husbands. Casting a backward glance to see if her daughters were escaping, she saw the Divine Presence and turned into a pillar of salt, for she had sinned by refusing to give her guests salt.

◄§ In the Merit of Avraham

וַיִּזְכֹּר אֱלֹהִים אֶת אַבְרָהָם — *God remembered Avraham* (19:29). God remembered Avraham and therefore saved Lot. He also remembered how Lot had done Avraham a favor and not told anyone that Sarah was his wife.

◄§ Lot Runs Further

וַיַּעַל לוֹט מִצּוֹעַר — *Lot went up from Tzoar* (19:30). Lot was afraid to stay in Tzoar because it was close to Sodom, and it too might be destroyed. *Chizkuni* writes that Lot thought that Tzoar was spared only because he had been unable to flee any further at the time, but now that he had more time he had to escape, for it too was to be destroyed.

⋘ Lot's Daughters

וַתֹּאמֶר הַבְּכִירָה אֶל הַצְּעִירָה — *The older daughter said to the younger* (19:31). Lot had two unmarried daughters. The older said to the younger, "Our father is old and may die suddenly, or will become unable to father children. There is no man left to make us pregnant." They thought that the entire world had been destroyed, as in the days of the Flood.

R' Bechaye writes that the daughters were modest and were ashamed to ask their father to have relations with them — which would have been permitted to the descendants of Noach. God placed wine in the cave in which they had hidden themselves. They gave him this wine, until he was too drunk to know that he had had relations with them.

Because the older daughter suggested it, in her case the Torah states explicitly, וַתִּשְׁכַּב אֶת אָבִיהָ — *and she lay with her father* (19:33), while in reference to the younger it says, less directly, וַתִּשְׁכַּב עִמּוֹ — *she lay with him* (19:35).

Our Sages say that Lot did not know when they slept together the first night, but when he awoke he realized what had happened. Even so, the next night he got drunk once again.

⋘ Moav and Ammon

וַתַּהֲרֶיןָ — *They became pregnant* (19:36). The elder had a son whom she named Moav (Moab), which means "from a father" (מֵאָב). Because she was immodest, God later gave Moshe (Moses) permission to disturb the nation of Moav, though he could not declare war on them. The younger was modest and called her son Ben-Ami ("son of my nation"), and did not clearly state his origin. Therefore God forbade Moshe from doing any harm at all to his descendants, the nation of Ammon.

⋘ Trouble in Gerar

וַיִּסַּע מִשָּׁם אַבְרָהָם — *Avraham journeyed from there* (20:1). Avraham saw that Sodom had been destroyed and no guests would be passing his way, so he left. Also, Lot's name had been tarnished because he had had relations with his daughters. Avraham was embarrassed, and traveled to the city of Gerar.

There Avraham said that his wife Sarah was his sister. Why did he not ask her to say that he was her brother, as he had done with Pharaoh? — Since Sarah had already been taken to Pharaoh as a result of this statement, Avraham knew that she would not want to say it again.

R' Bechaye asks why Avraham went to Gerar, when he had had such troubles and had needed great miracles to free Sarah from Pharaoh's palace. He answers that Avraham gave Sarah a divorce before going to Gerar. God told him that it was not legally binding for he had done it out of fear. Therefore an angel came to Avimelech, King of Gerar, to tell him וְהִיא בְּעֻלַת בָּעַל — *She is a man's wife* (20:3).

⋖§ Sarah is Taken

וַיִּשְׁלַח אֲבִימֶלֶךְ מֶלֶךְ גְּרָר וַיִּקַּח אֶת שָׂרָה — *Avimelech, King of Gerar, sent, and took Sarah* (20:2). When Avimelech took Sarah, an angel came to him that night in a dream and told him that he would die because the woman whom he had taken was married.

The author of *Toldos Yitzchak* asks why it says, in reference to Pharaoh, *the woman was taken to the house of Pharaoh*, whereas here it says *and he took Sarah*, not specifying that she was taken to his house. The answer is that Pharaoh was a greater king than Avimelech, as well as a wicked man. He had taken Sarah because of her great beauty. He wanted to make a lavish wedding before taking her, and he wanted to display his riches. Therefore, until the day of the wedding, he placed her in the home of one of his nobles. "The house of Pharaoh" refers to his household — his courtier's home.

Avimelech was righteous, and was not as wealthy. He took Sarah because of her fine family background, as the Torah says, *Avraham said of Sarah, "She is my sister," and Avimelech King of Gerar took Sarah.* Avimelech sent for her only because she was Avraham's sister. He did not take her for her beauty, for by this time she was not as beautiful as she had been. He did not intend to make a great wedding but simply to take her now as a wife.

⋖§ Avimelech's Righteousness

וַאֲבִימֶלֶךְ לֹא קָרַב אֵלֶיהָ — *Avimelech had not come near her* (20:4). The angel did not let Avimelech approach Sarah. In Pharaoh's case the Torah did not have to say this, for she had not even been taken to his palace, but was at a servant's home.

The author of *Toldos Yitzchak* gives another explanation. In the case of Avimelech, the Torah must say that he did not come near Sarah because she became pregnant immediately after the episode, and people would have said that she bore Avimelech's child.

The same author asks the following question. Why did an angel come to Avimelech and not to Pharaoh? Avimelech was righteous and Pharaoh was wicked, and God does not send angels to the wicked.

He raises another question. Why did God strike Pharaoh with leprous sores, and not Avimelech? God closed all of the openings in the bodies of Avimelech's household members, so that they could not give birth or attend to their bodily needs. Even the hens could not lay their eggs. God did this so that Avimelech would understand that this was his punishment for taking Sarah, and this was punishment enough for him.

Pharaoh, though, was a wicked man, and he caused men to speak ill of Sarah. God therefore punished him with sores and leprosy, which is the punishment of a person who speaks badly of another.

Even though people did say that Avimelech had made Sarah pregnant, this was not his fault. As soon as he found out that she was a married woman he did not want to touch her, whereas when Pharaoh found out that she was married he still wanted her as a wife. Therefore he was punished with leprosy.

Yet another question is raised by the author *Toldos Yitzchak.* Why did Pharaoh not ask Avraham for his excuses? Avimelech did ask him why he had said that Sarah was his sister. Further, why did Pharaoh tell Avraham to take his wife and leave the land, while Avimelech invited him to stay wherever he wished? The answer is that Pharaoh was wicked and did not want to hear Avraham tell him that he had feared he would be killed on account of his wife, so he did not ask him to explain himself. Moreover, he was afraid because his people were steeped in lasciviousness and might commit adultery. Avimelech, though, was righteous, and asked Avraham why he had lied.

Avraham answered that although Avimelech himself was righteous, he was afraid of Avimelech's people. Further, Avraham told him that he had not said this to Avimelech alone. Since he had left his father's house he had always told people that Sarah was his sister.

Avimelech was afraid that the angel had come to destroy his land as he had destroyed Sodom. He therefore asked Avraham to stay in his land, hoping that he would save it. Because of this the Torah says, וַיַּשְׁכֵּם אֲבִימֶלֶךְ בַּבֹּקֶר וַיִּקְרָא לְכָל עֲבָדָיו — *Avimelech rose early in the morning and called all of his servants* (20:8). Avimelech was afraid of the angel, and called together his servants to tell them what had happened. They too became terrified.

◄§ Avimelech's Defense

ה' הֲגוֹי גַם צַדִיק תַּהֲרֹג — *"Lord, will You kill even a righteous nation?"* (20:4). Avimelech argued: "If You kill a nation that is righteous, I will say that that is what You did in the time of the Flood."

R' Bechaye says that Avimelech also told God, "If You kill the nation (i.e., the king) You will also cause the death of the righteous (i.e., Avraham; גַּם צַדִּיק — lit., "also a righteous man"), because my people will kill Avraham in revenge." Avimelech asked, "Why am I to blame? Avraham told me that Sarah was his sister, and she said that he was her brother. I did not mean to sin, and I did not sin, for I did not touch her."

The angel told him, "I know that you did not intend to sin, and therefore I did not allow you to touch her. It was not your doing at all."

◆§ A Thousand Pieces of Gold

הָשֵׁב אֵשֶׁת הָאִישׁ כִּי נָבִיא הוּא — Return the man's wife, for he is a prophet (20:7). "Return his wife to Avraham. He is a prophet and knows that you have not touched her, so she will not be repulsive to him. Moreover, he will pray for you."

R' Bechaye writes that Avimelech told Sarah, "I have given your brother a thousand gold pieces, so that everyone will know that I did not touch you, and that I owe Avraham an apology. Had I given you the money everyone would have said that I gave it to you because you had relations with me."

וְאֵת כֹּל וְנֹכָחַת — Before all you are righted (20:16). These words of Avimelech mean the following: "With these (my gifts) you will be able to vindicate yourself and show that you left my house pure." [Since the root of וְנֹכָחַת means not only "to prove" but also "to rebuke,"] his words can also be translated as meaning, "You will be punished by God if you say that Avraham is your brother, for men will take you as a wife." The *Midrash Rabbah* writes that Avimelech gave Sarah a valuable dress which was worn only by the queen, and then said to her, הִנֵּה הוּא לָךְ כְּסוּת עֵינַיִם — Here it is for you, a covering of the eyes (20:16). All men will see this lovely dress and will be afraid even to look at you.

(The following [chapter 21] is read in the Torah on the first day of Rosh HaShanah.)

◆§ Sarah Deserves a Child

וַה' פָּקַד אֶת שָׂרָה — God remembered Sarah (21:1). The Torah placed this section immediately after the portion in which Avraham prayed that Avimelech's household should be able to give birth once again, to teach us that when a person prays for another, and he himself has the same request, God grants it to him even before he grants it to the one for whom he had prayed. Avraham had prayed that

Avimelech's household should be able to bear children, and now God allowed Sarah to become pregnant even before healing Avimelech's people.

The *Midrash* writes: Why did God remember Sarah? God said, "Sarah was in Pharaoh's house and in Avimelech's house and remained pure. Shall I not remember her, to give her a child?"

The author of *Toldos Yitzchak* asks why the Torah first says, וַה' פָּקַד אֶת שָׂרָה כַּאֲשֶׁר אָמָר — *God remembered Sarah, as He said He would,* and later, וַיַּעַשׂ ה' לְשָׂרָה כַּאֲשֶׁר דִּבֵּר — *God did to Sarah as He had said.* Why are both verses necessary? *God remembered Sarah* refers to the miracle that she became pregnant. *God did to Sarah as He had said* refers to the fact that she then gave birth to a son and had the milk to nurse him.

Being very modest, Sarah was embarrassed to uncover her breasts. Avraham told her that she must waive her modesty for a short time and not be ashamed. When she uncovered her breasts milk flowed from them as from two fountains, and all the nobles' wives asked her to nurse their children.

⊰§ Widespread Rejoicing

וַתֹּאמֶר שָׂרָה צְחֹק עָשָׂה לִי אֱלֹהִים כָּל הַשֹּׁמֵעַ יִצְחַק לִי — *Sarah said, "God has given me laughter. All that hear will laugh"* (21:6). Sarah rejoiced and everyone rejoiced with her, for many women who were childless were remembered together with Sarah, and many sick people were healed on the day that Yitzchak was born.

⊰§ A Miracle for the Aged

וַתֹּאמֶר מִי מִלֵּל לְאַבְרָהָם הֵינִיקָה בָנִים שָׂרָה — *She said, "Who would have said to Avraham that Sarah would nurse children?"* (21:7). The author of *Toldos Yitzchak* interprets thus: "Who will be able to speak to Avraham now? — For he may succumb to pride."

And why was it Sarah and not Avraham that spoke here of laughter? — Because it is more remarkable that a woman advanced in years should have children than a man, because a man might marry a young wife and have children.

⊰§ A Boast Reversed

וַיִּגְדַּל הַיֶּלֶד וַיִּגָּמַל וַיַּעַשׂ אַבְרָהָם מִשְׁתֶּה גָדוֹל — *The boy grew and was weaned. Avraham made a great celebration* (21:8). Avraham made a feast to celebrate when the child was weaned. Many nobles attended as well as Shem and Ever, Avimelech and Og.

The people turned to Og and said, "Liar! You said that Sarah would bear no children." Og answered that Yitzchak was as frail as a fly: he could crush him with one finger. God said, "Yitzchak's children will be as numerous as the sand by the sea, and you will be defeated by them."

◄§ Circumcision Feast

בְּיוֹם הִגָּמֵל אֶת יִצְחָק — *On the day that Yitzchak was weaned* (21:8). R' Bechaye asks: Why did Avraham not make a feast on the day he circumcised Yitzchak? The answer is that he waited for him to be weaned, for then he would bring him to a teacher to learn the Torah. He wanted to rejoice with the joy of the Torah.

Also, it is known that a person loves his children more after they are weaned, than when they are first born. A child then shows intelligence and can speak. Therefore he made a feast when he weaned Yitzchak.

The *Midrash* writes: The word *higamel* (הִגָּמֵל — "weaned") is made up of two parts: *hag* and *mal*. *Mal* means circumcised, while *hag* has the numerical equivalent of eight, meaning, on the eighth day he was circumcised, and Avraham made a feast to celebrate this. We learn from this that we should make a feast when a child is circumcised.

◄§ Yishmael's Plaint

מְצַחֵק ... וַתֵּרֶא שָׂרָה אֶת בֶּן הָגָר הַמִּצְרִית — *Sarah saw the son of Hagar the Egyptian ... making fun* (21:9). Sarah saw Yishmael mocking Yitzchak. She told Avraham to banish the maidservant and her son. The author of *Toldos Yitzchak* says that Yishmael had mocked the feast which Avraham had made for Yitzchak, and said, "Why is there such rejoicing? Why did they make Yitzchak a greater feast than they made for me? I am the eldest and will inherit a double portion."

And this was why Sarah went on to say, *For the son of this maidservant will not inherit with my son, with Yitzchak.*

◄§ Bread and Water

וַיַּשְׁכֵּם אַבְרָהָם בַּבֹּקֶר וַיִּקַּח לֶחֶם וְחֵמַת מַיִם — *Avraham arose early in the morning, and took bread and a bottle of water* (21:14). The author of *Toldos Yitzchak* asks: How could someone as wealthy as Avraham send them off with no food for the road, with just bread and water? The answer is that God told Avraham to do whatever Sarah asked him to do. Sarah said that he should exile them, so Avraham could do no more than what one customarily did for exiles, which was to give bread and water.

R' Bechaye writes that Avraham gave Yishmael only bread and

water because he saw that Yishmael's children would be great enemies of Israel.

Avraham put the bread and water upon her shoulders, as well as the child. Sarah had cast an evil eye upon the child, and he could not walk. The author of *Toldos Yitzchak* writes that Yishmael was wild and refused to obey his father and leave the house, so Avraham had to tie him up and place him on his mother's shoulders. Therefore the Torah does not say "he sent them away," but rather, וַיְשַׁלְּחֶהָ — *he sent her away.* He sent away only Hagar, for Yishmael was bound to her shoulders.

◄§ The Prayers of the Ailing

וַיִּכְלוּ הַמַּיִם — *The water was used up* (21:15). The water bottle was empty, for Yishmael was sick and a sick person drinks more than a healthy one. Hagar put him under a tree and sat at the distance of a bowshot from him, so that she would not see her child die. She began to cry.

וַיִּשְׁמַע אֱלֹהִים אֶת קוֹל הַנַּעַר — *God heard the voice of the child* (21:17). Our Sages learn from here that a sick person's prayers are heeded before the prayers of those who intercede on his behalf. The angel told Hagar not to be afraid.

◄§ The Angels Intercede

כִּי שָׁמַע אֱלֹהִים אֶל קוֹל הַנַּעַר בַּאֲשֶׁר הוּא שָׁם — *God has heard the youth's voice, there where he is* (21:17). The angels asked God: "Master of the Universe, how can you have mercy on Yishmael, when he will ultimately let the Jews die of thirst?" God answered that He judges a person "there where he is," in accordance with his present deeds, and not on the basis of evil which he will do in the future. At this time in his life Yishmael did not deserve death.

◄§ Hagar and the Angel

כִּי לְגוֹי גָּדוֹל אֲשִׂימֶנּוּ — *I will make of him a great nation* (21:18). The author of *Toldos Yitzchak* asks why the angel spoke at such length with Hagar, telling her that Yishmael would one day father a great nation. Would it not have been sufficient for God to show her the well? For then she would surely give her child water to drink. The answer is that Hagar intentionally left Yishmael to die. She said to herself, "His father shows him no mercy, why should I?" The Torah says earlier, וַתַּשְׁלֵךְ אֶת הַיֶּלֶד — *she thrust the boy under one of the bushes*, rather than וַתָּשֶׂם — "she placed the boy," to show that she mercilessly threw the boy under a tree, instead of laying him down gently.

The angel thought that now too she would let him die and therefore told her that he would one day father a great nation. She saw the well, filled the bottle and gave him water. God was with the youth and helped him. Later, his mother married him to an Egyptian.

⊷§ Avraham Swears

וַיְהִי בָּעֵת הַהִיא וַיֹּאמֶר אֲבִימֶלֶךְ — *It was at this time, Avimelech ... said* (21:22). Avimelech said, "Avraham has had great luck. He survived the destruction of Sodom, battled the four kings, and his wife gave birth to a son when she was already old." Avimelech therefore feared him. He came to Avraham and said, "Swear that you will not harm my children, for I have been good to you." Avraham swore. The author of *Toldos Yitzchak* writes that Avimelech had an idol, worn over his heart, and he wanted Avraham to swear by it. Avraham said, אָנֹכִי אִשָּׁבֵעַ — literally, "I shall swear," but here understood to mean "I shall swear by אָנֹכִי," as in the opening words of the Revelation at Sinai: *I (anochi) am the Lord your God.* That is to say, "I will swear by God alone."

⊷§ Avraham's Eshel

וַיִּטַּע אֶשֶׁל בִּבְאֵר שָׁבַע — *He planted a tamarisk tree in Be'er Sheva* (21:33). Avraham planted a beautiful garden with many fruits which he would serve to his guests. The Sages say the word *eshel* ("tamarisk") represents a house for guests. He built the house with four doors so that guests could arrive from all sides. Through this house he made God's Name known. When guests would thank Avraham for their food he would say, "You think you have eaten *my* food, but you are mistaken. Food and drink come from God, and it is Him Whom you should thank."

This is the meaning of the verse, וַיִּקְרָא שָׁם בְּשֵׁם ה' אֵל עוֹלָם — *And he called there on the Name of the Lord, the everlasting God* (21:33). For these words can be also understood to mean that through his hospitality Avraham *caused* people to call there on the name of the Lord.

R' Bechaye writes that *eshel* (אֶשֶׁל) is an acronym. The letter *alef* stands for eating (*achilah*), the letter *shin* for sleeping (*shechivah*), and the letter *lamed* for escort (*levayah*), for he escorted each guest homeward, telling him meanwhile of the One God.

(The following [chapter 22] is read in the Torah on the second day of Rosh HaShanah.)

⋘ The Ultimate Test of Faith

וַיְהִי אַחַר הַדְּבָרִים הָאֵלֶּה וְהָאֱלֹהִים נִסָּה אֶת אַבְרָהָם — *After these things, God tested Avraham* (22:1). Satan told God, "Avraham made a lavish feast and did not offer You a sacrifice!" God answered that he had made the feast in honor of his son, yet if He asked him to kill his son for the sake of God he would do it. This is what the words *after these things* refers to: after Satan's words, God told him to sacrifice his son Yitzchak.

Another meaning is that this was after the words of Yishmael, who boasted in Yitzchak's presence, saying, "My father circumcised me when I was thirteen years old, and I did not protest, while you were circumcised when you were eight days old, before you had the intelligence to protest." Yitzchak replied, "You praise yourself because of one organ of your body. If God should request my entire body, I would give it to Him." After this conversation, God told Avraham:

קַח נָא אֶת בִּנְךָ — *Take your son* (22:2). "Take your son and obey Me, I beg you, so that people should not say that the first tests of loyalty were worth nothing. Take your son and slaughter him as a sacrifice."

Avraham said, "I have two sons. Which shall I take?" God answered, אֶת יְחִידְךָ — *your only son.* Avraham said, "Yitzchak is an only son to Sarah, and Yishmael is an only son to Hagar." God said, אֲשֶׁר אָהַבְתָּ — *Whom you love.* Avraham answered, "I love them both." God finally said, *Yitzchak.*

Why did God not immediately tell him to take Yitzchak? — So as not to frighten him immediately, and in order to be able to give him a reward for each and every word which He said to him.

וְהַעֲלֵהוּ שָׁם לְעֹלָה — *Bring him as an offering there* (22:2). God never actually said that he should slaughter him, but only that he should bring him up, meaning that he could immediately take him down again from the altar. But Avraham thought that God had asked him to kill him there, as a sacrifice.

⋘ Avraham's Alacrity

וַיַּשְׁכֵּם אַבְרָהָם בַּבֹּקֶר — *Avraham rose early in the morning* (22:3).

Avraham awoke early in order to obey God's command, and saddled his donkey himself. He took Yishmael and Eliezer with him, so that if one should have to go to the fields to relieve himself, Avraham would not be left alone.

וַיְבַקַּע עֲצֵי עֹלָה — *He cut wood for the offering* (22:3). Avraham cut the wood in his house because he thought that there might be no wood available at the site of the sacrifice. R' Bechaye explains this differently: he took wood from his house to make certain that it was valid to bring as a sacrifice — wood from which no worms had eaten. In the merit of the wood which Avraham split for the sacrifices, God split the Red Sea for his children.

◆§ Both were Wrong

וַיַּרְא אֶת הַמָּקוֹם מֵרָחֹק — *He saw the place from afar* (22:4). When he saw the place in the distance he said to Yitzchak, "What do you see?" Yitzchak answered, "I see a lovely hill with a beautiful cloud rising above it." Avraham asked the other two what they saw and they answered that they saw nothing. So Avraham said, שְׁבוּ לָכֶם פֹּה עִם הַחֲמוֹר — *"Stay here with the donkey* (22:5), for you resemble the donkey."

Pirkei deR' Eliezer says that the two of them quarreled. Yishmael said that when Yitzchak was sacrificed he would be the heir, and Eliezer said that Yishmael would be exiled from his father's house and he himself would be the heir. A heavenly voice was heard saying, "Neither of you will inherit."

◆§ Satan Intervenes

וְנִשְׁתַּחֲוֶה וְנָשׁוּבָה אֲלֵיכֶם — *We will worship, and return to you* (22:5). Avraham told the others that they would pray and then return. *Rashi* writes that he spoke prophetically, in saying that they would both return. R' Bechaye writes that he meant that he would return with Yitzchak's bones which would remain after the burning, and for that reason said they both would return.

The *Midrash* writes that Avraham thought to himself, "Shall I not tell Sarah of this? If I sacrifice her son and she never sees him again, she will kill herself. But if I do tell her, she will not allow it, since women are light-minded."

He therefore told Sarah to prepare a lavish feast and be happy. He told her that he himself had recognized his Creator when he was three years old. Yitzchak was already thirty-seven years old, and it was time for him to become accustomed to obey the commandments. He told her that he was going to make a sacrifice on Mt. Moriah, and asked permission to take Yitzchak with him. Sarah gave permission. Avraham rose very early, while Sarah was still asleep, so that she would not change her mind, and when everyone else too was sleeping, so that they would not dissuade him from it.

Satan appeared before him, dressed as an elderly man, and asked him where he was going. Avraham answered that he was going to pray. Satan asked, "Why are you carrying the wood and the fire and that slaughtering knife?" Avraham answered that he would be away from home for several days, and would cook his food with the wood and the fire. Satan said, "You are an elderly man, with only one son born in your old age — and you want to kill him? How God will punish you!" Avraham answered that this was God's command.

Satan then went to Yitzchak and asked him where he was going. He answered that he was going to learn the commandments. Satan said to him, "Do you want to learn after your death or while you are alive? They want to slaughter you!" Yitzchak answered, "If God wants to kill me, I will allow Him to do it."

Satan then went to Sarah and asked her where Avraham and Yitzchak were. He told her that she would never see her son Yitzchak again, and she answered, "Let God do as He wills."

The *Midrash* writes that Satan then created a gigantic body of water in front of Avraham and Yitzchak. They walked into the water up to their necks. Then Avraham prayed, "Master of the Universe, You commanded that I sacrifice my son to You. Help me do it." And the water disappeared.

◄§ Father and Son

וַיֵּלְכוּ שְׁנֵיהֶם יַחְדָּו — *The two of them went together* (22:6). They went as one — Avraham, who knew that he was going to kill his son, as happy as Yitzchak, who knew nothing of it.

וַיֹּאמֶר יִצְחָק אֶל אַבְרָהָם אָבִיו וַיֹּאמֶר אָבִי וַיֹּאמֶר הִנֶּנִּי בְנִי — *Yitzchak said to his father Avraham, he said, "My father," and he said, "I am here, my son"* (22:7). This is difficult to understand. Why does the Torah say that Yitzchak called Avraham *my father*. We already know that Avraham was his father. Further, why does the Torah again tell us that he was *his father Avraham*?

R' Bechaye writes that he called out *Father, father!* in order to arouse Avraham's mercy. Another reason is that Yitzchak told Avraham that people would say that it was Avimelech who had made Sarah pregnant, because if Yitzchak had been Avaham's own son he would not have been able to kill him. Therefore Yitzchak asked, "My father?" — that is, "Are you really my father?" Avraham answered, "My son" — reassuring him that he really was his son.

Yitzchak said, "If I am your son, then where is the sacrifice?" Avraham answered, "God will show us the sacrifice, my son." Yitzchak then understood that it was he who was to be sacrificed.

The Torah then repeats the phrase, וַיֵּלְכוּ שְׁנֵיהֶם יַחְדָּו — *and the two of them went together* (22:8). Even when Yitzchak knew that he himself would be brought as a sacrifice they still walked on as one, whole-heartedly and with joy.

R' Bechaye asks who has the greater merit — Avraham, who was ready to lift his hand to kill his own son, or Yitzchak, who allowed himself to be sacrificed? Some Sages say that Avraham has a greater merit, for it is easier for a person to let himself be killed than for a father to kill his own child. Other Sages say that Yitzchak has the greater merit, because Avraham specifically heard God order him to slaughter Yitzchak, while Yitzchak had only heard it from Avraham, and still he allowed himself to be killed.

R' Bechaye adds that Avraham's achievement is the greater, because Yitzchak was duty-bound to obey his father's wish.

וַיִּבֶן שָׁם אַבְרָהָם אֶת הַמִּזְבֵּחַ — *Avraham built an altar there* (22:9). Avraham built the altar *there* — on the same place that Adam had built one.

◆§ Yitzchak's Request; Avraham's Test

וַיַּעֲקֹד אֶת יִצְחָק בְּנוֹ — *He bound his son Yitzchak* (22:9). Yitzchak asked Avraham to tie his hands and feet and to hide the knife from his sight so that he would not flinch, and thereby invalidate the sacrifice. He further asked his father not to convey the tidings of his death to Sarah while she was standing on a roof or next to a pit, in order that she should not fall to her death from mortal shock.

Avraham thereupon bound him, placed him on the pile of wood, and took up the knife to sacrifice him. As soon as the knife touched his neck his soul fled, but when a voice from the Throne of Glory commanded Avraham not to harm Yitzchak, the soul reentered the body. Avraham unbound him and said the blessing, בָּרוּךְ אַתָּה ה' מְחַיֶּה הַמֵּתִים — "Blessed are You, God, Who awakens the dead."

Chizkuni and *Imrei Noam* ask why God tested Avraham when He knew that he would obey Him. The answer is that the angels asked God why Avraham was greater than other righteous men, and deserving of all the miracles which had been done for him. God replied, "I will show you that even if I ask him to kill his son, he will obey Me."

Chizkuni asks further how Avraham could have believed that God wanted him to kill Yitzchak. Had God not told him, כִּי בְיִצְחָק יִקָּרֵא לְךָ זָרַע — *from Yitzchak you will have your progeny* (21:12)? If he would slaughter Yitzchak, how could he have children? The answer is that Avraham thought that perhaps Yitzchak had already

made a woman pregnant and had children. Yitzchak was thirty-
seven years old at the time.

⇜§ Avraham and the Angel

וַיִּקַּח אֶת הַמַּאֲכֶלֶת — *He took the knife* (22:10). He took the knife to
slaughter his son. A voice came from heaven and said, "Avraham,
do not slaughter Yitzchak."

Avraham asked, "And to let a drop of blood?"

The angel answered, *"And do him no harm."*

R' Bechaye writes that Avraham asked the voice, "Who are you?"

The voice answered, "I am an angel."

Avraham said, "It was God Himself Who commanded me to kill
my son. Let God Himself speak to me now!"

The angel appeared again and said, "God has sworn that He will
bless Yitzchak's children, who will be as countless as the stars, or the
sand by the sea."

Avraham said to God, "I have something to say. First, You told
me that my children would descend from Yitzchak; then You told
me to kill him; and now You command me not to do so."

God answered, "I do not change My words or lie. I told you only
to bring up your son as a sacrifice: I never asked you to kill him.
You have now brought him up, and you may now take him down."

Avraham said to God, "You have sworn. Now I too swear — that I
will not leave this place until You tell me that You will remember my
children when they sin, and let this be an atonement for them, as if I
had actually spilled my child's blood, just as if his ashes lay on the
altar."

The author of *Imrei Noam* asks why it is written that the angel called to Avraham from heaven, rather than coming down to him, while the angel came down to Hagar to show her the well. The answer is that the angel had to hurriedly call down to Avraham, for Avraham hastened to carry out God's command.

עַתָּה יָדַעְתִּי כִּי יְרֵא אֱלֹהִים אַתָּה — *Now I know that you fear God* (22:12). God told Avraham: "Now I have an answer for the angels as to why I do more for you than for other men."

≈§ Avraham's Ram; The Shofar of Rosh Hashanah

וַיִּשָׂא אַבְרָהָם אֶת עֵינָיו וַיַּרְא וְהִנֵּה אַיִל ... נֶאֱחַז בַּסְּבַךְ בְּקַרְנָיו — *Avraham looked up and saw a ram, caught in the thicket by its horns* (22:13). The ram was prepared for this moment during the Six Days of Creation. *Chizkuni* writes that because the ram was ensnared in the thicket, Avraham understood that God had sent it as a sacrifice in place of his son. Had the ram not been tangled there Avraham would have thought that it belonged to someone else, and would not have sacrificed it.

R' Bechaye writes that after a year during which God's People become heavy with sin and become distant from Him, they take in hand the horn of a ram on Rosh HaShanah, and by virtue of their *shofar* blast He forgives them all their transgressions.

≈§ Yitzchak's Mate is Born

וּבְתוּאֵל יָלַד אֶת רִבְקָה — *Besuel was the father of Rivkah* (22:23).

When Avraham left he thought to himself, "If Yitzchak had been killed he would have died without leaving children. I should have married him off to one of the daughters of Aner, Eshkol, or Mamre." Therefore God now sent him the news that his nephew Besuel had begotten Rivkah (Rebecca), who was destined to become Yitzchak's wife.

פרשת חיי שרה
Parashas Chayei Sarah
(23:1 — 25:18)

◆§ Sarah's Life

וַיִּהְיוּ חַיֵּי שָׂרָה מֵאָה שָׁנָה וְעֶשְׂרִים שָׁנָה וְשֶׁבַע שָׁנִים — *The life of Sarah was one hundred years and twenty years and seven years* (23:1). Our Sages say that during Sarah's lifetime her candles burned from one *erev Shabbos* to the next *erev Shabbos;* the dough she kneaded was blessed; and a cloud hovered over her tent. With her death, all of these things ceased, so everyone realized that they had happened in her merit. She merited death and burial in *Eretz Yisrael.*

The Torah specifies *one hundred years and twenty years and seven years* in order to show that she lived out all the years that she was destined to live.

Chizkuni writes that Sarah had no need of cosmetics. She was as lovely at twenty years as a young girl of seven.

R' Bechaye and *Chizkuni* write that the word *vayih'yu* (here translated "was") is numerically equivalent to thirty-seven. Sarah actually lived a real life for only thirty-seven years, from the time of Yitzchak's birth until the sacrifice, when he was thirty-seven years old. The years before his birth were not considered true life, for a person who is childless is compared to the dead. *Baal HaTurim* writes this as well.

◆§ Sarah's Death

וַתָּמָת שָׂרָה — *Sarah died* (23:2). The Torah ought to have written about Sarah's death immediately after the portion discussing Yitzchak's near-sacrifice, for when she heard how her son had been bound on the altar she was so overcome by fright that her soul fled from her body. Why does the Torah precede the account of her death with the news that Rivkah had been born? — To teach us that before one righteous person dies another is born into the world.

⋲§ The City of Four

בְּקִרְיַת אַרְבַּע — *In Kiryas Arba* (23:2). Why was the city called Kiryas Arba (lit., "City of Four")? Because four couples were buried there: Adam and Chavah, Avraham and Sarah, Yitzchak and Rivkah, Yaakov and Leah. Another interpretation is that it was called Kiryas Arba because four mighty giants lived there.

⋲§ Avraham's Weeping

וַיָּבֹא אַבְרָהָם לִסְפֹּד לְשָׂרָה וְלִבְכֹּתָה — *Avraham came to eulogize Sarah and weep for her* (23:2). Avraham came from Be'er Sheva. R' Bechaye asks why Sarah's name is mentioned here again, when we have just been told in this same verse, *Sarah died*. The explanation is that when eulogizing it is proper to mention the name of the deceased several times. R' Bechaye asks further, why it does not say that Yitzchak, too, mourned for his mother. The answer is that Yitzchak was not told of her death in order that he should not grieve that his mother had died because she had heard that he had been bound to an altar. Moreover, Yitzchak did not return after the sacrifice. Instead, he stayed on Mt. Moriah for three years, until he was forty years old, when he returned and married Rivkah. For this reason the Torah says, וַיָּשָׁב אַבְרָהָם אֶל נְעָרָיו — *Avraham returned to his young men* (22:19). He returned, but Yitzchak remained behind.

The author of *Toldos Yitzchak* asks: Generally a person weeps first and then eulogizes the dead. Why does it say the opposite here? The answer is that Avraham was very happy because Yitzchak had just been saved from the sacrifice and he had also heard the good news of Rivkah's birth, so that Yitzchak could look forward to marriage with a wife of good family. He therefore could not weep. First, he had to eulogize Sarah and enumerate all of her great deeds. Afterwards, he was capable of weeping somewhat. The word here translated *and to weep for her* (וְלִבְכֹּתָה) is written in the Torah with a small letter *kaf* to signify that he wept only a little, for he was still joyful and could not yet cry.

Baal HaTurim writes that he wept only a little because she was old and one does not weep excessively for the death of an old person. Another reason is that Sarah herself caused her death, by having earlier asked that God judge between her and Avraham. If one brings about his own death, people should not weep.

⋲§ Respect for the Dead

וַיָּקָם אַבְרָהָם מֵעַל פְּנֵי מֵתוֹ — *Avraham rose from before his dead* (23:3). Avraham asked the children of Ches (the Hittites) to give him a burial plot. *Baal HaTurim* writes that it is forbidden to speak in the presence of the dead. It shames the dead because everyone can speak but he. Therefore Avraham stood up from the body and went aside to speak with them.

◂§ Avraham's Request

גֵּר וְתוֹשָׁב אָנֹכִי עִמָּכֶם — *I am a stranger and a resident among you* (23:4). That is, "I am a stranger from another land, who has come to live among you." A second meaning is that Avraham said: "If you wish to sell me the land, very well — I will consider myself a *stranger*, and will buy it. If you do not want to sell it, I will consider myself a *resident*: God has promised me the land, and I can legally take a plot for myself."

The author of *Toldos Yitzchak* asks why Avraham had not bought a burial plot for himself and his wife earlier, since they were both elderly. The answer is that this was wise behavior on Avraham's part. He thought: "If Adam and Chavah were buried in the cave, it must be a place of importance. Efron, the owner of the property, may not know that Adam and Chavah are buried there, and probably thinks little of the land. If I should urge him to sell me the cave before Sarah's death, he will realize that there must be something there, since I want to bury my family on the land. He will investigate the matter and discover that Adam and Chavah are buried there, and will sell the land for an exorbitant price."

For this reason Avraham sent Sarah to Chevron when she was old. If she should die he could easily buy the cave from Efron. If Efron would ask why Avraham wanted the land he would be told that he needed it for a burial plot.

We also see Avraham's forethought in that he did not specify which cave he wanted. Rather he asked, "Who will sell me a plot of land?"

Chizkuni asks why the Torah specifies in which city Sarah died, when in the case of Avraham, Rivkah and Leah it is not mentioned. The answer is that Avraham had sent Sarah to Chevron so that she would be far from Mt. Moriah and would not immediately hear that Yitzchak had been sacrificed. When an angel came to her and told her that Yitzchak had almost been sacrificed she died. Some say that Sarah was sick, and Avraham sent her to Chevron because the air is healthy there. When she heard about Yitzchak, she died.

תְּנוּ לִי אֲחֻזַּת קֶבֶר עִמָּכֶם — *Give me a plot for burial with you* (23:4). R' Bechaye asks why Avraham said *with you*. The answer is that it was customary for each family to own its cemetery. When a stranger died they buried him alone in a field. Avraham therefore said, "Give me a plot for my family like your own."

◂§ The Children of Ches' Reply

נְשִׂיא אֱלֹהִים אַתָּה בְּתוֹכֵנוּ — *You are a prince of God among us* (23:6). The children of Ches told Avraham not to consider himself a humble stranger, for he was a holy ruler among them. They told him to choose the best of their plots to bury his dead, and promised that none would withhold his land from him.

Avraham told them that if they truly wanted him to bury Sarah wherever he wished:

◂§ Efron's Cave

וּפִגְעוּ לִי בְּעֶפְרוֹן בֶּן צֹחַר וְיִתֶּן לִי אֶת מְעָרַת הַמַּכְפֵּלָה אֲשֶׁר לוֹ — *Entreat for me to Efron son of Tzochar, that he should give me the Cave of Machpelah which he has* (23:8-9). It was called the Cave of Machpelah, from the word *kaful*, meaning double, because it consisted of two caves, one atop the other. Another reason that it was called the "cave of pairs" is because of the four couples that were buried there: Adam and Chavah, Avraham and Sarah, Yitzchak and Rivkah, Yaakov and Leah. Also, Adam was of such mighty stature that his body had to be laid there in a stooping position, as if doubled over.

Avraham said, "I will pay generously for your cave." Efron answered, "What is a piece of land which is worth four hundred silver coins between you and I, two such great friends? Bury your dead."

The wicked promise much and do nothing. First Efron said that he would give Avraham the land as a gift and later he asked an exorbitant price for it.

◂§ What Ages a Man

וְאַבְרָהָם זָקֵן בָּא בַּיָּמִים — *Avraham was old, advanced in years* (24:1). There are many people who age in appearance and grow grey because of their troubles and not because they are actually old. Avraham was rich and respected and had a son in his old age. He did not appear old because of his troubles but rather because he had lived many years.

Because he was old he began to wonder if he would die before finding Yitzchak a wife. He made his servant swear to find his son a wife from his own family.

Why did Avraham have his servant swear, rather than Yitzchak himself? Avraham was afraid that the servant might be unreliable and try to persuade Yitzchak to marry a Canaanite woman, so he made him take the vow.

The *Midrash* writes that four things age a man: fear, evil children, going to war, and a bad wife.

◆§ Avraham was Blessed with Everything

וַה' בֵּרַךְ אֶת אַבְרָהָם בַּכֹּל — *God blessed Avraham with everything* (24:1). He lacked for nothing, and had only one worry: to find his son a proper wife. R' Meir writes that God blessed Avraham by not giving him a daughter. If he would have had a daughter he would not have been able to find her a good husband, and she would have had to marry an idol worshiper and like all women would have come under his influence. R' Yehudah says that Avraham did have a daughter. Every man wants both sons and daughters, particularly when he is rich.

◆§ Avraham Adjures his Servant

עַבְדּוֹ זְקַן בֵּיתוֹ — *His servant, elder of his house* (24:2). *Chizkuni* writes that he sent Eliezer to find a wife for Yitzchak because Eliezer was the eldest in his household, and an older man is not as lustful as a younger one. Therefore he is called *elder of his house.*

שִׂים נָא יָדְךָ תַּחַת יְרֵכִי — *Place your hand under my thigh* (24:2). R' Bechaye, *Toldos Yitzchak* and *Chizkuni* write that in those days it was customary for a servant to place his hands beneath his master's feet to show his subservience.

וְאַשְׁבִּיעֲךָ בַּה' אֱלֹהֵי הַשָּׁמַיִם וֵאלֹהֵי הָאָרֶץ — *I will have you swear by the Lord, God of the heaven and God of the earth* (24:3). *Rashi* asks why later in the chapter it states *God of the heaven* and here it says both *God of the heaven and God of the earth.* The answer is that when God first brought Avraham out of Terach's house, He was not recognized as God by the people on earth. Only in heaven was He recognized as God and so, when discussing the God who took him from his father's house, He is called God of heaven. Later Avraham made everyone recognize God as both God of heaven and earth.

◆§ Matchmaking Advice

אֲשֶׁר לֹא תִקַּח אִשָּׁה לִבְנִי מִבְּנוֹת הַכְּנַעֲנִי — *Not to take a wife for my son from the daughters of Canaan* (24:3). This passage teaches us that a man should take a wife from his own family, as Amram did, in taking Yocheved for a wife, and as Avraham did for his son Yitzchak. When a man takes a wife from his own family there is peace between them, for one cannot taunt the other with a lack of family prestige.

The author of *Even Shoev* asks why Avraham himself took a maidservant and a concubine from among the Canaanite idol worshipers, while forbidding his son Yitzchak to do the same. The answer is that Yitzchak was sanctified on Mt. Moriah, and therefore was not allowed to take a concubine or marry a Canaanite. Avraham was not as holy and could take a concubine.

Because Avraham was permitted to take a concubine to bear children, he did not want to trouble God with prayers for his wife Sarah. The righteous do not like to trouble God with their prayers if they are not absolutely necessary. Yitzchak, though, could not take a maidservant, so he prayed that Rivkah would bear children.

The author of *Even Shoev* also asks why Avraham did not ask Yitzchak if he should send a servant to bring him a wife. — There was no need to ask, since Avraham knew that Yitzchak would obey him.

Chizkuni writes that Avraham did not want his son to marry a Canaanite woman, so that the Canaanites should not say that God did not want to fulfill His promise to give the land to Avraham's descendants, and they had to marry Canaanites to inherit the land. Avraham forbade his son to marry a Canaanite woman because he knew that God would give him the land without this.

⊸§ From His Father's House

וַיֹּאמֶר אֵלָיו הָעֶבֶד אוּלַי לֹא תֹאבֶה הָאִשָּׁה לָלֶכֶת אַחֲרַי — *The servant said to him, "Perhaps the woman will not want to follow me"* (24:5). Eliezer asked Avraham what he should do if the woman would not go back with him to Canaan. Avraham answered that if the woman did not want to go with him, he would be absolved of his vow, and could marry Yitzchak to one of the daughters of his friends Aner, Eshkol or Mamre.

Avraham then prayed, "Lord, God of heaven, who took me from my father's house, send an angel to precede Eliezer, to choose a wife for Yitzchak."

The author of *Toldos Yitzchak* asks why Avraham mentioned here that God had brought him from his father's house and homeland. The answer is that Avraham said in his prayer: "God, You took me from my father's house and homeland. I obeyed You and left my family. Now how can I find my son a wife from my family? It is only fair that You send an angel with Eliezer to help him bring Yitzchak a wife from my kin."

◄§ Avraham's Camels

וַיִּקַּח הָעֶבֶד עֲשָׂרָה גְמַלִּים מִגְּמַלֵּי אֲדֹנָיו וַיֵּלֶךְ וְכָל טוּב אֲדֹנָיו בְּיָדוֹ — *The servant took ten of Avraham's camels. He set out, and all of his master's goods were in his hands* (24:10). Avraham's camels were recognizable: he muzzled them so that they would not graze in other people's fields. Eliezer took with him a document in which Avraham gave over all his goods to Yitzchak. When Avraham's relatives would see that Yitzchak was rich, they would be more willing to send their daughter to marry him.

◄§ Eliezer's Prayer at the Well

וַיַּבְרֵךְ הַגְּמַלִּים מִחוּץ לָעִיר אֶל בְּאֵר הַמָּיִם — *He made the camels kneel down at the well of water at the outskirts of the city* (24:11). Eliezer came to the city of Nachor and let his camels kneel down at the well, so that they could drink. It was twilight, when the young women went to fetch buckets of water. Eliezer prayed:

וַיֹּאמַר ה׳ אֱלֹהֵי אֲדֹנִי אַבְרָהָם הַקְרֵה נָא לְפָנַי הַיּוֹם וַעֲשֵׂה חֶסֶד עִם אֲדֹנִי — *He said, "God, Lord of my master Avraham, be with me today, and show kindness to my master"* (24:12). "Let one woman come to the well, and offer myself and my camels water. Then I will know that אֹתָהּ הֹכַחְתָּ לְעַבְדְּךָ לְיִצְחָק — *her You have appointed for your servant Yitzchak* (24:14). Because she will act charitably at the well, I will know that she is worthy of being Yitzchak's wife, and of coming into Avraham's house, where they dispense charity to all. If You send a young woman from my master's family to the well, and she offers myself and my camels water, I will know that You have acted kindly towards my master."

Chizkuni asks why Eliezer wanted to meet the young girl at the well to see if she was kind; he could have met her at her father's house and seen whether she was pious and clever. The reason is that at a parent's house one cannot really discern if a child is bright. The child may be stupid, but parents show a child how to present himself in his best light in front of a guest. Eliezer therefore wanted to see her at the well, when she was by herself, to see if she would act properly of her own accord.

Chizkuni writes further that Eliezer took ten camels, so that he would have ten riders to make up a *minyan* (quorum) for the blessings of the marriage.

◄§ Divine Intercession

וַיְהִי הוּא טֶרֶם כִּלָּה לְדַבֵּר — *He had not yet finished speaking* (24:15). Before he finished speaking Rivkah, daughter of Besuel, arrived, her

Eliezer meets Rivkah

pitcher upon her shoulders. R' Bechaye asks why the word *he* (הוּא) is necessary (it would have been grammatically correct to delete the word, as it was clearly implied by the context of the sentence). The answer is that *he* refers here to God, as in the verse that says, הוּא עָשָׂנוּ — *He created us (Tehillim* 100:3). God sent an angel with Eliezer who helped him, and ensured that Rivkah would come down to the well at that moment.

⋙ Rivkah's Modesty

וְהַנַּעֲרָה טֹבַת מַרְאֶה מְאֹד בְּתוּלָה וְאִישׁ לֹא יְדָעָה — *The young girl was very beautiful, a virgin, and no man had known her* (24:16). The author of *Toldos Yitzchak* writes that this teaches us that God had listened to Eliezer's prayer and brought her to the well that day. She generally did not go down to the well because of the young men there. Even in her house she was rarely seen, because she was modest.

וַתֵּרֶד הָעַיְנָה וַתְּמַלֵּא כַדָּהּ וַתָּעַל — *She went down to the well, filled her pitcher, and came up* (24:16). The Torah does not say that she drew the water, only that she filled the pitcher. Our Sages learn from this that the water rose to greet her, so she did not have to draw it up. When Eliezer saw that the water rose he ran to her and asked for a little water to drink.

The author of *Toldos Yitzchak* writes that the verse *she filled her pitcher and came up* teaches us that because she was modest, she left the well as soon as she had filled the pitcher, unlike the other young women who would delay.

She gave Eliezer water, and then offered to give his camels water as well. Eliezer was astonished because he saw that God had begun to make his mission prosper.

◆§ Eliezer's Gifts to Rivkah

וַיִּקַּח הָאִישׁ נֶזֶם זָהָב — *The man took a golden ring ...* (24:22).
Chizkuni writes that concerning the valuable gift of jewelry the
Torah does not say "he gave it to the girl, " but rather *he took a
golden ring ...* to show that he readied them to be given to her, but
first ascertained who she was by asking, *Whose daughter are you?*
(24:23).

The same source also cites another opinion. He did indeed give
her the jewelry before he had asked her her identity, in order to
show her his master's wealth. But when he spoke with her father
Besuel and her brother Lavan (Laban) he told them that he had first
questioned her and only then given her the jewelry.

Rashi writes that he gave her the jewelry before questioning her
because he firmly believed that in Avraham's merit the young
woman he met would be a member of his family. He gave her a nose
ring which weighed one half of a shekel to symbolize that her
children would in future time give contributions to the Sanctuary of
one-half shekels, and two bracelets to allude to the Two Tablets of
the Law which her children would receive from God. They weighed
ten shekels to symbolize the Ten Commandments.

◆§ Hospitality to Eliezer; Eliezer's Refusal

הֲיֵשׁ בֵּית אָבִיךְ מָקוֹם לָנוּ לָלִין — *Is there room in your father's house for
us to sleep?* (24:23). Eliezer asked if there was room for him to sleep
at her father's house for one night. The word *lalin* ("to sleep") refers
to one night's sleep. Rivkah answered that there was room *lalun* ("to
sleep"), which implies sleeping there for many nights.

Toldos Yitzchak points out Rivkah's wisdom. She said that there
was room available to sleep for many nights. She did not specify
that he could sleep there, because she was not sure her father would
allow it.

Eliezer bowed down to God and thanked Him for having guided
him correctly. The girl ran to her mother, for generally a daughter
confides in her mother. When Lavan saw the jewelry which Rivkah
had received from Eliezer he ran to meet him. He invited him into
the house and assured him that they had cleared the house of all
their idols. Eliezer entered the house, they fed the camels, and
brought water so that Eliezer and his men could wash their feet.
Then they offered him food.

Eliezer however refused to eat until he had explained his mission.
R' Bechaye and *Baal HaTurim* write that his hosts poisoned his food
so that he would die and they would take his goods. They urged him

to eat, but Eliezer said that he was Avraham's servant: he could not eat until he had washed his hands and recited a blessing over the washing and over the bread. Eliezer felt that by virtue of the blessings he would be saved. At that moment, an angel came and turned around the common platter so that the portion with the poisoned food was now in front of Besuel. He ate of it and died. Later on we read, *They ate and drank, he and his men,* that is, Eliezer and his men. The verse does not mention Besuel's household, for they were in mourning for him and did not eat.

Eliezer awoke early and saw an angel waiting for him. He asked Rivkah's family not to hold him back, and to let him leave for home. When the day was two hours old Eliezer left Charan with Rivkah. The angel arranged that the trip to Chevron was completed on the same day, even though this was normally a journey of seventeen days. Likewise, when Eliezer traveled from Chevron to Charan it took him only three hours, as the verse says, *I arrived today at the well,* that is, "I left and arrived on the same day."

On their way back, they saw Yitzchak walking in a field. He had just left the Garden of Eden. Rivkah prophetically saw that one of her children would be wicked, and she fell off her camel.

◄§ Eliezer as a Matchmaker

וְהַ׳ בֵּרַךְ אֶת אֲדֹנִי מְאֹד וַיִּגְדָּל וַיִּתֶּן לוֹ צֹאן וּבָקָר ... וַעֲבָדִם — *God has blessed my master and he has become great; and He has given him sheep and cattle ... and servants* (24:35). Eliezer behaved like a matchmaker, pointing out that his master was rich in flocks, gold and silver, and servants. *Chizkuni* writes that the word *avadim* ("servants") is here spelled without a *yud* to show that Avraham actually had only one servant, Eliezer, who was as valuable to him as many men.

Eliezer told them that Sarah had given birth to a son אַחֲרֵי זִקְנָתָהּ, *when she was old* (24:36), to show that she would have no more children, and Yitzchak would thus be the sole heir.

The author of *Toldos Yitzchak* writes that Eliezer praised Avraham so that the others would not think: If Yitzchak is a good man and Avraham is so rich, why do they have to travel so far to find a wife for him? He should be able to find one in his own land. Eliezer therefore spoke at great length.

He said, "Do not think that my master is not as rich as he once was. My master is extremely wealthy, and Yitzchak is an upright, pious man. Miraculously, Sarah gave birth at the age of ninety. You may therefore rest assured that by a miracle God will certainly send you a fine son-in-law. And do not think that the camels and other riches which I show you have been borrowed from strangers, as is sometimes done for the sake of matchmaking, for *God has blessed my master, and he has become great.* He does not have to borrow from anyone to impress you. I was sent here only because my master Avraham does not want his son to marry a daughter of the Canaanites.''

⊷§ Eliezer's Secret Hope

וָאֹמַר אֶל אֲדֹנִי אֻלַי לֹא תֵלֵךְ הָאִשָּׁה אַחֲרָי — *I said to my master, "Perhaps the woman will not follow me"* (24:39). "When I asked my master what would happen if the woman would not want to leave her land, he said that God would send an angel with me to enable me to bring a wife for Yitzchak from his family.''

Rashi writes that the word אֻלַי, "perhaps," is written without a *vav*, because it can then also be read as אֵלַי, "to me." Eliezer was alluding to his hope that Yitzchak would marry his own daughter. Avraham answered that his son could not marry Eliezer's daughter because his son was blessed, while Eliezer was a Canaanite, belonging to a people who were cursed.

Chizkuni asks why the Torah hints to us here that Eliezer wanted Yitzchak to marry his daughter, while in the preceding verses, where he was entrusted with his mission, no mention is made of this desire. This shows us that Eliezer was acting like a professional matchmaker. Here he praised Yitzchak to Rivkah's parents, saying: "I would gladly have given my daughter as a wife to Yitzchak, but unfortunately, my master was not agreeable.''

⊷§ Eliezer Tells of his Journey

וָאֶשְׁאַל אֹתָהּ וָאֹמַר בַּת מִי אַתְּ ... וָאָשִׂם הַנֶּזֶם עַל אַפָּהּ — *I questioned her, and asked, "Whose daughter are you?" ... and I placed the ring on her nose* (24:47). Eliezer related everything that had happened to him, and how it had taken him only three hours to complete a journey of seventeen days.

Rashi writes that when speaking with her parents he said that he had first asked her name, in order that they should not ask him how he could be so foolish as to give presents to an utter stranger.

⊷§ The Proposal

וְעַתָּה אִם יֶשְׁכֶם עֹשִׂים חֶסֶד וֶאֱמֶת אֶת אֲדֹנִי — *Now, if you want to be kind and true to my master* (24:49). The author of *Imrei Noam* asks why Eliezer had to plead. Would they not want Rivkah to marry such a wealthy man? The answer is that they had heard that Avraham's children would be forced into exile, and so they did not want to give Rivkah to Yitzchak. This was why Eliezer had to beg and plead.

R' Isser'l asks why Eliezer asked them for truth and kindness. That expression is generally used in reference to a charitable act done for the dead — the most sincere form of charity, because it cannot be repaid. The answer is that this shows Eliezer's wisdom. He asked them to deal charitably with Avraham, and not to expect repayment for it.

וְאִם לֹא הַגִּידוּ לִי וְאֶפְנֶה עַל יָמִין אוֹ עַל שְׂמֹאל — *If not, tell me, and I will turn to the right or to the left* (24:49). Eliezer said that if they would not allow Rivkah to go with him he would have to marry Yitzchak to a daughter of either Yishmael or Lot.

⋖§ Made in Heaven

וַיַּעַן לָבָן וּבְתוּאֵל מֵהּ' יָצָא הַדָּבָר לֹא נוּכַל דַּבֵּר אֵלֶיךָ רַע אוֹ טוֹב — *And Lavan and Besuel answered, saying, "This thing comes from God. We are unable to speak to you of evil or good"* (24:50). Lavan and Besuel answered that this whole incident was obviously God's work, and they had no say in the matter. Lavan was wicked, and answered before his father, but since he was more clever at talking than his father, his father allowed him to do so. Since he was wicked the thing that first came to mind was *to speak of evil*, and only later, of good.

R' Bechaye writes that we can learn from here that all matches are from God. Indeed, the Sages say that forty days before a person is born an announcement is made in heaven that he shall marry so-and-so's daughter.

⋖§ Delaying Tactics

הִנֵּה רִבְקָה לְפָנֶיךָ קַח וָלֵךְ — *Here is Rivkah before you, take her and go* (24:51). When Eliezer heard these words he bowed and praised God. He took out gold and silver dishes and beautiful clothing, and gave them to Rivkah, and with them betrothed her to Yitzchak. He gave luscious fruits to her brother and to her mother, and they ate and drank and went to bed.

In the morning, the angel came to Eliezer, intending to escort him home. Eliezer asked Rivkah's family to let him return to his master. Her brother and mother protested that Rivkah should stay with them for a year or ten months, and then leave them. Besuel said nothing, for by then he had died of the poisoning.

Chizkuni asks why they had originally said that he could take Rivkah, and now they protested that she ought to stay with them for a year. The answer is that before they did not know that Eliezer had been appointed an agent to betroth her on Yitzchak's behalf. They therefore said that he should take her to Yitzchak for betrothal, for it was not proper for her to remain for a long period unbetrothed. But when they saw that Eliezer was an appointed messenger to betroth her to Yitzchak they said she should stay for a year, in order to prepare herself with clothing and jewelry.

The author of *Toldos Yitzchak* writes that Lavan was deceitful. First he told Eliezer to take Rivkah, so that Eliezer would agree to take her without a dowry. When he saw that Eliezer was thankful for the girl, even without a dowry, he offered to have her stay for a year, in order to outfit her with clothing and jewelry. He knew, then, that Eliezer would not acquiesce (and so made his offer, to appear generous).

◆§ Rivkah's Decision

וַיֹּאמְרוּ נִקְרָא לַנַּעֲרָה וְנִשְׁאֲלָה אֶת פִּיהָ — *They said, "Let us call the girl and ask her"* (24:57). Our Sages learn from this that one must ask an orphan if she wishes to marry the man chosen for her.

◆§ A Man and a Servant

וַיֹּאמְרוּ אֵלֶיהָ הֲתֵלְכִי עִם הָאִישׁ הַזֶּה וַתֹּאמֶר אֵלֵךְ — *They said to her, "Will you go with this man?" She said, "I will go"* (24:58). Rivkah said that she wanted to go, despite her family's wishes.

R' Bechaye asks why Eliezer is sometimes termed "the servant" (הָעֶבֶד) and at other times "the man" (הָאִישׁ), meaning, a man of importance. When Eliezer first arrived at the well, and had not yet seen the angel, he is called a servant. After he arrived at the well and saw the angel he is called a man. But as soon as Rivkah was given to Eliezer and the angel's task was completed, he is once again called a servant, as in the verses, *the servant took out silver vessels* (24:53); *the servant took Rivkah* (24:61); and *the servant told Yitzchak* (24:66).

But in that case, why did Lavan and his mother ask Rivkah (24:58), *Will you go with this man?* (The angel had already left, and Eliezer ought to have been referred to as a servant.) The answer is that they were embarrassed to call him a servant to his face. Moreover, out of consideration for Rivkah's feelings they referred to him in more respectful terms as אִישׁ, a man.

At this point the terms change.

וַתֵּלַכְנָה אַחֲרֵי הָאִישׁ וַיִּקַּח הָעֶבֶד אֶת רִבְקָה וַיֵּלַךְ — *They followed the man, and the servant took Rivkah and went* (24:61). This means that she followed the *angel*, who is referred to here as אִישׁ, a man, and Eliezer took them. *Ramban* asks why he had to take them. Was Rivkah not willing to go of her own accord? The answer is that Eliezer was afraid that the women who accompanied Rivkah, to escort her, would take her back with them, so he took her by the hand in order to protect her.

⇜§ Rivkah Meets Yitzchak

וְיִצְחָק בָּא מִבּוֹא בְּאֵר לַחַי רֹאִי — *Yitzchak was on his way, coming from Be'er LaChai Ro'i* (24:62). He was coming from the Garden of Eden.

וַיֵּצֵא יִצְחָק לָשׂוּחַ בַּשָּׂדֶה — *Yitzchak went out to meditate in the field* (24:63). Towards evening, Yitzchak went out into the field to pray the afternoon prayer of *Minchah*, when he saw camels approaching. Rivkah saw him in the distance walking about bashfully, and understood that this must be Yitzchak. She thought, "Everyone generally runs to see a bride. If this man is not running, he must be the groom." Realizing this, she too was overcome with bashfulness, and slipped off the camel. She nevertheless asked Eliezer who the man was, and when he answered that it was his master Yitzchak, she covered herself with a veil. The author of *Toldos Yitzchak* asks why Eliezer now called Yitzchak his master (הוּא אֲדֹנִי), when until now he had called him his master's son. The answer is that until Yitzchak was married he could not be considered a master; now that Rivkah had arrived he became a master.

⇜§ Sarah's Blessing in Rivkah's Tent

וַיְבִאֶהָ יִצְחָק הָאֹהֱלָה שָׂרָה אִמּוֹ — *Yitzchak brought her to the tent of his mother Sarah* (24:67). During Sarah's lifetime the candles burnt from *erev Shabbos* to *erev Shabbos*, her dough was blessed, and a cloud hovered over her tent. As soon as she died these things disappeared, but with Rivkah's arrival they began once again. Yitzchak therefore felt as if his mother was once again alive.

וַיִּנָּחֵם יִצְחָק אַחֲרֵי אִמּוֹ — *Yitzchak was consoled for his mother* (24:67). When a person's mother is alive he is generally close with her; when she dies, he becomes very close to his wife.

⇜§ Avraham Marries Keturah

וַיֹּסֶף אַבְרָהָם וַיִּקַּח אִשָּׁה וּשְׁמָהּ קְטוּרָה — *Avraham took another wife, and her name was Keturah* (25:1). R' Bechaye, *Toldos Yitzchak* and *Chizkuni* write: We learn from this that if a person's wife dies, he should not remarry until his children have married. If he remarries first, his children will not be able to make good matches, for people will assume that the children of the second marriage will inherit everything. Therefore Avraham first saw to it that his son was married, and then remarried.

Keturah is Hagar. After she was separated from Avraham she did not want to marry anyone else. She waited for Avraham, and eventually had many children with him, but they were not good men.

R' Bechaye writes that it is obvious from the verse itself that Keturah was Hagar. If translated literally, the verse says: *He continued to take another wife*, rather than "he took another wife." This shows us that Keturah was Hagar, and he had already been married to her.

Another proof that Keturah was Hagar is that Avraham gave all of his possessions to Yitzchak, and did not allow the children of Keturah to be his heirs, as the verse says, וַיִּתֵּן אַבְרָהָם אֶת כָּל אֲשֶׁר לוֹ לְיִצְחָק — *Avraham gave all that he had to Yitzchak* (25:5). Now the *Gemara* says that it is forbidden to take an inheritance away from one son in order to give it to another son, even if one is wicked and the other righteous. But Keturah was Hagar, Sarah's servant, and the children of a servant are servants themselves, and do not inherit.

Why was Hagar called Keturah? Because her deeds were as lovely as *ketores* (incense). But how can *Rashi* say this when he has stated above that she had served idols? — Because since then she had repented and had become a pious woman.

⇜§ Avraham's Bequests

וַיִּתֵּן אַבְרָהָם אֶת כָּל אֲשֶׁר לוֹ לְיִצְחָק — *Avraham gave all that he owned to Yitzchak* (25:5). Avraham gave Yitzchak a document saying that he was to inherit all of his possessions. It cannot be that at this point he already transferred all his property, for he did not know when he was to die, and would have to rely thereafter on being supported by Yitzchak. He gave the children of his concubines gifts. The word concubines *(pilagshim)* is written with only one *yud* to show that there was only one concubine, Keturah.

Rashi asks why the verse calls her a concubine, and then later calls her a wife. He explains that a wife is given a marriage contract, but a concubine is not. Hagar did have such a document, despite the fact that she was a concubine, and therefore she is sometimes called his wife. But in regard to her children's right of inheritance, she was considered a concubine, for a concubine's children do not inherit.

Rashi also asks: If Avraham had already given Yitzchak a document stating that he would inherit everything, before Eliezer left to find him a wife, why did he give him such a document again? *Rashi* answers, in the name of R' Nechemiah: This time Avraham gave him the blessings, so that anyone whom Yitzchak blessed would in fact be blessed.

◆§ Death of Avraham

וַיִּגְוַע וַיָּמָת אַבְרָהָם — *Avraham expired and died* (25:8).

The word *geviyah* (expired) signifies an easy death, quickly, without suffering, and *Rashi* says that it is used only in connection with the righteous. The author of *Toldos Yitzchak* raises a question: The same word is used in connection with the generation of the Flood! He explains, therefore, that when it is used in connection with the wicked this expression of haste shows that they died without leaving a will for their children, like the generation of the Flood. But in connection with the righteous it shows that they died without pain, having previously left a will.

◆§ Happy with His Lot

זָקֵן וְשָׂבֵע — *An old man, and satisfied* (25:8). Avraham died an old man. R' Bechaye asks why the Torah does not say שְׂבַע יָמִים — "full of days"? The answer is that Avraham did not pursue the passions of the earth, and did not lust for money. Many people die never having fulfilled half of their desires, as the verse says, אֹהֵב כֶּסֶף לֹא יִשְׂבַּע כֶּסֶף — *He who loves money will never be sated with money* (Koheles 5:9). Our Sages likewise say in the *Gemara* that a man dies not having half of what he had desired. If he had one hundred coins he wants two hundred. Avraham, however, was satisfied with whatever he had.

◆§ Yishmael Repented

וַיִּקְבְּרוּ אֹתוֹ יִצְחָק וְיִשְׁמָעֵאל — *Yitzchak and Yishmael buried him* (25:9). The order of their names shows us that Yishmael repented, giving the proper respect to Yitzchak and allowing him to go ahead because he was more righteous. If Yishmael had not repented God would not have allowed him to bury Avraham. This is what *Rashi* writes, as well as *Ramban* and R' Bechaye.

After Avraham's death, God blessed Yitzchak.

פרשת תולדת
Parashas Toldos
(25:19 — 28:9)

⋙ His Father's Son

וְאֵלֶּה תּוֹלְדֹת יִצְחָק — *These are the generations of Yitzchak* (25:19).
The Torah says, יִצְחָק בֶּן אַבְרָהָם אַבְרָהָם הוֹלִיד אֶת יִצְחָק — *Yitzchak
son of Avraham; Avraham was the father of Yitzchak.* This is ob-
scure: if Yitzchak was Avraham's son, obviously Avraham was his
father!

This passage speaks of Yaakov and Esav. Because of these two
children many people said that Sarah had become pregnant through
Avimelech, for they said that Yitzchak partially took after Sarah, in
her righteousness, and partially after Avimelech, in his wickedness,
and therefore his children were the righteous Yaakov and the
wicked Esav. God therefore made Yitzchak closely resemble
Avraham as a testimony that *Avraham was the father of Yitzchak.*

Toldos Yitzchak asks: If a woman is unfaithful, she usually is terrified of her husband, and has him on her mind constantly. The fact
that Yitzchak resembled Avraham, therefore, might not convince
people that he was his father; they might still say that Avimelech
had impregnated her [and Yitzchak resembled Avraham because he
was constantly on Sarah's mind, which affected the embryo]. *Devek
Tov* answers that although it is true that an unfaithful wife constantly fears her husband and thinks of him, Sarah had been taken
forcibly to Avimelech, and Avraham was aware of it. She had
nothing to fear from him. Therefore, when Yitzchak so closely
resembled Avraham, all knew that Avraham was his father.

Chizkuni writes that this verse praises Yitzchak, in that he was
born after his father's name was changed to Avraham, in contrast to
Yishmael, who was born before the letter *hei* from the Divine Name
was added. *Toldos Yitzchak* too writes this explanation.

⋙ His Rightful Match ...

וַיְהִי יִצְחָק בֶּן אַרְבָּעִים שָׁנָה בְּקַחְתּוֹ אֶת רִבְקָה — *Yitzchak was forty years
old when he took Rivkah* (25:20). *Rashi* asks why Yitzchak lived so
long without a wife. After all, the Sages say that one should marry at

the age of eighteen. The explanation is that Yitzchak had to wait until Rivkah, his rightful match, was old enough to marry.

◄§ ... Despite Her Environment

אֲחוֹת לָבָן הָאֲרַמִּי ... בַּת בְּתוּאֵל — *Daughter of Besuel ... sister of Lavan the Aramite* (25:20). *Rashi* asks why we are told that Besuel was her father and Lavan her brother, information which we have already been told. This shows us that despite the fact that both were wicked men, Rivkah did not learn from their evil deeds, and remained righteous.

וַיֶּעְתַּר יִצְחָק לַה' לְנֹכַח אִשְׁתּוֹ כִּי עֲקָרָה הִיא — *Yitzchak pleaded with God, opposite his wife, for she was childless* (25:21). He stood in one corner and Rivkah in the other and they prayed. God answered only Yitzchak's prayers because he was a righteous man, son of a righteous man. Rivkah was a righteous woman but the daughter of a wicked man.

◄§ The Rabbi and the Emperor

וַיִּתְרֹצְצוּ הַבָּנִים בְּקִרְבָּהּ — *The children struggled within her* (25:22). When she would pass by the doorway of a House of Learning, Yaakov fought to be born and enter it; when they passed by the doorway of a temple of idol worship, Esav fought to get out. Also, they battled over possession of both worlds — This World, and the World to Come.

Rivkah asked herself, "Why did I pray for children if the pain of bearing them is so great?"

She therefore went to the *beis midrash* (House of Study) of Shem and Ever to ask them why it was that her children fought so mightily. God told them to tell her that she carried two great nations in her womb.

The verse says she was carrying two *goyim* (lit., "nations"), but the word in its unusual spelling (גֹיִים) can here be read as *geyim*, meaning important men. This alludes to two men — one of Yaakov's descendants, Rebbe (R' Yehudah HaNasi), a ruler of the Jews; and a descendant of Esav, the Roman ruler Antoninus. Rebbe and Antoninus signed a treaty between themselves and maintained harmonious relations. *Rashi* writes that their tables were always laden with radishes and horseradish, both in winter and summer. This shows the extent of their wealth. Rebbe gave his servants so much to eat that they lost their appetites and had to eat radishes and horseradish to whet their appetites anew. Rebbe himself, however, never pursued pleasures, and indeed when he died he lifted up his fingers towards heaven and said: "Master of the Universe, You know that I have not had even one finger's worth of pleasure from This World."

◆§ Two Very Different Twins

וַיִּמְלְאוּ יָמֶיהָ לָלֶדֶת וְהִנֵּה תוֹמִם בְּבִטְנָה — *The time came for her to deliver, and there were twins in her womb* (25:24). *Toldos Yitzchak* asks why Yitzchak did not pray for Rivkah immediately, rather than waiting for ten years. The answer is that he did pray for her immediately, but God did not want to answer his entreaties, in order to delay the birth of the wicked Esav. Conversely, Moshe Rabbeinu was in his mother's womb for only six months and several days.

The word *tomim* ("twins") is spelled here without an *alef* to show that one of the twins was wicked; whereas when Tamar bore twins the word is spelled with an *alef* because both children, Peretz and Zerach, were righteous.

Some of our Sages ask why Rivkah did not ask Yitzchak himself why the children were clashing in her womb. After all, he too was a prophet. She was afraid that Yitzchak would tell her that if she was suffering more than most women, she must have sinned more than they, and would divorce her.

◆§ Rivals from Birth

וַיֵּצֵא הָרִאשׁוֹן אַדְמוֹנִי — *The first came out reddish* (25:25). The first was red-complexioned and full of hair, and was called Esav, because he looked like a child who had been born long before (from the word *asah*, meaning "made, completed"). Afterwards his brother emerged, his hand grasping the ankle of the first. He had held onto it in his struggle to be the first-born. He had been the first created within his mother, and wanted to be the first-born.

◆§ He Waited for Her

וְיִצְחָק בֶּן שִׁשִּׁים שָׁנָה בְּלֶדֶת אֹתָם — *Yitzchak was sixty years old when they were born* (25:26). *Rashi* asks why Yitzchak waited for twenty years before praying for children, when customarily one waits ten years. — Yitzchak first had to wait ten years until Rivkah became thirteen years old, and able to bear children. Then he waited another ten years, as was customary.

◆§ A Bow in His Hand; a Trap in His Mouth

וַיִּגְדְּלוּ הַנְּעָרִים וַיְהִי עֵשָׂו אִישׁ יֹדֵעַ צַיִד אִישׁ שָׂדֶה — *The children grew; Esav was a hunter, a man of the field* (25:27). While they were still young their characters were not apparent, but when they grew up Esav went to worship idols while Yaakov studied in the *beis midrash*.

Esav serves Yitzchak and his guests

Esav was hypocritical, and would ask his father how one gave a tithe of salt and straw [which do not have to be tithed at all]. Yitzchak therefore thought that he was very pious. Yaakov, on the other hand, was truly pious, and an artless scholar.

Yitzchak favored Esav because he hunted and brought food for him, while Rivkah favored Yaakov, because he learned Torah.

◀§ The Meal of a Mourner

וַיָּזֶד יַעֲקֹב נָזִיד — *Yaakov cooked a stew* (25:29). Esav came wearily from the field and asked Yaakov to give him the red lentils which he was cooking. Because of this he was called Edom (lit., "red"). Why was Yaakov cooking lentils? — His father Yitzchak was in mourning for his father, Avraham, who had died on that very day, so that he should not see his grandson Esav turn to evil. And for this reason Avraham died five years before his time. Why do we cook beans for a mourner? — To allude to the fact that just as beans are round, so death circles around, from one man to the next.

Yaakov asked Esav to sell him his birthright, for the sacrificial duties were to belong to the first-born and Yaakov felt that it was not right for an evil man to bring sacrifices. Esav answered that he did not want the birthright, for bringing the sacrifices improperly would be punishable by death.

R' Bechaye writes that in those days it was customary to show respect to the first-born upon the father's death, and place him in the father's seat. Esav said, "What good is that privilege to me? For that I must await my father's death, and who knows who will die first? I am often among wild beasts and they may very well kill me."

◆§ Anticipating the Torah

וַיְהִי רָעָב בָּאָרֶץ ... וַיֵּרָא אֵלָיו ה' וַיֹּאמֶר אַל תֵּרֵד מִצְרָיְמָה — *There was a famine in the land ... and God appeared to him and said, "Do not go down into Egypt"* (26:1-2). God told Yitzchak, "Unlike your father, who went down to Egypt during a famine, you were a sacrifice on My altar, and the lands outside the Holy Land are unworthy of your presence. Live in this land, and I will give it to your descendants. I will bless them, and they will be as numerous as the stars of the sky. This I will do, עֵקֶב אֲשֶׁר שָׁמַע אַבְרָהָם בְּקֹלִי, *because Avraham listened to My voice* (v. 5) and was pious."

Our Sages learn from this that Avraham recognized his Creator at the age of three. Avraham lived 175 years, while the word עֵקֶב ("because"), as in the above-quoted verse, is numerically equivalent to 172. This means that Avraham listened to God's voice for 172 years, from the time that he was three until his death. For Avraham and the other Patriarchs obeyed the entire Torah even before it was given.

R' Bechaye questions this: If the Patriarchs obeyed the entire Torah, how could Yaakov have been married to two sisters at the same time or Amram marry his aunt? These are relationships forbidden by the Torah!

Ramban and *Toldos Yitzchak* explain that the *mitzvos* ("commandments") are in fact given mainly for *Eretz Yisrael*. Yaakov married two sisters outside *Eretz Yisrael*, and Amram married his aunt in Egypt. The reason that Yosef (Joseph) kept *Shabbos* in Egypt was that *Shabbos* is the greatest commandment, equal to all the other commandments of the Torah.

R' Isser'l gives another explanation: Yaakov took two sisters because he thought, "The Torah forbids marriage to two sisters because when one has two wives jealousy flares up between them, and the Torah sought to avoid bringing jealousy and hatred between sisters. But I know that there can be no jealousy or hatred between these two sisters." Similarly, Amram married his aunt because he thought that the reason it was forbidden to marry an aunt was because one may not act properly towards her. But he knew that he would treat his wife respectfully.

⊷§ Yitzchak and Avimelech

וַיֵּשֶׁב יִצְחָק בִּגְרָר — *Yitzchak lived in Gerar* (26:6). The townspeople asked him who Rivkah was. He said that she was his sister, for she was beautiful and he was afraid that they would murder him and take her away. After he had lived there for some time Avimelech, looking out his window, saw Yitzchak in joyful union with Rivkah.

Avimelech reproached him: "What have you done to us, saying that she was your sister! What if someone would have lain with her? You would have brought a great sin upon us!" Avimelech warned that anyone who laid a hand on either Yitzchak or Rivkah would be executed.

Toldos Yitzchak asks why Avimelech said, *What have you done to us?* — while Pharaoh asked, *What have you done to me?*

What Pharaoh said was: "If you felt that my nation was wicked and would desire and take your wife, you would have been correct. But if you had told me, I would not have touched her." [This was therefore a personal insult to Pharaoh.] Avimelech, though, said: "Both I and my nation are moral. If you would have told us she was

Avimelech reproaches Yitzchak

your wife, none of us would have touched her."

Similarly, Pharaoh told Avraham to leave after the incident in Egypt, because it would have been to no avail to simply decree that it was forbidden to touch Sarah. Avimelech however did announce that anyone touching Rivkah would be killed for they were all afraid and dared not approach her.

Ramban asks: Did Avimelech not see that Yitzchak had two children with him? How could he not suspect that Rivkah was his wife? The answer is that he thought they were the children of another woman.

◆§ Count Your Blessings — and Tithe Them

וַיִּזְרַע יִצְחָק בָּאָרֶץ הַהוּא וַיִּמְצָא בַּשָּׁנָה הַהוּא מֵאָה שְׁעָרִים — *Yitzchak sowed in that land, and in that year reaped a hundredfold* (26:12). *Rashi* asks: Why did Yitzchak count his possessions? There is no blessing on something which has been counted.

The answer is that he had to count and measure in order to know how much to tithe. And in the merit of his tithe, blessing rested on his fields, despite the counting. From one measure of grain a hundred grew. Yitzchak became very wealthy, until it became proverbial that the dirt of his mules was worth more than Avimelech's gold. The proverb specified mules because generally by keeping mules one cannot grow rich but in Yitzchak's case even they brought him wealth.

◆§ Three Wells

וְכָל הַבְּאֵרֹת אֲשֶׁר חָפְרוּ עַבְדֵי אָבִיו בִּימֵי אַבְרָהָם אָבִיו ... — *The Philistines plugged up all the wells which his father's servants had dug, when his father Avraham was still alive* (26:15). The Philistines said that if soldiers would come and lay a siege on the town they could use the wells for water, whereas if they stopped them up the soldiers would be forced to retreat. Yitzchak opened the wells up. His servants also dug a new well, and Avimelech's shepherds disputed with them over it. It was named עֵשֶׂק, meaning dispute. Then they dug a second well, and once again the shepherds quarreled, so Yitzchak named it שִׂטְנָה, meaning enmity. The third time they dug the well there was no quarrel, and it was called רְחֹבוֹת, meaning "God has given us our space and brought peace."

◆§ Avimelech's Treaty

וַיַּעַל מִשָּׁם בְּאֵר שָׁבַע — *He went up from there to Be'er Sheva* (26:23). In Be'er Sheva God appeared to Yitzchak and told him not to be afraid, for He was with him and would bless him in the merit of

Avraham. Yitzchak built an altar and set up camp there.

When Avimelech and his nobles then came to Yitzchak he asked them why they had followed him, if they hated him and had sent him away. Avimelech answered that he had seen the many miracles which God had performed for him and his father, and they had come to sign a treaty. Yitzchak agreed.

⊷§ Impression of Piety

וַיְהִי עֵשָׂו בֶּן אַרְבָּעִים שָׁנָה — *When Esav was forty years old* (26:34). When Esav was forty years old he married two idol worshipers. He gave them Jewish names to give the impression that he was pious, but they were evil, and Rivkah and Yitzchak were not at all pleased with them.

⊷§ When One Ages

וַיְהִי כִּי זָקֵן יִצְחָק — *And it came to pass, when Yitzchak became old* (27:1). When Yitzchak was an old man his eyesight grew dim. He told Esav, "I am old, and do not know when I shall die."

Chizkuni writes that Yitzchak told Esav, "When I die you will have no money, no dominion, and no respect, because you sold your birthright. Therefore I will give you something while I am still alive, so that Yaakov will not be able to take it away from you."

Rashi writes that Yitzchak said, לֹא יָדַעְתִּי יוֹם מוֹתִי — *I do not know when I shall die* (27:2), because when a man reaches the age when his father or mother died, he ought to begin to be concerned about his own death.

⊷§ A Murderer's Slaughter

שָׂא נָא כֵלֶיךָ תֶּלְיְךָ וְקַשְׁתֶּךָ וְצֵא הַשָּׂדֶה וְצוּדָה לִי צָיִד — *Sharpen your weapons, your sword and bow, and go out to the field to hunt me game* (27:3). Why did Yitzchak instruct Esav to sharpen his weapons? So that there would be no imperfection in them, which would invalidate the ritual slaughter.

Chizkuni and *Imrei Noam* both ask how Yitzchak could have eaten meat slaughtered by Esav, an idol worshiper. Even if Yitzchak was not aware of it, would God not have protected him? God watches over even the animals of righteous men, making certain that they eat nothing forbidden. How much more so should God have watched over what Yitzchak ate!

The answer is that from the time that Esav began to worship false gods, God did watch over Yitzchak, and he never ate anything which Esav had slaughtered. In this particular case, when he wanted to eat Esav's meat, God protected him and sent Yaakov to bring him two kids.

Baal HaTurim says that the word *tzayid* ("game") is written here with an extra letter *hei* (צידה) to show that Yitzchak had cautioned him to beware of the five things which can invalidate a ritual slaughter.

Yitzchak told Esav to bring him something to eat, and then he would bless him. *Chizkuni* says that Yitzchak told him that since he had sold his birthright for food, he must regain his blessing through food. R' Bechaye writes that Yitzchak wanted him to bring him something to eat so that he would be cheerful, and in his joy he would be able to bless him, for our Sages say that prophecy never rests on a person when he is depressed.

R' Bechaye asks why Yitzchak ate in order to make himself happy. Could he not have listened to music, as our prophets did when they were unhappy? The answer is that Yitzchak wanted to be made glad through the same things with which he intended to bless Esav: that is, blessings מִטַּל הַשָּׁמַיִם וּמִשְׁמַנֵּי הָאָרֶץ וְרֹב דָּגָן וְתִירֹש — *from the dew of the sky, the fat of the land, and much grain and wine* (27:28).

וַיֵּלֶךְ עֵשָׂו הַשָּׂדֶה לָצוּד צַיִד לְהָבִיא — *Esav went out to the fields to trap game and bring [it] home* (27:5). The seemingly superfluous word "to bring" hints that if he did not succeed in trapping an animal he would steal one.

◁§ Rivkah's Ruse

וְרִבְקָה אָמְרָה אֶל יַעֲקֹב — *Rivkah said to Yaakov* (27:6). Rivkah told Yaakov: "Your father has asked Esav to bring him food so that he will bless him. Go to the flocks and bring me back two kids. I will cook a sumptuous dish for your father, just the way he likes it, so that he will bless you." Rivkah used the words "bring to me" to show that the two calves belonged to her. Yitzchak had written in her marriage contract that he would provide her daily with two calves.

וַיֹּאמֶר יַעֲקֹב אֶל רִבְקָה אִמּוֹ הֵן עֵשָׂו אָחִי אִישׁ שָׂעִר וְאָנֹכִי אִישׁ חָלָק — *Yaakov said to his mother Rivkah: "My brother Esav is hairy, while I am a smooth-skinned man"* (27:11). Yaakov protested: What would happen if his father would touch him, recognize the ruse, and curse him? His mother replied that the curse would be upon her.

Chizkuni writes that she knew he would not be cursed, for God had told her, וְרַב יַעֲבֹד צָעִיר — *the elder will work for the younger* (25:23). *Chizkuni* also says that Rivkah told Yaakov that Yitzchak would realize that she had instigated it, and would curse her and not him. Another explanation offered by *Chizkuni* is that she told Yaakov that if he did not obey her she would curse him, while

Yitzchak would most certainly not curse him because he had brought him food.

Imrei Noam explains that she meant to say that if Yitzchak would curse Yaakov she herself would suffer from the curse, because if he was disinherited she would give him her entire settlement from her marriage contract.

Rivkah took the clothing which Esav generally wore to the hunt and put it on Yaakov. She took the skins of the calves and placed them on his arms and neck, so that he would resemble Esav. Esav had placed these clothes in Rivkah's possession for safekeeping. Even though he had many wives he knew they were evil and did not trust them with his clothing.

Yaakov brought the food to his father. *Even Shoev* writes that Yaakov did not want to trick his father nor lie to him. He cried and protested bitterly against it, until Rivkah thrust the food into his hands. He still refused to go, until Rivkah told him that angels would accompany him to his father. When he stood by the door he felt weak, so God sent the angels Michael and Gavriel, who took him by the hands and brought him to his father.

Rivkah sent no wine, because Esav was known as the red one [and she wanted no connection at all with Esav at the time that the blessing was given]. The angel Michael however brought wine from the Garden of Eden.

As soon as Yaakov walked out the door, Esav walked in, but did not see him because Michael concealed him.

R' Bechaye and *Chizkuni* write that God so arranged things that Esav should sell his birthright so that Yaakov would be able to receive the blessings. Hence, when his father asked who he was, he answered אָנֹכִי עֵשָׂו בְּכֹרֶךְ — *I am Esav, your eldest*, meaning, "I am here instead of Esav, because he sold me his birthright."

Yaakov however also said, עָשִׂיתִי כַּאֲשֶׁר דִּבַּרְתָּ אֵלָי — *I have done as you have commanded me* (27:19). R' Bechaye therefore asks: Had Yitzchak asked Yaakov to bring him food? The answer is that the word אֵלָי ("to me") can be interpreted as meaning "for me." Yitzchak asked Esav to bring food while Rivkah was in earshot and this request was ultimately "for me." Another interpretation is that Yaakov was saying, "I have always done what you have asked me to do."

Yitzchak asked why he had returned from the field so soon, and Yaakov answered that God caused him to find animals quickly. Yitzchak thought to himself that this must be Yaakov, for Esav spoke rarely of God. This is difficult to understand, though, because at this time Yitzchak still believed Esav to be righteous. Why was it so astounding, then, that he mentioned God's Name, when the righteous always speak of God?

The answer is that Yitzchak thought that Esav rarely spoke of God because he was often hunting in the fields where it is unclean and forbidden to speak of Him. As a result he was unaccustomed to speaking of God, even at home. Now, when he mentioned God's Name, Yitzchak suspected that it was Yaakov, who did not wander through unclean fields and was accustomed to speaking of God.

◄§ The Voice of Yaakov; the Fragrance of Eden

וַיְמֻשֵּׁהוּ וַיֹּאמֶר הַקֹּל קוֹל יַעֲקֹב וְהַיָּדַיִם יְדֵי עֵשָׂו — *He touched him and said, "The voice is the voice of Yaakov, but the hands are the hands of Esav"* (27:22). He said, "It is Yaakov's voice, for he speaks quietly and Esav's voice is loud; but the hands are Esav's." *Chizkuni* writes that Yitzchak assured himself that he could not identify him by his voice, since a man's voice is changeable, but from his hirsute hands he could recognize with certainty that it was Esav.

Yaakov brought him wine in order to confuse him, to make certain that he would not be recognized. Yitzchak then smelled the pleasant smell of Yaakov's clothing. *Rashi* asks: The smell of goatskin is unpleasant. What then did he smell? The answer is that Yaakov had put on Esav's clothing which had been worn by Adam in the Garden of Eden, and for that reason they had a pleasant fragrance.

◄§ Yitzchak's Blessing to Yaakov

וְיִשְׁתַּחֲווּ לְךָ בְּנֵי אִמֶּךָ — *Your mother's sons will bow down to you* (27:29). *Devek Tov* asks why Yitzchak specified *your mother's sons* rather than "your father's sons." *Chizkuni* answers that Yitzchak felt that Rivkah was still a young woman and might remarry and have more children, and with these words he included them.

אֹרְרֶיךָ אָרוּר וּמְבָרֲכֶיךָ בָּרוּךְ — *Those who curse you will be cursed; those who bless you, blessed* (27:29). *Rashi* asks why, in the portion of Bilam, the Torah says *those who bless you will be blessed* before *those who curse you will be cursed*. The answer is that the righteous first suffer in this world and later enjoy the World to Come. Yitzchak therefore first mentioned the curse and then the blessing. But the evil live well and later are punished, so Bilam first spoke of blessing and later of curse.

Chizkuni writes that although Yitzchak thought that Esav was righteous, he recognized that he was combative and that men would hate him. He therefore said *those who curse you* before speaking of those who would bless him — for there would be more who would want to curse him than give him a blessing.

יָקָם אָבִי — *Get up, my father* (27:31). *Chizkuni* writes that Yitzchak was dozing after eating Yaakov's meal, and therefore Esav told him to wake up and eat. Yitzchak asked who he was, and he said, *I am your eldest son, Esav*.

◄§ Yitzchak Discovers His Error

וַיֶּחֱרַד יִצְחָק — *Yitzchak trembled* (27:33). The *Midrash* writes that Yitzchak was more frightened now than when he had been bound on the altar. For this reason, the Torah says here, עַד מְאֹד — "exceedingly."

מִי אֵפוֹא הוּא הַצָּד צַיִד וַיָּבֵא לִי ... גַּם בָּרוּךְ יִהְיֶה — *Who is it, then, that caught game and brought it to me ... He shall also be blessed* (27:33). Even after Yitzchak became aware of what had happened he said that Yaakov should remain blessed, in order to silence those who would say that Yaakov would not have been blessed if he had not deceived Yitzchak.

Chizkuni writes that Yitzchak said, "My mistaking Yaakov and Esav is perfectly natural, for I am blind. But God knows all. If He allowed the younger to take the blessing away from the elder, let the younger be blessed. My blessing was given out of reliance upon the knowledge of God. Moreover, it was obviously necessary that Yaakov receive the blessing. He bought the birthright from Esav, so it was only proper that he receive the blessings."

Chizkuni writes also that Yitzchak said Yaakov should remain blessed "because I blessed him by saying that those blessing him will be blessed, while those that curse him will be cursed. If I curse him now, I too will be accursed. Nor can it be suggested that I neither bless him nor curse him. Nay, *let him also be blessed*, for in blessing him, I too am blessed."

Esav cried loudly and bitterly and asked his father to bless him as well, but Yitzchak answered that his brother had cunningly taken the blessing. Esav said that fittingly indeed had he been named Yaakov (meaning "trickster") because he had tricked him out of his birthright and now his blessing.

Esav asked his father if he had at least one blessing left. Yitzchak answered that he had made his brother a master over him and had made all his brothers subservient to him, and had as well blessed him with corn and wine. What more could he bless him with?

Esav asked, "Do you have only one blessing?" — and began to sob, so Yitzchak blessed him, saying:

◄§ Yitzchak's Blessing to Esav

מִשְׁמַנֵּי הָאָרֶץ יִהְיֶה מוֹשָׁבֶךָ — *The fat of the land shall be your dwelling* (27:39). *Toldos Yitzchak* asks why Yitzchak said that he had already blessed his brother and so could not bless Esav. Is there no more than one blessing in this world? And in fact, we see that Yitzchak ultimately did give a blessing to Esav.

The answer is that Yitzchak said, "I cannot give you a blessing such as the one I gave to Yaakov." Esav had asked, בָּרְכֵנִי גַם אָנִי אָבִי — *Bless me also, my father* (27:38), not knowing what blessing Yaakov had been given. Yitzchak answered that Esav could never be equal to Yaakov; he had made Yaakov a master over him. Esav then told Yitzchak, "Even if I cannot be equal to him, at least give me the blessing of grain and wine."

Yitzchak then blessed him with wheat and wine, but Esav lamented, "What good does it do me to have these things? I want to rule over something." Yitzchak answered, וְעַל חַרְבְּךָ תִחְיֶה — *By your sword you shall live* (27:40). When Yaakov would not abide by the Torah, Esav would have dominion.

Imrei Noam writes that Avraham had a sword which had the Name of God inscribed upon it. He gave it to Yitzchak, who gave it to Yaakov. When Esav wanted to battle Nimrod, Yaakov sold him the sword in exchange for the birthright. Then they ate the lentils which Yaakov had prepared. Generally when two people complete a deal they eat together. When Esav complained that Yaakov had stolen his birthright, Yitzchak answered, *By your sword you shall live*, referring to the sword for which he had traded his birthright.

◄§ Unabated Anger

וַיִּשְׂטֹם עֵשָׂו אֶת יַעֲקֹב — *Esav hated Yaakov* (27:41). *Chizkuni* writes that Esav was relying on this blessing — *By your sword you shall live* — and hoped to kill Yaakov. Esav told himself, "*The days of mourning for my father are fast approaching and then I will kill my brother Yaakov* (27:41). I would not bring such sorrow upon my father during his lifetime." This is how *Rashi* understands the verse.

Chizkuni writes that Esav meant, "*The day of my father's death is approaching,* and then he will bear no more children. There will be no one to defend Yaakov, and I will murder him."

Rivkah was told through prophecy of Esav's plans. She called Yaakov and told him to run away to Lavan (Laban) and hide from Esav's wrath. She said she would send for him when his anger had abated.

❧ On the Same Day

לָמָה אֶשְׁכַּל גַּם שְׁנֵיכֶם יוֹם אֶחָד — *Why should I lose both of you in one day?* (27:45). Esav said that on the very day that Yitzchak would die he would kill Yaakov. Rivkah therefore thought, why should she lose both Yitzchak and Yaakov in one day. This is the interpretation of *Chizkuni*.

Rashi writes that Rivkah meant, "When Esav comes to kill you, and you kill him in self-defense, his children in turn will avenge him. I will lose both of you in one day." As a matter of fact, both did die on the same day.

❧ A Mother's Worry

אִם לֹקֵחַ יַעֲקֹב אִשָּׁה מִבְּנוֹת חֵת ... לָמָה לִי חַיִּים — *If Yaakov takes a wife from the daughters of Ches ... why should I go on living (27:46)?* Rivkah told Yitzchak that if Yaakov married a girl from the daughters of Ches, she would have no reason to live. *Chizkuni* writes that Rivkah told Yitzchak to forbid Yaakov from marrying such a woman. He would want to marry a daughter of a powerful man of the family of Ches to help him against Esav. Yitzchak thereupon called for Yaakov and told him to go to Lavan and marry one of his daughters.

❧ A Proper Match

וַיִּשְׁלַח יִצְחָק אֶת יַעֲקֹב וַיֵּלֶךְ פַּדֶּנָה אֲרָם אֶל לָבָן בֶּן בְּתוּאֵל הָאֲרַמִּי אֲחִי רִבְקָה אֵם יַעֲקֹב וְעֵשָׂו — *Yitzchak sent Yaakov, and he went to Padan Aram, to Lavan, son of Besuel the Aramite, brother of Rivkah, mother of Yaakov and Esav* (28:5). *Chizkuni* asks why the verse tells us she was their mother. And in fact, is it not remarkable that Yitzchak and Rivkah, who were both very righteous, could have a wicked son? The verse therefore says *Lavan, brother of Rivkah.* Her child, as is often the case, resembled her brother, and that was what made it possible for her to be *the mother of Yaakov and Esav.*

Another reason is that Rivkah sent Yaakov away to prevent him from killing Esav, and Esav from murdering him. She was mother of both of them, and felt compassion for both.

Toldos Yitzchak and R' Bechaye ask why Rivkah did not fear sending Yaakov to Padan Aram, which was quite close by. What if Esav should follow him there? The verse says however *mother of Yaakov and Esav*, with the name of Yaakov preceding that of Esav. In Padan Aram her relatives knew that the mother preferred Yaakov, and thus would save him from Esav.

Some of our Sages say that all twins are born in two sacs, but

Yaakov and Esav were born in one. Therefore it says *mother of Yaakov and Esav* — twins who were born together, in one sac.

Yaakov heeded his mother's words and went to Padan Aram. We later see that Yosef was lost away from home for twenty-two years and could not honor his father, because many years earlier Yaakov had likewise been away for twenty-two years without honoring his parents. R' Bechaye asks why Yaakov was thus punished, if Yitzchak and Rivkah had themselves told him to go. His answer is that Yitzchak had told Yaakov to marry Leah, Lavan's eldest daughter, and not stay away longer than was necessary. But Rachel appealed to Yaakov more, and because of her he lingered — and therefore in later years he was punished.

Imrei Noam explains that Yaakov hid in the *beis midrash* of Shem and Ever for fourteen years, until Esav's anger had abated. Before this, in his first year away from home, Rivkah had sent her nurse, Devorah, to summon him, and she found him in Lavan's house. But he did not return immediately, delaying instead for twenty-two years — and for this he was punished.

פרשת ויצא
Parashas Vayetzei
(28:10 — 32:3)

◆§ The City's Lights Fade

וַיֵּצֵא יַעֲקֹב מִבְּאֵר שָׁבַע — *Yaakov went out of Be'er Sheva* (28:10). *Rashi* asks why the Torah specifies that he went out of Be'er Sheva. Did we not know that this was where he had been? This shows us, however, that when a righteous man is in a city, he is its beauty and its illumination; when he leaves the city, the beauty and the illumination leave with him.

◆§ Moving Mountains

וַיֵּלֶךְ חָרָנָה — *And* [Yaakov] *went to Charan* (28:10). He journeyed from Be'er Sheva to Charan in one day. Our Sages say that it was a journey of seventeen days, yet it took him twelve hours. This is the reason the Torah uses the expression וַיִּפְגַּע בַּמָּקוֹם — *he encountered the place* (29:11): the place came to meet him.

The Sages point out further that the two Hebrew words וַיִּפְגַּע בַּמָּקוֹם can also be translated, "He prayed to God." When Yaakov reached Charan he greatly regretted that he had passed by Mt. Moriah without praying there. He began to retrace his steps, but God brought Mt. Moriah towards him, so that he would not have to walk far.

◆§ The Sun Sets Early

וַיָּלֶן שָׁם כִּי בָא הַשֶּׁמֶשׁ — *He slept there because the sun had set* (28:11). *Rashi* asks why the verse first says that he slept there, and then that the sun had set. It ought to have said that the sun had set, so he slept there. This means to tell us that he remained there because the sun had set early. The sun did not set at the proper time, in order to ensure that he remain at that particular spot for the night. If the sun had not gone down, he would have gone further, in order to put a greater distance between himself and Esav.

We learn from this that a person ought not travel at night, as our Sages say: "A person should always enter a town while there is yet sunlight and resume his journey in the sunlight."

◄§ The Dispute of the Stones

וַיִּקַּח מֵאַבְנֵי הַמָּקוֹם וַיָּשֶׂם מְרַאֲשֹׁתָיו — *He took some stones and put [them] at his head* (28:11). *Rashi* asks: Here our verse says that he took some stones, in the plural, while later it says וַיִּקַּח אֶת הָאֶבֶן — *he took the stone* (28:18), in the singular. Yaakov first took a number of stones and built a shelter around his head to keep out the wild beasts. But the stones quarrelled, each one saying, "Upon *me* shall this righteous man rest his head!" Hearing this dispute, God brought peace between them by making them all into one stone.

◄§ Yaakov's Dream

וַיִּשְׁכַּב בַּמָּקוֹם הַהוּא — *He lay down in that place* (28:11). *Rashi* says that the words *in that place* show us that he slept only in that place, and not while he studied in the *beis midrash* of Shem and Ever. During the fourteen years that he studied there, he did not sleep at all, and studied Torah day and night.

Yaakov dreamed of a ladder standing on the earth, with its top reaching up to the heavens, and upon it angels climbed up and down. *Rashi* questions: Since the angels reside in heaven, the verse ought to have said that the angels were climbing down and up. Yaakov was now on the border of *Eretz Yisrael*, prepared to leave it. The angels who had escorted him within *Eretz Yisrael* could not leave its borders, and had to return to heaven. They went up, and then other angels, who were able to escort him in other lands, came down to join him.

Chizkuni and R' *Bechaye* write that the image of Yaakov's countenance was engraved on God's holy throne. The angels who

Yaakov's dream

had been escorting him ascended heavenward to compare that image with Yaakov's appearance on earth, and then came down once again to rejoin him.

God appeared to Yaakov and told him: אֲנִי ה' אֱלֹהֵי אַבְרָהָם אָבִיךְ וֵאלֹהֵי יִצְחָק — *I am the Lord, the God of your father Avraham and the God of Yitzchak* (28:13). The *Baal HaTurim* asks why this verse calls Avraham his father, rather than Yitzchak. He does not offer an answer.

R' Isser'l, however, says that Yaakov was afraid that his father's blessings would not come true because he had received them through cunning, as Yitzchak had actually thought that he was blessing Esav. God therefore told Yaakov, "Avraham is your rightful father." Avraham had been loath to bless Yitzchak himself, knowing that Yitzchak would want to bless Esav, and for that reason Avraham asked God to bless Yitzchak. Yitzchak in turn wanted to bless Esav, rather than Yaakov, and therefore God told Yaakov that Avraham was his father, while Yitzchak could not be considered a father.

Rashi asks why the Torah says *God of Yitzchak.* As a rule God does not associate His name with that of a person who is still living, because he might change his ways and become evil. But Yitzchak was blind and housebound, and could be considered dead in the sense that his evil inclination had completely abandoned him. God could therefore mention His name in conjunction with Yitzchak's.

◄§ The Significance of Four Cubits

הָאָרֶץ אֲשֶׁר אַתָּה שֹׁכֵב עָלֶיהָ לְךָ אֶתְּנֶנָּה וּלְזַרְעֶךָ — *I will give the land which you are lying upon to you and your sons* (28:13). *Rashi* asks: What manner of gift is the four cubits of earth upon which a man lies? The answer is that God folded the entire *Eretz Yisrael* beneath Yaakov, to show him that the whole of the land would be conquered by his descendants, as easily as the four cubits which lay beneath him.

◄§ Stars and Dust

וְהָיָה זַרְעֲךָ כַּעֲפַר הָאָרֶץ — *Your descendants will be like the dust of the earth* (28:14). R' Bechaye asks why God did not say, according to an earlier promise, that they would be as numerous as the stars in the sky. The answer is that when Israel is virtuous God lifts them up but when they are, God forbid, sinners, God casts them down to the lowest depths, like dust which is trodden upon by all.

God told Yaakov that He would do אֵת אֲשֶׁר דִּבַּרְתִּי לָךְ — *what I have told you* (28:15). *Rashi* asks: We do not find that God had spoken with Yaakov previously. The answer is that the word לְךָ (here translated "to you") can also be understood to mean "about you." God refers to the times that He had spoken with Avraham and had told him that one of Yitzchak's sons would be his heir (21:12).

◄§ Yaakov's Condition

וַיִּיקַץ יַעֲקֹב מִשְּׁנָתוֹ — *Yaakov awoke from his sleep* (28:16). Yaakov awoke and said, "God is here and I did not know it; I would not have dared to sleep on such holy ground." He trembled and said, "This is the gate of heaven, through which people's prayers rise." He took the stone upon which he had slept and set it up as a monument, anointing it with oil. Then he vowed that if God stayed with him and protected him as He had promised, He would be his God.

One can raise the question: How can it be that Yaakov would say that his belief in God was conditional on whether or not God fulfilled His promises? The answer is that Yaakov was afraid that he would sin and God would not therefore fulfill all that He had promised him. He thus said, "If God helps and protects me I will worship Him on this very spot; if He does not, I will of course still worship Him, but not necessarily in this place."

◄§ Of Everything God Gives Me

אִם יִהְיֶה אֱלֹהִים עִמָּדִי — *If God will be with me* (28:20). "If God stays with me I will give tithes from everything which He gives me." Yaakov fulfilled this promise so fully that he even gave a tithe of his children — the tribe of Levi [who were dedicated to God's service, and could thus be considered his tithe to God].

וְנָתַן לִי לֶחֶם לֶאֱכֹל וּבֶגֶד לִלְבֹּשׁ — *And give me bread to eat and clothing to wear* (28:20). Rashi asks: Where did God promise to give Yaakov bread? — God promised not to abandon him, which implies that He would feed him, because a person left without food is considered abandoned. R' Isser'l asks: When did God promise him clothing? *Sifsei Chachamim* answers that when God promised him bread, this included a promise of clothing, because if He would not clothe him he would have to sell his food to buy clothes.

◄§ Yaakov and Rachel at the Well

וַיַּרְא וְהִנֵּה בְאֵר בַּשָּׂדֶה — *He saw a well in the field* (29:2). Yaakov saw a well in a field, with three flocks of sheep standing nearby. A large boulder covered the well. All of the shepherds would gather together to roll it off and give water to their sheep.

Yaakov asked the shepherds if they knew Lavan, son of Nachor. R' Bechaye and *Chizkuni* ask why he is here called Nachor's son,

when in fact Besuel was his father. But Besuel was an evil man and
Lavan did not use his name, preferring the name of his grandfather.
Since Nachor was Avraham's brother the whole family wanted to
show their relationship with him.

As they were speaking, Rachel approached, with her sheep.
Yaakov told the shepherds, "The day is still long, and it is not yet
time to give the sheep water. You are hired for the entire day; give
them water and go back to the pasture." Yaakov said this so that the
shepherds would leave and he would be able to speak with Rachel
privately.

The shepherds answered that they could not give the sheep water
until all of them had gathered together to roll the stone away. Just
then Rachel arrived at the well.

Chizkuni asks: Why did Leah not herd the sheep? — She had
weak eyes and the wind hurt her. *Ramban* points out as well that
because Leah was the elder sister, Rachel treated her with respect
and allowed her to stay at home.

וַיְהִי כַּאֲשֶׁר רָאָה יַעֲקֹב אֶת רָחֵל בַּת לָבָן אֲחִי אִמּוֹ וְאֶת צֹאן לָבָן אֲבִי אִמּוֹ ...
וַיָּגֶל אֶת הָאֶבֶן מֵעַל פִּי הַבְּאֵר — *When Yaakov saw Rachel, daughter of
his mother's brother Lavan, and the sheep of Lavan, his mother's
brother ... [Yaakov] rolled the stone from the mouth of the well*
(29:10). Yaakov did this to show his strength to Rachel. The
shepherds used to gather together and roll the stone off the well, as
it says, וְגָלֲלוּ — *and they would roll* (29:8). Because of its weight,
they were unable to lift it. But in Yaakov's case the Torah says וַיָּגֶל,
which means either *and he rolled* [from the root גלל], meaning that
he rolled it by himself, or *and he uncovered it* [from the root גלה, to
uncover or reveal], meaning that he lifted it as easily as one lifts a
cork from a bottle.

R' Bechaye asks why it says *Lavan, his mother's brother*, three
times. This shows us that Yaakov gave the wicked Lavan's sheep
water to drink only because he was his mother's brother.

◄§ No Gifts

וַיִּשַּׁק יַעֲקֹב לְרָחֵל וַיִּשָּׂא אֶת קֹלוֹ וַיֵּבְךְּ — *Yaakov kissed Rachel, and lifted
his voice and wept* (29:11). Why did Yaakov kiss Rachel? *Ramban*
answers: Because she was still very young. For this same reason
Lavan was not afraid to send her to the fields, since she was too
young yet for a man.

He cried because he saw prophetically that she would not be
buried next to him in the Cave, and because he had no gifts to give
to her. He said, "Eliezer, Avraham's servant, brought beautiful gifts
for Rivkah; I have brought nothing."

ı nis is difficult to understand. Is it possible that Rivkah sent him away with nothing? The answer is that Rivkah gave Yaakov money and gifts but Elifaz, Esav's son, pursued him, with the intent of obeying Esav's command and murdering him. When Elifaz caught up with him Yaakov told him to take everything which he owned, and then he would be considered dead [for a poor man is considered dead]. Then he could tell Esav that he had killed Yaakov.

◆§ A Match for Lavan

וַיַּגֵּד יַעֲקֹב לְרָחֵל כִּי אֲחִי אָבִיהָ הוּא וְכִי בֶן רִבְקָה הוּא — *Yaakov told Rachel that he was her father's brother [i.e., relative], and that he was Rivkah's son* (29:12). He explained that he had kissed Rachel because she was his relative.

Rashi writes that Yaakov was saying, "If your father is deceitful, then I am his brother: I too can be deceitful. If he is righteous then I too am righteous, for I am Rivkah's son."

Rachel went to tell her father. Why did she not run to her mother, as Rivkah had done? — Because Rachel's mother was dead. *Chizkuni* writes that because Yaakov had said that he was her father's brother, she ran to her father; Eliezer had not specified whose side of the family had sent him, so Rivkah told her mother. Also, Eliezer had given Rivkah a beautiful bracelet, which she wanted to show to her mother.

וַיָּרָץ לִקְרָאתוֹ — *[Lavan] ran to meet him* (29:13). Lavan thought to himself: "Eliezer, Avraham's servant, brought ten camels laden with precious goods. How much more will Yaakov bring with him!" When he saw no camels he thought to himself, "He must have great sums of money with him." He hugged Yaakov, to see if he was carrying any money. When he found no money he kissed him, to see if he had hidden any gems in his mouth.

Yaakov told Lavan that he was fleeing from Esav, in order to explain why he had brought nothing with him. *Chizkuni* writes that he told Lavan how he had received the blessings, so that Lavan would agree to give him his daughter.

◆§ A House of Idols

וַיֹּאמֶר לוֹ לָבָן אַךְ עַצְמִי וּבְשָׂרִי אָתָּה — *Lavan said to him, "Surely you are my bone and my flesh"* (29:14). Lavan told him, "I really do not have to take you into my house, since you have no money. But since you are my flesh and blood, my relative, stay with me for a month." Nor was the month's hospitality unpaid for: Yaakov watched Lavan's sheep for him.

Yaakov stayed with him for a month. Lavan did not want to hire him as a worker until he had seen what sort of person he was. *Imrei Noam* asks how Yaakov could have stayed in Lavan's home, which was full of idols. Even Avraham's camels would not enter Besuel's house until the idols were removed! The answer is that Yaakov wanted to discern if Rachel or Leah worshiped idols. He found out in one month, and left immediately afterwards, as it is written, וַיֵּשֶׁב עִמּוֹ חֹדֶשׁ יָמִים — *He stayed with him for a month of days (ibid.)*.

✑§ Lavan's Cunning

וַיֹּאמֶר לָבָן לְיַעֲקֹב הֲכִי אָחִי אַתָּה וַעֲבַדְתַּנִי חִנָּם — *Lavan said to Yaakov: "Just because you are my brother, should you work for me for nothing?"* (29:15). The author of *Toldos Yitzchak* writes: Lavan was cunning, and thought to himself that if Yaakov worked for him for nothing, he would not be liable for any damage incurred while he worked [the law is that an unpaid custodian is not generally liable for damage to the property]. Lavan therefore wanted to pay him, and thus Yaakov would be responsible for any damage. This explains why Lavan asked Yaakov how much he wanted for his work.

✑§ Yaakov Chooses Rachel

וְעֵינֵי לֵאָה רַכּוֹת — *Leah's eyes were weak* (29:17). They were weak because of her incessant crying. People used to say, "Leah is Lavan's elder daughter, so she will marry Esav, Rivkah's elder son; Rachel is the younger daughter, so she will marry Yaakov, Rivkah's younger son." This is what *Rashi* says.

Devek Tov writes that *Rashi's* question was why the Torah should here record Leah's handicap. Therefore *Rashi* explained that this actually showed Leah's righteousness: she cried her eyes out in prayer that she should not fall to Esav's lot.

R' Isser'l writes that the *Gemara* says: "If a bride has beautiful eyes one need not look at the rest of her body for any faults; if she does not, the entire body should be examined for other imperfections."

Yaakov thought: "I must obey my parents' command and marry one of Lavan's daughters. Had he had only one daughter, Leah, I would marry her. But Lavan also has Rachel, who is totally unblemished, so why should I marry Leah?"

Yaakov therefore told Lavan, אֶעֱבָדְךָ שֶׁבַע שָׁנִים בְּרָחֵל בִּתְּךָ הַקְּטַנָּה — *I will work for seven years for Rachel, your younger daughter* (29:18). *Rashi* asks: Why did Yaakov specify that she was his younger daughter? But Yaakov knew that Lavan was a deceiver, and thought to himself: "If I say that I shall work for Rachel, he will take any woman whose name is Rachel and will give her to me."

Therefore he specified that he wanted his daughter. Further, he feared that Lavan would rename Leah and call her Rachel, and give her to him. Therefore he specified the younger daughter. But none of this helped: Lavan gave him Leah anyway!

Chizkuni writes that Yaakov said: "I will marry Rachel because she is the younger. If I marry Leah, Esav will say that I took away not only his birthright and his blessings, but also the wife who rightfully belonged to him."

Chizkuni adds that Yaakov volunteered to work for seven years for Rachel because he felt that he would not be given such a beautiful woman for less. R' Bechaye writes that Yaakov offered to work for seven years because Rachel was only five years old at that time. He wanted to wait until she was twelve and of child-bearing age.

Lavan answered that he would rather have her marry Yaakov than someone else. The seven years flew by, and seemed to Yaakov to pass like a few days, because of his love for her.

This is a difficult statement to understand. As a rule when one loves a woman then each hour, each day, is long, until they can be together. Why does it say here that it seemed like a few days? The answer is that once the seven years were through, it then seemed to Yaakov that he had only worked a few days, because of his great love for her.

⋖§ The Waiting Period Ends

הָבָה אֶת אִשְׁתִּי כִּי מָלְאוּ יָמָי וְאָבוֹאָה אֵלֶיהָ — *Bring me my wife, for my days are complete, so that I may go to her* (29:21). *Rashi* asks: Why did Yaakov speak so bluntly, saying *so that I may go to her* (i.e., lie with her)? Even the most boorish man would not say such a thing. The answer is that he said, "I am already eighty-four years old, and I am destined to have twelve children. It is time for me to take a wife." His thoughts were only for his children.

Ramban asks: Why did Yaakov say that the days which his mother had told him to stay with Lavan had passed? Why should Lavan care? And *Ramban* answers that the words *for my days are complete* mean that the seventh year of his labor had already arrived. Yaakov then told Lavan that he should now give Rachel to him, despite the fact that seven full years had not passed. Lavan could be certain that Yaakov would stay with her for at least the remaining year. The meaning of the words *I may go to her* is thus, "I will take her now for a wife, and will not desert her."

⋖§ A Missed Hint

וַיֶּאֱסֹף לָבָן אֶת כָּל אַנְשֵׁי הַמָּקוֹם וַיַּעַשׂ מִשְׁתֶּה — *Lavan gathered all the* men of the place and made a feast (29:22). He told all the townspeople not to let Yaakov know that he was going to give him Leah. They all swore. Lavan asked for some sort of guarantee that they would keep their word. They gave him their clothing, and he pawned them to buy wine and delicacies. They became intoxicated and all that night joyously sang *Hilula!* With this word (Aramaic for "celebration") they hinted to Yaakov that his bride was actually Leah, for *hilula* brings to mind the two words *Hih Leah* ("She is Leah"). But Yaakov did not understand the hint.

❧ Rachel's Considerateness

וַיְהִי בָעֶרֶב וַיִּקַח אֶת לֵאָה בִתּוֹ וַיָּבֵא אֹתָהּ אֵלָיו וַיָּבֹא אֵלֶיהָ — *In the evening he took his daughter Leah, and brought her to him, and he came to her* (29:23). Lavan took Zilpah and gave her to Leah as a maidservant. Yaakov saw Zilpah, who was the youngest maidservant, and assumed that her mistress was Rachel, and that the older maidservant, Bilhah, had been given to Leah.

In the morning Yaakov realized that she was Leah. Yaakov had given certain passwords and signs to Rachel so that he should be certain that she would be his bride. When Rachel saw that they were leading Leah to him she realized that her sister would be humiliated in front of everyone because she would not know the passwords. She therefore told her all the signs to enable her to answer Yaakov, and so Yaakov did not recognize her until morning.

R' Bechaye writes: God rewards each person in kind. Yaakov sent Rachel gifts before the wedding, as all bridegrooms do. Lavan gave them to Leah, and Rachel said nothing. Therefore, in later years one of her children, Binyamin (Benjamin), did not tell his father that the brothers had sold Yosef (Joseph). Binyamin's descendant, King Shaul, did not reveal that Shmuel (Samuel) had anointed him as king. And Shaul's descendant, Queen Esther, did not reveal her family and her religion, and thereby brought about the redemption of Purim.

Yaakov protested to Lavan, "What have you done to me? I worked for Rachel and you gave me Leah!" Lavan answered that it was not customary in his town to marry off a younger daughter before an older one. But he could marry Rachel as well, after waiting for one week, in order not to lessen the joy of the first wedding.

❧ Love and Hate

וַיָּבֹא גַם אֶל רָחֵל וַיֶּאֱהַב גַם אֶת רָחֵל מִלֵּאָה — *He went to Rachel as well, and he loved Rachel more than Leah* (29:30). *Ramban* writes that generally a man loves his first wife most. Yaakov married Leah first;

why did he love Rachel more? The answer is that Leah deceived him. Although she had to obey her father's commands and go to Yaakov, she could have revealed her identity. She tricked him, pretending that she was Rachel, and therefore Yaakov hated her and wanted to divorce her. God understood that her intentions had been honorable, as she had wanted to marry a righteous man. Thus God helped her and gave her a child almost immediately, as the verse says, 'וַיַּרְא ה כִּי שְׂנוּאָה לֵאָה — *God saw that Leah was hated* (29:31). God gave her a child so that Yaakov would love her.

R' Bechaye and *Ramban* write that Yaakov did not hate her. It was only that when compared to his love for Rachel, his feelings toward Leah seemed like hatred.

◄§ Seven Faithful Years

וַיַּעֲבֹד עִמּוֹ עוֹד שֶׁבַע שָׁנִים אֲחֵרוֹת — *He worked with him another seven years* (29:30). The verse teaches us Yaakov's greatness. Even though he had worked for seven years for Rachel, and Lavan had cheated him and given him Leah, still he worked as faithfully for the next seven years as he had for the first seven.

◄§ Eleven in Seven Years

וַתַּהַר לֵאָה וַתֵּלֶד בֵּן — *Leah conceived and gave birth to a son* (29:32). R' Bechaye writes that soon after she conceived she gave birth to a son; she had each child after seven months of pregnancy. All of the twelve sons, except Binyamin, were born within the seven years of Yaakov's labor.

◄§ What's in a Name

עַתָּה הַפַּעַם יִלָּוֶה אִישִׁי אֵלַי — *This time my husband will join me* (29:34). When Leah gave birth to her third son she said, "This time my husband will be attached to me." She knew by prophecy that Yaakov would have twelve sons. Since he had four wives, each wife should have three children. She said, "I now have my portion, and so my husband will stay with me." She called the boy Levi (from the root לוה, "to accompany"; Rashi).

Chizkuni and *Toldos Yitzchak* say that when a woman has two children she can take one on each hand, but when she has a third child her husband must hold one. This is what Leah meant when she said her husband would have to join her. He would have to help her carry Levi, the third child.

The verse here says, קָרָא שְׁמוֹ לֵוִי — *he called him Levi*, while in reference to the other sons it says קָרְאָה or וַתִּקְרָא — *she called him* ..., because God sent the angel Gavriel to bring the baby to Him and

He gave him the name of Levi, for God had attached to him the twenty-four gifts of priesthood.

Despite this distinction Levi did not have many children, for his tribe was not enslaved in Egypt. Yaakov had instructed the priestly tribe not to bear his coffin, so the Egyptians saw that they were holy and did not enslave them. But for this reason they were not included in the blessing given to their enslaved brethren: וְכַאֲשֶׁר יְעַנּוּ אֹתוֹ כֵּן יִרְבֶּה וְכֵן יִפְרֹץ — *The more they afflicted them the more they increased and spread* (Shmos 1:12).

When Leah gave birth to her fourth son she said, "*This time I will praise God*" (29:35). She now had more than her portion of children, and so she named him Yehudah (Judah) meaning "thanks".

◄§ What did Rachel Envy

וַתֵּרֶא רָחֵל כִּי לֹא יָלְדָה לְיַעֲקֹב וַתְּקַנֵּא רָחֵל בַּאֲחֹתָהּ — *Rachel saw that she was not bearing children to Yaakov, and Rachel envied her sister* (30:1). *Toldos Yitzchak* asks why Rachel did not envy Leah her first three children. — She thought that her portion, too, would be three children. But when she saw that Leah already had four children she began to envy her for having the largest portion.

Rashi writes that she did not envy Leah her many children. This would be incomprehensible behavior on the part of such a righteous woman. Rather, she envied her good deeds, thinking that Leah must be very righteous to deserve a greater portion. And this it is permissible to envy.

וַתֹּאמֶר אֶל יַעֲקֹב הָבָה לִי בָנִים וְאִם אַיִן מֵתָה אָנֹכִי — *She said to Yaakov, "Give me children. If not, let me die!"* (30:1). She said, "Give me children or I am as good as dead! Your father Yitzchak prayed that Rivkah should have children; why do you not pray for me?" We learn from this that a person who has no children is likened to the dead.

◄§ Rachel's Request; Yaakov's Reply

וַיִּחַר אַף יַעֲקֹב בְּרָחֵל וַיֹּאמֶר הֲתַחַת אֱלֹהִים אָנֹכִי — *Yaakov was angry at Rachel and said, "Shall I take God's place?"* (30:2). He asked if she thought that he was God who had withheld children from her. His father had prayed for Rivkah because he had no children from other wives, but he already had children from Leah!

Ramban asks: How could Yaakov have answered her so? The righteous — such as Eliyahu and Elisha — even pray on behalf of total strangers. How much more should Yaakov have prayed for his own beloved wife! Further, it is difficult to understand Yaakov's anger, since Rachel had been justified in her request, for does God not accept the prayers of a *tzaddik?*

The *Midrash* says that God told Yaakov, "You did not reply properly to Rachel, and so your other children will be forced to bow down to her child Yosef." But the simple explanation is that Rachel frightened Yaakov. She knew how much he loved her and so warned him that she would die of sorrow if she would have no children, hoping that he would fast and wear sackcloth and plead with God until He granted her children. Yaakov was angered, for he realized that she had tried to frighten him so that he would pray, in her certainty that through his prayers she would have a child. This is why he replied, *Shall I take God's place?*

Rachel said, "Your grandfather Avraham had children from Hagar, and still he prayed for Sarah." Yaakov answered that his grandmother Sarah had of her own volition given Avraham her maidservant. It was then that Rachel said, "If so, *here is my maidservant Bilhah; come to her, so that perhaps in that way I will have children*" (30:3; *Rashi*).

R' Bechaye writes that Rachel said, "There is no letter of God's name in my name. Leah has a *hei*, a letter which appears in God's name, and therefore she has children. I will give you my maidservant Bilhah (בִּלְהָה), in whose name the *hei* appears twice. One *hei* will enable her to bear children, and the other will be for me."

◆§ Bilhah and Zilpah Conceive and Bear

וַתַּהַר בִּלְהָה וַתֵּלֶד לְיַעֲקֹב בֵּן — *Bilhah conceived and bore a son to Yaakov* (30:5). *Ramban* writes that the Torah says *to Yaakov* to show that even though they were the sons of maidservants, Yaakov loved them and considered them his sons. She called the boy Dan. She became pregnant once again, and had a son whom Rachel named Naftali, meaning, "God hearkened to my prayers."

When Leah saw that Rachel had given her maidservant to Yaakov, she too gave him her maidservant. *Toldos Yitzchak* asks why Leah did this, when she already had children.

Rachel gave her maidservant to Yaakov so that the maid would bear children, hoping that in the merit of her action she too would bear children. Leah, though, wanted to give birth to more children herself, not through her maid. When Zilpah gave birth, Leah was angry and said, "I did not want to have children through my maid; I wanted my own. Obviously, God did not listen to me, and the child was born through an act of mere fate." She therefore called him Gad, meaning luck. Because she said that the maid's son was born through luck and not through God's hand, she was punished and later gave birth to a bad daughter. She said, "Blessed is the true judge" (judge — *dayan*; the blessing is recited when a person hears bad news), and therefore named her daughter Dinah (from the same root — דִּין — as *dayan*).

וַתֵּלֶד זִלְפָּה שִׁפְחַת לֵאָה — *Zilpah, Leah's maidservant, gave birth* (30:10). The Torah does not say that she conceived, because she was very young and her pregnancy did not show. As mentioned above, Lavan had given the younger maidservant to Leah so that Yaakov would think that her mistress must be Rachel, the younger daughter.

Reuven, Yaakov's eldest son, *found dudaim* (mandrakes) *in the field* (30:14). He brought them to his mother Leah. *Ramban* and R' Bechaye write that this was a type of herb with a fragrant smell.

Rachel said to her, "Give me the mandrakes of your son," because she wanted to have children [and they promoted fertility]. Leah was angered, and answered, "You have taken away my husband; will you take my mandrakes as well?" Rachel answered, "In return for the mandrakes he will lie with you tonight, although he ought to have lain with me." Because she was contemptuous enough to sell marital relations with a *tzaddik*, she was adjudged unworthy of lying next to him in death, in the Cave of Machpelah.

◆§ Dinah

וַיָּבֹא יַעֲקֹב מִן הַשָּׂדֶה — *Yaakov came from the field* (30:16). As soon as Yaakov came in from the field Leah went to greet him, telling him to come to her tent that night, as she had earned his presence in exchange for her son's mandrakes. He lay with her that night, and she conceived a son whom she called Yissachar, meaning, God rewarded me (*sachar* — "reward"). She then had another son, named Zevulun, which means "a lodge" (זְבוּל), because she felt that after six children her husband would make his home with her. She then gave birth to a daughter, named Dinah.

Chizkuni writes: Why does the Torah not say that she became pregnant with Dinah? Because Dinah was actually Zevulun's twin sister. Another reason is that Leah was destined to give birth to another son, but she prayed that Rachel should have the son instead. God heeded her prayers, and as well gave her a daughter whom she named Dinah, because she had judged herself to have a daughter (from the root דִּין — "to judge").

◆§ Rachel is Remembered

וַיִּזְכֹּר אֱלֹהִים אֶת רָחֵל — *God remembered Rachel* (30:22). God remembered the compassion which Rachel had shown Leah by giving her the passwords which Yaakov had arranged with her. God also remembered how she had constantly cried, fearing that Yaakov would divorce her because she was childless and she would have to marry Esav. God remembered all of this and gave her a son.

Rachel said, אָסַף אֱלֹהִים אֶת חֶרְפָּתִי, *God has taken away (asaf) my shame* (30:23), meaning her humiliation before the people who had said that Yaakov would divorce her and she would marry Esav. For this reason she called the child Yosef.

Another explanation is that when a woman has a child, she can blame the child when a mishap occurs. Who broke the glass? — The child. Who ate up the figs? — The child. And so her shame is taken away.

יֹסֵף ה' לִי בֵּן אַחֵר — *May God grant me another son* (30:24). *Rashi* asks: Why did Rachel not ask for more than one more son? — She knew prophetically that Yaakov would have twelve sons. Eleven had already been born, so only one was left. She therefore prayed now that the one son left would be hers.

◄§ A Match for Esav

וַיְהִי כַּאֲשֶׁר יָלְדָה רָחֵל אֶת יוֹסֵף וַיֹּאמֶר יַעֲקֹב אֶל לָבָן שַׁלְּחֵנִי — *It was when Rachel gave birth to Yosef, Yaakov said to Lavan, "Let me leave"* (30:25). When Rachel gave birth to Yosef, Esav's nemesis, Yaakov no longer feared Esav and wanted to return home. *Toldos Yitzchak* asks: Why was Yosef such a formidable match for Esav? Because only he could stand and judge Esav, and ask him: "Why did you treat your brother Yaakov so grievously?" If Esav would answer: "Because he ill-treated me, by taking away my birthright and my blessing," Yosef could answer, "My brothers treated me badly and sold me as a slave, and yet I treated them mercifully." The other brothers could not ask Esav why he had been harsh to his brother, for they themselves had been wicked to their brother Yosef.

תְּנָה אֶת נָשַׁי וְאֶת יְלָדַי — *Give me my wives and my children* (30:26). Yaakov told Lavan, "I do not want to leave without your permission. Give me my wives and children and allow me to go home." Lavan answered, "If I have found favor in your eyes, I beg you to stay. I see that God has blessed me because of you. Before your arrival I had no sons, and was forced to send my daughter with my sheep to the fields. Once you arrived my wife bore sons."

Chizkuni asks how we know that Lavan had no sons before Yaakov's arrival. Perhaps he had sons, who were too young to go to the fields, and therefore he sent his daughter. R' Isser'l answers that if he would have had sons, even young ones, he would not have sent his daughters out. Rather, he would have sent out their maids Bilhah and Zilpah. But since he had no sons, his daughters were his heirs, and therefore he sent Rachel out, knowing that she would faithfully care for his sheep, for she would one day inherit them. He did not send the maids, as they were the children of concubines, and would not inherit, and so they would not watch the sheep carefully.

◄§ Spotted and Speckled

וַיֹּאמַר נָקְבָה שְׂכָרְךָ עָלַי וְאֶתֵּנָה — *Name your wages, and I will give them* (30:28). *Toldos Yitzchak* writes that since Lavan had more daughters, he was here making another offer: "I will give you a female [נְקֵבָה ("female") / נָקְבָה ("name")] as your wages, if you stay with me." Yaakov answered that he had enough wives.

Yaakov said to Lavan, "I have served you faithfully, and God blessed you because of me." Lavan asked, "What can I give you to reward you for the first years of work?" Yaakov replied, "I want nothing for the first years of work, for I was working for my wives. But if you want me to stay and work for you, come with me to the flocks of sheep, and separate all the spotted and speckled sheep. Any spotted or speckled sheep born to the remainder of the sheep shall be mine. If you find among my sheep one which is not spotted or speckled, you will know that I have stolen it from you."

וַיָּסַר בַּיּוֹם הַהוּא אֶת הַתְּיָשִׁים הָעֲקֻדִּים וְהַטְּלֻאִים — *He removed that day the goats that were spotted and speckled* (30:35). *Ramban* writes: Lavan was a swindler. Yaakov had requested that he take away all the spotted and speckled sheep, but Lavan took away any sheep with spots or streaks, even those which had white marks on their legs, or those which were mostly white. He took them away for a distance of three days' journey from the sheep which remained with Yaakov, so that it would be impossible for Yaakov to get any of the spotted or speckled sheep which Yaakov would, by terms of the agreement, keep for himself.

Yaakov, too, was forced to act with cunning. He took sticks of wood and peeled strips of bark off them, leaving white streaks. He placed them near the sheep's watering troughs, so that they would see them and later bear streaked lambs. He placed all the lambs which were born streaked in a separate flock near the other sheep, so that they would see them and bear still more streaked lambs. Yaakov placed the sticks only near the strongest of the sheep, and not near the sickly ones, so that the lambs born would be strong and healthy. Yaakov prospered, the sheep bore numerous lambs, and as a result he came to own many donkeys and camels, and servants and maidservants.

Yaakov overheard Lavan's children complaining that all of Yaakov's riches had been obtained from their father. God then appeared to him, telling him to go back to his land, and promising that He would be with him. Yaakov called to Rachel and Leah in the field and told them, "You know that I worked for your father faithfully, and he cheated me more than ten times, but God was with me and helped me."

⋙ Ten Times Cheated

אִם כֹּה יֹאמַר — *If he would say thus* (31:8). *Ramban* and *Toldos Yitzchak* ask: Why does the Torah say, *If he [Lavan] would say thus*, which is in the future tense, when Yaakov was speaking of what had taken place in the past? Lavan was a schemer who knew that God would give Yaakov whatever type of sheep they decided upon. If he would say that Yaakov should get all the spotted sheep, all the sheep would be born spotted. So, he schemed, once the sheep would conceive he would say that all the speckled sheep would belong to Yaakov, rather than the spotted sheep, as previously agreed upon. But God knew of all this, and therefore as soon as Lavan said he would give Yaakov the spotted sheep, intending all the while to give him the speckled, all the sheep carried with speckled lambs. Therefore the verse says, *When he would say thus*, meaning, he would say one thing, intending to say something else later.

Yaakov told Lavan, לֹא תִתֶּן לִי מְאוּמָה — *Do not give me a thing* (30:31), meaning, nothing which has been counted, for no blessing rests on something once it has been counted. "Rather," he continued, "I will go through your sheep. You will set apart all the spotted and speckled ones, and then any spotted or speckled sheep born to the flock will be mine as payment." *Toldos Yitzchak* writes that Yaakov told him, "You know full well that you won't give me whatever you promise me; allow me to watch your flocks, so that my reward will be under my protection."

⋙ The Angel Speaks

וַיֹּאמֶר אֵלַי מַלְאַךְ הָאֱלֹהִים ... שָׂא נָא עֵינֶיךָ — *An angel of God said to me, "... Lift your eyes"* (31:11-12). The angel told Yaakov, "Lift up your eyes and see the rams that are mounting your ewes; they are speckled and spotted. I have seen what Lavan is doing to you. I am God who appeared to you in Beth El; go to your native land."

R' Bechaye asks: How could the angel tell Yaakov to watch the goats as they mated? Does the *Gemara* not say that one may not watch birds or animals mate? The answer is that this was only a dream.

In this episode we see that even animals gave birth to lambs which reflected their impressions of the spotted sticks. From this we learn how a person must sanctify himself with pure thoughts during intercourse. Our Sages say that women, particularly, should think pure thoughts, as their thoughts during intercourse greatly affect the child to be conceived.

Rachel and Leah told Yaakov that they had no hope of inheriting their father's property, as he had sons, and moreover, וַיֹּאכַל גַּם אָכוֹל אֶת כַּסְפֵּנוּ — "He has devoured our money (31:15), which had been set aside as our dowry. Whatever wealth God has taken from our father belongs to us." They told him to do what God had commanded.

◄§ Children and Wives; Wives and Children

וַיָּקָם יַעֲקֹב וַיִּשָּׂא אֶת בָּנָיו וְאֶת נָשָׁיו — Yaakov arose and took his sons and wives (31:17). He first took his sons and then his wives, while Esav took his wives first (36:6), and then his sons. Yaakov was a righteous man whose intention in marriage was to have children, so his children were dearer to him than his wives. But the wicked Esav had wives only to satisfy his passions, so that they were more beloved than his children.

Chizkuni asks: In the portion of Shmos, we read that unlike Yaakov, Moshe took his wife and sons (וַיִּקַּח מֹשֶׁה אֶת אִשְׁתּוֹ וְאֶת בָּנָיו; Shmos 4:20). The answer is that Moshe's children were young and could not yet sit by themselves on the donkey. He therefore seated his wife on the donkey first, and then put the children in her lap. Yaakov's children were already older, and could ride by themselves on the camels, and so he sat them on the camels first, before his wives.

Another explanation is that because Yaakov was fleeing from Lavan, he was afraid that Lavan, pursuing him, would kill those whom he first captured. He therefore placed his wives last, in hope that Lavan would be merciful with his own daughters. But Moshe was approaching his enemies, not fleeing from them, for he had many enemies in Egypt. He therefore put his wife in the front, that the enemy would encounter her first, and deal mercifully with her.

◄§ An End to Idolatry

וַתִּגְנֹב רָחֵל אֶת הַתְּרָפִים אֲשֶׁר לְאָבִיהָ — Rachel stole her father's idols (31:19). She stole them in order to put an end to his idol worship, as Rashi says. Chizkuni and Toldos Yitzchak write that she stole them so that people would see that they had allowed themselves to be stolen, and were not divine.

R' Avraham writes: Why did Rachel not simply hide the idols from Lavan in his own house? Because there were many servants, maids and children there, and she was afraid that they would see her hide them.

◄§ Lavan Learns of Yaakov's Flight

וַיֻּגַּד לְלָבָן בַּיּוֹם הַשְּׁלִישִׁי כִּי בָרַח יַעֲקֹב — *It was told to Lavan on the third day that Yaakov had fled* (31:22). Lavan pursued him. It took the messengers three days to reach Lavan with news of Yaakov's flight, giving Yaakov a three-day start, so they were actually six days' journey apart [since Lavan had traveled a distance of three days' journey in the opposite direction]. Yet on the seventh day Lavan caught him. The journey which took Yaakov seven days Lavan completed in one.

Chizkuni writes that Lavan traveled speedily, as criminals generally do. But Yaakov traveled with much wealth, large flocks, and a great entourage, and so went slowly.

God appeared to Lavan in a dream and warned him not to speak to Yaakov *from good to bad* (מִטּוֹב עַד רָע; 31:24). *Rashi* writes that he was forbidden to speak even good, as the good of an evil man is bad for the righteous.

◄§ An Unwitting Curse

לָמָּה נַחְבֵּאתָ לִבְרֹחַ — *Why did you flee secretly?* (31:27). "Why did you run away without telling me? I would have sent you away with celebrations and merrymaking. Why didn't you allow me to kiss my daughters goodbye? I am capable of doing you great harm, but your father's God told me yesterday to desist from doing you evil." *Chizkuni* writes that Lavan said, "If your God came to caution me from doing you harm, you can imagine that I had the power to hurt you."

Lavan said, "Why did you steal my gods?" Not knowing that Rachel had stolen them, Yaakov answered that the person in whose possession he would find the idols should die. And indeed, *Rashi* writes that because of this curse Rachel died during the journey.

◄§ Lavan's Search

וַיָּבֹא לָבָן בְּאֹהֶל יַעֲקֹב — *Lavan came to Yaakov's tent* (31:33). Lavan first entered Yaakov's tent, which was also Rachel's, as his main dwelling was with Rachel. He searched there first, and afterwards he searched Leah's tent and the tents of Bilhah and Zilpah. Then he returned to Rachel's tent, because he suspected that she had stolen them, but he found nothing. Rachel had secreted the idols beneath the cushions of her camel, and she sat upon them. She told her father that she was menstruating and was too weak to stand up. *Ramban* and R' Bechaye write that as soon as Rachel told her father that she was menstruating he left her, for in those days men were very careful to stay away from menstruating women, and not to speak with them. Morever, the *Gemara* cautions one not to step in their footprints.

Yaakov was angry with Lavan and protested: "What piece of your property have you found among my things? I worked for you for twenty years, fourteen for your two daughters and six for your sheep. During that time your sheep and goats did not miscarry, and if a wolf or lion devoured them, I paid you for them. You repaid me by changing my salary ten times. I agreed to work for six years for the spotted sheep. The first year none were born, and in the last five years when they were born, twice a year you would change the terms of our agreement. As soon as the sheep would conceive, you would say something else."

Ramban asks: Yaakov himself had told him to search his possessions, so why was he so angry? The answer is that Yaakov thought that one of the children or his wives might have taken the idols. But when he saw that Lavan did not find them, he was angry at the seemingly false accusation. Lavan answered, הַבָּנוֹת בְּנֹתַי וְהַבָּנִים בָּנַי — *The daughters are my daughters, the sons my sons* (31:43).

R' Bechaye writes in the name of R' Chananel, that Lavan's claim that the children belonged to him was unfounded. Our Sages say that grandchildren born to a person's son are considered his own, but those born to a person's daughter are not. Also, when he said that the sheep were his he was lying, for Yaakov had earned them.

⋙ Two Camps

וַיִּפְגְּעוּ בוֹ מַלְאֲכֵי אֱלֹהִים — *God's angels met him* (32:2). Yaakov saw two encampments of angels, and called that place Machanayim, meaning "two camps." There were the angels from outside of *Eretz Yisrael* who had escorted him until he reached its borders, and there were the angels who were assigned to minister within *Eretz Yisrael*, who now came to meet him and accompany him.

פרשת וישלח
Parashas Vayishlach
(32:4 — 36:43)

✥§ Angelic Envoys

וַיִּשְׁלַח יַעֲקֹב מַלְאָכִים לְפָנָיו — *Yaakov sent messengers ahead of him* (32:4). R' Bechaye writes that the messengers whom Yaakov sent to his brother Esav were actually angels [the Biblical word for messengers being identical to the word for angels]. The Torah says, וַיָּשֻׁבוּ הַמַּלְאָכִים — *The messengers returned* (32:7), but does not say that they first traveled to Esav. Because they were angels, they flew to Esav and returned immediately to Yaakov.

R' Isser'l writes that we know that they must have actually been angels because Yaakov told them, כֹּה תֹאמְרוּן לַאדֹנִי לְעֵשָׂו — *So say to my master, to Esav* (32:5). Why would Yaakov have spoken so respectfully, unless Esav's angel was among them? He called Esav his master because he was afraid of Esav's angel.

✥§ Fulfillment of Torah in Lavan's House

עִם לָבָן גַּרְתִּי — *I dwelt with Lavan* (32:5). He told them to tell Esav, "You have no cause to hate me, for our father's blessings have not been fulfilled. Our father said that I would be a ruler, and instead I lived with Lavan as his servant."

The word גַּרְתִּי ("dwelt") is numerically equivalent to 613 [תַּרְיַ"ג]. Yaakov was hinting here that he had fulfilled all 613 commandments of the Torah during his sojourn with Lavan. Esav knew that he could dominate Yaakov only when Yaakov had not fulfilled the Torah's commandments, so Yaakov assured him that he had heeded the Torah, and Esav would not be able to rule him.

✥§ Yaakov's Flocks

וַיְהִי לִי שׁוֹר וַחֲמוֹר צֹאן וְעֶבֶד וְשִׁפְחָה — *I have come to own cattle, donkeys, sheep, servants and maids* (32:6). "But the blessing of our father was *the dew of the sky and the fat of the land.* What I have amassed comes neither from the sky nor from the earth, so our father's blessings have not been fulfilled."

R' Bechaye writes: Why did Yaakov first mention oxen and donkeys, and then speak of sheep, when in the case of both Avraham and Yitzchak it is written, וַיְהִי לוֹ צֹאן וּבָקָר — *He had sheep and cattle*, first mentioning sheep, the surest source of prosperity? [The word צֹאן, for conciseness' sake here translated "sheep," in fact means "flocks of sheep and/or goats."] The answer is that Yaakov wanted to avoid reminding Esav of the clothing of goatskin which he had worn on his arms and around his neck when he had received the blessings from Yitzchak. And indeed, after Esav had made peace with Yaakov, Yaakov enumerated his sheep and goats before his cattle and donkeys.

The *Midrash* writes that when speaking of the oxen Yaakov was referring to Yosef, who [in the blessings of Moshe Rabbeinu; *Devarim* 33:17] is referred to as an ox — and Yosef is Esav's nemesis. He wanted to show Esav that he did not fear him, for he had Yosef with him.

⋙ Esav's Feelings to Yaakov

בָּאנוּ אֶל אָחִיךָ אֶל עֵשָׂו — *We came to your brother, to Esav* (32:7). *Rashi* writes that here the angels were in fact telling Yaakov, "You said that he was your brother, but he is Esav, still nursing his hatred of you, and preparing to battle you."

R' Bechaye writes that Esav's angel joined him. *He is also going to meet you* (וְגַם הֹלֵךְ לִקְרָאתְךָ; 32:7) refers to the angel.

⋙ Yaakov's Fear and Defense

וַיִּירָא יַעֲקֹב מְאֹד וַיֵּצֶר לוֹ — *Yaakov was very frightened and distressed* (32:8). He was afraid that he would be killed, and distressed that he would be forced to kill others. This is what *Rashi* says.

R' Bechaye and *Chizkuni* write that "frightened" refers to his fear of Esav, while "distressed" refers to his feelings towards Esav's angel. *Even Shoev* and *Toldos Yitzchak* write that Yaakov was afraid that Esav would murder him, while he was distressed because he believed that his father was dead, as Esav had vowed to kill Yaakov only after their father's death. He was distressed that for some years now he had not shown his father the honor which was his due.

Yaakov split his encampment into two groups, saying, "Should Esav overcome one camp and kill them, his men will then be weary. They will then attack the second camp, which will be fresh, and they will be able to overpower Esav's men." This is what *Toldos Yitzchak* writes.

This teaches us the *Gemara's* dictum: "A man should always split his possessions into three: one third in land, one third in business, and one third in ready money." This is done for the same reason that we have written previously — if something happens to one portion, the others will remain.

The verse, וְהָיָה הַמַּחֲנֶה הַנִּשְׁאָר לִפְלֵיטָה — *and the camp which remains will escape* (32:9), shows us that God sends relief when disaster overtakes Israel, so that we survive.

◄§ Yaakov's Fear

קָטֹנְתִּי מִכֹּל הַחֲסָדִים וּמִכָּל הָאֱמֶת — *I am unworthy of all the kindness and faith that You have shown me* (32:11). Yaakov said, "I have already received many blessings from God; I am afraid that I am not worthy of further acts of mercy. Despite the fact that God promised to deal well with me, I am afraid that I have sinned."

כִּי בְמַקְלִי עָבַרְתִּי אֶת הַיַּרְדֵּן הַזֶּה — *For with my stick I passed over this Jordan (River)* (32:11). "When I fled from my brother Esav I had nothing but my stick, but now I have two camps." The *Midrash* writes that this means that Yaakov split the Jordan River with his staff, and passed over on dry land. R' Bechaye writes that we learn from this that when a man is fortunate he ought to recall the hard times of long ago, so that he will be grateful for what God has done for him.

Yaakov said that he was afraid *that he come and strike me, mother and children* (פֶּן יָבוֹא וְהִכַּנִי אֵם עַל בָּנִים; 32:12). He had no fear for his own safety, for God had promised to protect him from harm. He asked, "If Esav murders my children, how will the blessing which You gave me — *Your children will be as numerous as the sands of the sea* — come true?"

◄§ Yaakov's Tribute to Esav

וַיִּקַּח מִן הַבָּא בְיָדוֹ מִנְחָה לְעֵשָׂו אָחִיו — *He took from what he had in his hand as a tribute to his brother Esav* (32:14). This tribute included precious gems which a person can carry with him. R' Bechaye and *Toldos Yitzchak* write that, since he knew that Esav loved hunting, he brought him a bird, the falcon, which noblemen carry in their hands to help them hunt.

עִזִּים מָאתַיִם וּתְיָשִׁים עֶשְׂרִים — *Two hundred female goats and twenty male goats* (32:15). R' Bechaye asks why he placed the female goats before the other animals. It is customary to place them before other animals, because they bear more males than other animals. Next came the camels, for they are better than other animals. Then came the clean animals, and finally the unclean animals. Also, Yaakov placed them in accordance with the time that they carry their young; goats carry for five months, camels for six months, clean animals for nine, and horses and donkeys for twelve months.

Before this Yaakov had not wanted to show his goats to Esav as this might reawaken his anger, since he had stolen the blessings from him with the help of the goatskins which he had put on his arms. But once he had prayed he thought, "Now I am not afraid of you," and placed the goats in front.

He put the donkeys last to allude to the fact that ultimately *Mashiach* will come, of whom it is said, עָנִי וְרֹכֵב עַל חֲמוֹר וְעַל עַיִר בֶּן אֲתֹנוֹת — *a poor man, riding upon a donkey, upon a young ass* (Zechariah 9:9).

The number of animals totalled five hundred and fifty. *Baal HaTurim* writes that the Hebrew words, עִזִּים מָאתַיִם וּתְיָשִׁים עֶשְׂרִים רְחֵלִים מָאתַיִם וְאֵילִים עֶשְׂרִים — *female goats two hundred, male goats twenty, ewes two hundred and rams twenty* (32:15) each end with the letter *mem* (ם), to show that each of the animals which he sent was blemished (flaw — מוּם), and invalid as a sacrifice.

Rashi asks why it does not state how many male camels he sent. — Since camels conduct themselves modestly, the verse does not specify how many females there were for each male.

Toldos Yitzchak writes: Why did God not appear to Esav to warn him not to harm Yaakov, as he had done to Lavan? — God wants Yaakov's children to be pious. He did not forbid Esav from doing them harm, so that they would be afraid of him and hence God-fearing. *Toldos Yitzchak* also asks: Why did the angels abandon Yaakov, instead of protecting him from Esav? — God did this to show that the power of the righteous is greater than that of the angels. We see this also when Yaakov wrestled with an angel, and overpowered him.

Yaakov told the shepherds, וְרֶוַח תָּשִׂימוּ בֵּין עֵדֶר וּבֵין עֵדֶר — *Put a space between one flock and the next* (32:17), so that Esav would be led to believe that there were many animals. He told them, "When Esav meets you and asks to whom the animals belong, answer: 'They are a gift sent from your servant Yaakov, who is following us.' If Esav asks why I did not come immediately to greet him, answer that I felt that the gift would assuage his anger."

R' Bechaye writes that Yaakov asked God to place space between the flocks, meaning that when Israel faces adversity, this should not be followed by more trouble. Rather, let there be a distance between one misfortune and another.

Yaakov slept in the encampment that night, instead of his tent, so that he would be ready if Esav would launch an attack that night.

◆§ The River Crossing

וַיִּקַּח אֶת שְׁתֵּי נָשָׁיו וְאֶת שְׁתֵּי שִׁפְחֹתָיו וְאֶת אַחַד עָשָׂר יְלָדָיו — *He took his two wives, and his two maids, and his eleven children* (32:23). When he fled Lavan's house he put his wives last, so that when Lavan reached them with the intent of murdering them, he would meet his daughters and have mercy. R' Isser'l writes: Why did the wives go first in this case? Because the River Yabok split and the children were afraid of crossing. Similarly, we find when the Red Sea split, the people were afraid to enter, until Nachshon the son of Aminadav went in. And for this, by the way, he was richly rewarded.

Rashi asks: Why does it say his eleven children? Where was Dinah? Yaakov had concealed her in a box so that the evil Esav should not see her and desire her as a wife. God punished Yaakov for this, and she was abused by Shechem. Why? Because he ought to have given her to Esav in the hope that she would make him pious.

וַיַּעֲבֹר אֵת מַעֲבַר יַבֹּק — *He crossed the Yabok River shallows* (32:23). Yaakov first crossed the river by himself, to test the water, and then brought his household over. Yaakov then remained behind alone, for he had forgotten some small vessels and had returned to bring them over. We learn from this that money is precious to the righteous, for they do not steal.

Because he was alone an angel began to wrestle with him so violently that dust was raised. They wrestled until the morning star rose. The angel was Esav's guardian angel who was searching for a misdeed of Yaakov's with which to bring about his downfall.

Yaakov wrestles with an angel

Seeing that he could not overpower him, for he had no misdeeds, he touched Yaakov's thigh, thus alluding to his sin of having married two sisters, and was able to harm him somewhat. *Baal HaTurim* says that when the angel saw that he could not overpower him, he thought that Yaakov, too, was an angel.

The angel told Yaakov, שַׁלְּחֵנִי — *Send me away.* He had been sent to Yaakov by God and hence did not want to leave without obtaining Yaakov's permission.

◆§ Names and Their Significance

כִּי עָלָה הַשַּׁחַר --- *For the dawn has arrived* (32:27). Yaakov asked him, "Why are you afraid of the daylight?" The angel said, "Since I was created I have never sung hymns to God. My turn to sing comes when the dawn breaks." Yaakov answered, "I will not send you away until you have blessed me, that is, until you have given your consent to the blessings which my father gave me." The angel said, "Your name will henceforth be Yisrael, for you have overpowered (from the root שׂרֹר) Esav, Lavan, and angels. You will not be called Yaakov, whose meaning is deceit, hinting that you took the blessings through trickery; Yisrael will be your name, indicating that you struggled and gained dominion over the blessings." The angel then agreed to [allow Yaakov] the blessings. There is a verse that says, תִּתֵּן אֱמֶת לְיַעֲקֹב — *Give truth to Yaakov* (Michah 7:20), meaning that what Yaakov did to Esav and Lavan was done in truth, without trickery.

The *Midrash* writes that Yaakov's image is engraved on God's Throne of Glory. The angel told him, כִּי שָׂרִיתָ עִם אֱלֹהִים — *You have dominion with God,* that is, your figure is engraved on His Throne. *Chizkuni* writes that the angel told Yaakov, כִּי עָלָה הַשַּׁחַר — "*The morning is dawning* (32:27), and you need not fear, as demons and angels have no authority over humans during the day."

Yaakov asked the angel for his name. The angel replied, *Why ask for my name?* (32:30). An angel has no permanent name. Rather, his name reflects his current mission.

R' Bechaye writes that the angel said, "We do not divulge our names. We do not want to take pride in having accomplished anything by ourselves: we only do God's work."

Some say that the angel said, "Do not ask for my name. I could not overpower you and I am ashamed to let anyone know who I am." *Chizkuni* writes that the angel said, "You need not know my name. Why should one know the name of an angel? So that he can compel the angel by the calling of divine Names to do his bidding.

But you have been victorious over me without knowing the names of any angels.''

◆§ The Healing Sun

וַיִּזְרַח לוֹ הַשֶּׁמֶשׁ — *The sun shone upon* [or: *for*] *him* (32:32). *Rashi* asks: Did the sun shine only upon Yaakov? The sun shines on the entire world! The answer is that the sun began to shine earlier than it should have so that Yaakov's injury would heal faster. Similarly, we see that when Yaakov left Be'er Sheva the sun set before its time, for his sake alone.

◆§ Yaakov's Limp

עַל כֵּן לֹא יֹאכְלוּ בְנֵי יִשְׂרָאֵל אֶת גִּיד הַנָּשֶׁה — *Therefore the Israelites do not eat the nerve on the hip joint* (32:33). The children of Israel do not eat the hind parts of the animals until the sciatic nerve is removed, because the angel struck Yaakov's hip. *Chizkuni* asks: Why were the Jews penalized and forbidden to eat the animal's hindquarters? Because they let Yaakov remain alone in the field, and as a result he was wounded. *Toldos Yitzchak* writes: Why did the angel make Yaakov limp? So that he would thus appear to be constantly bowing down to Esav. The verse therefore says, וַיִּשְׁתַּחוּ אַרְצָה שֶׁבַע פְּעָמִים — *He bowed to the ground seven times* (33:3).

◆§ Battle Me First

וַיָּשֶׂם אֶת הַשְּׁפָחוֹת וְאֶת יַלְדֵיהֶן רִאשֹׁנָה — *He put the handmaids and their children first* (33:2). Yaakov placed Bilhah and her children first, followed by Zilpah and her children. Then came Leah and her children, with Rachel and Yosef in the rear, because he dearly loved Rachel. Yaakov stood in front of them all, thinking, ''Let Esav battle me first.''

Esav ran to greet him, and hugged and kissed him, and they both wept. The maids and their children approached and bowed. Then Leah and her children came forward and bowed, and finally Yosef and Rachel came forward. *Rashi* asks why the names of the mothers precede those of the children, except in the case of Rachel, where the verse says, יוֹסֵף וְרָחֵל — *Yosef and Rachel*. Since Rachel was very beautiful Yosef stood before her, blocking her from Esav's sight, so that he would not desire her.

◆§ He is Yaakov's Brother!

וַיֹּאמֶר מִי לְךָ כָּל הַמַּחֲנֶה הַזֶּה אֲשֶׁר פָּגָשְׁתִּי — *He said, ''This whole camp which I met: what is it of yours?''* (33:8). *Rashi* writes: Esav met numerous groups of angels. They struck his men, and then asked them, "Whom do you belong to?" When the men answered that they were Esav's troops, the angels fell upon them once again. The soldiers cried, "Esav is Yitzchak's son and Avraham's grandson!" But the angels only hit them again. The men said, "He is Yaakov's brother!" — and they ceased beating them, saying, "If so, you are one of us."

✍ Dividing Worlds

יְהִי לְךָ אֲשֶׁר לָךָ — *Let what is yours remain yours* (33:9). With these words Esav gave his consent to the blessings. At this point Yaakov had been blessed by Yitzchak, by the angel, and by Esav himself. Yaakov urged Esav to keep his tribute, saying that the sight of Esav's face was like seeing an angel. In this way Yaakov hinted to Esav that he had seen his angel. Why did Yaakov want to mention this to him? So that Esav would fear him, and think, "If he survived an encounter with my angel I certainly can do him no harm."

R' Bechaye writes that R' Yochanan said that it is permissible to flatter a wicked man out of fear, as Yaakov did, telling Esav that he resembled an angel, despite the fact that he hated him.

Yaakov said, "I like seeing your face, just as I like seeing the face of god," referring to Esav's gods. By this he meant: "Just as I hate your gods, so I hate you." Esav, naturally, thought he was referring to the true God.

Yaakov strongly urged Esav, until he accepted the tribute. Esav then said that he would favor Yaakov by escorting him. Yaakov answered that he could not travel with him, כִּי הַיְלָדִים רַכִּים — *for the children are weak* (33:13). R' Bechaye writes that the *Midrash* says that Esav told Yaakov to share the World to Come between them. Yaakov answered that his children were weak in fulfilling all the commandments, and could not bear the tortures of Gehinnom. Therefore, יַעֲבָר נָא אֲדֹנִי לִפְנֵי עַבְדּוֹ — *Let my master pass before his servant* (33:14), meaning, "You take this world as your portion; וַאֲנִי אֶתְנַהֲלָה לְאִטִּי — *and I will journey on slowly*" (ibid.): "I and my children will go into exile, עַד אֲשֶׁר אָבֹא אֶל אֲדֹנִי שֵׂעִירָה — *until I come to my master in Seir*" (ibid.).

On that day Esav returned alone on his journey towards Seir; the four hundred men who had accompanied him left him. God repaid them, and when David killed the men of Edom four hundred men were spared.

✍ Yaakov at Shechem

וַיָּבֹא יַעֲקֹב שָׁלֵם עִיר שְׁכֶם — *Yaakov came to the city of Shechem whole* [i.e., *safely*] (33:18). Yaakov came to Shechem whole in his Torah, for he had not forgotten the Torah during his stay with Lavan; whole in his purse, for he re-amassed all that he had given to Esav as a tribute; and whole in his body, for he was now healed of the angel's injury.

Yaakov purchased a part of a field from [the family of] Shechem and built an altar to God upon it.

◄§ What Dinah could have Accomplished with Esav

וַתֵּצֵא דִינָה בַּת לֵאָה — *Dinah, Leah's daughter, went out* (34:1). *Rashi* writes: Why does it specify that she was Leah's daughter, and not Yaakov's? To show that she was a forward girl, just like her mother, who had gone out to meet Yaakov and had told him to come to her tent. Dinah went to see the other women of the land and Shechem, son of Chamor, abducted her.

R' Bechaye writes that Yaakov was punished in this way because he had hidden Dinah from his brother Esav.

The *Midrash* states that a woman whose home is always kept warm by her presence atones for the sins of her entire household, just as the altar atoned for the sins of the entire world. The verse states, אֶשְׁתְּךָ כְּגֶפֶן פֹּרִיָּה בְּיַרְכְּתֵי בֵיתֶךָ — *Your wife shall be like a fruitful vine in the recesses of your home* (*Tehillim* 128:3). Just like the vine which grows within the house and sends its branches outside, so too should your wife grace her home from within, sending her children out into the world to study Torah.

Concerning her sons the Psalmist goes on to say, בָּנֶיךָ כִּשְׁתִלֵי זֵיתִים — *Your sons are like olive saplings* (ibid.). All trees other than the olive can be grafted with trees of other types. In the same way, if your wife is modest, not joining with other men, you will merit seeing your children anointed with holy oil. Moreover, just as an olive tree carries its fruit for nine months, so a modest woman will not deliver prematurely, and will be blessed with healthy children. Another reason the verse compares children to olives is that at the beginning olives are very bitter, but in the end they become sweet. Children, when they are young, are difficult to raise, but as they develop and flourish they become sweet.

◄§ An Ox and a Donkey

וַיֵּצֵא חֲמוֹר אֲבִי שְׁכֶם אֶל יַעֲקֹב לְדַבֵּר אִתּוֹ — *Chamor, Shechem's father, went out to Yaakov to speak with him* (34:6). The *Midrash* writes that Chamor said, "Your grandfather Avraham was a ruler. I, too, am a ruler, so give your daughter to a ruler's son." Yaakov answered, "My grandfather's name is connected with an ox, as it is written, וְאֶל הַבָּקָר רָץ אַבְרָהָם — *Avraham ran to the cattle* (18:7), while you are a donkey (*chamor*, lit., "donkey"). And the Torah commands us, לֹא תַחֲרֹשׁ בְּשׁוֹר וּבַחֲמֹר יַחְדָּו — *Do not plough with an ox and a donkey hitched together*" (*Devarim* 22:10).

Shechem was in love with Dinah. *R' Bechaye* writes that Dinah was eight years old at the time. Shechem seduced her, saying, "Your father has no fields. Come with me, and you'll have many fields."

◆§ The Brothers' Ruse

וּבְנֵי יַעֲקֹב בָּאוּ מִן הַשָּׂדֶה — *Yaakov's sons came from the field* (34:7). *Chizkuni* writes that as soon as Yaakov's children found out that their sister had been defiled they immediately returned from the field, weeping that such a shame should befall Yaakov's daughter. In those days even the idol worshipers would not do such a shameful deed, particularly to the daughter of such a notable man.

Ramban questions *Rashi's* assertion that in those times the idol worshipers were not lascivious, for the Torah says of the Canaanites, כִּי אֶת כָּל הַתּוֹעֵבֹת הָאֵל עָשׂוּ — *All of these abominations they have done* (*Vayikra* 18:27). *Toldos Yitzchak* answers that in Yaakov's times the idol worshipers were moral, for it was not long after the days of the Flood, when their lust led to their destruction. However in the days of Moshe Rabbeinu, to which the above verse refers, they had already forgotten the Flood, and followed their desires.

You may ask, if the idol worshipers at that time were moral, why did Avraham and Yitzchak fear for their wives? The answer is that Sarah and Rivkah were extraordinarily beautiful, and their husbands were therefore afraid.

Chamor came to Yaakov and his children and said, "Give your daughter to my son as a wife. I will give you as much money in the marriage contract as you ask for."

Yaakov could not answer, out of shame, and his sons had to reply. They answered with cunning. They felt that they could act deceitfully, since their sister had been defiled.

Yaakov's children told Chamor, וְנָתַנּוּ אֶת בְּנֹתֵינוּ לָכֶם וְאֶת בְּנֹתֵיכֶם נִקַּח לָנוּ — *We will give our daughters to you, and we will take your daughters* (34:16). *Rashi* writes that Yaakov's sons said to Shechem and Chamor, "We will give you whichever of our daughters we choose; and we will take whichever of your daughters we choose." When Shechem and Chamor went to the townspeople to persuade them to circumcise themselves, they said the opposite: "We will give them whatever daughters we choose and we will take whomever we choose for ourselves. We will have the right of choice, so let us circumcise ourselves."

⏺§ Circumcision of Shechem

וַיִּמֹּלוּ כָּל זָכָר כָּל יֹצְאֵי שַׁעַר עִירוֹ — *Every male was circumcised, all that
went out of the city gate* (34:24). *Chizkuni* asks why here the verse
says *all that went out of the city gate*, while earlier, when discussing
Sarah's funeral, it says בְּכֹל בָּאֵי שַׁעַר עִירוֹ — *all those who came inside
the city gate* (23:18). Shechem did not allow anyone from the city to
leave, and argued with them until they had circumcised themselves,
but they did not do so willingly and with good grace. In Sarah's case
they all came voluntarily, as an act of kindness towards her, and
therefore the Torah there says, *all those who came inside the city
gate.*

On the third day, when they were very weak, Shimon and Levi
took up their swords and attacked the city. They slew the townspeople, captured their womenfolk, took their gold and possessions, and
fled. R' Bechaye asks why they attacked on the third day after the
circumcision. That which is third indicates a weakening. Tuesday,
the third day of the week, is weakening to men, for its sign is the
Scorpion, and its star is Mars, whose redness indicates blood. Our
Sages in the time of the Temple did not require the members of the
Maamados, who were involved in the sacrificial service, to fast on
Sunday, because it is the third day from the creation of Adam, who
was created on Friday, and man is weak on that day. For this reason
too we smell the fragrant spices when *Shabbos* ends. Sunday is
beginning, and we wish to strengthen the soul with a savory smell.

⇜§ Yaakov's Distress

עֲבַרְתֶּם אֹתִי — *You have brought me trouble* (34:30). Yaakov told his sons, "You have distressed me, and have besmirched my name among the people in the land. They will now gather together and attack me." His children answered, "Can someone turn our sister into a prostitute with impunity?"

R' Bechaye writes that the justification which Yaakov's children had in killing the city of Shechem was that they were more lascivious and greater thieves than the rest of the world. Further, Dinah had told them that she had been told that they planned to kill Yaakov's household when they were healed from the circumcision.

⇜§ A Sacrifice to God

קוּם עֲלֵה בֵית אֵל — *Rise up and go to Beis El* (35:1). God told Yaakov to go to Beis El. *Rashi* writes: Why did God say *rise*? He told Yaakov, "You have delayed long enough in fulfilling your vow to bring Me a sacrifice; you have been punished and Dinah was abducted by Shechem. Now, stand up and go to Beis El to bring the sacrifice."

Chizkuni asks: *Rashi* had written previously that Yaakov had been punished because he had not given Dinah in marriage to Esav. Now *Rashi* writes that Yaakov was punished because he procrastinated in bringing the sacrifice. Actually, it was both things that caused his punishment.

Yaakov told his children, הָסִרוּ אֶת אֱלֹהֵי הַנֵּכָר — *"Remove the false gods* (35:2), for we are going to bring sacrifices and we do not wish it to be said that we are sacrificing to the idols; וְהַחֲלִיפוּ שִׂמְלֹתֵיכֶם — *change your clothes (ibid.);* remove the clothing of the idol worshiper." Yaakov secreted the idols under a tree, because he was too far from the sea to be able to throw them into it.

⇜§ Whom did They Fear

וַיְהִי חִתַּת אֱלֹהִים עַל הֶעָרִים אֲשֶׁר סְבִיבוֹתֵיהֶם — *The fear of God was upon the cities which surrounded them* (35:5). The people feared God and did not pursue Yaakov's sons. *Toldos Yitzchak* writes that the cities were angry with the people of Shechem for having circumcised themselves and for discarding their idols and thereby showing an affinity with the sons of Yaakov. For this reason too they did not pursue them. According to this interpretation, when the verse says *the fear of God* it alludes to their fear of the wrath of their own gods, their idols.

⇜§ A Double Share of Mourning

וַתָּמָת דְּבֹרָה מֵינֶקֶת רִבְקָה — *Devorah, Rivkah's nurse, died* (35:8). *Rashi* asks: How did Devorah become a part of Yaakov's household? Rivkah sent her to Lavan to summon Yaakov home. She died on the journey home, and Yaakov buried her. During the funeral he found out that Rivkah, too, had died.

The *Midrash* says that when Rivkah died everyone said, "Avraham is dead, Yitzchak is blind, and Yaakov is in Padan Aram. Who but Esav remains to bury her? She will be cursed by everyone for having such an evil son." She was therefore buried at night and her death is not openly mentioned in the verse. This also explains why Yaakov named that place אַלּוֹן בָּכוּת — the Oak of Weeping (35:8), the second Hebrew word implying a dual cause for mourning: his mother's death, and her undignified burial.

This matter is difficult to understand. What good would it do not to reveal her death? If people thought that she was still alive, would they not curse her still for having an evil son? The answer is that it is said, לֹא תְקַלֵּל חֵרֵשׁ — *Do not curse the deaf* (Vayikra 19:14), even though they cannot hear. But this stricture does not include the dead, so they refrained from announcing Rivkah's death.

God blessed Yaakov and comforted him in the mourning.

⇜§ Yaakov becomes Yisrael

שִׁמְךָ יַעֲקֹב לֹא יִקָּרֵא עוֹד שִׁמְךָ כִּי אִם יִשְׂרָאֵל יִהְיֶה שְׁמֶךָ — *Your name is Yaakov; your name will no longer be Yaakov, but Yisrael will be your name* (35:10).

"Your name will not be Yaakov, which means deceit, and alludes to the fact that you secured the blessings deceitfully. Rather, your name will be Yisrael, meaning dominion." R' Bechaye and *Chizkuni* write that this means, "Your name will be not only Yaakov: at times you will be called Yisrael. You will be called by both names."

⇜§ Rachel's Difficult Labor

וַתֵּלֶד רָחֵל וַתְּקַשׁ בְּלִדְתָּהּ — *Rachel was in childbirth, and had a difficult labor* (35:16). The midwife told her, אַל תִּירְאִי כִּי גַם זֶה לָךְ בֵּן — *Don't be afraid: this one will also be a son for you* (35:17). Our Sages say that a daughter was born with each of Yaakov's sons, and two daughters were born with Binyamin.

Midrash Rabbah tells a story of two students of R' Yehoshua who disguised themselves so that they would not be recognized as Jews, for at that time Jews who would not convert were being killed. A man found out their secret and said, "I know that you are Jews.

Why are you disguising yourselves, rather than sacrificing yourselves for God?" They answered that suicide was forbidden and they had to do what they could to conceal their identities.

The man told them, "Let me ask you something about your Torah. If you give me an answer I will not harm you. The verse says that Rachel had a difficult childbirth and her midwife told her not to fear because she had a son. Why did the fact that she had a son help her in her agony?" The students answered that a midwife must always speak of pleasant things to a woman giving birth with difficulty, in order to gladden her heart when she is in pain.

Yaakov buried Rachel on the road to Efras. Efras was just a short distance away and he wanted to bring her to the city, but since she had died in childbirth they buried her on the way and placed a monument on the grave. R' Bechaye writes that it is respectful to bury a woman at the place where she died, rather than carry her over fields.

◄§ Reuven's Tampering

וַיֵּלֶךְ רְאוּבֵן וַיִּשְׁכַּב אֶת בִּלְהָה — *Reuven went and lay with Bilhah* (35:22). When Rachel died Yaakov took his bed, which had been in Rachel's tent, and placed it in the tent of Bilhah. This distressed Reuven, who threw the bed out and asked Bilhah, "Do you want to be equal to my aunt Rachel? She was a mistress and you are a maidservant." Because he tampered with his father's bed, the verse describes him as having lain with Bilhah.

Ramban writes: Why did Reuven disturb the bed? Because he thought, "I am the eldest and am due to receive a double portion of my father's inheritance. Should he have more children, I will receive less." Leah was too old to have children, and Zilpah may already have been dead, so he tampered with Bilhah's bed.

וַיִּשְׁמַע יִשְׂרָאֵל — *Yaakov heard* (35:22). Yaakov heard that he had removed his bed, but was not angry with him, and when he enumerated his sons he named him before all the other children.

וַיִּהְיוּ בְנֵי יַעֲקֹב שְׁנֵים עָשָׂר — *Yaakov's children were twelve* (35:22). The verse shows us that they were all equally pious, and that Reuven had not sinned. The verse also emphasizes that after these twelve Yaakov had no more children.

◄§ Yaakov's Return

וַיָּבֹא יַעֲקֹב אֶל יִצְחָק אָבִיו מַמְרֵא קִרְיַת הָאַרְבַּע — *Yaakov came to his father Yitzchak, to Mamre, in Kiryas Arba* (35:27). Why does the verse not say that he returned to his mother? — Because she was dead. The verse does not want to state this explicitly, as we have explained above.

✎§ Yitzchak's Funeral

וַיִּקְבְּרוּ אֹתוֹ עֵשָׂו וְיַעֲקֹב — *And they buried him* (i.e., *Yitzchak*), *Esav and Yaakov* (35:29). *Chizkuni* writes: Why does Esav's name precede Yaakov's? Because Yaakov gave him honor, out of fear. Esav had said that when his father died he would kill his brother.

In the case of Avraham the Torah writes that *Yitzchak and Yishmael, his sons, buried him,* with Yitzchak preceding Yishmael, for he was the son of Sarah, the mistress, and Yishmael was the son of the concubine Hagar.

✎§ Esav's Idolatrous Wives

עֵשָׂו לָקַח אֶת נָשָׁיו — *Esav had taken his wives* (36:2). Esav took a wife named Ahalibama. *Rashi* writes that she was in fact Yehudis: Esau gave her this name to show that she was pious and kept the religion of the Jews (*Yehudim*), in order to deceive his father. He took another wife named Basmas, daughter of Yishmael, as well. In *Parashas Toldos,* where it is related that Esav married her, she is called Machlas, for marriage is one of three things which grant a person forgiveness from Above (*machal* — "forgive"; another is when one becomes elevated to greatness). That is to say, Esav's sins were forgiven when he married her.

וְתִמְנַע הָיְתָה פִילֶגֶשׁ לֶאֱלִיפַז — *Timna was a concubine of Eliphaz* (36:12). The verse shows that though she was of noble family she wanted to be with Eliphaz, even as a concubine, because he was a descendant of Avraham.

✎§ Mule Breeder

הוּא עֲנָה אֲשֶׁר מָצָא אֶת הַיֵּמִם בַּמִּדְבָּר — *This is Anah, who found mules in the wilderness* (36:24). Anah bred a donkey with a female horse and a mule was born. Because Anah was a bastard he was able to bring bastards to the world. Mules are called *yemim* because they put a great fear (*eimah*) into man, for one injured by a mule cannot be healed. *Chizkuni* asks: were there no mules in Yitzchak's time? We have said that people used to say that the refuse of Yitzchak's mules was worth more than Avimelech's gold and silver! The answer is that there were mules before this time, which mated with each other, but Anah was the first to mate donkeys with female horses. God's blessing to be fruitful and multiply does not include a creature bred from two different breeds.

פרשת וישב
Parashas Vayeshev
(37:1 — 40:23)

‏ܒ Strangers in this World

‏וַיֵּשֶׁב יַעֲקֹב בְּאֶרֶץ מְגוּרֵי אָבִיו — *Yaakov dwelt in the land where his father had sojourned* (37:1). R' Bechaye writes that this portion teaches us that a righteous man lives in this world as a stranger does, with neither relatives nor property. The righteous man always thinks of his impending death, preparing "provisions" for the journey — his deeds. When the verse says, *Yaakov dwelt in the land where his father had sojourned*, it tells us that he lived as his parents had lived, as sojourners, strangers in the world, thinking only of the World to Come.

In the last *parashah* the Torah told briefly of Esav. Now it speaks of Yaakov, and what happened to him, at great length. This can be likened to a person who loses a valuable pearl on the seashore, so he takes a sieve and fills it with sand. As soon as he discovers the pearl he throws all the sand away. So Esav is discarded in favor of Yaakov, the precious gem.

‏ܒ With the Children of Bilhah and Zilpah

‏אֵלֶּה תֹּלְדוֹת יַעֲקֹב יוֹסֵף — *These are the generations of Yaakov, Yosef* (37:2). Yosef was seventeen years old, and was raised together with the children of the maidservants, Bilhah and Zilpah. The verse says *and he was a lad (ibid.)*, meaning that it was no shame for him to be herding the sheep along with the maidservants' children, as he was still a youth. This is what *Chizkuni* writes. But *Rashi* says that this refers to his childish behavior; he primped and preened, and was always attending to his hair.

He was constantly with the children of Bilhah and Zilpah. The other children stayed away from them, and considered them inferior, but Yosef associated with them.

Rashi and R' Bechaye write: Why does the Torah say, *These are the generations of Yaakov, Yosef?* Because Yaakov's entire servitude to Lavan was for Rachel's sake, and Yosef was her son. Also, Yosef closely resembled Yaakov in appearance. Furthermore, all of the brothers' good traits were combined in Yosef: Reuven's birthright was given to him; the prophecy of Levi was given to Yosef, when he spoke prophetically to Pharaoh, telling of the famine; Yehudah's kingship was given to him, when he became a ruler in Egypt; the cleverness of Yissachar was given to Yosef, as it is written of him, אֵין נָבוֹן וְחָכָם כָּמוֹךָ — *There is no man as wise and clever as you (Bereishis 41:39).*

Further, everything which had happened to Yaakov happened to Yosef too: Esav planned to kill Yaakov, and the brothers wanted to kill Yosef; Yaakov's mother was barren and Yosef's mother was barren; Yaakov was born circumcised, as was Yosef; Yaakov's mother had a difficult childbirth, as did Yosef's mother; angels came to Yaakov, as well as to Yosef; a dream brought good fortune to Yaakov, and to Yosef likewise.

⊷§ Yosef's Misjudgment

וַיָּבֵא יוֹסֵף אֶת דִּבָּתָם רָעָה אֶל אֲבִיהֶם — *Yosef brought bad reports of them to their father* (37:2). Yosef would report to his father whatever he would see Leah's children do. *Rashi* asks: Why does the Torah here say, *Yosef brought bad reports,* but in reference to the spies it says, וַיּוֹצִיאוּ דִּבַּת הָאָרֶץ — *They took out evil reports of the Land (Bamidbar* 13:32)? Yosef was righteous and reported only what he had heard, but told no lies; the spies "took out" lies even from the things which they had not seen.

Yosef judged his brothers mistakenly. He saw them slaughter a cow and eat the calf which was within it without benefit of ritual slaughter. He was unaware that this is permissible, and told his father that they had eaten the meat of a living animal. They used to call the maids' children servants, and Yosef thought that this was forbidden. He saw them having business dealings with the gentiles' wives and assumed that they had a close relationship with these women.

Yosef was therefore punished in due course with these three things. Because he had accused them of eating a live animal, his brothers killed a kid and dipped his coat in its blood when he was sold; because he accused them of calling the maids' children servants, he himself was sold as a servant; and for saying that they had had a close relationship with the gentile women, his master's wife tried to seduce him.

⋖§ Yaakov Favored Yosef

וְיִשְׂרָאֵל אָהַב אֶת יוֹסֵף מִכָּל בָּנָיו — *Yisrael loved Yosef more than all his sons* (37:3). *Chizkuni* writes that all the brothers hated Yosef. Leah's children hated him because his father favored him over all the others, while the children of Bilhah and Zilpah hated him for speaking against Leah's children.

Ramban asks of *Rashi:* If Yosef had spoken ill of Leah's children only, why did the sons of the maids agree to kill him, and later, to sell him? There were four of them, and Reuven, too, did not agree, which made five. Yosef was the sixth, so they could conceivably have stood up against the remaining brothers. The answer is that the children of the maids hated him for he spoke ill of them as well. R' Bechaye and *Chizkuni* explain this in the same manner.

Toldos Yitzchak writes: Generally when one passes on gossip he makes himself liked. The verse however tells us that in this case Yaakov did not love Yosef because of his gossip, but only *because* כִּי בֶן זְקֻנִים הוּא לוֹ, *he was the son of his old age* (37:3), and the Sages interpret the word *zaken* to mean "one who has acquired (קנה) Torah wisdom" — that is, Yaakov loved Yosef only because he was a promising Torah scholar.

The brothers saw that their father favored Yosef and they hated him for it. *Toldos Yitzchak* asks: Is it right that because their father favored him, they should hate him? Was it his fault? The answer is that the brothers said, "If our father had not believed Yosef's tales it would not have bothered us, for Yosef would simply have made a fool of himself. But since we see that our father loves him, despite his gossip, this shows us that our father believes the gossip, so we hate him."

Their father sewed him a silken coat of many colors. All of his misfortunes came about because of the coat. Our Sages learn from this that it is forbidden to dress one child better than another, so as not to arouse jealousy.

The four letters of the word פַּסִים ("multicolored") allude to his misfortunes: the letter פ stands for Potifar, the letter ס for *socharim* ("merchants"), the letter י stands for Yishmaelim, and the letter מ stands for Midianim — these being the various people to whom Yosef was ultimately sold.

⋖§ Undisguised Hatred

וְלֹא יָכְלוּ דַּבְּרוֹ לְשָׁלם — *They could not speak peacefully with him* (37:4). *Rashi* writes that the verse shows us that the brothers were righteous. They could not speak words which did not come from their hearts. Since they hated him, they could not speak peaceably to him.

◄§ Dreams of Portent

וַיַּחֲלֹם יוֹסֵף חֲלוֹם וַיַּגֵּד לְאֶחָיו — *Yosef dreamed a dream and told it to his brothers* (37:5). He told it to them so that they should not hate him: it was through God's will that he would become a ruler, not his father's favoritism. *Chizkuni* writes that his first dream is not recorded because it was not true.

וְהִנֵּה אֲנַחְנוּ מְאַלְּמִים אֲלֻמִּים — *Here we were, binding sheaves* (37:7). "We were binding sheaves of wheat. My bundle stood up, and yours surrounded mine and began to bow down to it." *Toldos Yitzchak* writes that the sheaves had surrounded his sheaf but refused to bow down to it; they were however forced to, against their will. Another interpretation is that they surrounded the bundle just as a servant circles about his master, ready to wait upon him.

Your sheaves surrounded (תְּסֻבֶּינָה אֲלֻמֹּתֵיכֶם; 37:7) can also be interpreted as meaning "your sheaves grew smaller and smaller." The dream alluded to the fact that in the time of the famine all of the wheat which others saved would spoil, and all would be forced to turn to Yosef. The dream used wheat as its symbol, to show that it was because of wheat that the brothers would ultimately bow down to Yosef.

הֲמָלֹךְ תִּמְלֹךְ עָלֵינוּ — *Will you then be king over us?* (37:8). The brothers realized that the dream portended his rule over them. R' Bechaye writes that even though they hated Yosef, God caused them to interpret the dream in his favor.

His brothers hated him even more fiercely because of his dreams, and because he spoke of them and boasted over them. He had another dream, which he related to his father and his brothers — that the sun and the moon and eleven stars had bowed down to him.

His father rebuked him, and said, "Can your mother and I come to bow down to you, when your mother is dead? Your dream must be a lie!" Yaakov said this in order to assuage the brothers' hatred, though he knew that the dream was a true one. The moon, which symbolized his mother, represented Bilhah, who had brought him up as a mother. Our Sages say that in every dream there is some nonsense, even if the dream is true. So it was with this dream: even though it was true, the portion referring to his mother was nonsense. Yaakov knew this but wanted to quiet the brothers' animosity.

Toldos Yitzchak writes: Why did the first dream refer to sheaves of wheat, and the second to the stars? Because the first time the brothers set out to buy wheat, they went down to Egypt like any common folk, while the second time they arrived as honored guests, the stars in the second dream showing that this was an important event.

This explains too why in the first dream Yosef did not see the sun and the moon — because only the brothers went down to Egypt the first time; but the second time all of them came down, including Yaakov and Bilhah. Moreover, this explains why Yosef told the second dream to his father, and not the first; the first showed only that the brothers would bow down to him.

Imrei Noam asks why in the first dream the Torah writes, וַתִּשְׁתַּחֲוֶיןָ לַאֲלֻמָּתִי. *they bowed down to my sheaf* (37:7), while in the second it writes, מִשְׁתַּחֲוִים לִי, *bowing to me* (37:9), rather than "to my star." The first time the brothers did not recognize him, and they bowed only because they needed the wheat, so it says they bowed down to the sheaf. But the second time they knew already that it was Yosef and therefore the verse says *bowing to me:* by this stage they were bowing in his honor. Another reason is that the stars are in heaven and he could not say with certainty which was his star, but the wheat was held in his hands, so they could see which was his sheaf.

⊰§ Feeding the Sheep ... and the Shepherds

וַיֵּלְכוּ אֶחָיו לִרְעוֹת אֶת צֹאן אֲבִיהֶם — *His brothers went to pasture the sheep of their father* (37:12) — and to feed themselves as well. They ate of their father's sheep without his knowledge. The word אֵת is written in the Torah with two dots over it, to show that they, too, were fed. They did many wicked deeds here — they ate of their father's sheep and they sold their brother Yosef.

Yaakov told Yosef, "Your brothers are grazing the sheep in Shechem. Go to them, to see how they are faring." Yosef answered, "I am ready to go," despite the fact that he knew that they hated him and he was putting himself in danger. He went out of כְּבוֹד אָב, out of respect for his father's wishes.

וַיִּשְׁלָחֵהוּ מֵעֵמֶק חֶבְרוֹן — *He sent him from the valley of Chevron* (37:14). God brought about this series of circumstances so that the Israelites would ultimately go down to their exile in Egypt. He was fulfilling the deeply-founded promise that He had made to Avraham, who was buried in Chevron [hence the reference to the "valley" of Chevron, which is in fact in a hilly region] — that his children would be exiled in Egypt for 400 years.

Sefer HaYashar writes that because they had come late that day

from the fields, Yaakov was afraid that the men of Shechem had attacked them, and so Yosef was sent to hear of their welfare.

≈§ The Man Gavriel

וַיִּמְצָאֵהוּ אִישׁ — *A man found him* (37:15). This was the angel
Gavriel. *Toldos Yitzchak* writes: Generally, when a man is lost, he
stops and asks other people for directions; men do not stop and ask
him what he is looking for. Yet here the man asked Yosef what he
was seeking. We see that it must have been an angel, who wanted to
lead Yosef to his brothers to ensure that he would be brought down
to Egypt.

Another explanation is that Yosef asked the man, הַגִּידָה נָא לִי
אֵיפֹה הֵם רֹעִים — *Tell me where they are grazing the sheep* (37:16),
without previously having asked if he knew where they were. Obviously, then, Yosef understood that this was an angel.

We conclude moreover that it was Gavriel and not another angel,
for the verse says *a man found him,* and Gavriel is termed *a man*
(אִישׁ), as it is written, וְהָאִישׁ גַּבְרִיאֵל — *the man Gavriel* (Daniel 9:21).

≈§ No Longer Their Brother

וַיֹּאמֶר הָאִישׁ נָסְעוּ מִזֶּה — *The man said, "They have left here"* (37:17).
Rashi asks: Yosef had simply asked him if he knew where his
brothers were. Why did the man answer, *They have left here?* The
answer is that he was cautioning him: "Do not go to your brothers
for they have left you, that is, they have deserted you as a brother."
The word זֶה (here) is numerically equivalent to twelve, as if to say,
"They do not desire any more to be twelve brothers. They would
rather be eleven, and do not want you as a brother." Yosef however
did not heed these words of warning and continued to go after them,
out of filial obedience.

If Yaakov escorted Yosef at the commencement of the journey,
how could Yosef have met with misfortune? When one is escorted
he is saved from harm along the way. The answer is that Yaakov intended that Yosef should go only as far as Shechem, and he escorted
him with this in mind. But Yosef went further, and so the escort was
of no avail. God caused Yaakov to have in mind a journey only as
far as Shechem, so that Yosef would eventually go down to Egypt.

≈§ The Conspiracy; Reuven's Alternate Plan

וַיִּתְנַכְּלוּ אֹתוֹ לַהֲמִיתוֹ — *They conspired to murder him* (37:18). The
brothers did not want to kill him with their own hands, so they set
wild dogs upon him. God saved him, and so they said, לְכוּ וְנַהַרְגֵהוּ —
Now, let us go and kill him! (37:20). That is, "Since he was saved

from the wild dogs, we will have to kill him." God said [though in its plain meaning this verse is spoken by the brothers], *We will see what will become of his dreams* (וְנִרְאֶה מַה יִּהְיוּ חֲלֹמֹתָיו; 37:20). "His dreams show that you can do nothing to him, and he will rule over you."

When Reuven heard their plan he tried to save Yosef from their hands, and said, לֹא נַכֶּנּוּ נָפֶשׁ — *Let us not kill him* (37:21). Reuven wanted to prove to his brothers that he too hated Yosef, so that they would listen to him. He told them, "Even if he were a stranger it would not be right to kill him." He did not say, "Do not shed his blood," but rather, "אַל תִּשְׁפְּכוּ דָם — *Do not shed blood* (37:22); it is forbidden to spill the blood of any man, and God will punish you if you do. I do not say this because of any love which I harbor for Yosef, but rather because of my concern for yourselves."

Reuven thought to himself, "I am the eldest son, and my father will therefore be furious with me for not having saved him from them." R' Bechaye writes this.

Reuven then suggested, הַשְׁלִיכוּ אֹתוֹ אֶל הַבּוֹר הַזֶּה — *Throw him into this pit* (37:22). *Chizkuni* asks: Since there were venomous snakes at the bottom of the pit, of what avail would his suggestion be? The answer is that Reuven suggested that they throw him into a pit which had no snakes, and he intended to take Yosef out once his brothers left. But the brothers took him out of the empty pit and cast him into a pit full of snakes. This explains why we later read that when Reuven later returned he did not find Yosef in the pit.

They took off Yosef's coat, and Shimon threw him into the pit.

◆§ A Pit of Snakes

וְהַבּוֹר רֵק אֵין בּוֹ מָיִם — *The pit was empty; there was no water in it* (37:24). This is difficult to understand. If it says that the pit was empty, we surely understand that there was no water in it. Why does the Torah add that there was no water there? The answer is that the verse is here telling us that there was no water in the pit, but there were snakes. The brothers did not see the snakes, which were hidden in the crevices of the pit, and so they threw him in. Had they seen the snakes they would not have thrown him there.

Chizkuni likewise writes that if there would have been water in the pit they would not have thrown Yosef in it, for they said: וְיָדֵנוּ אַל תְּהִי בוֹ, *and our hand will not be upon him* (37:27). *Ramban* writes that the snakes hid in the crevices, because if the brothers had seen them in the pit, but causing Yosef no harm, they would have understood that Yosef was a *tzaddik* and would not have sold him.

They sat down at some distance from the pit to eat, in order not to

hear his cries. A group of Yishmaelim from Gilad passed, carrying
wax and resin and aged wine to Egypt. *Rashi* writes: Why does it
specify what cargo the caravan was laden with? To show us Yosef's
merit. Yishmaelim generally carried unsavory goods but it happened
here they were carrying goods with a fragrant smell, so that the
righteous Yosef would not have to smell anything foul.

The brothers agreed with Yehudah's suggestion that Yosef be
sold as a slave. They said, "Avraham's descendants are destined to
be exiled. Perhaps he will atone for us, as he is also one of
Avraham's children."

◆§ Sold and Resold

וַיִּמְשְׁכוּ וַיַּעֲלוּ אֶת יוֹסֵף מִן הַבּוֹר וַיִּמְכְּרוּ אֶת יוֹסֵף — *They pulled and lifted
Yosef out of the pit, and they sold Yosef* (37:28). *Rashi* writes that
the brothers took Yosef out and sold him to the Yishmaelim, and the
Yishmaelim sold him to the Midianim, and they sold him to the
Egyptians. But *Chizkuni* and R' Bechaye write that when the
Midianim traveled past the pit and heard Yosef's cries they took him
out and then sold him to the Yishmaelim. The Yishmaelim gave him
back to the Midianim as collateral, and then together they sold him
to the Egyptians. For this reason it says ... וְהַמְּדָנִים מָכְרוּ אֹתוֹ
לְפוֹטִיפַר, *the Midianim sold him ... to Potiphar* (37:36), and later,
וַיִּקְנֵהוּ פּוֹטִיפַר ... מִיַּד הַיִּשְׁמְעֵאלִים, *Potiphar bought him ... from the
hand of the Yishmaelim* (39:1). He was sold by both of them.

When at a later time Yosef revealed his identity to his brothers he
said, אֲשֶׁר מְכַרְתֶּם אֹתִי מִצְרָיְמָה, *whom you sold to Egypt* (45:4). He
was referring to the fact that because they had cast him into the pit
he was ultimately sold to the Egyptians. The brothers had not even

known what had become of him, and had assumed that he had fallen prey to a wild beast.

A third explanation is that Potiphar saw that Yosef was of too noble appearance to be a mere slave, and suspected that he had been kidnapped. He therefore demanded that the Midianim give him proof that Yosef had not been kidnapped. They brought the Yishmaelim to assure him of this, and the verse therefore says, *Potiphar bought him from the hand of the Yishmaelim,* meaning that he bought him because of the testimony of the Yishmaelim.

R' Isser'l writes that the Yishmaelim and the Midianim both bought Yosef from the brothers; the Yishmaelim paid, while the Midianim pulled him out of the pit. The Midianim then claimed that they owned him because he was in their possession. Since they could not reach an agreement, they brought him to Egypt and sold him there. The Yishmaelim received the money which they had paid for him, and the Midianim kept the rest.

Toldos Yitzchak writes that the Midianim, who were merchants, sold Yosef to the Yishmaelim. They pulled Yosef out of the pit in order to display his fine appearance, as is the usual procedure of merchants with their merchandise. The verse thus tells us, וַיַּעַבְרוּ אֲנָשִׁים מִדְיָנִים סֹחֲרִים וַיִּמְשְׁכוּ וַיַּעֲלוּ אֶת יוֹסֵף — *Midianite men, merchants, passed by, and they pulled out Yosef* (37:28). It was the Midianim who sold him to Potiphar (as it is written, *the Midianim sold him),* for they were expert middlemen; the Yishmaelim, who were the real owners, having asked them to assist in selling him on their behalf (as it is written, *Potiphar bought him from the Yishmaelim).* Some commentators explain the text in this manner.

Another interpretation is that the Yishmaelim paid for him and then told the Midianim, "The Egyptians will not want to buy him because he is circumcised and they will think that he is unable to father children." They told the Midianim to take Yosef as if they themselves owned him, and to sell him, while the Yishmaelim would bear witness to the fact that circumcision was a custom among their people as well, and it had not harmed them. With this interpretation too the two verses again fall into place.

The brothers sold him for twenty pieces of silver. *Chizkuni* and R' Bechaye write that God said, "You have sold Yosef, the first-born son [of his mother], for twenty pieces of silver, which is equal to five *selaim* of silver, and so you will have to redeem your eldest sons for five *selaim"* [referring to the ceremony of *pidyon haben,* in which the eldest son is redeemed from the priest, *Kohen,* for five silver coins].

⊰§ Reuven's Distress; Yaakov is Informed

הַיֶּלֶד אֵינֶנּוּ וַאֲנִי אָנָה אֲנִי בָא — *The child is not here, and I, where will I go?* (37:30). When Reuven returned to the pit and did not find Yosef, he rent his garments and cried, *"The child is not here, and I, where will I go?* How can I face my father? I am the eldest son and my father will lay the blame on me." *Chizkuni* writes that Reuven was afraid that his father would say, "You have killed him because the birthright was taken away from you and given to him."

Where was Reuven when the brothers sold Yosef? Every day another son served their father, and that day was Reuven's turn. On that day he repented for having moved his father's bed.

The brothers slaughtered a goat, pierced Yosef's coat, and dipped it into the blood, to make it appear that a wild beast had devoured him. *Chizkuni* writes that they sent (וַיְשַׁלְחוּ) a messenger with the coat because they were afraid to face their father's accusation of murder. *R' Bechaye* writes that we can see that they sent it with a messenger because the verse says, הַכְּתֹנֶת בִּנְךָ הִוא — *Is this the coat of your son?* (37:32). A son does not normally address his father in that manner; if the brothers had brought it themselves they would not have asked if it was Yosef's coat.

Yaakov recognized the coat and said, חַיָּה רָעָה אֲכָלָתְהוּ — *A wild animal has devoured him* (37:33). The *Midrash* says that he was speaking prophetically of Potiphar's wife, here compared to a wild animal, who libelled him and caused him to be thrown in jail.

Yaakov mourned for his son for many days, meaning, for twenty-two years. Because he spent twenty-two years at Lavan's — fourteen years' labor for his wives, six years for the sheep and two years of travel — and during that time did not have the opportunity to honor his parents, he was punished for twenty-two years.

His sons and daughters tried to comfort him. *R' Bechaye* writes that "daughters" refers to Dinah and Serach, Asher's daughter, but *Rashi* writes that a daughter was born with each son, and each son married the daughter who was born with him. So says *R' Yehudah*. *Ramban* writes that Leah's six children married the daughters who were born with the other six brothers, and the other six children [sons of Rachel, Bilhah, and Zilpah] married the daughters born with the sons of Leah. *R' Nechemiah* says that Yaakov's children married Canaanite women, and they are called daughters because a daughter-in-law is often referred to as a daughter.

Yaakov did not want to accept any words of consolation. *Rashi* asks: The *Gemara* says that God decreed that the dead will eventually be forgotten. Why then did Yaakov mourn for so long? The answer is that the decree refers only to a person who has died, but Yosef was still alive, and so was not forgotten. This poses a difficulty, however: since the dead are ultimately forgotten, when Yaakov saw that he could not forget Yosef, why did he not realize that this was an indication that Yosef was still alive? The answer is that Yaakov suspected that he was alive, but realized that he must be captured and in great misery, and therefore he wept.

◄§ Eternal Mourning

כִּי אֵרֵד אֶל בְּנִי אָבֵל שְׁאֹלָה — For I will go down to my son in mourning to the grave (37:35). "I will not forget his death until I, too, am dead." The word sheolah ("to the grave") can also mean "to Gehinnom." Yaakov said, "God assured me that none of my children would die during my lifetime, and this would be my sign that I will not go to Gehinnom. Now that Yosef is with us no longer, I am afraid that I will go to Gehinnom."

Even Shoev writes that Yaakov cried so over Yosef, because Yosef was not yet twenty years old, and before a man reaches the age of twenty he is not punished for his sins. Thus Yosef must have died because of his father's sins.

Devek Tov asks why Yaakov was not punished for the fourteen years which he spent in the beis midrash of Shem and Ever, when he was not fulfilling the command to honor his parents. The answer is that his parents wanted him to be studying Torah and so they freed him of his obligation to honor them. Why was he punished for going to Lavan? Did his parents not tell him to go there? Rivkah sent Devorah almost immediately to tell him to come home, but he delayed in Lavan's house in order to marry his daughters, and was therefore punished.

וַיֵּבְךְ אֹתוֹ אָבִיו — His father wept for him (37:35). His grandfather Yitzchak wept for Yaakov's misery. He knew that Yosef was still alive, but said nothing. God also told Binyamin that Yosef was alive, and he too kept the secret. The stone which represented Binyamin on the Urim VeTumim (High Priest's breastplate) was therefore called יָשְׁפֵה, a word which has the same consonants as יֵשׁ פֶּה, "he has a mouth" — and yet he did not reveal that Yosef was alive.

◄§ Yehudah and Tamar

וַיְהִי בָּעֵת הַהִיא וַיֵּרֶד יְהוּדָה מֵאֵת אֶחָיו — At this time, Yehudah went down from his brothers (38:1). When the brothers saw their father's sorrow they cast Yehudah down from his position of greatness, saying, "You were our leader. When you told us not to kill Yosef, we listened to you. If you had told us to bring him back to our father, we would have obeyed you."

Yehudah left his brothers, married the daughter of a merchant, and had three children. The eldest, Er, was evil in God's eyes, for he wasted his semen. He did not want his wife to become pregnant because she was very beautiful and he did not want her beauty marred. Therefore God killed him. We learn from this that one who wastes his semen will be killed. This was the sin of the generation of the Flood.

Yehudah told his second son, Onan, to marry Er's widow and have children with her who would bear his childless brother's name [i.e., according to the *mitzvah* of *yibum*, levirate marriage]. Onan thought to himself, "Why should I have children if they will bear my brother's name instead of my own?" He too did not want her to become pregnant, and God killed him as well.

Yehudah then told his daughter-in-law Tamar, "Remain a widow until my son Shelah will be old enough to marry you." Actually, he had no intention of given Shelah to Tamar because two men had already died after marrying her. He was afraid that whoever she would marry would die, and in fact the law is that when two men die after marrying a woman she ought not to marry a third time.

Ramban asks why Yehudah did not immediately tell her that he had no intention of giving her Shelah. The answer is that though Shelah was obligated to marry her, Yehudah felt that Shelah was still young and could not father a child. He was afraid that when the time came to marry his deceased brother's wife, he too would waste his semen and die, like his brothers.

Tamar saw that Shelah was growing older and she had not yet married him. She therefore took off her widow's garb and dressed herself in fine clothing. She put on a veil and sat down on a road which Yehudah would walk on, for she wanted to bear Yehudah's children. He passed her by and thought she was a prostitute. He did not recognize her because she had covered her face. This is what *Rashi* writes. Another explanation is that she had always kept her face covered in her father-in-law's house, for she was very modest, and that was the reason he did not recognize her as Tamar. We learn from this that a man ought to recognize his own relatives in order to avoid sinning with them.

Yehudah asked her to have relations with him. She answered, "What will you give me?" Yehudah said, "I will send you a goat." Tamar replied, "Give me something as a pledge." Yehudah asked, "What shall I give you?" and Tamar answered, "Give me your signet ring, your staff, and your *tallis* with your *tzitzis*." She hoped that when he took hold of his *tzitzis* they would brush against his face and serve him as a reminder of the *mitzvos*. This did happen once. A man gave a prostitute 400 gulden and as he approached her his *tzitzis* brushed against his face, and he left her without sinning.

Tamar took these things to show that her intentions were not to prostitute herself. Just as a pious woman is married with a *chupah* and a betrothal, she took a ring to indicate the betrothal, the staff for a pole to hold up the *chupah* ("wedding canopy"), and a *tallis*, with the *tzitzis* worked into it, as the canopy itself. In Germany to this day it is the custom to make the *chupah* out of a *tallis*.

Yehudah gave her all that she had asked for and had relations with her. She became pregnant. The verse says, וַתַּהַר לוֹ — *She conceived to him* (38:18), to show that her children were as righteous as he.

Tamar returned home and put on her widow's garb again. Yehudah sent a goat to her, and hoped to retrieve his security, but the messenger could not find the woman.

◄§ She is more Righteous than He

וַיֻּגַּד לִיהוּדָה לֵאמֹר זָנְתָה תָּמָר כַּלָּתֶךָ וְגַם הִנֵּה הָרָה לִזְנוּנִים — *Yehudah was told: "Your daughter-in-law Tamar has prostituted herself, and she is pregnant from her prostitution"* (38:24). Yehudah ruled that Tamar be burned to death. *Rashi* writes that she was Shem's daughter, and he was a priest. In those days the daughter of a priest was burned for such a sin. *Ramban* writes that in those days in certain lands when a women was convicted of adultery she was given to her husband, who could punish her as he liked. Tamar was considered married, for Shelah was obligated to marry her, and she was therefore sentenced to be burnt. She sent a message to her father-in-law, saying, "The one who owns these three items has made me pregnant." She thought that if Yehudah would confess, it would be well; and if not, better to be burned than to shame him by accusing him. Our Sages learn from this that it is preferable to throw oneself into the fire than to embarrass someone. *Baal HaTurim* writes that Yehudah did not order that Tamar be burnt; rather, he wanted them to burn a mark on her forehead indicating that she was an adulteress.

Tamar said, "Do you recognize whose ring, staff, and *tallis* these are?" Yehudah recognized them, and said, צָדְקָה מִמֶּנִּי — *She is more righteous than I* (38:26); that is to say: "צָדְקָה, *she is righteous*; מִמֶּנִּי, *by me is she pregnant*."

Rashi writes that a heavenly voice came and announced: "I [God] have allowed Yehudah to have relations with Tamar so that *tzad-*

dikim will be her descendants. Because she was modest in her father-in-law's house, kings shall issue from her." *Ramban* writes that *she is more righteous than I* alludes to the fact that his intention was to fulfill the commandment of levirate marriage *(yibum)*. In those days any relative could marry the widow of the childless man, even her father-in-law. *Chizkuni* writes this as well. Yehudah was thus not burned for having relations with his daughter-in-law, because she had no children and he was allowed to marry her, to perpetuate his son's name. That was customary at that time.

Chizkuni writes that since Tamar was still a virgin and therefore in a sense not yet the wife of his sons, Yehudah was allowed to marry her. Another explanation of the *Chizkuni*: Tamar was more righteous, for she wanted to have children. She feared that Shelah would act as his brothers did, and she would be left childless. Another interpretation of צָדְקָה מִמֶּנִּי is that Yehudah said, "She must remain innocent *on account of me*, for whatever judgment I give to her I must take upon myself as well."

וְלֹא יָסַף עוֹד לְדַעְתָּהּ — *He was not intimate with her any more* (38:26). Yehudah did not have relations with her again, fearing that she caused men's deaths. Further, he was embarrassed because she was his daughter-in-law. So writes *Chizkuni*.

◈ Tamar's Twins

וְהִנֵּה תְאוֹמִים בְּבִטְנָהּ — *Behold, there were twins in her womb* (38:27). The midwife told Tamar that she was giving birth to twins. One of the children stuck out his hand, and the midwife tied a red thread around it as a sign that he was the first-born. But suddenly the other came out first. They called him Peretz, meaning that he pushed himself over his brother, to come out first. Then the child with the red thread tied on his wrist emerged. They named him Zerach, meaning "shining", for the red thread shone upon him..

◈ Yosef's Success

וְיוֹסֵף הוּרַד מִצְרָיְמָה — *Yosef was taken down to Egypt* (39:1). Yosef came to Egypt, to the house of Potiphar. Everything which he did succeeded.

וַיַּרְא אֲדֹנָיו כִּי ה' אִתּוֹ — *His master saw that God was with him* (39:3). *Rashi* writes that this means that he saw Yosef constantly referring to God's name. Another meaning is that wherever Yosef went he spoke to himself, in the manner of a magician. His master asked him: "Aren't there enough witches in Egypt? Why do you practice magic?" God then placed a cloud near Yosef, to follow him wherever he went, so his master saw that God was with him.

He placed Yosef in charge of the entire household and its treasures. God blessed the house for Yosef's sake. His master relied on him entirely, and asked him for no accounting.

R' Bechaye writes that the words, בְּבַיִת וּבַשָּׂדֶה — *in the house and in the field* (39:5), shows that Yosef was in Potiphar's house for a period of one year. One works in the house for six months, and another six months in the fields. He was in jail an additional twelve years, because thirteen years passed from the time that he was in his father's house until he became a ruler. Yosef ought to have been away for eleven years. The eleven stars of his dream indicated the eleven years it would take until he would be a ruler. Because he relied on the king's wine steward to remind Pharaoh to free him, rather than relying on God, he had to remain in jail for another two years.

◆§ In Potiphar's Service

וַיַּעֲזֹב כָּל אֲשֶׁר לוֹ בְּיַד יוֹסֵף ... כִּי אִם הַלֶּחֶם אֲשֶׁר הוּא אוֹכֵל — *He left all that he had in Yosef's hands ... except for the bread that he ate* (39:6). *Rashi* writes that the master gave everything except for his wife into Yosef's hands. *Ramban* and *Chizkuni* write that the Egyptians do not let Jews touch their bread. They consider them to be unclean, as it says in *Parshas Miketz,* כִּי לֹא יוּכְלוּן הַמִּצְרִים לֶאֱכֹל אֶת הָעִבְרִים לֶחֶם — *for the Egyptians do not eat bread with the Hebrews* (43:32). Therefore it says that the master gave everything into Yosef's hands except for his bread.

Toldos Yitzchak writes that the words *God made successful in his hands* (39:3) mean that whatever Yosef touched prospered. A second explanation given by *Toldos Yitzchak:* A merchant must sometimes hold onto his merchandise for some time, in order to eventually sell it, but Yosef was lucky and his merchandise was always sold immediately.

Ramban explains the words *except for the bread that he ate* to mean that the master found that Yosef would take nothing from him, except the bread that a man must eat. He did not pursue luxuries, despite the fact that he had everything at his disposal, for he was loyal to his master.

◆§ Potiphar's Wife

וַיְהִי יוֹסֵף יְפֵה תֹאַר — *Yosef was handsome* (39:6). Because of his beauty Potiphar's wife wanted to have relations with him. The *Midrash* writes that Yosef, seeing that his master considered him important, began to feel vain and preen himself. God said, "Your father sits weeping for you, and you bedeck yourself? I will interest your master's wife in you, and you will find your way into jail!"

His master's wife told him to sleep with her. He refused, and told her, "My master is always with you; how can I sleep with you?" *Ramban* writes: Why does the verse call her here, אֵשֶׁת אֲדֹנָיו — *the wife of his master* (39:7)? To show us that even though she was his master's wife, and Yosef ought to have been afraid to disobey her, in this matter he was unafraid, and feared God alone.

R' Bechaye quotes a *Midrash* which says that a vision of his father's face appeared to Yosef, and his father spoke to him, saying, "Your brothers' names will be inscribed on the high priest's clothing when he brings sacrifices. If you commit adultery your name will not be inscribed among theirs." He therefore refused her advances.

Toldos Yitzchak writes that the words, וְלֹא חָשַׂךְ מִמֶּנִּי מְאוּמָה כִּי אִם אוֹתָךְ בַּאֲשֶׁר אַתְּ אִשְׁתּוֹ — *he has not kept anything from me, except for you, because you are his wife* (39:9), mean that Yosef told her: "My master placed everything into my care. When you need clothing or jewelry you must come to me, and I choose whether or not to give it to you. But you are his wife, and only he can lie with you. I cannot."

R' Bechaye and *Toldos Yitzchak* quote the *Midrash:* His master's wife told him, "Why won't you sleep with me? There is no one here." Yosef answered, "Your unmarried women and girls are forbidden to us. How much more so is another man's wife!"

Chizkunu writes that she said, "There is no one here," and he answered, וְחָטָאתִי לֵאלֹהִים — *"I will have sinned to God* (39:9), Who knows all." *Rashi* writes that Yosef told her that her religion, too, forbade adultery.

◆§ Companions in Gehinnom

לִשְׁכַּב אֶצְלָהּ — *To lie with her* (39:10). Yosef did not want to lie with her in This World, and then again be her companion in the World to Come. For he who lies with another man's wife goes to *Gehinnom* together with her.

R' Bechaye writes: There are three faithful people in this world: a landowner who is careful to give the correct tithes; an unmarried man who, when among prostitutes, does not sin; and a poor man who, given money to guard, returns it. Yosef was seventeen years old and was among the prostitutes of Egypt, yet he was faithful and did not sin.

Potiphar's wife tried to seduce him, adorning herself before him morning and evening, and flattering him, for she saw in the stars that she would bear Yosef's children. But the stars actually meant that her daughter would bear his children. For in time Yosef taught his master's daughter the faith of the Living God and eventually married her.

✦§ Defying the Evil Inclination

וַיְהִי כְּהַיּוֹם הַזֶּה — *It was, on a certain day* (39:11). *Rashi* writes that it was some sort of festival day for the Egyptians, and they all went to their temples. She said that she was too weak to attend, thinking that that day would be the time to seduce Yosef. She told him, "To-day there is no one here," and she grabbed his clothing and cried, "You must sleep with me!"

Yosef left the clothing in her hands and rushed out into the street. His evil inclination burned within him: she had almost convinced him to lie with her, for they were quite alone in the house. R' Bechaye writes that this shows Yosef's righteousness. He still treated his master's wife with respect, and did not wrest his clothes from her hands.

When she saw Yosef run out *she called to the men of her house* (וַתִּקְרָא לְאַנְשֵׁי בֵיתָהּ; 39:14). *Chizkuni* writes that she called to her household and claimed that Yosef had undressed and wanted to rape her. When he had heard her screams he left his clothing and fled. When the master came and had relations with her, she said, "כַּדְּבָרִים הָאֵלֶּה — *such things* (39:19) your servant tried to do to me, but when I started to scream he fled."

וַיִּתְּנֵהוּ אֶל בֵּית הַסֹּהַר — *And put him in prison* (39:20). *Chizkuni* writes: Why did they not put him to death? Because there were no witnesses. The *Gemara* says that they brought Yosef to trial and the angel Gavriel, disguised as a nobleman, said, "If we really want to know what happened, let us bring their clothing. If her clothes are torn, that is a sign that he wanted to violate her; if his clothing is torn, then it is she who wanted to force him to lie with her." They found that his clothing was torn, and realized that he was guiltless. But they said, "If we vindicate him completely it will be a great humiliation for the woman, and she will be accused by her husband of harlotry. Let him sit in prison." Because the priests judged him with wisdom, Yosef gave them ample bread during the famine.

They put Yosef in prison, in the illuminated area where the nobles were. God was with Yosef in prison.

✦§ Two Troubled Dreamers

אַחַר הַדְּבָרִים הָאֵלֶּה — *After these things* [lit. *words*] (40:1). After the accusation by Potiphar's wife, which had caused Yosef's incarceration, God caused the king's wine steward and baker to sin against the king, so that the public would speak of them, and stop talking about Yosef. The king thereupon threw them into prison. Ultimately, the wine steward was freed, for his sin was not grievous. A fly

Yosef interprets
the steward's
and the baker's
dreams

had been found in the cup of wine which he had served to the king,
which was really unavoidable. It was even possible that it had fallen
into the goblet when the cup was already in the king's hands. But
the baker had sinned more seriously. A piece of earth had been
found in the bread, which could have been avoided, and so he was
eventually hanged.

These two noblemen were put into prison in the same place as
Yosef. The warden of the prison commanded Yosef to serve them,
and they were there together for one year.

One night the two nobles dreamed of their own future, and also
dreamed of the correct interpretation of each other's dream. Yosef
came to see them the next morning, וְהִנָּם זֹעֲפִים — *and they were
troubled* (40:6). He asked them why they were melancholy, and they
said that they had both dreamed dreams which could not be interpreted since they were in prison. This is what *Chizkuni* writes.

Yosef asked them to tell him the dreams: perhaps God would help
him to interpret them. The wine steward said, "I dreamed that a
grapevine stood before me, with three branches which blossomed
before my eyes. I took the king's goblet and squeezed the grapes into
it and placed the goblet in Pharaoh's hand."

Yosef said, "The three branches are three days. In three days
Pharaoh will take you back and you will once again be his wine
steward, as before. Please, remember me and help me to get out of
prison, for I have been kidnapped from the land of the Hebrews."
Because he was not ashamed when among the Egyptians to admit
that he was from *Eretz Yisrael*, he was found worthy of burial there.
Moshe, on the other hand, did not reveal his roots, as it is written
that the daughters of Yisro (Jethro) described him as אִישׁ מִצְרִי, *an*

Egyptian man (Shmos 2:19) who saved them. Since Moshe did not avow his Jewishness, he did not merit burial in *Eretz Yisrael.*

◄§ Correct Interpretation

וַיַּרְא שַׂר הָאֹפִים כִּי טוֹב פָּתַר — *The baker saw that he had interpreted correctly* (40:16). *Rashi* writes that the baker saw this because he had dreamed the interpretation of the wine steward's dream.

The baker then told Yosef, "I dreamed that I was carrying three baskets of bread on my head. The top basket was filled with wonderful foods for the king. A bird sat, eating from the basket." Yosef answered that the three baskets represented three days. In three days Pharaoh would order that he be hanged, and the birds would prey on his body.

On the third day, which was the anniversary of Pharaoh's investiture as ruler, he made a great feast for his servants, and remembered his nobles in prison. He had the wine steward released and returned to his former position as head of the king's wine cellars, and the baker was hanged.

The king's wine steward did not remember the favor which Yosef had done for him, in interpreting his dream favorably, and his own promise to help him. Because Yosef had relied on the wine steward he remained in prison for two more years. One should rely on no one but God.

פרשת מקץ
Parashas Mikeitz
(41:1 — 44:17)

◄§ Pharaoh's Dream

וַיְהִי מִקֵּץ שְׁנָתַיִם יָמִים — *At the end of two years* (41:1). At the end of
the two years during which Yosef was punished for relying on the
wine steward, Pharaoh had a dream.

Chizkuni writes of Yosef's punishment that he ought to have had
twelve sons, like his father, but ten were taken from him and he had
only two. He ought to have been in jail for ten years, but two extra
years were added because he had relied on the wine steward.

After those two years Pharaoh dreamed that he was standing by
the Nile. R' Bechaye and *Toldos Yitzchak* note that during this entire episode Pharaoh is not called "king of Egypt" because his downfall came through the Nile, which was turned to blood during the
first of the Ten Plagues. Only when Yosef became a ruler does the
Torah say, בְּעָמְדוֹ לִפְנֵי פַּרְעֹה מֶלֶךְ מִצְרָיִם — *when he stood before
Pharaoh, king of Egypt* (41:46), to emphasize that he was the king,
and as such could appoint Yosef as a ruler. This verse also shows us
that Egypt survived the famine because it was Yosef who stood
before Pharaoh, and advised him.

It says that Pharaoh stood עַל הַיְאֹר — *on the river* (41:1), rather
than עַל שְׂפַת הַיְאֹר — "on the bank of the river." Pharaoh had deified
himself and claimed that he stood over the river, that is, that he had
created it.

God frightened Pharaoh with dreams and confused his wise men,
so that Yosef could come, interpret the dreams, and become a ruler.

In his dream Pharaoh saw seven cows emerge from the Nile, quite
fat and healthy. They were grazing on the bank of the river, when
seven scrawny cows followed them out of the river. They devoured
the seven fat cows but no trace of the seven fat cows could be seen
upon the bodies of the emaciated ones. Then Pharaoh awoke.

He fell asleep once again, and dreamed that seven full and large
ears of corn grew on a stalk, with seven meager ears growing up
after them. The meager ears devoured the healthy ones. *Pharaoh*

awakened and behold, it was a dream (וַיִּיקַץ פַּרְעֹה וְהִנֵּה חֲלוֹם; 41:7) — and it needed an interpretation.

Chizkuni asks why the Torah does not say after the first dream וְהִנֵּה חֲלוֹם — *Behold, it was a dream.* Did the first dream not bear interpretation as well? The answer is that the first dream, in which the healthy cows were devoured by the emaciated ones, was not so startling, for cows, after all, do have mouths. But ears of corn have no mouths, and so it was more disturbing when they devoured the other ears. For that reason Pharaoh was distressed.

◆§ Pharaoh and Nebuchadnezzar

וַיְהִי בַבֹּקֶר וַתִּפָּעֶם רוּחוֹ — *In the morning he was troubled* (41:8). In the morning Pharaoh was alarmed and his breath came violently [from a literal translation of the words וַתִּפָּעֶם רוּחוֹ, *his wind (or spirit) tolled like a bell* (פַּעֲמוֹן)].

R' Bechaye writes: Why did Pharaoh forget his dream? Years later, after a portentous dream, Nebuchadnezzar forgot it in the morning. The answer is that if he would have forgotten the dream the wine steward would not have thought of Yosef. He knew that Yosef could interpret dreams, but he would not have credited Yosef with the ability to know what the forgotten dream was. God therefore did not allow Pharaoh to forget.

Nebuchadnezzar did not want to relate his dream. He thought, "If I relate them my dream, numerous wise men will come, and each will interpret it differently. I will have no idea which is true. I will therefore not tell them what my dream was, and the one who can tell it to me will no doubt be the one who can also interpret it correctly." This is what *Chizkuni* writes, as well as *Toldos Yitzchak* and *Imrei Noam.*

Toldos Yitzchak and *Imrei Noam* propose still another explanation. Nebuchadnezzar's dream spoke of what would happen in future millennia. If Daniel had merely interpreted it, Nebuchadnezzar would not have believed him. He would have said, "How can you prove this is the true interpretation?" But since he now recalled what he had dreamed, he realized that Daniel's interpretation must be true. Pharaoh's dream, on the other hand, showed what would occur in the very near future. The interpretation could soon enough be proved true or false, so there was no need for Pharaoh to forget his dream.

Toldos Yitzchak also asks why Pharaoh did not order his wise men executed when they could not properly interpret the dream, while Nebuchadnezzar did execute his counselors. The answer is that Nebuchadnezzar had executed the Israelite priests *(Kohanim)* on the suggestion of the counselors. If he had not listened to them and killed them they could have interpreted his dream, using the *Urim VeTumim*. Nebuchadnezzar therefore said, "I killed the priests because of you. You had better interpret the dream, and if you cannot, you too will be executed."

⇜§ No Interpreters; Yosef is Remembered

וְאֵין פּוֹתֵר אוֹתָם לְפַרְעֹה — *There was no one to interpret them for Pharaoh* (41:8). No one could offer him an interpretation that his heart would accept. For he had dreamed the dream, together with its meaning. The dream he remembered, but could not remember the interpretation. His counselors told him that he would have seven daughters, and would bury all seven. But he would not accept that, for his heart still beat loudly from anxiety.

R' Bechaye and *Toldos Yitzchak* ask: Why did it not occur to his wise men to interpret the cows as a symbol of famine and abundance? For did the Egyptians not plow with oxen, and do the ears of corn not speak for themselves? The explanation is that God confused them, so that Yosef would interpret the dream.

The wine steward told Pharaoh, "When the baker and I dreamed while we were imprisoned, we were together with *a Hebrew boy, servant to the chief cook* (נַעַר עִבְרִי עֶבֶד לְשַׂר הַטַּבָּחִים; 41:12). *Rashi* says: The favors of wicked men are not done whole-heartedly. The wine bearer wanted to help Yosef emerge from prison, and yet described Yosef as "young — unfit for a position of authority; a Jew — who does not know the language of our country; a servant — who by our law cannot become a master."

Chizkuni writes that the wine steward was afraid that if Yosef would become a ruler he would be angry with him for letting him stay in prison for so long, and therefore he belittled him. *Chizkuni* also writes another explanation for the wine steward's unfavorable words. He was afraid that Pharaoh would be angry for having allowed an important person to sit in captivity.

Toldos Yitzchak writes just the opposite: The wine steward wanted to help Yosef become a ruler, and he told Pharaoh that Yosef was a wise man and a prophet. Even though he was still young and had not learned very much, he could interpret dreams, which showed that he undoubtedly was a prophet. "You may say that he is a magician — but then I say he is a Jew, and witchcraft is forbidden to them. If you think he is a noble who learned these arts, I say that he is a servant. And if you tell me that he may have learned the arts of dream interpretation in his master's home, I say that he was a servant of the chief cook, who would not know of such things.

◄§ Directing a Dream

בַּאֲשֶׁר פָּתַר לָנוּ בֵּן הָיָה — *As he interpreted it, so it was* (41:13). The *Midrash Rabasi* writes: A woman came to R' Eliezer and said, "I dreamed that a rafter in my house fell down." He told her, "You will have a son who will live." And so it was. Another time she came to R' Eliezer's *beis midrash* to ask his interpretation of another dream. He was not there, and his students asked her to tell them the dream. She said, "I dreamed that a rafter broke." They said to her, "Your husband will die." She began to cry, and R' Eliezer walked in and asked why she was weeping. His students answered, "We have interpreted her dream, and told her that her husband would die." R' Eliezer said, "You have killed her husband, for a dream follows its interpretation. It is fulfilled in the manner in which it is interpreted, as it is written, *as he interpreted it, so it was.*"

◄§ Out of the Depths

וַיְרִיצָהוּ מִן הַבּוֹר — *They rushed him out of the pit* (41:14). Our Sages learn from this that redemption comes speedily after misfortune: Yosef was made a ruler immediately after being released from prison.

He shaved and changed his clothing. *Rashi* writes that although he did not know that he was to be released from jail, he did this out of respect for majesty.

Pharaoh told Yosef that he had been told that *when you hear a dream, you can interpret it* (תִּשְׁמַע חֲלוֹם לִפְתֹּר אֹתוֹ; 41:15). Yosef answered that the wisdom was not his, but *God will answer Pharaoh's welfare* (אֱלֹהִים יַעֲנֶה אֶת שְׁלוֹם פַּרְעֹה; 41:16) — may God send me an answer concerning Pharaoh's well-being.

R' Bechaye writes that Pharaoh and his people thought that the world was controlled by seven planets, rather than by God. They therefore thought that the seven ears of corn represented the seven planets, which would bring on the famine. Hence Yosef first emphasized that God would speak of Pharaoh's welfare. He should not think that anything came through influence of the planets, for everything comes from God.

Pharaoh recited his dream to Yosef, saying he had seen seven cows that were בְּרִיאוֹת בָּשָׂר וִיפֹת תֹּאַר — *fat and beautiful* (41:18). R' Bechaye asks why Pharaoh describes them in this manner, when before the cows are described as יְפוֹת מַרְאֶה וּבְרִיאֹת בָּשָׂר — *beautiful and fat* (41:2). The Sages tell us that Yosef pointed out to Pharaoh that there were these and other discrepancies between what Pharaoh had said and what he had in fact dreamed. Pharaoh was amazed, and asked him, "Were you in my dream, that you know all the details?" For this reason the Torah says that Pharaoh said to him, אַחֲרֵי הוֹדִיעַ אֱלֹהִים אוֹתְךָ אֶת כָּל זֹאת — *since God has told you all of this* (41:39), meaning, "God let you know exactly what I dreamed."

⊷§ The Interpretation

חֲלוֹם פַּרְעֹה אֶחָד הוּא — *Pharaoh's dream is one* (41:25). "Do not imagine that because you first dreamed of seven cows and then of seven ears of corn, that these are two separate dreams; they are one. The seven healthy cows and ears of corn, and the seven emaciated cows and ears indicate that seven years of abundance will be followed by seven years of famine. You dreamed of it twice to show that God will bring this on in the near future."

Chizkuni asks: Yosef also dreamed two dreams concerning his brothers. Why did they not come true immediately? The difference is that unlike Pharaoh, he did not dream them both in one night.

⊷§ Yosef's Advice and Appointment

וְעַתָּה יֵרֶא פַרְעֹה אִישׁ נָבוֹן וְחָכָם — *Now Pharaoh should look for a wise and clever man* (41:33). Yosef said, "Now Pharaoh should seek a wise man who can govern the land, give the people sufficient bread for their needs, and sell whatever they do not eat. He must be knowledgeable in the means of storing wheat so that it does not spoil. Pharaoh ought to appoint this man to rule over all of Egypt, so that he can collect gold and silver for the king's treasuries. Pharaoh should appoint a man who will, in turn, appoint officers to gather the wheat. Each person should give a fifth of his crop to the king's treasuries. In the past, it was customary to give only one tenth, but in time of emergency the people should give more, to avoid starvation during the famine. They should store the wheat in all of Egypt."

Yosef's plan was most acceptable to Pharaoh. Pharaoh then asked, הֲנִמְצָא כָזֶה אִישׁ אֲשֶׁר רוּחַ אֱלֹהִים בּוֹ — *Can we find another man such as this, who has God's spirit within him?* (41:38). *Ramban* writes that because the Egyptians hated the Jews, they felt that if they touched their bread it became impure. Pharaoh thought, "In the face of such hatred the Egyptians will never consent to my making Yosef my second in command." He therefore had to point out that such a wise man could not be found among the Egyptians.

Pharaoh told Yosef, "*Since God has told you all this* (41:39) it is obvious that no wiser man can be found than you. You will be the ruler of my people." Pharaoh removed his signet ring and placed it on Yosef's finger, saying, "You will be the ruler, and *only by the throne will I outrank you*" (רַק הַכִּסֵּא אֶגְדַּל מִמֶּךָּ; 41:40).

Chizkuni writes that Pharaoh thought to himself, "I will test Yosef to see if he interpreted the dream correctly and honestly, or if he was just looking for a way to leave prison. I will make him ruler. If he did not interpret the dream honestly, he will refuse the offer, knowing that his solution will not work."

Pharaoh placed a golden necklace on his neck, and had him ride in the second royal chariot. The people announced before him, "Here rides the young ruler!"

Pharaoh told Yosef, וּבִלְעָדֶיךָ לֹא יָרִים אִישׁ אֶת יָדוֹ — *Without your consent, no man will lift up his hand* (41:44) — to take up a sword. He named him Tzafnas Pane'ach, meaning that like a prophet, "he reveals that which is hidden."

⋙ Yosef Marries Asnas

וַיִּתֶּן לוֹ אֶת אָסְנַת בַּת פּוֹטִי פֶרַע — *And he* [Pharaoh] *gave him Asnas, daughter of Poti-fera* [Potiphar] (41:45). Why was he called Poti-fera? Because he fattened (Hebrew — *pitem*) calves for sacrifice to idols.

Chizkuni writes that Yosef married Potiphar's daughter to prove that he had not had relations with Potiphar's wife, for in that case, he would have been forbidden from marrying her daughter.

Chizkuni and R' Bechaye write that Asnas was Dinah's daughter, whom she bore to Shechem. Her brothers wanted to kill the baby out of shame. Their father Yaakov, however, placed a necklace upon her which said that whoever married her was marrying into the family of Yaakov. He then cast her out of his house, and she hid among thornbushes. For this reason she was called Asnas, meaning "thornbushes" (*sneh*). The angel Gavriel brought her to Poti-fera's house, and his wife adopted her as a daughter. When Yosef rode through Egypt, the women of Egypt ran out to greet him and marvel at his great beauty. They threw their jewelry towards him. Asnas, having nothing else to throw, cast her necklace at him, which revealed that she was Yaakov's granddaughter. And because of this he married her. When Yaakov came down to Egypt and asked Yosef who his children were, he showed him this same necklace which had his message written on it.

⋙ Sharing His People's Plight

וּלְיוֹסֵף יֻלַּד שְׁנֵי בָנִים בְּטֶרֶם תָּבוֹא שְׁנַת הָרָעָב — *Two sons were born to Yosef, before the years of famine came* (41:50). The children were born before the years of hunger, for during a famine marital rela-

tions are forbidden. Even though Yosef had not fulfilled his obligation of having at least one male and one female child, and was hence
allowed to have marital relations, still, when he heard the anguished
cries of the hungry and saw their misery, he took it upon himself not
to have relations with his wife.

Chizkuni asks: Levi lived with his wife during the famine. We see
that Yocheved, his daughter, was born during the famine, by the
walls of Egypt. Yosef had to abstain because he visualized the misery of his father and brothers, while Levi knew that they actually
had enough and the famine had not affected them, and so did not
separate from his wife. As to the misery in which he must have supposed his long-lost brother Yosef to be, this was not sufficient
reason for him to separate from his wife, for this is done only for the
suffering of the many, not of an individual. *Devek Tov* writes that
Yosef separated because, as a result of his position as distributor of
grain, he knew better than anyone the misery of the people.

The famine first affected the poor, then the richer portion of the
populace. It grew worse in Egypt, and no matter how much they ate
they never felt satisfied.

⇜ Yaakov Sends His Sons to Egypt

וַיַּרְא יַעֲקֹב כִּי יֶשׁ שֶׁבֶר בְּמִצְרָיִם — *Yaakov saw that there was food in
Egypt* (42:1). The verse ought surely to have said that Yaakov had
heard — but he had seen, in prophecy, that hope lay for him in
Egypt. The word *shever* ("food") also signifies hope.

וַיֹּאמֶר יַעֲקֹב לְבָנָיו לָמָה תִּתְרָאוּ — *Yaakov told his sons, "Why are you
allowing yourselves to be seen thus?"* (42:1). Yaakov asked, "Why

are you growing lean and not going to Egypt?" This is what *Rashi* writes. Another explanation given by *Rashi:* "Why do you show yourselves as well-fed? Even though you have enough food at the moment, you have to go to Egypt to show the other people that you, too, need food." *Chizkuni* writes this as well.

R' Bechaye writes in the name of R' Chananel: Yaakov asked his children, "Why are you always seen together? Separate from each other." *Ramban* writes that Yaakov said, "Why do you want to be seen here, and not go for the wheat?" The *Midrash* writes that Yaakov warned them not to enter Egypt all together through one gate, so that no evil eye should be cast upon them, for they were all strong and handsome.

⊷§ To Ransom a Brother

וַיֵּרְדוּ אֲחֵי יוֹסֵף עֲשָׂרָה — *Yosef's ten brothers went down* (42:3). Why does the verse here call them Yosef's brothers, rather than Yaakov's children? Because they deeply regretted selling their brother, and they planned to ransom him if they would find him. R' Bechaye writes that ten of them went down so that they could pray in a *minyan* for God to send them their brother Yosef. *Ramban* writes that ten went in order to fulfill the first dream, in which only the brothers bowed down to him.

When Yosef saw that Binyamin was not with them, he realized that the dream would only come true if all eleven brothers were there. Until they would all stand before him, he would not reveal his identity. He therefore devised a stratagem so that they would be forced to bring Binyamin, the eleventh brother. The first dream would then be fulfilled and the second could begin to come true. If Yosef had not had this intention, he would never have so tormented his brothers and his father, and he would have immediately sent word to his father that he was alive and a nobleman in Egypt. After all, Yaakov lived only six days' journey away. Even if it had been one thousand miles Yosef would have sent a letter to his father, telling him that he was alive, to end his father's mourning. But he knew that the dream had to be fulfilled, and his father and brothers must bow down to him in Egypt. He saw that the famine was severe, and was certain that everyone from the entire region would ultimately come to him.

⊷§ The Brothers before Yosef

וַיָּבֹאוּ בְּנֵי יִשְׂרָאֵל לִשְׁבֹּר בְּתוֹךְ הַבָּאִים — *Yisrael's sons came to buy, among those that came* (42:5). They disguised themselves so that no one would cast an evil eye upon them.

וְיוֹסֵף הוּא הַשַּׁלִּיט עַל הָאָרֶץ — *Yosef was ruler of the land* (42:6). *Ramban* writes that Yosef himself sold the wheat. He commanded that all the treasure houses be locked up, and sold only that which was in one vault, to ensure that his brothers would come before him.

Ramban also gives an alternative explanation. Yosef himself did not sell the wheat. Rather, he instructed his officials to open a storehouse in each and every land. The representatives of each country had to come before Yosef to be confirmed as overseers of these storehouses. Yaakov's sons had been delegated by their countrymen to open a storehouse for the entire Canaan, and now stood before Yosef to receive his certification.

וַיַּרְא יוֹסֵף אֶת אֶחָיו וַיַּכִּרֵם — *Yosef saw his brothers and recognized them* (42:7). As soon as he saw his brothers he recognized them. He was afraid, however, that they too would recognize him, so he put a turban on his head, and with it covered his forehead and part of his face. He spoke harshly and angrily to them, and asked them where their homeland was. They answered that they were from Canaan. His recognition was confirmed, and that is why the Torah says a second time, וַיַּכֵּר יוֹסֵף אֶת אֶחָיו — *Yosef recognized his brothers* (42:8).

Chizkuni writes that he recognized them beyond doubt because he heard them call each other by name. Yosef was afraid to reveal his identity, lest they flee in fear and never return to their father; he now planned to have them bring Binyamin.

◆§ Two Types of Recognition

וְהֵם לֹא הִכִּרֻהוּ — *They did not recognize him* (42:8). They did not recognize him because he now had a long beard, whereas when he had been sold he had been beardless. So writes *Rashi*. *Ramban* writes that because Yosef expected the brothers to come, he recognized them; but the brothers were not looking for Yosef among the rulers, so they did not look carefully and recognize him. *Chizkuni* writes that because his name was Tzafnas Pane'ach they did not recognize him. They, however, were still called by the same names, so he could recognize them.

When his brothers fell into his power he recognized them as his brothers — he acted compassionately as a brother ought. But when Yosef fell into their hands they did not recognize their brotherly obligations, and they sold him.

◆§ The Dreams Come True

וַיִּזְכֹּר יוֹסֵף אֵת הַחֲלֹמוֹת — *Yosef remembered the dreams* (42:9). As soon as Yosef saw the brothers bow down to him he thought, "Today the dreams will come true." Yosef then accused them of having come as spies. The *Midrash* writes — and this appears too in *Rashi*, R' Bechaye, and *Chizkuni* — that Yosef ordered that no one be allowed into Egypt until he had given his name, his father's name, and his birthplace. Each night the guards would bring the list to Yosef, so that he would be aware of who had arrived in the city. When Yaakov's children arrived they each entered through a different gate, and wrote down their names and the name of their father. In the evening the list was brought to Yosef, and he saw his brothers' names. He ordered that all but one of the grain storehouses be shut, and instructed the official in charge of that storehouse to send his brothers to him when they arrived. The official waited for three days, and they failed to appear.

Yosef therefore took ten warriors of Pharaoh's household and told them to search for his brothers. When they were found, Yosef accused them of spying out ways of conquering the land, since they had entered the city through ten separate gates.

R' Bechaye writes that Yosef took a goblet, tapped on it, and said, "My goblet tells me that you are spies." They replied, "Our father commanded us not to enter together, through one gate." Yosef asked, "And what were you doing in the market?" They answered, "We had lost something and were searching for it there." Yosef then said, "My goblet also tells me that two of you murdered the entire town of Shechem." They became terrified and answered, "We are twelve brothers. Our father sent ten of us for wheat, because there are many thieves on the road, as a result of the famine. If we were so strong, two of us would have been sufficient to make the journey."

Toldos Yitzchak asks what manner of reply was this. In response to the accusation of spying, they said that they were the sons of one father. The answer is that they thereby said, "How can you believe that a father would send all of his sons into such danger? He would have sent only one to be a spy." But Yosef answered, *"It is as I have spoken* (הוא אֲשֶׁר דִּבַּרְתִּי; 42:14). You are spies. Spies will not take in a stranger for fear that he will be captured and, under torture, reveal all. But a brother will lose his life before betraying the others."

Another explanation is that because the brothers said, הַקָּטֹן אֶת אָבִינוּ הַיּוֹם וְהָאֶחָד אֵינֶנּוּ — *The youngest is today with our father, and one is gone* (42:13), Yosef said, "The young one must be righteous, and heeded his father's admonitions not to be a spy, but you are rebellious and do not heed your father. If you were not spies, then all of you would have come."

◄§ Yosef's Demand

חֵי פַרְעֹה — *By Pharaoh's life* (42:15). I swear by the life of Pharaoh that you will only leave from here if your youngest brother comes here. Yosef swore only by Pharaoh's life.

Yosef asked them, "If you would find your brother Yosef and were asked to pay a huge ransom for him, would you free him?" The brothers answered that they would pay any ransom whatever. Yosef continued, "And if they still would not want to give him to you, what would you do then?" They answered, "We would give our lives for his." Yosef then said, "*It is as I have spoken* (42:14); you are spies."

R' Bechaye writes that when he swore that they could not leave, he meant that all of them could not leave together, and that they would have to leave one behind as a guarantee of their return. Yosef said, "Send one of your number to bring your youngest brother Binyamin, while the rest of you stay in prison, and then we will see whether or not you are spies." He put them in prison for three days, and then told them, אֶת הָאֱלֹהִים אֲנִי יָרֵא — "*I fear God*" (42:18). I will therefore let all of you go, but one. Go to your father, bring him the wheat, and return with your youngest brother."

R' Bechaye says that the brothers said, "We consent. Choose whomever you wish to imprison." Yosef took Shimon and, before their eyes, placed him in fetters, in order to frighten them. As soon as they left he unbound him and gave him food and drink. Why did he choose Shimon? Because it was Shimon who threw him into the pit. Besides, he wanted to separate him from Levi, because they were both very powerful, and had killed the entire town of Shechem. He was afraid that they would kill him as well.

Chizkuni writes that Yosef had first intended to take Reuven, as he was the eldest and as such he should have been held accountable for the actions of the group. But Reuven had been the one who had cautioned them against killing him, and he had overheard Reuven and his brothers repenting for having sold him; he therefore decided not to take him. Finally, *He took Shimon from them* (וַיִּקַּח מֵאִתָּם אֶת שִׁמְעוֹן; 42:24), because the brothers would not willingly give over any of their number.

◄§ Confession

אֲשֵׁמִים אֲנַחְנוּ — *We are guilty* (42:21). The brothers said, "We are guilty of having seen our brother's suffering and having ignored his cries as he lay in the pit."

On this R' Bechaye comments that *tzaddikim* recognize their faults and repent over them.

We see here that the brothers did not sell Yosef, but threw him into the pit — because if they had sold him they would have been unable to repent until they had redeemed him.

Toldos Yitzchak asks why they did not repent while in jail, waiting instead until Yosef had released them. The answer is that at the time of their release Yosef told them that he feared God, and would not harm them. They then said to themselves, "This man is an idol worshiper, and yet he will not harm us. We are Jews, and Yosef was our own brother, and yet we harmed him."

◄§ But Yosef Did Understand

וַיַּעַן רְאוּבֵן אֹתָם לֵאמֹר הֲלוֹא אָמַרְתִּי אֲלֵיכֶם לֵאמֹר אַל תֶּחֶטְאוּ בַיֶּלֶד — *Reuven answered ... "Didn't I say to you, don't sin against the boy?"* (42:22). Reuven told his brothers, "I told you not to sin against the child, but you did not listen to me. Today his blood is being avenged. Even though we did not actually kill him, God considers it as if we had, for we knew that he was not accustomed to a hard life."

They said all of this in Hebrew, under the impression that Yosef did not understand them, *for the interpreter was between them* (כִּי הַמֵּלִיץ בֵּינֹתָם; 42:23). Yosef let his son Menashe stand between them, ostensibly as an interpreter, so they assumed that he did not know the language. When Yosef heard his brothers regret what they had done, he left them and wept.

Yosef commanded that their saddlebags be filled with quantities of wheat, and that their money be placed beneath it, without their knowledge. The second time he commanded that their money be returned to them openly, and he gave them food for the journey, to show that he bore them no ill will, and was only eager that they should bring their brother.

◄§ Yaakov Hears of Yosef's Demands

וַיִּפְתַּח הָאֶחָד אֶת שַׂקּוֹ — *One of them opened his sack* (42:27). On their way home, Levi opened his sack in order to feed his donkey, and saw his money. The brothers were frightened, and cried, "What has God done to us? The money is in our bags!" They came to their father and told him all that had happened. Their father said to them, "You are killing off my children! Yosef is not here, and Shimon is not with me, and now you want to take Binyamin?" He suspected that they had sold Shimon, and that they hoped to sell Binyamin as well.

Reuven answered, "You can kill my two sons (אֶת שְׁנֵי בָנַי תָּמִית; 42:37) if I don't bring Binyamin back safely. Give him to me, on my responsibility." Yaakov answered, "You are a first-born fool. If you do not bring Binyamin back, do you think I would kill my grandchildren as well? They are as dear to me as my own children!"

Toldos Yitzchak writes that Reuven said that he would kill his children, knowing that Yaakov would answer, "They, too, are my children." He then could tell Yaakov, "Binyamin is my brother. A brother is a closer relative than a grandchild. I will obviously make certain that Binyamin comes back safely." But Yaakov would not listen to his arguments.

Yehudah then said to his father, "If Binyamin goes with us, there is a chance that he will stay there, and there is a chance that he will return home; but if Binyamin does not come with us we cannot go for more food, and we will all die of hunger. It is wiser to send Binyamin with us."

◆§ Yehudah the Guarantor

אָנֹכִי אֶעֶרְבֶנּוּ — *I will be his guarantor* (43:9). Yehudah told Yaakov, "I will guarantee that he is brought back. If he is not, I will have sinned against you for the rest of my life. Had we not delayed this long we could have been there, brought back food, and come back twice already!" R' Bechaye notes that the brothers suffered through their hunger without coercing their father through loud arguments. They waited instead until their father finally told them to take Binyamin.

Yaakov then gave them five instructions: to take a tribute of fruits and aged wine as a gift to the Egyptian noble; to take double the amount of money which they had taken the first time, in case the price had gone up; to take back the money which they had found in their bags, in case the Egyptian had accidentally neglected to take it from them; to take Binyamin; and to pray.

◆§ Yaakov's Prayer

וְאֵל שַׁדַּי — *May God Almighty* (43:14). *May God give you the favor of the man, and have him send your other brother back.* Yaakov was referring to Shimon, but did not specify his name for he was still estranged from him over what had happened in Shechem. If he had had food he would not have sent Binyamin, and would rather have left Shimon in prison than risk Binyamin. So writes *Ramban. Rashi* writes that *your brother* (אֶת אֲחִיכֶם) refers to Shimon, while the additional word אַחֵר (the other) refers to Yosef. Yaakov thought, "Perhaps he is still living," and he prayed to God to send him back.

◆§ The Brothers at Yosef's House

וַיַּרְא יוֹסֵף אִתָּם אֶת בִּנְיָמִין — *Yosef saw that Binyamin was with them* (43:16). When the brothers came to Egypt, Yosef told the servant in charge of his household to bring them to his home. He told Menashe to slaughter an animal, since Yaakov's children would not eat without proper slaughter, and to remove the veins as was customary for the Jews, *for the men will eat with me at noon* (כִּי אִתִּי יֹאכְלוּ הָאֲנָשִׁים בַּצָּהֳרָיִם; 43:16).

The brothers were afraid when they were brought to Yosef's house, as it was not customary to bring guests there. They thought that it must be on account of the money which they had found in their saddlebags, and feared that he wanted to take them as slaves. They told the servant in charge of Yosef's house, "We have previously bought food and when we were on the road we found that our money was still in the bags. We have brought the money back, and money to buy still more food. We have no idea who placed the money in our bags." The servant told them, "Do not fear, Your God and the God of your fathers gave you the money. I can attest that I duly received the money from you."

Shimon was released, and the brothers prepared the gifts for Yosef. When he entered they bowed down to him and presented their tribute. He inquired into the state of their father's health and welfare, and they answered that he was well, and bowed down once again, because he had asked about their father. When he saw Binyamin, his mother's son, he asked if this was the youngest brother of whom they had spoken. They answered that it was he. He then told Binyamin, אֱלֹהִים יָחְנְךָ בְּנִי, *God grant you favor, my son* (43:29). He felt an urgent desire to weep, and left the adjoining room to cry. He then dried his eyes and ordered that the tables be set; one for him, a separate one for the brothers, and still another one for the Egyptian members of his household. The Egyptians would not eat with the Jews, for Jews eat lamb, the Egyptians' idol.

☙ Yosef Seats His Guests

וַיֵּשְׁבוּ לְפָנָיו הַבְּכֹר כִּבְכֹרָתוֹ וְהַצָּעִיר כִּצְעִרָתוֹ — *They were seated before him, in order of age* (43:33). Yosef took his goblet into his hand, tapped on it, and recited, "Reuven, Shimon, Levi, Yehudah, Yissachar, and Zevulun are the sons of one mother; let them sit together." He did the same with the rest. When he came to Binyamin's name he said, "You have no mother, and neither have I, so you will sit with me."

וַיִּתְמְהוּ הָאֲנָשִׁים — *The men were amazed* (43:33). *Toldos Yitzchak* writes that the brothers wondered what nation he could be from, since he would not eat with them, nor with the Egyptians.

Yosef gave each of the brothers gifts. Binyamin was given five times as many: Yosef gave him one portion above that which he had given all the brothers, and Asnas gave him one, and Menashe and Efraim, his sons, each gave him one.

The brothers drank with Yosef. Yosef had vowed not to drink wine until he had seen his brothers and had learned of his father's fate. The brothers, too, had vowed not to drink any wine until they had found Yosef. Although as yet they did not know Yosef's whereabouts they drank because they were afraid that if they would abstain Yosef would accuse them of spying, and say that they were afraid to drink because they might betray a secret.

Yosef instructed the manager of his household to fill their bags with as much food as they could hold, and to replace their money as well. He told him to tell the brothers that because they had been suspected of spying he wished to appease them now with the money. *Ramban* and R' Bechaye write that if the money had been placed in their bags without their knowledge, as was subsequently done with Yosef's goblet, the brothers could have said that just as they had not stolen the money, which had appeared in their saddlebags without their knowledge, so they had not stolen the goblet.

Yosef commanded that his goblet be placed in Binyamin's sack. *Chizkuni* writes: Why did he choose Binyamin? He thought, perhaps the brothers had taken an impostor and claimed it was Binyamin. If they offered to sacrifice their lives for his, he would be certain that this really was Binyamin.

◆§ Daylight Travel

הַבֹּקֶר אוֹר וְהָאֲנָשִׁים שֻׁלְּחוּ — *With the morning light, the men were sent on their way* (44:3). Our Sages learn from this that one should leave a city only once day has dawned, and one should enter a city while it is yet daytime.

The men had not gotten far from the city (לֹא הִרְחִיקוּ; 44:4) when Yosef commanded that they be brought back, so that they should not be forced to make a long journey back. He told his men to tell the brothers, "Why have you repaid kindness with malice, and stolen the goblet? That is the cup which Yosef drinks from, and one who steals an object from the table of a ruler has committed a capital crime."

◆§ The Charmed Goblet

וְהוּא נַחֵשׁ יְנַחֵשׁ בּוֹ — *He performs divination with it* (44:5). "That is why he is very fond of it." *Ramban* writes that the one who pursued them said, "My master asked the magicians, and they said that you had the goblet, so he ordered us to follow you." The brothers answered, "How could we possibly do such a vile thing, to steal his goblet, when we even returned the money which we had found in our bags? The one in whose bags you find it shall be killed, and the rest of us shall remain servants to your master." Their pursuer said, "Although it is true that if one finds that one person is a thief, the entire band deserves to be punished, still, I will be good to you. The one who has stolen the goblet shall remain a slave, and the rest can go free to their father."

Ramban writes that they answered, "If one finds stolen goods in possession of one of a group, and the rest did not know of the robbery, they should be set free. But we are ten brothers. If you find that one of us has robbed, the rest of us will also surrender ourselves as servants."

The pursuer answered, "*It will be according to your words* (כְּדִבְרֵיכֶם כֶּן הוּא; 44:10). When a robbery is discovered that has been committed by one of a group, you have said that the others should be set free. I will free all but the robber, who will be taken as a slave."

The pursuer began his search with the eldest and ended with the youngest, so that they would not suspect that he himself had placed the goblet with Binyamin. The goblet was indeed found in Binyamin's sack. The brothers were humiliated and lashed out at Binyamin, saying that he had been born a thief, like his mother Rachel, who had stolen Lavan's idols. But because they suspected him falsely, he was compensated by having the Beis HaMikdash built in his portion of the Land.

◄§ The Brothers are Brought Back

הִנֶּנּוּ עֲבָדִים לַאדֹנִי גַּם אֲנַחְנוּ גַּם אֲשֶׁר נִמְצָא הַגָּבִיעַ בְּיָדוֹ — *We will be servants to our master, both we and the one in whose hands the goblet was found* (44:16). Toldos Yitzchak asks: Why did they add, *the one in whose hands the goblet was found*? Could it be otherwise? The answer is that the brothers said, "God has punished us because we sold Yosef, and now we will all be enslaved. And not only us, but also the one in whose sack the goblet was found — Binyamin, who was not even with us when Yosef was sold." This also explains why they said גַּם אֲנַחְנוּ — *we too*, i.e., we who likewise had no share in the present offense.

Because they caused their father to tear his clothing for Yosef, they were punished and now tore their clothing. And Binyamin, who now tore his garment although he was guiltless, was found worthy of having Mordechai, who wore royal garments in the days of King Achashverosh, as a descendant.

The pursuer was actually Menashe. Because he caused the brothers to tear their clothing, his portion in the Land was torn and split in two, as he received half on one side of the Jordan River and half in *Eretz Yisrael* proper.

On their return to Egypt, the brothers fell to the ground before Yosef. Binyamin, too, fell down before him. Thus was fulfilled the prophecy that the brothers would bow before him, like the eleven stars.

"What can we say to my lord (מַה־נֹּאמַר לַאדֹנִי;44:16). That is, what can we say of the first time that the money was found in our sacks? *What can we speak, and how can we justify ourselves* (מַה נְּדַבֵּר וּמַה נִּצְטַדָּק; 44:16)? That is, what can we say of the goblet? God has found a means of punishing us for our sins."

Even Shoev asks: Why did Yosef want to send them back without Binyamin, causing his father grief? Why did he not reveal his identity immediately? The answer is that Yosef understood that it was hard for Yaakov to leave *Eretz Yisrael* for Egypt. He did not want to be the cause of his father's journey to Egypt. But when Yehudah spoke harshly to him he was forced to reveal himself, which led to Yaakov's coming down. Yosef felt now that it was God's will, and he was not to blame. Yaakov asked God if he should go down, and God replied, אַל תִּירָא מֵרְדָה מִצְרַיְמָה — *Do not fear going down to Egypt* (46:3).

God did not tell Yaakov that Yosef was in Egypt for twenty-two years. It was not yet the time for the exile of Egypt to begin, for Yitzchak was still alive. Yosef knew that Yaakov could not come down because of Yitzchak, and so earlier he had asked, הֲשָׁלוֹם אֲבִיכֶם הַזָּקֵן — *What is the peace of your aged father?* (43:27), which means, Is your grandfather still alive? — Because when he had accused them of being spies they had replied that they came of a fine family — the family of Avraham and Yitzchak. Now, in answer to his question, they answered, שָׁלוֹם לְעַבְדְּךָ לְאָבִינוּ עוֹדֶנּוּ חָי — *Peace to your servant, our father; he still lives* (43:28), in order that he understand that while their father was alive, their grandfather was not. They did not want to tell him the bad news explicitly. We learn from this that one should not explicitly tell bad news, but hint at it, as it says in the *Gemara:* R' Chiya asked Rav, "Is my father alive?" and he answered, "Your mother is living," so that he would understand that his father was not alive.

Yosef said, "Far be it from me to take you all as slaves. I will only take the one in whose bag the goblet was found, and the rest of you can return safely to your father."

פרשת ויגש
Parashas Vayigash
(44:18 — 47:27)

✍ Turning Away Wrath

וַיִּגַּשׁ אֵלָיו יְהוּדָה — *Yehudah approached him* (44:18). Yehudah approached Yosef with pacifying words; as the verse says, מַעֲנֶה רַךְ יָשִׁיב חֵמָה — *A soft answer turns away wrath* (Mishlei 15:1). He tried in his opening speech to arouse Yosef's mercy. In fact Yehudah prepared himself for judgment, for soft words, and for battle. For this reason he said בִּי אֲדֹנִי ("please, my lord"; however, these words can also be interpreted literally as "in me, my lord") — "You will find me prepared for everything: for judgment, soft words, or battle; and you will not be able to stand against me in any of these things." Another explanation is that Yehudah said, "Let the sin be considered *within me*, and I will become a slave. If you ask why I more than my brothers take this upon myself, I have *guaranteed for the boy* (כִּי עַבְדְּךָ עָרַב אֶת הַנַּעַר; 44:32). I guaranteed to my father that I would bring him home."

כִּי כָמוֹךָ כְּפַרְעֹה — *You are like Pharaoh* (44:18). "You are, in my eyes, as important as Pharaoh." Another explanation is that Yehudah was saying, "You will be punished for abducting Binyamin, just as Pharaoh was punished for abducting Sarah. He was struck with leprous sores, as you will be."

✍ The Debate Between Yehudah and Yosef

אֲדֹנִי שָׁאַל אֶת עֲבָדָיו לֵאמֹר הֲיֵשׁ לָכֶם אָב אוֹ אָח — *My lord asked his servants, "Do you have a father or brother?"* (44:19). "Why did you have to question us at all? Did we want to marry your daughter? But since you questioned us, we answered truthfully, that we had an old father and a younger brother, as well as a brother who was dead."

In *Parashas Mikeitz* they said that their brother was lost, rather than dead. They were afraid that if they would repeat that their brother was lost, Yosef would command them to find him and bring him to him. Therefore they said that they had been informed that he had died.

"You told us to bring our younger brother, and we answered that to take the youngster away from his father would cause his father untold grief, which would possibly kill him. But you said that we could not come into your presence without our younger brother. We came to our father and told him all that had occurred, and he said, שְׁנַיִם יָלְדָה לִי אִשְׁתִּי — 'Two sons my wife bore to me (44:27). My beloved wife Rachel had only two sons, Yosef and Binyamin. Yosef is no longer with me, and now you want to take Binyamin too? If something terrible befalls him on the journey, as happened to his brother, I will die of sorrow. When Binyamin is with me I am consoled for the loss of his mother and brother. If I lose Binyamin it will be as if all three died in one day.' "

R' Bechaye writes that Yehudah said to Yosef, "Beware of my father. He cursed Rachel, who stole Lavan's idols, and she died on the journey; he can curse you too. Binyamin is holy, for the Temple will be built in his portion; you must return him to us."

Yehudah continued, "I have guaranteed that I will bring him back. If not, וְחָטָאתִי לְאָבִי כָּל הַיָּמִים — I will have sinned to my father forever (44:32), both in This World and the World to Come."

Yosef answered, "I see in my goblet that you sold your brother. Why did you not guarantee his safety?" When Yehudah heard this he said to Naftali, "Go and scout out how many markets and streets there are in Egypt." Naftali returned and said, "There are twelve markets." Yehudah said, "I will take three markets, and the rest of you take one each to destroy." The brothers said, "If you destroy Egypt, it is as if you destroyed the entire world, for the entire world is now sustained by Egypt."

Yehudah thereupon resumed his debate with Yosef, saying, "You libeled us from the beginning, claiming that we were spies. Now you claim that we stole your goblet. I swear by my father, just as you swore by Pharaoh, that I will paint all of Egypt in blood." Yosef answered, "You have long been painters. You painted Yosef's coat in blood and told your father that a wild animal devoured him."

When they heard his words the brothers agreed to destroy Egypt. Yosef began to fear them, and so revealed his identity. First he commanded that everyone but his brothers leave the room, in order to spare them humiliation in front of the Egyptians who would learn that they had sold their brother. It would have been a painful embarrassment to him as well, to admit to having such brothers. Also, the Egyptians might not have allowed them to live in Egypt [had they known the truth]. Moreover, many courtiers interceded on Binyamin's behalf, and Yosef could not refuse their requests. For all these reasons he told those present to leave the room.

R' Shmuel bar Nachmani says that Yosef placed himself in great danger by commanding that the Egyptians leave, but he was not afraid that the brothers would murder him without anyone else knowing of it. The *Midrash* writes that Yosef told them, "You say that Binyamin's brother is dead, but I will show him to you." He began to call, "Yosef!" The brothers looked all around them, and Yosef said, "What are you looking for? *I am Yosef!*"

The brothers were dumbfounded when confronted with their sin by Yosef. How much more so will men be speechless, when on the Day of Judgment God will confront them with their sins!

◈§ I Am Yosef

אֲנִי יוֹסֵף הַעוֹד אָבִי חָי — *I am Yosef; is my father still alive?* (45:3). On this verse, R' Isser'l writes that Yosef meant to say: "Does my father still have the power of prophecy? If he does, would he not know that I am alive?"

Toldos Yitzchak writes: Why did Yosef ask if his father was still alive, when the brothers had previously told him that he was living? Yosef thought that the brothers may have been afraid that he would kill them because they had sold him, and so they had claimed that their father was still alive. Even the wicked Esav had not wanted to harm Yaakov during Yitzchak's lifetime, so as not to bring sorrow upon his father. How much more so would Yosef have refrained from harming them.

When he saw his brothers' fear he said, גְּשׁוּ נָא אֵלַי — *"Please come near to me* (45:4). I am Yosef, whom you sold. Do not be afraid: God sent me here to save you. You are not responsible for my being here; God is. This you can understand, because you sold me here as a slave, while God has made me a ruler here." Hearing this, the brothers approached him.

R' Bechaye writes that he said, "*I am Yosef your brother.* Even though you sold me I am still your brother, and will not rule over you."

Even Shoev writes that when *afterwards his brothers spoke with him* (וְאַחֲרֵי כֵן דִּבְּרוּ אֶחָיו אִתּוֹ; 45:15), they begged him not to tell Yaakov that they had sold him, for they were afraid that he would curse them. Yaakov did not know that the brothers had sold Yosef, even to the day of his death, as we will see in *Parashas Vayechi.* This is what *Ramban* writes.

If Yaakov had known that they had sold him, he would have requested on his deathbed that Yosef forgive them. Yosef did not let Yaakov know that he had been sold so that Yaakov should not curse his brothers, and also because the brothers had declared that they would excommunicate anyone who revealed what had happened. Although Yosef was not present at the time of that declaration, it was pronounced by ten men and he had to abide by it.

Yosef told them to go to their father immediately and tell him that God had made him a ruler in Egypt, and invite him to come and live in the finest portion of the land, Goshen. R' Bechaye writes that Yosef knew that Yaakov would not want to live in the royal city and so offered them Goshen.

◄§ Bring My Father Here

וְכִלְכַּלְתִּי אֹתְךָ ... פֶּן תִּוָּרֵשׁ — *I will provide for you... lest you become poor* (45:11). *Ramban* writes: Why did Yosef not support his father in Canaan, rather than asking him to move? He was afraid that the king and the Egyptians would suspect him of wishing to build storehouses in Canaan with the ultimate desire of leaving Egypt to live there.

עֵינֵיכֶם רֹאוֹת וְעֵינֵי אָחִי בִנְיָמִין כִּי פִי הַמְדַבֵּר אֲלֵיכֶם — *Your eyes see, and so do the eyes of my brother Binyamin, that it is my mouth that is speaking to you* (45:12). "Your eyes can see that I am your brother. I too am circumcised, and I speak the Holy Tongue." He spoke of them all equally, to show that just as he bore no hatred for Binyamin, who was not present when he was sold, so he bore the others no hatred either.

Chizkuni writes that Yosef told the brothers, "If you do not want to tell my father that I am alive, because of your vow never to do so, allow Binyamin to do it, for he has not sworn."

Toldos Yitzchak asks: How could Yosef use the fact that he spoke Hebrew as a sign of his identity, when many Egyptians could have spoken it? The answer is that Yosef actually said, "Go and ask my father to come here, for there will be five more years of famine. If you do not want to believe me, you can see with your own eyes that my dream of eleven sheaves of wheat bowing down to me has been fulfilled, for it alluded to the eleven brothers who would bow down to me. Why did I command that Binyamin be brought here? So that you should all be here to bow down. Just as that dream came true, so my prophecy of five more years of famine is true." The words, *My mouth that is speaking to you*, thus mean, "You can understand that what I say to you is the truth, and you must bring my father to me, so that I can support him."

◄§ Pharaoh Learns of Yosef's Brothers

וַיִּפֹּל עַל צַוְּארֵי בִנְיָמִין אָחִיו וַיֵּבְךְּ — *He fell on Binyamin's neck and wept* (45:14). He cried because the two Temples which would be built on

Binyamin's land would be destroyed. Binyamin in turn wept for the *Mishkan* of Shiloh which stood in Yosef's territory and was to be destroyed.

Yosef then kissed all of his brothers, to indicate that he bore them no hatred. Word got out to Pharaoh's household that Yosef's brothers had arrived. Pharaoh and his servants rejoiced. Until now they were embarrassed, thinking that Yosef, their ruler, had been a mere servant. Now they realized that he had notable brothers and a distinguished father, and it pleased them.

Pharaoh told Yosef to tell his brothers to load up their animals with wheat and return to Canaan. Pharaoh knew that Yosef was humble and faithful and would not send them the food of his own accord, and therefore he himself commanded it. He also told them to bring their father and his household to Egypt.

וְאִכְלוּ אֶת חֵלֶב הָאָרֶץ — *You will eat the fat of the land* (45:18). The Sages say that unwittingly Pharaoh was here prophesying that when the Jews would be released at the time of the Exodus they would take the best of Egypt with them.

⊷§ Yosef's Wagons and Calves

וַיִּתֵּן לָהֶם יוֹסֵף עֲגָלוֹת — *Yosef gave them wagons* (45:21). He sent a sign with them to Yaakov so that he would believe that he was really Yosef. Immediately before Yosef's departure, while Yaakov accompanied him as he set out on his mission to his brothers, Yaakov had taught him the importance of escorting a guest. This protects a guest from robbers along the highway. In this connection, the Torah commands that when the body of a slain man is discovered on a road, the people of the town closest to where the body is found must sacrifice a calf as an atonement. They must chop off its head and say, "We have not spilled the blood of this man, for we escorted him, and gave him bread for his journey."

Now the verse here says, *Yosef gave them wagons* (עֲגָלוֹת). The word עֲגָלוֹת is the plural form not only of עֲגָלָה ("wagon"), but also of עֶגְלָה ("calf", in reference to the עֶגְלָה עֲרוּפָה, the sacrificed calf mentioned above). By sending Yaakov עֲגָלוֹת, Yosef was thus giving his father a subtle but certain reassurance of his identity, for this sacrifice was the subject of their last conversation immediately before their separation.

⊷§ Yosef's Gifts

לְכֻלָּם נָתַן לָאִישׁ חֲלִפוֹת שְׂמָלֹת — *He gave to each of them changes of clothing* (45:22). He gave them each new clothing. They had torn their clothes in grief over the incident of the stolen goblet and they were ashamed to wear them. He gave Binyamin 300 pieces of silver, because he had not been present at the sale. He did not give the silver to his brothers, as a means of punishing them.

Toldos Yitzchak says that Yosef gave 300 pieces of silver because he had slandered his brothers over three issues. The law is that if one slanders another he must pay 100 pieces of silver. He did not give it directly to the brothers, however, as they had forfeited it by selling him.

He also gave Binyamin five sets of clothing: one because he had torn his own clothing; one because he was his brother from his mother's side as well as his father's; one because Yosef had placed the goblet in his sack, thus making him appear to be a thief; and two because he owed him double — the fine for theft — for having announced before everyone that he was a robber. *Chizkuni* writes this.

R' Bechaye and *Toldos Yitzchak* write that Yosef was alluding to the fact that Mordechai, one of Binyamin's descendants, would wear the five robes of King Achashverosh.

Yosef sent his father ten donkeys laden with food, fine aged wine and all manner of delicacies from all over the world, and luscious fruits. All of the brothers returned to their father. Yehudah traveled with Binyamin, as he had guaranteed his safe return, and had taken on excommunication if he would not return.

R' Bechaye writes that because of this excommunication, Yehudah's bones did not rest in their coffin for forty years. Despite the fact that he had in fact brought Binyamin home safely, and therefore ought not have suffered, he should not have taken such a commitment upon himself, for he could not know if Yosef would allow Binyamin to go free, and so he was punished.

Yosef told them, אַל תִּרְגְּזוּ בַּדָּרֶךְ — *"Do not fear along the way* (45:24), even though you are laden with many delicacies and there is a famine in the land, and robbery is rampant. I have sent you and I am feared all around." He also told them not to quarrel [*al tirg'zu*, "Do not fear," can also be interpreted as "Do not quarrel"] on the journey. One might accuse the other of having spoken ill of Yosef, and hence of causing his sale. In these words he also cautioned them against becoming too embroiled in scholarly argument along the way, lest they get lost.

Imrei Noam writes: Why did Yaakov not caution them likewise against excessive learning on the journey? The answer is that at that stage they had no food, and would have been unable to study; as our Sages say, אִם אֵין קֶמַח אֵין תּוֹרָה — "If there is no flour, there is no Torah." Some Sages say that by these words, Yosef meant to tell them, "If you study on the journey, be certain that you do not interrupt yourselves with small talk, and say things such as, 'What a lovely tree that is, what a fine field that is!' " This is the meaning of the words of the *Gemara* in interpreting Yosef's farewell injunction to his brothers: אַל תִּתְעַסְקוּ בִּדְבַר הֲלָכָה: "Do not busy yourselves in halachic discussions" — do not discuss irrelevant things while learning Torah.

Yosef also cautioned them not to travel too quickly, for this dims the light of the eyes. He felt that they might rush to tell their father the good news.

When Yaakov's children told him that Yosef was alive, *his heart grew faint* (וַיָּפָג לִבּוֹ 45:26). He did not want to believe them. But when they showed him Yosef's sign of the Torah passage which he had learned with his father regarding the duty of escorting guests, he believed the tidings.

◆§ Yaakov is Revived

וַתְּחִי רוּחַ יַעֲקֹב אֲבִיהֶם — *Their father Yaakov's spirit revived* (45:27). Once more the prophetic spirit rested upon him. The entire time that he was unaware of Yosef's fate the spirit of prophecy was withheld from him, for we see that for twenty-two years Yosef was only five days' journey away and yet Yaakov had no inkling of this. So writes *Midrash Tanchuma.*

◆§ Enough; My Son is Alive

רַב עוֹד יוֹסֵף בְּנִי חָי — *It is enough. My son, Yosef, is alive* (45:28). Even if he was not a ruler, it would be enough for me to know that he is alive. This is what *Chizkuni* writes.

Yaakov journeyed to Be'er Sheva, *and brought sacrifices to the God of his father Yitzchak* (וַיִּזְבַּח זְבָחִים לֵאלֹהֵי אָבִיו יִצְחָק; 46:1). Yaakov mentioned Yitzchak, his father, when bringing the sacrifices, rather than his grandfather Avraham. We learn from this that one is obligated to honor one's father more than one's grandfather.

Chizkuni writes: Why did Yaakov bring the sacrifices in Be'er Sheva? Because his father Yitzchak had also brought sacrifices there. This is the reason that Yitzchak is mentioned, rather than Avraham. And why did Yaakov bring sacrifices at all? Since he saw that his children were to be exiled in Egypt, he brought sacrifices and prayed that God would be merciful with them in their exile.

God appeared to Yaakov, and said: אָנֹכִי הָאֵל אֱלֹהֵי אָבִיךְ — *I am the God of your father* (46:3). "I forbade your father to leave *Eretz Yisrael,* but you should not fear going to Egypt." *Chizkuni* writes that Yaakov was afraid to go to Egypt because he would begin the exile which God had spoken of to Avraham. God told him, "Even though your children will be in exile, ultimately they will receive what I have promised, and in exile will become a great nation."

⋖§ Twelve, Seventy, Six Hundred Thousand

אָנֹכִי אֵרֵד עִמְּךָ מִצְרַיְמָה וְאָנֹכִי אַעַלְךָ גַם עָלֹה — *I will go down with you to Egypt, and I will surely bring you up* (46:4). "I will eventually bring your children out of there." God also promised Yaakov that he himself would be buried in *Eretz Yisrael*. The verse states, *I will bring you up, and bring you* (ibid.), meaning that the fathers of the Twelve Tribes too would be buried in *Eretz Yisrael*, and would be brought to the World to Come.

The word for "I" in this promise — אָנֹכִי — shows that it was by virtue of their acceptance of the Ten Commandments, which commence with this word, אָנֹכִי, that their descendants would be found deserving of entering *Eretz Yisrael* and ultimately the World to Come. Just as God was with the Jews in Egyptian exile, so was He with them during the Babylonian exile, and so He watches over us always. Because God was with the Jews in Egypt, seventy souls increased to six hundred thousand men.

R' Bechaye writes: A *rav* once gave a speech. The townspeople were not at all interested, and quite a number of them began to doze. He wanted to awaken them, and so he said, "There was a woman in Egypt who gave birth to six hundred thousand children at one time." All the people looked up, and asked who the woman was. He answered, "It was Yocheved. She gave birth to Moshe, whose deeds were equivalent to those of the six hundred thousand men of Israel."

⋖§ Yosef's Hands

וְיוֹסֵף יָשִׁית יָדוֹ עַל עֵינֶיךָ — *Yosef will place his hands on your eyes* (46:4). *Chizkuni* writes that this was God's promise — that Yosef would still be alive at the time of Yaakov's death, and would close his eyes with his own hands. It is a humiliation to leave a dead man's eyes open. God promised Yaakov that Yosef would bring him, with honor, to burial in *Eretz Yisrael*.

⋖§ The Value of Money

וַיִּקְחוּ אֶת מִקְנֵיהֶם וְאֶת רְכוּשָׁם — *They took their cattle and their goods* (46:6). Yaakov and his children took their animals, and the goods which they had amassed in *Eretz Yisrael*. That which they had amassed in Padan Aram they gave to Esav, as his portion, in place of his part in the ancestral burial ground. Yaakov said, "I do not want money which does not come from *Eretz Yisrael*." He placed a great heap of gold and silver before Esav and said, "Take this instead of your portion in the cave." This Yaakov did even though money was not worthless in his eyes, as we have seen that he once returned for some small jugs which he had forgotten; in fact honestly-gained money should be important, for that is difficult to earn.

◆§ The Sons' Wives

שָׁאוּל בֶּן הַכְּנַעֲנִית — *Shaul, son of the Canaanite woman* (46:10). The Torah enumerates Yaakov's descendants, and states that one of Shimon's children was called "Shaul, son of the Canaanite woman." This refers to the son of Dinah, who was abducted by Shechem, the Canaanite.

Dinah was reluctant to leave Shechem's house, for she was afraid that no man would ever want to marry her, so Shimon swore that he would take her as a wife. Despite the fact that she was his sister, he fulfilled his promise, and she bore him a son, Shaul.

A twin daughter was born with each of Yaakov's sons, and each took one of them as a wife. The Torah does not state explicitly that each brother married his twin. Rather, it says כָּל הַנֶּפֶשׁ הַבָּאָה לְיַעֲקֹב מִצְרַיְמָה יֹצְאֵי יְרֵכוֹ מִלְּבַד נְשֵׁי בְנֵי יַעֲקֹב — *all the souls that came to Egypt with Yaakov, that came from his loins, not counting the wives of Yaakov's sons* (46:26); this leads us to understand that the wives were also Yaakov's children, and each son married his twin sister. There were seventy souls, with Yaakov as the seventy-first, just as in Egypt there were seventy elders, and Moshe was the head over all of them. Similarly, there are seventy nations in the world, and Israel; and there are seventy angels surrounding the Holy Throne, with God ruling over them.

◆§ Seventy Souls

וּבְנֵי יְהוּדָה עֵר וְאוֹנָן — *The sons of Yehudah were Er and Onan* (46:12). *Chizkuni* writes that Er and Onan are included, even though they had died before Yaakov's arrival in Egypt, because Yehudah had caused all of them to go to exile. Had he stopped the brothers from selling Yosef, they would not have had to come to Egypt. Since he thereby caused his father great pain God said, "Even at the time that your father feels great happiness, we will mention your children who died, so that you shall feel pain [like that which you caused your father]."

בְּנֵי רָחֵל אֵשֶׁת יַעֲקֹב — *The sons of Rachel the wife of Yaakov* (46:19). Why is only Rachel singled out as *the wife of Yaakov?* — Because she was the one most beloved by him.

כָּל נֶפֶשׁ שִׁשִּׁים וָשֵׁשׁ — *All the soul was sixty-six* (46:26). Why does the Torah use the word for soul (נֶפֶשׁ) in the singular form? Because Yaakov and his progeny served only one God in the same manner, and so they are compared to one soul.

◀§ Showing the Way with Torah

לְהוֹרֹת לְפָנָיו — *To show before him* (46:28). Yaakov sent Yehudah ahead to show them the way to Goshen, in order to avoid the necessity of going through the metropolis of Egypt. This is what *Chizkuni* writes. *Rashi* writes that he sent him ahead to prepare a place to learn Torah (לְהוֹרֹת meaning both "to show," and "to teach").

◀§ Supremely Honored

וַיֶּאְסֹר יוֹסֵף מֶרְכַּבְתּוֹ — *Yosef prepared his chariot* (46:29). Yosef himself prepared it, out of respect and eagerness to meet his father. R' Yehudah says that two men were more honored than all others. One is Yaakov, for when Yosef went to greet him, all of Egypt's nobles went forth with great pomp. The second is Yisro (Jethro), for Moshe himself went out to greet him.

◀§ He Wept ...

וַיִּפֹּל עַל צַוָּארָיו וַיֵּבְךְּ — *He fell on his neck, and wept* (46:29). Yosef fell upon his father and wept. Yaakov did not fall upon his son, for he was reciting the *Shema*. Yosef however did not pray at that moment, for he was fulfilling the commandment of honoring his father, and so was exempt from the commandment of saying *Shema*.

Ramban says that Yosef could not have fallen on his father, for that would have been unseemly. Rather, he ought to have bowed before his father, in awe. His understanding of the verse is that actually Yaakov fell upon Yosef's neck.

◀§ ... and Wept

וַיֵּבְךְּ... עוֹד — *He wept ... more* (46:29). Yaakov wept even more. Just as he had wept upon losing him, now he wept because of his great joy — as elderly men generally do, both from misery and happiness.

Yaakov told Yosef, אָמוּתָה הַפָּעַם — *I will die at this time* (46:30). That is to say, "I know now that I will die only once. I thought that I would die twice, once in This World and once in the Next World. I thought God would punish me for having sent you away, and thereby causing your death. The Divine Presence left me. But today, since you are alive, I know that I will die only once — in This World." This is what *Rashi* writes. But *Toldos Yitzchak* writes that Yaakov said, "If I had not seen you alive, I could have been considered dead long ago, from the time that they showed me your bloody, torn coat. But today, seeing that you are alive, I will die only once, when my time comes."

◄§ Yaakov Meets Pharaoh

אֶעֱלֶה וְאַגִּידָה לְפַרְעֹה — *I shall go and tell Pharaoh* (46:31). Yosef said, "I will go and tell Pharaoh that my father and my brothers have arrived. When he asks you what you do for a living, tell him that you are shepherds in the field, just as your forefathers were. Say that you have many flocks of sheep, and you have no time to devote to other occupations."

Yosef took five of his brothers to present to Pharaoh. He took Reuven, Shimon, Levi, Binyamin and Yissachar, as they were the weakest of the brothers. Pharaoh asked them what they did for a living. They answered that they were shepherds and had come because of a dearth of pasture in Canaan, and asked permission to settle in the land of Goshen.

Pharaoh told Yosef, "Your brothers and their households may settle in Goshen, and you may settle your father wherever it pleases you. If there are strong men among your brothers, make them responsible for my flocks of sheep also. Shepherds must stay in the desert, where there are many wild beasts, and so they must be strong, valiant men."

Yosef also presented his father to Pharaoh, and Yaakov paid his compliments to Pharaoh. The king asked him how old he was, and Yaakov answered, "I am not elderly, but my sorrows have aged me. My forefathers were older than I, but I have been forced to live as a stranger all of my difficult life, wandering from place to place."

Chizkuni writes that God thereupon said to Yaakov, "I saved you from Esav, and from Lavan, and from Shechem, and gave you back Dinah and Yosef -- and yet you complain that you have lived short and difficult years? For the thirty-three words which you said to Pharaoh I will take away thirty-three years from the years of your forefathers [i.e., Yaakov was to live thirty-three years less than his father]." From this we learn that a man should love God, even when things do not go well for him. He should not speak against God, for God does everything for the man's own good.

Imrei Noam writes that because Yaakov said that he would stay in Egypt only as long as the famine persisted, and afterwards hoped to return to *Eretz Yisrael*, Pharaoh asked him how old he was, wondering if he thought that he would live long enough to return to *Eretz Yisrael* after the famine.

The *Midrash* writes that Pharaoh was lodging with Avimelech when Avraham was there. There was a low doorway in Avimelech's home, with an idol placed overhead, so that whoever walked through the door had to bend, and found himself bowing down to the idol. But when Avraham entered, the door lifted itself up, so that he would not have to bend. There was a similar door in Pharaoh's house, with an idol placed next to it. When Yaakov entered, this door likewise lifted itself up. Pharaoh therefore inquired as to Yaakov's age, thinking that he was Avraham.

Yaakov blessed Pharaoh. Since there is no rain in Egypt for the fields, his blessing was that the Nile should rise to greet him, overflow its banks, and irrigate them.

◆§ Yosef the Supporter

וַיְכַלְכֵּל יוֹסֵף אֶת אָבִיו וְאֶת אֶחָיו — *Yosef supported his father and his brothers* (47:12). He supported his father, brothers, and their households, with enough bread even for the children, who are wasteful.

Yosef amassed all of the money received from Egypt and Canaan in exchange for the wheat, and put it in Pharaoh's vaults. When there was no more money the people came to Yosef and begged for bread, saying, *Why should we die before your very eyes?* Yosef said, *Give me your animals.* They gave him their animals and Yosef gave them bread for a full year. And when the year ended Yosef took their fields and gave them bread in exchange.

Ramban writes: Why did the Egyptians tell Yosef that there was no more money in all of Egypt and Canaan? What difference would it make if there was money in Canaan? They told Yosef, "There is no money anywhere, and no one can buy any wheat. Why should we die of hunger for no reason? There is no one else who can buy the wheat."

◆§ Famine Postponed

וְתֶן זֶרַע — *Give [us] seeds* (47:19). They asked for seeds with which to sow their fields. Yosef had predicted a famine of five more years in which they could not sow, and if he was proved wrong he would be regarded as a false prophet. Nevertheless he now gave them the seeds, because when Yaakov came to Egypt the Nile rose to greet him and irrigated all of the fields, so all of Pharaoh's servants realized that the blessing on the land came because of a unique reason — Yaakov's presence there. *Ramban* writes that when Yaakov died the five remaining years of famine began again, but when Yaakov was there there was a blessing on the world.

קְנֵה אֹתָנוּ — *Buy us* (47:19). *Ramban* writes: Why does the Torah say a second time that Yosef bought only their fields? The Egyptians wanted to sell themselves as slaves to Pharaoh, and to sell their fields to him for his own use. Yosef said, "I will buy the fields only if I can buy you as well, as slaves to work the fields." It says that his main intent was to buy the fields, and he bought them only to work the fields.

Yosef said, "By rights, I should only give you one-fifth of the land for yourselves, and the other four-fifths should go to Pharaoh, since both the fields and you belong to him. But I will act kindly and will take a fifth of your land to Pharaoh, and leave you with four-fifths for yourselves. But you must serve Pharaoh, and work his fields."

Since Yosef was afraid that this duty might be forgotten in the course of time, and each farmer would only maintain his stake in his own field, he moved the people around from one region to the other.

As for the Egyptian priests, they were provided with bread from Pharaoh's table.

פרשת ויחי
Parashas Vayechi
(47:28 — 50:26)

◄§ Yaakov Lived

וַיְחִי יַעֲקֹב — *Yaakov lived* (47:28). King Solomon says in the Book of *Mishlei* (12:28), בְּאֹרַח צְדָקָה חַיִּים — *Life is on the path of charity.* It is known that a man's lifespan is contingent on many factors, such as the stars and constellations. With luck, a person lives long, without it a person does not. But charity is more powerful than the stars. Even if he was not destined to live a long life, if a man gives charity he lengthens his years. Our Sages have said that charity is so far-reaching that it extends up to the Holy Throne, meaning it rises above the constellations. We see this illustrated in this portion. Yaakov was not destined to have lived [for long, after he had been reunited with Yosef], yet because he supported Yosef for seventeen years of his life, until their separation, it was granted to Yaakov to live another seventeen years, while Yosef supported him, and he thus lived 147 years in all. God repays measure for measure.

This *parashah* is "closed" *(setumah)* meaning that in the *sefer* Torah there is no space left between it and the end of the *parashah* preceding it *(Vayigash)*. This is because Yaakov's death is discussed in this portion. With his death the eyes and hearts of all Israel were "closed", as a result of the agonies of exile. Another explanation: Yaakov intended to tell his children when the last exile would end, but the Divine Presence left him, so that he could not reveal when the *Mashiach* (Messiah) would come. Because of this obscurity, the *parashah* is blocked, or closed.

The *Midrash* says that Yaakov saw that the letters *ches* and *tes* were missing in the names of all of his children. Together these letters spell out *chet* ("sin"). Because they were free of sin he wanted to tell them when the end of the exile would be. But then he realized that their names were also without the letters *kuf* and *tzaddi*, which together spell the word *ketz*, or "end", and so he refrained from telling them when the exile would come to an end. For this reason too the portion is closed.

Even Shoev writes that for the entire seventeen years that Yaakov was in Egypt no woman miscarried, no one had a toothache, and no woman gave birth prematurely. *Even Shoev* also writes that the word וַיְחִי *(and he lived)* is numerically equivalent to thirty-four. Yaakov's real life was only thirty-four years: the seventeen years that Yosef lived with him until they were separated, and the seventeen years when he lived in Egypt. The other years were not real living.

◆§ Yaakov and Yisrael

וַיִּקְרְבוּ יְמֵי יִשְׂרָאֵל לָמוּת — *The days grew near for Yisrael to die* (47:29). Yaakov felt that his energy was dissipating, and he understood that soon he would die. He called for his son Yosef, to make him swear that he would carry him back to Canaan for burial. R' Bechaye writes: Why does the Torah first say *Yaakov lived,* and afterwards, *for Yisrael to die?* The name Yaakov alludes to bodily concerns, as is hinted in the word *akev,* "heel" — lowly things. The name Yisrael, derived from a root (שרר) meaning dominion, alludes to concerns of the soul — elevated things. When he came to Egypt the Torah called him Yaakov, for he came to allay his bodily need for food; now, when he grew weak and near death, when his soul was about to leave his body to go to the place of true life in the Next World, he is called Yisrael.

◆§ An Altruistic Favor

וַיִּקְרָא לִבְנוֹ לְיוֹסֵף — *Yaakov called for his son Yosef* (47:29). Even though Reuven was the eldest and Yehudah the ruler, he called for Yosef, because he governed Egypt and was in the best position to ensure that he be brought to Canaan for burial. Yaakov said, וְעָשִׂיתָ עִמָּדִי חֶסֶד וֶאֱמֶת — *Deal with me kindly and truthfully* (47:29). The kindness shown to a dead man is called חֶסֶד שֶׁל אֱמֶת, "true kindness," because there is no hope for repayment.

◆§ Not in Egypt

אַל נָא תִקְבְּרֵנִי בְּמִצְרָיִם — *Please do not bury me in Egypt* (47:29). "Do not bury me in Egypt, because the earth of Egypt is destined to be plagued by lice."

R' Bechaye adds a further reason. Yaakov was afraid to be buried in Egypt because he felt that the Egyptians would worship him as an idol, and God punishes those who worship idols. Since the earth of *Eretz Yisrael* atones for sins, as the verse says, הָעָם הַיּשֵׁב בָּהּ נְשֻׂא עָוֹן — *The nation who dwells within her, its sin is forgiven* (Yeshayahu 33:24), and since the gate of heaven, through which prayers arise, is located there, he wanted to be buried there, and from there his soul would ascend to heaven.

Yaakov said, וְשָׁכַבְתִּי עִם אֲבֹתַי — *I will lie with my forefathers* (47:30). R' Yitzchak learns from this that on the day that a man dies, he becomes aware of his final destination. For this reason he first said, *I will lie with my forefathers,* and afterwards asked to be carried back to Canaan. He knew that his soul would immediately go to his fathers. Even if a man dies in the middle of a desert, he joins his fathers.

Yaakov commanded that he be brought where his forefathers were buried. From this we learn that one ought to bury a righteous man next to another righteous man, and a wicked man next to another wicked man.

Yosef told him, אָנֹכִי אֶעֱשֶׂה כִדְבָרֶיךָ — *I will do as you have said* (47:30). This is to say, "Just as you have made me swear to take you to *Eretz Yisrael,* so I will have the others swear to bury me in *Eretz Yisrael.*"

וַיִּשָּׁבַע לוֹ — *He swore to him* (47:31). *Ramban* asks: Why did Yosef have to swear? Yaakov was afraid that Pharaoh would want him buried in Egypt, so that his merit would protect them. However, Pharaoh would not make Yosef break a solemn vow.

✒§ Yisrael Bows

וַיִּשְׁתַּחוּ יִשְׂרָאֵל עַל רֹאשׁ הַמִּטָּה — *Yisrael bowed at the head of the bed* (47:31). Yisrael bowed down upon hearing the good news. He bowed towards the head of the bed, because the Divine Presence lies over the head of a sickbed. This expression can also be read, "from the beginning of his bed," meaning, from beginning to end his bed was whole, and no one wicked was born to him — all his children were righteous. Even Yosef, who lived among the idol worshipers, was righteous.

This moment was the final fulfillment of Yosef's dream, for his father, too, now bowed down to him.

✒§ Yaakov Weakens ...

וַיְהִי אַחֲרֵי הַדְּבָרִים הָאֵלֶּה — *It was after these things* (48:1). Some time after this, Yosef was told that his father had weakened. *Chizkuni* writes that from the time the world was created until Yaakov's death, men did not become weak. They would simply sneeze and fall down dead, even on the street or on a journey. (For this reason one answers "Your health!" when someone sneezes.) Yaakov prayed that he should become weak before death, so that he should know when to leave his children his last will and testament.

God heeded his prayers, and he fell ill.

Yaakov sent Efraim, who was constantly at his side, to tell Yosef that he had become weak. *Even Shoev* writes that Yosef was careful not to be with his father, in order to avoid conversing with him about the circumstances of his sale to Egypt. He never told him what had happened, and used to say that he had lost his way. This was not true, but one may tell a white lie for the sake of peace.

◆§ ... Yisrael Strengthens Himself

וַיִּתְחַזֵּק יִשְׂרָאֵל — *Yisrael strengthened himself* (48:2). Yaakov gathered his remaining strength and sat up on the edge of his bed. Yaakov wanted to show his respect for Yosef who, although he was his son, was also a ruler. Similarly, Moshe later showed respect for Pharaoh despite his wickedness, because he was a ruler.

Chizkuni writes that Yaakov sat up to show that he was in full possession of his faculties. If a man who is sick gives a gift, he may live to regret it, if he is cured. We can say that he gave it without his full understanding. Yaakov therefore sat up to prove that he was not sick; he wanted to bless his children, and would not want to have any regrets later.

Yaakov said, "God promised that I would have another two tribes after Binyamin, but I had no more. I see, then, that one tribe must be split and take two portions in *Eretz Yisrael*. This gift I bequeath to Yosef: Menashe and Efraim, his sons, will each take a portion of *Eretz Yisrael*, equal to the portions of Reuven and Shimon." He decreed this out of respect for Rachel. Because Yosef was her eldest child, he gave him two portions.

Yaakov told Yosef, וַאֲנִי בְּבֹאִי מִפַּדָּן מֵתָה עָלַי רָחֵל — *When I came from Padan, Rachel died* (48:7), and so on. That is to say, "I know that you may hold it against me that I am troubling you to carry my body back to Canaan, while I did not do the same for your mother Rachel. She died during a journey, and I did not bury her in our ancestral burial ground, nor even in the city of Beis Lechem (Bethlehem), which was close to the place where she died. You should know therefore that God commanded me to do so. When the Jews go to exile in the time of Nevuzaradan, they will take the same road. Rachel will stand up in her tomb and pray to God, and God will listen to her."

Chizkuni writes: Why did Yaakov not bury Rachel in the Cave of Machpelah? Because at that time Esav was still disputing ownership of the cave, and she could not have rested peacefully there. But when the time came to bury Leah, Esav had waived his claim and had left the cave for Yaakov. Another explanation is that the land in which Rachel is buried lies in a portion of *Eretz Yisrael* which would belong to her son, which is a sign of respect for her. But the Cave of Machpelah lies in the portion of Yehudah, a son of Leah, and it would not have been proper to bury Rachel there.

Chizkuni and *Toldos Yitzchak* ask: *Rashi* says that she was not buried in *Eretz Yisrael*, but we find that she actually was! The answer is that she was not buried in any *city* of *Eretz Yisrael*; she was buried in a field. *Ramban* writes that Yaakov was ashamed to have two sisters buried together with him in the cave. Why did he choose Leah? — Because his marriage to her was of undisputed validity [whereas his marriage to Rachel, as the second sister whom he married, posed halachic problems].

◆§ The Divine Presence Retreats ...

וַיַּרְא יִשְׂרָאֵל אֶת בְּנֵי יוֹסֵף — *Yisrael saw Yosef's sons* (48:8). *Chizkuni* adds: If Yaakov's vision was impaired (48:10), how could he see Yosef's children? The answer is that he understood that they were Yosef's children, and he recognized Yosef himself by his voice. Yaakov wanted to bless Yosef's children, but the Divine Presence left him, because Efraim's descendants would include the wicked Yerovam and Achav, while Yehu and his children would descend from Menashe.

◆§ ... and Returns

וַיֹּאמֶר מִי אֵלֶּה — *He said, "Who are these?"* (48:8). Yaakov asked, "Who are these children, who are not worthy of receiving a blessing?" Yosef answered, "They are my children, born of a marriage performed with *chuppah* and *kiddushin*" (i.e., a halachically valid marriage). He showed Yaakov the marriage contract and prayed, and the Divine Presence returned to Yaakov. Yaakov then told Yosef to bring the children closer to him, so that he could bless them.

◆§ Sight and Insight

וְעֵינֵי יִשְׂרָאֵל כָּבְדוּ מִזֹּקֶן — *Yisrael's eyes had dimmed with age* (48:10). *Toldos Yitzchak* writes: Why does the verse tell us now that Yisrael could not see? Because, when one wishes to bless another, it is customary to look at the one receiving the blessing, so that the blessing will rest upon him. Yaakov could not see and thus requested that they be brought to his side where he could touch them, and in that way the blessing would rest upon them. Because nowadays few people have clear vision, we must bless with our hands.

Yaakov told Yosef, "I had thought I would not live to see you again. Now God has even allowed me to see your children." When

Yaakov kissed the boys, וַיּוֹצֵא יוֹסֵף אֹתָם מֵעִם בִּרְכָּיו — *Yosef brought them out from between his knees* (48:12). He placed them properly, with the elder, Menashe, on Yaakov's right, and Efraim, the younger, on the left. Yaakov then switched his hands. He understood that Yosef wanted to place Menashe on the right side and Efraim on the left, but he saw in prophecy that Efraim would have greater descendants than Menashe, and so he intentionally crossed his hands and placed his right hand on Efraim's head.

He did not want to humiliate Menashe by placing him on his left side, and so he allowed them to stand where Yosef had placed them. This explains the phrase here, כִּי מְנַשֶּׁה הַבְּכוֹר — *because Menashe was the first-born* (48:14).

When Yosef saw that Yaakov had placed his right hand on Efraim he was displeased, and removed his father's hands to replace them correctly. His father told him, יָדַעְתִּי בְנִי יָדַעְתִּי — *I know, my son, I know* (48:19). "I am aware that Menashe is the elder and will grow into a great nation, but the younger brother will be even greater. Menashe's descendant will be Gidon, through whom God will perform a miracle for Israel. But Yehoshua (Joshua) will come from Efraim, and he will help Israel inherit their land, and will teach them the Torah and battle the idol-worshiping nations. He will cause the sun to stand still in Givon and will lengthen the day so that he can destroy the idol worshipers, and he will stop the moon because of his battle in Emek Ayalon."

Ramban asks: Why was Yosef distressed when his father placed his right hand on Efraim's head? He thought that this indicated that his father had lost the gift of prophecy, and had placed his right hand on the head of the younger grandson in error. He therefore feared that the blessings, having been given in error, would not be fulfilled. Yaakov however reassured him, saying that he had not made a mistake, and knew which child was which.

Toldos Yitzchak writes: Why did Yosef wait until the end of the first blessing, before trying to move his father's hands? He thought that Yaakov wished to show equal regard for both children, by blessing Efraim with his right hand, and Menashe with a greater blessing. But when he saw that their blessings had been equal, he was disturbed that the right hand had been placed on Efraim.

It was to this train of thought that Yaakov answered, *I know, my son, I know.* That is to say, "I know two things. I know why I placed my right hand on Efraim's head and I know that I did not give Menashe the greater blessing. And indeed I will give Efraim a further blessing. When in time to come Jews will bless their children they will say, יְשִׂמְךָ אֱלֹהִים כְּאֶפְרַיִם וְכִמְנַשֶּׁה — *May God make you like*

Efraim and Menashe (48:20). Efraim's name will be said before that of Menashe."

R' Bechaye says: *"He placed Efraim before Menashe* (אֶת וַיָּשֶׂם אֶפְרַיִם לִפְנֵי מְנַשֶּׁה ;48:20) as a servant is placed before a master, in order to serve him." He said, "You are the younger and Menashe is the elder, so you must pay him respect."

After he had blessed Efraim and Menashe, Yaakov gave Yosef a separate blessing and told him of the exile and of the redemption which God would bring to the People of Israel.

◈§ Efraim and Menashe like Reuven and Shimon

שְׁכֶם אַחַד עַל אַחֶיךָ — *One portion above your brothers* (48:22). Yaakov told Yosef, "I have given you your birthright, so that you have one portion more than your brothers. Efraim and Menashe will have two portions, equal to Reuven and Shimon, in the land which you will take away from the Amorites. And because I have troubled you with my request to bring my body to Canaan, I give you the city of Shechem to be buried in."

◈§ Prophecy Turned to Blessing

בְּאַחֲרִית הַיָּמִים — *In the end of days* (49:1). Yaakov called for his children, wishing to speak to them of *the end of days*. He had wanted to reveal to them when the *Mashiach* would come, but the Divine Presence left him and he began to speak of other things.

◈§ Reuven's Blessing: Admonition and Forgiveness.

He said, רְאוּבֵן בְּכֹרִי אַתָּה כֹּחִי וְרֵאשִׁית אוֹנִי — *Reuven, you are my eldest, my first strength* (49:3), for until he had had relations with Leah, he had emitted no semen. "You ought to have had the priesthood, the kingship." *Toldos Yitzchak* writes that "first" refers to the fact that as the eldest Reuven ought to have had the priesthood, with all the gifts that go along with it: *terumah*, the first of the wheat; *challah*, the first of the dough; and the first of the sacrifices.

At the time of his marriage Yaakov had been very powerful. We see that he single-handedly took the rock off the well, a feat which was difficult for whole groups of men. He married Leah, and Reuven was born soon afterward, so he ought to have inherited that valor. Why did he not get it? Because his temper gushed like torrents of water, and he was therefore not worthy of kingship. He lost his birthright because he tampered with his father's bed, because of his fear that his portion would be lessened if his father had more children. Because he profaned his father's bed, he lost the priesthood, and was not singled out for sanctity.

Chizkuni writes that from the time that Reuven removed his father's bed from Bilhah's tent, Yaakov did not have relations with her.

יְצוּעִי עָלָה — *He climbed up on my bed* (49:4). Yaakov told his children, "Look, he went up upon the bed which was mine." R' Bechaye writes that מִשְׁכְּבֵי אָבִיךָ — *your father's bed (ibid.)*, refers to the two beds which Reuven had profaned (מִשְׁכְּבֵי implies a plural form) — the resting-place of the Divine Presence which hovered over Yaakov's bed, and Yaakov's bed itself.

The *Midrash* says that Yaakov told Reuven, "You will not be absolved of this shame until Moshe counts you first among those who will stand on Mt. Eval, at the time that the curses will be pronounced. At that time they will say, אָרוּר שֹׁכֵב עִם אֵשֶׁת אָבִיו — *Cursed is the one who lies with the wife of his father (Devarim 27:20)*, and that will be a sign to all of Israel that your sin has been forgiven, for you yourself will curse the others that commit that sin."

◈§ Shimon's and Levi's Blessing: Conspiracy, Teachers and Tithes

Yaakov then called to Shimon and Levi and said, שִׁמְעוֹן וְלֵוִי אַחִים — *"Shimon and Levi, brothers* (49:5) — brothers and conspirators in the killing of Shechem and in Yosef's sale." Another interpretation is that he meant, "You acted as brothers to Dinah, and were willing to sacrifice your lives for her honor, but you were not brotherly to Yosef, because you cast him into the pit and sold him." Why did Yosef put Shimon into jail in Egypt? — So that he could atone thereby for the sin of having sold him.

כְּלֵי חָמָס מְכֵרֹתֵיהֶם — *Instruments of violence are their wares* (49:5). Yaakov said, "You have stolen the sword which rightfully belongs to Esav."

בְּסֹדָם אַל תָּבֹא נַפְשִׁי — *Let my soul not enter their plot* (49:6). "Let my soul remain removed from the episode of Zimri. When the tribe of Shimon gather together to bring a Midianite woman to Moshe and ask if it is permissible to have relations with her; and when Moshe tells them that it is forbidden, and they retort, 'Who gave you permission to marry Yisro's daughter?' — do not mention my name in that episode." This request was fulfilled, as the verse there says, *Zimri, son of Salu, head of a clan in the tribe of Shimon (Bamidbar 25:14)*. It does not say, "Shimon, son of Yaakov."

"Likewise, in the episode of Korach, which will involve the tribe of Levi, do not mention my name." And indeed the verse states,

Korach, son of Yitzhar, son of Kehas, son of Levi (Bamidbar 16:1) —
and does not refer to Levi's father, Yaakov.

אָרוּר אַפָּם — *Cursed be their anger* (49:7). "Let their rage be cursed.
Let God not give them the opportunity to curse others, so that they
will be unable to harm others with their anger." So writes *Chizkuni*.
Rashi says that even when Yaakov rebuked them, he refrained from
cursing anything but their anger.

אֲחַלְּקֵם בְּיַעֲקֹב — *I will disperse them in Yaakov* (49:7). The tribe of
Shimon were teachers and scribes and as a result were spread out
through the Land; Levi was also dispersed, but in a more honorable
way. They were spread about the granaries throughout the Land in
order to be able to receive their tithes.

When Yehudah heard his father rebuke his brothers with harsh
words, he began to back away. His father called him back with reassuring words, saying, "You are not like your brothers. *You, your
brothers will praise* (אַתָּה יוֹדוּךָ אַחֶיךָ; 49:8). *Your hand will be on the
back of your enemies' necks (ibid.)*; you will defeat your enemies,
who will retreat before you. *Your father's children will bow down to
you (ibid.).*" Why did Yaakov say *your father's children* (בְּנֵי אָבִיךָ),
rather than calling them "your brothers"? Yaakov had had several
wives, and wanted to show Yehudah that all the children would bow
to him, even those who did not share the same mother.

◄§ Yehudah's Blessing: Brotherliness, Monarchy, Messiah

גּוּר אַרְיֵה יְהוּדָה — *Yehudah is a young lion* (49:9). Yaakov was here
referring to Yehudah's descendant David. In the days of Shaul
(Saul), David would be compared to a young lion, leading Israel to
victory. After Shaul's death he would be a grown lion, meaning, he
alone would be king.

מִטֶּרֶף בְּנִי עָלִיתָ — *You have risen from prey, my son* (49:9). "I
suspected that you killed Yosef, but it is not so. Actually, it was you
who saved him from death, by asking your brothers what benefit
could be derived from killing him. In the episode of Tamar you admitted that you were the father of her child, and thus saved her from
death. For this you will be found worthy of having King Solomon as
a descendant, and during his reign Israel will live in peace." This is
what *Rashi* writes.

Chizkuni writes that *You have risen from prey* means, "You will
be praised for destroying all of your enemies."

It can be asked of *Rashi*: Why was Yehudah praised for having
asked his brothers what they would gain out of murdering Yosef?
The *Gemara* says that it would certainly be an error to praise him for

having said, מַה בֶּצַע כִּי נַהֲרֹג אֶת אָחִינוּ — *What profit will we derive from killing our brother?* (37:26). For that implies that if there were a monetary benefit to be derived, it would have been permissible to kill him. Rather, his question means, "What would we get out of killing anyone?" — even someone who was not a brother. And, more specifically, אָחִינוּ — *our brother:* even if we would derive money from it, it would be forbidden to murder him.

Reuven's suggestion, that he be thrown into a pit to avoid shedding blood, was also an unworthy one, and to this Yehudah replied, — *"And we will cover his blood:* Can we cover the pit? His blood will scream from the earth!" The *Gemara* concludes that the question, *"What profit ...?"* was not praiseworthy, but for everything else which he said — "He is our brother and we ought not harm him, even if we were to get something out of it" — he was praised.

R' Bechaye writes that because Yehudah saved Yosef from death in the pit, Daniel — a descendant of Yehudah — was saved from the pit of the lions. Because Yehudah confessed that he had made Tamar pregnant and thus saved her and her two children from being burned, God saved three of Yehudah's descendants, Chananiah, Mishael and Azariah, from the furnace. Both Temples were built by Yehudah's descendants. Shlomo HaMelech built the first, and the second was built by Zerubavel, who was also Yehudah's descendant. And the third will be built by the *Mashiach*, also of the tribe of Yehudah.

לֹא יָסוּר שֵׁבֶט מִיהוּדָה ... עַד כִּי יָבֹא שִׁילֹה — *The scepter will not depart from Yehudah ... until Shiloh comes* (49:10). The kingship, and the leadership of the *nesi'im* in *Eretz Yisrael*, will not be taken away from Yehudah; they will remain his until the coming of the *Mashiach*, to whom kingship belongs, for then all will bring him tribute and sacrifices. R' Bechaye writes that this means that the kingship of Yehudah will last until the days of Moshe [who was from the tribe of Levi, and] who will rule Israel as a king; and concerning him the Torah says, וַיְהִי בִישֻׁרוּן מֶלֶךְ — *He was a king in Yeshurun (Israel)* (*Devarim* 33:5). Moreover, Shiloh (שִׁילֹה) is numerically equivalent to Moshe (מֹשֶׁה).

The *Midrash Rabbasi* says that God told Moshe, "Since you sacrificed yourself for Israel in Egypt, when Eliyahu leads Yisrael from the last exile you will be there too." And so the verse says, ה' בְּסוּפָה וּבִשְׂעָרָה דַּרְכּוֹ — *God's way is in gale and storm* (*Nachum* 1:3). "Gale" (סוּפָה) refers to Moshe who was thrown into the water, among the reeds, which are called סוּף; and "storm" (שְׂעָרָה) refers to Eliyahu, who rose alive to heaven in a great storm.

Another explanation offered by R' Bechaye: The kingship will not come to Yehudah until the Sanctuary (Mishkan) of Shiloh is destroyed. Afterwards Shmuel (Samuel) will anoint David as king.

Still another explanation given by R' Bechaye is that the kingship will rest with Yehudah — עַד (lit., "until"), i.e., to eternity. That is to say, once Shiloh (i.e., the Mashiach) comes, the kingship will be eternal. R' Bechaye also says that *until Shiloh comes* shows that just as Moshe led the Jews out of Egypt, so he will lead them out of the last exile, accompanied by Eliyahu (Elijah) — for Shiloh refers to Moshe, as mentioned above.

אֹסְרִי לַגֶּפֶן עִירֹה — *Loads his donkey with a grapevine* (49:11). Yehudah's land will grow such fruitful grapevines that a donkey will be needed to carry the harvest of a single grapevine.

חַכְלִילִי עֵינַיִם מִיָּיִן וּלְבֶן שִׁנַּיִם מֵחָלָב — *His eyes will be red with wine, his teeth white with milk* (49:12).

There will be so much wine in Yehudah's land that everyone's eyes will be bloodshot from drinking, and their teeth will be white from the milk which flows from his animals. Another meaning of this verse is that the hills in his territory will be red from the abundant wine of his grapevines, and the valleys white from the milk of his herds.

R' Bechaye writes that every letter of the *alef-beis* is included in Yehudah's blessing, with the exception of the letter *zayin*, to show us that the battles won by David's royal descendants will not be won with the help of arms (*klei zayin* — "arms"), but rather with the Name of God. And in fact Yehudah's own name includes all the four letters of God's Name, and in addition a *dalet* (fourth letter of the *alef-beis*), because he was the fourth son.

The kingship of Yehudah is likened to the sun, as the verse says, וְכִסְאוֹ כַשֶּׁמֶשׁ נֶגְדִּי — *And his throne is as the sun before me* (Tehillim 89:37). Just as the sun was created on the fourth day, so Yehudah was Yaakov's fourth son. Just as the sun, shining during the day, grows stronger and stronger, so will the kingdom of Yehudah grow ever stronger.

◄§ Zevulun's Blessing: Supporter of Torah

זְבוּלֻן לְחוֹף יַמִּים יִשְׁכֹּן — *Zevulun shall settle by the seashore* (49:13). Zevulun will be involved with shipping, and will support the tribe of Yissachar, who learns Torah. Zevulun's reward is greater than that of Yissachar, for if he would not provide him with sustenance, Yissachar could not learn at all. The Torah sets out Zevulun's blessing before that of Yissachar to teach us that the reward of one who enables others to study Torah for the sake of heaven (leshem *shamayim*), and gives food to students, is greater than the reward of those who study themselves.

⋖§ Yissachar's Blessing: Torah Study

יִשָּׂשכָר חֲמֹר גָּרֶם רֹבֵץ בֵּין הַמִּשְׁפְּתָיִם — *Yissachar is a large-boned donkey, resting between saddlebags* (49:14). Just as a donkey has large bones and little fat, so those who study Torah are generally thin. The study of Torah weakens men, and reduces their girth.

A donkey works night and day, and when he needs rest simply lies down among the city markets. Similarly, those who study Torah do not rest: they pursue their studies day and night, not sleeping on their own beds.

וַיַּרְא מְנֻחָה כִּי טוֹב — *He saw that rest was good* (49:15). Yissachar saw that tranquility is necessary for the proper study of Torah, and he could not live in the world of commerce or war. For this reason, in the daily *Shemoneh Esrei (Amidah* Prayer) we pray that God "return our judges as before, and our counsellors as at the beginning; take away our agony and sighs." This means, "God, bring us back to Yerushalayim (Jerusalem), and free us of our misery, so that our minds will be clear enough to learn Torah incessantly." And indeed, when *Mashiach* comes all will be able to study Torah; as the Prophet says, כִּי מָלְאָה הָאָרֶץ דֵּעָה אֶת ה' — *For the world will be filled with the knowledge of God (Yeshayahu* 11:9). The request, "Blow on the *shofar*" ("ram's horn"), therefore precedes the request, "Return our judges," to show that when the great horn will be blown, and *Mashiach* will arrive, everyone will have the proper state of mind for learning.

וַיֵּט שִׁכְמוֹ לִסְבֹּל — *He bent his back to the burden* (49:15). The scholar needs to accustom himself to the burden of his study. This means also that when a man learned in Torah is insulted or degraded, he must know how to bear the insult.

וַיְהִי לְמַס עֹבֵד — *And he became a worker for tribute* (49:15). Yissachar will pay his tribute to the People of Israel, by teaching them and judging halachic questions.

The *Midrash* says that the verse, *Yissachar is a large-boned donkey*, alludes to the fact that a donkey brought about (*garem* — "large-boned"; *garam* — "caused") the birth of Yissachar. When Yaakov returned from the fields on his donkey Leah heard the donkey's bray and went to meet him, and following this meeting she became pregnant with Yissachar.

⋐ Dan's Blessing: Shimshon

דָּן יָדִין עַמּוֹ — *Dan shall judge his nation* (49:16). The valiant Shimshon (Samson), a descendant of the tribe of Dan, will be a judge over Israel, and will rule them as a king. He will defeat the Philistines, not with arms, but with the jawbone of an ass, with which he will destroy thousands of men.

Why is Shimshon compared to a snake in this verse? Just as a snake crawls by itself silently, killing many men, so Shimshon went, without hue and cry, and killed many Philistines. Another reason is that a snake is full of fiery venom, and Shimshon burned the wheat of the Philistines. He caught three hundred foxes, tied firebrands to them, and drove them through the Philistines' wheat fields. When the Philistines found out they came to battle the Jews.

Three thousand Jews confronted Shimshon, hoping to bind him and hand him over to the Philistines, knowing that the Philistines wanted no one but him. Shimshon asked them to swear that they would not kill him, and then agreed to let them tie him up. They took two new, thick lengths of rope and bound him, and carried him to the Philistine camp. When the Philistines saw that they were carrying Shimshon they blew their trumpets and danced in a frenzy of joy. At that moment the spirit of God came to rest upon Shimshon. The fetters around his hands burst as if they were flax in a flame. He quickly took the jawbone of an ass and killed three thousand Philistines with it.

Afterwards he grew desperately thirsty, but could find nothing to quench his thirst. He prayed to God saying, "Lord of the entire world, You have saved me from all of the Philistines. Shall I now die of thirst, and fall into their hands?" God performed a miracle: the bone in his hand began to spurt water like a spring, and Shimshon drank the water and lived.

The *Midrash* writes further: Why does the verse compare Shimshon to a snake? A snake has no feet, and Shimshon limped.

לִישׁוּעָתְךָ קִוִּיתִי ה׳ — *I hope for your salvation, God* (49:18). Yaakov saw that Shimshon would be the last judge of the Jews. Even though in fact Shmuel followed him, he did not have to go to battle the way Shimshon did. Therefore Yaakov said, "Even though Shimshon is destined to die in battle, 'I hope for Your salvation, God,' and I hope that God continues to succor us against our enemies." This is what *Ramban* writes.

Rashi writes that it was Shimshon himself who said this verse as he grasped the pillars of the pagan temple and asked God for His help in bringing the temple down. It mattered not to him that in doing so he was going to kill himself — he wanted revenge on the Philistines. Thus, he cried, *"Let me die with the Philistines"* (Shoftim 16:30), as he pulled down the house on himself and the thousands of Philistines.

◄§ Gad's Blessing: Destroyer of Idolatry

גָּד גְּדוּד יְגוּדֶנּוּ — *Gad, raiders shall raid him* (49:19). Yaakov said that Gad, together with his brothers, would cross the Jordan River to battle the idol worshipers. He would destroy many of them, and then would return to his tribal territory on the eastern side of the Jordan River. He would return home safely, without losing any men in battle.

◄§ Asher's Blessing: Olive Oil

מֵאָשֵׁר שְׁמֵנָה לַחְמוֹ — *Asher will have the richest foods* (49:20). Asher will own lands rich with olive trees, and everyone will buy oil from him.

◄§ Naftali's Blessing: Beautiful Fruit; Beautiful Words

נַפְתָּלִי אַיָּלָה שְׁלֻחָה הַנֹּתֵן אִמְרֵי שָׁפֶר — *Naftali is a freed deer; he delivers beautiful words* (49:21). His fruit will ripen as swiftly as a deer runs. The "beautiful words" refer to the blessings of thanksgiving which will be made over his fruits.

In these words, Yaakov was also speaking prophetically of the ten thousand men of Naftali who would rally together as swiftly as a deer to battle Sisra. In this context the "beautiful words" refer to the praises of Devorah and Barak.

The *Midrash* says that Esav tried to prevent the sons of Yaakov from burying their father in the Cave of Machpelah. Because of his swiftness, Naftali was sent back to Egypt to bring the letter in which Esav had renounced his claim to the cave. But before he could return, Chushim, Dan's son, had killed Esav.

Ramban and *Toldos Yitzchak* write: Why is Naftali compared to a deer? Because people used to send deer to deliver messages. The "beautiful words" are these messages.

Imrei Noam writes that Naftali always went swiftly on his way undisturbed, and no man delayed him, because he would "give beautiful words," and answered each man whom he encountered with a kindly greeting.

◄§ Yosef's Blessing: Charm, Righteousness, Stone of Israel

בֵּן פֹּרָת יוֹסֵף ... בָּנוֹת צָעֲדָה עֲלֵי שׁוּר — *Yosef is a fruitful son ... daughters run along the wall* (49:22). Everyone who saw Yosef saw his special charm. Indeed, the Egyptian women would climb up on walls to gaze upon his beauty.

When Esav came to Yaakov and saw all his sons and wives, Yosef stood up in front of his mother, so that Esav should not see her and her especial beauty. Yaakov therefore told Yosef now, "Because you rose up and blocked your mother, all the women will gaze at your beauty."

בֵּן פֹּרָת עֲלֵי עָיִן — *A fruitful son by a fountain* (49:22). [*Alei ayin*, "by a fountain," can also be read as meaning "over an eye."] "You will transcend the Evil Eye; it will have no power over you."

R' Bechaye writes: Why does the verse call Yosef a *fruitful son* twice? To show that each of his two sons would multiply and increase within Israel, as Moshe Rabbeinu later said, וְהֵם רִבְבוֹת אֶפְרַיִם וְהֵם אַלְפֵי מְנַשֶּׁה — *They are the tens of thousands of Efraim and they are the thousands of Menashe (Devarim 33:17).*

Though the daughters of Egypt stepped upon the walls to gaze upon Yosef's beauty, he remained modest and refrained from looking at any woman, and was thus found worthy of being elevated to greatness. The *Midrash* writes that *ben poras* ("fruitful son") refers also to the cows (*paros*) which Pharaoh dreamed of, and through which Yosef ultimately rose to power.

וַיְמָרֲרֻהוּ וָרֹבּוּ — *They embittered him and quarreled with him* (49:23). Potiphar and his wife embittered him; his brothers quarreled with him.

וַיִּשְׂטְמֻהוּ בַּעֲלֵי חִצִּים — *The archers hated him* (49:23). This refers to his brothers, who were to share [from *chitzim* — "arrows"; *chetzi* — "half"] their inheritance with him, and who hated him.

וַתֵּשֶׁב בְּאֵיתָן קַשְׁתּוֹ — *But his bow remained firm* (49:24). This means that he became a powerful ruler.

וַיָּפֹזּוּ זְרֹעֵי יָדָיו — *His arms were decked in gold* (49:24). His hands were made splendid with the gold signet ring which the king himself placed upon his finger. Yosef was given all of this מִידֵי אֲבִיר יַעֲקֹב — *from the hand of the Mighty One of Yaakov (ibid.),* from God, by whose sanction he became a ruler of Israel (מִשָּׁם רֹעֶה אֶבֶן יִשְׂרָאֵל).

Toldos Yitzchak writes that the words *his bow remained firm* refer to the time that Potiphar's wife tried to seduce him, and he strengthened himself not to listen to her. As a result, he was found deserving of having *his arms ... decked in gold with* Pharaoh's ring. Why did Yosef not submit to her? *From the hand of the Mighty One of Yaakov* — he saw the image of his father, saying to him, "If you lie with her you will be known as the shepherd of prostitutes, but if you do not, you will be the shepherd of the stone of Israel, a leader of Israel."

Yosef is known as "Stone of Israel" for another reason as well. Each of the Twelve Tribes had a stone on the High Priest's breastplate *(choshen)*, with its name inscribed upon it. Yosef's stone was an onyx. On the shoulder bands of the apron *(efod)* of the *Kohen Gadol*, the High Priest, were two more onyxes inscribed with the names of all the Twelve Tribes. Since the onyx represented Yosef, and as well was used for the names of all of Israel, Yosef was called Stone of Israel, the stone on which all of Israel is inscribed.

מֵאֵל אָבִיךָ וְיַעְזְרֶךָ — *From your father's God, who will help you* (49:25). "All this happened because of God's intervention. He will continue to help you, because you clung to God and refused to sin with Potiphar's wife. You will be blessed with *blessings of the breast and the womb (ibid.).* There will be no miscarriages among your descendants, and they will be fruitful and bear many children."

בִּרְכֹת אָבִיךָ גָּבְרוּ עַל בִּרְכֹת הוֹרַי — *"The blessings which you receive from your father will be greater than those which I receive from my parents* (49:26) — for God gave me an unlimited blessing."

תִּהְיֶיןָ לְרֹאשׁ יוֹסֵף — *They shall be upon the head of Yosef* (49:26). May these blessings now rest upon your head.

◆§ Binyamin's Blessing: Shaul, Mordechai, Esther

בִּנְיָמִין זְאֵב יִטְרָף — *Binyamin is a preying wolf* (49:27). Yaakov spoke prophetically of the time that the tribe of Binyamin would abduct women as wives, after having been excommunicated over the incident of the concubine of Givah, when everyone refused to marry them. They abducted wives, like wolves.

בַּבֹּקֶר יֹאכַל עַד — *In the morning he will eat booty* (49:27). First King Shaul, of the tribe of Binyamin, would take the money and possessions of the idol-worshiping nations.

וְלָעֶרֶב יְחַלֵּק שָׁלָל — *And in the evening he will divide the spoils* (49:27). Later, Mordechai and Esther, also of the tribe of Binyamin, would take the money and possessions of the wicked Haman.

וְזֹאת אֲשֶׁר דִּבֶּר לָהֶם אֲבִיהֶם וַיְבָרֶךְ אוֹתָם — *This is what their father said to them, and blessed them* (49:28). This shows us that despite the fact that he rebuked some of his sons, ultimately he blessed them all equally.

⋙ Yaakov's Last Request

קִבְרוּ אֹתִי אֶל אֲבֹתָי — *Bury me with my ancestors* (49:29). Yaakov left a last command: "I will die, and let me be buried in the Cave next to my ancestors." *Ramban* writes that even though only Yosef had sworn to bring him back to the Cave, in fact all of the children carried him.

There in the cave *they buried Avraham and Sarah, his wife; and there they buried Yitzchak and Rivkah, his wife* (49:31). Why did Yaakov say that "they" buried Yitzchak, when he himself had performed the burial? Because Esav had assisted him, and he did not want to mention himself together with Esav. "There I buried Leah, so that I would have a claim to the land which Esav would not have." (There was no space for another couple to be buried there. For that reason, Yosef did not ask to be buried there.)

When they were carrying Yaakov back for burial, Tzfo, son of Elifaz and grandson of Esav, came with a large company and began to battle Yosef and his men. Yosef was victorious and did not lose a single man. He captured Tzfo and all of his soldiers and left him imprisoned in Egypt until his death.

⋙ Our Father Yaakov did not Die

וַיִּגְוַע וַיֵּאָסֶף אֶל עַמָּיו — *He breathed his last and was gathered into his people* (49:33). The *Gemara* asks: Why is the word "died" not mentioned in connection with Yaakov? Because Yaakov did not actually die. *Ramban, Toldos Yitzchak,* and *R' Bechaye* thereupon write: Since the body was embalmed with fragrant herbs in order to preserve it, he most certainly must have been dead. The explanation: Yaakov was very holy, and his soul was able to rejoin his body at times after his death, and this is what the *Gemara* means when it says that he did not die. We find likewise that Rebbe (R' Yehudah HaNasi) commanded that after his death his table be set every Friday, in honor of *Shabbos,* and the candles lit, for he was coming back on Friday evening to recite the benediction of *Kiddush* over the wine. And so it was. One day, the wife of a neighbor knocked on the door of the house where Rebbe was, and a maidservant came out and said, "Silence! Rebbe is here!" When he heard this he refused to return again, so that it should not become a well-known phenomenon, which would embarrass the other righteous men who could not return to their homes.

Another explanation is that Yaakov learned Torah with students. When they cite an exposition in his name, his lips move in the tomb as if he were still alive, and so the *Gemara* says that he did not die.

⋘ Mourning and Burial

וַיַּחַנְטוּ הָרֹפְאִים אֶת יִשְׂרָאֵל — *The physicians embalmed Yisrael* (50:2). The physicians instructed Yaakov's children in the art of embalming, and then his children embalmed him, not letting the physicians touch the body.

וַיִּבְכּוּ אֹתוֹ מִצְרַיִם שִׁבְעִים יוֹם — *The Egyptians wept for him for seventy days* (50:3). Forty days represented the time that it took to embalm the body; the actual period of mourning lasted thirty days.

בְּקִבְרִי אֲשֶׁר כָּרִיתִי לִי — *In the grave which I have dug for myself* (50:5). Yosef told Pharaoh, "Yaakov commanded that we bury him in the Cave which he bought." The word כָּרִיתִי ("dug") is reminiscent of the word כַּר ("a pile"). Yaakov piled gold and silver in front of Esav, and said, "Take this, in place of your portion in the cave."

Pharaoh told Yosef, "Go and bury your father, since he made you swear to do it. Had he not done so I would not have allowed you to go, but I cannot ask you to break your vow."

וַיַּעַל יוֹסֵף לִקְבֹּר אֶת אָבִיו — *Yosef went up to bury his father* (50:7).

Yosef went ahead alone, followed by several groups. First came Pharaoh's courtiers, then in turn came the elders of Israel, and the notables of Egypt. Then came Yosef's household, followed by his brothers and his father's household. Afterwards rode the chariots, and the common people brought up the rear.

וַיְהִי הַמַּחֲנֶה כָּבֵד מְאֹד — *It was a very great camp* (50:9). The same angels who had protected Yaakov during his lifetime now followed the people, and protected and accompanied Yaakov in death.

✑ The Kings Show Deference

גֹרֶן הָאָטָד — *The threshing floor of Atad* (50:10). The kings of
Canaan and Yishmael were in the midst of battling each other.
When they saw Yosef hang his crown on the coffin, they joined him
and out of deference hung their crowns there as well. For this reason
the place was called *atad* which means a thornbush, because the coffin was hung with crowns until it resembled a thornbush.

Yaakov's children carried him *as he had commanded* (50:12).
First, he had commanded that his grandchildren not carry the coffin,
because some of them were children of Canaanite and Egyptian
women. Second, he commanded that three of his children carry the
coffin on each side. The tribes in later years walked in the desert in
the same formation as their founding fathers when they carried the
coffin. Third, he commanded that Levi not carry the coffin, since his
children were destined to carry the Ark and the Tablets. Fourth, he
commanded that Yosef not carry the coffin, since he was a ruler;
Efraim and Menashe carried it in his stead.

✑ The Return to Egypt

וַיָּשָׁב יוֹסֵף מִצְרַיְמָה הוּא וְאֶחָיו — *Yosef returned to Egypt, he and his
brothers* (50:14). *Rashi* writes: Why, when the sons of Yaakov went
to bury their father, did the Egyptians precede them, while when
returning to Egypt the brothers went first? Because the Egyptians,
seeing that the other kings had hung their crowns up to show their
respect for Yaakov, now showed respect to his sons by allowing
them to travel first.

✑ Asking Forgiveness

וַיִּרְאוּ אֲחֵי יוֹסֵף כִּי מֵת אֲבִיהֶם — *Yosef's brothers saw that their father
had died* (50:15). They saw Yosef sit down to eat by himself, and
they thought that he hated them and planned revenge. Yosef did not
have this in mind. When Yaakov was alive they ate together at one
table, and Yaakov would make the blessing over the bread. With
Yaakov's death, it should have been Yosef's task to make the blessing, since he was the head of the household, but as he was the
second youngest he preferred to simply eat by himself, rather than
make the blessing for them.

Chizkuni writes that when they went to bury Yaakov they passed
by the pit in which they had thrown Yosef. Yosef stood in front of it
and made the blessing which one makes at the place where God performed a miracle, since God had helped him out of the pit and saved
his life. The brothers saw this and were afraid that this site would re-

mind Yosef of the anguish which they had caused him, and spark his vengeance. They therefore sent Bilhah's children to tell him that before his death their father had commanded that he forgive them for their deed. This was not true. Yaakov did not even know of the sale, and, further, he understood that Yosef was righteous and would not harm them, even if they had treated him badly. For the sake of peace it is permissible to tell a white lie, provided that it harms no one.

Toldos Yitzchak asks why they asked him to forgive *the servants of the God of your father* (50:17). They wanted to remind Yosef that he himself had told them, when revealing his identity to them, that it was not they who had sent him to Egypt: it was God's doing. They were thus telling him, "We were simply servants and messengers of God in selling you, and we have not sinned."

R' Bechaye writes that the brothers asked his forgiveness, but we do not see explicitly that he forgave them. The *Gemara* says that if one sins against someone else, even if he is truly penitent, the sin is not absolved until he has been forgiven. The brothers died without his having forgiven them, and for this reason ten important Sages in a later generation died.

They said *the servants of the God of your father* to remind him that though his father had died, they were still the servants of the living God of their father.

✦§ Their Fears are Allayed

וַיֵּבְךְ יוֹסֵף בְּדַבְּרָם אֵלָיו — *Yosef wept when they spoke with him* (50:17). Yosef wept. The brothers then approached him and fell before him, crying, "We are your servants!" Yosef told them, "Do not fear. Am I God? Even if I wanted to harm you I could not do so without God's approval, just as you could not harm me. You tried to, but everything ended otherwise, and I was able to save you from the famine. Do not fear, I will support you and your households." From this we learn that with Yaakov's demise the famine began once again. When Yaakov came to Egypt it had stopped in his merit, and with his death it began again. Yosef therefore assured them now that he would support them through the famine.

Yosef told his brothers, "Because of you I became a man of fine lineage. Before you came the entire world thought I was merely a slave, and now they realize that I am a noble. Should I have you killed people would say, 'He was only flattering himself with them. They are not his real brothers, or he would not have killed them.' "

וַיְחִי יוֹסֵף מֵאָה וָעֶשֶׂר שָׁנִים — *Yosef lived 110 years* (50:22). He saw his son Menashe's grandchildren, and raised them. The verse shows us that they must have been righteous, since they grew up in Yosef's home, and learned from him.

◆§ Raised from the Nile

וַיַּשְׁבַּע יוֹסֵף אֶת בְּנֵי יִשְׂרָאֵל — *Yosef bound the sons of Yisrael with an oath* (50:25). He bound them with an oath to carry him to *Eretz Yisrael*, when they would leave Egypt. And in fact Yosef merited having Moshe himself carry his bones. All the tribes carried the bones of their forefathers — Reuven's children carried his bones, the children of Shimon carried his remains, and so on.

When Israel left Egypt, Yosef's coffin was deep in the Nile River, for the Egyptians had said, "Let the river be blessed by his merit." Moshe took a silver platelet and inscribed on it the words עֲלֵה שׁוֹר עֲלֵה שׁוֹר — "Rise up, ox; rise up, ox!" — referring to Yosef, whose strength was likened to that of an ox *(Devarim 33:17)*. But the coffin did not rise. Moshe then cried, "Israel is leaving Egypt, and the Holy Spirit is awaiting you! Do not delay, come out from the river. If you do not arise, then we will no longer be bound by your oath!"

At these words, the coffin floated upwards. And because Moshe in person occupied himself with the transfer of Yosef's remains, he was found worthy of having God Himself bury him. From this we learn that when one fulfills a commandment by himself, and not through a messenger, his reward from God is great.

הפטרות
Haftoros

HAFTORAH

Bereishis

(Yeshayahu/Isaiah 42:5 — 43:10)

Thus said the Lord, Who created the heavens and stretched them out, Who spread forth the earth and all that comes from it (כֹּה אָמַר הָאֵל ה' בּוֹרֵא הַשָּׁמַיִם וְנוֹטֵיהֶם רֹקַע הָאָרֶץ וְצֶאֱצָאֶיהָ ;42:5). During the days of the prophet many people claimed that the world had been created of its own volition, and not by God. Therefore, the prophet here attests to the fact that God created the world, spreading the sky over the earth as one pitches a tent. He spread out the land and drew the various fruits, trees, and vegetables from it. Then He gave a soul to the men who populate the earth, and breathed the spirit of life into the earth's other creatures.

God assures us that "Since I am the God Who created everything, I have the power to release you from exile. Therefore, when the time comes, *I am God, Who will call you with righteousness* (אֲנִי ה' קְרָאתִיךָ בְצֶדֶק; v. 6), to take you out of exile, and you will be a light to the other nations. I will call you *to open blinded eyes* (לִפְקֹחַ עֵינַיִם עִוְרוֹת; v. 7) — your eyes, which until now were blinded by sorrow."

"I am God, and that is My Name (אֲנִי ה' הוּא שְׁמִי; v. 8). My Name signifies that I am Master of the entire world, and will no longer allow My honor to be directed to another. Until now I did not render to the wicked what they deserved, and so they refused to recognize Me, preferring their idols. But when I mete out justice to the wicked the whole world will recognize that I alone am God. The reverence which is rightfully Mine shall no longer be shown to false gods."

The prophet continues: *"The first ones have come* (הָרִאשֹׁנוֹת הִנֵּה בָאוּ; v. 9). The first prophecies which I delivered, concerning the fate of Sancheriv (Sennacherib), have been fulfilled. Now, when new events are about to sprout forth, I shall tell you of them."

Sing a new song to God (שִׁירוּ לַה' שִׁיר חָדָשׁ; v. 10). In the days of *Mashiach* (Messiah) the praises of God will pervade the entire world. Men on the sea and on far-off islands will give praise to Him. In the desert and in the cities, in barbaric countries, in mountainous regions and on cliffy crags, all will loudly praise God.

The Lord will go forth as a mighty man, stirring up jealousy as a warrior (ה' כַּגִּבּוֹר יֵצֵא כְּאִישׁ מִלְחָמוֹת יָעִיר קִנְאָה; v. 13). He shall go forth to bring salvation, and to wreak vengeance against His enemies. He will say, "Until now *I have held my peace* (הֶחֱשֵׁיתִי מֵעוֹלָם; v. 14), but now I will scream as a woman does during the pain of childbirth. I will devour them all."

God compares His enemies to high mountains, and to grass, and to mighty rivers, warning that "*I will destroy mountains and hills* (אַחֲרִיב הָרִים וּגְבָעוֹת; v. 15), and make the grass wither, and dry up the mighty waterways. I will lead the blind upon the proper path (v. 16). No matter how dark the way, I will illuminate the path for them."

They will be turned back, they will be ashamed (נָסֹגוּ אָחוֹר יֵבֹשׁוּ בֹשֶׁת; v. 17). Those who put their trust in heathenish ideas will be cast back and put to shame.

Listen, you who are deaf; and look, blind men, so that you see (הַחֵרְשִׁים שְׁמָעוּ; v. 18). God tells Israel: "You make yourselves deaf and refuse to hear. You blind yourselves and will not see, and then you say that it is My prophets, who rebuke you, who are deaf and blind. You say of My servant, 'Who is as blind as the prophet?' — but in truth *Who is as blind as those who have been repaid?* (מִי עִוֵּר כִּמְשֻׁלָּם; v. 19). You have suffered terribly, yet will not consider why you have been punished. Your ears are open but you will not listen to the prophet; you have made yourselves blind and deaf."

God desired, for the sake of [Israel's] righteousness, to make the Torah great and glorious (ה' חָפֵץ לְמַעַן צִדְקוֹ יַגְדִּיל תּוֹרָה וְיַאְדִּיר; v. 21). With the arrival of *Mashiach*, however, Israel will be endowed with great wisdom, enabling them to learn the Torah. God will give them this understanding because of His great goodness, rather than Israel's worthiness.

For they are a despoiled and burglarized nation (וְהוּא עַם בָּזוּז וְשָׁסוּי; v. 22). "Even if you conceal yourselves in your houses and cellars you will be robbed, and no one will speak up on your behalf or turn away those who raid your houses. But none among you will listen to what the prophet says (v. 23); you are not interested in what will be."

Who gave Yaakov for booty? (מִי נָתַן לִמְשִׁסָּה יַעֲקֹב; v. 24). "Which of you recognize the sin which caused Yaakov's downfall? If you truly understood, you would realize that all has befallen you because you ignored God's commands and His Torah. As a result *He poured upon [you] the fury of His wrath* (וַיִּשְׁפֹּךְ עָלָיו חֵמָה אַפּוֹ; v. 25), engulfing Israel in flames, though no one will understand that their own sins are the reason for it!"

But God, the Creator, says: "Have no fear, Yaakov (43:1). Just as I redeemed you in the days of Sancheriv, so in time to come shall I release you from Bavel (Babylon). I will call you by name for you are Mine, and you will recognize Me."

When you pass in the water, I am with you (כִּי תַעֲבֹר בַּמַּיִם אִתְּךָ אָנִי; v. 2). Thus says God: "When Sancheriv, who has been compared to a great body of water, attempted to engulf you, I was there. I rescued you from the fire, to which he has also been likened. When you are caught between fire and water, only I can save you — *for I am the Lord your God, the Holy One of Israel* (כִּי אֲנִי ה' אֱלֹהֶיךָ קְדוֹש יִשְׂרָאֵל; v. 3)."

Before Sancheriv attacked Yerushalayim he fought the King of Cush and Seva and the King of Egypt, and was victorious. He arrived at Yerushalayim with his booty in tow, thinking that victory would come easily, since Israel were few in number and weak. But God showed him that despite his victory over the mighty, he could not overcome Israel. So in future time mighty nations will rally and do battle with each other, and then wage war against Israel — but God will save you. "Because you are dear to Me you will be honored (v. 4) among those nations, and they will be your ransom money."

Do not fear, for I am with you (אַל תִּירָא כִּי אִתְּךָ אָנִי; v. 5). "I will take you and your children, even the tiniest infant, and lead you all safely to *Eretz Yisrael*." God will command the four directions — north, south, east and west — to bring the Jews back to their land. "I will bring back this people who are blind though they have eyes, and deaf though they have ears" (v. 8).

All the nations gather together (כָּל הַגּוֹיִם נִקְבְּצוּ יַחְדָּו; v. 9). "They gather together, but none can foresee what will be in the days of *Mashiach*, just as none foresaw Sancheriv's fate. Let them bring testimony to prove that their foresight was trustworthy! But my prophecies concerning Sancheriv did prove to be true, so you may well believe that the new prophecies concerning the future will likewise come true."

The *Midrash* explains that the verse *You have not called upon Me, Yaakov* (וְלֹא אֹתִי קָרָאתָ יַעֲקֹב; v. 22) refers to one who does not pray in a synagogue. He finds the time and energy to talk freely and carry on his business all day, but is too tired to pray where he should. A person should make a point of offering his prayers in the synagogue.

HAFTORAH

Noach

(Yeshayahu/Isaiah 54:1-9)

Sing, barren woman, who did not give birth (רָנִּי עֲקָרָה לֹא יָלָדָה; v. 1). The prophet says: "Sing, Yerushalayim, who in your years of exile was likened to a woman who never bore a child. Sing, for now there will be many children in the city, the city which in its desolation was like a woman whose husband has forsaken her."

Enlarge the place of your tent (הַרְחִיבִי מְקוֹם אָהֳלֵךְ; v. 2). The prophet tells Yerushalayim to prepare many places for the numerous children who will be coming home. Together with the other cities of the Holy Land, she must extend her tents, strengthening them with ropes and pegs, in preparation for the return of her children.

"You will spread forth to right and to left, and your children will inherit *Eretz Yisrael*, inhabiting the abandoned cities. Fear not, for you will be shamed no longer. There will be such bounty that all former humiliation will be forgotten, your widowhood remembered no more."

For your husband is your creator (כִּי בֹעֲלַיִךְ עֹשַׂיִךְ; v. 5). "Your husband, your Creator, whose name is God, is your redeemer." The prophet says further: "You are not like a woman whose husband is dead, but rather *like an abandoned wife* (כְּאִשָּׁה עֲזוּבָה; v. 6) whose husband, in a fit of rage, has left her, but who may return at any moment. A man may leave the wife of his youth, but soon remembers her and returns in a kindlier mood."

God promises: "You will feel that the exile passed in the blink of an eye, because of the great things which will befall you in the days of *Mashiach* (Messiah), for with great mercy will I redeem you. In my wrath I hid My face from you, but I will have mercy upon you with My everlasting charity."

For like the waters of Noach (כִּי מֵי נֹחַ זֹאת לִי; v. 9). The exile can be compared to the waters of Noach. "Just as I swore never to bring such a flood to the world again, so I swear that [after the arrival of *Mashiach*] I will never again show anger to Israel. *Mountains may disappear and hills collapse* (v. 10) — but My promise is eternal." So says God.

In the *Gemara*, Tractate *Sanhedrin*, R' Yehudah tells his son R' Yitzchak that a man discovers true happiness only with his first wife, as is indicated in the verse, *For your husband is your creator* (v. 5). R' Shmuel says, in the name of Rav, that a woman gives her whole heart only to the first man who married her.

HAFTORAH

Lech Lecha

(Yeshayahu/Isaiah 40:27 — 41:16)

Why do you say, Yaakov, and speak, Israel (לָמָה תֹאמַר יַעֲקֹב וּתְדַבֵּר יִשְׂרָאֵל; 40:27). Why do the people of Yaakov say that God has forgotten them, and cares for them no longer? They claim that He did not plead their cause. But *Do you not know? Have you not heard?* (v. 28). Your own understanding should have led you to the conclusion, or else your Sages should have told you, that God, Who created the entire universe with truth, is the judge of the world. How can you say that He is unjust?

The verse tells us that *He does not grow faint, nor does he tire* (לֹא יִיעַף וְלֹא יִיגָע; v. 28). He created the entire world with His strength, and has not grown weary. We cannot comprehend God's wisdom: He alone knows the meaning of what He does.

He gives strength to the weary (נֹתֵן לַיָּעֵף כֹּחַ; v. 29), while those who are lacking in the performance of the *mitzvos* will grow faint. Men who put their faith in God, no matter how weakened their state, will gain new strength, just like an eagle who grows new feathers every ten years, for a span of a century. They may walk, or run, but never grow weary.

Be silent before Me, islands; nations, renew your strength (41:1). "Let the nations strengthen themselves so that they can confront Me with their complaints. They can approach and have their say, if they have something to discuss." So says God.

The prophet continues: *Who awakened from the east?* (מִי הֵעִיר מִמִּזְרָח; v. 2). Who aroused Avraham and brought him up from the east, from Aram? Wherever he went he called to the people around him to take up the belief in the true God. "Who was it that gave him the courage to do so, if not I, God? I delivered nations and kings into his hands, despite the minuteness of his forces. With his sword he felled pagans numerous as dust motes, with his bow he brought down, like mere straw, hordes of idol worshipers. *He pursued them, and passed safely* (v. 3), returning home in peace, despite the strangeness of the land."

Who has wrought and done it? (v. 4) — if not God, who created all of mankind, beginning with Adam. "I, God, saved Avraham, and I am the same God who will save you. The nations gazed upon the wonders I wrought for you, and were afraid."

Each man helped his neighbor (אִישׁ אֶת רֵעֵהוּ יַעֲזֹרוּ; v. 6). They helped each other, encouraging one another to build idols. *The carpenter encouraged the goldsmith* (v. 7) to cover the idols with metal. They said that the glue was strong, and fixed the foil in place with nails. All this they did to strengthen themselves in their idol worship.

"But you, Israel, were not like this. You served Me. You have been acquired by Me since the days of your fathers Avraham and Yaakov. You are the seed of Avraham, who served Me with selfless love. I chose you as My servants and have not discarded you, as I did reject others long ago. Have no fear. Let your heart not melt like wax, for I, God, will strengthen you and aid you, upholding you with My right hand of justice."

Those that were wrathful against you will be ashamed and humiliated (v. 11). "The pagans who taunted you will be shamed. You will seek, to no avail, those who fought with you, for it will be as if they never existed. I, God, take your right hand and vow to help you; fear not!"

Fear not, worm of Yaakov (אַל תִּירְאִי תּוֹלַעַת יַעֲקֹב; v. 14). Israel is compared here to a worm, whose entire strength is in its mouth. Similarly, our strength lies in our mouths, in the Torah which we learn and the prayers which we say.

Lo, I have made you a new threshing board with sharp teeth (v. 15). "You will go to the pagans, though they are as mighty as mountains, and cut them down as wheat. You will scatter them and they will be wafted away by the wind. And as for you, you will rejoice in your God and praise Him."

☙ ☙ ☙

In this *Haftorah* the following verse appears: וְקוֹיֵ ה' יַחֲלִיפוּ כֹחַ — *Those that hope in God shall renew their strength* (40:31). This refers to a man's younger years. Concerning one's old age we have the promise of a different verse: עוֹד יְנוּבוּן בְּשֵׂיבָה — *In their old age they will yet yield fruit* (Tehillim 92:15).

The *Gemara*, in *Sanhedrin*, *Perek Chelek*, says that the verse, *Those that hope in God shall renew their strength*, refers to the words of Eliyahu (Elijah), who said that the righteous people resurrected by God in the days of *Mashiach* will live eternally. If you wonder what will become of them during the seventh millennium, when God destroys the world, the answer is that God will grant each righteous man the wings of an eagle, and they will soar over the water. But will they suffer anguish? No, for *those that hope in God shall renew their strength*.

The *Gemara*, in the last chapter of Tractate *Shabbos*, refers to the verse, *Who raised from the east [the one whom] righteousness met wherever he set his feet?* (41:2). Rav teaches there that prayer and charity can change a person's destiny from bad to good, as the Torah says in this week's *parashah*, וַיּוֹצֵא אוֹתוֹ הַחוּצָה — *He took him outside* (15:5). That is to say, God raised Avraham out of his destiny.

Avraham told God, "I see that my fate is to be childless," and God replied, "Leave your fate behind, for the righteous can change their destiny by prayer and acts of kindness. You have seen that your sign in heaven is called *tzedek* ["righteousness", the Hebrew name for the planet Jupiter]; it is situated in the frigid west. This destiny dooms you to childlessness. But I will draw your star eastward, to warmer realms, and then you will bear children."

For this reason the verse says, *Who awakened from the east, righteousness* ... God awakened the planet called "righteousness" *(tzedek)* and caused it to rise in the east, so that Avraham could have children.

The *Gemara* continues and tells a story of Shmuel (Samuel), which also proves that *tzaddikim* can rise above their fate. Shmuel was sitting with an astrologer by the name of Avalet. The stargazer told Shmuel: "That man who is passing through the field is destined never to return. He will be bitten by a snake and die." Shmuel retorted: "If he is righteous he will live."

As they sat, the man returned from the field safely, carrying a load of wood. He put the load on the floor, and they found, hidden beneath a board, the remains of a snake. The man knew nothing of it.

Shmuel asked him, "What righteous deed have you performed?" Answered the man: "I belong to a group of men who eat together, and each day one of us collects the bread from all the members. One day, though, one of our group had no bread. I thought to myself, 'He will be humiliated,' and so I volunteered to collect the bread that day. When I came to the man I pretended to take his bread, and I placed an extra serving of my own bread into the communal container."

Hearing this, Shmuel said, "You have certainly performed a *mitzvah*," and he went straight to the *beis midrash* and there taught: צְדָקָה תַּצִּיל מִמָּוֶת — *Charity saves from death* (Mishlei 10:12).

R' Akiva had a daughter who according to the astrologers was destined to die of a snakebite received while she stood under a *chuppah*, getting married. R' Akiva was naturally very anxious about her wedding day. On that day she took a golden pin from her hair and stuck it into the wall. It happened to pierce the eye of a snake which was lurking there, killing it. The next morning, when she went to get the pin, she pulled the snake out with it.

Her father asked her, "What righteous deed have you performed?" She answered: "Yesterday, a beggar came asking for bread. Everyone was busy with the festive meal, and ignored him, so I gave him my portion of food."

Her father said, "You did a righteous deed and were therefore saved from death." He likewise went to the *beis midrash* and taught the people there that *charity saves from death*.

From R' Nachman bar Yitzchak, too, we see that the righteous can rise above their fate. Astrologers warned his mother that he was destined to be a thief. She never allowed him to walk bareheaded, constantly warning him to keep his head covered, to pray to God that his evil inclination not rule over him, and to be always conscious of the fear of God. R' Nachman had no idea why his mother behaved so, until one day, as he was learning, the hood of his cloak fell off his head. He raised his eyes and saw a date tree, and the evil inclination aroused in him a burning desire to eat. He climbed the tree and bit off a cluster of dates — they were not his — thus becoming a thief, as the stars had destined.

We can learn from this story that a poor man must not despair of changing his destiny. Through his deeds he can indeed change his fate.

If a man is born on a Tuesday he is fated to be prosperous, for the grains and fruits were created on that day. So writes the *Gemara*, in Tractate *Shabbos*. But in Tractate *Chullin*, we find that the destiny to be a rich man is not an unalterable one. The *Gemara* there quotes Abbaye as saying that poverty is a result of letting crumbs of bread fall to the ground.

The story is told there of a man who was constantly pursued by the angel of poverty. The angel could not harm him, for the man was scrupulously careful not to drop a breadcrumb. One day the man was sitting outside, eating on the grass, and the angel said, "Today I will succeed in impoverishing him, for it is impossible to pick up the crumbs from the grass." When the man had finished eating, he tore out the grass around him, which contained some fallen crumbs, and threw them into the river. The man then heard the angel's anguished cry: "I can do nothing against this man. He is too cautious!"

We see from this story that if a person is born with a fate of riches, he can still lose his wealth through his deeds. Conversely, if he is fated to be poor, he can change his destiny by living piously and giving charity. This we see in the *derush* of the Sages on the verse עַשֵּׂר תְּעַשֵּׂר (*Devarim* 14:22). Literally this means *You shall surely tithe* [your yearly harvest], from the root עשר, meaning "ten." But since the root עשר means "to grow rich," the Sages read this verse on the non-literal level of *derush* as follows: עַשֵּׂר בִּשְׁבִיל שֶׁתִּתְעַשֵּׂר — "Tithe in order that you grow rich." They taught, moreover: Give charity and you will have wealth enough to give a tenth once again.

God has said explicitly, "Test Me with charity and with tithes, to see if I will repay you richly" (cf. *Malachi* 3:10). In brief, the rule is that good deeds and charity can change an unfortunate fate.

There is a story told of Nachum Ish Gamzu, who was so termed because no matter what happened to him, good or bad, he would always say, "*Gam zu letovah*" ("This, too, is for the best").

The Jews once sent a chest full of precious stones as a tribute to their king, and chose Nachum, the renowned miracle worker, as their messenger. While he was spending the night at a wayside inn, the innkeepers opened the chest and substituted earth for the precious gems. Nachum came to the king and presented the chest. Upon his discovery of the earth, the king ordered Nachum put to death.

The prophet Eliyahu appeared in the guise of a noble and told the king, "Perhaps this is the earth which their father Avraham used to defeat the mighty warriors." Now there was a certain fortified city which the king had for years tried to conquer, to no avail. In order to test the earth, a bit was sprinkled upon the city's walls, and the walls immediately collapsed. The king then commanded that Nachum's chest be filled with gold as a token of appreciation, and sent him home with great honor.

On his way home, Nachum Ish Gamzu arrived at the inn once more. The hostelers asked how his mission had gone, and he told them the whole story. They eagerly took more earth and brought it to the king, thinking that they would be given gold in exchange for it. But the king commanded that it be tested, and when it proved to have no magical properties, they were severely punished.

The *Midrash Tanchuma* makes a comment on the verse which appears in this *Haftorah*, קֹרֵא הַדֹּרוֹת מֵרֹאשׁ — *He calls the generations from the beginning* (41:4): When men were pious God Himself gave them names, as we see in the cases of Avraham, Yitzchak, and Yaakov, who each were given good names by God. And in fact God likewise names many righteous men.

When R' Meir would meet a person, he would know from his name the type of person he was. Once, in an inn owned by a man named Kidor (כִּידוֹר), he warned his students against the owner.

One day the students went to wash themselves, leaving their clothing with the owner. Kidor took their belongings and fled. The students later came to R' Meir and told him what had happened, and he answered, "Didn't I warn you to beware of him?"

The students asked him how he had known, and he answered, "From his name, Kidor, which is reminiscent of the verse, *Ki dor tahapuchos hemah (For they are a perverse generation; Devarim 32:20)."*

The *Midrash* says that the verse in the *Haftorah, the carpenter encouraged the goldsmith* (וַיְחַזֵּק חָרָשׁ אֶת צֹרֵף; 41:7), refers to Shem, who was a carpenter, and who built the Ark. Noach's son Shem "strengthened the goldsmith" — the goldsmith Avraham, who was thrown into the fire, just as a goldsmith works with fire. *They say the soldering is good* (אֹמֵר לַדֶּבֶק טוֹב הוּא; *ibid.)* — this refers to the pagans, who learned that it is better to cleave to the God of Avraham than to Nimrod.

HAFTORAH

Vayera

(Melachim II/II Kings, chapter 4)

The narrative opens with the plaint of *a certain woman, of the wives of the sons of the prophets* (וְאִשָּׁה אַחַת מִנְּשֵׁי בְנֵי הַנְּבִיאִים; v. 1).

A righteous man by the name of Ovadiah concealed one hundred prophets in two caves, because Izevel (Jezebel), wife of King Achav (Ahab), was persecuting and murdering all prophets. He had no money to buy them food, so he borrowed money at a high rate of interest from Yehoram (Jehoram), the son of Achav. Because Yehoram held his hands out to take interest, he was ultimately shot by an arrow in the heart, *between his arms* (*II Kings* 9:24), for taking interest is a most reprehensible sin.

The severity of the sin is illustrated by the prophet Yechezkel (Ezekiel), who succeeded in resurrecting thousands of dead men, but who could not revive one particular man. He asked God the reason for it, and God answered that it was because in his lifetime that man had charged interest on loans.

In the days of *Mashiach*, when the dead are resurrected, those men who have charged interest will likewise not be revived.

The *Haftorah* states that Yehoram came to collect the money which he had lent. Ovadiah was already dead, and Yehoram wanted to take two of his children as payment. Ovadiah's widow therefore came to Elisha, crying to him that Yehoram wanted to take two of her sons for slaves.

Elisha said to her, "What shall I do for you?" (וַיֹּאמֶר אֵלֶיהָ אֱלִישָׁע מָה אֶעֱשֶׂה לָּךְ; v. 2). He asked her what she had in her house, and she answered that she had nothing in her house but a small jar with a bit of oil in it. Elisha then commanded her to borrow empty jars from her neighbors — *and come in and close the door* (וּבָאת וְסָגַרְתְּ הַדֶּלֶת; v. 4), to show respect for the miracle, which should happen quietly, with no one there to witness it.

He further commanded her, *"Pour oil into these empty vessels* (v. 4), and when each vessel is full, put it to one side. Do not move the jar of oil from its place, for it will be like an immovable well."

The woman heeded him, locked the door, and with only herself and her children in the house, filled all the vessels with oil.

When the vessels were full, the woman said to her son (וַיְהִי כִּמְלֹאת הַכֵּלִים וַתֹּאמֶר אֶל בְּנָהּ; v. 6). The *Gemara* says that after she had filled all of the jars, the woman told her son to collect all of the shards of broken jars and place them next to each other, and "the God Who commanded that the empty jars be filled with oil will also command that the shards cleave to each other, creating whole, unbroken jars which can be filled with oil." Her son did as she requested, collecting the broken pieces and placing them next to each other. The jars became whole again, and she filled them with oil.

When all of the jars were filled, and the son said that there were no empty vessels left, the oil immediately ceased flowing.

She came and told the man of God (וַתָּבֹא וַתַּגֵּד לְאִישׁ הָאֱלֹהִים; v. 7). She came to the prophet Elisha and asked for his advice, wanting to know if she should wait with the oil until the prices rose. Elisha told

The miracle
of the oil

her to sell the oil, and she would have enough to pay her debts and support herself and her children.

It was on a day, Elisha passed on to Shunem (וַיְהִי הַיּוֹם וַיַּעֲבֹר אֱלִישָׁע אֶל שׁוּנֵם; v. 8). In the city of Shunem lived a woman of importance, sister of Avishag of Shunem, who had been chosen to be the companion of King David in his old age. This woman begged Elisha to eat at her home, and he agreed and dined with her. From that time on whenever he would pass that way he would dine at her home.

She told her husband, *I know that he is a man of God, and he is holy* (וַתֹּאמֶר אֶל אִישָׁהּ הִנֵּה נָא יָדַעְתִּי כִּי אִישׁ אֱלֹהִים קָדוֹשׁ הוּא; v. 9). "I have known this for some time. Since he comes to us often it is only right for us to build a small attic, furnished with a bed, a table and chair, and a lamp. Each time he comes to stay with us he can stay there."

One day Elisha came and lay down on his bed in the attic. He told his servant lad Gechazi to call the Shunamite woman, his hostess. When he brought her, Elisha said, "You have troubled yourself so much on our behalf, and have built a separate room. How can I repay you? Have you something to ask of a king or of a noble? Tell me, and I will speak on your behalf."

The woman answered, "*I live among my people* (בְּתוֹךְ עַמִּי אָנֹכִי יֹשָׁבֶת; v. 13), and if I have something to say my family speaks for me."

Elisha later turned to his servant and asked how they could repay her kindness.

And Gechazi said, "She has no son, and her husband is old (וַיֹּאמֶר גֵּיחֲזִי אֲבָל בֵּן אֵין לָהּ וְאִישָׁהּ זָקֵן; v. 14). If you think she may still give birth, you should know that her husband is old and may die quite soon."

Elisha commanded Gechazi to bring the hostess again. He called her, and she stood in the doorway.

And he said, "At this time, in the coming year, you will embrace a son" (וַיֹּאמֶר לַמּוֹעֵד הַזֶּה בָּעֵת חַיָּה אַתְּ חֹבֶקֶת בֵּן; v. 16). *She answered, "Please, holy man of God, do not make fun of your handmaid — by giving me a gift that will not last. You tell me that I will embrace a son. What use is that, if he will die soon afterwards? If you want to pray for me, pray for a son who will live."*

The woman became pregnant and gave birth to a son at the time that the prophet had predicted. The child grew older, and one day, during harvest time, he went to his father in the field.

He said to his father, "My head, my head! (וַיֹּאמֶר אֶל אָבִיו רֹאשִׁי רֹאשִׁי; v. 19). *My head is aching."* His father asked a young man to carry him home to his mother. The child lay in his mother's lap until noon, when he died.

She went up and laid him on the bed of the man of God (v. 21), and then told her husband, "Send a servant lad and a mule, and I will go to the prophet. I will return shortly." She did not tell her husband that their son was dead.

Her husband asked her, *Why are you going to him today? It is neither Rosh Chodesh (New Moon) nor Shabbos* (לֹא חֹדֶשׁ וְלֹא שַׁבָּת; v. 23). We learn from this that people used to go to visit a prophet or a *Rebbe* on *Shabbos* and Rosh Chodesh.

The woman assured her husband that everything was in order, not wanting to tell him of their son's death until she had seen the prophet.

She saddled the mule and commanded the young man to hasten to the prophet on Mount Carmel. Upon seeing her, Elisha ordered Gechazi to go ahead and greet her, and find out if all was well.

And she came to the man of God, to the mountain (v. 27), and fell down before him. Gechazi tried to push her away, but Elisha told him, *Leave her be, for her soul is grieved within her, and God has hidden [this] from me and not told me [of it].*

She said, "Did I ask for a son from my lord? Did I not say, 'Do not deceive me?' " (v. 28).

Elisha ordered Gechazi: "Prepare yourself. *Take my staff in your hand, and set out. If you see any man, do not greet him, and if he greets you, do not answer him. Put my staff on the child's face"* (v. 29). He commanded this so that Gechazi would not waste any time.

The *Midrash* writes that Gechazi laughed about the staff, and said, "Can a staff raise the dead back to life?"

The boy's mother said, "As the Lord lives, and by your life, I will not leave you (v. 30). You yourself must come with me." Elisha then accompanied her home.

Gechazi reached the house before them, and laid the staff on the face of the child, who did not stir. He then returned to meet Elisha and told him that the child had not awakened. Elisha entered the house and found the child lying dead on the bed.

He came and shut the door upon the two of them (v. 33), and prayed to God. Then he laid himself down upon the child, placing his mouth upon the child's mouth, his eyes upon the child's eyes, his hands upon the child's hands. He stretched out his entire body on the child's body, warming him through his mouth. Then the prophet paced to and fro in the room. Afterwards, he again spread himself out and warmed the child.

The child sneezed seven times and opened his eyes. Elisha then called his servant Gechazi and told him to bring the child's mother. When she came he told her to take her son. She fell at Elisha's feet, prostrating herself on the ground. Then she took her son and left.

Pirkei deR'Eliezer says of this *Haftorah:* R' Yehoshua ben Korcha says that in the merit of charity the dead will be resurrected in the days of *Mashiach.*

We find that no woman could look at Elisha's face. Any woman who did look him in the face would die. Elisha was forced to hide himself from women, roaming from one mountain to the other, from one cave to the next. When he came to Shunem, the notable woman spoken of above told her husband, "It is known that women cannot look this godly man directly in the face. Let us therefore build him a separate room." They did so, and he slept there.

One day he called the Shunamite woman, and she stood on the threshold, afraid to approach him lest she look at him. Later, when her son was revived from the dead, this happened in the merit of the charity which she had bestowed upon him.

The *Gemara,* in Tractate *Berachos,* says of the verse, *She said to her husband, "I know that he is a man of God, and he is holy"* (v. 9): R' Yosei ben Chanina says that we learn from this that a woman can better recognize if her guests are pious than a man.

R' Yosei ben Chanina also said, in the name of R' Eliezer ben Yaakov, that when a person is hospitable to a Torah scholar in his home, and gives him food, drink, and gifts, it is as praiseworthy as if he had offered a *korban tamid* (daily sacrifice). This is hinted at in the words of the Shunamite woman to her husband: *He passes by us always* (הוּא עֹבֵר עָלֵינוּ תָּמִיד; v. 9; *tamid* — "always").

In this *Haftorah* it is written that the Shunamite woman put a bed, a table, a chair, and a candlestick in Elisha's room. This shows that one who takes guests into his home is like one who builds a sanctuary *(mishkan)* for the Divine Presence to dwell in. Indeed, the initials of the words for: bed (מִטָּה), table (שֻׁלְחָן), chair (כִּסֵּא), and candle (נֵר), together spell out the word מִשְׁכָּן, *sanctuary*.

Bereishis Rabbah asks: Why does the verse say, in Avraham's case, *This time next year I will return to you* (לַמּוֹעֵד אָשׁוּב אֵלֶיךָ; *Bereishis* 18:14), while, in the case of the Shunamite woman, the word for *I will return* (אָשׁוּב) does not appear, and the verse says only, *at this time, in the coming year, you will embrace a son* (v. 16)? The answer is that Avraham received his promise from an angel, who lives eternally, and so he could promise that he would return. But Elisha, who was a mortal man, could not promise to return in a year. He simply promised that anyone who was living would see her embrace a son.

HAFTORAH

Chayei Sarah

(Melachim I/I Kings chapter 1)

The king, David, was old, advanced in years (וְהַמֶּלֶךְ דָּוִד זָקֵן בָּא בַּיָּמִים; v. 1). David was seventy years old. He had been anointed king when he was thirty years old, and had reigned for forty years.

It is difficult to understand why he is here called "old," when he was still relatively young. The answer is that he was as weak as an old man of one hundred, because all of his life had been spent battling various enemies.

He was covered with many layers of clothing, but to no avail; he never felt warm. The *Midrash* writes that one who does not treat another's clothing properly will never be kept warm by his own clothes. This we see in the case of David. Because he tore off a piece of Shaul's (Saul's) garment, his own clothing did not keep him warm.

The Sages also say that King David once saw the Angel of Death, and was so stricken with fear that from then on he could not stay warm. In his older days, this feeling of cold grew worse.

His servants said to him, "*Let there be sought for our lord the king a young virgin* (v. 2), in order to keep him warm." They searched for a beautiful young girl in all of the borders of Israel, and found Avishag of Shunem. She was brought to the king to serve him. He had no relations with her; she merely warmed his bones.

Adoniah ben Chagis exalted himself, saying, "I will be king" (וַאֲדֹנִיָה בֶן חַגִּית מִתְנַשֵּׂא לֵאמֹר אֲנִי אֶמְלֹךְ; v. 5). Adoniah, David's son by Chagis, flattered himself by saying that he would reign after his father's death. His father never rebuked or grieved him by questioning him.

Adoniah, who was born after Avshalom, David's son, flattered himself on his beautiful appearance. He built himself a chariot, appointing fifty men to run before him.

He used to confer with Yoav ben Tzruyah (v. 7), who agreed to help him win the kingship. Yoav had killed Avner ben Ner, Amasah, and Avshalom, and David was furious with him. He refrained from killing him only because he was his chief general, but he planned to leave a command to his successor to take vengeance on Yoav after his death. Yoav therefore supported Adoniah's bid for the kingship and sought his favor, hoping that Adoniah would ultimately ignore his father's command to kill him.

Evyasar the priest, too, agreed to help Adoniah become king, because David had taken the high priesthood away from him and replaced him with the priest Tzadok (Zaddok).

Tzadok, Benayahu (Benaiah), the prophet Nasan (Nathan), Shimi, Reyi, and all of David's mighty warriors did not support Adoniah.

Adoniah slaughtered sheep and oxen and fatted cattle (v. 9) at the stone of Zocheles. This was a boulder which the young men used to test their strength, seeing who could lift the stone. The stone stood by the side of the spring Ein Rogel, where the women would bathe.

Adoniah invited his brothers, and the people of the tribe of Yehudah who served the king; he did not invite Nasan the prophet, nor Benayahu, nor his own brother Shlomo (Solomon).

Nasan told Bas Sheva (Bathsheba), Shlomo's mother, "*Have you not heard that Adoniah is reigning, and our master David does not know of it? Now, let me give you some advice, so that you can save your life and the life of your son Shlomo* (v. 11-12). Your son will surely want to rule after David's death, as God has promised him. If Adoniah proclaims himself king, Shlomo will be forced to fight for the kingship. Further, you yourself will undergo the humiliation of having to serve Adoniah. I suggest that you go to the king and complain to him that he promised that your son would rule — so why has he allowed Adoniah to reign?"

Now why in fact had David sworn that Shlomo would be king? Who persuaded him to do so? The answer is that when the first son whom Bas Sheva bore to David died, everyone said that it was a punishment for David's treatment of Uriah, Bas Sheva's former husband. Bas Sheva cried out to David, saying, "Even if my children were to live, everyone would humiliate them and treat them with disrespect. I will not live with you any more, nor bear your children." It was then that David swore that the first son she would bear him would become king. That son was Shlomo.

Nasan knew of all this through the prophecy, and so he counselled her to go to David. He promised to follow her and speak on her behalf.

Bas Sheva came to the king's chamber (וַתָּבֹא בַת שֶׁבַע אֶל הַמֶּלֶךְ הַחַדְרָה; v. 15). Though no one was allowed to enter the king's chamber without permission, because she was a queen Bas Sheva went in. She bowed down to the king, who asked her why she was prostrating herself. She answered, "My master, my king, you swore to me that your son Shlomo would be king, and would sit on the throne, yet now Adoniah has been crowned king, without your knowledge. He has slaughtered many animals, and invited all of the king's children, together with the priest Evyasar and your general Yoav, and yet he did not invite Shlomo. It is clear that he wants to become king and invited those who would help him. My master, my king, you know that all of Israel wait for your words, to know whom you would appoint as your successor. *When my master, the king, shall sleep with his ancestors, I and my son Shlomo will be left with nothing"* (v. 21) — that is, left without the kingship.

Some of our Sages translate this verse literally, that is, "I and my son Shlomo will be thought to be sinners (חַטָּאִים; v. 21). People will say that because David took Uriah's wife, his son Shlomo did not become king." Others say that the mention of sin refers to David himself. She warned him that if he did not give Shlomo the throne he would have sinned by breaking his vow to her.

As they were speaking Nasan came and asked for an audience with the king. Permission was granted. Nasan entered, bowed to the ground, and said, "My master, my king, have you announced that Adoniah will be king? I have heard that he has slaughtered many sheep and oxen and has made a great feast to which he invited the king's sons, the general Yoav, and Evyasar the priest. They are all eating and drinking and toasting the long life of the new king Adoniah. Tzadok and Benayahu and Shlomo and I were not invited, and so now I turn to you to find out if Adoniah is really the king. I am surprised that the king has not, until now, let me know who will rule."

The king said, "Call Bas Sheva to me" (v. 28). As soon as Nasan arrived Bas Sheva had left, so that no one would realize that they had spoken with each other prior to their visits.

She now came again before the king, who said to her, "As God lives (v. 29), I swear by God who saved me from so many sorrows, that just as I swore to you that Shlomo would be king, so will I do this very day." Bas Sheva bowed low twice and said, "May King David live forever!"

❦ ❦ ❦

Midrash Tanchuma writes of this verse, *The king, David, was old, advanced in years* (v. 1): Why is it granted to a person to live to a ripe old age? And the *Midrash* answers: There is a verse concerning old age that says, בְּדֶרֶךְ צְדָקָה תִּמָּצֵא — *It is found in the way of righteousness* (Mishlei 16:31). This is exemplified in the life of Avraham, who *gave charity and trained his children likewise, so that they watch the path of God, to act charitably and with justice* (וְשָׁמְרוּ דֶרֶךְ ה׳ לַעֲשׂוֹת צְדָקָה וּמִשְׁפָּט; *Bereishis* 18:19). As a result of this he was granted a long life, as it is written, *and Avraham was old, advanced in years* (וְאַבְרָהָם זָקֵן בָּא בַּיָּמִים; *Bereishis* 24:1). In David's case it is likewise written, *He acted charitably and with justice to his entire nation* (וַיְהִי עֹשֶׂה מִשְׁפָּט וּצְדָקָה לְכָל עַמּוֹ; *Divrei HaYamim I*, 18:14), and therefore he was found worthy of becoming an old man, advanced in years (זָקֵן בָּא בַּיָּמִים).

In *Koheles (Ecclesiastes)*, Shlomo says: *Cast your bread upon the waters, for after many days you shall find it* (שַׁלַּח לַחְמְךָ עַל פְּנֵי הַמָּיִם כִּי בְרֹב הַיָּמִים תִּמְצָאֶנּוּ; 11:1). Give your bread to the poor, like one who throws bread into the water, with no thought of getting it back or being rewarded, and you will see many days — that is, you will live a long life.

When a person gives charity with the intention of being rewarded with prosperity, God so rewards him. But if he does it for the sake of God he lives a long life.

The *Gemara* says, in Tractate *Megillah*, that R' Yaakov said in the name of R' Yochanan: Shlomo was permitted to take Avishag as a wife, because he was a king and therefore allowed to take another king's wife. Further, Avishag was not really his father's wife, since David had never consummated a marriage with her. Adoniah, on the other hand, was not permitted to marry her, since he was for all intents and purposes a commoner, and she was a queen.

The *Gemara* in Tractate *Sanhedrin* comments on the words in this *Haftorah, the girl was very beautiful* (וְהַנַּעֲרָה יָפָה עַד מְאֹד; v. 4). R' Chanina bar Papa learns from a comparison of two verses that Avishag was not half as beautiful as Sarah. The passage describes her as being beautiful עַד מְאֹד (literally, "*until* very much"), but does not say she had as it were attained the degree of beauty which the Torah ascribes to Sarah, who is described as *very beautiful* (יָפָה הִיא מְאֹד; *Bereishis* 12:14).

The *Talmud Yerushalmi* says, in Tractate *Pe'ah:* R' Shmuel bar Nachmani says, in the name of R' Yonasan, that although speaking ill of a person *(lashon hara)* is a very serious sin, it is permissible to speak evil of one who causes controversy and conflict. We learn this from Nasan the prophet, who spoke ill of Adoniah in order that he should not usurp the throne.

The *Gemara* says in Tractate *Bava Kama* on the verse, *But me, me — your servant, and Tzadok the priest, he did not invite* (v. 26): Sixty kinds of toothache come to one who sees someone eating while he does not eat, as Nasan complained, "All of the servants were invited to eat, and I was not invited." Some say that we see this in Avraham as well. When Avraham saw Yitzchak marry he grew jealous, and soon afterwards he married, as it says, *And Avraham again took a wife* (וַיֹּסֶף אַבְרָהָם וַיִּקַּח אִשָּׁה; *Bereishis* 25:1). Because Yitzchak had taken a wife, he did the same.

HAFTORAH

Toldos

(Malachi 1:1-2:7)

The burden of the word of God to Israel, by the hand of Malachi (מַשָּׂא דְבַר ה' אֶל יִשְׂרָאֵל בְּיַד מַלְאָכִי; v. 1). This is the prophecy of God's words which were communicated to Malachi to tell Israel. These prophecies had long been in Malachi's hands. Our Sages learn from this that all the prophets stood on Mount Sinai and were given their prophecies, which they would later tell in their own time.

I have loved you, says God (אָהַבְתִּי אֶתְכֶם אָמַר ה'; v. 2). "If you wonder how I show My love, I will tell you. Although Esav was Yaakov's brother, I favored Yaakov and gave him the good land, *Eretz Yisrael. I shall lay his mountains waste* (וָאָשִׂים אֶת הָרָיו שְׁמָמָה; v. 3), so that they will not be comparable to the mountains of *Eretz Yisrael*; and Mount Seir, which belongs to Esav, will be inhabited only by snakes."

If Edom says, "Yes, *we were impoverished* (v . 4), but now we are rich, for we have looted Yerushalayim; we can now return and rebuild our destroyed cities" — God answers: "They will build and I will destroy. They will be called a wicked country, this people with whom I am eternally angry."

"Your eyes will see (v. 5), and you will testify, that God has become great throughout the borders of Israel and has shown that He is our God."

A son honors his father (בֵּן יְכַבֵּד אָב; v. 6). God says: "If I am your Father, where is the honor due Me? If I am your Master, where is the fear which you should feel for Me?"

God then tells the priests who have despised His name: "You may ask, 'How have we despised You?' Let me tell you, then, that you have brought unclean bread to My altar. If you ask, 'How, then, have we made the bread disgusting?' I tell you, it is by the way you have divided the sacrifices among yourselves."

They used to say, "Let this priest take this sacrifice, and that priest take that one." This is prohibited; rather, each sacrifice must be divided among all of the priests. This is a tedious procedure, since each time one gets a portion the size of an olive — but it is the proper way.

If you bring the blind for sacrifice (v. 8). "If you priests bring a blind sheep as a sacrifice, is this not an evil thing? If you bring a lame or sick animal, is this not disgusting? Just take such an animal to your governor as a gift! Would he be satisfied? Would he favor you and refrain from punishing you? Yet you bring Me such a sacrifice!" So says God, Your master.

And now, beseech God that He be gracious toward us (v. 9). "How can you priests think that you can be messengers for Israel and plead on their behalf? Do you think that I will listen to your prayers, when you anger Me so?"

Who is there among you who would close the doors? (v. 10). "Who among you is still good, and will lock the doors of My Temple, to prevent you priests from lighting a fire on My altar and bringing such sacrifices? I will not accept them from your hands!" So says God, the Lord of Hosts.

"From the rising of the sun until its setting (כִּי מִמִּזְרַח שֶׁמֶשׁ עַד

מְבוֹאוֹ; v. 11) — from one side of the earth, where the sun rises, to the other, where it sets, My name is revered among the people. In all lands they burn incense and bring sacrifices and pure offerings to Me, yet you profane Me by speaking with contempt of the altar and its food" (v. 12).

And you say, "What a burden!" (v. 13). "You say, 'We are poor, and cannot afford to bring a well-fed animal as a sacrifice.' Instead, you bring a sickly animal, and distress Me with it." So says God. "You bring a stolen animal, or an animal which is weak and sick. Shall I accept this from you?"

Cursed be the deceiver, who has in his flock a male (v. 14). "Cursed be the man who claims that he has no fine animal in his flock, while in truth he has a ram worthy of being sacrificed. He vows to bring a sacrifice and slaughters a blemished animal. He should not have done this, for I am a great King, and My Name is feared among the nations."

And now, priests, this commandment is for you (2:1). "I command that you no longer sacrifice imperfect animals upon My altar. If you do not heed Me, and do not show respect for My holy name," says God, "I will send a curse upon you. I will curse your grain harvest, which ought to have been blessed. It is already accursed, but it shall be even more so, for you do not revere Me."

"I will rebuke your seed (v. 3), and destroy the seeds which you plant. I will spread dirt upon your faces, the dirt of the animals which you sacrifice on the festivals — that is, you will receive no reward for the sacrifices. Conversely, they will bring shame and evil to you. You will become as disgusting as the refuse and carried away with it, if you show disrespect for My name by sacrificing blemished animals."

"Know then, priests, that I have given the prohibition against sacrificing a flawed animal to you, for My covenant is with the Tribe of Levi. *My covenant was with him, for life and peace* (בְּרִיתִי הָיְתָה אִתּוֹ הַחַיִּים וְהַשָּׁלוֹם; v. 5). Long ago I made My covenant with Aharon (Aaron), and later with Pinchas (Phineas), both members of the tribe of Levi. It was a covenant that they should live, and be at peace, as it is written, *Behold, I give to him My covenant of peace"* (הִנְנִי נֹתֵן לוֹ אֶת בְּרִיתִי שָׁלוֹם); *Bamidbar* 25:12).

"I placed within Aharon the fear of My name. *The Torah of truth was in his mouth and iniquity was not to be found on his lips; he walked with Me in peace and righteousness, and turned many people back from sin* (תּוֹרַת אֱמֶת הָיְתָה בְּפִיהוּ וְעַוְלָה לֹא נִמְצָא בִשְׂפָתָיו; בְּשָׁלוֹם וּבְמִישׁוֹר הָלַךְ אִתִּי וְרַבִּים הֵשִׁיב מֵעָוֹן; v. 6) — for not one man of the tribe of Levi took part in the sin of the Golden Calf."

For the priest's lips should guard knowledge (כִּי שִׂפְתֵי כֹהֵן יִשְׁמְרוּ
דַעַת; v. 7). The priest's lips must guard the wisdom of the Torah, for
they are asked questions about the Torah. It has been taught to them
so that they will be able to teach its laws to Israel. The priest is God's
messenger, for like an angel he can go into the Holy of Holies to
serve God, a privilege accorded no one else.

HAFTORAH

Vayetzei

(Hoshea/Hosea 12:13 — 14:10)

Shabbos Teshuvah

(14:2 — 14:10)

And Yaakov fled to the field of Aram (וַיִּבְרַח יַעֲקֹב שְׂדֵה אֲרָם;
12:13). He fled to Aram and served Lavan for the sake of a woman,
and for the sake of a woman he tended Lavan's flocks; and God
protected him.

God brought Israel out of Egypt through a prophet, and through
a prophet he watched over them — and yet now they mock their
prophets.

Efraim angered Him (v. 15). Efraim infuriated God by mocking
His prophets, and will come to a bitter end. The blood spilled by
Yeravam (Jeroboam), of the tribe of Efraim, when he caused the
Jews to worship idols, will overpower him. God will also punish
Yeravam for having publicly humiliated Shlomo (Solomon), who
was less sinful than he.

When Efraim spoke, there was trembling (כְּדַבֵּר אֶפְרַיִם רְתֵת; 13:1).
When Yeravam, motivated by his zeal for God, first rebuked King
Shlomo, he trembled before the king's greatness, but spoke
nevertheless. Because of this he was found worthy of being granted
the kingship of Israel. But when, after achieving greatness, he
sinned and worshiped false gods, he and his family were doomed to
death and destruction.

And now they sin even more (v. 2). The household of King Yehu, despite their having seen all this, sin even more, building themselves silver idols.

Sacrificers of man, kiss the calves (זֹבְחֵי אָדָם עֲגָלִים יִשָּׁקוּן; v. 2). Worshipers of the idol Molech (Moloch), who believe in human sacrifice, say that those who sacrifice their own children are worthy of kissing the golden idols which Yehu's household have built for themselves.

Therefore they will be like a morning cloud (v. 3). The household of Yehu will be like a cloud which is soon dispersed, like the dew which soon evaporates, like the chaff which is blown away by the gale, and like smoke which disappears up the chimney.

"*And I am God, your Lord* (v. 4) who took you out of Egypt. You are not permitted to worship any god but Me. I have no assistant, and you should not have rebelled against Me."

"*I knew you in the desert* (v. 5). I gave you My heart, supplied you with all of your needs in the barren desert. But when you came to *Eretz Yisrael*, where you were sated with everything you wished for, you forgot Me. Therefore, *I will be to them like a lion* (v. 7), and like a leopard that lies in wait. This is how I will gaze at you, in My anger."

"*I will meet them like a bereaved bear* (אֶפְגְּשֵׁם כְּדֹב שַׁכּוּל; v. 8), which lashes out and kills humans. I will break open their hearts like a bear who thrusts his paws into a man's breast and reaches for his heart. I will prey on them like a lion; the beasts of the field will devour them."

"*You have destroyed yourself, Israel* (שִׁחֶתְךָ יִשְׂרָאֵל; v. 9), by rebelling against the help which God always granted."

"*Where is your king?* (אֱהִי מַלְכְּךָ אֵפוֹא; v. 10). I, God, will stand at a distance to see where your king is, and how he can help you in all your cities. Where, then, are the judges that you asked for, when you said, 'Give us a king and master'? *I gave you a king in My anger* (v. 11), and in even greater wrath will I take him away from you."

"*The sin of Efraim is bound up* (צָרוּר עֲוֹן אֶפְרָיִם; v. 12). It is stored away; I have not forgiven it."

"*The pangs of a travailing woman shall come upon him* (חֶבְלֵי יוֹלֵדָה יָבֹאוּ לוֹ; v. 13), for he is an unwise son."

"*I redeem them from the grave* (מִיַּד שְׁאוֹל אֶפְדֵּם; v. 14). I, God, have always saved you from death and hellfire, but today I speak to you of death, and pronounce the decree of purgatory. There will be no mercy in My eyes; I will not regret My anger."

"*For he prospered among his brothers* (כִּי הוּא בֵּין אַחִים יַפְרִיא; v. 15). Before he sinned, Efraim grew among his brothers; that is, he grew to be more important than they — in the words of Yaakov's blessing, *but his younger brother will be greater than he* (וְאוּלָם אָחִיו הַקָּטֹן יִגְדַּל מִמֶּנּוּ; *Bereishis* 48:19). But now that he has sinned with golden idols, an eastern wind will come out of the desert, a mighty wind which meets no obstacles, and it will dry up his wells and his springs and destroy all his precious vessels."

"*Shomron (Samaria) will be desolate* (תֶּאְשַׁם שֹׁמְרוֹן; 14:1) because she rebelled against her God. Her people will fall by the sword, her women and children will be torn open."

(The following section of this Haftorah constitutes the major portion of the Haftorah of Shabbos Teshuvah.)

"*Return, O Israel, unto the Lord, your God* (שׁוּבָה יִשְׂרָאֵל עַד ה' אֱלֹהֶיךָ; v. 2).

"*You have stumbled on account of your sins — therefore repent.*" Our Sages say that repentance is so lofty that it reaches up to the very throne of God, as it is written, ... *unto the Lord your God. Take with you words, and return to the Lord* (קְחוּ עִמָּכֶם דְּבָרִים וְשׁוּבוּ אֶל ה'; v. 3).

Say to God: "Forgive us for our sins and consider only our good deeds when You judge us. *We will offer [the words of] our lips, instead of [the sacrifices of] oxen* (וּנְשַׁלְּמָה פָרִים שְׂפָתֵינוּ; v. 3). *Ashur will not save us; we will no longer ride horses* (אַשּׁוּר לֹא יוֹשִׁיעֵנוּ עַל סוּס לֹא נִרְכָּב; v. 4). We will no longer depend on the help of Ashur (Assyria) and Egypt [who used to supply Israel with horses], nor will we worship the work of our hands; rather, You, our God, will be our only hope, *for in You the fatherless find compassion* (אֲשֶׁר בְּךָ יְרֻחַם יָתוֹם).

The prophet says, in God's name: "*I will heal their backsliding, and love them charitably* (אֶרְפָּא מְשׁוּבָתָם אֹהֲבֵם נְדָבָה; v. 5). Even if they do not deserve it, I will love them and My anger will abate. I will be like the dew to them (אֶהְיֶה כַטַּל לְיִשְׂרָאֵל; v. 6), and they will flourish as roses do, and strike roots vigorously, as in the forests of Lebanon."

"*His branches will spread* (יֵלְכוּ יֹנְקוֹתָיו; v. 7). Israel shall have many children, as beautiful as the oil of the *Menorah* and as sweet as the incense of the Temple" (וְרֵיחַ לוֹ כַּלְּבָנוֹן) — the Temple being called Levanon, because it whitens *(lavan)* the sins of Israel through the sacrifices which they offer there.

"*They who live in his shadow shall return* (יָשֻׁבוּ יֹשְׁבֵי בְצִלּוֹ; v. 8). Those that once sat in the shadow in the Temple, and were exiled from it, will return. They will be richly nourished with their harvests, and will blossom as the grapevine does. The memory of their prosperity will linger like the lingering notes of the *shofar* blasts which were sounded to accompany the offerings of wine on the altar."

"*Efraim will say, 'What have I to do with idols any more?* (אֶפְרַיִם מַה לִּי עוֹד לָעֲצַבִּים; v. 9). I will serve them no longer.' Then God will answer his prayers and end his tribulations."

"*I am like a leafy green tree* (אֲנִי כִּבְרוֹשׁ רַעֲנָן; v. 9). I, God will be like a tree whose branches bend earthward, so that anyone can grasp them. I will allow Myself to be found by anyone who longs for Me. All your fruits come from Me, all goodness comes from Me."

"*Who is wise, and will understand these?* (מִי חָכָם וְיָבֵן אֵלֶּה; v. 10). Who among you is wise enough to pay heed to these words and return to God? For *God's ways are right; the just shall walk in them and transgressors will stumble in them* (יְשָׁרִים דַּרְכֵי ה' וְצַדִּקִים יֵלְכוּ בָם וּפֹשְׁעִים יִכָּשְׁלוּ בָם; v. 10).

❀ ❀ ❀

In Tractate *Sanhedrin*, the *Gemara* amplifies the words, *idols according to their own understanding* (כִּתְבוּנָם עֲצַבִּים; 13:2). R' Yitzchak says that each Jew made himself an idol and kept it in his pocket, and whenever he was reminded of it he would take it out and kiss it.

R' Yitzchak says further that the verse זֹבְחֵי אָדָם עֲגָלִים יִשָּׁקוּן (13:2; translated above as *sacrificers of man, kiss the calves*) refers to the priests of the idols, who robbed the wealthy through extortion. They would take the calves which were worshiped and deprive them of food. Then they sculpted the figure of a wealthy man, and placed it next to the calves' trough. Finally, they would set the calves free, and the animals, seeing a figure resembling that which had stood next to their trough, would follow the rich man and lick him, mistaking him for the form.

The priests would then claim that the calves had chosen the rich man as a sacrifice, and would extort huge sums of money in order to redeem the man's life. This, then, is another meaning of the words זֹבְחֵי אָדָם עֲגָלִים יִשָּׁקוּן: the priests claimed that the men "kissed" — or licked — by the calves must be sacrificed.

The *Gemara* says in Tractate *Yoma* that R' Shimon ben Lakish says: "Repentance is a great thing. When a man repents, God considers the intentional sins as if they were unintentional, as it is written, *Return, O Israel, to the Lord, your God, for you have stumbled* (כִּי כָשַׁלְתָּ) *in your sins* (14:2). Your sin will be considered as if you had unintentionally tripped over something which you were not aware of.

R' Yitzchak says that it is said in *Eretz Yisrael,* in the name of Rabbah bar Mari: "Come and see the difference between God and man: When two men quarrel, and one wants to appease the other, he does not know how to go about it; perhaps he should appease him with a gift, perhaps through cordial words. But when we sin against God, He is appeased by our words alone, as it is written, *Take with you words, and return to the Lord* (קְחוּ עִמָּכֶם דְּבָרִים וְשׁוּבוּ אֶל ה'; 14:3). Moreover, one who repents in words is likened to one who has built an altar and offered a sacrifice on it, as it is written (*ibid.*), וּנְשַׁלְּמָה פָרִים שְׂפָתֵינוּ — *We will offer [the words of] our lips instead of [the sacrifices of] oxen.*"

HAFTORAH

Vayishlach

(Ovadiah/Obadiah)

This is the vision of Ovadiah (חֲזוֹן עֹבַדְיָה; v. 1). Ovadiah spoke solely of Edom. This was because he was a convert, originally of Edom. God said to Himself: "I will punish Edom at the hands of the Edomites themselves. So let Ovadiah, who lived with two wicked people, Achav and Izevel (Ahab and Jezebel), but did not learn from their ways, foretell the punishment of Edom, whose progenitor Esav lived with two righteous people, Yitzchak and Rivkah, but did not learn from their ways."

This was his prophecy to Edom: "We prophets have heard tidings from God. A messenger has been sent among the pagan nations, telling them to gather together and encourage one another to rise up and battle Edom."

"I have made you the smallest of the nations" (הִנֵּה קָטֹן נְתַתִּיךָ בַּגּוֹיִם; v. 2). Edom did not have its own alphabet or language, and was despised, for it did not have a hereditary monarchy.

The prophet tells Edom: *"The evil in your heart has deceived you* (זְדוֹן לִבְּךָ הִשִּׁיאֶךָ; v. 3), convincing you to speak badly of your own brother Yaakov. *You dwell in the clefts of the rocks* (שֹׁכְנִי בְחַגְוֵי סֶלַע; v. 3); that is, you are depending on the merits of your ancestors, like one who hides among the lofty rocks for shelter, and thinks to himself, 'Who can touch me?' Therefore God says, *If you rise like an eagle, if you build your nest among the stars, from there will I cast you down* (אִם תַּגְבִּיהַּ כַּנֶּשֶׁר וְאִם בֵּין כּוֹכָבִים שִׂים קִנֶּךָ מִשָּׁם אוֹרִידְךָ; v. 4).

So says God: "*When thieves came upon you* (v. 5), how did you sleep so soundly? They stole as much as they desired, without difficulty. If grape pickers came to you, they would at least have left the poor, rotten grapes, but the thieves who came to you, Edom, have left nothing at all."

"How were all of your hiding places discovered, Esav? The allies with whom you had treaties escorted you until the borders (v. 7) where your enemies were massing, persuading you to go out to war. But they abandoned you when they reached the border, leaving you alone to face the enemy."

They have caused your bread to become a pain in your place (לַחְמְךָ יָשִׂימוּ מָזוֹר תַּחְתֶּיךָ; v. 7); that is to say, "Because your brother Yaakov gave you bread and lentils, you, Esav, despised your birthright, and now this causes you pain. Esav, you lack wit and understanding."

On the day that the punishment came to Edom, says God, "*I will destroy the wise men of Edom, and [men of] understanding from Esav's mountains* (וְהַאֲבַדְתִּי חֲכָמִים מֵאֱדוֹם וּתְבוּנָה מֵהַר עֵשָׂו; v. 8). Your mighty men will be broken and will flee to the land of Yemen, because of the great massacre which will take place among them. Because you robbed your brother Yaakov you will be totally humiliated, cut off eternally."

"*On the day that you stood aloof, on the day that strangers captured his wealth* (בְּיוֹם עֲמָדְךָ מִנֶּגֶד בְּיוֹם שְׁבוֹת זָרִים חֵילוֹ; v. 11). When strangers robbed all of your brother Yaakov's cherished possessions, when they stood at his very gates and cast lots for Yerushalayim, so as to divide it up between them, you, Edom, stood to a side and did not come to your brother's assistance. Therefore, you too are considered to be one of Israel's enemies. You ought not to have stood to one side, gazing upon Yaakov's downfall; you should not have rejoiced when Yehudah's children were defeated; you should not have scoffed at them on the day of their great anguish. You should not have approached them on the day that they were defeated; you should not have come to see them and to thrust your hands into their booty."

"*You should not have stood at the crossroads, to cut off his refugees* (וְאַל תַּעֲמֹד עַל הַפֶּרֶק לְהַכְרִית אֶת פְּלִיטָיו; v. 14). You cut off Israel's escape routes; you delivered them into their enemy's hands.

You should not have done this; rather, you should have thought to yourself that *the day of God upon all the nations is near* (כִּי קָרוֹב יוֹם הי' עַל בָּל הַגּוֹיִם; v. 15). The day of punishment approaches, when God will repay measure for measure, giving each nation what it deserves."

"*For just as you drank on My holy mountain* (כִּי כַּאֲשֶׁר שְׁתִיתֶם עַל הַר קָדְשִׁי; v. 16). Just as you rejoiced at the calamity that overcame My mountain," says God, "you together with all those nations will soon drink from the cup of punishment; you will drink and be destroyed."

"*On Mt. Zion will be deliverance; it will be holy* (וּבְהַר צִיּוֹן תִּהְיֶה פְלֵיטָה וְהָיָה קֹדֶשׁ; v. 17). The household of Yaakov will inherit the booty which the nations stole from them. *The house of Yaakov will be fire, the house of Yosef (Joseph) a flame* (וְהָיָה בֵית יַעֲקֹב אֵשׁ וּבֵית יוֹסֵף לֶהָבָה; v. 18), while Esav will be the straw which will be consumed. Nothing will be left of him."

"The Jews who live in the south will take over Esav's mountain in the south; those who live on the plain shall inherit the land of the Philistines. The fields of Efraim and of the Shomron will belong to them. The tribe of Binyamin (Benjamin) will be given the land of Gilead, which formerly belonged to the tribe of Menashe, while Menashe will take land even further eastward of *Eretz Yisrael*."

"*And this exile of the host, of the Children of Israel* (וְגָלֻת הַחֵל הַזֶּה לִבְנֵי יִשְׂרָאֵל; v. 20). The Ten Tribes that were exiled among the Canaanites as far as Tzarfas and the exiles from Yerushalayim, who are of the Ten Tribes of Yehudah, who were sent to Sefarad, will possess the cities in the south of *Eretz Yisrael*."

"*And deliverers shall ascend Mt. Zion to judge the mountain of Esav* (וְעָלוּ מוֹשִׁעִים בְּהַר צִיּוֹן לִשְׁפֹּט אֶת הַר עֵשָׂו; v. 21). Esav will be judged for the evil which he did to Israel. And at that time, וְהָיְתָה לַה' הַמְּלוּכָה; (v. 21) — *the kingdom shall be God's*."

HAFTORAH

Vayeshev

(Amos 2:6 — 3:9)

So says God, "I have forgiven Israel three sins, but will not turn away [the punishment of] the fourth" (כֹּה אָמַר ה' עַל שְׁלֹשָׁה פִּשְׁעֵי יִשְׂרָאֵל וְעַל אַרְבָּעָה לֹא אֲשִׁיבֶנּוּ; v. 6). After three offenses the time has certainly come to punish them; how much more so since they persist in sinning.

"I will punish them *because they sold the righteous for silver* (עַל מִכְרָם בַּכֶּסֶף צַדִּיק; v. 6). Their judges sell justice for a bribe, proclaiming the righteous guilty. They twist the poor man's verdict in order to force him to sell land which he owns adjacent to their own fields. Since this results in a forced sale the judges buy up the land cheaply, and thus gain a monopoly on continuous tracts of land."

The judges are evil men *who pant after the dust of the earth on the heads of the poor* (v. 7). They want the land which they tread upon and scheme to find ways of stealing it from the poverty-stricken, by perverting justice. Moreover, *a man and his father go to the same girl, thereby profaning My holy Name (ibid.).*

They lay themselves upon clothing (v. 8). "They sleep in clothing which has been given as a pledge. They cause the poor to put themselves in debt, taking their clothing as security, and then mis-handling it. They spread the clothing on their beds and sleep on it, and use it at the meals which they eat next to the altars of their idols and at their wine revelries." This means that they tax and fine the poor and use the proceeds for their own gluttony.

I destroyed the Emori before them (וְאָנֹכִי הִשְׁמַדְתִּי אֶת הָאֱמֹרִי מִפְּנֵיהֶם; v. 9). "They were as tall as cedars and as strong as oaks, and yet I, God, destroyed their fruits — their defending angels in heaven — and their roots, their warriors on earth."

And I brought you up from Egypt and led you through the desert for forty years, so that you would inherit the land of the Emori (v. 10). *And I raised up prophets from among your sons* (וָאָקִים מִבְּנֵיכֶם לִנְבִיאִים), and men to turn away from this world and study Torah. *Was it not so, Children of Israel? So says God* (v. 11).

"And how did you repay My kindness? *You gave the nazir* [an ascetic who has taken certain vows of abstinence] *wine* (v. 12), so that, being drunk, he would be unable to study Torah or judge; you commanded the prophets to cease their prophesying. Therefore I, God, will burden you as a loaded wagon is burdened. *Flight will vanish from the swift* (וְאָבַד מָנוֹס מִקָּל; v. 14), the mighty will be unable to fight, the archer shall not do battle, and the courageous shall retreat."

You alone have I known of all the families of the earth (רַק אֶתְכֶם יָדַעְתִּי מִכֹּל מִשְׁפְּחוֹת הָאֲדָמָה; 3:2); *therefore will I punish you for all your iniquities.*

God further rebukes Israel for having forbidden the prophets to deliver their teachings. He tells them: When two men walk together, did they not make plans to meet beforehand? Similarly, the prophets do not speak of their own accord; rather, all is planned by God. How can they refrain from speaking?

Will a lion roar in the forest if he has no prey? (הֲיִשְׁאַג אַרְיֵה בַּיַּעַר וְטֶרֶף אֵין לוֹ; v. 4). A lion does not roar unless it has caught an animal or beast. This refers to God, whose voice is like the roar of a lion, and the verse means to say that a vision of warning will come to a prophet only if the punishment has been decreed by God.

Will a young lion cry out of his den if he has snared nothing (הֲיִתֵּן כְּפִיר קוֹלוֹ מִמְּעֹנָתוֹ בִּלְתִּי אִם לָכָד; *ibid.*). Would God cry out and speak of evil decrees if He had not found His People sinning?

Can a bird fall into a snare upon the ground without being entrapped? (v. 5). Can one sin without becoming ensnared thereby?

If a shofar is blown in the city by the scout who was appointed to sound an alarm before the enemy, *will not the people be afraid* (אִם יִתָּקַע שׁוֹפָר בְּעִיר וְעָם לֹא יֶחֱרָדוּ; v. 6)? Similarly, one should tremble at the words of the prophets, and flee from wrongdoing.

Can it be that evil befalls a city, and God has not caused it? (v. 6). When evil comes to you, you should know that God brought it upon you, because you did not heed the words of the prophets. *For the Lord God does nothing without [first] revealing His secret to His servants, the prophets* (v. 7). If therefore you would only listen to them, you would be saved from disaster.

The lion has roared; who will not fear? The Lord God has spoken; who can but prophesy? (אַרְיֵה שָׁאָג מִי לֹא יִירָא ה' אֱלֹהִים דִּבֶּר מִי לֹא יִנָּבֵא; v. 8).

❧ ❧ ❧

In Tractate *Yoma*, the *Gemara* expounds the verse, *For three sins of Israel* ... (עַל שְׁלֹשָׁה פִּשְׁעֵי יִשְׂרָאֵל; 2:6). "R' Yosei says, 'When a man sins, God will forgive him three times — but not the fourth time, as it says, וְעַל אַרְבָּעָה לֹא אֲשִׁיבֶנּוּ, *and on the fourth I will not turn away (ibid.).'"*

The *Gemara*, in Tractate *Chullin*, speaks of the verse, *The lion has roared; who will not fear?* (אַרְיֵה שָׁאָג מִי לֹא יִירָא; 3:8). A great noble once told R' Yehoshua ben Chananiah, "Your God is likened to a lion. How can that be, when a hunter can sometimes kill a lion?" R' Yehoshua answered, "He is not likened to the lions which we are used to. Rather, He is compared to the lion of the great forest of Elai." The man said, "You must show me such a lion."

R' Yehoshua prayed, and the great lion began to leave his habitat and run towards them. When he was four hundred miles away he gave a mighty roar. All the pregnant woman nearby miscarried and homes began to collapse. Three hundred miles from the city he roared once again. Men lost their teeth, and the noble fell off his chair. He turned to R' Yehoshua and begged, "Pray that he return home." R' Yehoshua prayed and the lion turned back.

One time the man told R' Yehoshua, "I want to see your God." R' Yehoshua answered, "Come and I will show Him to you." He pointed to the sun that was blazing in the midsummer month of Tammuz and said, "Look in there and you will see Him." The man answered, "But I cannot look directly at the sun." R' Yehoshua said, "The sun is just one of the many servants of God, and you cannot look at it. Yet you want to see God Himself?"

On another occasion the noble told R' Yehoshua, "I want to make a meal for your God." R' Yehoshua answered, "You cannot, for He has a great escort with Him. You will not have enough room for all his hosts. But if you insist upon it, go and prepare a place for them by the sea."

For six months of summer the man toiled, and then a great rain came and swept everything into the sea. He worked another six months of winter, again preparing a meal, and a wind came and blew everything into the sea. The noble asked R' Yehoshua what was happening, and he answered, "That is the vanguard which travels before God, sweeping up the land before Him." The noble finally admitted, "If this is so, I cannot make a meal for your God."

HAFTORAH

Mikeitz

(Melachim I/I Kings 3:15 — 4:1)

And Shlomo awoke, and behold, it was a dream (וַיִּקַץ שְׁלֹמֹה וְהִנֵּה חֲלוֹם; 3:15). Shlomo (Solomon) awoke and understood that his dream had revealed the truth. He understood, too, the message of the dream, and as a result he went to Yerushalayim, stood before God's Holy Ark, and brought sacrifices. In his joy he made a festive meal for all of his servants, for he knew that his dream would come true.

Then two harlots came to the king (v. 16).
When Shlomo was still in Yerushalayim two harlots came to him for judgment. They stood before him, and one woman said: "Please, my lord, this woman and I live in one house. I gave birth when she was in the house. Three days later, she gave birth as well. The two of us were all alone; there was no one with us.

"The other woman's son died that night, when she accidentally lay upon it in her sleep. She awoke during the night and took my son from me. As I slept she took my child to her bosom and placed her dead son on my bosom.

"When I woke up that morning to nurse my child, I saw that he was dead! I looked closer, and saw that it was not my son at all!"

The other woman said: "It is not as you claim. My son is the living child, and your son is dead. What you say is not true. My son is alive and yours is dead!"

Then the king said: "This woman claims that the living son is hers and the dead one is not; the other woman says your son is dead and hers is alive." We learn from these words that a judge must sum up the complaints of the litigants before handing down a verdict, to show them that he has understand their case fully and will be able to judge correctly.

The king continued, "Bring me a sword." They brought him a sword and he commanded that the living child be cut in two pieces, one half for one woman and one half for the other. Then the woman who was the mother of the living child, because her pity was aroused, said, "I beg you, my lord, give the child to the other woman, but do not kill him!" But the other woman said, "He will not belong to you, nor to me; cut him!" (גַּם לִי גַם לָךְ לֹא יִהְיֶה גְּזֹרוּ; v. 26).

The king then said: "Give that woman the living child, and do not kill him, for she is his mother."

The *Midrash* says that the words הִיא אִמּוֹ — *She is his mother!* — were not said by Shlomo; it was a heavenly voice that rang out and said: "This is his mother; Shlomo has judged correctly."

And all of Israel heard of the judgment which the king had judged and they stood in awe of the king, for they saw that he had God's wisdom within him for judgment (כִּי רָאוּ כִּי חָכְמַת אֱלֹהִים בְּקִרְבּוֹ לַעֲשׂוֹת מִשְׁפָּט; v. 28). They were afraid to do evil, even secretly, for they felt certain that in his wisdom he would find them out, as he had found out which woman was the true mother.

Shlomo ruled over all of Israel, and the people, seeing his wisdom, rejoiced in his kingship.

We learn from this *Haftorah* that women are given to light-mindedness, for the woman wished to have the child cut in half for no reason. So said Shlomo in the Book of *Koheles (Ecclesiastes* 7:28): וְאִשָּׁה בְּכָל אֵלֶּה לֹא מָצָאתִי — *and a [good] woman among all these, I did not find.*

HAFTORAH

Vayigash

(Yechezkel/Ezekiel 37:15-28)

The word of God came to me, saying, "You, son of man, take a piece of wood, and write upon it the words, 'For Yehudah and the Children of Israel, his companions'" (לִיהוּדָה וְלִבְנֵי יִשְׂרָאֵל חֲבֵרָו; v. 16). This inscription referred to Yehudah, and his companion, the tribe of Binyamin, which joined Yehudah in his kingdom.

And take another stick, and write on it, "For Yosef, tree of Efraim, and all the House of Israel, his companions" (לְיוֹסֵף עֵץ אֶפְרַיִם וְכָל בֵּית יִשְׂרָאֵל חֲבֵרָו; v. 16). This inscription referred to Yosef, and more specifically to Efraim, the tribe descended from his son, and towards the other nine tribes who joined the [Northern] kingdom, a kingdom separate from that of Yehudah and Binyamin.

The kingdom of the Ten Tribes was called by Efraim's name because Yerovam (Jeroboam) the son of Nevat, their first king, was a member of the tribe of Efraim.

"And join them one to the other to make one stick. Miraculously, they will become one in your hand (וְהָיוּ לַאֲחָדִים בְּיָדֶךָ; v. 17).

"If the people ask you why you are doing these things, tell them that God, the Master, says: 'I will take the stick of Yosef, which is in the hand of Efraim, together with the tribes of Israel, his companions, and I will unite them with the stick of Yehudah. *I will make them into one stick and they will be one in My hand* (v. 19); that is, they will no longer be divided into two kingdoms. *And these sticks on which you write shall be in your hand before their eyes* (v. 20).

"Say to them, so says God, the Lord: Behold, I will take the Children of Israel from among the nations among which they have gone, and I will gather them from every side, and bring them to their land (הִנֵּה אֲנִי לֹקֵחַ אֶת בְּנֵי יִשְׂרָאֵל מִבֵּין הַגּוֹיִם אֲשֶׁר הָלְכוּ שָׁם וְקִבַּצְתִּי אֹתָם מִסָּבִיב וְהֵבֵאתִי אוֹתָם אֶל אַדְמָתָם; v. 21). *I will make them one nation in the land* (וְעָשִׂיתִי אוֹתָם לְגוֹי אֶחָד בָּאָרֶץ) *upon the mountains of Israel* (v. 22). They will have one king (וּמֶלֶךְ אֶחָד יִהְיֶה לְכֻלָּם לְמֶלֶךְ; *ibid.).* They will no longer be two separate nations, and they will never again be split into two kingdoms.*"

"They will no longer defile themselves with their idols and abominations, and with all their sins. I will save them in all their dwelling places where they have sinned ... I will be their God (וְהוֹשַׁעְתִּי אֹתָם מִכֹּל מוֹשְׁבֹתֵיהֶם אֲשֶׁר חָטְאוּ בָהֶם ... וַאֲנִי אֶהְיֶה לָהֶם לֵאלֹהִים; v. 23).

"And David, My servant, will be king over them, and they shall all have one shepherd (וְעַבְדִּי דָוִד מֶלֶךְ עֲלֵיהֶם וְרוֹעֶה אֶחָד יִהְיֶה לְכֻלָּם; v. 24). They will listen to My laws and heed them. *They will dwell in the land* which I promised to give to My servant Yaakov, a boundless inheritance, the land in which their ancestors lived. *They will live there, they and their children and their children's children, eternally, and David, My servant, shall be their prince (nasi) forever* (v. 25).

"I will make a covenant of peace with them (וְכָרַתִּי לָהֶם בְּרִית שָׁלוֹם; v. 26), an eternal covenant. I will give them their land, they will multiply, and My Temple will stand eternally among them; (וְיָדְעוּ הַגּוֹיִם כִּי אֲנִי ה' מְקַדֵּשׁ אֶת יִשְׂרָאֵל בִּהְיוֹת מִקְדָּשִׁי בְּתוֹכָם לְעוֹלָם — v. 28). *And the nations shall know that I, God, sanctify My People, Israel, when my Sanctuary will be in their midst for evermore.*

HAFTORAH

Vayechi

(Melachim I/I Kings, chapter 2)

v. ‎;וַיִּקְרְבוּ יְמֵי דָוִד לָמוּת *And the days of David's death drew near* (‎לָמוּת דָוִד יְמֵי וַיִּקְרְבוּ). David called his son Shlomo (Solomon) and told him, "I will die, as is the way of the world. You must be a man, and conquer your desires. Heed the laws of God, your God. Walk in His ways, obey His laws, commandments, and statutes, as set forth in His Torah, so that you will prosper in all your endeavors, and *so that God will fulfill His words* (v. 4) to me. He promised that if my children heed His ways and follow Him with all their hearts, the kingship will be theirs eternally."

"Moreover, you know what Yoav ben Tzruyah did to me — to two captains of the hosts of Israel, Avner ben Ner and Amasa ben Yeser (v. 5). He killed them as if at war, in time of peace; that is, he killed them when they considered themselves at peace with him, and thus were unwary."

He murdered them with his sword upon his loins (v. 5). He placed the sword in such a way that it would fall out of its scabbard, and when he approached Amasa the sword did, indeed, fall out. He bent down to pick it up. Amasa paid no heed to him, thinking that he was simply retrieving his sword. Then Yoav stood up and swiftly murdered him.

He killed Avner *with the shoes on his feet (ibid.)*, in the following way. He asked how a woman with no hands goes through the ceremony of *chalitzah* (in which a shoe is untied). Avner stooped down to show him how to untie a shoe with one's teeth. When he was thus bent over, Yoav drew his sword and murdered him.

Midrash Tanchuma writes that the words *what Yoav has done to me* (v. 5) refer to the letter which David sent, commanding Yoav to put Uriah in the heat of battle to ensure that he would be killed. Yoav did as he was told, and let him be killed. When others complained of this, he showed them the letter. *What he has done to me* thus means "to me personally," that is, "He harmed and humiliated me by displaying the letter."

"Do according to your wisdom (‎וְעָשִׂיתָ כְּחָכְמָתֶךָ; v. 6), and do not

let him die a peaceful death of old age. Do not let Yoav go to the grave in peace."

Although Yoav was the son of David's sister, David commanded that he be executed, in order that his sins be atoned for and he be allowed to enter the World to Come.

King David continued his instructions: *"Show kindness to the sons of Barzillai of Gilead"* (v. 7), and let them be guests at your table, for they fed me when I was fleeing from your brother Avshalom (Absalom)."

Midrash Rabbasi writes that the name Barzillai of Gilead is written in the *Haftorah* five times, to show that one who offers a righteous man food at his table is like one who has studied the Five Books of the Torah.

"You have with you Shimi ben Gera (v. 8), of the tribe of Binyamin, from the city of Bachurim. He once cursed me grievously, on the day when I went to Machanayim; but later he came down to me at the Jordan River and I swore not to kill him with the sword. *But now, do not hold him guiltless* (v. 9). You are clever. Find within him a sin for which he deserves death, and bring him down to a bloody grave."

And David slept with his fathers, and was buried in the City of David (v. 10). He ruled for forty years — seven years in Chevron (Hebron), and thirty-three years in Yerushalayim.

Shlomo sat on the throne of David his father, and his kingdom was firmly established (v. 12).

Midrash Rabbah writes that when the Torah says, in reference to a righteous man, *the days of ... drew near that he should die* (וַיִּקְרְבוּ יְמֵי ... לָמוּת), this is a sign that the man did not live as long as his father did. In David's case the verse states, *the days of David grew near that he should die* (v. 1), and he lived to only seventy. His ancestors Boaz, Oved, and Yishai each lived for four hundred years.

The *Gemara* records, in Tractate *Berachos*, that R' Shmuel bar Nachmani says on the verse, *the days of David's death drew near:* "The days of a righteous man die, but the righteous man himself lives eternally — in the other world."

Midrash Rabbasi asks why the verse says *the days of David* (יְמֵי דָוִד), rather than "the days of King David." With a man's death, his dominion ends. Similarly, on the day of Yaakov's death he was very humble, begging his son Yosef to bury him in *Eretz Yisrael.*

R' Yehoshua says, in the name of R' Levi: "On the day of Moshe's death, God hid the trumpets which he had made in the desert, so that no one would see he had once been a ruler. It is as the

Book of *Koheles* (*Ecclesiastes* 8:8) says: וְאֵין שִׁלְטוֹן בְּיוֹם הַמָּוֶת — There is no kingship on the day of death."

HAFTORAH

Shabbos Rosh Chodesh

(Yeshayahu/Isaiah, chapter 66)

"*So says God: The heaven is my throne and the earth My footstool* (כֹּה אָמַר ה' הַשָּׁמַיִם כִּסְאִי וְהָאָרֶץ הֲדֹם רַגְלָי; v. 1). I have no need for your Temple. Can you build a house great enough for My spirit? Where can I rest, when I Myself created both heaven and earth?

"I have rested My Presence among you because you have heeded Me. I look always to the poor and broken in spirit and to those who eagerly listen to Me. But today this is no more."

❧ ❧ ❧

The prophet shows us in this passage how a person should conduct himself in his home — giving charity, showing respect for the poor, and feeding them. He must consider his home as belonging, not to himself, but to God. The prophet here says that God tells us: "What house can you build for Me, when I dwell in heaven? If you want to build a house for Me to live in, take in the poor and show them respect, and then I will live with you."

The *Gemara* says: "One who wants his possessions to remain with him, let him plant within them the Mighty One" (יִטַּע בָּהֶן אָדָר; lit., Adar: a kind of tree); i.e., God, who is called mighty (אַדִּיר). A man must declare that his house belongs, not to him, but to God.

In *Parashas Metzora* the Torah says, *The one whose house is his* (וּבָא אֲשֶׁר לוֹ הַבַּיִת; *Vayikra* 14:35), referring to one who does not welcome guests or lend assistance to neighbors. To such a house God sends *tzaraas* (a disease similar to leprosy).

In the days of the Temple the *Kohen* would come to such a stricken home and order that all the dishes and clothing be carried out, in order to avoid impurity. The possessions were all placed in the street, so that everyone could see that the owner had lied when he had told his neighbors that he did not have them available to lend. God does all of this because the owner did not want to take guests or lend his possessions.

In the Book of *Tehillim (Psalms* 127:1) it is written: *If God does not build a house, its builders have worked in vain* (אִם ה' לֹא יִבְנֶה בַיִת שָׁוְא עָמְלוּ בוֹנָיו בּוֹ). If someone does not admit that God has built the house, he builds for nothing, for it will not have permanence.

A man must know that he is like a person who has rented a home for a year or some such period. God is his landlord.

It is known that renting a place to live in another's house is problematic for three reasons: first, the tenant may not be able to run his business properly, if it competes with the landlord's, and he may as well be afraid to show the landlord how much money he has, because of taxes; second, he may not be able to rent the rooms he needs because he has a large family and the landlord may feel that the children clutter up the whole house; third, he may be afraid that the landlord will tell everyone how he conducts himself in private. If he is greedy, for instance, the landlord will let everyone know. For all of these three reasons, a man may not want to rent and will, instead, build his own home.

The verse makes mention of all three problems. First, although God is the landlord, the renter does not have to worry about his business, for God gives everyone their sustenance, as it is written, *It is vain for you to rise early* (שָׁוְא לָכֶם מַשְׁכִּימֵי קוּם; *Tehillim* 127:2). Rising early in order to make more money helps not at all, if God does not help. But one who relies on God to send him sustenance will be helped, even while he sleeps, as it is written, *For to His beloved He gives sleep* (כֵּן יִתֵּן לִידִידוֹ שֵׁנָא; *ibid.*).

Second, he must not fear that because he has a large family the landlord will complain. On the contrary: the same Psalm says, *Children are a heritage of God, and the fruit of the womb is a reward* (הִנֵּה נַחֲלַת ה' בָּנִים שָׂכָר פְּרִי הַבָּטֶן; *Tehillim* 127:3). God is the landlord, and all children belong to Him, as the *Gemara* says: There are three partners in a person — God, the father, and the mother. When a person dies God says, "You people take your portion, the body; I will take mine, the soul." Because God has a portion in every person, they are like His own children, and He never finds them offensive. Therefore, a person does not have to worry about his large family when God is his landlord.

The third fear is that the landlord will reveal to everyone that he is miserly, or that he is a glutton. But when God is one's landlord one need not fear, for He will not tell. We find that a wise man once told a person who had mocked and humiliated him: "We must thank God day and night, for He knows all of our sins and tells no one. When a person sees a tiny fault in his friend he tells everyone and embarrasses him, as the verse says, *When they speak with enemies at the gate* (כִּי יְדַבְּרוּ אֶת אוֹיְבִים בַּשָּׁעַר; *Tehillim* 127:5). Men often speak about one another, and if they know of a fault — how someone eats, or drinks — soon everyone *at the gate*, in the market, and in the streets, speaks of it. The verse, *as arrows in the hand of a warrior* (כְּחִצִּים בְּיַד גִּבּוֹר; *Tehillim* 127:4), refers to the gossip which men spread when they gather together in the market. Slander is like an arrow shot from afar, striking its victim in the distance. But when God is the landlord, He does not reveal His tenant's faults."

Since we have shown that a person should consider his house as belonging to God, it must always be open to God's relatives — the poor. In the verse, *When you lend money to My people, to the poor* (אִם כֶּסֶף תַּלְוֶה אֶת עַמִּי אֶת הֶעָנִי; *Shmos* 22:24), the poverty-stricken are termed "God's people." In *Yeshayahu*, too, it is stated that *God will comfort His nation, and will have pity on His poor* (כִּי נִחַם ה'; עַמּוֹ וַעֲנִיָּו יְרַחֵם; 49:13). Again, the poor are called "His nation."

Generally, if a prosperous man has rich relatives he tries to draw closer to them, but when his relatives are poor he avoids them. God, though, does the opposite, drawing the poor closer to Him, as it is written in our *Haftorah*, *I will look ... to the poor and broken in spirit* (וְאֶל זֶה אַבִּיט אֶל עָנִי וּנְכֵה רוּחַ; *Yeshayahu* 66:2).

The *Midrash* says that the poor man stands on your threshold, and God stands at his right hand. If the poor man comes into a house, God accompanies him. One who drives away a poor man from his house is like one who has driven away God, the landlord.

In *Pirkei Avos* (Ethics of the Fathers 1:5) the Sages say: "Let your house be open wide, and let the poor be members of your household" (יְהִי בֵיתְךָ פָּתוּחַ לִרְוָחָה וְיִהְיוּ עֲנִיִּים בְּנֵי בֵיתֶךָ). It is difficult to understand why we are told that the door should be open wide; how could the poor be inside if it were closed? The answer is that the verse is telling us that the door should be opened wide and Satan should not be allowed to block it.

When Satan stands in the doorway he blocks it. No one can enter, for it is dangerous to pass him by. But if the poor are in a house, Satan stays away, and the Divine Presence is there instead.

The idea that Satan cannot stand in the same door as the poor is found in the *Zohar, Parashas Bereishis*. It says there that at every festive meal Satan stands at the door, watching to see if there are any poor people in the house. If there are no poor men in the house God grows angry.

We find this in the case of Avraham, who made a meal for his son Yitzchak, and invited many guests. He served them personally. Sarah, too, was very busy, nursing the children of the nobles. These nobles did not believe that Sarah had borne a child in her old age. They said that she had taken someone else's child and claimed it as her own. They therefore brought their nursing children with them, to see if Sarah had milk in her breasts to suckle them. Sarah was therefore nursing all the children.

At this time Satan came in the guise of a poor man and stood by the door, asking for a piece of bread. No one paid him any attention, for neither Avraham nor Sarah had time. Satan then confronted God, saying, "You love Avraham very dearly, yet today I begged bread from him and he gave me nothing. He has no poor men in his home."

As a result, God destroyed Avraham's tranquillity by commanding him to sacrifice Yitzchak. And Sarah subsequently died of fright at the news that her son had nearly been killed.

We learn from this that when there are no poor people in a home Satan stands in the doorway and makes trouble, so that it is dangerous to enter. Our Sages therefore cautioned us to keep our homes wide open, and drive away Satan by bringing in the poor.

❀ ❀ ❀

He slaughters an ox and kills a man (שׁוֹחֵט הַשּׁוֹר מַכֵּה אִישׁ; v. 3). The people may bring an ox as a sacrifice, but first they murder its owner and steal the ox. *They sacrifice a lamb and behead a dog* (זוֹבֵחַ הַשֶּׂה עֹרֵף כֶּלֶב; *ibid.*). Such men are like people who chop off a dog's head as sacrifice. Their meal offering is like an offering made of pig's blood (מִנְחָה דַּם חֲזִיר; *ibid.*); he who brings incense is as if he brought a gift of wrongdoing. *"They have chosen their ways,* says God, and I shall choose their punishments, bringing upon them all that they dread. This will happen because I called to them, by means of My prophets, and told them to return to Me, but no one answered and said, 'I will return' (יַעַן קָרָאתִי וְאֵין עוֹנֶה; v. 4). I spoke but they ignored Me, and they did what was evil in My eyes."

Says the prophet: *"Hear the words of God* (v. 5). Righteous men, listen to God's words. Those who have misled you by claiming that you are unclean and that God will have nothing more to do with you are mistaken. We will live to see your joy, and their humiliation. *There is a voice of tumult from the city, a voice from the Temple* (קוֹל שָׁאוֹן מֵעִיר קוֹל מֵהֵיכָל; v. 6). God is aware of the evil deeds done in His city, Yerushalayim. A heavenly voice rings out, indicting those who have destroyed His city. God's voice will ring out and avenge the destruction."

"Before she travailed she gave birth (בְּטֶרֶם תָּחִיל יָלָדָה; v. 7). Before Tzion (Zion) begins to feel her labor pains, she will give birth; that is, her children, who have been cast far away from her, leaving her forlorn, will return to her. Tzion will then have a son — the king, Mashiach."

So says Yeshayahu: *"Who has heard such a thing?* (מִי שָׁמַע כָּזֹאת; v. 8). Who has heard such wonders? Can a woman give birth in one day to such a multitude of children? Can an entire nation be born in one moment? But, in truth, it is no wonder, for *shall I bring to the birth, and not bring forth a birth?* (הַאֲנִי אַשְׁבִּיר וְלֹא אוֹלִיד; v. 9). Shall I, God, put a woman on a birthstool and not give her a child? Will I begin something and not bring it to its conclusion? I, God, am the one who brings forth all the newborns. Shall I not allow Tzion to give birth?"

God says, *"Rejoice with Yerushalayim, and be happy with her, all you who love her ... all those who mourn her [destruction]* (שִׂמְחוּ אֶת יְרוּשָׁלַיִם וְגִילוּ בָהּ כָּל אֹהֲבֶיהָ שִׂישׂוּ אִתָּהּ מָשׂוֹשׂ כָּל הַמִּתְאַבְּלִים עָלֶיהָ v. 10). You will drink deeply at the breast of her consolation, and delight in the abundance of her glory (v. 11)."

God promises: "I will bring peace to Yerushalayim, and will restore her glory with the swiftness of a rushing torrent. You will drink in her goodness and play in her lap, as a child plays (v. 12). *Like a man whom his mother consoles, so will I console you, and in Yerushalayim will you be consoled* (כְּאִישׁ אֲשֶׁר אִמּוֹ תְּנַחֲמֶנּוּ כֵּן אָנֹכִי אֲנַחֶמְכֶם וּבִירוּשָׁלַיִם תְּנֻחָמוּ; v. 13)."

You will see, and your heart will rejoice (וּרְאִיתֶם וְשָׂשׂ לִבְּכֶם; v. 14). Your bones will find new strength and flourish like grass. God's might will finally be revealed to His servants, the righteous, as He wreaks vengeance upon the evil men and pours His wrath upon His enemies.

For God will come in fire (v. 15), and in stormy winds. *Those that sanctify themselves and purify themselves in the gardens* (v. 17), for the purpose of idol worship, shall be destroyed.

So says God: "I know their deeds and thoughts (v. 18) and must destroy them. I will leave over a mere remnant of their people, to attest among the nations to My glory. *They will bring all your brethren from among all the nations as an offering to God ... to my holy mountain. Yerushalayim* (v. 20). *From them too will I take Kohanim and Levites* (v. 21) — for even though they be assimilated among the nations, I know their origins. Just as the new heavens and the new earth which I shall make shall remain before me (v. 22) and exist forever, so the Children of Israel will stand before Me eternally."

Midrash Tanchuma writes of a gentile who once asked R' Yosei ben Chalafta, "It says in your Torah that Israel will live for as long as the sky and the earth exist. Yet Yeshayahu has said that the heavens will be destroyed. Won't Israel therefore be destroyed as well?"

R' Yosei explained, "What Yeshayahu said was that the sky will be renewed, for when *Mashiach* comes, God will revive the sky with a great light."

And it will come to pass that on every Rosh Chodesh and every Shabbos, all flesh will come to bow down before Me. So says God (v. 23).

They will go out and see the bodies of the people who rebelled against Me. The worms which eat at them will never die; their hellfires will never be extinguished, and they will be an abhorrence to all flesh (v. 24).

Midrash Tanchuma writes that evil men suffer in Hell for twelve months, just as the Egyptians suffered the plagues for twelve months.

In Tractate *Rosh Hashanah* the *Gemara* says, "The fires of Hell were created on Monday." They are never extinguished. Evil men go down into Hell and are sentenced to a period of twelve months. After twelve months their bodies are destroyed and their souls burn into ash, which the wind spreads under the feet of the righteous.

It is from this that we get the folk expression: "If you are higher than I am in *Gan Eden* (Heaven), you will throw ash into my eyes."

God tells Israel, "You go to My Temple three times a year, but with the coming of *Mashiach* you will go every month, as it is written, מִדֵּי חֹדֶשׁ בְּחָדְשׁוֹ (v. 23) — *on every Rosh Chodesh.*"

HAFTORAH

Machar Chodesh

(Shmuel I/I Samuel 20:18-42)

(When Rosh Chodesh falls on a Sunday, the following Haftorah is read on the preceding Shabbos.)

Yehonasan (Jonathan) said to him (David): "Tomorrow is the New Moon" (וַיֹּאמֶר לוֹ יְהוֹנָתָן מָחָר חֹדֶשׁ; v. 18). The nobles used to eat at the king's table on Rosh Chodesh. Therefore, Yehonasan told David, "When my father (Shaul) sees that your place is empty, he will remember you and ask about your whereabouts. You must hide yourself securely, for they will search for you, and after three days, return to this place where you have been hiding on the working day (בְּיוֹם הַמַּעֲשֶׂה; v. 19). Yehonasan was referring to the day preceding Rosh Chodesh, when men would normally work. On Rosh Chodesh itself women do no work. It was given to them as a festival as a reward for their refusal to give their jewelry for the Golden Calf.

Yehonasan continues: "You must stay near the Ezel stone (a stone used a signpost for travellers). I will shoot three arrows towards the rock. Then I will send a lad to find the arrows. If I tell him that they are on this side of him, you can come out of your hiding place, take the arrows, and come to me without fear, for there is peace and nothing to be afraid of. But if I tell the lad that the arrows are beyond him, you must flee. It is a sign that God wants you to run away and save yourself from my father. God Himself will bear witness to the eternal oath which we have vowed to each other."

And David hid himself in the field (v. 24). On Rosh Chodesh, the king sat down to eat at his accustomed place. Yehonasan stood up, it being ill-mannered to recline at the table next to his father (for in those days it was customary to eat while reclining on couches).

Normally, David sat between Yehonasan and Shaul. With David's absence, Yehonasan left his place empty, and Avner sat down next to Shaul, though leaving David's place vacant. Yehonasan then sat next to Avner.

On the first day Shaul paid no attention to David's absence, assuming that David was ritually impure and had not immersed in a *mikveh* and was therefore unable to attend, since he did not want to render the food impure. *And it was on the day after the New Moon* (v. 27), when David's place was still empty, that Shaul asked his son Yehonasan why the son of Yishai (Jesse) had not appeared at the festive meal.

Yehonasan answered, "He received permission from me to go to Beis Lechem (Bethlehem), to attend a family sacrifice there. His elder brother Eliav had requested his presence there."

Shaul's anger burned against Yehonasan (v. 30), and he told him, "You are the son of a perverse and rebellious woman (בֶּן נַעֲוַת הַמַּרְדּוּת). I know that you have chosen Yishai's son. What a disgrace to your mother! People will say that since you love my enemy, you can be no son of mine!"

❀ ❀ ❀

Shaul's calling Yonasan's mother a "perverse and rebellious woman" is a reference to an event which occurred once when a certain man took a woman as a concubine. He was a Levite, living on Mount Efraim, and she was a native of Beis Lechem.

One day the concubine, angry with the man, returned to her father's home in Beis Lechem. She had lived there for four months when her husband came after her, taking a young servant and a pair of donkeys with him.

He came to his father-in-law, who received him very cordially. He stayed for three days. The father-in-law then insisted that he stay on one day more. Finally, on the fifth day, he left with his concubine and his young servant.

They arrived at the town of Givah and wandered through the streets there, for no one invited them in. Finally, an old man invited them to stay in his house overnight. They ate and were merry inside, but the people of the town in the meantime assembled outside the house, demanding that the old man send out his guest, whom they hoped to sodomize.

The owner of the house begged the people not to do such a humiliating act, and offered his own daughter and his guest's concubine instead. He then sent out the concubine, and the men raped her. When day finally arrived, she dragged herself to the threshold of the door and died.

Her husband brought her body to his home town on his donkey. He cut it into twelve pieces and sent a piece to each of the Tribes of Israel. They were dismayed, saying that such a thing had not occurred among them since the Exodus from Egypt.

All of Israel then assembled in the city of Mitzpeh, four hundred thousand men with drawn swords. The man told the assemblage the story, and they vowed not to go home until the matter had been investigated.

Messengers were dispatched to the tribe of Binyamin to ask why they had done such a disgraceful deed. They ordered them to give over the wicked men of the city of Givah for execution. The tribe of Benjamin demurred, and instead assembled in Givah in order to fight the rest of the nation. There were twenty-six thousand of them, and another seven hundred men of Givah.

They all set out from the town of Givah and killed twenty-two thousand men of Israel. The people of Israel wept and lamented, and went to question the *Urim VeTumim* (the priest's breastplate) of the *Kohen Gadol* to learn if they should continue the fight. God told them to go out once again. This time Binyamin killed another 18,000 men.

All of Israel regrouped, repentant and fasting, and offered sacrifices to God. Then Pinchas ben Elazar, the priest, again questioned the *Urim VeTumim*. "Today you will go after Binyamin and defeat them," God answered.

The men of Israel stationed soldiers behind the city, so that when Binyamin would leave they could burn it down. Then they pretended to be retreating. The tribe of Binyamin left the city to pursue them, and the soldiers hiding nearby set the city ablaze.

The whole tribe of Binyamin was killed, with the exception of six hundred men. The men of Israel vowed never to give their daughters to the men of Binyamin in marriage. Soon afterwards, though, they repented of their vow, saying, "What have we done? We have doomed an entire tribe to destruction."

The city of Gilead had not come to Israel's aid during the battle. The men of Israel therefore dispatched twelve thousand men there, and they killed all of the men of the city, and all of the married women. They found four hundred unmarried girls there, whose lives they spared, taking them to Shiloh.

Then they sent messengers to the survivors of Binyamin, inviting them to come and make peace. They gave them the four hundred girls of Gilead as wives. Still this did not suffice, since there were six hundred men, so they proposed a new scheme.

Every year there was a festival in Shiloh, when the young girls would dance in the vineyards. They told the men of Binyamin to go to the vineyards and choose themselves wives. If the girls' fathers would complain, they would appease them.

The tribe of Binyamin did thus, taking the young girls from the dance. King Shaul had been one of those survivors. Being tall and handsome, he attracted the girls' attention, and they all sought to catch his eye. But Shaul was quite shy and was too embarrassed to dance.

One young girl was not ashamed. She took hold of Shaul and danced with him. He subsequently married her and she bore him Yehonasan. Shaul therefore called him *the son of a perverse and rebellious woman,* implying that he had inherited his mother's trait. Just as she had unashamedly taken him to dance, so Yehonasan, without shame, had shown favor to his father's enemy.

♛   ♛   ♛

Shaul went on to say: "So long as the son of Yishai lives, your kingdom will not be established. Bring him to me, for he shall surely die!" (v. 31).

"What has David done to deserve death?" Yehonasan replied to his father. Shaul then raised his javelin at him (v. 33), to strike him. From this Yehonasan understood that his father was determined to have David killed.

Yehonasan rose from the table in fierce anger (v. 34), and did not eat, for he was grieved for David, because of the humiliation that his father had inflicted upon him.

And it was in the morning (v. 35), Yehonasan went out to the field to meet David at the appointed time, taking a young servant with him. He told the young boy to run after his arrows. Yehonasan then shot an arrow quite a distance from the lad, who ran after it. Yehonasan shot another arrow, and told the boy, "The arrow is beyond you." He told the boy not to tarry, so the boy collected all the arrows and brought them to his master.

The young boy knew nothing of this signal, but Yehonasan and David understood.

Yehonasan then gave his weapon to the lad and told him to bring it to town. The lad obeyed, and David came out of his hiding place on the southern side of the stone. He fell to the earth and bowed three times. They embraced each other, and cried, and David cried more bitterly than the other.

Yehonasan said to David: "Go in peace (לֵךְ לְשָׁלוֹם; v. 42), and the oath which we have both sworn in God's name will be witnessed by God, between you and me, between your children and mine, eternally."

HAFTORAH

Shabbos Chanukah

(Zechariah 2:14 — 4:7)

(This Haftorah is also read on the Shabbos of Parashas Behaaloscha.)

Sing and be joyous, daughter of Tzion, for behold I will come and dwell in your midst. So says God (רָנִּי וְשִׂמְחִי בַּת צִיּוֹן כִּי הִנְנִי בָא וְשָׁכַנְתִּי בְתוֹכֵךְ נְאָם ה'; 2:14). The prophet says: "On the day of the redemption, many nations will cling to God and worship Him. They will be His, but He will live among Israel. Israel will then recognize that God sent His prophecies through me. On that day, *God will once again choose Yerushalayim* (וּבָחַר עוֹד בִּירוּשָׁלָיִם; 2:16)."

Addressing all of creation, the prophet says: *Be silent, all flesh, before God, for He has aroused Himself from His holy abode* (הַס כָּל בָּשָׂר מִפְּנֵי ה' כִּי נֵעוֹר מִמְּעוֹן קָדְשׁוֹ; 2:17).

In *Bereishis Rabbah*, the *Midrash* says, R' Pinchas says in the name of R' Reuven: "David said the words *Rise up, God* (קוּמָה ה') five times. 'You can ask Me one thousand times,' answered God, 'but I will not rise. I will rise up only when injustice is done to the poor and stricken, as it is written, *Because of robbery from the poor and the outcry of the needy, now will I rise, says God* (מִשֹּׁד עֲנִיִּים מֵאֶנְקַת אֶבְיוֹנִים עַתָּה אָקוּם יֹאמַר ה'; *Tehillim* 12:6).' "

This is the meaning of our verse: All flesh will be silent, in fear and trembling, when God rises to defend the poor and weak.

He showed me the High Priest, Yehoshua (3:1). God showed me (the prophet, Zechariah) the High Priest, Yehoshua, standing before one of His angels. To his right stood Satan, eager to speak against him, because Yehoshua's children had married daughters of neighboring nations. But the angel turned to Satan and told him, *God will rebuke you, ... for [Yehoshua] is a firebrand saved from the fire* (הֲלוֹא זֶה אוּד מֻצָּל מֵאֵשׁ; 3:2). Yehoshua is worthy of the High Priesthood because of his salvation from the fire.

❀ ❀ ❀

This was what happened: The *Gemara* says, in *Perek Chelek*, that two false prophets once lived during the Babylonian exile. One was called Tzidkiah ben Maaseyah, and the other was named Achav ben Klayah. Tzidkiah approached Nebuchadnezzar's daughter and told her that God had sent a command to her to lie with Achav; Achav told her the same story about Tzidkiah.

The girl told her father what had happened, and he told her, "When they come to you, send them to me." She did as he asked, and sent the two of them to her father.

When they stood before him, he asked them, "Why did God give you such a message, while he did not say this to Chananiah, Mishael and Azariah?" The men answered: "They were not real prophets, but we are."

"Then I will test you as I tested them," retorted Nebuchadnezzar, "by placing you in a fiery oven."

"There were three of them," protested the false prophets, "and so they had a greater combined merit than the two of us, and that merit was sufficient to save them."

"So pick another to join you," commanded Nebuchadnezzar.

The two of them chose the High Priest, Yehoshua, certain that in his merit they would all be saved. The three of them were placed in the fire, and the two false prophets were burned up. Yehoshua was saved; only his clothing was burnt.

Nebuchadnezzar now questioned him: "I know that you are a righteous man. How was it, then, that your clothing was burnt, whereas the clothing of Chananiah, Mishael and Azariah remained unharmed?"

"There were three of them, and only one of me," explained Yehoshua.

"But Avraham was also alone in the oven," returned Nebuchadnezzar, "yet he survived, with his clothing intact."

"In Avraham's case," Yehoshua answered, "the fire was not permitted to burn at all. But here, because the fire was permitted to burn Tzidkiah and Achav, it could burn my clothing as well. Further, if two dry sticks catch fire, a third stick nearby will also be scorched, even if it is damp."

But the truth was that Yehoshua had sinned by allowing his children to marry divorcees, although they are forbidden to priests — and that was why his clothing was burnt.

🌑 🌑 🌑

Yehoshua was wearing dirty clothing (3:3), that is, he still had his sons' sins upon him. The angel then turned to other angels standing nearby and said, *"Take the dirty clothing off him —* cleanse Yehoshua of sin by having his sons divorce their unlawful wives, and God will forgive him."

The angel then addressed Yehoshua as follows: *"Look, I have taken your sins away from you, and have clothed you in festive garments"* (3:4). And he proceeded to address him, in the name of God: "If you follow My ways, and will be a ruler of My house, and its guardian, I will give you access among the angels — that is, your children will, in the future, walk among angels."

"*Hearken, Yehoshua* (3:8), and let your friends Chananiah, Mishael and Azariah, who sit before you, listen as well, for I wrought miracles for them too. I will bring the *Mashiach*, who is called Tzemach (lit., "that which sprouts"; כִּי הִנְנִי מֵבִיא אֶת עַבְדִי צֶמַח).

"*For here is the stone which I have placed before Yehoshua* (3:9), a stone with seven facets. The foundations of the Temple which were laid in the days of Coresh (Cyrus), and which your enemies have kept from completion, seemed small in your eyes. But I will rebuild them to seven times the size of the First *Beis HaMikdash*. I will break open your enemies' schemes against your Temple. I will destroy their plans. So says God."

"I will remove all sin from the land, in one day. There will be peace. Each man will invite his fellows to join him under his grapevine and under his fig tree (אֶל תַּחַת גֶּפֶן וְאֶל תַּחַת תְּאֵנָה; 3:10), to enjoy their fruit in unity."

The prophet continues: *The angel ... returned, and woke me* (4:1), as a man awakens from a deep sleep, and asked me what I saw.

"I told him: *I see a golden Menorah (candelabra), with a bowl at its topmost point* (רָאִיתִי וְהִנֵּה מְנוֹרַת זָהָב כֻּלָּהּ וְגֻלָּהּ עַל רֹאשָׁהּ; 4:2). It has seven branches which are filled with oil, and seven wicks, and seven tubes in which the oil flows from the bowl to the branches. Near the *Menorah* stand two olive trees, one on its left, and one on its right.

"Then I asked the angel who had spoken to me: 'How is it that the olive trees themselves are pressing the oil which flows into the bowl, without a person's help?'

"He answered: 'It is a sign. Just as the oil is being squeezed of its own volition, so the Temple will be rebuilt *not by might, nor by power, but by My spirit, says the Lord of Hosts* (לֹא בְחַיִל וְלֹא בְכֹחַ כִּי אִם בְּרוּחִי אָמַר ה' צְבָאוֹת; 4:6). I will put My will upon Daryavesh (Darius), and he will decree that you be given all that you need for the rebuilding, and all you need to sustain yourselves. You will have to look to no one for help.' "

Who are you, great mountain, who before Zerubavel has become a plain? (מִי אַתָּה הַר הַגָּדוֹל לִפְנֵי זְרֻבָּבֶל לְמִישֹׁר; 4:7). The nobles from across the river who, until now, managed to foil any plans for rebuilding the Temple, will today no longer have any dominion over Zerubavel. They will be crossed as easily as a flat plain. Zerubavel himself will take the measurements, and he himself will supervise the builders. They will follow his plans, and he will put the headstone in place; they will build a beautiful edifice, praised by all for its beauty — תְּשֻׁאוֹת חֵן חֵן לָהּ — *with shouts of "Grace, grace to it!"*

❀ ❀ ❀

The *Gemara* says: R' Yehoshua ben Levi said that the Angel of Death once warned him, "Do not stand in front of women returning from a funeral, for I dance and spring in front of them and am permitted to harm anyone whom I meet." Anyone who does meet these women should recite the verse, *God said to Satan, "God will rebuke you, Satan"* (3:2).

Why does the Angel of Death dance in front of these women? Because if Chavah (Eve) had not sinned, people would have lived eternally and the Angel of Death would have had no one to kill. Therefore he rejoices when he sees women in the presence of a corpse.

The author of *Pardes Rimonim* writes that one should not walk before the women at a funeral because women generally cry at the sight of the dead, and their faces become flushed. If a man looks at them his evil inclination may tease him. He may have evil thoughts, because the Angel of Death is also the evil inclination.

When *Mashiach* comes, however, God will take all power away from the Angel of Death, as it is written, בִּלַּע הַמָּוֶת לָנֶצַח (*Yeshayahu* 25:8) — [God] *will destroy death forever.*

HAFTORAH

Second Shabbos Chanukah

(Melachim I/I Kings 7:40-50)

(This Haftorah is also read on the Shabbos of Parashas Vayakhel.)

And Chirom made the basins (וַיַּעַשׂ חִירוֹם אֶת הַכִּיּרוֹת; v. 40). Chirom (Hiram) made the basins, and the copper shovels with which the ashes were put into the pots, and the bowls for the blood of the sacrifices. He made four hundred pomegranates, and ten bases, with ten lavers on them, also made of copper. He made a "sea" of copper, and twelve copper oxen underneath it. All the vessels which Chirom made for King Shlomo, for use in the house of God, were made of pure, clean copper.

The vessels were all cast in the thick earth of the Jordan plain; that is, molds were made of the hard earth, and within these the vessels were formed. They cast the molds between the cities of Succos and Tzarasan, because the earth there was very hard.

And Shlomo left all the vessels (v. 47). Shlomo ceased trying to calculate the weight of the vessels because there were so many of them. As a result, the weight of the copper was never ascertained.

Shlomo made all the vessels (v. 48) in the House of God. He made the golden altar, and the golden table upon which the *lechem hapanim* ("showbread") rested.

There were five *Menoros* ("candelabra") to the right of the *Menorah* made by Moshe (Moses) and five to the left of it. The *Midrash* asks: Why did Moshe make one *Menorah*, and Shlomo ten? Moshe was in the desert, and there was no need for harvests, because everyone ate the *man* ("manna"); thus, one *Menorah* was sufficient. But Shlomo lived in *Eretz Yisrael*, where it was important for the crops to flourish. He therefore built ten *Menoros*, and said: In the merit of the five candelabras standing on the right side, may God grant dew and rain in their proper time; in the merit of the five standing on the left side, may He keep away the harmful dew, which brings evil things to this world.

The ten *Menoros* symbolized the Ten Commandments. Each *Menorah* had seven branches, making a total of seventy, for the seventy nations. As long as all seventy branches burned, the nations had no authority over Israel; if the lights were extinguished, they gained power over them.

Shlomo first put the *lechem hapanim* on the table which Moshe had made in the desert, which was in their possession; similarly, he first had Moshe's candles lit, and then his own.

The twelve copper oxen standing underneath the "sea" symbolized the twelve constellations of the heavens.

The Story of Chanukah

In the city of Nineveh lived King Antiochus, ruler of Assyria. He was very ambitious, and hoped to conquer many lands and kings. He sent messages to many countries, demanding that they accept his dominion, but these were ignored and his messengers humiliated. The king, in a fury, vowed vengeance.

He convened a meeting of his councillors, and gathered together his warriors and his general, Holofernes (Eliforni, in its Hebrew form), for the purpose of waging war against these nations.

Holofernes went with his entire army, which numbered 120,000 marching men and 12,000 riders. With them, they took huge numbers of beasts and camels, great quantities of wheat, gold and silver, wagons and horses. There were so many of them that they covered the earth.

They traveled to many lands and fortified cities, conquering them all. Holofernes took the best warriors of each vanquished country with him. Soon, the entire world cringed in fear before him, paying him tribute and showing him great respect. Many sought to make peace with him, and gave their lands into his hands.

When Antiochus saw that he had conquered the world, he commanded that Holofernes destroy the temples of each conquered country, so that they would worship only him as a god, and he would be god of the entire world. Thus did Holofernes do, destroying the palaces of the idols and commanding that everyone worship King Antiochus.

He then decided to proceed with his entire army to *Eretz Yisrael.* When the Jews heard that Holofernes was coming, they trembled for their Temple, fearing that he would, God forbid, destroy it, as he had done to so many other places of worship. All of *Eretz Yisrael* thereupon prepared to fight him.

The High Priest wrote to all the Jews throughout *Eretz Yisrael,* telling them to come to Yerushalayim to prepare to fight against the invader. They cried out to God, and they and their families fasted. The priests clothed themselves in mourning, as well as the small, sinless children; even the altar was draped in sackcloth. The Jews prayed that God not send them and their families into captivity, not desecrate or destroy their beloved Temple, not humiliate them in the eyes of the nations of the world, nor devastate their cities.

Mattisyahu (Matthias), the High Priest, went among the people and exhorted: "Beloved brothers, do not stop pleading with our holy God. If you beg Him He will come to your aid, as He has done in the past. When Amalek came to fight the Jews, the Jews relied upon their own strength, but Moshe did not. He prayed to God, and God rescued him from his enemies. You have begun to plead with Him, and you must continue without cease, and He will help you."

At these words all the Jews renewed their weeping, with an earnest prayer to God. The priests poured ashes upon their heads and brought many sacrifices upon the altar, pleading mightily for succor.

Meanwhile, the general Holofernes had been informed that Israel planned to resist him, and had built fortifications against him on all their hills. Greatly incensed, he asked the people of Amon, "What manner of men are these, who will resist me more than any other nation?"

The chief of Amon, a man by the name of Achyor, answered, "My lord, I will tell you what manner of men they are. Their ancestors served their God piously, but when they turned to other gods they became downtrodden and humiliated. When they show regret for their sins and return to their God, He helps them against their enemies. Therefore, my lord, find out if they have sinned. If so, we will be able to overrun their land and conquer them. But if they have not sinned against their God, we will not be able to defeat them. Their God will come to their aid and we will be a laughingstock throughout the world."

Holofernes' officers were greatly angered by Achyor's words, and wanted to shoot him. As for their general, he told Achyor angrily that Antiochus alone was the god of the world, and commanded that he be brought to the city of Beis Cholia, in order to execute him there, together with the city's Jewish inhabitants. The city's defenders saw Achyor arriving and thought he was a spy. Meanwhile, the soldiers had bound Achyor to a tree. The Jewish fighters left the city to investigate and found him tied up. They released him and brought him to their city, where they questioned him.

He explained that Holofernes had brought him there to the Jews because he had told Holofernes that their God could save them. He told them too that his punishment was to die with the Jews of the city.

The chief of the city, Uzziah of the tribe of Shimon, listened to his words. When he had finished speaking, Uzziah and all of the Jews of the city fell prostrate to the ground, weeping and praying to God. They called to God, beseeching Him to see the confidence of their enemies and their own isolation. "Look kindly at us," they cried, "and let the whole world see that You have not abandoned those who rely on You, and that You destroy those who rely on their own prowess."

Thus they cried. They also comforted Achyor, assuring him, "The God in whom you have placed confidence will repay you, and you will see your enemy's defeat."

After a day of fasting, Uzziah invited Achyor to a meal together with the city's elders. They were all cheerful and merry. At the meal's end they called together the entire populace, and they prayed through the night.

The next morning Holofernes commanded his army to fall upon the city of Beis Cholia. They were a huge company. Seeing their approach, the Jews began wailing to God, placing ash upon their foreheads, and asking God for mercy.

As Holofernes surveyed the approaches to the city, he noticed that there were wells only outside the city. Water was pumped from these wells into the city through pipes. Someone suggested that before they began to fight they destroy the Jews' water supply. "The Jews are not warriors," he was assured, "and they will not take the offensive. They have all hidden in the mountains. If we cut off their water, they will be forced to surrender."

Holofernes commanded that the pipes be destroyed. Guards were posed at the smaller wells to ensure that no Jew drew water from them. This situation lasted for twenty days. The amount of water in the town was small, and such water as there was was sold in the market.

The populace implored the town's leaders to surrender to Holofernes, before they and their wives and children died of thirst. "Better to surrender and stay alive and be capable of serving God, than see our children and wives die before our eyes," they said.

There was a loud outcry, and all wept. Some of them cried to God, saying: "God, we and our ancestors have sinned, but You are merciful. Have pity on us. Punish us Yourself, if You wish, but do not let us fall into the hands of our enemies, who know You not. Do not let them say, 'Who is this God of the Jews?' "

As they cried, their leader Uzziah addressed them. "Beloved brothers," he said, "wait for five more days. Let us wait for God's help. Perhaps He will come to our aid and glorify His name. And if, God forbid, He does not help us in those five days, we will surrender to the enemy."

In the city lived a pious woman, a widow, by the name of Yehudis, of the tribe of Shimon. She had been a widow for three and a half years. She had a special room in her house for prayers. She fasted every day, making an exception only for *Shabbos* and holidays. She was very beautiful, quite wealthy, and had earned a good reputation.

When Yehudis heard Uzziah's words she called together the town's elders and said, "Uzziah's suggestion is not a good one. He wants to test God, to see if He can help us. You have given Him a deadline. Because you are testing Him, He will not come to your aid. God wants us to plead with Him. We must pray and cry for vengeance against our enemies. Beloved friends, you are the eldest in the town. You must comfort the people. Our ancestors were tested with many difficulties, in order to make them serve God whole-heartedly. Remind the people how our father Avraham was tested with so many sorrows, and yet believed in God, and God called him His friend. Yitzchak, too, and Yaakov, and Moshe, and all who loved God, were tested in their turn, and accepted their pains with love and not rancor. Those who did rail against God were horribly punished. And so, dear brethren, do not test God. Realize that this is a punishment — and a merciful one, when compared to our sins. We must believe that though God punishes us, He will not destroy us."

Uzziah and the elders answered: "What you have said is true. But please, join us in prayer, for we see that you are a righteous woman."

"Since you feel that my words are from God," Yehudis replied, "hearken, my brothers, to a plan which I have thought of, and may God let it succeed. Tonight, my maid and I shall go out of the city, into the hands of the enemy. You must all pray, until I return and tell you what must be done."

Uzziah answered: "Go in peace, and may God help you." And Uzziah and the elders left her.

Yehudis entered her home, put ashes on her head, and prostrated herself on the floor, and prayed. "You are the God who controls the battle, from its beginning to its end. You alone are God. I ask You, my God, stretch out Your holy hand to help Israel through me. They flatter themselves and say that they will desecrate Your Temple and destroy Your altar. Punish them with their own swords. If Holofernes sees me, let me find favor in his eyes, so that I can ultimately take revenge upon him. Strengthen my heart so that I do not show fear before him. If I can bring about his downfall, Your name will be glorified, for he will have met defeat at the hands of a woman. You, God, can help even without great armies, for You do not rely on the might of arms or horses. Heed my prayers, my God, for I rely on no one but You."

When she had ended her prayer, she called to one of her maids. She took off her widow's clothing and donned exquisite clothes embroidered in silver. God gave her great charm, and she appeared very beautiful to all who saw her. She gave her maid wine and oil, figs and bread, all that she would have to eat, and together they went through the city. They met Uzziah and the elders, who escorted her out, saying: "May God grant you grace so that you accomplish all that you plan; may Israel rejoice in you." And everyone answered: "Amen."

The next morning Yehudis reached the mountain where Holofernes and his army were encamped. The guards who had been posted there asked her where she had come from, and she answered, "I have fled from the Jews, who wanted to kill me. I have come to tell your general about the weak points in their fortifications, and how he can overpower them."

Holofernes' officers were standing nearby, and all admired her great beauty. They led her to his tent; she entered, and prostrated herself at his feet. He ordered that she stand, and assured her, "Fear not, for never have I harmed anyone who accepts the yoke of King Antiochus. Now, why have you come?"

"My lord," answered Yehudis, "I beg you to listen to me. If you do as I say, God will grant you fortune. Your name is known and feared throughout the world. We are well aware of what Achyor told you, and his punishment. You should know, then, that God is furious with us, because of our sins. He has already told us, through our prophets, that He will punish us.

"The Jews, in their great fear, are undergoing terrible hunger and thirst. Soon they will be forced to drink the blood of their animals and eat the flesh of their sacrifices, both of which have been forbidden by God. I fled from them, for I know for certain that if they do so they will be defeated.

"God has told me that He is angry at them, and commanded me to tell you this. I have always been a God-fearing woman, and still remain so. Now, let me go out into the fields and ask God to reveal to me the most propitious time to destroy Israel. I will tell you what He says, and lead your troops into the midst of Yerushalayim."

Her words greatly pleased Holofernes and his servants, and they all marveled at her wisdom and beauty. Holofernes himself assured her, "You will be greatly cherished by Antiochus, should everything you have said come true."

He then took her into a tent in his living quarters, and ordered that food be given her from his own table. Yehudis replied, "I do not need your food; I can eat from that which I brought with me." She also asked for permission to go past the sentries and into the fields every morning and evening, in order to pray to her God. Holofernes thereupon called his servants and ordered them to allow her to go and pray whenever she wished.

Yehudis went to a body of water near Beis Cholia, immersed herself, and prayed for God's help. Afterwards she entered Holofernes' quarters, careful to keep herself pure and free of sin. This situation lasted for three days.

On the fourth day Holofernes made a festive meal, inviting all of his officers and servants. He told one of his servants, "Go and persuade Yehudis." The servant approached her, and said, "My dear woman, go to his table, eat with him and be merry." She stood up, dressed beautifully, and went to join her host.

Her beauty enchanted Holofernes, and he told her, "Come and join us, eat and drink with us." He was very jolly indeed, drinking much more wine than he was accustomed to. As night drew on, his officers left him alone with her. He tottered into his bedroom, and his valet led Yehudis in as well. Holofernes lay on the bed, in a drunken stupor.

Yehudis had ordered her servant to wait for her on the other side of the door. Now Yehudis began to pray once again, saying: "God of Israel, strengthen and help me, for I rely solely upon You. Help Your city, Yerushalayim."

Yehudis approached his bed, and saw a sword standing nearby. Taking it into her hand, she gave two mighty blows to his neck, and chopped off his head. She rolled the body onto the floor and, taking the head wrapped in a sack and his blanket with her, she walked out of the room.

She and her maid then left the camp, as usual, to say their prayers. They passed by the sentries without interference, for everyone was certain that they were off to pray. The walked towards the city of Beis Cholia. As they approached the city's gates, she shouted to the watchmen, "Open the gates, for God is with us now!"

When they heard her voice they quickly called together all of the city's elders. They opened the gate and joyfully went to hear what she had to relate. A hush descended upon the crowd, and Yehudis spoke. "My brothers," she said, "thank and praise God, Who does not abandon those who rely on Him. God has destroyed the enemy through me today!"

She showed them Holofernes' head, and said, "This is the head of our foe, the Assyrian general, and this is the blanket which he lay upon. Give thanks to God, who used a woman to save us."

The people all thanked God and told Yehudis: "May you be most blessed among women. Blessed be God who gave you good fortune and allowed you to kill the general of our enemies. Let all who praise God praise you as well, for you risked your life for your people."

They called for Achyor, and Yehudis told him: "See how the God whom you believed in has helped us! He has destroyed Holofernes. Here is the head of the man who hoped to destroy you and the people of Israel."

When Achyor saw the head he trembled with happiness and fell at her feet. He told her, "May you be blessed by God and all of Israel. The God of Israel will now be revered by all the people of the world."

Yehudis then addressed the people. "My beloved people," she said, "hear what I say. When day breaks, hang up the invader's head on the city's tower. Take up your arms and storm the enemy camp. Terrified, they will run to their master Holofernes for instructions. When they realize that he is dead they will panic and will not know what to do. It will be a total rout."

And so it was. As soon as day came the Jews hung the head on their tower and noisily invaded the army encampment. When they heard the noise his men ran to their commander's headquarters and demanded to know what to do, but no one answered them. His servant banged on the door of his bedroom — still no answer. Finally, he opened the door and saw the body of their leader on the floor, headless, gushing blood. He ran to Yehudis' tent and found it deserted. The servant then wailed, "A Jewish woman has humiliated the entire nation of Antiochus! Our leader Holofernes is dead!"

His officers rent their garments and wailed and screamed, until they were all thoroughly terrified and alarmed. Without a commander to lead them against the Jews they were helpless, and they retreated. The Jews pursued them hotly, killing many of them.

Uzziah sent a message to the other Jews of *Eretz Yisrael*, urging them to pursue the fleeing army. The people of Beis Cholia hurried out to the army's encampment, and took the many possessions which the retreating army had left behind — gold and silver and wheat. Other Jews who pursued them further also took their treasures, and the people grew very wealthy.

Achyor, seeing God's help to the Jews, abandoned his own idol worship and believed thenceforth in God. He had himself circumcised, and he and his children became part of the Jewish people.

The High Priest Mattisyahu, together with an entourage of many priests, came to Beis Cholia to see the pious woman, Yehudis. They showed her great honor, and told her, "You are Yerushalayim's crown, a credit to your people, for having done such a deed. May you be blessed eternally by God." And the people answered, "Amen."

They divided the spoils for thirteen days. Yehudis was given the best of everything which Holofernes had owned, gold and pearls and precious gems. The Jews rejoiced, dancing and singing and praising God.

Yehudis herself sang a hymn to God. She said: "Exult with drums and harps. Sing a song to God. Rejoice and call upon his name. God is a great warrior against the people of Assyria. There were so many of them that they covered the earth. They hoped to destroy our land, kill our men, enslave our women and children. But our Almighty God delivered their general into the hands of a woman. With her beauty she defeated the people of Medea, of Persia, of Assyria. They fled before the Jews. Therefore, sing a new song to God. You are a mighty God, You do great things. What You decree must come about. Mountains tremble before You, stones melt at Your words as wax in fire. You come to the aid of those who fear You, for You love the God-fearing more than You desire sacrifices. You wreak vengeance upon those who plague Your nation."

The people of Beis Cholia travelled to Yerushalayim together, and prayed there. They cleansed themselves and brought sacrifices. Yehudis hung Holofernes' arms in the Temple, and donated all of the priceless spoils which she had received. For three months Yehudis and the people rejoiced, and each day was a holiday, with no work done.

Finally, the people returned to Beis Cholia. Yehudis' name was renowned throughout *Eretz Yisrael.* She never remarried, and lived in her husband's home until her death at 105 years of age. She was buried next to her husband, Menashe, and the people mourned for her for seven days. Her wealth was divided between her husband's heirs.

During her lifetime, no enemy dared to raise arms against Israel. As to the date of her daring exploit, it was proclaimed an eternal day of praise to God.

❀ ❀ ❀

Antiochus, king of Greece, captured numerous kingdoms and destroyed them by fire, taking many prisoners whom he left in captivity until their death. He built a great city by the seashore which he named Antioch, and built a huge palace for himself there.

In the twenty-third year of his reign, that is, 233 years after the construction of the Second Temple and the return of the Jews to their land, the king chose to once again torment Israel. He called together his councillors and said, "You know that the Jews whom we have captured do not believe in our gods or abide by our rules. They constantly pray for our downfall. We must stop them, by prohibiting observance of the commandments of *Shabbos*, of sanctification of the new month, and of circumcision. These are their three most important commandments."

The king sent his chief of staff, Nikanor, together with a great army, to besiege the city of Yerushalayim. They outlawed observance of the three commandments, but the Jews did not heed them. As a result, many of the people were executed.

One of the soldiers abducted the daughter of the High Priest Mattisyahu, a girl renowned for her beauty and assaulted her on a Torah scroll. The Greeks put a stone in the Holy of Holies in the Temple, and there slaughtered a pig, bringing its blood into the Temple.

When Yehudah, eldest son of Mattisyahu, heard of these doings, he was furious. He concealed a large sword under his cloak, and went to call on Nikanor. He told the sentry at Nikanor's palace that Yehudah, son of the High Priest Mattisyahu, wished an audience with the chief of staff. Nikanor gave the order to let him in.

Nikanor asked him, "Have you, too, rebelled against the king and me?"

"Yes, yes, I admit that I have sinned," he answered. "Yet today I have come willingly into your power; do what you will with me."

Answered Nikanor: "Because of your actions, I will forgive you, and will not have you executed. But I will test your loyalty thus: you must bring a pig as a sacrifice upon the altar which we have placed in the Temple. If you do so, I will forgive you completely, and will dress you in the apparel of royalty. You will ride through the streets on the king's own horse, with music played before you."

Yehudah told him: "My lord, the Jews are embittered and downtrodden. If I do such a thing in front of them, they will undoubtedly stone me to death. But I will willingly do the deed on a stone in front of you. Just dismiss all of your servants, so word of my action does not leak out to the Jews."

Nikanor ordered his servants to leave them. When Yehudah saw that the two of them were alone, he lifted his eyes to God and uttered a silent prayer. Swiftly, he snatched the sword out from under his cloak, and stabbed Nikanor.

Yehudah fled out into the street, crying, "Whoever believes in God, join me!" The mightiest of the Jews came to him, and he ordered them: "Pursue the enemy. They will retreat before you, for I have slain their leader!"

The Jews turned upon the enemy, killing 7,772 men, in addition to those whom the Greeks, in their panic, killed themselves.

From that day on Yehudah was known by the name "Maccabee," which means "great warrior" in the Greek language.

In the meantime, Antiochus heard that his commander in chief had been murdered. In a fury, he called to the evil man Bagrus, and appointed him in Nikanor's stead.

"You have heard what the Jews have done, destroying my army and killing my officers. Go and punish them."

Bagrus assembled a huge army and entered Yerushalayim with them, killing many Jews. He once again prohibited the observance of the commandments of *Shabbos*, circumcision, and the announcement of the new month.

One day Bagrus' servants came to him with a Jew who had circumcised his child. He ordered the man, his wife, and the child hanged. On that same day another woman took her newly circumcised son, climbed onto the city wall, and shouted, "We will not give up the commandment of circumcision!" She then threw the child down and jumped to her death after him.

At that time a thousand Jews concealed themselves in a cave, in order to be able to properly observe *Shabbos*, for the king had deemed Sabbath observance a capital crime. Bagrus was told of this, and he dispatched his troops to the area. They stood at the entrance to the cave and shouted, "Jews, come out, and save your lives. After all, we all have one father, one god. Why do you not join us, so that we can be one people?" The Jews in the cave kept silent and made no response.

The Greeks made another attempt, crying, "Jews, come out to us. Eat our bread and drink our wine. If you do not come out, this cave will be your tomb!"

The Jews then replied, "You will not succeed. We would rather die here than abandon our God and desecrate His *Shabbos.*"

The Greeks then brought flaming pieces of wood and threw them into the cave. All of the Jews were burned alive.

❈ ❈ ❈

The High Priest Mattisyahu had five sons. Yehudah was the eldest, Shimon was the second, Yochanan the third, Yonasan the fourth, and Elazar the youngest. When the five young men heard of these deeds, they were greatly troubled. They strengthened themselves and began to fight Bagrus' men. They killed many of them, but Bagrus escaped, together with a large army, and eventually arrived at Antiochus' court.

"You have been foolish," he told the king, "in sending me to fight the Jews and in prohibiting observance of their commandments. No one can stand against the five sons of Mattisyahu. They are stronger than lions and swifter than eagles. The only possibility is to gather together all of your armies, wherever they may be dispersed, for with a small army you will achieve nothing, and will be humiliated besides."

The idea appealed to the king, who dispatched letters to all of his nobles, in all of his lands. He commanded them to gather together in his palace on a certain day, bringing with them great masses of soldiers, all armed and ready for battle.

And the wicked Bagrus once again came to besiege Yerushalayim. He first broke through the city walls, and then breached the Temple walls in thirteen places. "Now they will not dare fight against me," he thought to himself, "because of my huge army. I will do with them as I desire."

But the Lord, blessed be He, had other plans. The five sons of Mattisyahu came to the city of Mitzpe Gilead, gathering great numbers of Jews with them. They decreed a day of fasting and mourning, even rolling in ashes, begging God for mercy. Their shouts reached up to Heaven and God, with pity on His people Israel, rose up to protect His land.

The next day Mattisyahu blessed the assemblage, each person individually. He told them, "Now, my sons, go out and take vengeance on God's foes."

That day they fought the enemy, killing huge numbers of them. But Yehudah the Maccabee, the eldest son of the High Priest Mattisyahu ben Yochanan, was killed in battle. When his brothers saw his death, they panicked and returned to their father.

He asked them why they had returned so early, and they told him that their brother's death had terrified them. Mattisyahu, the High Priest, did not discuss their news, and showed no sign of grief; rather, he comforted the four brothers.

"Your brother died fighting God's foes," he told them, "so why are you weeping? I myself will accompany you to the fray. Heaven forbid if we sin against God by avoiding the battle and not fight for our people and our land. Strengthen yourselves, be men, and God will give us good fortune. If you do not go to war, know then that we are all lost."

On that day Mattisyahu and his four sons went to battle, and God delivered the enemy into their hands. They killed all of their officers and riders, and masses of soldiers. Those who survived fled beyond the seas, and Bagrus himself was burned to death.

Elazar, Mattisyahu's youngest son, was trampled to death in the course of the fighting.

When Antiochus heard the news of his soldiers' rout and Bagrus' fiery death, he grew afraid and fled to a small island in the sea, where he became known as "the retreater." From that time on, all memory of his rule was eradicated.

On the 25th day of Kislev, Mattisyahu and his sons returned from battle and entered the Temple. They repaired whatever the Greeks had destroyed, and cleansed the Temple courtyard. They next searched for oil with which to light the *Menorah* (candelabra), but found only one vial which still had the seal of the High Priest, an indication that it had not been desecrated. A great miracle occurred, for the oil, which was sufficient for only one day, burned for eight days. In remembrance of the miracle the Jews took upon themselves and their descendants the celebration of the eight-day festival of Chanukah, beginning with the 25th day of Kislev, when the battle finally ended.

On these eight days we light candles, eat festive meals, give charity generously, and recite the entire *Hallel* prayer of thanksgiving and praise, so that everyone will be aware of what the great God did for us. Eulogies are prohibited during these eight days, as well as fasts, but work is allowed.

From that time on the sons of the *Chashmonaim* (Hasmoneans) ruled over Israel for 206 years, up to the destruction of the Second Temple.

May God grant that the next Temple be built speedily, *in our days*, Amen.

ספר שמות

Sh'mos / Exodus

פרשת שמות
Parashas Sh'mos
(1:1 — 6:1)

◆§ The Benefits of Rebuke

וְאֵלֶּה שְׁמוֹת בְּנֵי יִשְׂרָאֵל — *These are the names of the sons of Israel* (1:1). King Solomon says, in *Proverbs:* נֶזֶם זָהָב וַחֲלִי כָתֶם מוֹכִיחַ חָכָם עַל אֹזֶן שֹׁמָעַת — *Like an earring of gold, and an ornament of fine gold, so is a wise reprover upon an ear that listens (Mishlei 25:12).* Just as a ring beautifies the body, so is a person improved by listening to a sage's words of rebuke. The most important rebuke is that given to a child when he is still young. At that point in his life he seeks only pleasures, not having developed an inclination towards goodness. That inclination is first evident when the child reaches the age of thirteen. For this reason, rebuke is vital for a child. Solomon tells us: חוֹשֵׂךְ שִׁבְטוֹ שׂוֹנֵא בְנוֹ וְאֹהֲבוֹ שִׁחֲרוֹ מוּסָר — *He that spares his rod hates his child, but he who loves him chastises him early (ibid. 13:24),* either by words or action, so that he will become righteous.

King David forbore from chastising his son Avshalom (Absalom), so that ultimately he became evil, and was even guilty of misconduct with his father's wives, eventually forcing his father to flee Yerushalayim (Jerusalem) out of fear. Yaakov (Jacob), on the other hand, did chastise his children, and so they all grew up righteous. This is what is implied in the words, *These are the names of the sons of Israel* — because of their upbringing they resembled him in righteousness.

◆§ Righteous Descendants

Rashi writes: Why does the verse here enumerate Yaakov's children, after having listed them in the portion of *Vayigash?* The answer is that just as God counts the stars as He sends them out to illuminate the dark, and again when He takes them back in, so the children of Yaakov are counted during their lifetime, as well as after their death.

Tzror HaMor and *Toldos Yitzchak* write: Why are the righteous compared to stars? To teach us that just as the stars shine more brightly at night than during the day, so the righteous receive more recognition in the World to Come than in This World.

R' Bechaye, *Chizkuni*, and *Imrei Noam* write that this verse teaches us that Yaakov married off all of his sons and grandchildren, so that they would not marry the Egyptians, whom he hated.

◂§ With His People in Exile

אִישׁ וּבֵיתוֹ בָּאוּ — *Every man and his household came (ibid.).* The *Midrash*, R' Bechaye and *Tzror HaMor* write that this shows us that God is with Israel in their exile. God, who is called אִישׁ מִלְחָמָה — *a Man of War* (15:3), had pity on them, and came with them to redeem them.

◂§ The Children of Israel

R' Bechaye writes: Why are the maidservants' children listed between Binyamin (Benjamin) and Yosef (Joseph)? To show that the children of Leah and Rachel should not rule over the children of the maidservants; they are to be considered just as important as Yosef and Binyamin, the children of Yaakov's most beloved wife Rachel. And why is Yosef mentioned last? To show that despite the fact that he was a ruler, he conducted himself with humility. The more greatness the righteous achieve, the more humble they become.

R' Bechaye writes: Why does the verse say, וַיָּמָת יוֹסֵף וְכָל אֶחָיו וְכֹל הַדּוֹר הַהוּא — *Yosef died, and all of his brothers, and all of that generation* (1:6)? To indicate that even though they had all died, God in heaven lives on eternally.

The Torah writes, וּבְנֵי יִשְׂרָאֵל פָּרוּ וַיִּשְׁרְצוּ — *The Children of Israel were fruitful, and increased greatly* (1:7), because each woman gave birth to six children at one time. Moreover, no woman miscarried or was barren. So writes *Toldos Yitzchak.*

Tzror HaMor says that the Children of Israel are enumerated twice in order to emphasize that though they began as 70 souls, in a short time they increased to many tens of thousands. *Tzror HaMor* also writes that they are termed *souls that came out of Yaakov's loins* (יֹצְאֵי יֶרֶךְ יַעֲקֹב) (1:5), with *yerech*, the word for loins (lit., "thigh"), in the singular — to teach that his offspring numbered only seventy because the angel had wounded him in the thigh. Had he not been wounded he would have had more children.

וְיוֹסֵף הָיָה בְמִצְרָיִם — *Yosef was in Egypt* (1:5). *Rashi* writes: Why does the verse tell us that Yosef was in Egypt, a fact which we had previously known? To emphasize that despite the fact that he was in Egypt, among idol worshipers, he was unchanged in his piety.

וַיִּרְבּוּ וַיַּעַצְמוּ בִּמְאֹד מְאֹד — *They multiplied abundantly ... and they were very, very strong* (1:7). R' Avraham said: I once saw a woman give birth to quadruplets. Generally, if a woman gives birth to twins, they are weak, for the strength which would have gone to one child is divided between two. How much more so, when divided among six children! Therefore the verse says that *they were very, very strong*, even though six were born at one time.

◂§ New King: New Decrees

וַיָּקָם מֶלֶךְ חָדָשׁ — *A new king arose* (1:8). *Chizkuni* writes that because the verse says *a new king arose*, rather than "the king died," it is implied that this was the same king as before, but he issued new decrees. He forgot the benefits which Yosef had brought to Egypt. Thus writes *Rashi*. In the *Gemara* there is a dispute between Rav and Shmuel as to whether this was a new king in actuality, or the same king issuing new decrees.

הִנֵּה עַם בְּנֵי יִשְׂרָאֵל רַב וְעָצוּם מִמֶּנּוּ — *Behold the people of the Children of Israel are greater and more mighty than we are* (1:9). The new king said: "There are three reasons why we must destroy the Jews. First, they are accustomed to miracles: I remember what Yaakov did to his brother Esav (Esau). Esav approached him with four hundred men and could not defeat him. Second, I remember how his two children destroyed the entire city of Shechem. Thirdly, they acted wickedly by selling their own brother. Besides, they are very mighty."

הָבָה נִתְחַכְּמָה לוֹ — *Let us deal wisely with them* (1:10). "We must scheme against them, and craftily choose the means of their destruction. Their God repays in kind. Therefore, we will throw their children into the water. Their God has sworn never to bring a flood on the world, so He will be unable to punish us through water."

They did not understand that God had merely vowed not to engulf the entire world, but He could most certainly drown them!

Chizkuni tells us that the *Gemara* says that Bilaam was one of the conspirators against the Jews. It is difficult to understand how Bilaam could have lived for so long. He fought against the Jews in the desert, during the war with Midian, and was killed by Pinchas (Phineas). Further, we find in the *Gemara*, in *Perek Chelek*, that

Bilaam lived only thirty-three years. The answer is that there were two men named Bilaam, a father and a son. The father was one of Pharaoh's schemers, but it was the son whom Pinchas killed.

וְנוֹסַף גַּם הוּא עַל שֹׂנְאֵינוּ — *They too will join our enemies (ibid.).* *Toldos Yitzchak* writes that the Egyptians feared that if they would be attacked the Jews would surrender immediately in order to save themselves, as happens in battle, thus allowing the enemy to conquer their cities.

∽§ The Bondage Begins

וַיָּשִׂימוּ עָלָיו שָׂרֵי מִסִּים — *They set taskmasters over them* (1:11). Pharaoh appointed foremen to collect the taxes, rather than supervise this himself, to show that he did not hate them.

The *Gemara* says that three men were involved in Pharaoh's decree. The first was Bilaam, who advised killing everyone. Because of this, he was later killed by the Jews in the desert. The second was Iyov (Job), who remained silent. He was punished with pain and suffering. The third was Yisro (Jethro), who ran away when he heard the plan. He was therefore found worthy of having descendants who were members of the Sanhedrin.

After the Jews' first day of toil Pharaoh commanded that the work accomplished be tallied up. He saw that many bricks had been made, because they were still strong, and commanded that henceforth the same amount of bricks be made every day. Men were appointed to count the bricks and if the quota was not reached the overseers were beaten for not having adequately forced the Jews to work. The overseers themselves were Jews, and allowed themselves to be beaten. They would not reveal who had not fulfilled his quota, in order to protect their fellow Jews. These men ultimately became the Sanhedrin of Israel. They were the same seventy elders who accompanied Moshe (Moses) when he performed his miracles before Pharaoh.

On the words, וּבְכָל עֲבֹדָה בַּשָּׂדֶה — *and in all kinds of work in the fields* (1:14), *Yalkut* writes that Pharaoh commanded that they sleep in the fields, in order to separate them from their wives and prevent the birth of children. But the wives brought food to their husbands in the fields, comforting them with assurances that God would redeem them from the bitter exile. This heartened the men, and they had relations with their wives in the field, and the women became pregnant. God later repaid the wives by giving them gold and silver taken from the bodies of the Egyptians which were cast out of the sea.

✦§ Mothers and Children

The *Gemara* says that the merit of the righteous women in Egypt allowed Israel to be redeemed. When a woman went to draw water, God filled the bucket halfway with fish. The woman cooked the fish and warmed up the water, then brought it to her husband in the field. There she washed and anointed him, and gave him the fish.

When it was time to give birth she went into a field, under the apple trees, and had the child by herself, without the aid of a midwife. God Himself cleaned the child and cut the umbilical cord. God sent two stones to each child. One gushed oil, the other honey, and the child nursed from them.

When Pharaoh became aware of this, he sent men to kill the children in the fields. Miraculously, the earth swallowed them. Pharaoh commanded that the fields be plowed, but God saved them once again by placing them deeper within the earth. God allowed the children to grow up in the earth, and after they had grown they rose from the earth like grass, in their tens of thousands. These children later recognized God at the splitting of the sea, and said, זֶה אֵלִי וְאַנְוֵהוּ — *This is my God, and I will glorify Him* (15:2).

וַיֹּאמֶר מֶלֶךְ מִצְרַיִם לַמְיַלְּדֹת הָעִבְרִיֹּת — *The king of Egypt said to the Hebrew midwives* (1:15). Pharaoh secretly commanded the Jewish midwives to kill all of the male children. *"You must look upon the birthtable* (1:16) to see in what manner the child leaves his mother's womb. If its face looks towards the earth, it is a sign that it is a male, and it should be killed immediately. The mother will suspect nothing, certain that the child was stillborn. If its face is turned upwards, it is a female and can be allowed to live."* *Chizkuni* wrties thus, quoting the *Gemara*.

Rashi writes that Pharaoh commanded that the males be killed because his astrologers had predicted that a male child would be born to free Israel. *Chizkuni* writes that he commanded that all the males be destroyed because they would be the ones who would go to war.

✦§ The Midwives

R' Bechaye writes, quoting the *Gemara:* Why is the bench upon which a woman gives birth called *avnayim* (from the root word *even* — "stone")? When a woman goes into labor her legs and other organs become as cold as stones. Pharaoh taught the midwives this sign: when a woman's legs become cold, she will be giving birth immediately.

One midwife's name was Shifra. This was Yocheved. She was called Shifra because she cleaned and beautified the child (from the root שפר, "to beautify"). The other was named Puah, and this was Miriam, Yocheved's daughter. Why did they call her Puah? Because she whispered (from פעה, "to murmur") and soothed the child when it cried. Not only did these two allow the children to live, they also fed them.

Chizkuni, Toldos Yitzchak and Imrei Noam say that these two were the head midwives, and they were in charge of many other midwives. It is not reasonable to think that two midwives sufficed for all of Israel. Imrei Noam writes that the Egyptians offered the midwives a huge bribe to entice them to kill the children, but they refused it, because they feared God.

וַיֹּאמֶר לָהֶן מַדּוּעַ עֲשִׂיתֶן הַדָּבָר הַזֶּה — And he (Pharaoh) said to them (the midwives), Why have you done this thing? (1:18). That is, why have you let the children live? The midwives answered that the women of Israel were like beasts (חַיּוֹת) of the field, giving birth without the assistance of midwives. Another explanation is that they said that all of the women were midwives (חַיּוֹת) in their own right.

וַיַּעַשׂ לָהֶם בָּתִּים — He made them houses (1:21). Rashi writes, quoting the Gemara, that God rewarded the midwives by making them the founders of the houses of priesthood and royalty: Yocheved's descendants became Kohanim and Levites, and Miriam's descendants were kings.

R' Bechaye writes that He made them houses refers to Pharaoh, who placed an Egyptian between every two Jewish houses, to listen for when a male child would be born. Chizkuni says that Pharaoh built homes for the pregnant women in order to ensure that all the children be thrown into the water.

R' Bechaye writes: Why is the word lahem ("to them," in the masculine form) used, instead of the word lahen (in the feminine form), as if one were speaking of males? This shows that God rewarded them just as He rewards men who faithfully fulfill His commandments [for there are certain commandments which only men are obliged to observe].

◄§ The Astrologers

וַיְצַו פַּרְעֹה לְכָל עַמּוֹ — Pharaoh commanded all of his people (1:22). Rashi and Tanchuma write that the astrologers told Pharaoh that a redeemer of Israel would be born on a certain day, but they could not tell if he would be a Jewish or an Egyptian child. The redeemer would meet his downfall through water. Pharaoh therefore commanded that even the Egyptians cast their children into the sea on that particular day.

The astrologers did not prophesy correctly. Moshe was punished because he did not heed God's command to tell a certain rock to give forth water. Rather, he struck the rock. Because of this, he was punished and not allowed to enter *Eretz Yisrael*.

⋘ Amram and Yocheved

וַיִּקַּח אֶת בַּת לֵוִי — *He took a daughter of Levi* (2:1). The *Gemara* says that Amram was the greatest man of his generation. When Pharaoh decreed that the children be cast into the water, Amram divorced his wife, and many other righteous men followed his lead. His daughter Miriam reproached him, and said, "Your decree is harsher than that of Pharaoh. Pharaoh decreed only that the males be killed, and has let the females live; you are causing us to lose both males and females!" Amram took his wife back, and the others returned to their wives as well. Thus it says, *He took a daughter of Levi*. He made a *chuppah*, a wedding canopy, to remarry his wife.

At that time Yocheved was 130 years old. Why is she called a "daughter," implying youth? To show that she became pregnant, just as a young girl does, and gave birth with no pain. We can learn from this that the righteous woman does not suffer during childbirth.

Pirkei deR' Eliezer writes that all the children who were thrown into the water were cast out by the water into the desert.

⋘ Birth of Moshe Rabbeinu

Yocheved gave birth to a son, Moshe, whom she hid for three months.

וַתֵּרֶא אֹתוֹ כִּי טוֹב הוּא — *She saw him, that he was good* (2:2). As soon as he was born Yocheved saw that he was an exceptional infant, because the house was radiant with light, and she saw that he had been born circumcised. She was determined to save him.

וְלֹא יָכְלָה עוֹד הַצְּפִינוֹ — *She could no longer hide him* (2:3). The Egyptians had counted nine months from the time that Amram had returned to her, and then they came to search for a child. But Moshe was actually born after six months and one day, so she could conceal him in her home for three months. Three months after his birth the Egyptians came, asking, "Where is your child?" She answered, "We have thrown him into the water."

Moshe was born on the seventh day of the month of Adar, and remained hidden until the sixth day of Sivan. Because he was destined to bring down the Torah on the 6th day of Sivan, the Torah rescued him from drowning. This is what R' Bechaye and *Chizkuni* write.

Yocheved built a basket and smeared it with clay and tar, placed the child within and put the basket on the water. Pharaoh's daughter came to bathe in the river and noticed the basket. When she commanded her handmaidens to bring it out, they demurred. Therefore, they all died at once. Then, miraculously, her hand stretched and she was able to reach it. When she saw it she sensed the Holy Presence with the child. The child wailed loudly, and Pharaoh's daughter said, "Undoubtedly it is a child of the Jews whose mother placed him in the basket to spare him from drowning."

✑ Miriam's Prophecy

The child's sister, Miriam, had prophesied that her mother would give birth to a son destined to lead Israel out of Egypt. She stood nearby, to see if her prophecy would be fulfilled. Pharaoh's daughter called many Egyptian wetnurses to nurse the child, but the child would not suckle from them, because the mouth that was destined to speak with God could not suckle from the breast of an idol worshiper. Miriam then said to Pharaoh's daughter, "Shall I bring you a Jewish woman to nurse the child?" Pharaoh's daughter replied, "Go and bring one." Miriam called the child's mother and

Moshe in the basket in the river

Pharaoh's daughter said, "Take him," She spoke unawares with the spirit of prophecy, for the word הֵילִיכִי ("Take him") is reminiscent of the two words הֵא שֶׁלִיכִי ("Here is yours").

She said, "I will pay you, but you must not nurse any other child." We learn from that that when a woman is nursing she ought not nurse another. R' Bechaye writes that God deals mercifully with the righteous. Not only did He return her child to her, but she was compensated for nursing him as well!

When the child was weaned, Yocheved brought him to Pharaoh's daughter, who regarded him as her own son. She fondled and kissed him, and Pharaoh played with him as one does with a young child. Pharaoh's daughter called him Moshe, for she had drawn him (meaning "I drew him") from the water. God had placed within her the thought of calling him Moshe, so his name was never changed.

⸗§ The Anguish of his Brethren

When Moshe grew older he went to the fields and saw his brethren toiling. One day he saw an Egyptian striking a Jew. The Egyptian was a judge, who had one day awoken a Jew and sent him off to work. He had then returned to the Jew's house and had had relations with his wife, who thought that he was her husband. She became pregnant and gave birth to a wicked son who ultimately was stoned in the desert for having "blessed the name of God" [a euphemism for blasphemy]. When the Jew returned home he found out what had happened. The Egyptian, realizing that the Jew knew all, beat him mercilessly during his working hours.

Moshe knew of what had occurred, and saw that no good would ever come out of the Egyptian. He killed him by using the Holy Name, and hid him in the sand.

The next day, when Moshe was walking outside, he saw Dasan and Aviram quarreling. He rebuked one of them: "Wicked man, why would you hit (לָמָה תַכֶּה) your brother?" Since the verb is not in the past tense (הִכִּיתָ), we can learn from this that when one Jew only lifts his hand to beat another Jew, without having yet struck him, he is already termed wicked (רָשָׁע).

Dasan and Aviram answered: "Who made you our master and our judge? You are too young to be a judge!" (Moshe was only twelve years old at the time.) "Do you want to murder us as you murdered the Egyptian?"

Upon hearing these words, Moshe grew very frightened. Pharaoh soon became aware of the incident, because Dasan and Aviram told him of it, and wanted to execute Moshe. Rendering himself invisible by uttering the Holy Name, Moshe fled. The *Midrash* says that he was given to an executioner for beheading, but the sword would not penetrate his neck.

◄§ In Midian

Moshe fled to the land of Midian and stood by a well. Yisro, a great noble of Midian, had at that time abandoned idol worship and as a result had been excommunicated. Because of the excommunication, no one would herd his sheep. He had no sons, so his daughters were forced to act as shepherds. They went to give the sheep water, but the other shepherds drove them away from the well. Moshe appeared and protected them from the shepherds, and gave their sheep water.

When they returned to their father Yisro, he asked them how they had managed to return so speedily. They told him that an Egyptian had protected them from the shepherds and had drawn the water, which rose to meet him.

Why does the Torah call Moshe an Egyptian? Because his killing of an Egyptian had forced him to flee to Midian.

Yisro asked, "Why did you let him leave you? He could have married one of you! If the water rose to meet him, he undoubtedly is a descendant of Yaakov!"

◄§ Yisro's Daughter

וַיּוֹאֶל מֹשֶׁה — *Moshe was agreeable* (2:21). Moshe was willing to live with Yisro and married his daughter. R' Bechaye writes: Why did Moshe marry Yisro's daughter? Because he was afraid that Pharaoh's men would pursue him and find him. Moshe came to Yisro because he was aware that he had seven daughters. He thought to himself: he will undoubtedly allow me to marry one of them.

Moshe swore to Yisro that he would not leave his land without permission, and Yisro gave him his daughter Tzipora as a wife. Why was she called Tzipora? Tzipora means a bird, and her name shows that she ran to Moshe as quickly as a bird. Another interpretation is that she was called Tzipora because she gave forth light just like the morning star *(tzafra)*.

Very soon, Tzipora became pregnant. She gave birth to a son, whom Moshe named Gershom because he was a *stranger there (ger sham)*, in a foreign land.

וַיָּמָת מֶלֶךְ מִצְרַיִם — *The king of Egypt died* (2:23). The king of Egypt became leprous, and each day Jewish children were slaughtered and he bathed in their blood. Israel was deep in misery. God heeded their anguished cries and remembered the merit of their righteous forefathers.

◆§ The Shepherd

וּמֹשֶׁה הָיָה רֹעֶה אֶת צֹאן יִתְרוֹ חֹתְנוֹ — *Moshe tended the flocks of his father-in-law Yisro* (3:1). The righteous often used to be shepherds, apart from other men, because many sins, such as talebearing, jealousy, and hatred, are committed when a person lives among men.

He herded the sheep in the desert (אַחַר הַמִּדְבָּר; 3:1) to ensure that he would not feed his flock in a stranger's pasture.

The Sages say that Moshe lived in Egypt for 40 years, in Midian for 40 years, and in the desert for 40 years. Similarly, R' Akiva was in commerce for 40 years, studied Torah for 40 years, and then for 40 years headed a yeshivah.

◆§ The Burning Bush

Moshe came to Mount Chorev (or Sinai), where the Torah was ultimately to be given. God appeared to him in the form of fire, within a bush, but the bush was not consumed by the fire. *Chizkuni* and R' Bechaye ask: Why did God appear through fire? Because when the Torah would be given it would be accompanied by flames.

Moshe said, "I will go to see why that bush is not consumed."

The burning bush is not consumed

God called to him, "Moshe, Moshe," and he replied, "I am here." God then told him, "Remove your shoes from your feet, for the earth upon which you are standing is holy."

Why did he hear his name twice? Because the voice of heaven is very powerful, and sounds like two separate voices. Another reason is because the first time a man hears a heavenly voice he is overwhelmed and is rendered speechless, so he must be called a second time.

God told him, *I am the God of your father* (3:6). With this He informed him that his father was dead, because God does not couple His name with the name of a person still living. Why did God tell him that his father was dead? Because God knew that out of deference Moshe would refuse to assume any authority as long as his father was alive.

◄§ Beginning of a Mission

Moshe covered his face and was afraid to speak with God. God told him, "I have seen the anguish of Israel, and have come to save them and bring them to a good land, a land flowing with milk and honey. You, Moshe, must go to Pharaoh and tell him to release My people."

Moshe answered, "Who am I to speak with a king? And what merit does Israel have to be released from bondage? Who am I, to free such a worthy nation? And even if the bondage ceases, they will not want to go to Canaan, when they are so afraid of the mighty idol worshipers living there."

God replied: "Your fear of speaking with Pharaoh is unfounded, for I will be with you the entire time. As to your question regarding what merit the people of Israel have to be freed, I know that they will eventually accept the Torah on Mount Sinai. Because of this merit they will be released from Egypt. The fire which you see is a sign for you, not to fear Pharaoh; and an omen for Israel, that they must not fear the Canaanite idol worshipers, for I will destroy them with fire."

Moshe then asked: "When Israel asks me for the name of God, Who shall release us, what shall I say?" Answered God: "I will be Whom I will be," meaning, I will be with them in this exile and in their other exiles as well.

לֵךְ וְאָסַפְתָּ — *Go and assemble* (3:16). "Go and assemble the elders of Israel and tell them that the God of their forefathers has sent you to free them. Use the words, *I have surely remembered you* (פָּקֹד

פָּקַדְתִּי אֶתְכֶם: 3:16). They will then have trust in you, because Yosef too said, *God will surely remember you* (פָּקֹד יִפְקֹד; *Bereishis* 50:24-25).

"Go to Pharaoh and say, '*God of the Hebrews has appeared to us* (3:18), and has commanded that we go to the desert to bring Him sacrifices.' I know that Pharaoh will not allow you to go. I will be forced to reveal My mighty hand and bring the plagues upon him, and finally he will allow you to leave. I will cause you to find favor in the eyes of the Egyptians, who will lend you their gold and silver. You will empty the entire land of Egypt." R' Bechaye says that in fact they did not have to borrow from the Egyptians; rather, they so charmed them that they were given the gold and silver.

⋙ Signs

Moshe asked God: "What if Israel refuses to believe that You have sent me?" God answered, "What is that in your hand?" (4:2). Moshe replied: 'It is a rod." Said God: "Fling it to the earth." Moshe cast it down and it became a snake. Moshe fled from it. God then commanded him to grab it by the tail, and when he did so it changed back into a stick. *Rashi* writes that God changed the stick into a snake to show Moshe: "You have spoken ill of the Jews, saying that they would not believe you, just as as the snake spoke ill of Me [in the Garden of Eden]."

God then told Moshe to place his hand next to his chest. When he did, his hand became leprous. With this God taught him that one who speaks ill of another will ultimately be stricken with leprosy. God then commanded him to place his hand on his chest again, and it was healed.

God told Moshe to show these signs to Israel. Should they not believe him after the first sign, the rod changing into a snake, he would show them the second, the leprous hand, to show them that he had been punished for speaking ill of them. It was common knowledge by then that one who harmed Israel was struck with leprosy, as when Pharaoh abducted Sarah and was cursed with it.

If they did not believe both signs, Moshe was commanded to take water from the Nile, and spill it onto the earth, and it would turn into blood.

⋙ Not a Man of Words

Moshe then said, "I beg of You, my God, I am no orator and cannot speak." When Moshe as a young boy had taken Pharaoh's crown off his head, his astrologers said, "We have told you many times that someone would be born to redeem the Jews from exile. This must be that boy." Pharaoh consulted with Iyov (Job), Yisro and Bilaam for their judgment. One said that the child should be executed; another said that he was but a child. They brought a bowl of gold and a brazier full of burning coals, to see which he would take. If he took the fiery coals they would know that he had taken Pharaoh's crown without intent; if he preferred the gold it would be a sign that his mind had already developed, and he had taken the crown purposely, and he would be executed.

Moshe wanted to take the gold, but an angel came down and pushed his hand towards the fire. He placed the fiery coal into his mouth and burned his tongue, and that is why he could never speak properly.

R' Bechaye asks: Why did God not heal him? Because he did not pray to be healed. And why did he not pray? So that he would have an excuse to give to God, and could say that he could not speak clearly.

God answered him: "You hesitate because you cannot speak well. *Who places the mouth into a person?* (4:11). Who gave you the power to speak before Pharaoh, at the time when he tried to execute you? *Who makes a man mute?* (4:11). Who then silenced the adviser, so that he did not order your immediate execution? *Or deaf?* (ibid.). Who deafened his servants, so that they did not hear his order to kill you? Who made them blind, so that they could not see your escape? All this I have done for you — and I can also make you speak clearly to Pharaoh."

ᐸᔞ Aharon the High Priest

Moshe answered: "Send Aharon (Aaron). He is older than I am. Since it is destined that I cannot accompany Israel to *Eretz Yisrael*, send messengers who can bring them all the way into the land."

Angrily, God replied, "Because of your words, you will not be a priest *(Kohen)*, and your brother Aharon shall. You will be a Levite. Aharon will speak to Pharaoh for you.

"Rest assured that your brother will come to meet you, and will be glad you have merited leadership. He will not envy you. Because he will be truly happy in his heart, he will be found worthy of wearing the *Choshen*, the breastplate full of precious gems, upon his heart. Go to Aharon and tell him all that I have told you. You will be his master, and he will speak to Pharaoh for you. And take with you the rod with which you will show the signs."

◆§ Moshe Prepares to Return

וַיֵּלֶךְ מֹשֶׁה וַיָּשָׁב אֶל יֶתֶר חֹתְנוֹ — *Moshe went and returned to Yisro, his father-in-law* (4:18). Moshe went to obtain permission from his father-in-law to return to Egypt. He said, "I want to go to see the welfare of my brothers." Yisro replied, "Go in peace."

God told Moshe, "Return to Egypt, for Dasan and Aviram, who spoke against you to Pharaoh, are dead." God said that they were dead, even though they actually were still living, because they had become impoverished, which is comparable to death. They were no longer in a position to speak against him, for their words would not be heeded.

Moshe took his wife and children and placed them on the same donkey upon which Avraham had placed Yitzchak when going to the *Akedah*, Yitzchak's near-sacrifice. And on that same donkey *Mashiach* will ride upon his arrival.

God told Moshe: "You will show Pharaoh all of My signs with the staff which you hold in your hand. I will harden his heart and he will not send Israel from his land, so that I can perform even more miracles. Tell Pharaoh, 'The God of Israel has sent me to tell you, *Israel is My first-born* (4:22). They are My most esteemed nation, and you must release them to serve Me. *If you refuse to release them, I will kill your first-born son.'*" Although this was actually the last plague, it was spoken of first in order to terrify him, for it was the most awful.

◆§ The Circumcision

וַיְהִי בַדֶּרֶךְ בַּמָּלוֹן — *And it was on the way, in the inn* (4:24). During Moshe's journey, while he was in an inn, an angel accosted him and tried to kill him, because he had failed to circumcise his son Eliezer.

R' Yosei says: Heaven forbid that we should believe that Moshe did not fulfill the commandment of circumcision. He had thought to himself: "If I circumcise him before I go on my way, then travel is dangerous. Shall I wait for three days while the circumcision heals? God Himself commanded me to go to Egypt; I am forbidden to delay."

The angel would therefore not have harmed him, for he was not to blame. But when he came to the inn he busied himself with his own affairs rather than with the circumcision, and then the angel came to kill him. Tzipora understood, and she took a sharp stone and circumcised her son. With that, the angel left him.

R' Bechaye writes, in the name of R' Chananel: Moshe did not

perform the circumcision himself because he was not nearby. R'
Bechaye writes further that the Torah does not say the angel "went
away from him" (וַיֵּלֶךְ מִמֶּנּוּ) but rather, *he let him alone* (וַיִּרֶף מִמֶּנּוּ;
(4:26), for Tzipora made the cut, but did not do the *priyah*, the
peeling back of the foreskin. The angel therefore stood and waited
until she did it. Tzipora alluded to this with her words, חֲתַן דָּמִים
לַמּוּלֹת, *You are a bridegroom of blood, for the circumcisions* (4:26),
using the plural form of the last word, in reference to these two
stages of the circumcision.

The *Midrash* says that the child was circumcised with a stone,
rather than with a knife, because that was the custom at the time.
When King David threw a stone to kill Goliath the Philistine who
was protected by an iron helmet, the angel who is the patron of
stone told the angel who is the patron of metal: "Let the stone which
David casts pierce your metal so that it will hit the Philistine's head.
In return I will give you a reward: until now, circumcision has been
performed with a stone. Henceforth it shall be done with a knife."
The angel agreed and so today we circumcise with a metal knife.

◆§ The Elders are Apprehensive

וַיֹּאמֶר ה' אֶל אַהֲרֹן לֵךְ לִקְרַאת מֹשֶׁה — *God told Aharon, Go to meet
Moshe* (4:27). Aharon met Moshe, who told him of the signs which
God had shown him. They gathered the elders together and showed
them the sign of the staff. Israel believed in them, prostrating
themselves at the joyous news of their redemption.

The elders however left them, fearing to confront Pharaoh,
leaving only Moshe and Aharon. As a result, the elders did not merit
accompanying Moshe on Mount Sinai.

◆§ Confronting Pharaoh

Moshe and Aharon told Pharaoh: "The God of Israel has appeared to us and has bidden us tell you to release His nation for a
holy day in the desert." Answered Pharaoh: "I have never heard of
your God."

The *Midrash* says that Pharaoh owned a book which listed the
names of all the idols which were worshiped. He said, "Your God's
name does not appear in the book!"

R' Bechaye writes that Pharaoh was very knowledgeable, and
knew the name of every single ruler, and over what kingdom he
ruled. He said, "I do not know of your God, for He rules over no
land." What he did not realize was that God is the ruler over all the
mortal kings.

Our Sages liken this to a *Kohen* with a foolish servant. The priest went away, and the servant set out to find him. He went to the cemetery and asked if his master was there. "Fool," answered the townspeople, "your master is a priest. How could he possibly be here in the graveyard?"

Similarly, Moshe told Pharaoh, "Why are you seeking God among the idols who are dead and powerless, when ours is the living God, King over all kings?"

Pharaoh asked, "What can your God do?" Moshe replied, "He created heaven and earth and all creations. He brings rain and causes everything to grow. He anoints rulers on the earth — and deposes them."

Pharaoh retorted: "I am master of the world. I created myself and the Nile River." God told Moshe, "Because Pharaoh prides himself on his river, you will change the water of the river to blood."

Pharaoh continued, "I don't have to obey God, for He never appeared to me, even when I abducted Sarah. Yet He appeared to Avimelech when he abducted her."

Moshe and Aharon said, "Release us or you will be punished with pestilence and the sword." Pharaoh's answer was, "Make certain that you do not interfere with the people's work. The Jews will hear your words and cease working."

⇐§ The Tribe of Levi

לְכוּ לְסִבְלֹתֵיכֶם — *Go to your burdens* (5:4). "Go, Moshe and Aharon, to your work, and do not interfere with the people." But Pharaoh did not command them to go to *his* labors, because the tribe of Levi was not enslaved.

Pharaoh had commanded that the tribe of Levi be left free to study the Torah, so that they could teach the people the commandments. *Chizkuni* writes that Levi did not have to work because at the beginning Pharaoh worked together with the Jews in order to induce them to work; and the tribe of Levi did not go to work from the beginning, because Yaakov had commanded that Levi not carry his coffin, since in the future they would carry the Ark *(aron)* and the holy vessels of the Tabernacle; they likewise refused to work with Pharaoh on the first day, and thus remained free.

⇐§ The Burden is Increased

וַיְצַו פַּרְעֹה בַּיּוֹם הַהוּא אֶת הַנֹּגְשִׂים בָּעָם — *On that day Pharaoh commanded the taskmasters of the people* (5:6). Pharaoh commanded that they not be given any straw with which to make the bricks. They would have to collect the straw themselves. But their quota of bricks was not lessened. He did this to make their work even more difficult, so that they would not speak of freedom.

The Jews dispersed to gather straw. The Egyptians beat the Jewish overseers who were responsible for making certain that the Jews worked. These overseers became the Sanhedrin of Israel because they were beaten on behalf of their fellows and yet they refused to strike them to force them to work harder.

וַיִּרְאוּ שֹׁטְרֵי בְנֵי יִשְׂרָאֵל אֹתָם בְּרָע — *The overseers of Israel saw themselves in trouble* (5:19). The overseers saw that Israel was forced to toil cruelly. They saw Moshe and Aharon leaving Pharaoh's palace, and told them, "God will judge you for having caused the toil to become even more difficult." Moshe turned to God and said, "Why have You worsened the lot of Israel? Their work is difficult, and they blame me for being Your messenger! Pharaoh has refused to release them."

God replied, "You are not like Avraham. I told him that his most esteemed son would be Yitzchak, and afterwards commanded him to sacrifice him, and yet he did not importune against Me, while you are again complaining. *Now you shall see* (עַתָּה תִרְאֶה; 6:1): the miracles which I perform now with Pharaoh you shall see, but not what I shall do to the thirty-one kings of *Eretz Yisrael*."

R' Bechaye writes that Moshe asked, *Why have you dealt badly?* (לָמָה הֲרֵעֹתָה; 5:22). Why is it that all is well with Pharaoh and his people, who are so wicked, while Israel suffers? For suffering comes either as punishment for sin, or in order that one should enjoy the rewards of the World to Come. What then is the reason for the present suffering?

God answered, "*You shall see* (6:1) the downfall of Pharaoh very soon, as their joy comes to an end. And why did I deal so harshly with Israel? In order to reward them doubly, for having endured their troubles with loving patience."

❧   ❧   ❧

The *Haftorah* of *Parashas Sh'mos* may be found on p. 471.

פרשת וארא
Parashas Vaera
(6:2 — 9:35)

◈§ A Fourfold Promise of Redemption

וָאֵרָא אֶל אַבְרָהָם — *I appeared to Avraham* (6:3). God said, "I appeared to Avraham, Yitzchak and Yaakov, and revealed My Name as the Almighty. I fulfilled all that I promised, using that Name. How much more so, when I swear by the [Four-Letter] Name of God itself; I will most certainly do all that I have said. Go and tell Israel that I will fulfill the oath which I swore to their forefathers, and I will redeem them from Egypt."

R' Bechaye writes that the verse speaks with four different expressions of redemption: וְהוֹצֵאתִי — *I will bring forth*; וְהִצַּלְתִּי — *I will rescue*; וְגָאַלְתִּי — *I will redeem*; וְלָקַחְתִּי — *I will take* (6:6-7). These four phrases show us the four things which God promised Israel. First, He told them that they would be free from their toil, as He said: *I will bring you forth from the burdens of Egypt* (וְהוֹצֵאתִי אֶתְכֶם מִתַּחַת סִבְלֹת מִצְרַיִם; 6:6). Our Sages tell us that the work ended six months before the redemption. They stopped laboring on Rosh HaShanah, and they were liberated from Egypt on the 15th day of Nissan.

The second thing which God promised was that they would no longer be under the sway of the Egyptians. Of this He said, *I will rescue you from their work* (וְהִצַּלְתִּי אֶתְכֶם מֵעֲבֹדָתָם; 6:6), meaning, "By Nissan you will no longer be under their authority."

The third thing which He said was that He would split the sea for them, as it says, *I will redeem you* (וְגָאַלְתִּי אֶתְכֶם; 6:6). So long as the master is alive the slave trembles that the master will come and enslave him once again. But the Egyptians drowned when the sea was split, so everyone understood that they were truly free.

The fourth promise of God was that they would receive His Torah, as He said, *I will take you to Me as a nation* (וְלָקַחְתִּי אֶתְכֶם לִי לְעָם; 6:7). We became God's nation through the Torah, serving Him and no other.

וְנָתַתִּי אֹתָהּ לָכֶם מוֹרָשָׁה — *I will give it to you as a heritage* (6:8). R'
Bechaye writes: Why does the Torah use the word *morashah*
("heritage," or "bequest") rather than *yerushah* (inheritance)? This
shows that these people themselves would not inherit the land. They
were destined to perish in the desert, bequeathing *Eretz Yisrael* as
the heritage of their own children.

When Moshe came to Israel and said that he had come to end their
exile, *they did not pay heed to Moshe* (6:9) because of their great
troubles: their breath was short on account of their hard labor. God
told Moshe, "Go to Pharaoh and tell him to release Israel from
Egypt." Moshe answered, "If Israel themselves pay no attention to
me, and to the good news which I bring them, why will Pharaoh
listen?" God once again told Moshe to go to Pharaoh, and
commanded him to treat him with respect, despite his wickedness,
because he was a ruler. He also warned him not to speak angrily
with the Jews.

⋑ The Lineage of Israel

אֵלֶּה רָאשֵׁי בֵית אֲבֹתָם — *These are the heads of their fathers' houses*
(6:14). Because the time of Israel's release had arrived, the Torah
now traces their lineage, in order to show that they were not like the
Egyptians, who had no clear lineage. It further traces the lineage of
Moshe and Aharon, who were the sons of noble parents. It begins
with the tribe of Reuven, and continues until it comes to Levi,
Moshe's tribe.

The verse says that Levi was 137 years old at his death, in order to
teach us that so long as one of Yaakov's sons was alive, the people
were not enslaved. Levi lived longer than any of the others, and the
enslavement began with his death.

אֲחוֹת נַחְשׁוֹן — *The sister of Nachshon* (6:23). Aharon married
Elisheva, daughter of Aminadav, and Nachshon's sister. Why does
the verse mention Nachshon? To show that when one wants to take
a wife he should investigate what sort of brother she has, because
children often resemble the mother's brothers.

הוּא אַהֲרֹן וּמֹשֶׁה — *These were Aharon and Moshe* (6:26). The verse
sometimes mentions Moshe's name before Aharon's (v. 27), and
sometimes Aharon precedes Moshe, to show that they were equals.
Aharon was of important status because he was the elder, and
Moshe was notable because of his prophecy.

God told Moshe to go to Pharaoh, and Moshe replied, *But I am a
man who stammers* (הֵן אֲנִי עֲרַל שְׂפָתָיִם; 6:30). R' Bechaye writes:

Why did Moshe not protest earlier that he stammered, when God first sent him to Pharaoh? At that time God spoke to Aharon as well, so Moshe thought that Aharon would speak to Pharaoh. Now, however, God told him alone to go to Pharaoh, so he protested that he could not speak properly.

Chizkuni writes: Why did God have Moshe and Aharon descend from Amram, a man who had married his aunt, a relationship forbidden by the Torah? In order that there exist something to taunt them with. If ever they would become haughty, the people could say, "Look where you come from — from a relationship forbidden by the Torah!"

⇥ Pharaoh is Unimpressed

God told Moshe, "When Pharaoh tells you to give him a sign, take your staff and throw it down before him. It will become a snake."

R' Bechaye asks: Why did it become a snake? Because Pharaoh is compared to the snake, which spoke against God and caused Adam's sin. Similarly, Pharaoh asked scornfully, "Who is God, that I should pay heed to him?" Further, just as a snake writhes from one side to the other, so Pharaoh, when suffering from the plagues, would agree to release the Jews, and after the plague would end he would refuse to let them go.

לִפְנֵי פַרְעֹה וְלִפְנֵי עֲבָדָיו — *Before Pharaoh and before his servants* (7:10). Aharon threw his staff down before Pharaoh and his servants, and it became a snake. Pharaoh called for his wizards, and using magic they turned their wands into snakes. Aharon's snake

Aharon's snake and the wizards' snakes

then turned back into a stick, and devoured the wizards' wands. This was an allusion to the time when because of Israel the Egyptians would be devoured by the sea.

R' Bechaye writes that regarding their feat the Torah says, וַיִּהְיוּ לְתַנִּינִם (7:12), the letter *lamed* here implying that "they became *like* snakes": the wizards' snakes were mere illusions, not actual snakes.

⊰§ The First Plague: Blood

וַיֶּחֱזַק לֵב פַּרְעֹה — *Pharaoh's heart was hardened* (7:13). He refused to send the Jews out. God told Moshe, "Go to Pharaoh (7:15) early in the morning, and you will find him at the Nile River." Pharaoh had deified himself, and claimed that he neither ate nor drank, nor had bodily needs. Every morning he would go the Nile and take care of his bodily needs when no one could see him. God told Moshe to accost him at the Nile and demand that he release Israel.

"I know that he will not release them until I have punished him with the plague of the first-born. Tell him that I will punish him with this staff which is in your hand. The water of the Nile will turn to blood, and the fish will die. The Nile will reek of their stench, and the water will become undrinkable."

God further told Moshe, "Go to Aharon and tell him to take his staff and hold it out over the water of Egypt, over all of its rivers and streams. All the water will turn to blood, even the water in their clay and wooden vessels."

Why did Aharon, and not Moshe, strike the river? Because the Nile had been kind to Moshe, when he had been concealed there as an infant, so he was forbidden to strike it. Similarly, the plague of frogs was brought by Aharon, rather than Moshe, because they arose from the water. So too Moshe did not bring the plague of lice to the earth, because the earth had saved him when he buried the Egyptian whom he had killed.

The wizards, too, were able to change water into blood. R' Bechaye writes that they dug until they struck water, and they turned it into blood. All the other water in Egypt had already been stricken by Aharon.

וַיִּבְאַשׁ הַיְאֹר — *The river was foul* (7:21). The river became rancid, and all of its fish died. The Egyptians dug for water from near the river to drink.

וַיִּמָּלֵא שִׁבְעַת יָמִים — *Seven days passed* (7:25). The plague ended after seven days, and Pharaoh refused to release the people. Each plague likewise lasted seven days, just as a woman is considered

ritually impure for seven days after her menstrual flow has ceased. Pharaoh then had a hiatus of twenty-one days before the onset of the next plague, during which time Moshe gave him due warning of the plague to come.

◄§ The Second Plague: Frogs

God told Moshe, "Go and tell Pharaoh that if he does not release you I will strike *all your borders with frogs* (7:27). They will be in your homes, in all of your rooms, and in your beds. They will be in your nobles' homes, and in the homes of your servants. You will find them in your ovens and in your dough."

R' Bechaye writes that Pharaoh had been quarreling with the King of Cush (Ethiopia), claiming that he had annexed some of his land across a common border. When the plague of frogs struck they could see exactly where the borders of Egypt ended, because the frogs took over the entire land, exactly up to the borders. Peace then reigned between the two kings.

וּבְכָה וּבְעַמֶּךְ — *Within you and within your nation* (7:29). The frogs will literally be within you, croaking from within your intestines.

וַתַּעַל הַצְּפַרְדֵּעַ — *The frogs arose* (8:2). The frogs arose from the water and filled the land. The wizards, too, caused frogs to appear. Pharaoh begged Moshe and Aharon to pray for the frogs' disappearance the next day.

Ramban, Chizkuni, and R' Bechaye ask: Why did Pharaoh ask them to pray that the frogs disappear the next day, rather than on that very day? Because he thought that they might disappear that day of their own accord. He would show that Moshe was a liar, because they had disappeared without his prayers. Therefore Pharaoh asked that all the later plagues likewise disappear "tomorrow," and Moshe would pray for that.

Chizkuni and *Baal HaTurim* write that with Moshe's prayers, all the frogs died, with the exception of those which had entered the ovens, facing the fire at God's command. These remained alive, and returned to the water.

Imrei Noam asks why first it is written, *the frogs shall depart* (8:7), and later *the frogs died* (8:9). The answer is that those frogs which were within the people themselves, as well as the ones in Pharaoh's home, disappeared, out of respect for majesty; those in the other people's homes died.

וַיִּצְעַק מֹשֶׁה אֶל ה' — *Moshe cried out to God* (8:8). *Imrei Noam* writes: Why did Moshe cry to God during this plague? Prior to this he had said to Pharaoh, *Challenge me* (הִתְפָּאֵר עָלַי; 8:5). Because he spoke proudly God did not answer his prayers immediately, and he was forced to cry out to God.

R' Isser'l writes that the plague of blood included water in wooden and stone vessels, but not those in iron vessels, teaching us that at the time of the equinox iron should be placed in vessels of water to avert harm.

✌§ The Third Plague: Lice

God told Moshe, "Because Pharaoh refuses to release Israel, tell Aharon to stretch out the staff and strike the earth. Lice will emerge from it."

The wizards tried to create lice, but were unable to, because magic has no power over things smaller than a grain of barley.

R' Bechaye writes that the magicians could make the blood because it was not a new creation. It was made out of the water which was changed into blood. Similarly, the frogs already existed in the water, and just had to be brought out. The lice were wholly new creations and so the magicians could not create them.

Chizkuni writes: Why were the wizards unable to create the lice? Because the lice were so thick that one could not stand firmly on the ground, and if a wizard does not have his feet planted on the ground he cannot perform his sorcery.

The magicians recognized the hand of God from this plague, and thereafter Pharaoh did not bother calling them to imitate the other plagues. The lice attacked the men, the beasts, and the entire land.

◆§ The Fourth Plague: Wild Beasts

אֶת הֶעָרֹב — *The beasts* (8:17). God told Moshe, "Because Pharaoh will not release Israel and has hardened his heart, I will send wild beasts to the houses in all of Egypt, with the exception of Goshen, where Israel lives."

R' Bechaye writes that if a man wants to harm his enemy he keeps his plans secret so that his enemy cannot defend himself; but God always warned Pharaoh of the impending plagues. He could not protect himself anyway.

וְשַׂמְתִּי פְדֻת — *I will make a division* (8:19). "I will make a separation between My people and his. When a Jew walks through Egypt, near the wild beasts, they will not dare harm him." And so it was.

Pharaoh told Moshe and Aharon to "*Go and sacrifice to your God* (8:21). Make the sacrifices here, but do not go to the desert." Moshe and Aharon answered, "How can we slaughter the sacrificial animals here in this land? If we destroy that which the Egyptians worship, they will stone us." Answered Pharaoh: "I will let you go, but do not go far. And pray for me!" Moshe replied, "When I leave the city I will pray that the animals and ferocious beasts disappear tomorrow, so that you will know that they did not disappear of their own accord. But do not have second thoughts and refuse to release us."

וַיָּסַר הֶעָרֹב — *He removed the beasts* (8:27). The beasts disappeared. Why did they not simply fall down dead, as the frogs did? So that the Egyptians would derive no benefit from their furs.

Pharaoh hardened his heart *this time also* (גַּם בַּפַּעַם הַזֹּאת; 8:28), and refused to release the Jews. R' Bechaye asks: Why does the verse specify *this time also*? Because in the case of the first three plagues, the sorcerers induced him to harden his heart. But when they could not create the lice they admitted that the plague was God's doing. The verse therefore says *this time also*, meaning that even though the sorcerers did not persuade him this time, still he himself hardened his heart, without the counsel of the sorcerers.

◆§ The Fifth Plague: Pestilence

God told Moshe, "Go to Pharaoh and tell him that if he does not release the Jews, *Behold the hand of God will be upon your cattle in the field*" (9:3).

R' Bechaye says that the verse states *in the field* because the majority of animals graze in fields; but those animals in the houses were also struck.

Ramban writes that the verse specifies *in the field* because the Egyptians, who worshiped the animals, did not want to keep their animals in their cities. They placed them in the fields away from the cities, close to the land of Goshen. Although the animals of the Jews were kept nearby, not one of them perished. Though Pharaoh sent out messengers to confirm that this was so, he still remained obstinate and did not allow Israel to leave.

✑§ The Sixth Plague: Boils

God then commanded Moshe and Aharon to take ashes from a furnace into their hands, throw them towards the sky, in front of Pharaoh, and all of the men and animals would be covered with boils. Moshe and Aharon each took two handfuls of ash, and Moshe miraculously placed all of it into one hand, throwing it up towards the sky. This too was a miracle, for as a rule one cannot throw ash up high, as it is immediately dispersed in the air.

וַיְחַזֵּק ה' אֶת לֵב פַּרְעֹה — *God hardened Pharaoh's heart* (9:12). R' Bechaye writes: Why does the Torah say concerning this particular plague that it was God Who hardened Pharaoh's heart? During the first plagues the sorcerers had hardened his heart. But during this plague they too were covered with boils. They were ashamed to enter Pharaoh's palace, and could not harden his heart.

Rashi asks: It is written that the boils affected the animals; where did they get the animals? The Torah says clearly that all of the animals of Egypt were killed during the previous plague. The answer is that the animals in the fields were killed, while those in the homes remained alive, and were subsequently struck with boils.

✑§ The Seventh Plague: Hail

God told Moshe, "Go and tell Pharaoh that if he does not release the Jews I will send down a mighty hailstorm which will destroy all of the trees and crops. Bring all of your animals in from the fields, and all of your people, so that the hail will not destroy them as well." R' Bechaye writes that even though all of the animals had already been killed, the Egyptians had bought new animals from other nations, and these animals had to be brought in. Also included were animals owned jointly by Egyptians and Jews, which had been spared during previous plagues.

R' Bechaye writes that the hail was composed of water, with fire in its center. The fire burned the roots in the earth, and the water did not extinguish the flames. A parable: a noble had two servants who

loathed each other. One day he had to go to battle, and needed both servants, so he made peace between them. Similarly, in order to strike Pharaoh, God made peace between fire and water. At the same time God made peace between the angels Gavriel (Gabriel) and Michael. Gavriel is responsible for fire, Michael for water.

The hail destroyed all the vegetables growing in the fields, all the flax and barley, and men and beasts as well. Only in the land of Goshen, where the Jews lived, was there no hail.

Pharaoh called for Moshe and Aharon and said, "God is just. My nation and I are wicked for not having allowed the Jews to leave. Pray to God to stop and thunder and the hail, and I will release the Jews." Moshe answered: "I will leave the city to pray, and the thunder and hail will cease, so that you will recognize that God reigns over all the idols."

Moshe had to leave the city to pray, for the city was full of idols. *Chizkuni* writes that Moshe went out to the fields to show that despite the fact that the hail was hardest there, he had no fear of it.

Chizkuni also asks why Moshe warned the Egyptians to take their animals in from the fields during the hailstorm, while during the plague which destroyed the animals God did not warn them to bring them to the city. During the plague of hail, men too died, so God ordered them to bring in their animals for the sake of [warning] the men. But the other plague destroyed animals alone, so God issued no warning.

R' Bechaye writes: Why did Moshe, during the plague of hail, lift his hand and pray harder than for any other plagues? Because during that plague both animals and men were killed. There was a piteous outcry, and so he prayed more fervently.

וַה' נָתַן קֹלת וּבָרָד — *God gave thunder and hail* (9:23). He first brought the thunder, killing the men, and then hail fell.

וּמָטָר לֹא נִתַּךְ אָרְצָה — *Rain did not fall on the earth* (9:33). R' Bechaye writes that the hail remained suspended between heaven and earth for 41 years, until Yehoshua (Joshua) battled the 31 kings. The hail then struck them and their people. The thunder remained suspended until Elisha's time. The king of Aram advanced toward Shomron with a great camp, hoping to capture the city. God loosed the thunder on the people and they fled in fear and panic, leaving their property unguarded in their tents, so that the Jews could come and claim the booty.

וַיֹּסֶף לַחֲטֹא — *He continued to sin* (9:34). As soon as the hail stopped, Pharaoh sinned once again. When he is suffering the wicked man becomes righteous and loves God. But once his misery is alleviated he becomes evil once again. The righteous, however, are always humble. They are respected for this reason, as the verse says (*Mishlei* 29:23), וּשְׁפַל רוּחַ יִתְמֹךְ כָּבוֹד — *The humble in spirit shall be supported by honor.*

❧ ❧ ❧

The *Haftorah* of *Parashas Vaera* may be found on p. 473.

פרשת בא
Parashas Bo
(10:1 — 13:16)

◆§ The Eighth Plague: Locusts

בֹּא אֶל פַּרְעֹה — *Go to Pharaoh* (10:1). God told Moshe, "Go to Pharaoh. Warn him that I will punish him if he does not release the Jews."

King Solomon says, in *Proverbs:* אַשְׁרֵי אָדָם מְפַחֵד תָּמִיד — *Happy is the man who fears constantly (Mishlei 28:14).* A man who is constantly in a state of caution as to the outcome of his actions will not turn to evil. Man is called *adam* (אָדָם) to show that even though he comes from the earth (אֲדָמָה), he can use his mind to act righteously. When he wants to eat and drink his intention should not be to satisfy his bodily desires. Rather, the intention ought to be to strengthen his body so that he can serve God. The verse continues: וּמַקְשֶׁה לִבּוֹ יִפּוֹל בְּרָעָה — *but one who hardens his heart will fall into evil,* just as Pharaoh did. He set his heart against God, and suffered much anguish. Because he set himself against God, God later hardened his heart so that he would prolong his punishment. God leads men along the path which they themselves choose. If a man wants to be good, God leads him toward goodness; if he wants to travel an evil road, God helps him to do that too.

God told Moshe to go to Pharaoh's palace and tell him, "Because you refuse to recognize My wonders, I am sending a plague of locusts such as your forefathers have never seen. They will cover the earth, and devour all of your trees and crops. Your house will be full of them."

R' Bechaye writes: God warned Pharaoh twice — once on the banks of the river, because he had boasted that he had created the Nile; and once in his house, because he had prided himself on the beauty of his palace. God humbled him in both places. Similarly, because Nevuchadnetzar thought too highly of himself and claimed he was a god, God humbled him by turning him into an animal who ate grass in the wilds for seven years.

◆§ Sequence of the Plagues

R' Bechaye writes that the plagues followed one another in this manner. On the 15th day of Nissan God appeared to Moshe from within the bush and ordered him to go to Pharaoh. On the 21st day of Nissan Moshe asked his father-in-law's leave to go back to Egypt to warn Pharaoh to release the Jews. This warning lasted eight days, until the end of Nissan. For the next three months, Iyar, Sivan, and Tammuz, Moshe was in hiding; the plague of blood began on the first day of Av. The plague lasted seven days, and Pharaoh then had three weeks of peace before the onset of the next plague. This was the pattern of all ten plagues. The plague of the first-born was in the month of Nissan, and Moshe had warned Pharaoh of it in the preceding Nissan. The period of the plagues totalled twelve months: they suffered for twelve months, just as the wicked are judged in *Gehinnom* for a twelve-month period.

◆§ An Ominous Star

וַיִּפֶן וַיֵּצֵא מֵעִם פַּרְעֹה — *He turned and left Pharaoh* (10:6). As soon as Moshe left Pharaoh, his servants turned to him and implored: "How much longer will the Jews stand in our way? Let them go and serve their God! Do you not yet realize that Egypt is already lost because of the plagues?" Pharaoh thereupon sent for Moshe and Aharon and said, "Go serve your God. But tell me, who of you will go?" Moshe answered, "We must all go, old and young, women and children. This is a festival of God." He was referring to *Shavuos*, when they would receive the Torah. Said Pharaoh: "Why must the children go, too? Let the men go alone. You claim that you must bring sacrifices, but women and children do not slaughter animals. I see that you must be planning to escape to the desert. It will end badly for you, for I see an evil star hanging over you in the desert, a bloody star signifying your death. The name of the star is Ra'ah, because it causes harm (רָעָה) to men."

As a matter of fact, Pharaoh had read the stars correctly. When the Jews soon after created the Golden Calf, God did want to kill them, and only Moshe's intercession caused Him to exchange the blood of their destruction for the blood of the circumcision in the desert. For before their entry into *Eretz Yisrael* Yehoshua circumcised them all.

At that time, Moshe said in his prayers: "If You kill Israel the Egyptians will claim that they warned us when we were being released that You brought us out of the land under the sway of the ominous star Ra'ah (בְּרָעָה הוֹצִיאָם; 32:12). All of Your miracles will then be forgotten."

Pharaoh ordered Moshe away from his palace. God told Moshe, *Stretch our your hand over Egypt [to bring] the locusts* (10:12). Moshe stretched his hand out and God sent a powerful easterly wind which howled for an entire day and an entire night. The wind brought the locusts and they covered the whole land, darkening it. They devoured all the grasses and crops in the fields.

The word for locust (אַרְבֶּה) is mentioned seven times in this passage because there were seven types of locust: large ones, small ones, red, black, white, green and brown ones.

Pharaoh confessed to Moshe and Aharon: "I have sinned to your God and to yourselves, for I called for you and then ordered you away from my house. Now, I beg of you, take away this bitter, deadly plague of locusts!"

R' Bechaye writes that the locusts gouged out the Egyptians' eyes, causing their deaths. Pharaoh begged them to end this death. Moshe prayed and God sent a westerly wind which carried away all the locusts to the sea. *Imrei Noam* says that God sent the locusts to the sea so that if the Egyptians would pursue the Jews into the sea, the locusts could attack the pursuers. All of the plagues with which they were smitten in Egypt were repeated at the sea as well.

לֹא נִשְׁאַר אַרְבֶּה אֶחָד — *Not one locust remained* (10:19). Even the locusts which had been pickled in Egypt suddenly came to life and flew away, so that the Egyptians could derive no benefit from them.

R' Bechaye writes: Moshe's prayers are efficacious forever. Because he prayed that God clear Egypt of locusts, no locusts ever appear there, even though they do sometimes appear in *Eretz Yisrael*. And even if they pass by the land, they do not harm its vegetation. Similarly, since Moshe prayed that the frogs remain in the water, one gigantic frog remains there. It climbs out onto dry land and devours three people in one gulp. It cannot be harmed, as it is very poisonous. Even if one strikes it one dies from the venom.

◄§ The Ninth Plague: Darkness

God told Moshe, "Stretch your hand towards heaven and a heavy darkness will engulf the land. When the darkness of night begins to disappear and daybreak appears, it will become dark once again, so that this will be recognized as God's plague."

Rashi writes: Why did it become dark? Because there were wicked men among the Jews who did not wish to leave. They were killed in the days of darkness, so that the Egyptians would not witness their deaths and say, "They are being punished just as we are."

The darkness was thick and palpable. If a person was sitting he was unable to stand up. It lasted only six days. The seventh day of darkness was reserved for the time that the Egyptians pursued the Jews at the sea, and were engulfed in darkness.

אוֹר בְּמוֹשְׁבֹתָם — *Light in their homes* (10:23). There was light for Israel. Why does the Torah specify *in their homes*, rather than "in the land of Goshen," where the Jews lived? To show that if a Jew was in the house of an Egyptian, the Egyptian was in darkness and the Jew was in the light.

Pharaoh told Moshe and Aharon, "Go to the desert, all of you, and serve your God. Only your animals must remain behind as a guarantee of your return." Moshe replied, "You will even give us *your* sheep, for we do not know how many sacrifices God will ask of us." Pharaoh retorted, "Go away and let me see your face no more!" Moshe answered, "Your answer is both true and timely: you will indeed see me no more."

God told Moshe, "I will bring one more plague onto the Egyptians and then Pharaoh will send you away from here. Tell the Jews to borrow silver and gold from the Egyptians so that they can leave with it. I promised Avraham that they would leave wealthy. Because they slaved for the Egyptians, let them take their valuables from them."

◈§ The Tenth Plague: Death of the First-born

Moshe told Pharaoh, "God has said, 'In the middle of the night I will kill all of your first-born, whether the eldest of the mother or the father. The first-born of the nobility, and of the animals too are included' — for they were worshiped by the Egyptians. 'The night will be rent with screams and there will be no house without its dead within.'" Only Pharaoh, though himself a first-born son, remained alive, so that he would be a witness to the wonders that took place on the sea and attest to it to other idolatrous nations.

Moshe told Pharaoh, "Your servants will come to me during the night and beg me to leave with the Jews. Only then will I leave." Moshe then left Pharaoh, full of wrath.

God spoke to Moshe and Aharon outside of the city. Because it was full of idols, He did not want to appear in such a place to tell them of a commandment.

He told them that they must sanctify the month (קִדּוּשׁ הַחֹדֶשׁ) each time that the moon begins a cycle. Our Sages say that if the Jews would have been given no commandments other than their sanctification of the new moon, it would be sufficient. We receive the moon lovingly, as one receives a great noble. This is why we stand when sanctifying the moon. The moon represents the fact that God created the world, just as He renews the moon each month.

וּלְכֹל בְּנֵי יִשְׂרָאֵל לֹא יֶחֱרַץ כֶּלֶב לְשֹׁנוֹ — *To all the children of Israel no dog will whet his tongue* (11:7). At the time of the tenth plague, no dog howled at the Jews, for there were no corpses among them. Our Sages say that when dogs rejoice, it is a sign that Eliyahu (Elijah) the Prophet is in the city. He killed four hundred false prophets and gave their bodies to the hounds. When they see him, they rejoice, thinking that he has more meat for them.

Chizkuni writes that as a rule dogs bark when someone passes them at night holding a stick. The Jews went out at night, and each held a staff, and yet the dogs were silent. God repaid them by decreeing that the carcasses of non-kosher animals should be given to them [cf. 22:30].

◄§ The Pesach Sacrifice

God commanded that they take a lamb for the Pesach sacrifice, *a lamb for each of their father's homes* (שֶׂה לְבֵית אָבֹת; 12:3), one lamb per household. This was on the 10th day of Nissan. They tied the lamb up for four days, until the 14th day of Nissan, the day preceding Pesach (Passover). All of the Jews brought the Pesach sacrifice. God said, "If a lamb is too much for one household, let them share it with a neighbor." This teaches us not to waste.

R' Bechaye writes: Why did God command them to slaughter a lamb? Because the constellation for the month of Nissan is a lamb. In this way the Jews could not think that their astronomical sign helped them; only God had released them. Also, God commanded that they slaughter a lamb because the Egyptians worshiped the lamb. They roasted it, rather than cook it, because that gives off a strong smell, and it was done whole on a spit, to ensure that the Egyptians recognize that it was a lamb, yet they were powerless.

God said, "You shall eat the sacrifice in Egypt, but be ready to begin your journey. Let your belts be tied, your shoes be on your feet, and your sticks be in your hands.

◄§ Defying Idolatry

שֶׂה תָמִים — *An umblemished lamb* (12:5). "Take for yourselves a whole lamb, without a blemish, so that the Egyptians shall not be able to say that you take a flawed lamb which could not have been used as an idol, so they need not be angry with you." For this same reason the Torah specifies *of one year* (בֶּן שָׁנָה; *ibid.*): once the lamb was a year old, it was unquestionably eligible for the Egyptians' idolatry.

The lamb stood bound for four days so that the Egyptians would hear their idols bleating, and would be unable to do anything about it.

בֵּין הָעַרְבָּיִם — *At dusk* (12:6). They must slaughter the sacrifice between day and night, when everyone is returning from work and can see their idol being slaughtered. The blood must be smeared over the door and on its two sides, to show the miracle to the entire world. The blood smeared on the two sides and the top resembled the letter *ches* (ח), which stands for חַיִּים — "life."

They were to eat the lamb with bitter herbs in order to embitter the Egyptians.

וּבְכָל אֱלֹהֵי מִצְרַיִם אֶעֱשֶׂה שְׁפָטִים — *I will execute judgments against all the gods of Egypt* (12:12). God said, "I will destroy the idols of Egypt." He then commanded that they clean up all of the leaven, and eat unleavened bread *(matzos)* for seven days. A person who would eat leavened bread would be liable for the punishment of *kares*, being cut off from the world. He also commanded that they take a sprig of a certain herb, the hyssop, dip it into the blood of the lamb, and sprinkle the blood over their doors. "During the night that I kill the first-born, let none of the people of Israel leave their home. I will see the blood on the door and will pass over the house and no one will die within."

R' Bechaye writes that it was not the blood which saved them, but the fact that the Jews smeared the blood on their homes, without showing fear of Pharaoh for having slaughtered his god. They relied on God and were thus found worthy of staying alive.

כִּי אֵין בַּיִת אֲשֶׁר אֵין שָׁם מֵת — *There was no house where there was not someone dead* (12:30). In a house with no first-born, the eldest of the house was killed. Because of this the eldest in every house fasts on the day before Pesach.

Even if the first-born was long since dead, it was customary among the Egyptians to carve a likeness on the wall as a memorial. On that night the images were destroyed, and thus it seemed as if the first-born had died on that very night.

וַיִּקְרָא לְמֹשֶׁה וּלְאַהֲרֹן לַיְלָה — *He called for Moshe and for Aharon by night* (12:31). Pharaoh called for Moshe and Aharon and searched for them from house to house. He told them, "Get out, all of you, with your animals, and go and serve your God as you have requested."

⇥ Measure for Measure

R' Bechaye writes that God brought ten plagues upon the Egyptians, representing measure for measure the ten evil deeds which they perpetrated. They forced Israel to draw water for their animals, and so God turned their water to blood and the animals could not drink; they forced them to awaken early, leave their beds and go to work, so God sent frogs into their beds and they would not let them sleep; they kept the Jews from washing themselves, and thus they became full of lice — and so too did the Egyptians; they forced the Jews to hunt for them, so they were plagued with hordes of wild animals; the Jews had to watch their animals, so the animals were smitten with a plague; they would not allow the Jews to warm water to wash themselves and so the Jews became dirty, as a result God sent boils upon the Egyptians; when the Egyptians saw a Jew they threw stones, so God threw hailstones upon them from heaven; the Jews had to fertilize their fields and cover them with manure, so the locusts covered their fields; they put many Jews in the darkness of prison, and so God brought darkness upon them. Finally, they wanted to destroy Israel, who are called God's first-born [cf. 4:22], so God destroyed their eldest children.

⇥ Military Tactics

The *Midrash* writes that God brought the plagues upon them in the manner that a warrior lays siege upon his enemy's city. First he attacks the water supply, hoping that without water they will be forced to surrender. Similarly, God turned all of Egypt's water to blood. Next, the warrior has his army make a fearful noise in order to make the populace panic, and so too God sent the noisy army of frogs. Third, the warrior commands that they be attacked with arrows, and so God brought lice, which prick the body like arrows. Fourth, he sends squads of soldiers to the city to capture it, as God sent hordes of wild animals. Fifth, he sends wild horses to destroy all of the city's animals. Similarly, God sent a plague to destroy the Egyptians' livestock. The warrior then captures men of the city and tortures them with fire so that they will reveal the city's weaknesses. God burned their bodies with boils. The seventh step is when the invader commands that gigantic stones be hurled at the city walls, and so God sent the hailstones. Next, the soldiers enter the city, as the locusts overwhelmed Egypt. Ninth, the commanding officer captures prisoners and places them in dark dungeons, and so God placed darkness upon Egypt. Finally, God destroyed all of the first-born Egyptians.

◄§ Pharaoh Eats his Words

וַתֶּחֱזַק מִצְרַיִם — *The Egyptians were urging* (12:33). The Egyptians urged the Jews to leave because they had been struck with ten plagues and had no choice. Before this, Pharaoh had said to Moshe, "Who is your God? All the other gods have written me letters, and yours has not, so I do not recognize Him." Pharaoh had also called his counselors, and they had told him, "We have heard that their God is a son of their sages." God retorted, "You call Me a son of wise men? Soon all of your wisdom will be destroyed. And you, Pharaoh, claim that you do not recognize Me nor know Me? Soon you will proclaim that God is just. You claim you will not release the Jews? Soon you will beg them to leave Egypt."

This situation is analogous to a noble who sent his servant to buy fish. He bought fish which were rotten and smelled foul. Angered, the noble told him, "Choose one of these three punishments. Either you must eat the fish, receive one hundred lashes, or pay a fine of one hundred gulden." The servant chose to eat the fish, but after he began he could not go on, they were so rotten. He then said that they should strike him instead. But as soon as they began to flog him he cried that he would rather pay the hundred gulden. In this way he suffered all three punishments! He ate the fish, was flogged, and ultimately paid the fine. Similarly, the Egyptians were struck with ten plagues, their wealth was taken away by the Jews, and they still were forced to release them from bondage! It was their evil hearts that caused all of this.

◄§ Preparations for the Exodus

The Jews carried their dough upon their shoulders, bound in sheets. Although they had a great many animals, they carried it by themselves because of their love of the commandments.

The Jews took *silver vessels and gold vessels and clothing* (כְּלֵי כֶסֶף וּכְלֵי זָהָב וּשְׂמָלֹת; 12:35) from the Egyptians. R' Bechaye writes that the clothing was more valuable than the silver and the gold. The verse says silver and then gold to teach us that that which is mentioned last was the most valuable.

Chizkuni writes that the day on which the Jews took a lamb as the Pesach sacrifice, the tenth of Nissan, was a *Shabbos* (Sabbath). They bound it without a tight knot, as tying a permanent knot is forbidden on *Shabbos*. Even so the lamb did not free itself, which was a miracle in itself. Another miracle was that the Egyptians were unable to protest when their idols were bound to the beds in a most degrading manner. For this reason the *Shabbos* which precedes Pesach every year is known as *Shabbos HaGadol*, the great *Shabbos*, because great miracles took place on that day.

וְעֶצֶם לֹא תִשְׁבְּרוּ בוֹ — *Do not break a bone of it* (12:46). The lamb had to be eaten after they were already sated. If they would have broken a bone in order to reach the marrow, it would have appeared as if they were still hungry.

וְגַם צֵדָה לֹא עָשׂוּ לָהֶם — *They also had not prepared any food for themselves* (12:39). The Jews had not taken along with them any food for the journey. They relied on God to provide for them, even in the barren desert.

⧉§ Sanctifying the First-born

God told Moshe to *sanctify each first-born to Me* (קַדֶּשׁ לִי כָל בְּכוֹר; 13:2), the first-born of each mother.

R' Bechaye asks: Why did God command the sanctification of the mother's first-born, and not the father's, even though in Egypt the first-born of the father was also killed? Because only in the case of the mother can we be absolutely certain that the child is a first-born.

⧉§ The Promised Land

God told the Jews, "If you heed my commandments I will bring you to Canaan." R' Bechaye asks: Why is it called the land of the Canaanites, when there were seven nations living there? Because the Canaanites had been cursed with slavery [cf. *Bereishis* 9:15], and whatever a slave owns belongs to his master. God therefore called the land Canaan to show that the land was not theirs; rather, it belonged to their masters, Israel.

Chizkuni says that it is called the land of Canaan because when they heard that God intended to give it to the Jews they abandoned it and left it for them. God said, "Because you left of your own accord I will give you a good land, the land of Africa, and I will call *Eretz Yisrael* by your name, the land of Canaan."

◆§ Redeeming the Donkey

וְכָל פֶּטֶר חֲמֹר — *The first-born of every donkey* (13:13). When a donkey has its first foal it must be redeemed with a lamb. Why was only the donkey redeemed, and not other impure animals? Because the donkeys helped to carry the gold and silver from Egypt. Each Jew had ninety donkeys carrying his gold and silver.

One of the reasons for which the Jews had carried their dough on their shoulders was that their donkeys were so laden with treasures.

◆§ The Mitzvah of Tefillin

לְאוֹת עַל יָדְכָה — *As a sign on your hand* (13:16). The *tefillin* will be put on your left hand, because the right hand is used for work and may be dirty. R' Shimon ben Lakish says that a person who wears *tefillin* lives a long life.

❦ ❦ ❦

The *Haftorah* of *Parashas Bo* may be found on p. 476.

פרשת בשלח
Parashas Beshalach
(13:17 — 17:16)

◈§ Tests of Faith

וַיְהִי בְּשַׁלַּח פַּרְעֹה אֶת הָעָם — *And it was when Pharaoh sent away the nation* (13:17). When Pharaoh sent the people away God did not want to lead them through the land of the Philistines, even though it was the closest way to *Eretz Yisrael*. God wanted to test the Jews to see if they would enter the desert, together with their wives and children, despite the deadly snakes which infest it.

Moreover, He led them through the desert so they would be unable to return to Egypt when forced to encounter battle. For this reason, too, God brought them to the other side of the sea.

R' Chananel writes that God always wants to perform miracles for the righteous. He wanted to display His miracles to Israel in the desert — the miracle of the manna (מָן), the miracle of the quail, the miracle of the water-giving rock. For this reason He led them through the desert. Similarly, when Chananiah, Mishael and Azariah were thrown into a fiery furnace, God could have simply extinguished the fire. Instead, He made it blaze even more fiercely, and yet not a hair on their heads was scorched. He did this in order to maximize the miracle. When Daniel was thrown into a lions' den, God could have killed the lions. Instead, He let them remain alive but sealed their mouths so they could not harm Daniel. Thus, He displayed His wonders.

In this same manner, God performed miracles in the desert, and split the sea for them. Later, when they arrived at Marah, where the water for many years had been sweet and drinkable, God made it bitter, so that Israel could not drink of it. God then commanded Moshe to throw a bitter tree into the water. Miraculously, it became drinkable once again. God did this to test His people to see if they would rely on Him or not.

God did the same thing with the manna. He sent one portion

every day, rather than send enough for a long period of time, so that they would have to turn to Him every day for their daily bread.

∾§ Avoiding Philistia

Chizkuni adds that God did not want to bring Israel through the land of the Philistines, lest the Philistines think that they were coming to do battle with them, in vengeance for the Philistines' murder of the people of Efraim. These people had incorrectly calculated the end of the Egyptian exile, and had left several years too early. Had the Jews traveled through the land of the Philistines, they would have assumed that they were coming to avenge their brothers' deaths, so God avoided that route.

Another explanation of the words, *God did not lead them through the land of the Philistines because it was near* (13:17), is that since Avimelech, king of the Philistines, was related to Pharaoh (כִּי קָרוֹב הוּא — "because it was near," can also be translated as "because he was a relative"), God was loath to bring the Jews through his land. If the Egyptians would pursue them, the Philistines would have joined them, out of kinship, and together they would have fought Israel.

∾§ Helping Those who Help Themselves

וַחֲמֻשִׁים עָלוּ בְנֵי יִשְׂרָאֵל מֵאֶרֶץ מִצְרָיִם — *The Children of Israel went up, armed, from Egypt* (13:18). They left as warriors, even though they had no need to go to war, since God fought against the Egyptians for them. This shows us that a man must ready himself for whatever he must do. Only then will God help him, as it says in *Proverbs: The horse is readied for the day of war, but salvation comes from God* (סוּס מוּכָן לְיוֹם מִלְחָמָה וְלַה' הַתְּשׁוּעָה; *Mishlei* 21:31).

The *Midrash* says that the word *chamushim* ("armed") can be translated as "one-fifth" (*chamesh* — "five"). One-fifth of the people left Egypt, while four-fifths died during the plague of darkness, because they did not want to leave Egypt. Why did they die during that particular plague? So that the Egyptians should not see what was happening and say, "They are being punished, just as we are."

Another explanation is that the word *chamushim* refers to fifty. They left Egypt in order to receive the Torah fifty days later. There are fifty days between Pesach and Shavuos.

∾§ An Old Vow Fulfilled

וַיִּקַּח מֹשֶׁה אֶת עַצְמוֹת יוֹסֵף עִמּוֹ — *Moshe took Yosef's bones with him* (13:19). Yosef had asked the Jews to swear that they would take his bones with them and bury them in *Eretz Yisrael*. All of the Jews were preoccupied with borrowing gold and silver, but Moshe went to do a *mitzvah* — to fulfill the vow. Because Yosef buried his own father with great pomp and respect, he merited having Moshe, who was greater than he, bury him. Moshe in turn merited having God, Who of course is greater than he, bury him. No man knows the location of his tomb because God Himself buried him.

The sea split by virtue of Yosef. As soon as his coffin reached the sea, and the sea saw whose coffin it was, its waters split and *fled* (וַיָּנָס; *Tehillim* 114:3), because Yosef had *fled* (וַיָּנָס; *Bereishis* 39:12) from his master's wife and refused to sin with her.

◄§ In the Wilderness

וַה׳ הֹלֵךְ לִפְנֵיהֶם יוֹמָם בְּעַמּוּד עָנָן — *God went before them, by day, in a pillar of cloud* (13:21). During the day God led a cloud before them, to show them the way. At night He led them with a pillar of flame, to illuminate their way and to scorch the Egyptians.

לָלֶכֶת יוֹמָם וָלָיְלָה — *That they might go by day and by night (ibid.).* They traveled by day and by night in order to receive the Torah as quickly as possible. The pillar of the day would wait for the pillar of the night to arrive before disappearing, and vice versa.

God commanded that the Jews return towards Egypt, to the city of Pisom.

וְיָחֲנוּ לִפְנֵי פִּי הַחִירֹת ... לִפְנֵי בַּעַל צְפֹן — *They shall encamp before Pi Hachiros ... before Baal Tzephon* (14:2). "They shall encamp before the idol called Baal Tzephon, so that Pharaoh will believe that they are lost and wandering through the desert, not knowing where to go." Why did God specifically command that they encamp before the idol? Because the Egyptians would believe that the mighty idol would not allow the Jews to escape. Their hearts would be hardened and they would pursue the Jews, even though they had urged them to leave. Now they would say that the Jews were stranded in the desert, with no idea of where to go.

The Jews heeded God's words and returned towards Egypt.

◄§ Pharaoh is Alerted

וַיֻּגַּד לְמֶלֶךְ מִצְרַיִם כִּי בָרַח הָעָם — *It was told to the king of Egypt that the people had fled* (14:5). On the third day Pharaoh was told that the people had escaped. The Jews had told Pharaoh in Egypt that they wanted to spend three days in the desert and then return. Pharaoh sent his emissaries with them to make certain that they returned in three days, but the Jews refused to return. In one day the emissaries journeyed the distance which had taken the Jews two days, because they were not so heavily laden nor such a great multitude.

The emissaries told Pharaoh of the Jews' refusal. Pharaoh and a great army then went to pursue them. Even though the Jews were heading back towards Egypt they were still two days' journey from there, for they had only returned a short distance. God performed a miracle for them and despite their great number they traveled in one day the journey that took Pharaoh two days. They reached the sea on the seventh day of Pesach, in the evening, and sang God's praises there. For this reason we read these praises (שִׁירַת הַיָּם) on the seventh day of Pesach every year.

◈ The Egyptians in Pursuit

וַיֶּאְסֹר אֶת רִכְבּוֹ — *He prepared his chariot* (14:6). Pharaoh himself prepared his chariot, in order to inspire and strengthen his people to pursue Israel. He opened all the vaults which were full of the treasures which he had amassed, and divided them among his people. They took all of this with them to the battle.

He took with him six hundred select charioteers, with fine Egyptian steeds. But if the hail destroyed all the animal life, where did Pharaoh get the horses? The animals of those Egyptians who had feared God's warning and had brought their animals inside had not been destroyed. However, though they feared God, still they gave their horses to Pharaoh for war.

וַיְחַזֵּק ה' אֶת לֵב פַּרְעֹה — *God strengthened Pharaoh's heart* (14:8). He was wavering in his decision to pursue them, so God hardened his heart. The Jews had proudly and high-handedly left Egypt. The Egyptians found them near their idol Baal Tzephon, so that they should think that God could not harm the Egyptians.

וּפַרְעֹה הִקְרִיב — *When Pharaoh drew near* (14:10). Pharaoh drew near to the Jews. A second explanation [because of the causative form of the verb] is that Pharaoh drew the hearts of the Jews near to their God, when they prayed to Him for help. Similarly, when Haman's threat of destruction hung over their heads, the Jews repented and became pious.

◈ Four Reactions

וְהִנֵּה מִצְרַיִם נֹסֵעַ אַחֲרֵיהֶם — *And behold, the Egyptians traveled after them* (14:10). The verse says *traveled* (in the singular) because they all went with one intention: to destroy the Jews. The *Midrash* says that the singular form is used to show that the Egyptians' guardian angel, who is called Azah, was also pursuing them. The Jews grew very frightened and said to Moshe, "Are there not enough graves in Egypt? Did you take us out in order to see us die in the desert?"

R' Bechaye writes that there were four opinions among the Jews. One group cried to God, one group urged battle, one group pleaded to return to Egypt, and one group advised leaping into the sea.

Moshe told the Jews, "*God will do battle for you* (ה׳ יִלָּחֵם לָכֶם; 14:14). The Egyptians saw that God had destroyed their first-born sons, yet they do not repent. Since they are thereby challenging God, He will fight them, and you shall remain silent." He added, "You must be silent, or else God will punish you, for you too worshiped idols in Egypt."

מַה תִּצְעַק אֵלָי — *Why do you cry to me?* (14:15). God told Moshe, "Now is not the time to pray at length, because the Jews are facing great troubles." Another explanation is that God said, "Why are you crying to Me? I am fully aware that everything is now contingent upon Me. Tell Israel to approach the sea and it will split before them, in the merit of their forefathers and in the merit of the trust which they will have in Me in the desert."

⇜§ Lift your Staff

הָרֵם אֶת מַטְּךָ — *Lift your staff* (14:16). "You, Moshe, lift your stick and split the sea." The *Midrash* says that Moshe told the sea to split, and the sea answered, "You have no authority over me. Go to the Nile River, where you are the ruler." Moshe told God what had happened, and God answered, "When a servant refuses to obey his master, he beats him with a rod. Lift your staff and strike the water and it will split." Moshe struck the sea, which adamantly refused to split. Then God Himself came down. When the sea recognized God's approach it split immediately and flowed counter-currently. Moshe then asked the sea, "Why are you flowing away?" [Cf. *Tehillim* 114.] The sea answered, "Moshe, you are mistaken. You think that I am running away from you, but in reality I am fleeing from God, the world's Creator."

R' Bechaye writes that *lift your staff* means, "Moshe, remove the stick from your hand. People have said that you can perform no wonders without your stick. Leave it, and tell the sea to split."

וְלֹא קָרַב זֶה אֶל זֶה כָּל הַלָּיְלָה — *One did not come near the other, all through the night* (14:20). Even though the Egyptians and the Jews were close by each other, they did not approach each other that entire night. The cloud which would lead the Jews during the day and disappear by night did not disappear on that day. It went behind the Jews and left the Egyptians in total darkness.

⋑§ The Sea Splits

וַיִּבָּקְעוּ הַמָּיִם — *The waters split* (14:21). All of the waters of the world split. There were ten wonders performed by the sea: first, the sea split; second, the waters were like a cave, sheltering all of Israel, with water overhead and on both sides; third, the land beneath them was dry and hard, so that they would not dirty their feet in mud; fourth, when the Egyptians advanced the earth became muddy and they sank within it; fifth, the water was solidified; sixth, the water did not solidify like a single rock, but rather hardened in many places, like pebbles; seventh, the water split twelve ways so that each tribe had its own path; eighth, the water was as clear as glass, so that each tribe could see the other tribes walking nearby; ninth, the water of the sea became sugar-sweet, so that the Jews could drink it. When they wished to drink the water liquefied for them, and when they had finished it immediately hardened again, so their feet would not get wet. Finally, *Chizkuni* says that the tenth wonder was that only one third of the water on the bottom became hard. If the entire sea, until the bottom, had dried up, there would have been a great pit and it would have been difficult for them to climb down and climb back up.

R' Bechaye writes that God grew many assorted fruits in the sea. When a child cried its mother would give him an apple or a pomegranate.

וְהַמַּיִם לָהֶם חוֹמָה — *The waters were a wall for them* (14:22). The *Midrash* says that Israel had a merit for each side. On the right they had the merit of the Torah. The left side had the merit of their *tefillin*. In front of them was the merit of the commandment of circumcision, and beneath them was the commandment of *tzitzis* ("fringes") which hang underneath the *tallis*.

וַיָּסַר אֵת אֹפַן מַרְכְּבֹתָיו — *He removed the wheels of their chariots* (14:25). God burned all the wooden fittings of their chariots, using the fiery pillar. The cloud turned the ground underneath them into mud, while the fire heated it, so that their horses became unshod.

וַיָּשָׁב הַיָּם לִפְנוֹת בֹּקֶר לְאֵיתָנוֹ — *The sea returned, as morning appeared, to its strength* (14:27). This happened when the Jews came out of the sea, and the Egyptians entered it. The Egyptians tried to retreat, but God confused them, and they ran into the sea.

⋖§ Miracles Built into Creation

R' Bechaye writes that the word לְאֵיתָנוֹ ("to its strength") also suggests another meaning: "The sea returned to fulfill the condition (תְּנַאי — 'condition') which God stipulated at the time of its creation" — that it would split for Israel when they would leave Egypt. Similarly, God made a condition with the sun, that it would stand still in the days of Moshe, and that both the sun and the moon would come to a halt in the days of Yehoshua.

⋖§ The Egyptians in the Sea

וּמִצְרַיִם נָסִים לִקְרָאתוֹ — *The Egyptians fled towards it* (14:27). The water flowed towards them, pulling them into the sea. *Chizkuni* writes that the Egyptians pursued the Jews through the sea, thinking that they, too, would pass through. While in the middle of the sea the water began to liquefy. They tried to retreat, but were unable to.

וַיַּרְא יִשְׂרָאֵל אֶת מִצְרַיִם מֵת עַל שְׂפַת הַיָּם — *Israel saw the Egyptians dead on the seashore* (14:30). The sea cast them out so that the Jews would see that they had drowned, and not say, "Just as we came out on one side, so the Egyptians came out on another side, and they will come and fight us." Another reason that the sea cast them out was to allow the Jews to take the gold and silver which the Egyptians had carried with them.

וַיַּרְא יִשְׂרָאֵל אֶת הַיָּד הַגְּדֹלָה — *Israel saw the great hand which God brought upon Egypt* (14:31). They saw God strike the Egyptians on the sea with His entire hand. In Egypt the Torah says, *It is the finger of God* (אֶצְבַּע אֱלֹהִים הוּא; 8:15), meaning that with one finger He struck them with the ten plagues. When on the sea He struck them with His entire hand — with five fingers, so to speak — they were struck with fifty plagues, five times ten.

⋖§ The Song of the Sea

אָז יָשִׁיר מֹשֶׁה וּבְנֵי יִשְׂרָאֵל — *Then Moshe and all the Children of Israel sang* (15:1). Even the nursing infants and the unborn children joined in the song, saying, "God is greater than all the masters in the world."

This is what they sang:

"God kept the rider mounted upon his horse, and the water threw both up and down, together. This is my God and I will extol Him. He is the God of my forefathers, and I will exalt Him with acclaim. God battles on behalf of Israel, and sustains the entire world with His holy Name. Unlike man, at the same time that He does battle He still sustains the world.''

ה' אִישׁ מִלְחָמָה ה' שְׁמוֹ — *God is a Man of War, God is His Name* (15:3). God does not battle with a sword or a gun. Rather, because His Name is God, He battles with His holy Name.

טֻבְּעוּ בְיַם סוּף — *Drowned in the Red Sea* (15:4). The Egyptians drowned in the Red Sea. Why did it become muddy beneath them? God repays in kind. Because they forced the enslaved Jews to make bricks out of clay, they themselves now sank into the muddy clay.

יָרְדוּ בִמְצוֹלֹת כְּמוֹ אָבֶן — *They went down into the depths like a stone* (15:5). The evil Egyptians were like straw which floats upon the water. They too floated, and did not drown immediately, enduring great misery and pain, as it says, *It consumed them as straw* (15:7). The less evil among them were like stones, which quickly sink to the bottom. Their death was quick, as it says, *they went down into the depths like a stone.*

◆§ The Role of the Waters

נֶעֶרְמוּ מַיִם — *The waters were piled up* (15:8). The waters solidified. R' Bechaye tenders another explanation; the waters became wise (from the similarity between the words נֶעֶרְמוּ — ''piled up,'' and עָרְמָה — ''cunning'') for they understood that they must become solid for Israel, and liquid for the Egyptians.

The song continues:

''Pharaoh, the enemy, told his people: 'I will pursue Israel, and upon capturing them we will share the booty.' Who is like our God, Who keeps His silence until He repays the wicked, and does not strike them immediately? God is awesome to praise, for one cannot praise Him properly.''

Of the words, *they sank as lead* (צָלֲלוּ בַּעוֹפֶרֶת; 15:10), *Imrei Noam* writes that there were many Egyptians who were versed in the magical arts. They flew out of the water towards heaven. Gavriel and Michael thereupon came down and struck them on the heads, and they fell back in the water, sinking like lead.

תִּבְלָעֵמוֹ אָרֶץ — *The earth swallowed them* (15:12). The earth swallowed up the Egyptians. They merited this burial because they finally admitted, *The Lord is just* (9:27). R' Bechaye writes: Why did they merit burial? Because the Egyptians accompanied Yosef when he went to bury Yaakov, and God repays measure for measure.

נָטִיתָ יְמִינְךָ — *You stretched out Your right hand* (15:12). "You stretched out Your hand to swear." The earth did not want to accept the Egyptians, for it had been cursed for having accepted the blood of Hevel (Abel). God then swore that He would not punish the earth for its actions.

Imrei Noam writes: The words אָז יָשִׁיר — *Then they sang* (15:1), literally mean, "Then they will sing," in the future tense. This shows us that God will reanimate the dead in the days of *Mashiach*. The *Gemara* says: There are three keys in God's hand alone, which were never given over to an angel. The first is the key of a woman giving birth; the second is the key of rain; and the third is the key of awakening the dead.

◄§ The Nations Tremble

שָׁמְעוּ עַמִּים יִרְגָּזוּן — *The nations have heard, and are afraid* (15:14). The Philistines were terrified, as mentioned above, thinking that the Jews would avenge their murder of the children of Efraim who had left Egypt thirty years before the proper time of redemption. The nobles of Edom were frightened, because they thought that the Jews would take revenge for Esav's ill treatment of Yaakov. The nobles of Moav (Moab) were afraid, thinking that the Jews would take revenge because Lot's shepherds had quarreled with Avraham's — and Moav is a descendant of Lot. And the inhabitants of Canaan were panic-stricken, knowing that the Jews would come and take their land.

◄§ Looking Ahead

עַד יַעֲבֹר עַמְּךָ ה' עַד יַעֲבֹר עַם זוּ קָנִיתָ — *Until Your people pass, God, until the people which You have bought have passed* (15:16). "God, help us until after we have crossed the Arnon River, until after we have crossed the Jordan and entered *Eretz Yisrael*." When the time came for them to pass over the Jordan the *Kohanim* stood in the water, together with the Ark. The waters of the Jordan remained standing upright, and the river was dry until the Jews had crossed.

The people which You have bought means that when Israel accepted the Torah they became God's possession eternally, to serve Him as a servant does a master.

תְּבִאֵמוֹ וְתִטָּעֵמוֹ — *You will bring them in and plant them* (15:17). "You, God, will bring *them* to *Eretz Yisrael*." Moshe did not say "us." He was hinting, prophetically, that he would not be found worthy of entrance to *Eretz Yisrael*.

הי יִמְלֹךְ לְעֹלָם וָעֶד — *God shall reign forever* (15:18). "God will be King eternally, just as He is King now, rewarding the righteous and destroying the wicked." The word יִמְלֹךְ ("shall reign") is spelled incompletely — missing the letter *vav* — to show that in reigning God does not place an unbearable burden on man. He demands only as much as man can give.

R' Bechaye writes that there are 18 verses in the Song, alluding to the 18 parts of a man's back, all of which will come to life and praise their Creator when *Mashiach* comes.

◄§ Praise by Women: Praise of Women

כִּי בָא סוּס פַּרְעֹה — *When the horses of Pharaoh came* (15:19). The Jews sang praises while the Egyptians were entering the sea, and they were leaving it, completely dry. At that time *the prophetess Miriam, sister of Aharon, took the drum in her hand* (15:20) and sang hymns. Why is she called Aharon's sister? To show that even before Moshe's birth, when she was Aharon's sister only, she prophesied that her mother would bear a son who would redeem the Jews from Egypt. Another reason that she is called Aharon's sister, rather that Moshe's, is that Aharon's name was not mentioned before, in the entire Song, and so it is mentioned here.

R' Bechaye writes that we should not wonder at the fact that a woman was a prophetess, for women, too, are of course human beings. Indeed, Sarah was a greater prophetess than Avraham himself.

R' Bechaye continues, saying that one should not hold women in low esteem. They are just as worthy as righteous men. Avigail (Abigail) was a prophetess who alone exhibited the truth of the World to Come, which is not otherwise explicitly stated in the Torah. Chanah showed us the impending Awakening of the Dead, which also is never overtly alluded to in the Torah. One must hold women in high esteem, for when a woman is righteous, her goodness is boundless.

The *Gemara* says, in Tractate *Megillah*, that were were seven prophetesses: Sarah, Miriam, Chanah, Devorah, Chuldah, Avigail and Esther.

בְּתֻפִּים וּבִמְחֹלֹת — *With drums and dances* (15:20). Miriam took a drum in her hand and played, while the women danced with joy. Why did she choose to play a drum? So that the sound of the drum would cover the sound of the women's singing. It is sinful for a man to listen to a woman's singing. In our days, when women sing at a wedding it is customary for them to clap their hands, so that the men will not hear their voices, for when a man hears a woman's voice, he thinks evil thoughts. When women pray overly loud they can disturb a man's prayers. We can learn from Chanah, who prayed silently, soundlessly, moving only her lips, and God answered her prayers immediately. Our Sages learn from this that prayer should not be shouted.

⇜§ Booty at the Sea

וַיַּסַע מֹשֶׁה אֶת יִשְׂרָאֵל — *Moshe led Israel* (15:22). *Rashi* and *Imrei Noam* write that Moshe forcibly led them away from the sea. They were procrastinating, in order to take still more gold and silver from the dead Egyptians. They took more from the dead in the Sea than they did from Egypt itself.

You may ask, what of the verse, *and they emptied Egypt* (וַיְנַצְּלוּ אֶת מִצְרָיִם; 12:36) by borrowing everything which the Egyptians owned? How, then, was there still more gold and silver? The answer is that they had taken only the wealth that was in the Egyptians' homes. When Pharaoh wanted to pursue the Jews he opened his treasure vaults, as mentioned earlier, and gave his soldiers all that he had amassed, both gold and silver, in order to convince them to pursue the Jews.

⇜§ From Bitter to Sweet

וְלֹא מָצְאוּ מַיִם — *And they did not find water* (15:22). They traveled through the desert and found no drinkable water. This was in the month of Nissan, when it is quite hot, and it is difficult to live without water. God did this to test whether or not they would speak out against Him. They arrived at Marah and could not drink the water there, since it was bitter.

R' Bechaye writes that the water had been sweet previously, and God turned it bitter in order to test the Jews. They complained, and in particular the pregnant women and the children could not stand being without water. They cried to God, who commanded Moshe to *take a bitter tree and cast it into the water. The water will become sweet.*

God performs one miracle within the other: He commanded that a bitter tree be thrown into bitter water, and the water became sweet. This shows us that man ought to rely on God, even in bitter times, for God can change his bitterness into sweetness.

⋅⧉ Law and Order

שָׁם שָׂם לוֹ חֹק וּמִשְׁפָּט — *There he gave him a statute and a law* (15:25). There, in Marah, Moshe was made a king over Israel, and there introduced legislation regarding their behavior to one another. Moreover, many idol worshipers had brought fruits to sell to the Jews, and Moshe taught them how to act towards the idol worshipers in order to ensure that there were no dishonest dealings.

⋅⧉ Medicinal Herbs

R' Bechaye writes that Moshe showed them which herbs were medicinal and which were harmful. For this reason the Torah says, immediately afterwards, *and there they tested him* (וְשָׁם נִסָּהוּ; *ibid.*), hinting that they tested Moshe to see if his words were truthful. Immediately following are these words: *If you listen to the voice of the Lord, your God* — to teach us that even though the herbs are helpful for healing, you must not rely on them. Rely, rather, on God, who can heal you from your sickness. Pray to God, and He will heal you, *for I am the Lord, who heals you* (כִּי אֲנִי ה' רֹפְאֶךָ; 15:26). I am the one who heals, not the herbs.

King Chizkiyahu concealed the Book of Medicine, within which was written the medicinal power of every herb, so that people would pray to God for a cure, rather than rely on the medicine.

The *Midrash* writes that the Tree of Life stood next to the water. Satan removed it, hoping that Israel would then speak against God. God then revealed the tree to Moshe, and he threw it in, foiling Satan's plan.

אִם שָׁמוֹעַ תִּשְׁמַע לְקוֹל ה' אֱלֹהֶיךָ — *If you listen to the voice of the Lord* (15:26). "If you heed God's commandments you will not fall ill." *Baal HaTurim* writes that the word מַחֲלָה ("sickness") is an anagram of the word הַלֶּחֶם ("the bread") and הַמֶּלַח ("the salt"), to show that man's body is sensitive to 83 illnesses (the numerical value of the letters of the word מַחֲלָה), and they can all be cured with bread, salt, and water. The word *machalah* follows the incident of the well, to show that sickness is cured through bread, salt, and water.

וַיָּבֹאוּ אֵילִמָה — *They came to Elim* (15:27). They arrived at Elim and saw twelve wells, for each tribe had a well of its own. There were seventy date trees, so that each of the seventy elders who had accompanied Moshe had a tree of his own. The water was very sweet. In a place where date trees grow, the water is generally sweet and good.

◄§ Food from Heaven

Israel ate the dough which they had brought with them from Egypt for thirty days, until the 15th day of the month of Iyar. When the dough ran out the Jews cried, saying, "It would have been better to be in Egypt, sitting over our pots of meat, than starving of hunger here." God then sent them manna (מָן) from the sky, on the 16th day of Iyar.

The manna first fell on a Sunday. God told them, *I will rain bread from the sky for you* (16:4), for they made bread out of the manna. It was like a coriander seed, and was white and honeysweet. R' Eliezer says that it fell in piles sixty *amos* high.

It fell at night when the Jews were at home, asleep, and in the morning they went to collect it. God furnishes the righteous with the best of everything while they sleep.

When the Temple stood, rain fell only on Saturday night and Tuesday night, when people generally were not about, so as not to interfere with their work. Similarly King Chizkiyahu pleaded with God: "Master of the Universe, I have not the power to fight the idol worshipers, or to chase them, and I do not know how to sing Your praises. I only want to sleep in my bed, while You come to my aid." God did as he willed and sent an angel by night to destroy the Assyrian encampment, while Chizkiyahu slept.

A verse in *Psalms* says, *He will give sleep to His beloved friend* (כֵּן יִתֵּן לִידִידוֹ שֵׁנָא; *Tehillim* 127:2). God grants those whom He loves good fortune while they are asleep. Conversely, He does not aid the wicked, even after they have awakened.

The manna was digested so perfectly that they had no need for excreting, as is hinted in the verse, *Men* (lit., "the man") *ate the bread of the mighty* [i.e., of the angels (*Rashi*)] (לֶחֶם אַבִּירִים אָכַל אִישׁ; *Tehillim* 78:25). This was a bread which was digested perfectly by the organs [— a play on the similarity between the words אַבִּירִים — "mighty," and אֵבָרִים — "organs"].

◄§ Day by Day

דְּבַר יוֹם בְּיוֹמוֹ — *A day's portion every day* (16:4). Each day enough manna fell to last for one day. As explained earlier, God could certainly have sent enough for a longer time, but He wanted them to pray every day, and then be certain that there would be food on the morrow. R' Eliezer says that a person who has food for today, and wonders what he will eat tomorrow, is lacking faith in God. God ordains food for each person at the proper time.

R' Shimon says: The manna did not fall in a quantity sufficient for an extended period of time so that each man of Israel, together with his wife and children, would lift his eyes to God and ask for his food. Another explanation is that it happened this way so the Jews would eat it fresh every day. Still another explanation is that if a large amount would have fallen at one time it would have been difficult for them to carry when they journeyed from one place to another.

The manna fell directly in front of the houses of the righteous, so that they would have it immediately. The middling person had to walk further to get it, and the wicked still further.

◈ Preparing for Shabbos

לְמַעַן אֲנַסֶּנּוּ הֲיֵלֵךְ בְּתוֹרָתִי אִם לֹא — *So that I may test them, whether they will walk in My Torah or not* (16:4).

God said, "I will give Israel manna to test them, to see if they will heed My commandments." What were the commandments concerning the manna? The people could not leave over from one day to the next; they were not to gather it on *Shabbos*; they were to gather a double portion on Friday. They took it on Friday without measuring, but when they came home they found double the amount that they had had on the other days!

וְהָיָה בַּיּוֹם הַשִּׁשִּׁי וְהֵכִינוּ אֵת אֲשֶׁר יָבִיאוּ — *On the sixth day, they will prepare that which they bring in, and it will be double* (16:5). Moshe told the Jews: "On the sixth day, Friday, prepare the manna for *Shabbos*." Moshe further admonished: "Your complaints are not against us; they are against God." We learn from this that one who quarrels with a rabbi or sage is like one who quarrels with God.

עֶרֶב וִידַעְתֶּם כִּי ה' הוֹצִיא אֶתְכֶם מֵאֶרֶץ מִצְרָיִם — *At eve, you will know that God brought you out of the land of Egypt* (16:6). Moshe and Aharon told the Jews, "You will become aware that God led you out of Egypt, and we did not, even though you have said 'You brought us to die in the desert.' This evening God will give you meat. You did not act properly by asking for meat, for you can live without it. Therefore He will bring it to you by night." Since they were justified in their request for manna, God gave it to them in the morning, so that they had time to prepare it.

◈ Tests for All Men

R' Bechaye writes that the manna was given to the Jews to enable them to study Torah. Similarly, priests (*Kohanim*) and Levites were in later days given *terumos* and *maosros* (the priestly gifts and tithes), as well as meat from the sacrifices, so that they would be free to study Torah. God tested the Jews with the manna to see if they would study Torah.

God tests a person even though He knows the ultimate result. He wants to show other people that the righteous man has passed the test so that they will learn from him. For this reason, God strikes the righteous. People will learn from them that one must not speak against God, even when He brings ill fortune. We must love God, even in time of suffering.

He tests the wealthy, to see if they will act properly and charitably with their money. He also tests the poor, to see if they accept poverty without railing against Him. God tests the soul within the body, to see if it will follow the inclination towards goodness or the inclination towards evil. And he who stands firm in the test receives a great reward from God.

וּבַבֹּקֶר תִּשְׂבְּעוּ לָחֶם — *And in the morning you will be sated with bread* (16:12). "In the morning you will be sated with bread, and then you will recognize that I am God, your God." We learn from this that we are obligated to make a blessing after eating. Moshe said, "When you are sated with bread you must know that it was God who provided it, and you must bless Him."

וַיְהִי בָעֶרֶב וַתַּעַל הַשְּׂלָו — *It was in the evening, and the quail came up* (16:13). In the evening, tasty birds came to the Jews. They ate these birds all forty years in the desert. Why does the Torah specify only that they ate the manna for forty years, without mentioning the birds? Because it was a new creation, and was surrounded by miraculous events, while the birds were not something unique.

The *Midrash* writes that the manna fell as follows: First dew fell, smoothing the ground. Then came the food itself, followed by a covering of more dew. On *Shabbos* we spread a tablecloth, place the *challah* upon it, and then cover these braided loaves with another cloth, in the very manner that the food from heaven lay in the desert. The Jews called it מָן, which means a gift (as in מַתָּנָה) from heaven.

◄§ Collecting the Manna

לִקְטוּ מִמֶּנּוּ אִישׁ לְפִי אָכְלוֹ — *Gather from it, each man to his food requirement* (16:16). Moshe told the Jews: "Have no fear that the strongest will forcibly take a lot, while the weaker will have to settle for a small amount." The Torah says *each man to his food*

Manna from heaven

requirement, an omer per head (ibid.). Whoever eats his portion will stay healthy, but one who eats more will be considered a glutton, and will become weak.

אִישׁ לַאֲשֶׁר בְּאָהֳלוֹ — *Every man for those in his tent (ibid.).* Each man will collect for his wife, who is called his tent, for she sits in her home. From here we learn that a man is obligated to sustain his wife and young children.

וַיִּלְקְטוּ אֹתוֹ בַּבֹּקֶר — *They gathered it in the morning (16:21).* The manna lay on the ground for the first four hours of the day. As the sun rose higher it melted away. If a man procrastinated the others would each give him some, like a beggar, so that he would have something to eat throughout that day.

◈§ More Miracles

There were many wonders and miracles performed in connection with the manna. It revealed many mysteries and secrets to the people, in the way that a prophet knows them. If a servant of one Jew ran away to another Jew's home, and they disputed ownership over him, one saying he had legitimately bought the servant and the other denying it, the truth would be revealed through the manna. Whichever house had an extra portion of food, that was the house to which the servant belonged, for enough of it fell to feed all of the members of each household. If a woman would quarrel with her husband, and return to her father's house, and they disputed over who was the guilty party, Moshe would say, "Judgment will be rendered in the morning." When morning arrived they would see if the portion of manna had fallen in her husband's house. If so, they would know that she was guilty. Conversely, if it would appear at her father's house, they would know that the husband was guilty.

If a woman remarried less than three months after the death of her husband, or after her divorce, and just over six months later bore a child, they could not tell if it was her first husband's child, born after nine months, or her second husband's child, born prematurely at six months. But they would see where the extra portion of manna would fall. If it fell near the first husband's house they realized that it was his child, and if it fell at the house of the second husband they knew that it was his.

Baal HaTurim writes: When the manna dissolved it formed rivers from which many animals drank. Other nations ate of these animals, and tasted the flavor of the manna. In wonder, they felt the excellent taste of the meat and said, "What a great deed God did for the Jews in the desert, with such food!"

וְרִמָּה לֹא הָיְתָה בּוֹ — *There was no worm within it* (16:24). Even though, during the week, if it was left overnight it became wormy, when they left it over from Friday to *Shabbos* it remained clean. We learn from this that the dead, too, rest on *Shabbos*, and the worms cease devouring them, just as they refrained from eating the manna. This is what R' Bechaye writes.

◆§ Shabbos Meals

אִכְלֻהוּ הַיּוֹם — *Eat it today* (16:25). Moshe told the Jews: "Eat the manna today, on *Shabbos*, for today you will find none in the field." The verse repeats the word *today* three times to show that one ought to eat three meals on *Shabbos:* one on Friday evening, one on *Shabbos* morning, and one after the afternoon prayer. It is a meritorious deed to faithfully eat these three meals.

רְאוּ כִּי ה' נָתַן לָכֶם הַשַּׁבָּת — *See that God has given you Shabbos* (16:29). The *Midrash* writes: Everything on *Shabbos* is doubled. There were double portions of manna on *Shabbos*. The sacrifice of *Shabbos* is double the weekday offering — two sheep are sacrificed. One who desecrates the *Shabbos* is referred to be a dual expression of death: *Its desecrators shall surely die* (מְחַלְלֶיהָ מוֹת יוּמָת; 31:14). Conversely, a person who observes it properly receives a doubled reward. And on *Shabbos* we each have two souls.

◆§ A Memorial for Posterity

לְמַעַן יִרְאוּ אֶת הַלֶּחֶם — *So that they may see the bread* (16:32). They hid away a jar full of manna for the days of the *Mashiach*, as an exhibit of the bread which our forefathers ate in the desert. Aharon's staff was also hidden, and the ark with its rods, and many of the vessels of the Temple. They were hidden in a cave beneath the *Beis HaMikdash*. It was King Yoshiahu who secreted these things within the cave.

When the prophet Yirimeyahu (Jeremiah) rebuked the Jews for not learning Torah, they retorted, "And how will we eat?" He took out the jar of manna and showed it to them, saying, "Do you see? God sustains those who study Torah. There is no need to worry about food."

◆§ Forty Years

וּבְנֵי יִשְׂרָאֵל אָכְלוּ אֶת הַמָּן אַרְבָּעִים שָׁנָה — *The Children of Israel ate the manna for forty years* (16:35). R' Bechaye writes: Even though they lost one month, for they began to eat manna in the middle of Iyar, and it ceased falling in the middle of Nissan, we still consider it forty years, for one month is insignificant.

Moshe died on the seventh day of Adar, and Yehoshua (Joshua) began leading the Jews. The manna fell in his merit for an additional thirty-eight days, until the middle of Nissan.

Rashi however writes that they ate manna for the entire forty years. The *matzos* which they had brought from Egypt tasted like manna, and this was what they ate from the middle of Nissan until the middle of Iyar. The manna, *Rashi* says, stopped falling immediately after Moshe's death, but on the day before his death enough fell to last until the middle of Nissan, and so they ate for a full forty years.

וְהָעֹמֶר עֲשִׂרִית הָאֵיפָה הוּא — *An omer is one tenth of an ephah* (16:36). The measure which is called an *ephah* is comparable to 432 eggs. One tenth would equal forty-three and one-fifth eggs. This was the size of a portion of manna, and it is the minimum size of dough from which *challah* must be taken. When baking *matzos* for Pesach, it is forbidden to knead more than this amount at one time.

◆§ Water in the Desert

וַיִּצְמָא שָׁם הָעָם לַמַּיִם — *The people thirsted there for water* (17:3). When the Jews came to Refidim they were parched and had nothing to drink. They told Moshe: "Why did you take us out of Egypt, to kill us with thirst?" Moshe cried out to God that the Jews were ready to stone him, and God answered, "Go before the Jews and see if they can stone you. Firstly, I will protect you. Moreover, you should not suspect them of such an intention."

וּמַטְּךָ אֲשֶׁר הִכִּיתָ בּוֹ אֶת הַיְאֹר — *And the staff with which you struck the river* (17:5). "Strike the stone with the same rod which struck the Nile and turned it into blood, and good water will begin to flow from it."

R' Bechaye writes that the rod was never held in the hand of any other prophet. Even Yehoshua, Moshe's disciple, did not have it. During battle he had only a lance. A staff signifies dominion, while a lance only indicates a warrior who himself goes out to battle.

Why did God tell him to take his rod? Because the Jews had been saying that it had only the power to bring plagues and harm. God told Moshe, "Take the rod and strike the stone and water will flow, so that the Jews will see that the rod can bring forth blessings too."

R' Bechaye writes that the stone which was in Refidim was the same one that was later in Kadesh. This was also the well which accompanied the Jews for forty years in the desert, giving them sufficient water for their needs.

∝§ The Battle with Amalek

וַיָּבֹא עֲמָלֵק — *And Amalek came* (17:8). God sent Amalek to attack Israel, because they had sinned by saying that God was not always with them. They prayed to Him and He saved them, thus showing that He was with them constantly.

בְּחַר לָנוּ אֲנָשִׁים — *Choose us men* (17:9). Moshe told Yehoshua: "Choose men for both of us, by yourself." We learn from this that a teacher ought to consider his student as important as he.

R' Bechaye writes that the people of Amalek were stargazers and very wise, and chose men who were destined not to die that year, so that the Jews would be unable to defeat them. Therefore Moshe ordered Yehoshua to choose men who had the power to defeat them. For this reason the Torah later states, *Yehoshua weakened Amalek* (וַיַּחֲלֹשׁ יְהוֹשֻׁעַ אֶת עֲמָלֵק; 17:13). He could not kill them because they were destined to live out the year.

Rashi writes that Amalek was full of magicians, so Moshe told Yehoshua to choose men who could battle the magic.

וְצֵא הִלָּחֵם בַּעֲמָלֵק — *And go out and battle Amalek* (17:9). "Leave the protection of the cloud and go to battle Amalek." There was a cloud surrounding the Jews, through which none could harm them. But the cloud pushed away the wicked among the Jews so that Amelek could strike them.

וּמֹשֶׁה אַהֲרֹן וְחוּר — *And Moshe, Aharon and Chur* (17:10). These three went up to pray. When Moshe would lift his arms towards heaven the Jews grew stronger, and when his arms began to fall the Amalekites began to overcome them. When his arms grew too heavy to lift towards heaven Aharon and Chur took a stone and placed it underneath him. Moshe sat upon it, and Chur and Aharon each held up one of his arms, one on each side.

Why did his arms grow heavy? Because he did not go to the battle himself, and sent Yehoshua in his stead. Why did they put a hard and uncomfortable stone, rather than a cushion, beneath him? Because the Jews were suffering and he wanted to suffer with them.

עַד בֹּא הַשֶּׁמֶשׁ — *Until the sun set* (17:12). Moshe held his hands up until the sun "changed." There were certain astrologers among the Amalekites who knew which hours were propitious for battle. Moshe made the sun and the moon change their usual times, so that the enemy could not plan their battle through astrology.

וַיַּחֲלֹשׁ יְהוֹשֻׁעַ אֶת עֲמָלֵק — *Yehoshua weakened Amalek* (17:13). Yehoshua killed all of their valorous men, leaving only the weak ones. God then told Moshe to *write this as a memorial in the book* (17:14), write down in the Torah that Amalek acted cruelly towards the Jews, and therefore the Jews must seek eternal revenge. R' Bechaye writes that God told Moshe to write a separate book describing the entire incident of Amalek, but the book was lost in the course of the generations before us.

❦ ❦ ❦

The *Haftorah* of *Parashas Beshalach* may be found on p. 479.

פרשת יתרו
Parashas Yisro
(18:1 — 20:23)

⋖§ Recognizing God's Existence

וַיִּשְׁמַע יִתְרוֹ — *Yisro heard* (18:1). King Solomon says, in *Proverbs* (15:4): מַרְפֵּא לָשׁוֹן עֵץ חַיִּים — *A healing tongue is a tree of life.* The tongue can heal a sick soul. Transgressions are a sickness of the soul, particularly if one does not believe fully in God. The tongue, though, can heal the sickness, by affirming that God is the only true God, who repays the righteous with their due reward.

Our Sages tell us that a rare gem hung around Avraham's neck. When someone ill looked at it, he was healed. When Avraham died, God hung the gem on the sun.

With this our Sages were hinting that Avraham spoke wise words, persuading people to serve the true God. After his death there was no one left to convince mankind to serve the true God, and so the rare gem was hung in the sun. This alludes to the fact that proof of God's existence can be found in the sun, which each day rises in the east and sets in the west. There must be a God Who regulates such an ordered world.

Similarly, Yisro recognized the existence of the true God through the worthy words of Moshe, as he recounted God's wonders and miracles. The verse tells us that *Yisro heard all that God had done for Moshe and Israel* (18:1) and as a result he recognized God's existence.

⋖§ Yisro's Arrival

R' Bechaye writes that certain Sages say that Yisro approached Moshe after the bestowal of the Torah upon Israel, as is hinted in the verse, *I tell them the laws of God, and his Torah* (18:16). Since Moshe here told Yisro that he had taught the people the Torah, we can infer that the Torah had already been given. Further, the Torah later states that *Moshe sent away his father-in-law* (18:27). Had the

Torah not already been given, he undoubtedly would not have sent him away, to miss the sight of God's revelation on Mt. Sinai.

R' Bechaye then asks: How could it be that Yisro arrived after the Giving of the Torah, and yet Moshe spoke to him of the miracles of Egypt, and not of the wonders of the thunder and the fire which surrounded Mt. Sinai during the Giving of the Torah? We must therefore assume that Yisro arrived before the Giving of the Torah, and for this reason Moshe did not speak of the wonders to come. Yisro might not have believed him, but the miracles which had already occurred had been witnessed by the entire world. When the sea split, all the waters of the world split as well, and during the war with Amalek the sun stood still, and this was seen by the entire world.

This is the reason that *Rashi* writes that the words *and Yisro heard* (18:1) refer to the splitting of the sea and the battle of Amalek. These two events were known throughout the entire world, so Yisro believed what he was told of them.

As for Moshe's words to Yisro, saying that he taught God's laws to the Jews, he was actually referring to the commandments which had been given prior to the Giving of the Torah, such as the precepts of *Shabbos* and circumcision, and certain other commandments. Moshe sent Yisro away and did not keep him there until after the Torah was given because Yisro had gone to make the rest of his household aware of God's existence. He returned soon afterwards, and found all the Jews at Mt. Sinai.

⋅§ Amalek

The portion discussing Yisro directly follows the portion concerned with the war of Amalek to show that Amalek, who was our relative, a descendant of Esav (Esau), harmed us, while Yisro, a stranger to our nation, befriended us and gave us valuable assistance.

The Torah states that we must obliterate the name of Amalek. No one dared fight the Jews, with the exception of Amalek. And just as in that battle the principals were Moshe, of the tribe of Levi, and Yehoshua, of the tribe of Ephraim, so too in the days of the last battle the principals will be the prophet Eliyahu, of the tribe of Levi, and *Mashiach*, the son of Yosef, of the tribe of Ephraim.

⋅§ The Order of the Passages

Why is the description of the Giving of the Torah placed in *Parashas Yisro?* In order to show that when *Mashiach* comes, the

Torah will bring wisdom to Israel just as it did to Yisro. And the coming of *Mashiach* will be followed by the Day of Judgment.

And why does *Parashas Mishpatim*, with all its laws, follow *Parashas Yisro*? Because when *Mashiach* comes, God Himself will give laws to all of humanity.

Yisro had seven names. First, he was called Yeser. When he recognized the true God, God added the letter *vav* to his name, now calling him Yisro.

לְמֹשֶׁה וּלְיִשְׂרָאֵל — *To Moshe and to Israel (ibid.)*. The way these words appear together hints that Moshe Rabbeinu, by virtue of all his righteous deeds, is reckoned as being equal to the entire House of Israel.

◆§ Moshe Rabbeinu's Family

אַחַר שִׁלּוּחֶיהָ — *After he had sent her away* (18:2). Yisro brought Moshe's wife back to him after he had sent her away. When God commanded Moshe to return to Egypt he took his wife and his two children with him. Aharon came out to greet him and asked who they were. He replied, "These are my wife and children." Asked Aharon: "Where are you taking them?" Moshe replied, "To Egypt." Aharon then said, "We have enough anguish over the women and children already in Egypt. Why do you want to bring more in?" Moshe immediately sent his wife and children back to Midian, to her father Yisro. Now Yisro brought them back to Moshe.

The first son was named Gershom for, in Moshe's words, גֵּר הָיִיתִי בְּאֶרֶץ נָכְרִיָּה — *I was a stranger (ger) in a foreign land* (18:3). The second was called Eliezer for, again in Moshe's words, אֱלֹהֵי אָבִי בְּעֶזְרִי וַיַּצִּלֵנִי מֵחֶרֶב פַּרְעֹה — *The God (El) of my father was my succor (ezer), and saved me from Pharaoh's sword* (18:4).

Why did Moshe not name the first child Eliezer? Because Yisro had stipulated that the first-born son woud be retained for idol worship, so Moshe did not want to put God's Name in his name.

Why did Moshe not circumcise him? Because of his fear of Yisro. As a result the angel tried to kill him, so ultimately Tzipora circumcised him, and Yisro forgave her.

Moshe's words, *I was a stranger in a foreign land*, were thus his excuse for not having circumcised his son. He was a stranger in Yisro's home and was afraid, because he had forbidden the circumcision.

The explanation for Eliezer's name is given less explicitly, without the words בִּי אָמַר ("for he said"), because Moshe did not want to publicize the fact that he had been saved from Pharaoh's sword.

Chizkuni notes that the verse says *the name of one was Eliezer* (18:4) when it actually should have said "the name of the second was Eliezer." Though he was in fact the second son, the first one ought to have been called Eliezer, since the miracle through which God saved Moshe from Pharaoh's sword occurred *before* Moshe became a stranger in a foreign land. The verse thus says *the name of one* because he was considered the first, in the sense that his name reflected the first miracle.

וַיֹּאמֶר אֶל מֹשֶׁה אֲנִי חֹתֶנְךָ יִתְרוֹ בָּא אֵלֶיךָ — *He said to Moshe: "I, Yisro, your father-in-law, have come to you"* (18:6). Even though no one could penetrate the cloud which surrounded Israel, Yisro shot an arrow through it, with a message attached. Moshe read the note, which said, "I, your father-in-law Yisro, have come to you. Come out to see me, for my sake. If you do not wish to do it for me, do it for the sake of your wife. If you do not wish to do it for her sake, do it for the sake of your children."

Moshe left the cloud. Seeing him leave, Aharon and his sons Nadav and Avihu joined him. Seeing Moshe and Aharon going out, all of Israel followed them. Thus Yisro was greeted with great pomp and respect. Moshe bowed to his father-in-law and kissed him.

◄§ Yisro Rejoices

וַיִּחַדְּ יִתְרוֹ — *And Yisro rejoiced* (18:9). Yisro rejoiced over the great deeds which God had done on the Jews' behalf, and at the same time grieved that so many idol worshipers had met their destruction. Then he said, "Now I know that your God is greater than all of the idols of the world. Because the Egyptians schemed to drown all the Jewish children, God saved the children and drowned the Egyptians."

Yisro made a feast to celebrate his own circumcision and ritual immersion, which together marked his conversion to Judaism. Why did he make a feast? In order to satisfy his body, and please it, so that a spirit of holiness would rest upon him.

Godliness does not rest upon a grieving body. We find that when Yitzchak wished to bless his son he asked him to bring him good food to cheer him, so that the Divine Presence would be present at the blessing.

The words *before God* (18:12) show that the meal was a godly one. This teaches us that if a person takes part in a meal together with Torah scholars it is as if he had enjoyed it with God.

ᨀ Judging the People

וַיְהִי מִמָּחֳרָת — *And it was on the next day* (18:13). It was the day after Yom Kippur, the Day of Atonement, and Moshe sat down to judge the people. The people stood before him as before a king. When Yisro saw this he was disturbed that Moshe was holding the honor of the Jews so lightly, and he said, "Why are you sitting, when all the rest stand?"

Chizkuni writes: Why did Yisro ask Moshe why he was sitting? The law is that a judge sits while the plaintiffs stand. Further, how could Yisro dare rebuke a man of Moshe's stature? The answer is that Yisro actually asked Moshe: "Why are you sitting all alone? Appoint more judges to help you judge the people." He was not rebuking him for sitting while the others stood, for he was aware that the claimants must stand. Moshe misunderstood and answered that they were all waiting to be judged and thus were standing.

מִן בֹּקֶר עַד עָרֶב — *From morning to evening* (18:14). *Rashi* asks: Is it possible that Moshe sat in judgment the entire day? When did he find time to teach the people Torah? We learn from this that when a man judges fairly for one hour, it is comparable to having learned Torah for an entire day. This also teaches us that when a judge is fair it is as if he helped God create heaven and earth, as here the Torah states, *from morning to evening,* and in reference to the Creation it is written, *and it was evening, and it was morning.* The world exists because of fair judgment.

נָבֹל תִּבֹּל — *You will wilt away* (18:18). Yisro told Moshe, "You will not be able to handle judging all of the people by yourself. You will come to grief and, Heaven forbid, the Jews will suffer with you. Even if Aharon and Chur were to help you, it would be insufficient. How much more so, now that Chur is long since dead, since the incident of the Golden Calf. It is a burden on the people as well, making them wait for one another to be judged."

R' Bechaye writes that Moshe replied, "Many of the people come to me. Some come to ask me to pray that their sickness be cured, others ask me to tell them if they will discover things which they have lost, and others come for me to sit in judgment." Answered Yisro: "Pray for the Jews, and teach them Torah — but you cannot judge them all by yourself. You must choose other wise men from among the Jews to sit as judges."

◆§ Choosing the Judges

R' Bechaye writes further: Why is the word *techeze* ("seek out") used, rather than the more common word, *tivchar* ("choose")? *Techeze* connotes the use of prophecy. To choose wise men who are also righteous is difficult, and can be done only with the use of prophecy. The word *techeze* also indicates that one can see in their faces if they are qualified. Moshe was very wise and could recognize if a person was righteous or not just by looking at him. The verse therefore says *you will seek* (18:21), for Moshe alone could choose them, through his wisdom in discerning a righteous man.

אַנְשֵׁי חַיִל — *Men of valor* (18:21). That is, those who have the qualities of character necessary for a good judge. He must constantly feel that a sword is dangling over his neck and the gates of Hell are open beneath him, and only by judging fairly can he be saved from both fates.

שֹׂנְאֵי בָצַע — *Loathers of gain* (18:21). The judge must be one who hates wealth. Even if someone threatens to burn his house down, he must not be afraid to judge honestly.

◆§ Counting the Judges

שָׂרֵי אֲלָפִים — *Leaders of thousands* (18:21). Moshe chose one judge for each thousand men, aged twenty to sixty. Since they numbered six hundred thousand there were six hundred of these judges. He then chose judges with authority over each hundred people, and there were six thousand of those. Then he chose judges for each fifty — twelve thousand judges. Then he chose one judge for each ten, or sixty thousand judges.

Chizkuni questions: By this reckoning the number of judges was 78,600. But then the population would not number six hundred thousand, since many of them were judges [and thus not included in the count]. The answer is that the judges were all older than sixty years of age and so were not included in the census. The Jews thus numbered 600,000, excluding the judges.

Chizkuni tenders still another explanation: The judges were part of the six hundred thousand. The judges of the thousand were included with their thousand, the judges of the one hundred were included with their hundred, and so on.

וְשָׁפְטוּ אֶת הָעָם בְּכָל עֵת — *And they shall judge the nation at all times* (18:22). "Other judges will be able to judge the people at all times, but you, Moshe, have not the time. You must often speak with the Divine Presence. Besides, the nation is too numerous for you alone to judge."

◄§ Arriving at Sinai

בַּחֹדֶשׁ הַשְּׁלִישִׁי — *In the third month* (19:1). In the third month, which is Sivan, the Jews came to the Sinai Desert. They travelled on the same day from Refidim and came to rest across from the mountain. Why in 2:2 does the Torah say וַיִּחַן ("he encamped," in the singular), rather than וַיַּחֲנוּ ("they encamped," in the plural)? This shows that at Sinai they encamped with one heart and one intention, as one person, to receive the Torah. All the other encampments found them full of differing opinions, and quarrels.

R' Bechaye writes that the first day of Sivan fell on a Monday. They arrived at the mountain on Tuesday and God gave them certain commandments. On Wednesday Moshe told God that the Jews were prepared to receive the Torah with their whole hearts. On Thursday God commanded that Moshe tell the people to separate from their wives for a three-day period, through *Shabbos*, the sixth day of Sivan. God bestowed the Torah on *Shabbos*. We recite the prayer *Yismach Moshe* ("Moshe rejoiced") on *Shabbos*, because the Torah was given to us through Moshe on that day.

◄§ The Women of Israel

כֹּה תֹאמַר לְבֵית יַעֲקֹב — *Thus shall you say to the House of Yaakov* (19:3). God told Moshe: "Go and gently tell the women certain commandments." Why did God command that the wives be told first? Because the women lacked the understanding to receive the entire Torah at once, and so they were first given certain commandments.

R' Bechaye explains this differently: It is the women who assist in learning Torah, by bringing their children to school to learn from a Rebbe, and by encouraging their children, who are generally in the home, with motherly words of love. When a woman lights the candles of *Shabbos* she ought to pray that God grant her children who will illuminate the world with Torah, because prayer is more readily accepted when offered in conjunction with the fulfillment of a commandment. For this reason, God directed that the women be given certain *mitzvos* first.

God first told the people that He repaid each person with his just reward. He told Israel that if they heeded His commands they would be duly rewarded, and whoever did not listen would be punished.

◄§ God and His People

אַתֶּם רְאִיתֶם — *You have seen* (19:4). "You have seen that I took you out of Egypt because you were destined to receive the Torah. And I punished the Egyptians for their evil."

וָאֶשָּׂא אֶתְכֶם עַל כַּנְפֵי נְשָׁרִים — *And I carried you on eagle's wings* (19:4). "I carried you in My hands, just as an eagle carries its nestlings upon its wings."

Most birds carry their young from one nest to another between their feet. They are afraid to set them upon their wings, because a bird of prey which flies higher than they may dart down upon the nestlings. But an eagle does bear its young upon its wings because no other bird flies higher. It does not carry them with its feet, to avoid having them shot from below, preferring that an arrow pierce it rather than its children. Similarly, God surrounded His children with a cloud, saying, "Better that My cloud be shot at, than My children."

וִהְיִיתֶם לִי סְגֻלָּה — *You will be My chosen* (19:5). "You will be more beloved to Me." The people are here called a treasure of rare gems, which a king holds close to him.

כִּי לִי כָּל הָאָרֶץ — *For all the world is Mine (ibid.)*. Accordingly, I am able to reward richly all those who serve Me faithfully.

◄§ Accepting the Torah

וַיִּקְרָא לְזִקְנֵי הָעָם — *He called to the nation's elders* (19:7). Moshe called together the elders and told them all that God had said. The Jews answered in unison: We will accept all that God has said. Moshe then went to God to tell Him that the Jews were willing to accept the Torah.

R' Bechaye asks: The *Gemara* says that God held the mountain above them and said, "If you accept the Torah, good; if not, I will bring the mountain crashing down upon you and you will be buried beneath it." And yet the verse explicitly states that they willingly accepted the written Torah! The explanation is that they willingly accepted the *Chumash* (the Pentateuch). But the Oral law with its unwritten laws and *halachos*, they were averse to accepting, because it is full of numerous difficult commandments. At that point God poised the mountain over their heads and told them that they must accept them.

וַיַּגֵּד מֹשֶׁה אֶת דִּבְרֵי הָעָם אֶל ה' — *Moshe told God the people's words*

(19:9). Moshe told God what the people had said, that is, that they wished to hear God's voice itself, that they wanted to see their King in person. God then told Moshe, *"Behold, I will come to you in a thick cloud (ibid.),* so that all Israel will recognize Me. You will come into a cloud of fire, and all of Israel will hear how I speak with you. The whole nation will be prophets. They will hear Me speak and fear Me eternally. They will learn that God can speak to a man, and the man can remain alive. And should someone come and claim that he is a greater prophet than Moshe, they will bear witness that there can be no greater prophet than he, for they themselves witnessed Moshe in a fiery cloud, speaking to God."

God told Moshe to go into the cloud himself, so that all of Israel would believe that he was a true prophet.

⋇§ Preparations

וְקִדַּשְׁתָּם הַיּוֹם וּמָחָר — *And you shall sanctify them today and tomorrow* (19:10). Make the Jews holy today and tomorrow. They must separate from their wives, wash their clothing, and immerse themselves.

אִם בְּהֵמָה אִם אִישׁ — *Be it beast or man* (19:13). Neither man nor beast may approach the mountain. R' Bechaye writes that this verse refers to the wicked, who are likened to beasts, and to the righteous. Neither was permitted to step near the mountain. Any one who touched it was to be stoned. Moshe was ordered to set a boundary around the mountain, indicating how close they were allowed to approach it.

⋇§ The Shofar

בִּמְשֹׁךְ הַיֹּבֵל — *When the ram's horn is blown long* (19:13). "When a long note is blown on the *shofar* they will be permitted to climb onto the mountain, as that will be their sign that the Divine Presence has left."

The *shofar* came from the ram which had been sacrificed in place of Yitzchak. R' Bechaye questions: Was that ram not burnt, together with its horns, skin, and flesh? How could this be the source of the *shofar* that was blown on Mt. Sinai? The answer is that God created a new ram out of the ashes.

Pirkei deR' Eliezer writes that the ram's bones were made into the foundation for the Altar in the Temple. Its sinews were used as the strings on King David's harp, and its skin was made into a belt for Eliyahu. Its left horn was blown as a *shofar* on Mt. Sinai, and its right horn will be blown to herald the coming of *Mashiach.*

The right horn was larger than the left, and thus, concerning the days of *Mashiach*, it is written: וְהָיָה בַּיּוֹם הַהוּא יִתָּקַע בְּשׁוֹפָר גָּדוֹל — *And on that day a large shofar will be blown* (*Yeshayahu* 27:13).

לֹא תִגַּע בּוֹ יָד — *Let no hand touch him* (19:13). R' Bechaye writes that it is written, *Whoever touches the mountain shall be put to death* (19:12), and afterwards, *Let no hand touch him*, to teach that the people should not lay their hands on whoever touches the mountain. They could thus not strangle or behead him; rather, they must stone him.

◆§ At the Mountain

וַיְהִי קֹלֹת וּבְרָקִים — *There was thunder and lightning* (19:16). There was the sound of angels accompanying God to the mountain, and other angels blazing with lightning and fire. God put a huge cloud between Israel and the angels so that the Jews should not see them and be terror-stricken.

וַיּוֹצֵא מֹשֶׁה אֶת הָעָם לִקְרַאת הָאֱלֹהִים — *Moshe brought out the people to meet God* (19:17). Moshe brought the nation towards the angels' encampment, closer and closer to the mountain. Twenty-two thousand angels accompanied God, just as twenty-two thousand Levites accompanied the Tabernacle, in which the Divine Presence rested.

The *Midrash* says that on the day of the Giving of the Torah the sun stood still in the sky. Many Jews died of fright, but they were resurrected by God.

The sun stood still five times in Moshe's lifetime: when the people left Egypt; at the Red Sea; during the battle with Amalek; at the Giving of the Torah; and at the Arnon River.

וַיִּתְיַצְּבוּ בְּתַחְתִּית הָהָר — *And they stood at the foot of the mountain* (19:17). They stood by the sign which had been placed to mark off the boundary of the mountain. God was at the summit, and Moshe entered the cloud in which God alone rested.

וַיַּעַל עֲשָׁנוֹ כְּעֶשֶׁן הַכִּבְשָׁן — *Its smoke rose, like the smoke of a furnace* (19:18). With God's arrival at Mt. Sinai came a great flood of smoke, like that of a furnace. There was thunder and lightning and a large cloud of fog. The mountain itself shook and trembled, while other mountains danced and cavorted. Israel too trembled, because the earth beneath them rocked. They withdrew far away from the mountain, in fear and trepidation.

Moshe on the mountain

מֹשֶׁה יְדַבֵּר וְהָאֱלֹהִים יַעֲנֶנּוּ בְקוֹל — *Moshe spoke, and God answered him aloud* (19:19). The Jews stood three miles away, and still they heard clearly each word which Moshe said when he spoke on the mountain. Even though the *shofar* was blowing loudly, it did not overpower Moshe's voice, for God gave him the strength to speak loudly enough so that all Israel would hear him.

וַיֵּרֶד ה' עַל הַר סִינַי — *God came down on Mt. Sinai* (19:20). God came down to Mt. Sinai in a great cloud of flame. God told Moshe: "Go and caution the Jews not to touch the mountain or they will be killed. Warn the *Kohanim*, too, not to approach the mountain, and tell them not to rely on their status [to save them]." Moshe answered: "I cautioned them three days ago not to touch the mountain."

אַל יֶהֶרְסוּ לַעֲלוֹת — *Let the people not break through to come up* (19:24). God told Moshe: "Tell Israel and the *Kohanim* that they must not gaze at the cloud in which I am resting."

God then uttered all of the Ten Commandments by Himself. What of our Sages, however, who said that He only said the first two commandments? The truth is that God said all of the Ten Commandments, but the Jews understood unaided only the first two. The others required clarification from Moshe.

◄§ I: I am the Lord, your God

אָנֹכִי ה' אֱלֹהֶיךָ — *I am the Lord, your God* (20:2). God said: "You must know within your heart that I am God who took you out of Egypt. Therefore, it is appropriate that you accept Me as your God.

You have seen by yourselves the wonders which I performed in Egypt."

Why did God not say that He was the God who had created heaven and earth? Because they had not witnessed that with their own eyes. But the miracles of Egypt they had seen, and from that they could infer that God had created the world, and He paid heed to men's actions, rewarding richly those who serve Him. "I have dealt kindly with you, and that is why you ought to accept the Torah, and I have punished Pharaoh for his wickedness to Me."

מִבֵּית עֲבָדִים — *From the house of slavery* (20:2). "It is only fair that you become My servants, since I released you from a house where you were in bondage."

◄§ II: You Shall Have No Other Gods

לֹא יִהְיֶה לְךָ אֱלֹהִים אֲחֵרִים עַל פָּנָי — *You shall have no other gods before Me* (20:3).

"You must not serve another god. You must not worship angels, or the constellations." They are called אֲחֵרִים ("other," "strange") because they are foreign to those who worship them. Their worshipers pray to them for help which they cannot provide.

Why does it say "to you" (לְךָ) in the singular form, rather than the plural (לָכֶם)? To give Moshe an excuse, at the incident of the Golden Calf, when he would tell God: "Why are you blaming the Jews? You said 'You shall have no other gods,' in the singular form. Actually, You had only forbidden *me* to worship false idols, and not Israel!"

עַל פָּנָי — *Before Me* (20:3). "*While I exist* you cannot serve false idols. Do not think that I have forbidden idol worship only to you who stand here at Mt. Sinai, and future generations may worship them. 'Before Me': while I exist idol worship is forbidden — eternally."

לֹא תַעֲשֶׂה לְךָ פֶסֶל — *Do not make an image for yourself* (20:4). "You are not to make yourself an image [to worship]. Do not think that because I told you 'you shall not have' I only meant that you may not worship idols, but you may make them. This too is forbidden.

"You may think that it cannot be sinful to carve the form of the sun or moon or an angel. You may say to yourself that through this form you will realize how God rules the world. You will remember that the sun always rises in the east and sets in the west, which proves that there is a Being who orders the sun. In this way you will think about God.

"Perhaps you may feel that this is comparable to the building of a *sukkah* to remind yourself how God surrounded us with a cloud in the wilderness, or the *matzah* which you eat to remember that God took His people out of Egypt. You may think that this figure, too, will remind you of God's existence.

"Therefore I caution you, *Do not make an image for yourself.* You must not make it, even if you have no intention of worshiping it, because ultimately you will worship it as a god.

"You must not create an image of the things *which are in heaven (ibid.),* that is, the angels; the things *which are on earth (ibid.),* man, animal, or wild beast; and that *which is in the water, beneath the earth (ibid.),* the demons inhabiting that water."

There are three types of demons: those of the atmosphere, which bring dreams to mankind; those on earth, which cause men to sin; and those underground. If those in the abyss below were allowed to escape to the earth they would destroy it.

אֵל קַנָּא — *A jealous God* (20:5). God remembers the sin of the idol worshiper, and does not forgive him.

פֹּקֵד עֲוֹן אָבֹת עַל בָּנִים — *Remembering the sins of the fathers upon their children (ibid.).* God punishes children for their father's sins if they continue following their father's evil deeds.

וְעֹשֶׂה חֶסֶד לַאֲלָפִים — *Showing kindness to the thousands* (20:6). When the father is righteous God remembers his merit for his children for two thousand generations. We learn from here that God's attribute of goodness is five hundred times as powerful as His attribute of stern justice. If a man is wicked God keeps his evil in consideration for four generations; if he is righteous the merit is counted for two thousand generations, or five hundred times four.

◄§ III: Do not Take the Name ... in Vain

לֹא תִשָּׂא אֶת שֵׁם ה' אֱלֹהֶיךָ לַשָּׁוְא — *Do not take the name of the Lord, your God, in vain* (20:7). You shall not swear falsely. R' Bechaye asks: The verse ought to have said "Do not take My name," since God Himself was speaking. *Ramban* gives an answer, saying that God Himself said only the first two commandments, as they are the essential ones, the core — to worship God and not worship idols. Moshe then said the remaining commandments in God's stead. Therefore it does not say "My name," for it was Moshe who was now speaking.

Why does the prohibition against swearing in vain appear

immediately after idol worship? To show that one who swears in vain is likened to an idol worshiper. If he swears that "by the truth of God, so my words are truthful," and yet is lying, he shows that he considers God to be a lie, heaven forbid. Thus we see that Shaul was ready to kill his son Yehonasan (Jonathan) for breaking a vow, as he would have killed an idol worshiper, and only the Jews' defense of him, that he had not heard the vow being made, saved him.

Similarly, God brought a great famine to *Eretz Yisrael* because King Shaul broke the promise which the people had sworn to the Givonim not to harm them. As soon as the guilty ones were punished the famine ceased.

One who swears falsely is also likened to an adulterer, as it is written, *God will not overlook the guilt* (כִּי לֹא יְנַקֶּה ה'; 20:7) of one who swears falsely, and the same language is used to describe an adulterer.

No [specific] reward or punishment is mentioned in the Ten Commandments, with the exception of the commandment to honor one's parents. The Torah promises that one will live long if he honors his parents. It also warns in the commandments against idol worship and swearing in vain that God will harshly punish transgressors. This shows that swearing falsely is comparable to idol worship. People sometimes feel that this is not a weighty prohibition, when in actuality it is. One cannot often commit murder or adultery, because of the fear of man's retribution, but a person can swear falsely a thousand times in a day because he need not fear other men. And even if swearing falsely were the only sin committed by Israel, it would be no surprise if *Mashiach* did not come.

◆§ IV: Remember the Shabbos Day

זָכוֹר אֶת יוֹם הַשַּׁבָּת — *Remember the Shabbos day* (20:8). You must remember to keep the *Shabbos*. God first commanded that we hold Him in esteem, and not worship other gods, and now He commanded that we rest on the day that He rested when He created the world, so that we remember that He is indeed the Creator.

You must keep the *Shabbos* holy. Do not think of bodily or financial matters; rather, study Torah. One who properly keeps *Shabbos* is forgiven for his sins.

The Sages relate that Turnus Rufus once met R' Akiva on *Shabbos* and queried, "What makes this day better than any other?" R' Akiva answered: "Why are you more important than other people?" Answered Turnus Rufus: "I have been rendered more important [by the emperor]." R' Akiva retorted: "And God has made *Shabbos* more important."

Turnus Rufus then asked: "If God wants to make this day more important, why does He do work on it? He lets the rain fall and brings the clouds from great distances, all on *Shabbos!*" R' Akiva answered: "You are well versed in our Torah, and must be aware that when two men share one courtyard they must set up an *eruv* to enable them to carry. But if a man owns the courtyard by himself no *eruv* is necessary and carrying is permitted. Similarly, God owns the entire world, and shares ownership with no one, so He may bring rain and move clouds.

"Further," continued R' Akiva, "the *manna* did not fall on *Shabbos*, and the Sambatyon River rests on that day." Turnus Rufus answered: "Do not bring me the *manna* as proof, nor the Sambatyon, for I have never seen them." Then R' Akiva told him, "Go to your father's grave and try to raise him from the dead by magical means. You will see if you can do it on *Shabbos*." The remainder of this incident is narrated above in the portion of *Bereishis*.

The wicked in Hell rest on *Shabbos*. On Friday evening a heavenly voice rings out, commanding that the wicked be allowed to rest. When *Shabbos* ends, and the Jews have said the prayers *Viyehi noam* and *Ve'atah kadosh*, the angel Dumah, who punishes the wicked during the week, cries out: "Wicked ones, return to Hell, for the Jews have just finished their prayers!"

שֵׁשֶׁת יָמִים תַּעֲבֹד — *Six days you shall work* (20:9). You shall work for six days, and on *Shabbos* you must feel as if you have completed all of your work. You should not give it another thought.

◆§ V: Honor your Father and your Mother

כַּבֵּד אֶת אָבִיךָ וְאֶת אִמֶּךָ — *Honor your father and your mother* (20:12). First God commanded that we honor Him, our first father. In addition, a person must hold his parents in esteem, as they helped to bring him into the world. Just as swearing falsely in God's Name is forbidden, so it is forbidden to swear falsely in the name of one's parents. Just as we must not honor God in order to receive material wealth, so we must not honor parents for the sake of their inheritance. A person is obligated to give his parents food and drink, just as he must serve God with his money, through charity and tithes.

Why does the Torah explicitly state in connection with this

commandment alone, that one who honors his parents lives a long life? Rabbeinu Saadiah says that it is because at times a father lives a long life, and it is difficult for his son to honor him properly. Therefore the Torah assures us that if we honor our parents we will live long. Complaining about your father's longevity means complaining about your own, for you will live long *because* you honor him.

Toldos Yitzchak writes that this means that if you honor your parents you will merit a long life and will be honored in turn. People will stand up for you and do all the other things that are done for the elderly.

"*Honor your father*" is the fifth commandment, because a man is created from five things: his parents, and the four elements: earth, water, air, and fire. He then has to spend nine months in his mother's body.

God gives the soul and the mind and the power of speech. The father contributes the white portion: sinews and bones. The mother gives the red in a person — blood, flesh and hair — and in addition the pupils of the eyes.

There are five types of creations: man, beast, bird, fish, and reptile. The Torah says *on the earth* (עַל הָאֲדָמָה; 20:12) in connection with the fifth commandment because there are five kinds of growing things: wheat and other grains; grapes; onions and turnips and other vegetables; trees and their fruits; and the forest trees grown for wood. There are also five types of metal in the earth: iron, lead, copper, silver and gold.

◄§ VI: Do Not Kill

לֹא תִרְצָח — *Do not kill* (20:13). Even though there are so many people in the world, one is not allowed to reduce this number by one.

This is the sixth commandment. There are six reasons why a man might, heaven forbid, murder: jealousy, passion, enmity, anger, insanity, and drunkenness. Also, man was created on the sixth day.

◄§ VII: Do Not Commit Adultery

לֹא תִנְאָף — *Do not commit adultery* (20:13). Lest a person think that though it is forbidden to decrease the number of people in the world one may be allowed to increase it by means of adultery, it is written thereafter, *Do not commit adultery*. This explanation comes from R' Bechaye.

This is the seventh commandment because there are seven kinds of forbidden relationships: with another man's wife; a man's wife, when she is menstrually impure; a widow; a virgin; bestiality; homosexuality; and, in the case of a strange woman, seven forbidden actions: intercourse; kissing; touching her; extended conversation; *yichud* (being alone with a woman in an empty house); listening to her singing; and gazing at her.

◀§ VIII: Do Not Steal

לֹא תִגְנֹב — *Do not steal* (20:13). Further, continues R' Bechaye, a person must not think that though murder is forbidden, it is permissible to abduct a person and sell him abroad into slavery, and so the Torah now continues, *Do not steal,* an admonition against abduction and kidnapping.

This commandment is listed eighth because there are eight kinds of robbery. First, there is robbery through dishonest billing; second, by false measures; third, by giving false weight; fourth, by refusing to return lost property to its rightful owner; fifth, kidnapping and selling a person; sixth, actual theft of cash; seventh, misleading someone *(gneivas daas;* e.g., inviting someone knowing that he cannot accept the invitation, in order to gain his favor); eighth, marrying an orphan left in one's care to one's son, in order to keep her money in the family. This, too, is considered stealing.

◀§ IX: Do Not Bear False Witness

לֹא תַעֲנֶה בְרֵעֲךָ עֵד שָׁקֶר — *Do not bear false witness against your neighbor (ibid.).* This prohibition also relates to a gentile.

Here too R' Bechaye explains the sequence of the commandments. A person might want to think that it is indeed forbidden to steal outright or to cause bodily harm, but one may steal someone's money by giving false testimony. Hence the admonition, *Do not bear false witness* — one may not harm another with words.

◀§ X: Do Not Covet

לֹא תַחְמֹד — *Do not covet* (20:14). Finally, a person may think that he can, at the very least, harm another in his own thoughts, so we are warned, *Do not covet.* Even in one's thoughts it is not permitted to want someone else's possessions.

Do not envy your friend's prosperity. This is a sin of the heart, and is a very grave one. These commandments do not include an admonition against theft because if we know that we are prohibited even from coveting another's possessions, how much more so is it prohibited to steal them!

There is only one thing which is permitted to covet, and that is, if a person sees his friend learning Torah, doing good deeds, and causing other to study Torah, it is permissible to envy these accomplishments, in order to be spurred on to similar deeds. It is also permitted to covet a friend's daughter as a wife for one's son. So writes R' Bechaye.

◈ The People Tremble

וְכָל הָעָם רֹאִים — *All the people saw* (20:15). *All of the people saw,* for everyone was healed [at the time of the Giving of the Torah]. There were no blind among them. The deaf, too, were healed, as we see from the verse, *We will do and we will hear.* The mute were likewise healed, as we see from the verse, *The entire nation answered* — everyone could speak.

וַיַּרְא הָעָם וַיָּנֻעוּ — *The people saw and trembled (ibid.).* They saw the thunder and lightning and were frightened. They fled twelve miles away, until angels came to lead them back to Mt. Sinai. Then they turned to Moshe and pleaded, "Speak to us, and let God not speak to us directly, or we will die." Moshe answered, "Fear not, for God is testing you and wants you to fear Him forever."

They stood some distance away and Moshe entered the cloud and received the Torah. God told Moshe to tell Israel that because they had heard Him speak with him, they should not worship the angels.

◈ Gods of Silver

לֹא תַעֲשׂוּן אִתִּי אֱלֹהֵי כֶסֶף — *Do not make with Me gods of silver ...* (20:20). Do not appoint a judge or community head just because he is wealthy. A judge is called *elokim*, a god. Another interpretation of this verse is: Do not worship Me when you are wealthy, and then abandon Me when things do not go well. Whether you are prospering or times are bad, you ought to revere Me as your God and love Me.

◈ Building an Altar

מִזְבַּח אֲדָמָה תַּעֲשֶׂה לִּי — *Make Me an altar of earth* (20:21). R' Bechaye writes that a great miracle was performed in connection with the altar. It was made of copper as thin as a gold coin, while under the copper was wood, and under that, earth. Yet the fire of the altar did not burn up the wood or the copper.

Moshe was anxious lest the copper would burn, so God told him: "You were on Mt. Sinai where there were terrible flames. I was there and you were not burned up. Now I will also save the copper and wood of the altar, and they will not burn."

לֹא תִבְנֶה אֶתְהֶן גָּזִית — *Do not build them* (the altar stones) *of hewn stone* (20:22). It is not proper that tools of iron, which shortens men's lives, be raised up against the very altar that lengthens their years. Also, the altar brings peace between God and man and it is not proper to raise up iron against it, since it is used in war and kills men.

If God commanded that no iron be raised up against the altar because iron brings war and the altar makes peace between God and mankind, how much more will a man be saved from harm if he brings peace between man and wife, or two feuding families, or quarreling friends.

R' Bechaye writes that it was prohibited to hew the stones of the altar because they were holy, and the unused portions might be discarded in public thoroughfares. *Imrei Noam* says that God asked for an altar of earth rather than hewn stone, because an altar of proud hewn stone would cost a great deal of money, and to build it one might be forced to steal or lift a sword and rob others. This would desecrate the altar, because God loathes a sacrifice brought through robbery, as it is written, *If you lift a sword to it, you will desecrate it (ibid.).*

וְלֹא תַעֲלֶה בְמַעֲלֹת עַל מִזְבְּחִי — *Do not go up on steps to My altar* (20:23). Do not build steps to climb up to the altar. If there were steps you would be forced, when climbing them, to separate your legs, exposing yourself to the altar.

Even though the vestments of the *Kohen* included trousers it was forbidden to build steps. Instead, a smooth ramp was constructed. Our Sages learn from this that if it is forbidden to expose oneself to stones, how much more so is it forbidden to do so to other people, who are capable of thought and were created in God's image.

❧ ❧ ❧

The *Haftorah* of *Parashas Yisro* may be found on p. 487.

פרשת משפטים
Parashas Mishpatim
(21:1 — 24:18)

⋈§ Judges and Justice

וְאֵלֶּה הַמִּשְׁפָּטִים אֲשֶׁר תָּשִׂים לִפְנֵיהֶם — *These are the laws which you shall place before them* (21:1). Shlomo HaMelech (King Solomon) says in *Mishlei:* גַּם אֵלֶּה לַחֲכָמִים הַכֵּר פָּנִים בְּמִשְׁפָּט בַּל טוֹב — *This, also, to the wise men: it is not good to show favoritism in judgment* (24:23). A person who judges fairly establishes God's throne in its rightful place; one who judges unfairly pushes God's throne aside.

Justice brings peace to the world. Yisro gave advice regarding the judicial system, and that is why he said of the people of Israel: עַל מְקֹמוֹ יָבֹא בְשָׁלוֹם — *it will come in peace to its rightful place* (18:23). The Jews were given their laws to enable them to bring peace to the world, for when there is peace, then and only then can the world survive.

The words *you shall place* (21:1) show us that a judge must personally tell the litigant his verdict, and give him a written rationale for his judgment.

The listing of laws which begins here follows the laws at the end of the preceding *Sidra* — in order to teach that the judges are to convene next to the *Beis HaMikdash.*

R' Eliezer says that when justice is done on earth, heaven suspends judgment and does not mete out punishment. But when there is no justice, heaven sits in judgment and sends down punishment. Indeed, our Sages say that the Jews have been cast out of their land because they did not judge fairly.

The word *tasim* ("put") shows that judgment, when executed fairly, is the elixir *(sam,* similar to the root of *tasim)* of life for the judge; when judgment is unfair, it is his venom *(sam)* of death.

⋈§ The Hebrew Bondman

כִּי תִקְנֶה עֶבֶד עִבְרִי — *If you buy a Hebrew bondman* (21:2). The Torah begins this code of laws with the particular law of buying a

Jewish servant, because it is related to the first commandment: אָנֹכִי ה' אֱלֹהֶיךָ אֲשֶׁר הוֹצֵאתִיךָ מֵאֶרֶץ מִצְרָיִם — *I am the Lord, your God, Who brought you out of the land of Egypt* — that is, to serve *Me*, and not to work as a servant to [My] servants!

Just as we rest on *Shabbos* to commemorate the fact that God created the world in six days and rested on the seventh, so shall a bondman serve his master for six years and go free in the seventh. This shall be a commemoration of the seventh day, the day of God's cessation from work.

שֵׁשׁ שָׁנִים יַעֲבֹד — *He shall serve for six years* (21:2). The verse refers to a bondman who has been sold by the *beis din*, the rabbinical court, because he robbed and did not have the money to repay his theft. Despite this, his master must not give him difficult or dirty labor, nor force him to work at night.

חִנָּם — *For free* (21:2). After six years he shall be liberated "for free," that is, if he had been sick during his servitude, the master cannot deduct money for the time that he was unable to work or for medical expenses which the master had incurred on his behalf. But if the servant was ill for more than three years, he is obligated to repay his master.

◆§ His Wife and Children

אִם בְּגַפּוֹ יָבֹא — *If he came in by himself* (21:3), without a wife, the master must not marry him to a Canaanite slave girl. But if he had previously been married to a Jewess, she too shall be set free.

Rashi questions: Who brought his wife into servitude, so that she must be freed? She had not been a servant at all! The answer is that this shows us that one who purchases a Jewish servant is obligated to feed the servant's wife and children for the entire period of servitude. This we learn from the words, וְיָצְאָה אִשְׁתּוֹ עִמּוֹ — *his wife shall go out with him* (ibid.).

If the bondman had been married prior to his servitude, his master may marry him to a Canaanite wife, in order that she bear children who remain servants of the master.

◆§ Choosing Slavery

Should the bondman say, אָהַבְתִּי אֶת אֲדֹנִי — *"I love my master, and my wife and my children* (21:5), and I have no desire for freedom,"* his master must pierce his ear with an awl by a doorpost, and he remains his bondman until *yovel* (Jubilee, the fiftieth year of the Sabbatical *shemittah* cycle).

Why does he pierce his ear? His ear heard God say on Mt. Sinai that Israel is His servant, and must not serve another, and yet this man chose to remain a bondman. Why is the piercing done next to a door? The door bore witness in Egypt. God watched over the doors of the Jews on the night that He struck the Egyptian first-born, and it was on that night that God proclaimed us His servants.

וְרָצַע אֲדֹנָיו אֶת אָזְנוֹ — *His master shall pierce his ear* (21:6). His master himself must do the action, rather than a son or a messenger. The man to whom he has sold himself must personally inflict the humiliation.

Why is he called "a Hebrew bondman" rather than "an Israelite bondman"? Because *Yisrael* is a superior name, which the Jews were called after God released them from their Egyptian bondage to serve Him and receive the Torah. But when they were enslaved in Egypt they were called Hebrews, as it says אֱלֹהֵי הָעִבְרִיִּים — *God of the Hebrews* (3:18). Someone who has sold himself into slavery is likened to the Jews of Egypt, and so is termed "Hebrew".

Why do they spill a drop of blood from his ear? He has rejected the memory of the blood which was sprayed on the doorposts when God freed our forefathers from slavery.

The *Midrash* says: Says God, "I have opened a door for him to be free after six years of bondage, and he does not want to walk through it." For this reason the piercing is done by a doorway.

~§ The Jewish Maidservant

וְכִי יִמְכֹּר אִישׁ אֶת בִּתּוֹ לְאָמָה — *If a man sells his daughter as a maidservant* (21:7). The Torah permits a man to sell his daughter to a Jew as a maidservant while she is still very young. However, unlike a gentile maidservant, who is freed in the event that her master knocks out a tooth or an eye, the Jewish maidservant receives a monetary indemnity and continues working for him.

One who takes in a Jewish maidservant ought to marry her, but does not give her money as a settlement for the *kiddushin*, or betrothal. The money which he had previously paid to her father is sufficient and is considered her settlement.

אִם רָעָה בְּעֵינֵי אֲדֹנֶיהָ — *If she displeases her master* (21:8). If she does not please him and he does not want to marry her, he must ease her way to freedom. For example, if he bought her services for six years, for a total of twenty-four gold pieces, that is, four pieces per year, then (in the event that someone will redeem her) he must deduct from the price four gold pieces for each year that she has served, despite the fact that during the first years she did less work as she was inexperienced.

לְעַם נָכְרִי לֹא יִמְשֹׁל לְמָכְרָה — *He shall have no power to sell her to a strange nation* (21:8). A man is prohibited from selling his daughter as a maidservant to a pagan because he will undoubtedly defile her.

✅ A Canaanite Wife

Toldos Yitzchak raises several questions. Why does the Torah permit a servant who is married to a Jewess to be mated with a Canaanite woman, while a single servant may not be so mated? How can he be given a Canaanite? Though a servant, he is still a Jew, and is not supposed to marry her. Further, how can any father sell his own daughter as a maidservant?

The answer is that when a Jewish thief who is unable to repay his theft is being sold by the court, if he has a wife and children no one will be willing to buy him, for the master is obligated to feed the wife and children despite the fact that they do no work. Therefore the Torah allows the master to give him a Canaanite maidservant to bear him children, who then belong to the master. In this way, his ultimate sale is ensured, despite the family which he brings with him. Since the master will gain many servants from him, it is worthwhile to buy him.

If the man is single, however, they will readily find a buyer for him, so his master is not permitted to give him a Canaanite maidservant. He must not marry him to a Jewish woman either, for then the children will not belong to the master, yet he will be obligated to feed them.

Another reason is that if the servant was previously married he will probably not grow to love the Canaanite woman, for a man's true love is usually his first wife. He will most certainly leave the Canaanite. But if a man was not married first, and then was given a Canaanite woman, he may very well come to love her and will never leave her. If he keeps her as his wife she will persuade him to be evil. Therefore, the Torah prohibited the master from giving a Canaanite woman to an unmarried servant.

As to the question of why a father would sell his own daughter, the answer is that the father hopes that the master will marry her, particularly since no settlement money other than that originally paid the father is necessary. The father is simply hoping to find his daughter a husband, and has no real intention of making her into a maidservant.

✍ The Thief as a Bondman

Toldos Yitzchak asks: If we pierce the servant's ear because he had heard, and chose to ignore, God's announcement of our servitude to Him alone, why do we not pierce him as soon as he sells himself into bondage? The answer is that he was actually sold by the court because he was a thief, and was not responsible for the sale. But at the end of the period of servitude he himself chose servitude.

If he was a thief, how is it possible that the master will want to keep him on in his household? It can only be that he is a thief no longer. He did not steal from his master, who now considers him trustworthy.

✍ Closing One's Ears

A person's ear is compared to a door — at times it must be shut, to avoid hearing evil words. Our Sages ask: Why is the entire ear hard, with the exception of the lobe, which is soft? Because when a man hears evil words he must cover his ears with the lobe to shut the words out.

✍ Rights of the Maidservant

כְּמִשְׁפַּט הַבָּנוֹת יַעֲשֶׂה לָּהּ — *According to the rights of the daughters he shall deal with her* (21:9). If the master's son decides to marry the maidservant, rather than the master himself, he must treat her as a wife who had been the daughter of a landowner (i.e., one who had not first been sold as a maidservant). Should he then marry another woman, he must still feed her, clothe her, and take care of her needs, and he may not hold the other wife in greater esteem just because his first wife had been sold as a maid to his father.

If they have not done one of the three things with her — that is, the master has not married her, nor the master's son, and her own father has not freed her — then she is freed when she reaches puberty, that is, at the age of twelve years and one day.

✍ Manslaughter and Murder

מַכֵּה אִישׁ וָמֵת ... וַאֲשֶׁר לֹא צָדָה — *Who kills a man ... and who had no intent* (21:12-13). If a man accidentally kills someone, only because God had planned such a fate, and not through his own intent, the man must be exiled to one of the "cities of sanctuary." Once there he must not be harmed. In the desert, where there are no such cities, an accidental killer would flee to the Levites' camp, and there was sure from harm.

If a man intentionally murders another he must be killed.

מֵעִם מִזְבְּחִי תִּקָּחֶנּוּ לָמוּת — *Take him from My altar to die* (21:14). Even if the murderer is a priest in the midst of the sacred service on the altar he must be taken away to die. He may not be a priest, but may have fled to the altar for sanctuary, as Yoav did. Yoav fled to the *Beis HaMikdash* after Shlomo HaMelech (King Solomon) had sentenced him to death, hoping that by grasping the altar he would escape. But the truth is it is to no avail. The murderer is taken from the altar and executed.

⊰ Kidnapping

וּמַכֵּה אָבִיו וְאִמּוֹ מוֹת יוּמָת. וְגֹנֵב אִישׁ וּמְכָרוֹ ... מוֹת יוּמָת. וּמְקַלֵּל אָבִיו וְאִמּוֹ מוֹת יוּמָת — *He that wounds his father or mother must die* (21:15) ... *He that steals a man and sells him ... must die* (21:16) ... *And he that curses his father and mother must die* (21:17). A kidnapper who sells his victim must be put to death. This law is followed by the law that a person who curses his father or mother is stoned.

R' Bechaye asks why the two laws concerning parents are separated by the law concerning kidnappers. Ought the two laws governing behavior to parents not have appeared one after the other, followed by the kidnapping law? R' Saadiah answers that it was more common to kidnap youngsters because of the difficulty of kidnapping adults. It might happen that a child would be kidnapped and eventually come to his parents' hometown and, not recognizing them, would curse or strike one of them. The Torah uses this order to show that the kidnapper caused this situation.

Ramban says that the kidnapping law follows that of one who strikes his parents because they have identical means of death: strangulation. A person who curses his parents, however, is killed by stoning, which is a more painful means of death. It is simple to curse someone and therefore the Torah assigns it a very severe death, to ensure the greatest caution against doing so. Moreover, this offender had invoked God's name in the course of his sin.

⊰ Workers' Compensation

וְנָפַל לַמִּשְׁכָּב — *And he is bedridden* (21:18). If a man hits someone and as a result he is bedridden and cannot do his work, the attacker is imprisoned until the victim is up and about. He must also pay for the missed work.

If he cut off a limb the court must reckon how much less the man is worth now as a result of his disability, and the attacker must pay the difference, his earning power being calculated as if he were the watchman of a vegetable garden.

✑ Medical Expenses

וְרַפֹּא יְרַפֵּא — *He must surely heal him* (21:19). He must hire a doctor to cure his victim. But if the victim does not want to be healed, preferring the money, the attacker is not obligated to pay. So says *Ramban*.

R' Bechaye says that when the word יְרַפֵּא appears in the Torah, the letter *pei* appears with a dot within it (and is now called a "hard" letter), yet when it speaks of God's *refuah* (healing), there is no dot (and it is thus pronounced *fei*, which is a "soft" letter). This is because healing through the hands of man is difficult and painful — thus, the hard letter. God's healing is swift and painless, and so is written as a "soft" letter.

Rashi writes that "he must pay the doctor's fee." If the assailant brings a doctor who will take the case without charging, the victim has a right to say that a doctor who works without payment will be careless. If the attacker himself is a doctor the victim can refuse his services, and can say that he cannot tolerate the thought of his enemy healing him.

✑ The Assailed Bondman

וְכִי יַכֶּה אִישׁ אֶת עַבְדּוֹ — *If a man hits his servant* (21:20). If a man hits his servant or maid with a rod and the servant dies under his hand, the master is killed by sword, even if the servant were a Canaanite. But should the servant live for a day or two, the master is not executed.

✑ Woman with Child

וְיָצְאוּ יְלָדֶיהָ — *And she loses her children* (21:22). If two men quarrel and push a pregnant woman, so that she loses her child, the judges decide the amount of the fine, on the basis of the husband's request. Why not the woman's? Because the child belonged to the man. It is as if the child were in the woman's keeping until the time that she can give it to him. If the father asks for an exorbitant sum, the judges must decide.

If the woman dies, however, as a result of the violence, some Sages are of the opinion that the person responsible should be put to death. Others say that since the deed was unintentional, he must merely pay indemnity, as decided by the court.

◄§ The Assailed Canaanite Slave

וְכִי יַכֶּה אִישׁ אֶת עֵין עַבְדּוֹ — *If a man should hit his servant's eye*
(21:26). If a man knocks out the eye or the tooth of a Canaanite
slave or maidservant, he must set him free.

R' Bechaye writes that the Canaanites are destined for slavery
because their forefather Cham used his mouth to sin, when he spoke
ill of his father to his brothers. If a Canaanite's tooth is knocked out,
the pain which he undergoes atones for that sin and he must be
freed.

◄§ Injury by a Dangerous Animal

וְכִי יִגַּח שׁוֹר אֶת אִישׁ — *If an ox gores a man* (21:28). If an ox gores a
man to death the ox is stoned, and no profit may be had from the ox.
The ox's owner is exempt from punishment. But if there had been
previous warnings of the ox's dangerous tendencies, and the owner
had been told three times to be careful with it and had ignored the
warnings, then if the ox gores a man or woman it is stoned, and God
will kill the owner.

R' Bechaye asks: Why is the word *yigach* ("gore") used in
connection with men, and *yigof* ("hurt") used when discussing an
ox which gores another animal? The word *yigach* connotes the use
of strength. A man has a certain supervisory destiny *(mazal)*, and an
ox cannot readily gore him unless it is so destined. Therefore, the
word *yigach* is used, connoting strength. But animals have no
special destiny and so it says *yigof*, meaning that no effort is needed;
as soon as the ox sees the other animal it may gore it.

If an ox gores three men in three days it is considered a *muad*,
meaning, a goring ox. (This is not so if he gores three times in one
day.) If the owner does not watch it, he is liable. Even though
nowadays we do not punish when an ox gores a man, we punish one
who keeps a dangerous animal or dog which harms people.

◄§ Damage in Public Property

A person should also take care not to leave dirty things in areas
where men pass by, lest someone trip or dirty himself. The pious
men of bygone days used to pick up broken glass lying in the street
and bury it in the ground so that no one could harm himself through
it.

A story is told of a man who cleared stones from his field and
threw them into the adjoining public thoroughfare. A pious man
approached him, and asked, "Why are you throwing stones from a

stranger's field into your *own?"* The man mocked him, thinking him a simpleton.

Not much later the man sold his fields and walked through the communal property, hurting himself on the stones. "How right the pious man was," he lamented. "I threw stones from a stranger's field — for I have been forced to sell to a stranger — into my own field, because everyone has a portion in the communal property."

We learn from this that a person should not spill dirty water onto the street where men pass by for it may cause damage. God will then mete out punishment, just as he punished the man by forcing him to sell his fields.

וְכִי יִפְתַּח אִישׁ בּוֹר — *If a man opens a pit* (21:33), or if he digs a hole in a public place, and does not cover it, and an ox falls in, he must pay the ox's owner for damages.

✦§ Fines for Theft

כִּי יִגְנֹב אִישׁ שׁוֹר — *If a man steals an ox* (21:37), he must repay five oxen in its stead. If he steals a sheep he must repay four sheep for it. *Rashi* writes in explanation that an ox can be led by its horns, and thus is not difficult for the thief to take, and so he must repay five times the amount of theft. A sheep, however, must be hoisted onto the thief's shoulders, thus proving a burden and a humiliation. Therefore the fine is lessened to four sheep.

A second explanation is that an ox plows a field and is useful for other work. Since the thief has disturbed this work, he must pay five times the amount of the theft. A sheep, on the other hand, does no work, so the fine is only four times the theft.

R' Bechaye writes: When a man steals clothing or money from a house he must pay the owner double, but when he steals an animal from the field, a much simpler theft to arrange, he pays double that fine — or four times the amount of the theft. This is because God punishes a sin which is easily committed more harshly, so that people will be doubly cautious. Since an ox can be stolen even more easily than other animals — since the shepherd cannot keep oxen herded together — the thief must pay five times the amount.

✦§ The Thief and the Burglar

A thief, who breaks in stealthily, must repay double the amount of his theft, while a burglar, who does so openly, does not. The reason is as follows: the thief is afraid of men but not of God, and steals secretly, when no one sees him, unafraid that God, who sees all, knows what he has done. The burglar, on the other hand, does not fear men more that God, and so is not obligated to pay double.

⇜§ Five Punishments

The *Midrash* says that the Children of Israel "stole" an ox — that is, they made the Golden Calf — and therefore they had to repay five times: there were five punishments for the sin. Many were killed by the Levites' swords; a plague broke out and killed many others; their faces turned green and yellow after they drank the water which Moshe gave them, in the manner of the *sotah*; the *Beis HaMikdash* was destroyed as a result of the sin; and finally, God bears the sin in mind in every generation, meting out punishment for it.

⇜§ Four Hundred Years' Exile

וְאַרְבַּע צֹאן תַּחַת הַשֶּׂה — *Four sheep to compensate for the [one] sheep* (21:37). The Jews were in exile for four hundred years, because they sold Yosef, who is likened to a sheep.

⇜§ The Magical Arts

מְכַשֵּׁפָה לֹא תְחַיֶּה — *Do not let a witch live* (22:17). R' Bechaye asks: Why did the Torah forbid magic? Because the Jews had learned it in Egypt. This prohibition was made to ensure that they did not return there.

Why does it say, *Do not let a witch live?* To show that you may kill her with any means possible.

Why does it speak of a *mechashefah* ("witch"), rather than a *mechashef* ("warlock")? Because women are better versed in the magical arts. The magic of Ov, in which the dead are raised back to life, can only be done if a woman is present.

⇜§ As Widows and Orphans

כָּל אַלְמָנָה וְיָתוֹם לֹא תְעַנּוּן — *Do not torment any widow or orphan* (22:21). "For," says God, "they have no one to take their part. If someone hurts them they cry out to Me. I will hearken to them and kill their oppressor, leaving his wife a widow and his children orphans."

Rashi asks: If it says that the oppressor's wife will be widowed, why does the Torah add that his children will be orphaned? Is that not obvious? The answer is that this shows that the husband will disappear to an unknown fate, leaving his wife a permanent widow, not permitted to remarry, and his children eternal orphans, unable to receive their inheritance.

כָּל אַלְמָנָה — *Any widow* (22:21). Do not take advantage of any widow, even a wealthy one, for widows cry profusely and their tears are not shed in vain. One must not cause them pain, or even tax the wealthy, for if a woman has no husband her riches have no meaning.

Yirmeyahu (Jeremiah) likened Yerushalayim to a widow: "She was like a widow" who "cries at night." Even if she is rich and has many pleasures, at night she cannot forget her husband.

◄§ Lending to the Poor

אִם כֶּסֶף תַּלְוֶה אֶת עַמִּי — *When you lend money to My people* (22:24). R' Bechaye writes: King Solomon said, מַתָּן בַּסֵּתֶר יִכְפֶּה אָף וְשֹׁחַד בַּחֵק חֵמָה עַזָּה — *A secret gift pacifies anger; a bribe in the bosom brings on great wrath* (Mishlei 21:14). A person who gives charity pacifies God's anger, but a person who takes bribes brings God's fury down upon him. If a person takes his own money and gives it to charity, God gives him back twice as much.

אִם כֶּסֶף תַּלְוֶה אֶת עַמִּי אֶת הֶעָנִי — *When you lend money to My people, to the poor* (ibid.). The Torah tells us this in order to teach us that if a rich man and a poor man come to you, you should first lend the money to the poor man.

אֶת הֶעָנִי עִמָּךְ — *The poor man that is with you* (ibid.). This shows that if a poor man from your hometown and a poor man from another city come to you, precedence should be given to the man from your home. Similarly, if one is a member of your family and the other is not, first lend the money to the relative.

This verse also warns that if you do not lend money to the poor, you will become impoverished yourself. And once you have lent him money you must behave as if he owes you nothing.

◄§ Interest on Loans

You must not charge him interest for that is a major sin. This was illustrated in the case of Ovadiah, an appointee in the court of Achav, king of *Yisrael*. He gave all of his money to sustain one hundred prophets who were being persecuted by Achav, hiding them in two caves. During a time of famine Ovadiah's money came to an end, and he approached Achav's son Yehoram for a loan, promising him interest, while having no intention of paying it, for the sin of paying interest is as great as the sin of charging it. God sent Yehu to shoot Yehoram, and the arrow struck him between his arms, because he had stretched out his arms to take interest.

⇜ My People are the Poor

עַמִּי — *My people (ibid.).* The poor are called God's people, as it says, כִּי נִחַם ה׳ עַמּוֹ וַעֲנִיָּו יְרַחֵם — *For God has comforted His people, and has mercy on His poverty-stricken ones (Yeshayahu* 49:13). A wealthy person is ashamed of his poor relatives but treats his rich relatives with respect; God does the opposite, hating the rich when they are evil and loving the poor.

⇜ Mercy Need Not be Merited

אִם חָבֹל תַּחְבֹּל — *If you take as a pledge* (22:25). If you take someone's clothing as security, and he must wear it during the day, you must leave it with him all day, and may take it as security at night.

You must not think to yourself: "The poor man whose security I am holding is not overly pious, and even if I do not return it I will not be sinning." For this reason the Torah says, כִּי חַנּוּן אָנִי — *I am gracious* (22:26), and have mercy on men even when they do not merit it. If you take advantage of him, I will punish you."

⇜ Cursing a Judge

אֱלֹהִים לֹא תְקַלֵּל — *Do not curse a judge* (22:27). This is forbidden, even if he rules against you in court. You may also not curse a king because of his judgment.

⇜ Rewards for Dogs

וְאַנְשֵׁי קֹדֶשׁ תִּהְיוּן לִי — *Be men of holiness to me* (22:30). Eat no animal which has been killed in the field; it must be given to the dogs.

When God killed Egypt's first-born sons the dogs barked at the Egyptians who were burying their dead, but they did not bark at the Jews, although they were traveling at night, sticks in their hands, and dogs usually bark at such sights. For this reason the dogs are given animal carcasses.

⇜ Judicial Procedure

לֹא תִשָּׂא שֵׁמַע שָׁוְא — *Do not bring about a false report* (23:1). Do not administer an oath to a person who may very well lie. Also, do not listen to one litigant's complaints without the presence of the other. He will probably lie and later it will be hard for you to forget what he has said, because his words will lie embedded in your heart. But if the other litigant is at hand and immediately denies the allegations, you will be able to discern the truth.

This verse also teaches us to stay away from slander and gossip.

לֹא תִהְיֶה אַחֲרֵי רַבִּים לְרָעֹת — *Do not follow a majority for evil* (23:2). Do not follow a crowd if they are doing wrong, even if they are a majority.

Our Sages also learn from this verse that we do not follow a majority of one for a verdict of guilty. There were seventy-one members of the Sanhedrin. If thirty-six said a man was guilty and should be put to death, and thirty-five said not guilty, he was not put to death. Only a majority of at least two was sufficient. However, if a majority of one proclaimed him innocent, it was so decided.

וְלֹא תַעֲנֶה עַל רִב לִנְטֹת — *Do not complain in a conflict* (23:2). A judge is not allowed to coach the litigant in his argument, nor is he allowed to complain on his behalf. Only the litigant can state his complaint, and his fellow litigant can answer him.

וְדָל לֹא תֶהְדַּר בְּרִיבוֹ — *Do not show preference to the poor in his suit* (23:3). If a poor man and a rich man come to court you must not justify the poor man in order to force the rich man to give him charity in a respectable manner. This is forbidden.

⋙ Helping an Enemy

עָזֹב תַּעֲזֹב עִמּוֹ — *You shall surely help him* (23:5). If you see a person's donkey laboring under a load and on the verge of falling, you must help him unburden the animal, even if the man is your enemy. If you see your enemy's ox wandering away, and it will get lost, you are obligated to return it to him.

⋙ Verdicts

וְנָקִי וְצַדִּיק אַל תַּהֲרֹג — *Do not kill the innocent and the righteous* (23:7). If a man has been pronounced guilty and sentenced to death, and is being led out of court, and another person comes with evidence which may acquit him, he is brought back to the court, for he may be innocent. But if a person has been pronounced not guilty and someone comes with evidence proving his guilt, he is not judged again, and remains free. This is the meaning of the words, *Do not kill the righteous* — if he has been pronounced innocent by the court he cannot be executed [despite new evidence to the contrary].

כִּי לֹא אַצְדִּיק רָשָׁע — *I will not acquit the guilty (ibid.).* God assures us, however, "If he really should be killed, I will do the deed. You may not execute him."

⋺§ Meat and Milk

לֹא תְבַשֵּׁל גְּדִי בַּחֲלֵב אִמּוֹ — *Do not cook a kid in its mother's milk* (23:19). This verse is stated in the Torah three times to show that we are not allowed to eat milk and meat together; to derive enjoyment or benefit from mixing meat and milk; nor to cook them together.

Why does the Torah write only that we should not cook them together, and does not explicitly state that we should not eat them? To show that if a person ate meat and milk together without deriving enjoyment, for instance, if he cooked hot meat and milk and burned his throat, he is still guilty and liable for a flogging. This differs from certain other prohibitions in which flogging is not mandatory if there has been no enjoyment.

Toldos Yitzchak says that pagans used to cook meat and milk and put it near the roots of trees so that their fruit would grow more speedily. For this reason the prohibition against cooking meat and milk is in the same verse as רֵאשִׁית בִּכּוּרֵי אַדְמָתְךָ — *The first fruits of your land* (23:19), which refers to wheat. This shows that we must not cook meat and milk together even for crops: God will make our crops flourish.

⋺§ Angelic Escort

הִנֵּה אָנֹכִי שׁוֹלֵחַ מַלְאָךְ לְפָנֶיךָ — *Behold, I send a messenger before you* (23:20). God told Moshe: "Israel will sin with the Golden Calf, and will not be worthy of having My Presence with them. I will therefore send an angel to accompany them."

Moshe prayed that during his lifetime no angel should accompany them, only God himself. God heeded him and He alone accompanied the people as long as Moshe was alive. Immediately after Moshe died and was succeeded by Yehoshua (Joshua), an angel began to accompany them.

R' Chananel writes that the angel who accompanied Yehoshua was Michael.

לֹא יִשָּׂא לְפִשְׁעֲכֶם — *He will not pardon your sin* (23:21). God cautioned them not to sin while with the angel for the angel did not have the power to forgive them. Only God can forgive sins. If they listened to what the angel told them, their enemies would fall before them and the angel would bring them to *Eretz Yisrael*.

⋺§ Illness and Remedy

וַהֲסִרֹתִי מַחֲלָה מִקִּרְבֶּךָ — *I will remove sickness from within you*

(23:25). God said: "If you heed the Torah I will take all illness away from you."

R' Bechaye says that many illnesses are a result of too much food and drink; others come from the air itself. But learning Torah cures all illnesses.

⛤ The Hornets

וְשָׁלַחְתִּי אֶת הַצִּרְעָה לְפָנֶיךָ — *I will send the hornets before you* (23:28). "I will send hornets [or some other type of killer insect, not necessarily still existing — *Trans.*] to blind the Hivites, Canaanites, and Hittites."

Rashi writes that the hornets did not cross the Jordan River. The Canaanites and Hittites lived on one side of the Jordan, and the hornets attacked and blinded them, and then they died. As for the Hivites, who lived on the other side of the river, they were blinded by the poison which the hornets flung over the water.

God said: "I will not exile the nations of *Eretz Yisrael* all at once, for there are not enough of you yet to totally populate the land, and wild animals will breed there if the land is left empty."

⛤ Moshe Ascends the Mountain

God told Moshe, "*Go up to God, you and Aharon*" (עֲלֵה אֶל ה'; אַתָּה וְאַהֲרֹן; 24:1). This passage was said before the Giving of the Torah.

On the fourth day of Sivan Moshe alone went up to Mount Sinai, within the clouds. He then descended and told *Yisrael* all that he had heard from God, and the people answered, נַעֲשֶׂה וְנִשְׁמָע — *We will do and we will hear* (24:7). Moshe then wrote down the Torah, beginning with Creation and continuing to the point of the Giving of the Torah.

He ascended once more on the fifth of Sivan in the early morning. Moshe had built an altar at the foot of the hill and the first-born sons brought sacrifices.

R' Bechaye writes that these first-born sons were all young men, unmarried and pure. With their sacrifice Israel entered into a covenant with God in which they promised to keep the Torah.

⛤ Covenant and Conversion

Israel entered the covenant through three actions: circumcision, immersion (for they all immersed themselves before the Giving of the Torah), and this sacrifice. Similarly, a convert in *Eretz Yisrael* had to fulfill three conditions: circumcision, immersion, and bringing of a sacrifice.

Prior to his conversion each convert is told of several of the commandments, in order to discourage his conversion, for converts were liabilities to the Jews. Converts are often not serious and not careful with the commandments, and Jews learn from them and are punished. We see this with the *erev rav*, the mixed multitude who converted when the Jews left Egypt, and who later made the Golden Calf, causing the death of thousands of Jews.

Converts are told some of the commandments so that they cannot say afterwards that if they had known how many commandments there were they would not have converted. And as to the *Gemara's* saying that converts are bad for Israel, that is because God sees how they left behind their mother and father and entire family to cleave to God, and He then punishes Israel because they are not as pious.

וַיִּקַּח מֹשֶׁה חֲצִי הַדָּם — *Moshe took half the blood* (24:6). That is, the blood of the sacrifice. An angel came and split the blood into two equal halves. Moshe put half into a basin and sprinkled it on Israel: he poured the other half on the altar.

⊷§ The Vision

Moshe, Aharon, Nadav, Avihu, and the seventy elders climbed up Mount Sinai and saw God's Holy Throne, and, lying beneath Him, כְּמַעֲשֵׂה לִבְנַת הַסַּפִּיר — *something like a sapphire brick* (24:10), which God had placed before Him as a reminder of the brickmaking which the Egyptians forced the Jews to do and from which He had redeemed them.

Chizkuni writes that there was a woman in Egypt named Rachel who was helping her husband make cement, causing her to abort her child. The fetus fell into the cement and she could not find it. They cried out to God, who sent the angel Michael. He made a brick of the cement in which the fetus had fallen, and placed it beneath the Holy Throne.

The seventy elders were the overseers appointed over the Jews in Egypt. They made their burden easier for them, unknown to Pharaoh, and so were rewarded by seeing God's throne and being appointed the elders of *Yisrael.*

וַיֶּחֱזוּ אֶת הָאֱלֹהִים — *They beheld God* (24:11). At such a time, the elders and Nadav and Avihu ate and drank, and as a result deserved to die. God did not want to disturb the rejoicing and so waited until the eighth day of Nissan to kill Nadav and Avihu. The elders were killed in the desert, when the people spoke against God, as a result of this sin.

⋙ Second and Third Ascents

עֲלֵה אֵלַי הָהָרָה — *Come up to Me to the mountain* (24:12). God told this to Moshe after giving the Torah. Moshe went up and learned the entire Torah, all 613 commandments. Yehoshua, his disciple, accompanied him to the foot of the mountain. He set his tent at the foot of the mountain and remained there for the forty days that Moshe was on the mount.

Moshe told the elders to stay with the people and act as their judges. He also told Miriam's son Chur to judge them.

When Moshe went up the mountain a cloud covered it, remaining until the sixth day of Sivan, when God gave the Torah. Immediately after the Giving of the Torah he went up the mountain again, remaining there for forty days and forty nights. We are told this to show Moshe's greatness. He was like an angel who neither eats nor drinks.

Because Moshe was on the mountain for forty days learning Torah, his face was so luminous for forty years that no one could look directly at him, and he covered the radiance with a veil. This radiance remained with him until his death.

For every day that he remained on the mountain, he lived for one year. We see that he was on the mountain three times, for forty days each time, totaling 120 days. And indeed he lived to one hundred and twenty.

For the six days preceding the Giving of the Torah Moshe was covered by a cloud. On the seventh day God made a path through the cloud, and Moshe followed it and spoke to God.

※　※　※

The *Haftorah* of *Parashas Mishpatim* may be found on p. 492.

פרשת תרומה
Parashas Terumah
(25:1 — 27:19)

◆§ How to Give Charity

וְיִקְחוּ לִי תְּרוּמָה — *Take for Me an offering* (25:2). King Solomon says, in *Proverbs:* (קְחוּ מוּסָרִי וְאַל כָּסֶף) — *Take my rebuke, and not money (Mishlei* 8:10). This means that a person should take the Torah's words of rebuke to heart, rather than simply amass wealth. Through the Torah one can possess this world and the next, while material possessions lead to nothing but worry and aggravation.

Take my rebuke — with zeal and not with laziness. If a person fulfills a commandment without any pure thoughts or happiness it is worth nothing. Similarly, when giving charity one must have good intentions. There are many people who give no charity unless they are cajoled into it, and they do not do it for the sake of God. This charity is worth little.

This is why the verse says, וְיִקְחוּ לִי תְּרוּמָה — *Take for Me an offering:* take *for Me,* and not to flatter yourself with it. The words *for Me* also teach that when a person gives charity it should be done quietly, with no one but God knowing it.

It says "take" rather than "let them give" to show that a person should cause others to give charity, collecting the money and dividing it among the needy. One who causes other to give charity fulfills a greater commandment than one who gives himself. Our Sages say in the *Gemara,* גָּדוֹל הַמְעַשֶׂה יוֹתֵר מִן הָעוֹשֶׂה — "He who causes a good deed to be done is greater than the one who does it."

It also says *Take for Me* to teach that God reassures us that "if you give charity you take Me to yourself. When the poor man stands next to you, I stand next to you too." Thus in *Psalms* it is written, כִּי יַעֲמֹד לִימִין אֶבְיוֹן — *For He stands to the right of the impoverished (Tehillim* 109:31). God stands by the right hand of the needy.

⋑ Cleaving to God

Why does the portion discussing charity follow that of the Giving of the Torah? To show that God's spirit rests in a place where people learn Torah, and in a place of charity.

Baal HaTurim writes that the words *Take for Me an offering* imply that if you learn the Torah, which was given at the end of forty days, you take God to yourself [based on the numerical value of the word לִי, "for Me," which is forty].

Toldos Yitzchak writes that in saying the words וְיִקְחוּ לִי — *they shall take unto Me* — God is telling the people of Israel that by giving *tzedakah* they are, as it were, betrothing God unto themselves, just as a bridegroom betroths a bride through a gift. Hence the word *take*, and not *give*.

Finally, it says "take", instead of "give", because one who gives charity takes a reward from God which exceeds the amount he gave.

תְּרוּמָתִי — *My offering* (25:2). Why does the verse use this word? God is saying, "Charity is Mine: it is I that have given you the money." A man should realize that God has merely appointed him as a trustee to give his money to others.

אֲשֶׁר יִדְּבֶנּוּ לִבּוֹ — *Whose heart prompts him* (25:2). Each man shall give as much as his heart desires. *Toldos Yitzchak* asks why charity is connected with the heart, rather than another organ. This shows that just as the heart nourishes all the other organs, and is the sole organ which receives no nourishment from others, so one who gives charity will be rewarded. He will always be in a position to give, and never have to receive.

The verse specifies לִבּוֹ — "*his* heart," because there are people who, when they see others giving charity, give also, but their hearts do not really prompt them to do so. They give only because they are shamed into it. Men should really give because their own heart prompts them to do so.

⋑ The Best Merchandise

Midrash Tanchuma writes: *Take for Me an offering* because I have sold you the Torah, which is called "good merchandise." Why is the Torah so termed? Take, for example, two merchants, one of pepper and one of ginger. They trade their merchandise and, in the end, the pepper merchant is left without pepper and the ginger merchant without ginger.

Not so the Torah. If one learned man knows one chapter, and

another man knows another, and they trade their merchandise by teaching each other, in the end both own both chapters!

Another reason the Torah is called "a good purchase" is that it cannot be lost. The story is told of a wise man who traveled on a ship, together with some merchants. The merchants asked him: "Where are your goods?" He answered, "My goods are the best goods one can possibly have." The merchants searched the entire ship, to no avail. They could not locate his merchandise, and so they all made fun of him.

Later, pirates boarded the ship and ransacked it of its entire cargo. The merchants made their way to a nearby city, impoverished and hungry. The learned man entered the local *beis midrash*, where he was treated with respect because of his vast learning. When the other merchants saw this, they begged him to intervene with the local populace on their behalf.

The wise man told them: "Didn't I tell you that my merchandise was the best? Your merchandise was taken away from you, but mine stays with its owner always."

The *Yalkut* quotes Tractate *Sanhedrin* which states that a non-Jew asked R' Avin: "Your God is a *Kohen* (priest), for He has asked you to bring Him a *terumah*, or offering, just like a *Kohen*, who is entitled to a *terumah* from the yearly crop. But after He buried Moshe Rabbeinu, where could he immerse Himself [to purify Himself, as a priest must]? What water would suffice for Him?"

R' Avin answered: "He purified Himself in fire, as it says, כִּי הִנֵּה ה' בָּאֵשׁ יָבוֹא — *For behold, God will come in fire (Yeshayahu* 66:15).

⌘ The Building Materials

וְזֹאת הַתְּרוּמָה — *This is the offering* (25:3). *Rashi* writes that there were three types of offerings: first, the half-shekel donated by each person, from which they constructed the bases for the Tabernacle's panels; second, a half-shekel donated by each person for the purpose of purchasing the animals for sacrifice; and, finally, each person's voluntary donation of thirteen kinds of goods, as much as they wished — gold, silver, copper, blue and purple wool, linen and red threads, goats' hair, red-dyed sheepskin, furs of a *tachash*, cedar wood, olive oil and spices.

The *Gemara* says that God sent the animal called *tachash* to Moshe in the desert, in order to make a covering for the Tabernacle from it. The animal's pelt was multicolored, and seemed to give off light. It had one horn on its forehead, and has since disappeared, not to be seen again.

There was no silk in the Tabernacle, for it is made by worms, which are impure. R' Bechaye asks: What about the red threads, which are dyed in the blood of impure worms? The answer is that it was not dyed with the actual blood, but with the grains in which the worms grow.

R' Bechaye points out that they took linen threads and mixed them with woolen cloth, despite the fact that this is *shaatnez*, the mixture of linen and wool which is ordinarily forbidden. In the Tabernacle it was permitted.

וַעֲצֵי שִׁטִּים — *Cedar wood* (25:5). The *Midrash* asks: Where did Moshe find cedar wood in a desert? The answer is that Yaakov prophetically saw that his descendants would built a Tabernacle in the desert. He therefore planted cedars in Egypt and gave instructions that they should take the wood when they left the country.

R' Bechaye and *Toldos Yitzchak* quote a *Midrash* which says that gold is mentioned as the first gift to show that God had forgiven them the sin of the Golden Calf. For the same reason it says later, in connection with the sacrifices, "an ox, sheep, or goat," with ox mentioned first. This shows, too, that the sin of the Golden Calf, which is a young ox, was forgiven.

◄§ The Mishkan and Redemption

Although the sin of the Golden Calf took place on the 17th day of Tammuz, and the Tabernacle was built close to Yom Kippur, the Day of Atonement, the construction is discussed first to teach that God prepared the means of atonement before the sin, for He prepares the cure before the illness.

שֶׁמֶן לַמָּאֹר — *Oil for light* (25:6). These words hint at *Mashiach*, who will illuminate the world as pure oil does, as it is written, עָרַכְתִּי נֵר לִמְשִׁיחִי — *I have prepared a candle for My anointed* (Tehillim 132:17).

Why is *Mashiach* alluded to in the portion of *Terumah*, which tells of the donations which are to be given to the Sanctuary? To teach that if Jews give charity while in their bitter exile, it will surely come to an end.

Similarly, in *Parashas Ki Seitzei*, Rashi writes that the Torah commands us to deal with honest weights and measures, and immediately afterwards describes the massacre of many Jews by

Amalek — to show us that if we deal dishonestly with others, an enemy will (heaven forbid) attack us, killing and despoiling our nation.

The *Midrash* teaches us that while the Temple stood it saved us from exile. Now that it has been destroyed only charity can save us. For this reason all four exiles are hinted at in this portion.

⚞ The Names on the Gems

אַבְנֵי שֹׁהַם וְאַבְנֵי מִלֻּאִים — *Onyx stones, and stones for setting* (25:7). R' Bechaye writes that they took uncut gems. The spiritual value (*segulah*) of a stone lies in its wholeness, and not when it is cut.

You may then ask how they carved the letters on to the gems: they would not then be whole. The answer is that the letters were not engraved in the gems. Instead, the letters were written on the stones in ink, and then the worm called *shamir* was placed upon them. Through this, the letters were embossed upon the stones.

The names were inscribed upon the gems, which were set upon gold, to show that the Torah stands above gold and silver.

⚞ Encompassing the Infinite

וְעָשׂוּ לִי מִקְדָּשׁ — *Let them make Me a sanctuary* (25:8). *Yalkut* quotes a *Pesikta* which says that Moshe heard three things from God which left him stricken with terror. First, God told him to build a sanctuary where He would rest. Moshe answered: "Can all of the gold, silver, and wood in the world suffice for You, when You encompass all of the universe?" Answered God: "It is not as you think. Build a mere twenty boards on the northern side, twenty on the southern side, and eight on the western side and I will rest there."

The second time that he was taken aback was when God commanded him to bring sacrifices. Moshe said: "If I should bring all of the animals and birds in the world as sacrifices, would they suffice?" God replied: "It is not as you think. Bring Me just two sheep a day, one in the morning and one in the evening."

The third time was when God told him that a person must redeem himself. Moshe was terrified, saying: "Can all the gold in the world redeem a person?" Answered God: "It is not as you think. Each person must give a mere half-*shekel* to redeem himself."

This situation is analogous to a man with a daughter. When she is still young the father speaks with her freely outside, but when she grows up he grows modest and speaks to her only in their home.

Similarly, when the Jews were in Egypt God appeared openly to them, as it is written, וְעָבַרְתִּי בְאֶרֶץ מִצְרַיִם — *I shall pass through the* land of Egypt (12:12). Later, He spoke to them at the Red Sea. But after they received the Torah on Sinai they became more esteemed. God then said: "It is not proper to speak to them openly." He therefore commanded that a Tabernacle be built from where He would speak to them.

⋖§ Sanctuary, Universe, Man

R' Bechaye writes that the Tabernacle had three parts. First, deep inside, behind the curtain, were the Ark, the Tablets, and the Cherubim. This was parallel to heaven, where the angels, full of wisdom and understanding, reside. Similarly, the Ark contained the Torah, symbol of wisdom and understanding. The parallel in man is the head, which holds within it the brain, center of knowledge, and the mouth, which speaks with wisdom, for a person can be recognized as wise or not by what he says.

Second was the Ohel Moed, which held the Table, the Menorah (candelabra), and the altar of the incense. All of these are important items, though not of the same sanctity as those inside. This parallels the world of the spheres and heavenly bodies — the sun, moon, and stars. These are certainly important, but not as the angels are. In man, this is analogous to the heart, which provides man with his life, as the sun and moon provide life to the earth by illuminating the day and night.

Third was the outer area (chatzer) where sacrifices were slaughtered. This parallels the mortal world, in which everything is destined to die. In man, this is comparable to the organs which digest food and drink.

This shows us that a person who is righteous is compared to the three worlds — the angels, the heavenly bodies, and the mortal world. The world itself is compared to the Tabernacle, for the Divine Presence rests upon both.

⋖§ The Torah Ark and Torah Scholars

וְעָשׂוּ אֲרוֹן עֲצֵי שִׁטִּים — They shall make an ark of cedar wood (25:10). R' Bechaye asks: Why in connection with the Ark does the Torah say They shall make, in the third person plural form, while in reference to the other items constructed, the second person singular form וְעָשִׂיתָ is used? The answer is that the Torah is in the Ark, and everyone must build an ark for the Torah — that is, everyone should learn the Torah, for everyone has a part in it. So write Imrei Noam and Baal HaTurim.

R' Bechaye gives another reason for the use of the third person plural (וְעָשׂוּ) in connection with the Ark. This shows that everyone must support Torah learning. If a person is not capable of learning, he should support others and enable them to learn. If he does so, his merit is as great as those who learn.

Why does the Torah command the construction of the Ark first, and the other furnishings afterwards? To teach that a person should begin the day by regularly learning Torah for an hour or two, and then proceed to his work.

אַמָּתַיִם וָחֵצִי אָרְכּוֹ וְאַמָּה וָחֵצִי רָחְבּוֹ וְאַמָּה וָחֵצִי קֹמָתוֹ — *Its length is to be two cubits and a half, its width a cubit and a half, its height a cubit and a half* (25:10). Why *half*-cubits? To show that a learned man should consider himself low and incomplete, without pride or haughtiness.

וְצִפִּיתָ אֹתוֹ זָהָב טָהוֹר — *Cover it with pure gold* (25:11). This shows that God will make a shelter for Torah scholars and those who support their efforts, as it is written in *Koheles (Ecclesiastes)*: בְּצֵל הַחָכְמָה בְּצֵל הַכֶּסֶף — *In the shelter of wisdom, in the shelter of silver* (7:12). God places a protective canopy over those who learn His Torah and over those who support them. In *Mishlei (Proverbs)* we are told, עֵץ חַיִּים הִיא לַמַּחֲזִיקִים בָּהּ — *It is a tree of life to those who grasp it* (3:18). The Torah grants long life to those who support it, even if they are not capable of learning themselves.

מִבַּיִת וּמִחוּץ תְּצַפֶּנּוּ — *Within and without you shall cover it* (25:11). *Toldos Yitzchak* writes that these words show that a learned man should be as pure inside as he is out. There are many learned men who speak as if they were very good and pious, while in their hearts they are not so. Our Sages say that a learned man must be a mirror which reflects the same image from within and without.

Imrei Noam says that the Ark was made of wood covered with gold to teach us that we should cover the poor but learned man with gold.

◆§ Kingship, Priesthood, Scholarship

וְעָשִׂיתָ עָלָיו זֵר זָהָב — *Make upon it (the Ark) a crown of gold* (ibid.). R' Bechaye and *Toldos Yitzchak* point out that here the Torah says *upon it*, while in connection with the Table and the Altar it states וְעָשִׂיתָ לּוֹ — *make for it* a golden crown. The Table represents the crown of majesty and wealth, as the word לוֹ ("for it", or "for him") is used in connection with majesty: וְכָתַב לוֹ — *He [the king] shall* write for himself [a Sefer Torah] (Devarim 17:18). The Altar represents the crown of the priesthood, for there the Kohanim performed their divine service; and the word לוֹ (for him) is used in connection with the priesthood: וְהָיְתָה לוֹ — It shall be for him and his sons after him (Bamidbar 25:13). These two, the kingdom and the priesthood, are hereditary positions. If a father is a priest, the son is a priest; if the father is a king, his son inherits the kingship.

Not so with the Torah. There are times when the son of a learned man will be ignorant. For this reason the Torah here says עָלָיו [which also means "upon him"] — it is incumbent upon each man to make a crown for himself. A man must decide for himself to learn Torah, for it is not an inheritance from a father.

The Midrash says that the word עָלָיו (upon it) also shows that God's Torah stands above all other wisdom.

⇒§ The Cherubim

וְעָשִׂיתָ שְׁנַיִם כְּרֻבִים — You shall make two golden cherubim (25:18). R' Bechaye writes: Why is the word shnayim ("two") used, rather than the more common form, shnei? To show (by its dual form) that the two cherubim were not identical; one had the likeness of a maie, and the other of a female. When speaking of the Tablets the Torah says shnei, because they were identical.

At another time the Torah says מִבֵּין שְׁנֵי הַכְּרֻבִים — between the two cherubim (Bamidbar 7:89), using the word shnei. This shows that the cherubim showed us God's love for us, like the love of a man for a woman. The Gemara tells us that when our forefathers came to the Beis HaMikdash for one of the three yearly festivals the curtain was taken off the Ark, revealing the golden cherubim, to remind them that God loved them as a man loves a woman.

⇒§ The Table and its Loaves

וְעָשִׂיתָ שֻׁלְחָן — Make a Table (25:23). God commanded that they build a Table in the Tabernacle on which to place bread which was later eaten by the priests. A piece of bread the size of a chickpea would satisfy a person.

Why is a table called a shulchan, which means "sender" (from the root שלח, "to send")? Because God sends His blessings upon the table.

The Table was to be made of the wood of שטים (cedar), which is an acronym for שָׁלוֹם (peace), טוֹבָה (goodness), יְשׁוּעָה (salvation), and מְחִילָה (forgiveness). These blessings came because of the Table.

The same word is used in connection with the Ark and the Altar, because they, too, bring these blessings to the world. The Table is thus like the Altar, in that it atones for sin just as a sacrifice does.

In France the custom is to take the table of a righteous man who has died and built it into a coffin, to show that a person takes nothing to the next world except the charity which he has done with the food on his table.

וְעָשִׂיתָ קְּעָרֹתָיו — *You shall make its dishes* (25:29). They made iron pans on which they placed the bread when it was in the oven. After taking the bread out it was transferred to golden pans, where it was kept until *Shabbos* morning, when it was placed on the Table.

⋙ The Golden Menorah

וְעָשִׂיתָ מְנֹרַת זָהָב — *You shall make a golden Menorah* (candelabra) (25:31). God commanded that a golden *Menorah* with seven arms be built in order that a person coming to the Temple feel awe and reverence at the sight of the burning lamps. It was placed outside the curtain, before the people, to show that God Himself did not need the light, but had placed it there for the sake of the people.

It is known that when the soul sees illumination it derives great pleasure, for the soul comes from heaven, which is full of light. For this reason Shlomo HaMelech likened the soul to a candle, as it says, נֵר ה' נִשְׁמַת אָדָם — *Man's soul is a candle of God (Mishlei* 20:27).

The seven arms of the *Menorah* paralleled the seven stars which influence the world. It stood in the southern part because the people who live in the south have much Torah learning and wisdom, which are compared to candles, as it is written, נֵר מִצְוָה וְתוֹרָה אוֹר — *A mitzvah is a candle, and the Torah is light (Mishlei* 6:23). The Table, which symbolized wealth, stood in the north, for that is the source of wealth, as it is written, מִצָּפוֹן זָהָב יֶאֱתֶה — *Gold comes from the north (Iyov* 37:22). The *Menorah* stood near the table to show that you cannot learn Torah if you have no food.

Baal HaTurim notes that the letter ס does not appear in the portion containing the *Menorah*, to show that Satan does not appear where there is light. For this reason people should take care wherever possible to go out at night with a light.

⋙ Discord on Friday

The *Midrash* and *R' Bechaye*, in *Parashas Bereishis*, write that it is known that Satan has his greatest strength on *erev Shabbos*, Friday. The *Gemara* tells us that Satan would incite two men to fight every *erev Shabbos*. R' Meir came and on three occasions made peace between them. The people then heard Satan screaming: "R' Meir forced me out of my home by making peace between them. I cannot reside with them now!"

Why is his power great on *erev Shabbos*? Because God created demons late on *erev Shabbos*, they are most powerful then. On Friday evening we recite the prayer of *Magen Avos* to protect us from demons. We should be careful to hear the *chazan* (reader) say the blessing, and refrain from speaking during that time.

In his prayer book, R' Herz tells of a *rav* who, after his death, came to his disciple in a dream. The disciple saw that the *rav* had a stain on his forehead, and asked the reason. The *rav* answered that it was a punishment for not having cut his nails on *erev Shabbos*. (The *Sefer Hagan* warns that one should not cut one's nails on Thursday because they will begin to grow back on *Shabbos*.)

Women light candles on *erev Shabbos* because Satan was created together with the woman, and the candle drives Satan away.

✑§ Making the Furnishings

וּרְאֵה וַעֲשֵׂה בְּתַבְנִיתָם — *See, and make them in the pattern* (25:40). God had shown Moshe a *Menorah* of fire and told him to make an identical one of gold. Moshe was unable to imitate it, though, so God told him to throw gold into fire, and a *Menorah* came out of it.

R' Bechaye says that was *in the pattern* (בְּתַבְנִיתָם) rather than כְּתַבְנִיתָם, *like the pattern*, to show that Moshe was unable to do as God showed him, because our fire is unlike the fire of heaven, which is a spiritual thing.

The Table represents the riches of the world, and the *Menorah* represents the World to Come, which is full of light. The boards of the Tabernacle resemble the disciples who surround their *rav*, as the boards surround the Tabernacle. The curtains symbolize the working people who support Torah learning, as the curtains sheltered the Tabernacle from wind and rain.

❈　❈　❈

The *Haftorah* of *Parashas Terumah* may be found on p. 495.

פרשת תצוה

Parashas Tetzaveh

(27:20 — 30:10)

◄§ Oil and Incense

וְאַתָּה תְּצַוֶּה — *And you will command* (27:20). R' Bechaye writes that King Solomon said, in *Proverbs:* שֶׁמֶן וּקְטֹרֶת יְשַׂמַּח לֵב וּמֶתֶק רֵעֵהוּ מֵעֲצַת נָפֶשׁ — *Oil and incense gladden the heart, and so too the sweetness of a friend's wise counsel* (Mishlei 27:9). The verse teaches us that we should give food to strangers and to the poor, and speak warmly to them. Food is likened to oil and fragrant incense to teach that we should honor a pauper by serving him delicacies, succulent and fragrant, in order to gladden his heart. The words *sweetness of a friend* mean that we should speak sweetly to a pauper, just as if he were a close friend. We should speak sincerely, not like some people, who with cordial phrases invite the poor to come and eat, but do not really mean it.

On the words *Oil and incense gladden the heart*, the *Midrash* says that the oil of the *Beis HaMikdash* and its fragrant incense bring as much joy to God as the creation of the world did, as it is written, יִשְׂמַח ה' בְּמַעֲשָׂיו — *God rejoices in His creations (Tehillim* 104:31).

God created man after everything else, for man was the most important of the creations. Similarly, God commanded the High Priest to light the *Menorah* and burn the incense after the construction of the *Mishkan*, for these duties were the most important of all.

From the words *And you will command* we also learn that you (Moshe Rabbeinu) shall command them to light the *Menorah* with olive oil, rather than oil of sesame or nuts. The first oil pressed from the olives was used for the *Menorah;* the remainder was used for the *minchah* sacrifice.

✑§ Destruction and Curse

כָּתִית לַמָּאוֹר — *Pounded for light* (27:20). The first *Beis HaMikdash* stood for 410 years, and the second for 420 years — a total of 830 years. This is the numerical equivalent of the word כָּתִית ("pounded"), to show that the two Temples would be pounded and destroyed after 830 years. The Third *Beis HaMikdash*, however, which will be built when *Mashiach* comes, will stand forever, and the word לַמָּאוֹר hints at the everlasting light which he will radiate.

Baal HaTurim asks why Moshe's name is not mentioned in this entire *parashah*. When Moshe interceded because God wanted to destroy His people after the sin of the Golden Calf, Moshe told God: "If You destroy them, erase my name from Your Book." As a result, his name was not mentioned in this *parashah*. A righteous man's curse is never uttered in vain.

✑§ Light and Blessing

Tzror HaMor writes that the Jews are like olive oil; the Torah which they learn illuminates their way like the light of burning oil.

Why does the verse say וְיִקְחוּ אֵלֶיךָ — *take to you* (27:20)? This shows that if you keep the Torah properly, and heed its commandments, it will belong to you in this world and the next. No one can take it away from you.

It also says that the *Menorah* should be lit אֵלֶיךָ — *to you*, to show that God says: "I have no need for light. There is sufficient light in heaven" (i.e., the light is for the people, not for God). This can be likened to a person who leads a blind man, and tells him: "Light a candle for me." The blind man retorts, "I took you to light my way and lead me on the right path, and now you tell me to light a candle for you?" The man answers him: "I want you to light the candle, so that you do something for me, too."

God's people are like the blind man walking in the dark, with God lighting their way. He tells them to light a candle so that they will do something to serve Him, and as a result they will be found worthy of receiving many blessings.

✑§ The Priestly Vestments

וְאֵלֶּה הַבְּגָדִים אֲשֶׁר יַעֲשׂוּ — *These are the clothes which they shall make* (28:4). The High Priest is compared to an angel, and must have special garments to do his work. Just as an angel is pure, so must the *Kohen Gadol* be pure as he accomplishes his tasks.

The *Gemara* says that just as the sacrifices atoned for sins, so too

did the priestly vestments atone for sins. The breastplate, the *choshen*, was next to the heart, and atoned for sins committed against commandments connected to the heart. The *efod*, the apron, atoned for idol worship. The outer coat, the *me'il*, atoned for the sin of slander, and the coat which was worn underneath it, the *ksones*, atoned for accidental murder. The *mitznefes*, or hat, atoned for haughtiness. The *avnet*, which was a belt, atoned for evil feelings of the heart. The *tzitz*, a golden platelet for the High Priest's forehead, atoned for stubbornness; the trousers, *michnasayim*, atoned for lasciviousness.

R' Bechaye asks: Why are only six garments enumerated in this portion, when the High Priest actually wore eight garments? Because this *parashah* refers only to the garments in which Moshe Rabbeinu clothed him. The High Priest himself put on his trousers in private; and the *tzitz* was a platelet of gold worn on his forehead: it was an accessory rather than an article of clothing, and so was not mentioned here.

◦§ The Efod and the Choshen

וְעָשׂוּ אֶת הָאֵפֹד — *They shall make the efod* (28:6). R' Bechaye asks: Previously, the *choshen*, or breastplate, was mentioned before the *efod*. Why is the *efod* now placed before the *choshen*? The answer is that this is a list of the priestly garments, and the *efod* was more of a garment than the *choshen*. But previously the *choshen* was discussed first, because it bore the holy names upon it. There were twelve stones upon the *choshen,* and each stone bore the name of one of the Tribes.*

The *efod* was like a skirt, wide as a man's back and reaching from under a man's arm until his ankles. It had two straps at the shoulders. (R' Bechaye describes it as being worn like the undergarment with *tzitzis,* which is known as *arba kanfos.*) Each strap had an onyx set in gold attached to it, and the names of the Tribes were inscribed upon these stones, six on each. There were four rows of stones in the *choshen,* with three stones in each row, twelve stones in all. Each stone was inscribed with the name of a Tribe; the names Avraham, Yitzchak, and Yaakov and other holy names were also inscribed.

Each stone had six letters, totaling seventy-two, representing the hours in the six days of the week (excluding the nights). This was to show that the world, which was created in six days, exists in the merit of the twelve Tribes.

The names inscribed upon the stones of the *choshen* were called the *Urim veTumim.* Where there was a question to be answered, they would go to the High Priest. He would look at the *choshen* upon his heart to see which letters had shone, and then composed a word out of them and understood its meaning. He did not answer everyone's questions; he answered only the king or the entire community.

◂§ The First Row: Reuven, Shimon, Levi

R' Bechaye writes that the twelve stones were the most precious gems in the world. One stone, known as an *odem,* was a ruby. It was red, and it had Reuven's name inscribed on it, because he was humiliated and red-faced when he disturbed his father's sleeping quarters. The *segulah,* or distinctive spiritual influence, of a ruby is such that when a pregnant woman wears it, she does not miscarry. This, too, hints at Reuven, who found certain mandrakes of the field which promote fertility.

Shimon's name was inscribed on the stone *pitdah,* a topaz. It is green and yellow, because Shimon turned green and yellow during the sin with the Midianite women. Its *segulah* is that it cools the ardor of the body. The stone is found in great numbers in the land of Cush, where it is torrid and hot, and so the people are full of desires. They use the stone to cool their lust.

---

* In naming the twelve stones of the priestly vestments, we have followed the Yiddish of *Tz'enah Ur'enah.* There are, however, many other opinions among the commentators.

The name of Levi was on the stone *barekes*, a garfinkel, which gives off light like a candle. Noach (Noah) kept this stone in the ark for illumination. Because Levi was a great scholar, illuminating the eyes of Israel with Torah, his name was inscribed upon such a stone. Its charm is that it makes men clever.

◄§ The Second Row: Yehudah, Yissachar, Zevulun

The name of Yehudah (Judah) was inscribed on the stone *nofech*, carbuncle, which is green, because his face turned green with shame when he had relations with his daughter-in-law Tamar. When a person goes to war and wears this stone, his enemies fall before him. In the days of King David, the tribe of Yehudah was always victorious in battle.

Yissachar's name appeared on a *sapir*, or sapphire, which is pure white, because Yissachar studied Torah. Moshe carved off pieces of a sapphire for the Tablets and wrote the Ten Commandments on them. The sapphire from which the Tablets were taken stands under the Holy Throne. For this reason, one who learns Torah comes, after death, beneath the Throne. And so too is the Torah a cure for the body.

The name of the tribe of Zevulun was inscribed upon a *yahalom*, or mother-of-pearl. This indicates riches. It brings great luck when worn upon a person. It also helps induce sleep, since with Zevulun's birth, his mother said, הַפַּעַם יִזְבְּלֵנִי אִישִׁי — *Now my husband will dwell with me (Bereishis* 30:20), and sleep in my tent at night.

◄§ The Third Row: Dan, Naftali, Gad

Dan's name was inscribed upon a *leshem*, or jacinth, which has the form of the back of a man, to show that Dan left God to worship idols.

The name of Naftali was on a *shevo*, an agate, which brings a charm to its wearer — if one on horseback wears it, he does not fall off. The name Naftali means "clasped," for the stone causes a person to clasp and cling to his horse without falling. For this reason, his name appeared upon the stone.

Gad's name was on an *achlamah*, or crystal, which is found and recognized world-wide. Everyone knew the tribe of Gad, because they were so numerous. Also, Gad's victims in war were easily recognizable, because Gad would remove their victim's head and arm with one blow. Crystal strengthens a person's heart, so that he is not afraid in battle.

◆§ The Fourth Row: Asher, Yosef, Binyamin

The name of the tribe of Asher appeared on a stone called *tarshish*, a beryl.

The name of Yosef was on a stone called *shoham*, an onyx. It gives great charm to the wearer, just as Yosef was pleasing to everyone. One who wears the stone finds that people listen to him and accept what he says.

Binyamin's name was on a *yashpeh*. It is a three-colored stone: red and black and green. Its charm is that it stems the flow of blood, just as Binyamin stemmed the flow of his words, by not letting his father know that the brothers had sold Yosef. He was given the stone *yashpeh* because it can be separated into two words, *yesh peh* — "there is a mouth." Although he possessed a mouth, he did not reveal that his brothers had sold Yosef.

R' Bechaye writes that they had to keep these precious stones very clean, for if they were not spotless, they would lose their power.

◆§ The Shamir

The *Gemara* writes, in Tractate Sotah, that the *shamir* was a worm which they used to engrave the Tribes' names on the stones. It was as small as a grain of barley, and was created during the Six Days of Creation. The worm was kept in wool in a lead vessel, together with husks of barley. When the worm was placed on a stone or on iron or another hard material, the *shamir* would crack it.

◆§ A Mother of High Priests

Apropos High Priests: The *Yerushalmi* says, in Tractate *Yoma*, that there was once a woman named Kimchis, with seven sons, each of whom served as a High Priest in the *Beis HaMikdash*. The Sages asked her what she had done to be deserving of this privilege, and she answered that for all of her life she had never shown her hair to anyone, not even revealing it to the beams of her ceiling.

We find many righteous women who raised pious children because of their prayers and modesty. We see that when Chanah prayed in the *Beis HaMikdash* for children, God heard her prayers and she gave birth to a great son, the prophet Shmuel, or Samuel.

◆§ The Robe

וְעָשִׂיתָ אֶת מְעִיל הָאֵפוֹד — *You shall make a robe for the efod* (28:31). This too was for the High Priest, and on its lower hem were seventy-two bells, so that everyone would hear when he entered the *Beis*

HaMikdash — just as one does not enter the chamber of a great ruler unannounced.

Although God was certainly aware of who was entering, this was done in order to warn the angels inside that they must leave and allow the High Priest to enter and perform his tasks without harming him. When he left he also rang the bells so that the angels would return to serve God. He would ring as he entered for permission to come in, and as he left, for permission to exit.

৶ The Gold Platelet

וְעָשִׂיתָ צִּיץ זָהָב — *And you shall make a platelet of gold* (28:36). This was placed upon the forehead of the High Priest, and reached to his ears. There were holes in each end, with silk threads inserted inside. These were tied behind his neck, so that the plate stayed firmly upon his forehead.

৶ The Ordinary Kohanim

R' Bechaye points out how astounding it was that the *Kohanim* were able to function. They did the work in the Temple wearing one shirt, barefoot, and they bore severe cold both in summer and in winter. Because of this wise men were placed among them to check who was becoming weakened, as a result of the frequent immersions in cold water during the course of their work.

৶ Sacrifice and Prayer

וְזֶה הַדָּבָר אֲשֶׁר תַּעֲשֶׂה — *This is the thing which you shall do* (29:1). This refers to the offering of the sacrifices.

R' Bechaye writes: Why is the word *davar* ("thing") used here? To show that after the destruction of the *Beis HaMikdash*, when sacrifices could no longer be brought, words of prayer would be accepted by God in their stead. *Davar* shares the same root as *dibur*, the spoken words which would replace the sacrifices.

৶ The Levites' Daily Psalm

The Levites recited a different chapter from the Book of *Psalms* for each day. On the first day of the week they said *Psalm 24*: לַה׳ הָאָרֶץ וּמְלוֹאָהּ — *God's is the earth, and all of its fullness* — for the earth was created on the first day.

On the second day they recited *Psalm 48*: שִׁיר מִזְמוֹר לִבְנֵי קֹרַח — *A song of praise for the sons of Korach* — because they were Levites, separated from the rest of Israel by God, just as, on the second day of creation, God separated the water of the earth from the water of heaven, which is closer to Him.

On the third day of the week they said *Psalm* 82: בְּקֶרֶב אֱלֹהִים יִשְׁפֹּט — *He judges among the judges* — because on the third day God created the fruit with which He would judge man, the fruit which he would eat and which would cause his banishment from Eden.

On the fourth day of the week they said *Psalm* 94: אֵל נְקָמוֹת ה' — *The Lord is a God of vengeance* — because He punishes those who worship the sun and the moon, which were created on that day.

On the fifth day of the week they said *Psalm* 81: הַרְנִינוּ לֵאלֹהִים עוּזֵנוּ — *Sing aloud to God our strength*. In this Psalm God is called הַמַּעַלְךָ מֵאֶרֶץ מִצְרָיִם — *the One Who brought you out from the land of Egypt* (v. 11), out of the hands of Pharaoh. Pharaoh is likened to a great fish, which was created on the fifth day.

On the sixth day of the week they said *Psalm* 93: ה' מָלָךְ גֵּאוּת לָבֵשׁ — *God reigns; he is clothed in majesty* — like man, who was created on the sixth day, in the image of God. When man is righteous, he reigns over all of the world's creations.

On *Shabbos* the Levites said *Psalm* 92: מִזְמוֹר שִׁיר לְיוֹם הַשַּׁבָּת — *A song of praise for the Shabbos day*. God rests on *Shabbos*, and we, too, should rest.

❧ ❧ ❧

The *Haftorah* of *Parashas Tetzaveh* may be found on p. 498.

פרשת כי תשא
Parashas Ki Sisa

(30:11 — 34:35)

✑§ Length of Days

כִּי תִשָּׂא — *When you take the count* (30:12). Shlomo HaMelech says, in *Proverbs: Fear of God prolongs one's days, but the years of the wicked are shortened* (יִרְאַת ה' תּוֹסִיף יָמִים וּשְׁנוֹת רְשָׁעִים תִּקְצֹרְנָה; *Mishlei* 10:27). This shows us that every day God wreaks miracles for people, of which they are wholly unaware. It is known that fear shortens life, yet the righteous man fears God and lives long. This is miraculous. It is known that when a person eats well, he lives long, yet when the wicked eat well God still shortens their days.

Although we do find that some pious men do not live long, and some wicked men do, this is because the one was not entirely righteous nor the other entirely wicked. God may shorten the days of a righteous man in order to give him greater pleasure in the World to Come. A man must believe that God is making unseen miracles for him. One who does not so believe does not believe in the Torah; nor does he have real faith.

✑§ Counting Individuals

Why have our Sages told us that there is no blessing on something unless it remains uncounted? Because God conceals His miracles. For this reason, our Sages have said that when one counts or measures something, and then begs God to bless it, it is a vain prayer. An evil eye lurks over a thing which has been counted or measured.

For this reason God commanded that Israel not be counted, except by means of the coins called *shekalim*. Each person was told to give a one-half *shekel* coin, and then the coins were counted, so that the number of the population was then known.

The verse thus says that *each man shall redeem his soul* (30:12) with a half-*shekel* coin, וְלֹא יִהְיֶה בָהֶם נֶגֶף — *and there will be no plague (ibid.)* and no death. If they would have actually counted the people, then as each person was counted individually, God would have seen his sins and evil deeds and would have killed him. But when the community is united there are many good deeds between them, and one man protects the other.

◦§ The Holy Shekel

מַחֲצִית הַשֶּׁקֶל — *Half a shekel* (30:13). They must each give a half a *shekel* coin. When Moshe was ruler he had a silver coin minted. It was known as the *holy shekel* because it was used in the weighing of the various holy vessels. A first-born was redeemed with five *shekalim*. Other commandments were also fulfilled with the coin, and since these commandments are written in the holy Torah, it was called the *holy shekel*.

◦§ The Holy Tongue

The language of the Torah is called the Holy Tongue (לְשׁוֹן הַקֹּדֶשׁ), because in this language God spoke to Moshe, and because God's seventy Names and the names of His angels are in the Holy Tongue. The world was created with this language, and when the *Mashiach* (Messiah) comes, all will speak it, as it is written: *For then I will turn over to the nations a pure language* (שָׂפָה בְרוּרָה), *so they may call in God's Name (Tzephaniah* 3:9).

◦§ Atonement and Incense

Why did God command that they use half a *shekel*? Because when Israel fashioned the Golden Calf they transgressed the laws of the Ten Commandments. They were therefore told to give half a *shekel*, which contains ten halves [i.e., ten *gerah*; one *shekel* equaled twenty *gerah*], as an atonement for the Ten Commandments which they had contravened. Further, it served as an atonement for the sin of the Golden Calf, which was made at midday [lit., "at half-day"].

Tzror HaMor writes: Why does the portion of *Ki Sisa* follow that of the incense? Because the lighting of incense prevents plague, and taking a census causes plague. This shows us that by using the method of census involving the half-*shekel* they would not be harmed.

✑ Charity and Forgiveness

The verse tells us, וְנָתְנוּ אִישׁ כֹּפֶר נַפְשׁוֹ — *each man shall redeem his soul* (30:12), so that he will not be harmed by a plague resulting from the census. In the days of the *Beis HaMikdash*, it was the incense which prevented epidemic. With its destruction, charity acts to protect people from plague, as it is written, *Charity saves from death* (וּצְדָקָה תַּצִּיל מִמָּוֶת: *Mishlei* 10:2).

In the last verse of the preceding *parashah* (30:10) we learn that God forgives transgressions once a year, on Yom Kippur. And the opening words of our passage (כִּי תִשָּׂא) may also be understood to mean, "when You will forgive." Our verse regarding the half-*shekel* thus constitutes a prayer: "Forgive us our sins by virtue of the charity we give."

Why did God specifically command that we give *half* a coin? To show that God does not demand a great amount of charity — no more than half a *shekel*, from rich and poor alike.

R' Bechaye writes that they gave half a *shekel* to show that a person should not give his body his all, but only half of what he has, by not eating or drinking to excess; half should go to his soul, for the service of God.

From the *shekalim* which Israel gave were built the bases of silver in which the boards of the Tabernacle stood. This was done so that they would serve as an atonement for the sin of the Golden Calf. A penitent should hold himself low and humble, like a base or step which is trodden upon.

✑ The Basin

The portion discussing the wash basin follows that of the *shekalim*. The *shekalim* hint at charity, and the basin hints at the fact that one must wash his hands before eating. This shows that the greatest of all merits lies in giving a poor man something to eat.

Another reason that the description of the basin follows that of the *shekalim* is because one who does not give charity, like one who does not properly wash his hands before eating, is destined to poverty. Our Sages say that one who washes his hands with a generous amount of water will be given ample blessings.

The priests washed their hands and feet together in the basin. They placed their hands upon their feet and let water run over them.

There were twelve pipes in the basin, so that twelve priests could wash simultaneously, for all twelve were needed for the daily sacrifices. The priest who slaughtered the sacrifice, however, was not obligated to wash.

⇜ The Anointing Oil

שֶׁמֶן מִשְׁחַת קֹדֶשׁ יִהְיֶה זֶה לִי — *It shall be a holy anointing oil to Me* (30:31). R' Bechaye writes, in the name of *Ramban:* Why does the Torah say that the oil will be "to Me," to God? It ought to have said that the oil was for the *Kohanim,* used to purify them. The answer is that the oil was not used solely to anoint priests. Kings, including David, were anointed with that same oil.

⇜ Spice and the Variety of Life

The Torah then commanded that Israel make incense. They took eleven varieties of fragrant spices and burned them in the *Mishkan.* Among the spices was *chelbenah,* galbanum, which has a foul smell. This shows that God does not humiliate wicked men, once they have repented, if they consort with the righteous, and pray and fast.

Our Sages have said that if a congregation prays and fasts, but no sinners are among them, their prayers are not accepted. God has pleasure only when the wicked repent and join the righteous. If there are no wicked men among them, in the process of repentance, the righteous are cursed, for all of Israel is responsible for one another.

In the four *minim* (varieties of plants) used on the festival of Sukkos we see this same idea, similarly expressed. One of the four varieties is *aravah* (willow), which has neither good taste nor fragrant smell. This parallels the wicked, who have neither Torah learning nor observance. All of the other varieties have some quality — the *esrog* (citron) is fragrant and tasty, the *hadas* (myrtle) fragrant, and the *lulav* (palm frond) grows on a date tree, and dates are tasty. Yet we bind the *aravos* together with the others, to show that God wants the wicked to be included among us, so that they will repent and be counted as part of the community of the righteous.

⇜ Making the Vestments

God said: רְאֵה קָרָאתִי בְשֵׁם בְּצַלְאֵל — *See, I have called Bezalel by name* (31:2). This teaches us that there was no one among them who knew how to work with gold, silver, and silk. When they were in Egypt they learned only how to make bricks. Bezalel was twelve years old at the time. God then prophetically gave him the knowledge of working with gold, silver, silk, and other materials.

אֹתוֹ וְאֵת אָהֳלִיאָב בֶּן אֲחִיסָמָךְ לְמַטֵּה דָן — *And with him Ahaliav, son of Achisamach, of the tribe of Dan* (31:6). "Together with Bezalel, you shall take Ahaliav of the tribe of Dan, although he is from a lowly tribe and Bezalel is from the prestigious tribe of Yehudah (Judah)."

This teaches us that a person should not think too much of himself. If he is from a fine family he should link himself with people from a lowly one, because rich and poor are equal in God's eyes.

The people were told to make vestments for the High Priest. These are called בִּגְדֵי שְׂרָד, which means "garments of office," but the root שׂרד also means "left over." Because of the priestly garments, Israel were saved and were "left over" in the world.

⋘ Alexander the Great

The *Gemara,* in Tractate *Yoma,* tells the following story. When Alexander of Macedonia came to conquer Yerushalayim, Shimon HaTzaddik, the High Priest, went out to meet him, dressed in the garments which he wore in the *Beis HaMikdash.* When the ruler saw him he stood up from his chariot and bowed down before him. He let the city remain free.

When his servants questioned him to find out why he had treated a Jew so respectfully, he said: "Whenever I go fight a battle, I see the image of a person dressed exactly as he was, and then I am victorious." Actually, an angel had revealed himself to Alexander during the course of battle, an angel dressed in the garments of the High Priest.

⋘ Observing Shabbos

אַךְ אֶת שַׁבְּתֹתַי תִּשְׁמֹרוּ — *But keep My Sabbaths* (31:13). This teaches us that although God commanded that we build a Tabernacle, we must keep the *Shabbos.* We are not allowed to desecrate it in order to do more work on the Tabernacle.

Our Sages say that the word אַךְ ("but") is limiting: it comes to show that sometimes we must desecrate the *Shabbos* — when there is danger of death.

We should know that *Shabbos* was the first commandment which Israel was given, before the Giving of the Torah. *Shabbos* is considered equal to the entire Torah. Our Sages have said that

Yerushalayim was destroyed because the people did not keep *Shabbos* properly. They have also said that if Israel would keep two *Shabbosos* correctly, *Mashiach* would come.

וּשְׁמַרְתֶּם אֶת הַשַּׁבָּת — *You shall keep the Shabbos* (31:14). The Torah repeats again that we must keep the *Shabbos* properly, to show that we should receive the *Shabbos* even before nightfall on Friday, and cling to it even after it has gone. We should try to prolong the *Shabbos* by adding some of the weekday time to it.

מְחַלְלֶיהָ מוֹת יוּמָת — *Her desecrators will surely die* (31:14). Whoever does work forbidden on *Shabbos*, in front of witnesses and after proper warning, shall be sentenced by the Sanhedrin to stoning. If someone has not been warned, or if there were no witnesses, God Himself cuts off the desecrator.

לַעֲשׂוֹת אֶת הַשַּׁבָּת — *To make the Shabbos* (31:16). On *erev Shabbos* (the day before *Shabbos*; i.e., Friday) we must prepare everything for *Shabbos*. God bestows his blessing upon a person's money because of his *Shabbos* preparations.

Tzror HaMor asks: Why does the Torah twice state that we must keep the *Shabbos*? Because of two special *Shabbosos*: *Shabbos HaGadol* ("the Great *Shabbos*"; i.e., the *Shabbos* prior to Pesach), when the body was liberated from the slavery of Egypt, and *Shabbos Teshuvah* ("the *Shabbos* of Repentance"; i.e., the *Shabbos* prior to Yom Kippur), when the soul is cleansed of all sin. "Because of these two *Shabbosos* it is only right that you keep My *Shabbos*, remembering the miracles which I have done for you."

◆§ Shabbos as a Sign

The *Gemara* says, in Tractate *Beitzah:* R' Shimon bar Yochai says that all the commandments were given openly, but the *Shabbos* was given in a hidden manner, as it is written, *It is a sign* (אוֹת הִיא) *between Me and the Children of Israel* (31:17); that is, given between God and the Jews alone.

R' Bechaye asks: How can it be said that *Shabbos* was given in a concealed way? Was it not mentioned as part of the Ten Commandments, which were given openly? Actually, the *Gemara* means to say that *Shabbos* was given to our souls, which are hidden within the body. Not only need the body rest, but the soul, too, will rest by learning Torah, for this gives repose to the soul.

⋅§ Spiritual Re-creation

This is the reason that our Sages say that *Shabbos* should be [to borrow a phrase properly pertaining to *Yom-Tov*] "half to God and half to yourselves." Half the day should be devoted to food and drink, in order to give joy to the body; half the day should be given over to learning and the observance of the commandments, in order to give the soul its happiness. This is not what some people, who spend the day in idle talk, actually do.

For this reason the verse says, בֵּינִי וּבֵין בְּנֵי יִשְׂרָאֵל — *Between Me and the Children of Israel* (31:17). It is solely between God and Israel; that is, they can learn Torah, and eat and drink — but they should speak of nothing else.

Why does the verse say "to make" the *Shabbos*? To show that we should "make" our repentance on *Shabbos*, by studying Torah and thinking of the service of God. During the course of the week a person does not have the leisure to do so, because of his job or business.

⋅§ The Dignity of a Scholar

Tzror HaMor says that "to make" can be understood as explained by the *Gemara*: even if a person has one hundred servants, he himself should prepare for *Shabbos*. We find that R' Yosef was a respected communal leader, with many servants, yet he himself cleaned the head of a calf over the fire for *Shabbos*. Rava, too, was a prominent citizen, and head of a large household of servants, yet he himself salted the fish for *Shabbos*.

⋅§ Teaching and Learning

וַיִּתֵּן אֶל מֹשֶׁה כְּכַלֹּתוֹ לְדַבֵּר אִתּוֹ — *And He gave to Moshe, when He had finished speaking to him* (31:18). God gave Moshe the tablets when He had finished speaking with him. The word כְּכַלֹּתוֹ ("when He had finished") shows that God gave Moshe the tablets as a gift, as one gives a gift to a bride (for the word also suggests another meaning — "like his bride"). It was difficult for Moshe to master the entire Torah in such a short time, in forty days, but God granted him the wisdom and strength to do so.

Resh Lakish says: When a person tells Torah to others, and it is not sweet to them, better that they should not have been created. But when Israel accepted the Torah, it was sweet to them, just as a bride is beloved to her groom.

R' Shimon says: Just as a bride is bedecked with 24 ornaments, so should a learned man bedeck himself with the 24 Books of Torah, Prophets, and Writings.

Tzror HaMor says: The Torah stresses *when He had finished* to show that Israel, thinking that Moshe had delayed, were wrong. As soon as God finished speaking with him Moshe came down with the tablets. For this reason, God punished them.

✑§ The Two Tablets

שְׁנֵי לֻחֹת הָעֵדֻת — *The two tablets of testimony (ibid.).* God gave Israel two tablets which bear witness to the fact that His Presence rests among them. The tablets were like a king's message to his people announcing that he is among them.

R' Bechaye writes: Why did God not write the Commandments upon one tablet? Because they were to bear witness [and two witnesses are always needed in court]. The tablets were made of stone, which comes from the earth, while the writing was divine, so that both heaven and earth would bear witness when Israel would not observe the Torah properly, as it is written, *I will call heaven and earth as witnesses against them* (וְאָעִידָה בָּם אֶת הַשָּׁמַיִם וְאֶת הָאָרֶץ; *Devarim* 31:28). When they do not heed the Torah the sky does not give its rain nor the earth its wheat.

The tablets were made of stone because the punishment for most of these transgressions was by stoning.

✑§ A Momentous Mistake

וַיַּרְא הָעָם כִּי בֹשֵׁשׁ מֹשֶׁה — *The people saw that Moshe delayed* (32:1). Moshe went up on Mt. Sinai on the seventh day of Sivan, telling them that he would be there for forty days, descending on the fortieth, after six daylight hours had elapsed. He did not count the day which he ascended in the reckoning, and therefore expected to descend on the seventeenth day of Tammuz, after six hours. The twenty-three remaining days of Sivan and seventeen of Tammuz would total forty days.

The people thought that the seventh day of Sivan, too, was counted, so they expected Moshe to arrive after six hours on the sixteenth day of Tammuz.

When they saw that Moshe did not come as expected, they said that he was delayed, and that the six hours had passed [a play on the similarity between the words בֹשֵׁשׁ — "delayed", and בָּא שֵׁשׁ — "the six have come"]. They said that he must have disappeared.

The *Midrash* says: That day Satan came and brought darkness to the world. He showed them an image of a bier being carried in heaven, so that they would think that Moshe had died while in heaven.

◈§ Chronology

They made the Calf on the sixteenth of Tammuz, in the afternoon, and on the morning of the seventeenth they brought sacrifices to it. After six hours Moshe descended from the mountain. Immediately upon seeing the Calf, he broke the tablets.

On the eighteenth of Tammuz he executed those who had worshiped it, and he ascended again on the nineteenth in order to pray for forgiveness for Israel's sin. He remained for forty days once again — the ten remaining days of Tammuz and the entire month of Av, which has thirty days. The forty days thus ended on Rosh Chodesh Elul.

Moshe then ascended again in order to receive the new set of tablets. He remained for an additional forty days — the entire month of Elul, and ten days of Tishrei — which ended on Yom Kippur, the Day of Atonement. At the end of that forty-day period, God forgave the Jews and told them to give their contributions to the *Mishkan*. Immediately after Yom Kippur they brought gifts of gold and silver, silk and gems. We see from this that the incident of the Calf actually took place before the construction of the *Mishkan*.

◈§ The Making of the Calf

וַיַּעֲשֵׂהוּ עֵגֶל מַסֵּכָה — *He made it a molten calf* (32:4). R' Bechaye writes, in the name of *Ramban:* Why did Aharon form the shape of an ox? Because there is the figure of an ox on the left side of the holy throne, facing north, and much harm comes out of the north. This was particularly true in the desert where Israel were, a barren and evil wasteland. Aharon fashioned the shape of an ox, as if to ask that God should help His people, and send them a favorable wind from the left side of the holy throne.

וַיֹּאמֶר אֲלֵהֶם אַהֲרֹן פָּרְקוּ נִזְמֵי הַזָּהָב — *He said to them: Take off the golden rings* (32:2). Aharon told them: "Take your wives' earrings and I will make a god of them." He thought that the wives would not give over their jewelry so readily, thus allowing Moshe more time to return.

Aharon himself knew that Moshe was to return the next day, but

Israel, in their wickedness, refused to listen to him. Aharon feared that they would kill him as they had killed Chur, his nephew.

They had first approached Chur, asking that he fashion an idol for them. When he had demurred they murdered him. Aharon feared that they would kill him, too, but his intentions were honorable. He hoped to prevent Israel from idol worship by suggesting that they gather together the women's jewelry.

The women were pious and refused to give their earrings, so the men took their own rings and brought the gold to Aharon. Aharon took the gold and flung it into the fire, wrapped in a scarf. The magicians from among the *erev rav* (Egyptians who had joined the Jews during the Exodus) used their magic, and a calf came out of the fire.

Some of our Sages say that it was made by a person by the name of Michah, who had been taken out of the cement in Egypt. When the Jews failed to make their quota of bricks, their children were placed in the cement. Moshe protested to God: "Perhaps the Jews have sinned, but their children have not!" Answered God: "Those children are all wicked. See for yourself — take one of the children and let him live. You will see if he grows up wicked." Moshe then rescued a child and named him Michah, from the root מוך, meaning "crushed," because he had been compressed within the cement bricks.

This Michah was very wicked. It was he who took a silver plate upon which Moshe had written the name of God. Moshe had used this plate to bring up the casket of Yosef (Joseph) from the depths of the Nile River. After Yosef's death, the Egyptians had placed his body in an iron coffin and put it in the Nile. When the time came for the people to leave Egypt, they could find no trace of the coffin. Moshe took a silver plate and wrote upon it the words עֲלֵה שׁוֹר ("Rise up, ox"), because Yosef is referred to as an ox (cf. *Devarim* 33:17). He threw the plate into the river and the casket floated up.

This plate Michah now took and threw it into the fire. As a result a calf came out of the fire, a calf which Israel revered as a god.

⋖§ Aharon's Stratagem

וַיַּרְא אַהֲרֹן — *And Aharon saw* (32:5). He saw that the Calf was alive and prancing, and he was unable to persuade Israel not to worship it. He built an altar for it, thinking that he would stall until the arrival of Moshe. Had all of Israel built it, each would have contributed a stone, and it would have been quickly completed.

Therefore, he alone built the altar, so that it would take longer.

He was afraid that if they killed him as they had killed Chur, there would be no atoning for their sin. "Better that I commit one sin, which God will forgive," he thought.

R' Bechaye writes that Aharon said to himself: "My intentions are purely for the sake of God. My only sin is in the actual construction of the idol, which is a transgression of the prohibition, *Do not make for yourselves an image* (לֹא תַעֲשֶׂה לְךָ פֶסֶל; 20:4). One is not obligated to let oneself be killed for this transgression."

⋙ Frivolity

וַיָּקֻמוּ לְצַחֵק — *They rose up to make merry* (32:6). They broke out in dancing and frivolity.

Tanna deVei Eliyahu writes: R' Akiva says that mirth and hilarity bring a person to many sins and to immorality, as it is written: *Hearken to the words of God, you scoffers ...* (שִׁמְעוּ דְבַר ה' אַנְשֵׁי לָצוֹן; *Yeshayahu* 28:14ff). God tells Israel: "My children, for 974 generations before the creation of the world I studied Torah. Since the day that I created the world I sit on My throne for eight hours a day studying Torah; I judge the world for eight hours each day; and for eight hours a day I sustain the world. I do not laugh, except when a wicked person schemes against the righteous, as it is written, זֹמֵם רָשָׁע לַצַּדִּיק — *The wicked man plans harm for the righteous* (*Tehillim* 37:12). This is followed by the verse, ה' יִשְׂחַק לוֹ — *God laughs at him*, letting no evil befall the righteous. But other than that, I do not laugh at all. Yet you busy yourselves with hilarity."

⋙ Moshe Intercedes

God told Moshe: לֶךְ רֵד — "*Go, descend* (32:7) from the mountain, for your people have ruined everything." Moshe answered: "Today you call them my people, but when they were enslaved in Egypt you said, 'I will free *My* people, they are *My* children.'"

Moshe prayed on Israel's behalf, and said: "If they deserve to be burnt, remember the merit of Avraham, who allowed himself to be thrown into a fiery furnace. If they deserve death at the sword, remember the merit of Yitzchak, who stretched his neck out on Your altar, to let himself be slaughtered for Your sake. If they deserve exile, remember the merit of Yaakov, who was exiled in Lavan's house because of Esav."

אֲשֶׁר נִשְׁבַּעְתָּ לָהֶם בָּךְ — *To whom You swore by Yourself* (32:13). Moshe said: "You swore by Your Name that You would not allow

Israel to be destroyed. You did not even swear by heaven and earth. It is therefore not right for You to break Your promise."

This situation is analogous to a king who plants a vineyard with precious vines. After the first year the king tests the wine, and finds it sour. He wants to destroy the entire vineyard, but a knowledgeable gardener assures him that though the first year's wine is not good, it will improve the next year. This is what Moshe was saying to God: Israel will become more righteous with time.

Moshe also told God: "You promised that You would make them more numerous than the stars in the sky, and that You would give them *Eretz Yisrael*. You must keep Your word."

God was appeased by his words, and forgave their sin.

◆§ Among the Angels

וַיִּפֶן וַיֵּרֶד מֹשֶׁה — *Moshe turned and went down* (32:15). He descended from the mountain, keeping his face turned toward God. We too do this, at the conclusion of the prayer of *Shemoneh Esreh*. We walk backwards, as though God is standing before us.

Yalkut writes: Moshe wanted to go down from the mountain, when he was accosted by five evil angels, who wanted to kill him. Terrified, he clutched at God's throne. God protected him, and spread His cloud over him.

We see from this the immensity of sin. Before Israel sinned, Moshe walked through heaven unscathed, but once they had transgressed he stood terrified before the five angels.

The angel's names were Af, Ketzef, Mashbis, Mashchis, and Chemah [which are five words denoting anger and destruction]. With Moshe's mention of Avraham, Yitzchak, and Yaakov, three of the angels disappeared, leaving over two, Af and Chemah. Moshe then asked God: "Take one angel, and I will fight the other one." This is hinted at in the verse, קוּמָה ה' בְּאַפֶּךָ — *Rise, God, in Your anger* (אַף — "anger"): that is, "Stand up, God, next to Your angel called Af."

◆§ The Two Tablets

וּשְׁנֵי לֻחֹת הָעֵדֻת בְּיָדוֹ ... כְּתֻבִים מִשְּׁנֵי עֶבְרֵיהֶם — *The two tablets of testimony in his hand ... written on both sides* (32:15). It was possible to read the tablets from both sides. This was a miracle — how is it possible for a person to write something which is readable from both sides? For when you turn the writing to the other side, it is backwards!

וְהַלֻּחֹת מַעֲשֵׂה אֱלֹהִים הֵמָּה — *The tablets were the work of God*
(32:16). They were created for His glory. They are termed God's
work because He busies Himself with the Torah and revels in it both
day and night.

R' Bechaye asks why the Torah describes the glory of the tablets
here. Ought it not have described them in the previous portion,
when we were told that they were first given to Moshe? The answer
is that this shows us that despite the glory of the tablets, Moshe
unhesitatingly broke them when the Jews sinned.

R' Bechaye raises another question: How could Moshe possibly
break the tablets on his own, when they were God's holy writings?
Even though Israel had sinned and were not worthy of receiving
them, he did not have to break them. He could have merely returned
them to God, and asked for God's instructions.

This can be likened to a master who sends a letter bearing his seal
to his servants, in the hands of a messenger. If the servants refuse to
accept the letter, he returns it to the master. Similarly, Moshe ought
to have brought the tablets back to God.

The answer is that Moshe saw that the letters of the tablets flew
out of them. When a master sends a letter without his seal, it is
worthless. Similarly, the tablets without their writing had lost their
value, and he could break them.

The letters of the tablet are likened to its soul, while the tablets
themselves are its body. When the soul deserts the body, the body is
ready for burial. When Moshe saw the letters fly off, he broke the
tablets.

Our Sages say that the tablets became very heavy in Moshe's hands after the letters flew off, just as a man becomes heavier after his death, when his soul departs. For this reason, it first says that the tablets were בְּיָדוֹ — *in his hand* (32:15), while after Israel worshiped the Calf, it says, וַיַּשְׁלֵךְ מִיָּדָו אֶת הַלֻּחֹת — *he flung the tablets from his hands* (32:19) — that is, from both his hands, for even with both hands he was unable to hold them.

✍ Moshe Descends

וַיִּשְׁמַע יְהוֹשֻׁעַ — *And Yehoshua heard* (32:17). He heard the shouts of Israel, as they danced and sang. Yehoshua was not part of their camp; he was awaiting Moshe. God sent him manna to eat separately.

Yehoshua told Moshe: "There is a loud noise in the encampment, like the sounds of a battle."

"These are not the words of battle," said Moshe. "After a battle the victors shout in exultation and the vanquished wail in their despair. What I hear is shouts of frivolity and laughter."

When Moshe came to the people and saw that they were worshiping the Calf, he was furious with them and broke the tablets. He said to himself: "One who worships idols is forbidden to eat the Pesach sacrifice. How much more, then, are they unworthy of receiving the tablets, which contain with them all of the Torah." And he broke the tablets.

Toldos Yitzchak writes: Why did Moshe not break the tablets while still in heaven, immediately upon hearing from God that Israel had made the Calf? Because he thought that they might have already regretted their actions. But when he came among them and saw them dancing around the Calf, with no regrets, he broke the tablets.

Tzror HaMor writes that he broke them in front of the people in order to emphasize to them that their sin had lost them the beautiful tablets made of precious stones.

Moshe took the Calf and burnt it down to ashes. These he threw into the water and had the people drink of it. Moshe was testing to see which of them had served the Calf with his entire heart, just as a *sotah*, a woman suspected of adultery, is given water from the *Beis HaMikdash*. If it does not harm her, it is a sign that she is guiltless.

✍ Punishment

Those who publicly worshiped the Calf were put to death by Moshe; those who rejoiced in their hearts turned green and yellow after drinking the water. The Sages say that those who worshiped the Calf before witnesses, after having been properly warned not to, were killed by sword. Those who worshiped before witnesses, without having received due warning, were killed by God in a plague. Those who had no witnesses as well turned green and yellow from the water.

Although God did not need the proof of the water, men might have said that the deaths were due to sickness, rather than the sin. Therefore the people were given the water to drink, to show that it was the water of the Calf which turned them green.

וַיַּעֲמֹד מֹשֶׁה בְּשַׁעַר הַמַּחֲנֶה — *Moshe stood in the gate of the camp* (32:26). He announced: "Whoever wishes to serve God, come to me." The men of the tribe of Levi gathered around him, for they had not served the Calf. Moshe commanded that they take their swords and kill all of those who had served the Calf, even if they were relatives, even if they were their fathers or sons. The sons of Levi then killed three thousand men of Israel.

Moshe now pleaded with God for forgiveness. "If You will not forgive them," he said, "*erase me, please, from Your book which You have written*" (מְחֵנִי נָא מִסִּפְרְךָ אֲשֶׁר כָּתָבְתָּ; 32:32).

"I will forgive them," answered God, "but I will repay them slowly." There is no sorrow which comes upon Israel that does not contain a bit of the punishment for the sin of the Calf.

וַיִּגֹּף ה' אֶת הָעָם — *God struck the people* (32:35), killing those who had worshiped the Calf before witnesses, but without benefit of due warning.

◆§ Stripped of Divine Grace

וַיִּשְׁמַע הָעָם אֶת הַדָּבָר הָרָע הַזֶּה — *The people heard this evil thing* (33:4). They heard the news that God was stripping them of their ornaments, and they grew frightened and wept. For when they had received the Torah, God had given each person two ornaments. Now the people had to take them off.

R' Bechaye writes, in the name of R' Chananel, that God told them: "Now, *take off your ornaments from you* (וְעַתָּה הוֹרֵד עֶדְיְךָ מֵעָלֶיךָ; 33:5), that is, the clothing which you wore at Mt. Sinai. Now that you have sinned, you must remove it."

R' Bechaye raises a question. In an earlier verse it is written, *No man put his ornaments upon himself* (וְלֹא שָׁתוּ אִישׁ עֶדְיוֹ עָלָיו; 33:4): the people themselves had removed this clothing. Later, it says that

God commanded them to take it off. The answer is that first they had removed their clothing out of respect, but now it had become a command, and they were forced to remove it.

Even Shoev also asks why the Torah first says that the people shed the clothing and later that God commanded them to take it off. The answer is that these were the luminous garments that an angel wears when he reveals himself to the pious and the wise. In heaven an angel wears no clothing, for he is composed of fire, but when he reveals himself on earth he puts on clothing. Such clothing did God give to Israel on Mount Sinai. Even the Angel of Death could not harm them while they wore it.

After they had made the Calf they were ashamed to openly wear such garb, and so they put other clothing on top of it, as it says, וְלֹא שָׁתוּ אִישׁ עֶדְיוֹ עָלָיו — *No man put his ornaments upon himself* (33:4): they did not wear them openly. Then God told them that they must take off the clothing altogether, and so it says, וַיִּתְנַצְּלוּ בְנֵי יִשְׂרָאֵל אֶת עֶדְיָם — *the Children of Israel stripped themselves of their ornaments* (33:6). All of this they lost because of the Calf.

Moshe took the clothing away. Nevertheless, we find a few righteous men over whom the Angel of Death has no sway, even generations after the sin of the Calf.

⋅§ Rabbah and the Angel of Death

The *Gemara* tells us, in Tractate *Bava Metzia*, that certain wicked men once slandered Rabbah bar Nachmani, claiming he was harming the government by assembling all of the Jews for his speeches on Rosh HaShanah and Pesach, so that they could not be found in their homes. When Rabbah became aware of the libel he fled, so the local ruler sent a servant to search for him.

The servant came to the inn where Rabbah had concealed himself. The landlord set a table before him, with two cups of wine for him to drink. Suddenly, the servant's face became paralyzed on one side. The members of the household came to Rabbah to find out how to heal the man, and he told them to set the table before him once again, and give him another cup of wine. They did as they were advised, and the man was cured.

The servant then said: "I know that Rabbah must be here." He searched, found him, and locked him in a fortress. "I will not reveal Rabbah's hiding place," he said, "even if they kill me for the information. But if they use torture, I will be forced to confess and bring him out to them."

Rabbah prayed and the wall split. He fled to a field, sat on a tree stump, and studied Torah.

At that time, a scholarly disputation was taking place in heaven on the law governing a leprous sore which a man had contracted before his hair turned white. The man remains clean, argued God, while the rest of the Heavenly Yeshivah argued that he was thereby rendered unclean. Finally, they decided to ask Rabbah Bar Nachmani: his ruling would be decisive.

They sent the Angel of Death for Rabbah but the angel could do nothing to him because he was studying Torah. The angel then caused the leaves to rustle. Rabbah thought that the authorities were coming after him.

"I would rather die at God's hand than at the hands of men," he thought — and the Angel of Death took him.

With his death he ruled that the sore did not render the man impure, and a heavenly voice rang out: "Happy are you, Rabbah, whose soul went out on the word 'pure.' "

A letter fell into the town of Pumbedisa, announcing that Rabbah had been taken to the Heavenly Yeshivah. Abbaye and other rabbis searched for the place where he had died, in order to bury him, but they did not know where his body was. Then, from afar, they saw a flock of birds floating next to each other, sheltering his body with the shadow of their wings so that it would not grow foul. In this way they were able to find him.

They eulogized him for three days and nights, and then a letter fell from heaven announcing that anyone who left the eulogy would be excommunicated. They continued their eulogies for another seven days, and then a heavenly message announced that they could return home.

We see from this incident that the Torah can save a person from the Angel of Death.

In Tractate *Shabbos*, in the chapter beginning *Bameh Madlikin*, the *Gemara* tells a similar story regarding King David, and how the Angel of Death could not harm him as he learned Torah.

◄§ R' Shimon ben Chalafta

Another story is told, of how R' Shimon ben Chalafta once went to the town of Tzippori, accompanied by many other rabbis, for a circumcision. After they had finished eating the child's father asked them all to make merry.

"Just as I have merited giving you wine for the circumcision," he said, "may I merit to give you wine at the child's marriage." And everyone answered Amen.

When the rabbis left they met the Angel of Death looking very depressed. They asked him the reason for his sadness, and he answered: "I have a letter authorizing me to kill the child after thirty days, and you have just annulled the decree by answering Amen to the father's blessing."

"Do you have a decree concerning us?" asked R' Shimon. "If so, show us."

"You learn Torah and fulfill the commandments," said the angel. "I have no power to harm you."

Answered R' Shimon: "Just as you have no power over us, so shall you have no power over our words, and over the Amen which we answered. May we indeed merit to drink wine at the child's marriage!"

We see that the righteous can annul a decree made by God. God decreed that men shall dwell on earth and the angels in heaven. Then came Moshe, a man who went to heaven, and who caused God to come down to earth, to Mount Sinai, accompanied by angels.

God created the angels in such a manner that they did not eat. Yet when the angels visited Avraham they were forced to dine. God created man with the necessity for food, yet Moshe was in heaven without food for forty days. God created the sea to be wet; Moshe came and dried it. God created day to be day and night to be night; Yaakov came and changed day into night and night into day, for the day became longer than it should have been.

◄§ The Torah among Mortals

Our Sages say that after the Torah was given, God's holy name was placed over Israel and even the Angel of Death had no domination over them. This is hinted at in the words חָרוּת עַל הַלֻּחֹת — *engraved upon the tablets*, which can also be read as "free, because of the tablets" [from the similarity between the words חָרוּת — "engraved", and חֵרוּת — "freedom"]. They were freed from the Angel of Death because of the Torah, which is contained within the tablets.

With the construction of the Calf, however, God removed His name from them. Moshe alone took the glory and the crown of all Israel. This is the reason that it is written after, וּמֹשֶׁה יִקַּח אֶת הָאֹהֶל — *and Moshe would take the tent* (33:7). The word *ohel* ("tent") also suggests a connotation of light, as in the words, בְּהִלּוֹ נֵרוֹ (*Iyov* 29:3). That is, Moshe took all of the light.

◆§ Moshe's Tent

Moshe placed his tent 2,000 cubits away from the people, for it was as if they had been excommunicated. *And whoever sought God* (וְהָיָה כָּל מְבַקֵּשׁ ה'; 33:7), whoever wanted to learn His Torah, went out to Moshe's tent.

Our Sages learn from this that whoever went out to Moshe was like someone who went to search for God. This shows that one who goes out to greet a scholar or sage is like one who greets God Himself.

When Moshe went into his tent all of Israel stood in the doorways of their homes until he had entered. Then a cloud came from heaven and remained poised in front of the door of his tent. All of the people then bowed down, each in front of his tent, towards the Divine Presence which rested within the cloud.

The *Tanchuma* writes that *whoever came to find God* (וְהָיָה כָּל מְבַקֵּשׁ ה'; 33:7) includes the angels. An angel who wished to leave heaven in order to do his task had to first go to Moshe's tent to get permission from God, Who was to be found there. When the sun and the moon wished to go out and illuminate the world, they too had to go to Moshe's tent for God's permission.

פָּנִים אֶל פָּנִים — *God spoke to Moshe face to face* (33:11). He spoke to him openly and publicly. After speaking with Him, Moshe would go to the encampment and teach the people what he had learned from God. He did this from Yom Kippur until Rosh Chodesh Nissan. After Rosh Chodesh Nissan, when the *Mishkan* was built, God did not speak with Moshe in his tent; He spoke in the *Mishkan* instead. In explanation of this change, the *Midrash* says that God told Moshe: "I am angry with Israel, and you are angry with Israel. Who, then, will bring them back lovingly? Return, therefore, to your tent among them."

◆§ Moshe's Request

Moshe told God: רְאֵה אַתָּה אֹמֵר אֵלַי הַעַל אֶת הָעָם הַזֶּה — "*See, You tell me, 'Bring up this nation'* (33:12). You have not told me, however, whom You will send with me; that is, You told me that You would send an angel with me, but I do not consent to that. Better it would be for You Yourself to accompany me. You have said that I will be found more worthy than all other men, and that I have found favor in Your eyes. Therefore let me know what reward You give to those whom You favor. You have said, 'I will make you into a great nation,' and that You would destroy Israel. This I do not want, for Israel has been Your nation for a long time."

He said: "My Presence will go with you" (וַיֹּאמַר פָּנַי יֵלֵכוּ; 33:14). God told him: "I Myself will accompany you, instead of an angel." Answered Moshe: "That is good; now all will know that You love us."

◌§ A Lesson in Prayer

When Moshe saw that God was granting his requests, he asked Him: *Show me, please, Your glory* (הַרְאֵנִי נָא אֶת כְּבֹדֶךָ; 33:18). God answered: "I will reveal Myself somewhat. You must do as I say, and you can see no more. I will teach you, too, to pray to Me. Do not be afraid that when the merit of the forefathers ends there will be no hope, heaven forbid, for Israel. I will teach you how to pray, so that Israel will have hope."

"You shall hide within a cave," God continued, "and I will reveal Myself upon a nearby rock. I will wrap Myself within a *tallis*, as a *chazzan* does, and will show you how to pray. Then you will teach Israel to say: ה' ה' אֵל רַחוּם וְחַנּוּן אֶרֶךְ אַפַּיִם וְרַב חֶסֶד וֶאֱמֶת נֹצֵר חֶסֶד לָאֲלָפִים נֹשֵׂא עָוֹן וָפֶשַׁע וְחַטָּאָה וְנַקֵּה — *God, the Lord God, merciful and gracious, long-suffering, full of goodness and truth; remembering acts of lovingkindness to the thousandth [generation], forgiving iniquity and transgression and sin, and cleansing*" (34:6-7). This is what God told us to say in our prayers.

◌§ Seeing the Divine Light

לֹא תוּכַל לִרְאֹת אֶת פָּנָי — *You cannot see My face* (33:20). God warned Moshe thus, for no man can live after seeing such a sight.

The *Yalkut* tells of Hadrian, who asked R' Yehoshua: "You say that your God created the sky and the earth. Why does He not reveal Himself, say twice a year, so that mankind will fear Him?"

"Look at the sun," said R' Yehoshua.

"How can I possibly look at the sun?" answered Hadrian.

"If you cannot look at the sun, which is merely God's servant," retorted R' Yehoshua, "how do you want to look at God Himself, Who gives off so much more light?"

When the *Mashiach* comes God will reveal Himself to mankind, as it is written, וְנִגְלָה כְּבוֹד ה' — *God's glory will be revealed*

(*Yeshayahu* 40:5). And when a man's soul leaves his body, he sees God.

The *Yalkut* writes further: God revealed many great treasures to Moshe. "To whom does this treasure belong?" asked Moshe. "To those who give charity," answered God. "And to whom does this one belong?" questioned Moshe. "To those who support orphans." And thus did God answer him on each treasure.

Finally, Moshe came to a certain treasure, and asked, "To whom does this belong?" "This belongs to one who has no merit of his own. I give him this treasure unearned," answered God. This is referred to in the words, וְחַנֹּתִי אֶת אֲשֶׁר אָחֹן — *I will be gracious to those to whom I will be gracious* (33:19) — I will give freely to those who lack merit.

◆§ Moshe Carves the New Tablets

God told Moshe: "*Carve for yourself two stone tablets* (פְּסָל לְךָ שְׁנֵי לֻחֹת אֲבָנִים; 34:1) of sapphire, and I will write the Ten Commandments upon them."

The *Gemara* says, in Tractate *Shabbos*: Why was the first set of tablets made by God Himself in heaven, and the second made by Moshe? This can be likened to a master who went to sea. While there, he heard that his wife had been unfaithful to him, together with his maidservants. A servant quickly tore up their *kesubbah* (marriage contract) so that if the master, in his rage, would want to kill his wife, the servant could say, "Without a *kesubbah*, she is not your wife."

When the master returned home he found that his wife had indeed not been unfaithful; only the maidservants were guilty. The servant then told the master to write a new marriage contract, because the old one had been torn up. "Write it yourself," said the master, "since you tore it up, and then I will sign it."

The master represents God, the servant, Moshe. The wife is Israel and the maidservants the *erev rav*. The tablets were the *kesubbah* and since Moshe broke them, God told him: "*Carve [the tablets] for yourself* (פְּסָל לְךָ; 34:1), since you broke the first ones."

God told Moshe: "Go up on Mount Sinai, *and no man shall ascend with you* (וְאִישׁ לֹא יַעֲלֶה עִמָּךְ; 34:3)." The first tablets were given amidst great furor, and as a result an evil eye was cast upon them, and they were broken. "But now I will give the tablets quietly, so that they will last."

◌§ Patience for Sinners

Moshe carved out the tablets and early in the morning ascended the mountain, tablets in hand. God came to Moshe within a cloud and, as explained above, taught him to pray, directing him to mention in his prayers the words, הֵן וְחַנּוּן רַחוּם אֵל 'ה 'ה — *God, God, merciful and gracious*, having pity upon men both before they sin and after they have sinned and repented; *long-suffering* (אֶרֶךְ אַפַּיִם), holding back His wrath and not immediately punishing the sinner, giving him time to repent.

The *Gemara* says, in Tractate *Sanhedrin:* When Moshe learned that God extends his patience both to the righteous and the wicked, he said: "Why not let the wicked be destroyed?" Answered God: "There will come a time when you will need the patience."

And indeed, when Israel made the Calf, Moshe begged God to be patient and withhold His anger, and God retorted: "But you yourself told Me not to have patience with the wicked."

"But You promised that You would be patient with them as well," answered Moshe.

This exchange is hinted at in Moshe Rabbeinu's intercession for the people after the return of the Spies: כַּאֲשֶׁר 'ה כֹּחַ נָא יִגְדַּל וְעַתָּה דִּבַּרְתָּ — *And now let God's power wax great as You have spoken* (*Bamidbar* 14:17); that is, "as You once promised me."

The *Yerushalmi* says of the words, עָוֹן נֹשֵׂא — *forgiving* (lit., "taking up") *iniquity:* God allows certain sins to be taken off the scales of judgment, so that the merit will outweigh the sins.

R' Huna says, in the name of R' Avihu: Although God forgets nothing and remembers all, He sometimes acts as if He has forgotten certain sins. Some Sages say that God lifts up the side with the sins, so that the merits on the other side of the scales will outweigh them.

◌§ Idolatry Today

In Tractate *Pesachim*, in the chapter beginning *Arvei Pesachim*, it is written that the words, תַעֲשֶׂה לֹא מַסֵּכָה אֱלֹהֵי — *You shall make no molten gods* (34:17), are placed next to the commandment to *keep the festival of matzos* (תִּשְׁמֹר הַמַּצּוֹת חַג אֶת; 34:18), to show that one who works on a festival in order to avoid monetary loss, or one who does not want to give out money to honor the festival, *worships gold*, and hence is likened to one who worships false gods.

◌§ The Pilgrim Festivals

זְכוּרְךָ כָּל יֵרָאֶה — *All your males shall appear* (34:23). They shall come to Yerushalayim on the festivals, to be seen by the Divine Presence. Women were not so obligated, nor were the blind.

R' Bechaye asks why women did not go, nor a maimed person. It was because the cloud within the *Beis HaMikdash* reflected like a mirror, and it was not proper that the reflection of a woman or of a maimed man be seen within the *Beis HaMikdash.*

◄§ The Written and the Oral Law

עַל פִּי הַדְּבָרִים הָאֵלֶּה — *By these words* (34:27). That is, by these words God has made a covenant with His people. Our Sages learn from this that it is forbidden to learn the written Torah by heart, without the words in front of one. Likewise, those laws which God taught Moshe orally were to be studied only by heart, and not written down.

R' Bechaye asks: Why did God not command that we write down the laws which are a commentary upon the *Chumash* (Pentateuch), so that we could understand it correctly? In order to separate us from the rest of the nations. We, and only we, can correctly interpret the Torah, for we know the proper explanations.

During the Persian exile, however, Israel underwent great tribulations, and were dispersed, and so they were not able to properly learn the laws by heart. It was then that Rebbe (R' Yehudah HaNasi) wrote down the laws in concise form, in the *mishnayos,* so that they would not be forgotten in the exile.

◄§ In Heaven Again

וַיְהִי שָׁם — *And he was there* (34:28). Moshe remained together with God on Sinai for forty days and forty nights.

R' Bechaye asks: While in heaven, how did Moshe know the difference between night and day? In heaven, after all, it is always light, and never dark. The answer is that when the angels said "Holy," he knew it was day; when they said "Blessed," he knew it was night.

Another answer is that when Moshe saw the sun bowing down, he knew that it was day, and when the moon bowed down he knew that it was night.

◄§ A Luminous Countenance

וְהִנֵּה קָרַן עוֹר פָּנָיו — *Behold, the skin of his face was luminous* (34:30). When Moshe descended from heaven, his face radiated light.

R' Bechaye asks: Why did Moshe merit giving off such a light with the second set of tablets? Because with the first tablets all of Israel saw the miracles which accompanied them, and so no sign of their divine origin was necessary. But with the second set, Moshe alone went to heaven to receive them, and so he needed a sign that they were from God.

Another explanation of why God did not give him the light with the first set of tablets is that God knew that they would not last and would ultimately be broken, and so He did not want to give Moshe the distinction of this radiance. But since God knew that the second set would last eternally, He gave the light to Moshe.

The *Midrash* writes that Moshe merited this light because when he was in the cave, God Himself covered his face with His hand. From this moment Moshe's face began to glow.

Some Sages say that his face shone because God spoke with him face to face.

❧ A Veil is Needed

וַיִּירְאוּ מִגֶּשֶׁת אֵלָיו — *They were afraid to approach him* (34:30). Our Sages say: How terrible was the sin of the Calf! Before they made the Calf, Israel could look through seven fiery walls without fear. Yet once they had sinned they could not even look at Moshe's radiance, though it was far smaller than the light of God.

Moshe placed a veil upon his face so that the light would not blaze forth and harm people. When he went into the *Mishkan* he would take the veil off, and likewise when he left the *Mishkan* and taught Israel the Torah and the commandments which God had told him there, he would speak without wearing the veil. When he had finished speaking of Torah and the commandments, he once again donned it.

❧ Aharon and His Disciples

Aharon knew that he would gain great merit if he would teach the Torah to Israel, and so he taught them all. He taught those ignorant of prayer how to pray; those who did not know how to learn he taught Torah.

This great merit does not belong to Aharon alone. Anyone who teaches another Torah or prayer, or rebukes him so that he will better himself, has a great merit. God will help him to understand the wisdom of the Torah.

❧ The First Yom Kippur

During the last forty days that Moshe was on the mountain the people fasted and lamented. On the very last day they fasted both day and night. They then went to the mountain to meet Moshe. They all cried, and Moshe too joined them in their tears. God thereupon had mercy upon them and forgave them for the sin of the Calf.

God told them: "Let your tears become joy and happiness. This day shall be a day of forgiveness for your sins all through the years." That day is Yom Kippur.

⇜§ The Power of Intercession

When Moshe had broken the tablets, God decreed that Israel would have to learn Torah in sorrow and exile, wandering from one town to another as penitents do, learning in poverty (for one who is wealthy cannot learn Torah), and becoming weak through Torah study. But when *Mashiach* comes these same people will experience great joy, both in this world and the next.

The *Yalkut* writes that Moshe told God: "Master of the world, I will judge those who worshiped idols myself." He went down and burned the Calf, and announced that those who worshiped God should join him.

When they had killed the idol worshipers, Moshe prayed: "Master of the world, three thousand men worshiped the false god whole-heartedly; do you want to kill six hundred thousand?" Then God had pity on them.

This situation is analogous to a king who grew angry with his eldest son, and handed him over to one of his courtiers. The courtier brought him to another town, and said nothing of it to the king.

After thirty days the king made a great feast and was very merry, but upon remarking his eldest son's absence, he grew sad and remorseful. No one but that one courtier alone knew the reason for the king's sorrow. He quickly went and brought the son back to the king, and the king became merry once again, richly rewarding the servant.

So, too, did Moshe save Israel from death four or five times, by praying for them. Therefore, God took the crown of Torah and gave it to Moshe as a gift.

⇜§ The Radiance of the Righteous

וְרָאוּ בְנֵי יִשְׂרָאֵל אֶת פְּנֵי מֹשֶׁה — *The Children of Israel saw the face of Moshe* (34:35). Though they saw it they could not gaze upon it because of the radiance which resembled the light of the sun. This glow stayed with him even after his death, as it is written, *His eyes did not grow dull* (לֹא כָהֲתָה עֵינוֹ; *Devarim* 34:7). His face was luminous even after his death.

In the next world, God lights up the face of the scholar who learns both day and night, as it is written of David, *The soul of my master will be bound in the bond of life with the Lord, your God* (וְהָיְתָה נֶפֶשׁ אֲדֹנִי צְרוּרָה בִּצְרוֹר הַחַיִּים אֶת ה' אֱלֹהֶיךָ; *I Shmuel* 25:29). The soul of a righteous man is with God, and gives forth God's light.

❧　❧　❧

The *Haftorah* of *Parashas Ki Sisa* may be found on p. 501.

פרשת ויקהל
Parashas Vayakhel
(35:1 — 38:20)

◆§ The Sanctuary Completed

וַיַּקְהֵל מֹשֶׁה — *Moshe gathered together* (35:1) all of Israel, one day after Yom Kippur. He descended from heaven with the Second Tablets on Yom Kippur, which was on a Thursday. He had gone up on Rosh Chodesh Elul, which was on a Monday. For this reason, we fast on [certain] Mondays and Thursdays. God forgave Israel's sins on those days, and we hope that He will forgive our sins as well.

Moshe now gathered all of Israel together and commanded that they build the *Mishkan,* the Sanctuary.

The author of *Even Shoev* writes that as soon as Moshe built it he recited the verse from *Psalms* (90:17) which begins with the words, וִיהִי נֹעַם — *And may the pleasantness of the Lord our God be upon us,* so that the Divine Presence would rest within it.

◆§ The Divine Presence Retreats ...

The *Midrash* writes that R' Levi says: "At first, the Divine Presence rested mainly on the earth, as it is written, וַיִּשְׁמְעוּ אֶת קוֹל ה' אֱלֹהִים מִתְהַלֵּךְ בַּגָּן — *And they heard the voice of the Lord God walking about in the Garden (Bereishis* 3:8). When Adam ate from the Tree of Knowledge the Divine Presence withdrew to the first level of heaven. When Cain murdered Hevel (Abel) the Divine Presence retreated further, to the second level. During the generation of Enosh, which worshiped idols, it ascended to the third heaven, and in the time of the wicked generation of the Flood it again recoiled, and went up to the fourth level. When the people built a tower to heaven the Divine Presence ascended to the fifth level; when Nimrod deified himself it went up to the sixth; and in the days of Sodom it went up to the seventh.

◆§ ... and Returns

Then a righteous man was born — Avraham — and the Divine Presence descended again to the sixth level. Avraham was followed

Moshe brings the second Tablets from heaven

by Yitzchak, and the Divine Presence came down to the fifth heaven; in Yaakov's day it came down to the fourth level. In Levi's day it came down to the third; and in the time of Kehas it came down to the second level. Then came Amram, and the Divine Presence descended to the first heaven, and finally Moshe brought the Presence of God back to earth, into the *Mishkan*. It was Moshe whom God commanded to build the *Mishkan*, since it was he who had brought the Divine Presence back to earth.

✑§ Shabbos and the Mishkan

שֵׁשֶׁת יָמִים תֵּעָשֶׂה מְלָאכָה — *Six days shall work be done* (35:2). The phrase reads "shall work be done" — of its own accord. Whoever keeps *Shabbos* properly will have his work done for him by others.

The Torah warns that *Shabbos* must be kept before speaking of the construction of the *Mishkan* — to show that even the Sanctuary of God could not be built on *Shabbos*. How much more so must a man take care not to work on his own affairs on *Shabbos*!

Baal HaTurim writes: The Torah speaks of *Shabbos* immediately after telling of the light which Moshe gave forth to show that on *Shabbos* God bestows a gracious light upon the faces of those who observe it properly.

לֹא תְבַעֲרוּ אֵשׁ — *Do not kindle a fire ... on Shabbos* (35:3). Why did the Torah specifically point out the kindling of fire, rather than the other prohibitions? Because most of the other prohibitions make use of fire. For this reason, when *Shabbos* ends and the prohibitions are lifted, we make *Havdalah*, the ceremony marking the end of the *Shabbos* or festivals, with fire.

Also, when God created the world, the first creation was light, which is like fire, and so fire is the first prohibition mentioned.

◄§ A Time to Speak

The Torah tells us not to work with fire, to teach women — who attend synagogue especially on *Shabbos* — not to discuss their cooking while there, as they are wont to do, thus disturbing their own prayers and those of others. For this reason this commandment appears next to the passage on the *Mishkan* — for in the synagogue, as in the *Mishkan*, one is forbidden to indulge in idle talk.

The *Gemara* says, in Tractate *Kiddushin:* "Ten portions of speech were given to the world; women took nine portions, leaving one for the rest of the world."

R' Huna says: "When the *Sefer* Torah is opened for the Torah reading it is prohibited to speak, even words of Torah." Even when not in synagogue one should avoid pointless talk, as *Menoras HaMaor* says: Our Sages have said that a person can be recognized through his speech. One who speaks much is a fool; one who speaks little is wise and undoubtedly of good family.

The *Gemara* says, in Tractate *Kiddushin*, that the way to discern if a person is of an honored family is this: When two men argue, the one who falls silent first is from a good family. Rebbe (R' Yehudah HaNasi) says: The noble lineage of the scholars of Babylonia consists of their ability to hold their peace.

As far as Torah is concerned, however, a person should speak as much as he can. Still, there are times when one is not allowed to speak even of Torah, such as during the recital of *Shema* or *Shemoneh Esreh*, or during *Hallel* or the Torah reading.

The *Gemara* says that a person who spoke during prayers was ordered to leave the ranks before a battle. When Israel went to battle other nations, they sent away anyone with many sins, lest he cause his fellows to fall into enemy hands. One who spoke during prayers, too, had to go home, for that is a grievous sin.

We see that though speaking of Torah is a great thing, the Sages forbade us to do so during prayer. How much more so, then, is common talk during prayer forbidden! But people are not careful and speak much during prayer. This is quite a serious offense, particularly on *Shabbos*, since the *Gemara* admonishes us that our speech on *Shabbos* should not be like that of the rest of the week.

The *Midrash Vayikra Rabbah* says that the mother of R' Shimon bar Yochai once spoke at length on *Shabbos*. When he told her "Today is *Shabbos*," she grew silent.

Baal HaTurim writes, on the words *Do not kindle a fire:* God says, "Since My flames in Hell cease for you sake on *Shabbos*, so too should your flames cease."

◆§ Learning to Give

Toldos Yitzchak writes that the reason the Torah asks for donations of gold and silver for the *Mishkan* immediately following the discussion of *Shabbos* is that *Shabbos* resembles the heavenly world, in which there is no labor. If a person understands that This World means nothing in comparison with the next, he will not be miserly with his gold and silver.

קְחוּ מֵאִתְּכֶם תְּרוּמָה — *Take from yourselves an offering* (35:5). The words "from yourselves" show that one should not say that he will wait until he is rich to give his donation. Rather, he should take from what God has given him now.

כֹּל נְדִיב לִבּוֹ יְבִיאֶהָ אֵת תְּרוּמַת ה׳ — *Whoever has a willing heart shall bring it, the offering of God* (35:5). *Toldos Yitzchak* asks: Why did Moshe command that they themselves bring the donations, rather than have someone take it from them? The answer is that Moshe had originally planned to appoint people to go from house to house collecting whatever the people gave, but when they brought their gold for the Calf by themselves, he said: "Because you yourselves brought gold for the Calf, you must also bring your offerings to the *Mishkan* by yourselves, so that it shall serve as an atonement for the sin of the Calf."

◆§ Charity from Women

וַיָּבֹאוּ הָאֲנָשִׁים עַל הַנָּשִׁים — *And the men came, after the women* (35:22). *Ramban* writes that because most gold and silver jewelry belongs to women, the Torah here says that they preceded the men; that is, first the women brought their gold and silver jewelry, and then the men brought their rings.

Toldos Yitzchak asks: The Sages have said that it is not permitted to take more than small sums from women, to be given to charity — so how could they take so much gold and silver? Further, a woman is not permitted to give away the gold and silver which she has brought from her father's house, nor that which her husband has given her. The answer is that the women came together with their husbands.

We see from this that a woman is not allowed to give a great sum for charity, though she may give small amounts independently of her husband. The *Gemara* says that a woman may give food from her home to a poor man or a guest.

⋖§ A Visit to Abba Chilkiah

The story is told in the Talmud of a time when rain was desperately needed. The Sages sent two rabbis to Abba Chilkiah, to ask him to pray for rain. The rabbis went to his house and did not find him there; they went out to the field and found him. They greeted him, and he made no reply.

With nightfall, he put wood on one shoulder and his clothing on the other, and walked home barefoot. When he came to a body of water he put on his shoes, and when he walked through thorns he picked his clothing up and went barefoot. When he approached the town his wife met him, wearing her best clothes. He came home and let her enter the house first. Then he entered, followed by the rabbis. He sat down to eat but did not invite his guests; he gave his elder son one piece of bread and his younger, two pieces.

After eating, Abba Chilkiah turned to his wife and said: "I know that these men have come to me to pray for rain. Come to the attic and let us pray now, so that the rabbis will not realize that the rain will fall as a result of our prayers."

They went to the attic, he in one corner and she in another, and prayed. A cloud came forth first over the corner in which his wife was praying, for her prayers were answered more readily.

Then he went down and asked the rabbis why they had come. "So that you should pray for rain," they answered.

"Well, then, thanks be to God that you need me no longer," he answered, "since it seems that it is starting to rain without my intervention."

"We know very well that the rain came because of your prayers," they answered. "But please, answer our questions. Why didn't you respond to our greeting?"

"Because I was hired as a day laborer and did not want to waste any of my master's time," Abba Chilkiah replied.

"Why did you put your clothing on one shoulder and your wood on the other, instead of putting the wood on top of the clothing?"

"Because I borrowed the clothing to wear, and not to carry wood upon."

"And why did you walk barefoot on the earth, and put on your shoes when walking through the water?" they continued.

"On the road I can be careful of stones or thorns," he answered, "and so I will not hurt my feet. But in the water where I cannot see, I put on shoes."

"Why did you lift your clothing when you walked through thorns, instead of protecting your feet?"

"Because if I scratch my feet they will heal, but if I tear the clothing it will not."

"Why was your wife dressed up?"

"So that I should not have thoughts of other women."

"And why did she enter the house first, and then you, and only then did you let us in?"

"Because," he answered, "I did not know if you were pious, so I put myself between my wife and you."

"Why didn't you invite us to eat?"

"Because I didn't have enough bread in the house for my own household. I didn't want to mislead you by extending an invitation that was not whole-hearted."

"And why did you give your elder son one piece of bread, and the younger two pieces?"

"Because the elder is always at home, and eats when he wishes; the younger is in school all day, where he cannot eat."

"Why did a cloud come first over the corner in which your wife stood?"

"Because when she gives charity," he replied, "she gives cooked and baked goods, and so the poor man has immediate pleasure. But I give money, and so the poor man must first buy the food."

We see from this that a woman may give food for charity without her husband's knowledge, as Abba Chilkiah's wife did. If she had done it with his knowledge, it would have been considered as if he had given it, and thus the cloud would have come first from his corner.

We also see from this that a poor man must also give charity. Abba Chilkiah was certainly impoverished — he was forced to hire himself out as a day laborer — and yet he gave charity.

◄§ Mar Ukva and his Wife

The *Gemara* also says, in Tractate *Kesubbos:* Mar Ukva had a neighbor, a poor man. Each day, Mar Ukva placed four gold coins under the man's door, so that the man would not know who had given it to him.

One day the poor the man said, "I must find out who is giving me this." When Mar Ukva and his wife placed the four gold coins under his door that day, the poor man followed them. Mar Ukva and his wife fled, until they came to a fiery oven. They ran into it, and Mar Ukva burned his feet.

His wife told him: "Put your feet upon mine, and they will not burn." Her feet were not burned because she had given charity from cooked and baked goods, which the poor enjoyed immediately.

Why did they jump into an oven? Because it is better to burn oneself than to embarrass another person.

We see from this story that a woman should give prepared foods to the poor. Incidentally, it is preferable to give charity to a woman, rather than a man, for a woman is more ashamed of asking for charity.

Charity saves a person from two things: from the Angel of Death, and from Hell.

⇜§ In Praise of Women

וַיֵּצְאוּ כָּל עֲדַת בְּנֵי יִשְׂרָאֵל מִלִּפְנֵי מֹשֶׁה — *All of the congregation of the Children of Israel departed from the presence of Moshe* (35:20). R' Bechaye writes: This verse teaches us that the people had a great desire to bring gold and silver for the *Mishkan*. The women had the greatest yearning of all, and therefore the verse says, וַיָּבֹאוּ הָאֲנָשִׁים עַל הַנָּשִׁים — *The men came, after the women* (35:22). When the men came, they found the women already there.

The fact that the women had refused to give their jewelry for making the Calf, and yet willingly gave it now to the *Mishkan*, shows their particular stature.

Pirkei deR' Eliezer writes that this is the reason that women especially were given Rosh Chodesh as a holiday, celebrated with fine clothes and an avoidance of hard work. Further, God will repay them richly in the next world, and then they will rejoice.

King Shlomo referred to this in *Koheles (Ecclesiastes 7:28)* when he said: וְאִשָּׁה בְּכָל אֵלֶּה לֹא מָצָאתִי — *But a woman among all of these I have not found.* There was no woman among the worshipers of the Golden Calf. The word אֵלֶּה ("these") refers to the Calf, as it is written, אֵלֶּה אֱלֹהֶיךָ יִשְׂרָאֵל — *These are your gods, O Israel (Shmos 32:4)*.

⇜§ The Daughters of R' Nachman

The *Gemara* says, in *Perek HaShole'ach*: The daughters of R' Nachman used to stir a boiling pot with their bare hands, with no cooking utensils. R' Ilish saw this and said: "King Shlomo has said that among a thousand women he could not find one who was pious; how is it, then, that fire has no power over the daughters of R' Nachman?"

It happened once that the daughters of R' Nachman were captured, and R' Ilish, too, was captured with them. He found himself together with a Jew who understood the language of the birds.

A raven came by and shrieked, and R' Ilish asked the man what he had said.

"He says: 'R Ilish, flee, and you will reach safety.' "

Said R' Ilish: "The raven is a liar and cannot be believed."

A dove then came and chirped, and the Jew said: "The dove, too, says R' Ilish should flee and be saved."

"Israel is compared to a dove," said R' Ilish, "and so this is a sign that God will miraculously save me from captivity. For if the dove told lies, Israel would not be compared to it."

Then R' Ilish said to himself: "Let me go and see if the daughters of R' Nachman are as pious as they used to be. If so, I will take them with me."

He approached them secretly, and overheard one say to another: "Why should this bother us? We have husbands here, as good as the ones we had there." They did not miss their husbands, for they were living with the robbers! "Let us tell the robbers to take us further away," they said, "so that our husbands won't find us and ransom us."

R' Ilish then fled, taking along the other Jew. They reached a great river and God miraculously helped R' Ilish cross it. The other Jew was not so fortunate, and was murdered by their pursuers.

The rabbi reached home safely. Later, the daughters of R' Nachman did so as well, and once again they were able to stir boiling pots with their bare hands.

R' Ilish then said: "Shlomo was right — there is not one pious woman in a thousand [i.e., they are no longer pious]. And as for retaining their ability to touch boiling water with their bare hands, that must be a form of *kishuf* [witchcraft or magic]."

We see from this that women must be very careful not to go among strange men [for they may easily succumb to temptation, as the daughters of R' Nachman did].

◄§ Offerings of Silver and Gold

כָּל מֵרִים תְּרוּמַת כֶּסֶף — *Whoever made an offering of silver* (35:24). In the case of offerings of silver, the word מֵרִים (the usual word for making an offering) is used, while when gold was brought, the verse says הֵנִיף (35:22), lit., "raised" an offering of gold. This shows that whoever brought an offering of gold to the *Mishkan* lifted it up, and the one accepting the offering lifted it up as well, to indicate that this was a generous donation.

⇜ The Offerings of the Princes

וְהַנְּשִׂאָם הֵבִיאוּ אֵת אַבְנֵי הַשֹּׁהַם — *And the princes brought the onyx stones* (35:27) for the *Choshen*, the High Priest's breastplate. This was because princes and communal leaders are usually haughty, and so the *nesi'im* brought the stones that were worn over the heart of the *Kohen Gadol*, which atoned for the sin of pride, which lurks in a man's heart.

The princes had said that all of Israel should bring their offerings first, and then they would complete whatever was lacking. But when they saw that the people had brought more than enough, and no more gold or silver was needed, they had to bring the precious stones.

The verse spells *nesi'im* ("princes") without the letter *yud* because these leaders delayed in bringing the offering. Although their intentions were pure, the Torah here points out their disgrace. We learn from this that a person should not delay in fulfilling a commandment or giving a donation. The faster he does it, the greater will be his reward.

Some of our Sages say that clouds rained down the precious stones, for no such gems could otherwise be found. In the Torah, the word נְשִׂיאִים sometimes means "clouds." Other Sages say that the gems fell down in the desert, together with the *man* (manna), and the people gathered them together.

⇜ The Artisans

וַיְמַלֵּא אֹתוֹ רוּחַ אֱלֹהִים — *And He filled him with the spirit of God* (35:31). God prophetically showed Bezalel how to fashion the vessels, although he had never done it before. God wanted to show that He gives everyone knowledge, if they truly want to do good. Indeed, even the animals were given a measure of understanding, as will be explained below.

In one day, the people brought more gold and silver than was needed for the entire *Mishkan*. The artisans then came to Moshe and told him that there was more than enough, to show that they were honest workers. Moshe did not want more gold and silver, and directed that an announcement be made that no further offerings were needed, since there was enough.

⋖⋗ The Ark

וַיַּעַשׂ בְּצַלְאֵל אֶת הָאָרֹן — *And Bezalel made the ark* (37:1). He actually made three arks: first, an ark of gold, then an ark of wood, which was placed within the golden ark, and finally another ark of gold, which was placed within the wooden ark. The upper edges were then coated with gold.

Why was there wood in the ark? To show that one should give respect to a needy scholar, and surround him with gold. The broken tablets were placed within to show that an impoverished scholar should also be treated with respect.

⋖⋗ The Basin

בְּמַרְאֹת הַצֹּבְאֹת — *Of the mirrors of the women who congregated* (38:8). The women of Israel brought their pure copper mirrors to the *Mishkan*. God ordered that a washbasin be made of them for the hands. It was from water taken from this basin that a woman suspected of adultery without witnesses was made to drink. If she was guilty her stomach swelled up from the water, because, unlike the women who had brought the mirrors, she was not righteous.

R' Bechaye writes that the older women brought the mirrors, for they did not preen themselves any more, instead spending evening and morning in prayer.

⋖⋗ Constructing the Sanctuary — Then ...

Even Shoev writes that the goats came to the women of their own accord, so that they could spin their hair into curtains for the *Mishkan*. But they did not come on *Shabbos* and on Rosh Chodesh. This was a mark of a special instinct on the part of the animals, to recognize the days when no work was done. The women spun the hair directly off the animals, which is a great talent.

⋖⋗ ... and Now

R' Bechaye writes that it is very important to learn the details of the *Beis HaMikdash*, its measurements and its vessels, although it has been destroyed. Our Sages have said that one who earnestly studies the laws of the sacrifices is considered as one who has himself brought a sacrifice. Similarly, when a person studies the details of the *Beis HaMikdash*, he is rewarded as if he had built it. May we soon merit that God rebuild the *Beis HaMikdash*, so that His Presence will reside there, Amen!

⚘ ⚘ ⚘

The *Haftorah* of *Parashas Vayakhel* may be found on p. 504.

פרשת פקודי
Parashas Pekudei

(38:21 — 40:38)

⋘ An Honest Penny

אֵלֶּה פְקוּדֵי — *These are the accounts* (38:21). There is a verse in *Mishlei* (15:16) that says: טוֹב מְעַט בְּיִרְאַת ה' מֵאוֹצָר רָב וּמְהוּמָה בוֹ — *Better a little, with the fear of God, than a great treasure, with confusion.* On this R' Bechaye comments: It is better to have just a little money, obtained with the fear of God, properly, than an entire treasure obtained through foul means, through thievery or usury. And the next verse states: טוֹב אֲרֻחַת יָרָק וְאַהֲבָה שָׁם מִשּׁוֹר אָבוּס וְשִׂנְאָה בוֹ — *Better a dinner of herbs, when love is there, than a fatted ox, with hatred (ibid. 15:17).* It is better to eat a meal of cabbage, and be beloved by all, never having stolen, not having lent money out at interest, and never swearing falsely, than to eat the most succulent meats, but bearing the hatred of people for having swindled them or having lent money out at interest. Stealing is the worst of all sins.

Our Sages have said that a full measure of sins is not so terrible, until that of robbery is included. God only seals a decree against men because of that particular sin. We see that God drowned the generation of the Flood because of their robbery, even though they had also committed the sins of adultery and idol worship. It was their robbery that was their undoing.

Better a little, with the fear of God ... This shows that a person should realize that just as it is better to eat vegetables without meat together with a good friend or loving wife, rather than eat meat in a place of enmity, so it is better to be thrifty with a penny that is honestly earned, than generous with a dollar stolen from others. Of course, one should not be miserly, relying only on his money; he should have faith that God will give him more money if he needs it. As the *Mishnah* says: "Who is rich? He who is content with whatever God has given him." Such a man has faith that God will continue providing for him.

✑ Miserliness

It is written, כָּל יְמֵי עָנִי רָעִים — *All the days of a poor man are bad* (*Mishlei* 15:15). The *Midrash* says that this verse refers to an intentional poor man, that is, a miser, one who does not eat enough because of his fear that he will eat up his money. All of his days are dark, and he will never be satisfied. Ultimately he will steal, for he will never have enough money to suit him.

The same verse goes on to say: וְטוֹב לֵב מִשְׁתֶּה תָמִיד — *but the happy of heart has a continual feast* (ibid.). He who trusts in God's succor is always merry, eating and drinking in joy, and never turning to thievery.

✑ Delaying a Salary

As the *Gemara* says, in Tractate *Bava Kama:* If one man robs another, even of a tiny sum, it is as if he stole his soul. This is true even if the other owes him his salary, and delays payment. And in Tractate *Bava Metzia* the *Gemara* says that when one owes another his salary, and delays paying it even for one day, it is as if he stole the other's soul.

✑ Gilding a Theft

There are many people who steal and then give generously to charity. Of them the *Gemara* says the following, in Tractate *Sotah.* R' Yochanan quoted R' Shimon: "It is written: שֹׂנֵא גָזֵל בְּעוֹלָה — *He hates thievery in sacrifice* (*Yeshayahu* 61:8). God despises a sacrifice brought with stolen money."

Similarly, it is prohibited to make a blessing upon something which has been stolen. The *Gemara* says this in Tractate *Sanhedrin.* R' Eliezer ben Yaakov says: When a person steals wheat, makes dough of it and takes *challah* from it with a blessing, he angers God, as it is written, וּבֹצֵעַ בֵּרֵךְ נִאֵץ ה' — *And the greedy one who blesses, angers God* (*Tehillim* 10:3).

Stealing from a non-Jew is even worse. The *Gemara* says, in Tractate *Bava Kama*, that to steal from a non-Jew is a greater sin than to steal from a Jew, for then the sin also desecrates the name of God.

Because theft is so grievous a sin, Moshe wanted to clearly show that there was no reason to suspect him of stealing any of the gold brought for the *Mishkan*. This is why he rendered a full accounting.

The *Midrash* states that the word *Mishkan* appears twice (in

38:21) to indicate that two temples would be destroyed by the nations of the world.

⊷§ Evidence of Forgiveness

מִשְׁכַּן הָעֵדֻת — *The Tabernacle of testimony* (38:21). The *Mishkan* testified to the fact that God had forgiven the people the sin of the Golden Calf, by bringing His Presence down into the *Mishkan*.

⊷§ Justice in the Eyes of Men

וְאֵת הָאֶלֶף וּשְׁבַע הַמֵּאוֹת וַחֲמִשָּׁה וְשִׁבְעִים — *And the one thousand seven hundred and seventy five* (38:28).

R' Bechaye writes that when Moshe gave a full accounting of all the gold and silver, he found that he had forgotten what had been done with 1,775 shekels of silver. A heavenly voice called out and said that hooks had been made of that silver, and there was no reason to suspect Moshe, a trustworthy warden.

We see from all this that a person should justify himself in the eyes of men, and not only in the eyes of God. Moreover, God helps the righteous man be believed and trusted.

⊷§ Erection of the Sanctuary

וַיְהִי בַּחֹדֶשׁ הָרִאשׁוֹן — *And it was in the first month* (40:17) that Moshe erected the *Mishkan*.

The *Midrash* writes that on that day Moshe put the *Mishkan* up three times. He put it together the first time when they wanted to bring the daily sacrifice in the morning, and then he took it apart. The second time was when the *nesi'im* brought their offering for the inauguration of the altar. And the third time, he put it together for the daily sacrifice of the afternoon.

The *Midrash* also says that all of the skilled artisans who worked on the *Mishkan* were unable to put it together, so they brought their completed work to Moshe. Moshe was distressed because he had not worked on the *Mishkan*, and so God told him: "No man will be able to put it up. You will take it, and it will become constructed of itself, and it will seem as if you have put it up."

The *Yalkut* writes that there were many miracles in the *Mishkan*. The courtyard was no wider than fifty cubits, and yet 600,000 people stood within it. When they bowed down, there was a space of four cubits between each person and the next. Also, all of Israel saw a heavenly fire come to the courtyard of the *Mishkan* and enter the Tent of Communion, the *Ohel Moed*, rising upon the altar, consuming the sacrifices, and remaining on the altar.

৵§ When God Returns to Zion

R' Bechaye writes that God said: "Today I am causing My Presence to rest among you; if you sin, My Presence will leave you. But when *Mashiach* comes, My Presence will remain with you permanently. Now you see the Divine Presence through fire, but with the advent of *Mashiach* you will see it clearly revealed, as it is written (*Yeshayahu* 52:8): כִּי עַיִן בְּעַיִן יִרְאוּ בְּשׁוּב ה׳ צִיוֹן — *For eye to eye shall they see when God returns to Zion.*

❀ ❀ ❀

The *Haftorah* of *Parashas Pekudei* may be found on p. 505.

הפטרות
Haftoros

HAFTORAH
Sh'mos
(Yirmeyahu/Jeremiah 1:1 — 2:3)

דִּבְרֵי יִרְמְיָהוּ בֶּן חִלְקִיָּהוּ — *The words of Yirmeyahu, son of Chilkiyahu* (1:1). Yirmeyahu was a descendant of Rachav. God decreed: Let the pious Yirmeyahu, who stems from the harlot Rachav, rebuke the wicked people of Israel, who stem from the pious matriarchs.

Yirmeyahu was one of the priests living in the city of Anasos. God first spoke to him in the thirteenth year of the reign of Yoshiyahu ben Amotz, king of Yehudah. He prophesied in the days of Yehoyakim, son of Yoshiyahu, continuing until the end of the eleventh year of the reign of Tzidkiyahu, Yoshiyahu's son. That was the year of the exile of the people of Yerushalayim, in the fifth month, the month of Av.

Says Yirmeyahu: "These were God's words to me (v. 5): 'Before I created you in your mother's womb, I knew you..Before you left her womb, I prepared you to be a prophet to the peoples.'

"I protested to God: 'I cannot speak! I am young and not worthy of rebuking Israel. Moshe rebuked them before his death, after he had won their respect by wreaking many miracles — bringing them out of Egypt, splitting the sea, bringing them *man* (manna) and meat and water, and bringing down the Torah. Shall I now begin my mission by rebuking them?'

וַיֹּאמֶר ה' אֵלַי — *Then God said to me* (v. 7): "Do not say that you are young, too young for My mission. What I tell you to tell them you shall say. Fear them not, for I am with you."

וַיִּשְׁלַח ה' אֶת יָדוֹ — *And God put out His hand* (v. 9) and touched my mouth. Then he said: "I have put My words into your mouth. Behold, I have today appointed you over the kingdoms of the Chaldeans and Philistines, to uproot and destroy and overthrow them; while Israel, if they heed you, will build and plant."

God's words came to me: "What is that you see, Yirmeyahu?"

"I see the stick of an almond tree," I said.

Then God told me: "You have seen properly. Just as an almond tree blooms quickly, earlier than other trees, so shall I quickly keep My promises."

The *Midrash* says that twenty-one days elapse between an almond's first blossoms and its ripening. Similarly, there are twenty-one days between the 17th of Tammuz, when the walls of Yerushalayim were breached, and the 9th of Av, when the *Beis HaMikdash* was destroyed.

God's word came to me a second time (v. 13), and He said: "What do you see?"

I replied: "I see a boiling pot facing northward."

Then God said: "This shows that from Babylonia, on the northern side of *Eretz Yisrael*, evil will come to the land. I will call to the tribes and kingdoms of the north to come and set their thrones at the gates and walls of Yerushalayim and of the other cities of Yehudah. *And I will tell My judgment to them* (v. 16), My people, for having left Me and burned incense to false gods, for bowing to idols which they themselves made. Gird your loins, arise, and tell them all that I command you. Do not fear them, lest I make you as nought before them.

"*For behold, today I have made you* (v. 18) a fortified city, a pillar of iron, a wall of bronze, against the kings of Yehudah and their nobles, their priests, their people. They will be able to do nothing against you. *They will fight against you, but will not prevail* (v. 19), for I am with you, to protect you." So said God.

וַיְהִי דְבַר ה׳ אֵלַי לֵאמֹר — *God's word came to me, and said* (2:1): "Go and cry out in the ears of the populace of Yerushalayim, and tell them God's words: זָכַרְתִּי לָךְ חֶסֶד נְעוּרַיִךְ אַהֲבַת כְּלוּלתָיִךְ לֶכְתֵּךְ אַחֲרַי בַּמִדְבָּר בְּאֶרֶץ לֹא זְרוּעָה — "*I remember the lovingkindness of your youth, the love which I felt when I brought you under the chuppah,* [i.e., the wedding canopy], when you followed Me [i.e., My messengers, Moshe and Aharon], *into the desert, into a land which was not sown,* taking no food for the journey, because you had trust in Me. For this I love you. I would love to have mercy upon you, if only you would repent."

קֹדֶשׁ יִשְׂרָאֵל לַה׳ — *Israel is hallowed to God* (v. 3), just as the first of the wheat crop, which, before the *Omer* offering was brought, could not be eaten. Those who devour Israel, like those who eat the forbidden wheat, will be held guilty; great harm will befall them.

❦ ❦ ❦

Midrash Rabbasi writes on the verse, בְּטֶרֶם אֶצָּרְךָ בַבֶּטֶן יְדַעְתִּיךָ — *Before I formed you in the belly I knew you* (1:5): It can be seen if a child will be righteous or wicked while it is still in the mother's womb, as it is written, וַיִּתְרֹצְצוּ הַבָּנִים בְּקִרְבָּהּ — *The sons contended within her (Bereishis 25:22).* When Rivkah passed a *beis midrash,* a house of Torah study, Yaakov struggled to be born, and when she passed by a pagan temple, Esav strove to be born.

The story is told of a pregnant woman who smelled a certain food on Yom Kippur and had a strong craving for it. When R' Chaninah was asked what to do, he suggested that they remind her that it was Yom Kippur. If that did not check her desire, she should be given the food.

This was done, and her craving did not abate, and ultimately she was given the food. Of this incident, R' Chaninah quoted the verse, זֹרוּ רְשָׁעִים מֵרָחֶם — *The wicked are estranged from the womb* *(Tehillim* 58:4). And indeed, she bore a wicked son.

Another story is told of a pregnant woman who craved food on Yom Kippur. R' Yosef said she should be reminded that it was Yom Kippur, and when this was done her craving ceased. Of her, R' Yosef said: *"Before I formed you in the belly I knew you —* knew that you would be righteous." And it was R' Yochanan who was born from this woman.

HAFTORAH

Vaera

(Yechezkel/Ezekiel 28:25 — 29:21)

כֹּה אָמַר ה' — *Thus said God* (28:25): "I will gather in the household of Israel from wherever they are scattered. In this way I shall be sanctified in the eyes of the nations, by means of the wonders and miracles which I shall wreak. And they shall live in their land, the land which I gave My servant Yaakov, when I promised him a boundless heritage.

וְיָשְׁבוּ עָלֶיהָ לָבֶטַח — *"And they shall live there in security* (v. 26), building homes and planting vineyards. This will happen once I have judged those who tormented or robbed them; they will now know that I am their God."

בַּשָּׁנָה הָעֲשִׂרִית — *In the tenth year* (29:1) of Tzidkiyahu's reign, in the tenth month, which is Teves, on the 12th day of the month, this is what God told me, Yechezkel: בֶּן אָדָם שִׂים פָּנֶיךָ עַל פַּרְעֹה מֶלֶךְ מִצְרָיִם — "*Son of man, set your face* (v. 2) to receive a prophecy concerning Pharaoh, king of Egypt. *Speak and say* (v. 3) to them: 'So said God, the Master — I will send My wrath upon Pharaoh, the giant fish lurking in the middle of his river.' "

God compared Pharaoh to a fish because all of Egypt's greatness and prosperity are due to the Nile, which rises and fills its canals, and irrigates the entire land. The people of Egypt are compared to smaller fish.

God tells Pharaoh: "You are a great fish which says: '*The river is mine* (v. 3), sufficient for all of my needs. I do not need rain from heaven. I alone, with my courage and my wisdom, have made my nation great.' "

וְנָתַתִּי חַחִים בִּלְחָיֶיךָ — "*I will put hooks in your jaws* (v. 4). I will make the other fish in the river cling to your scales; I will bring you up from your river, with the other fish in tow." This means: I will place within your heart and the heart of your warriors the desire to go out and fight, and in that battle you shall all fall.

וּנְטַשְׁתִּיךָ הַמִּדְבָּרָה — "*I will cast you into the desert* (v. 5), you and all of your fish. Just as fish, when cast onto dry land, soon die, so Pharaoh and his people shall die. They will fall on the battlefield, and know no burial. I shall give them to the beasts and birds of prey. Then all of Egypt will recognize that I am God, punishing them for being a staff of reeds for Israel." A staff of reeds is soft, and bends whenever anyone leans on it. When Israel depended on Egypt's help, in the days of Sennacherib [of Assyria] and in the days of Nebuchadnezzar [of Babylonia], Egypt could not be relied upon.

בְּתָפְשָׂם בְּךָ בַכַּף תֵּרוֹץ — "*When they took hold of you by the hand* (v. 7) and leaned upon you, Egypt, you broke beneath them and caused them harm." It was as if a person leaned upon a cane, and the cane broke. Not only did the man fall, but the splinters from the broken cane caused further damage.

"When Israel relied on you, you could not be depended upon, and you forced them to stand up to the nations by themselves. It was like a man leaning on a person who himself was weak, and who deserts the one who looks to him for support.

"Therefore" (v. 8), says God, the Master, "I will bring warriors upon you who will kill with their swords. They will destroy your people and livestock, leaving Egypt a barren ruin. The people will recognize that I am God, Who pays what is due.

"Your king has said that the river belongs to him, and that he needs no one. Therefore, I will send My wrath upon Pharaoh, and upon his river, and the land will be barren, from the tower of Sveneh to the border of Cush.

לֹא תַעֲבָר בָּהּ רֶגֶל אָדָם — *"No man's foot shall pass through it* (v. 11), nor shall animals pass through it, it shall be such a wasteland; *for forty years it shall be uninhabited."*

Rashi writes: Forty-two years of famine were decreed for Egypt, by means of Pharaoh's dreams, which are retold three times in the Torah. The first time it says that he saw seven thin cows and seven lean sheaves; the second time it repeats what he told Yosef; and the third time Yosef repeats the dream. This totals forty-two sheaves and cows, symbolizing forty-two years of hunger.

Only two years of famine had passed when Yaakov arrived, as the verse says, כִּי זֶה שְׁנָתַיִם הָרָעָב — *for the famine has lasted two years* (Bereishis 45:6). With Yaakov's arrival, the famine came to an end, as the people told Yosef: וְתֶן זֶרַע וְנִחְיֶה — *Give us seeds and we will live* (ibid. 47:19). There were forty years left, which were repaid when the land lay barren for forty years.

וְנָתַתִּי אֶת אֶרֶץ מִצְרַיִם שְׁמָמָה — *"I will make the land of Egypt desolate* (v. 12), one of the world's wastelands, its cities one of the world's barren cities. The people of Egypt will be scattered among all the nations and lands."

כֹּה אָמַר ה' — *For so says God* (v. 13): "At the end of the forty years I will gather in the Egyptians from the lands where they were scattered, and will return them to Pasros, the land where they originated. There they will be a humble and lowly kingdom. I will keep them small and low, so that they cannot rule over the other nations as they used to do.

וְלֹא יִהְיֶה עוֹד לְבֵית יִשְׂרָאֵל לְמִבְטָח — *"[Egypt] will no longer be a source of security for Israel* (v. 16), for they are a constant reminder of sin, of Israel's desire to return to Egypt despite God's prohibition against returning there. Then Egypt will recognize that I am the Lord, with the ability to do what I desire."

וַיְהִי בְּעֶשְׂרִים וָשֶׁבַע שָׁנָה — *It was in the twenty-seventh year* (v. 17) of the reign of Nebuchadnezzar, in the first month, the month of Nissan, on the first day of the month, when God spoke to me, to

Yechezkel, and said: "Son of man! Nebuchadnezzar sorely overworked his army in the city of Tzor (Tyre). Each man lost his hair, the skin of each shoulder was torn, under the heavy burdens of wood which each carried upon his head and shoulders, in order to build a siege-tower with which to capture the city. Yet Nebuchadnezzar and his army saw no reward for their labors, for after they had looted the city the sea came and flooded their booty, carrying it away. It had been decreed that the city of Tzor and its booty be lost at sea.

לָכֵן כֹּה אָמַר — *"Therefore," says God* (v. 19): "I will give the land of Egypt to Nebuchadnezzar. He will carry the masses of its people into exile, and take its booty. This shall be his reward, and the reward of his army, for their toil in Tzor, which was done at My behest, for so did I desire. I will give him the land of Egypt, who treated Me unfaithfully by pledging to Israel their false assistance." So says God, the Master.

בַּיּוֹם הַהוּא אַצְמִיחַ קֶרֶן לְבֵית יִשְׂרָאֵל — *"On that day I will cause the horn of the House of Israel to flourish* (v. 21). On the day when Egypt's forty years of ruin shall end, I, God, shall cause the fortunes of Israel to prosper. At that time the downfall of the Babylonian kingdom will begin, and the kingdom of Persia shall begin its ascent. This will be of great import for Israel, for it will be Coresh (Cyrus) of Persia who will build the *Beis HaMikdash* and send Israel out of exile.

"And to you, Yechezkel, will I give at that time the opportunity to speak to Israel unhampered. You will be able to speak freely, for they will see that your prophecies were fulfilled. At that time they will see that I am God, who fulfills My promises."

HAFTORAH

Bo

(Yirmeyahu/Jeremiah 46:13-28)

הַדָּבָר אֲשֶׁר דִּבֶּר ה' אֶל יִרְמְיָהוּ הַנָּבִיא — *The words which God spoke to Yirmeyahu the prophet* (v. 13) regarding Nebuchadnezzar's forthcoming attack on Egypt:

הַגִּידוּ בְמִצְרַיִם — *"Tell in Egypt* (v. 14), announce in the city of

Migdol, declare in Nof and in the city of Tachpanches; tell them to prepare for battle, for the sword of destruction surrounds them. Why have their mightiest warriors been swept away? None of them could remain standing, because God thrust them down.

הִרְבָּה כּוֹשֵׁל — *He caused many to fall* (v. 16); then they gathered together and said: "Arise, and let us return to our people and our native land which we left in order to battle, because of the sword of the enemy.

"Cry out in the battle, announce that Pharaoh has missed the time which he appointed to come and fight with Nebuchadnezzar; that deadline has passed and he has not come." This was a humiliation for Pharaoh, for he always used to pride himself in battle.

חַי אָנִי נְאֻם הַמֶּלֶךְ ה׳ צְבָאוֹת — *"As I live," says the King, Lord of Hosts* (v. 18): "Just as it is true that Mount Tavor stands among other hills, and Mount Carmel looks out to the sea, so truly shall this come onto Egypt."

כְּלֵי גוֹלָה עֲשִׂי לָךְ יוֹשֶׁבֶת בַּת מִצְרָיִם — *"Make for yourself equipment for exile, daughter of Egypt"* (v. 19). A person who goes on the road takes along a flagon and a pitcher to scoop up water. For the city of Nof will be a barren wasteland, abandoned and empty.

עֶגְלָה יְפֵה פִיָּה מִצְרָיִם — *Egypt is a lovely kingdom* (v. 20), but destruction will come to her from the north, and come quickly.

גַּם שְׂכִרֶיהָ בְקִרְבָּהּ כְּעֶגְלֵי מַרְבֵּק — *"Her nobles, too, are like fatted calves* (v. 21), not wanting to go to war. They look only to flee and hide, are not capable of standing and fighting. But their day of doom fast approaches, the day when their sins are remembered."

קוֹלָהּ כַּנָּחָשׁ — *Her voice shall go as a serpent's* (v. 22). Egypt's voice will travel from one end of the world to the other, just like the serpent's, when God cursed him and chopped his feet off. When he cried his voice was heard throughout the world.

The Chaldeans will come with a great army, carrying axes like wood choppers.

כָּרְתוּ יַעְרָהּ — *They cut down her forest* (v. 23). The Chaldeans have the power to cut down the entire forest of Egypt, for they are more numerous than the countless locusts.

הֹבִישָׁה בַּת מִצְרָיִם — *The daughter of Egypt is humiliated* (v. 24). The city is shamed, for she has fallen into the hands of the enemy from the north, the Chaldeans.

אָמַר ה' צְבָאוֹת אֱלֹהֵי יִשְׂרָאֵל — *The God of Hosts, God of Israel, says* (v. 25): "I shall remember the sins of the ruler of the city of Noe (this is Alexandria), and the sins of Pharaoh and Egypt, her idols and her kings, and all who rely on her, and I will deliver them into the hands of those that seek their deaths, into the hands of Nebuchadnezzar, king of Bavel (Babylonia), and his servants. But after forty years Egypt will once again be as it was before." So says God.

וְאַתָּה אַל תִּירָא עַבְדִּי יַעֲקֹב — *"And you, do not fear, My servant Yaakov* (v. 27), do not worry, Israel." This refers to the righteous who were in Egypt, exiled there against their will. "I, God, will help you from afar, you and your children, in the land where you are imprisoned. Yaakov will return, in peace and serenity, and none shall make him afraid. Do not fear, my servant Yaakov, for I, God, am with you. When I destroy the pagans among whom you have been exiled, I will not destroy you. I will punish you in My judgment, but will not destroy you."

❧ ❧ ❧

The *Tanchuma* writes that there were four people in the world who proclaimed themselves gods, three pagans and one Jew: Hiram, king of Tyre; Nebuchadnezzar; Pharaoh; and Yoash of Israel. God punished them all.

Nebuchadnezzar made himself into a god, and God brought him down very low. He had to flee his kingdom into the forest for seven years, eating grass like a beast. Hiram too placed himself over seven heavens and proclaimed himself a god, and afterwards met his downfall. Pharaoh also had his downfall, as we have seen in the above passage.

Yoash too made himself into a god. For six years he had been hidden in the Temple, in the room where the High Priest dared enter only on Yom Kippur. There he hid, together with his nurse, from the time that he was born, until he was crowned king.

Because he had left unharmed, the people approached him and said: "You must be a god. This holy place did you no harm, while even the High Priest dares enter it only once a year, on Yom Kippur, and when he leaves safely he celebrates with a joyous feast. Therefore, you must be a god." He let them persuade him of it, deified himself, and they bowed down to him.

❧ ❧ ❧

The *Gemara* says, in Tractate *Megillah*, on the verse כְּתָבוֹר בֶּהָרִים — *as Tavor is among the mountains* (v. 18): On the day that the Torah was given to Israel two mountains, Tavor and Carmel, came to God, each asking that the Torah be given on him. God rewarded them by allowing them to be in *Eretz Yisrael*.

How much more, then, can we be certain that the *batei midrash* in which Torah is studied, and the synagogues in which people pray, will ultimately come to rest in *Eretz Yisrael!*

HAFTORAH
Beshalach
(Shoftim/Judges 4:4 — 5:31)

וּדְבוֹרָה אִשָּׁה נְבִיאָה אֵשֶׁת לַפִּידוֹת — *Devorah, a prophetess, a woman of Lapidos (wicks)* (4:4). Devorah was a prophetess who made wicks for the *Menorah* (candelabra) in the *Beis HaMikdash*. She judged Israel at this time, sitting beneath a palm tree located between Ramah and Beis-El, on Mount Ephraim, and there the people would come to her for judgment.

Targum Yonasan writes that Devorah lived in the city of Ataros, and her means of support were date trees which she owned in Yericho (Jericho), vineyards in Ramah and olive trees in Beis-El, for this was fertile earth. She also owned a plot of white soil on King's Mountain, which is Mount Ephraim.

This *haftorah* reflects very well on women. R' Bechaye writes in this portion that we must not wonder at the fact that a woman can be a prophetess. We find that Sarah had a greater gift of prophecy than Avraham, as it says in the verse, *In all that Sarah tells you, listen to her voice*, that is, listen to the voice of the Divine Spirit within her.

Miriam, too, sang a hymn by herself, and Moshe and all of the righteous woman joined her in a song of praise. Avigail was a prophetess, and Chanah too, as the *Gemara* says in Tractate *Megillah*: the seven prophetesses were Sarah, Miriam, Chanah, Devorah, Chuldah, Avigail and Esther.

This *haftorah* parallels the song of praise which Moshe chanted at the Red Sea, to show that Devorah and her song have the same importance as Moshe and his song.

There was a time when a decree forbade obeying the Torah of Moshe. As a result, it was impossible to read the Torah in the synagogue on *Shabbos*. The Sages feared that the Torah might (heaven forbid) be forgotten, and so they searched the twenty-four books of the Prophets and Writings for passages which resembled the weekly portions. These were read in place of the weekly Torah readings, and ultimately became read as the *haftorah*.

The story of Devorah and her song was chosen to substitute for Moshe's song, showing that Devorah's song has the same importance.

Why did she sit beneath a date tree, rather than in a house? So that no suspicion should fall upon her that she was alone in a house with a strange man. For this reason, too, she sat in an open field.

We see from this that a woman should be careful not to enter unguarded into a stranger's home, so that no suspicion should fall upon her. Even if she is righteous, she ought not rely on her piety. Devorah, after all, was a prophetess, yet she was careful not to allow suspicion to fall upon her.

וַתִּשְׁלַח וַתִּקְרָא לְבָרָק בֶּן אֲבִינֹעַם מִקֶּדֶשׁ נַפְתָּלִי — *She sent and called to Barak, son of Avinoam, of Kedesh-Naftali* (v. 6), and she said to him: "Go and tell the people that they must be rid of the seven Canaanite nations in *Eretz Yisrael*." And she told him further: "Go to Mount Tavor, taking with you by means of persuasion ten thousand men of the tribes of Naftali and Zevulun.

"God says: וּמָשַׁכְתִּי אֵלֶיךָ אֶל נַחַל קִישׁוֹן — *I will bring to you, to the Kishon Brook* (v. 7), Sisera, the commander of all of Yavin's armies, with his chariots and warriors. I will deliver him into your hands.'"

וַיֹּאמֶר אֵלֶיהָ בָּרָק — *Barak told her* (v. 8): "I will go if you accompany me, but if you refuse, I too will not go."

וַתֹּאמֶר הָלֹךְ אֵלֵךְ — *And she said: "I shall indeed go* (v. 9), but it will not be an attractive prospect for you. God shall deliver Sisera into the hands of a woman — that is, everyone will say that it was in my merit that Sisera fell, rather than yours."

Devorah then stood up and went to Kedesh with Barak.

וַיַּזְעֵק בָּרָק אֶת זְבוּלֻן וְאֶת נַפְתָּלִי קֶדְשָׁה — *And Barak summoned Zevulun and Naftali to Kedesh* (v. 10), bringing with him ten thousand men. Devorah too went with him.

Sisera was told that Barak ben Avinoam was on Mt. Tavor. Sisera assembled all of his iron chariots, nine hundred of them, and all of his men, to advance with him from the town of Charoshes Goyim, to the Kishon Brook.

Sisera was thirty years old at the time, and extraordinarily mighty. He had conquered the entire world, and there was no city whose walls could withstand him. All were terrified of his valor and strength, and armies were helpless before his cry, they were in such terror of him.

וַתֹּאמֶר דְּבֹרָה אֶל בָּרָק — *Devorah said to Barak* (v. 14): "Get up, for today is the day when God shall deliver Sisera into your hands, for God goes out in front of you." At these words, Barak descended from Tavor, followed by his ten thousand men.

וַיָּהָם ה' אֶת סִיסְרָא — *The Lord confused Sisera* (v. 15) and all of his charioteers, and the entire encampment fell before Barak's sharp swords. Sisera himself abandoned his chariot and fled on foot.

וּבָרָק רָדַף אַחֲרֵי הָרֶכֶב — *Barak pursued the chariots* (v. 16) until they reached the town of Charoshes Goyim, when the entire army was routed by Barak's swords. No one remained.

Sisera fled to the tent of Yael, wife of Chever the Kenite. There was peace between Chever and Yavin of Hazor.

וַתֵּצֵא יָעֵל לִקְרַאת סִיסְרָא — *And Yael came out to meet Sisera* (v. 18) and told him: "Please come in. Have no fear."

He went into her tent, and she covered him with a blanket. He asked her: "Give me a drink of water, for I am thirsty." She opened a flask of milk and gave him some, and covered him.

Rashi writes that she gave him milk because it makes a person sleepy, to ensure that he would sleep soundly.

"Stand in the doorway of the tent," he told her, "and if anyone approaches and asks if you have seen a man, say no."

Some of our Sages say that Sisera did not touch Yael, and that this is the meaning of the word "blanket" *(semichah)*. God himself testified [cf. *Radak* on this verse] to the fact that Yael was pious and did not have illicit relations with Sisera. We learn from this that a woman must be careful not to go into a house by herself, for people will suspect her and not believe that she is innocent. Even though Sisera fled and Yael actually killed him, still people suspected that she and Sisera had had illicit relations, and God Himself had to testify to her innocence.

וַתִּקַּח יָעֵל אֵשֶׁת חֶבֶר — *Yael, wife of Chever, took* (v. 21) a tent-peg and a hammer and pierced his temple with it as he slept, and he died.

וְהִנֵּה בָרָק רֹדֵף אֶת סִיסְרָא — *Behold, as Barak pursued Sisera* (v. 22),

*Yael shows
Barak the
dead Sisera*

Yael came out to meet him and said: "Come, I will show you the man whom you are seeking." He went with her and saw Sisera, lying dead, the tent-peg in his temple.

On that day God subdued Yavin king of Canaan. The people of Israel grew stronger and stronger, until they destroyed Yavin.

וַתָּשַׁר דְּבוֹרָה וּבָרָק בֶּן אֲבִינֹעַם — *Then Devorah and Barak the son of Avinoam sang* (5:1). "When God metes out punishment upon Israel, this is because they have forsaken him, but as soon as their hearts bring him back to Him in repentance, He helps them, and they thank Him.

"*Hearken, kings* (v. 3), listen, for I am God's prophetess, and I will sing praise to God, the God of Israel."

The *Midrash* says: Why is the word *anochi* ("I") repeated twice on Mt. Tavor, and on Mt. Carmel the words *God is the Lord* are repeated twice *(Melachim I* 18:39), while on Sinai the words *I am the Lord your God* are said only once *(Shmos* 20:2)? The answer is that on the day the Torah was given, Mt. Tavor and Mt. Carmel came and asked that God give the Torah upon them. God demurred, but instead gave them a double reward: on Sinai the word "I" is said once, while on Tavor it is said twice; on Sinai the words "I am the Lord your God" are said once, and on Carmel the words "God is the Lord" are said twice.

ה' בְּצֵאתְךָ מִשֵּׂעִיר — "*God, when You went out of Seir* (v. 4), when You marched from the fields of Edom to offer the Torah, the Edomites did not want to receive it. At that time the earth trembled and the heavens dripped with the dew that will, in the future, revive the dead. The clouds, too, dripped water."

God had told the heaven and earth that if the Torah was not accepted, they would be destroyed. When Edom refused the Torah the heaven and earth trembled, for they feared imminent destruction.

Why did Devorah begin her song with praise for the Torah? To show its great goodness, and how we should cleave to it, since it was given in trembling and might. How terrible it is to abandon it! When Israel abandoned it, they fell into their enemy's hands, but when they became righteous and began to learn Torah, God helped them once again.

הָרִים נָזְלוּ מִפְּנֵי ה' — "Mountains melted before God" (v. 5), and Mt. Sinai, too, the mountain of which the Torah tells that it had smoke upon it, and lightning and thunder. All of this was for fear of God, the God of Israel.

בִּימֵי שַׁמְגַּר בֶּן עֲנָת — "In the days of Shamgar, son of Anas (v. 6), in the days of Yael (for Yael, too, was a judge in Israel), in those days the people stopped walking on the roads of the idolaters. If forced to travel, they avoided the direct routes and traveled circuitously, in order to avoid the idol worshipers.

"Israel stopped living in open cities (v. 7), and those cities were abandoned — until I, Devorah, stood up to be a mother of Israel.

יִבְחַר אֱלֹהִים חֲדָשִׁים — "They chose new gods (v. 8). When Israel chose new idols, they then were forced to fight in their cities. But today, when they have repented, was there a shield or spear raised against the 40,000 men of Israel? The most seasoned troops of Sisera did not fight, for God confused them with stars and with the Kishon Brook [see below on v. 21].

"My heart goes to the lawgivers of Israel (v. 9), the scholars who give of themselves to the nation, enjoining them to praise God for His salvation, and to return to Him.

רֹכְבֵי אֲתֹנוֹת צְחֹרוֹת — "Those that ride white donkeys (v. 10), the merchants and lords who can now ride their white donkeys with no fear of the pagans, the judges who can now sit in judgment, and the travelers on the roads — these should now tell each other of God's aid.

מִקּוֹל מְחַצְצִים — "From the sound of the archers (v. 11) who lurked among the water carriers, that is, by the wells (where archers had formerly disturbed the people's peace), God has today helped you here too, and therefore the merchants and people should tell of His goodness and the favor which He has shown Israel. The people can now live in unfortified cities.

אָז יָרְדוּ לַשְּׁעָרִים — "Then the people of the Lord went down to the gates (v. 11), back to their unfortified cities; God's nation, who had formerly fled before the pagans."

The sound of the archers (v. 11) may also mean "the sound of the pebbles" (חָצָץ), the pebbles by the river. When a person would walk to the river for water, the pebbles would make noise, alerting the pagans. As a result, the people used to be afraid to go. But now that God has helped them, they can go down to the water without fear, and so there they should sing God's praises.

עוּרִי עוּרִי דְּבוֹרָה — "Awaken, awaken, Devorah (v. 12), sing your song. Stand up, Barak, and take your captives, son of Avinoam."

Our Sages say that because Devorah praised herself — until I, Devorah, stood up to be a mother in Israel — her gift of prophecy left her, and she was forced to say "awaken" four times, enjoining her prophetic spirit to return.

אָז יָרַד שָׂרִיד לְאַדִּירִים עָם — "Then He gave dominion to a remnant (v. 13) of Israel. God gave Israel dominion over the powerful pagans. Out of Ephraim (v. 14) came their root" — Yehoshua (Joshua), of the tribe of Ephraim, began the fight with Amalek; "and later, one from the tribe of Binyamin" — this refers to Shaul (Saul). Binyamin came "among your people" — for Shaul came with 200,000 foot soldiers. The word בַּעֲמָמֶיךְ also suggests that he would extinguish his enemies like failing coals (עמם = "dull").

מִנִּי מָכִיר — "From Machir (v. 14) the nobles also went to war, capturing numerous cities. And from the tribe of Zevulun went even those who write with their pens — the scribes and scholars — not to mention the common people. All went to war.

וְשָׂרַי בְּיִשָּׂשכָר — "And the princes of Yissachar (v. 15), that is, the scholars, were always with Devorah, teaching Israel Torah and justice. The other men of Yissachar accompanied Barak and did his bidding. Into the valley they rushed forth, at his feet (v. 15), to conscript their brethren and see to the needs of the battle.

"But בִּפְלַגּוֹת רְאוּבֵן — the divisions of Reuven (v. 15), the heart of the tribe of Reuven, separated itself from Israel by refusing to go to battle.

"Great are the thoughts of the heart," says Devorah. "Why did you, Reuven, sit between the borders during the war? Did you want to hear the noise of battle, in order to know which side was winning, which side to join? Reuven, in my heart I felt your splitting yourself off from battle, for I know the reason behind it.

גִּלְעָד בְּעֵבֶר הַיַּרְדֵּן שָׁכֵן — *"Gilad dwelt on the other side of the Jordan* (v. 17), together with Reuven, and also did not join the battle. Tribe of Dan, why did you collect your money and your ships, in preparation for flight? The fact that Asher did not join is understandable, though, for they dwell near the sea, in unfortified cities close by the enemy, and they could not leave them undefended.

"But Zevulun (v. 18), you were a tribe which scorned your life, welcoming death in battle with Barak. You too, Naftali, offered your life on the high fields, on Mount Tavor.

בָּאוּ מְלָכִים נִלְחָמוּ — *"The kings came, they fought* (v. 19). The kings fought and then encamped in the town of Taanach, their numbers so large that they extended all the way to the waters of Megiddo. These kings who came to help Sisera took no money; they offered their services without charge.

מִן שָׁמַיִם נִלְחָמוּ הַכּוֹכָבִים — *"The stars fought them from heaven* (v. 20), from their orbits they fought Sisera."

Rashi writes that because the kings came to help Sisera, refusing to take money, God struck them with an army which also accepted no payment — the stars.

נַחַל קִישׁוֹן גְּרָפָם — *"The Kishon Brook swept them away* (v. 21), out of this world. When the stars began to burn them up they jumped into the waters of the Kishon to cool off, and they drowned.

תִּדְרְכִי נַפְשִׁי עֹז — *"My soul trod the strong nations* (v. 21). *Then the horses' hoofs* (v. 22) stamped with the fury of the leaping of Sisera's men." *Rashi* writes that the stars heated up the earth and the horseshoes of Sisera's mounts fell off, and thus their hoofs stamped.

אוֹרוּ מֵרוֹז — *"Curse Meroz* (v. 23), the city of Meroz, says the messenger of God." This is Barak. "Cursed be its inhabitants, because they did not come to the aid of God against the mighty."

Some of our Sages say that Meroz is the name of a star which did not join the battle as the other stars did; others say that this was a man of importance who did not give assistance to Barak.

תְּבָרֵךְ מִנָּשִׁים יָעֵל — *"Blessed above women shall be Yael, wife of Chever the Keni* (v. 24). Let her be more blessed (see end of verse) than the women of whom it is written *in the tent* — that is, Sarah, Rivkah, Rachel and Leah. Let Yael be more blessed than they." True, they gave birth and brought up the tribes of Israel, but had Yael not killed Sisera he would have destroyed all of Israel.

A second reason that the words "in the tent" appear in Yael's blessing is because she was a pious woman who dwelt modestly in her tent, rather than in the open streets.

מַיִם שָׁאַל חָלָב נָתָנָה — *"Water he asked for, milk she gave"* (v. 25). Sisera asked for water and she gave him milk in order to see if he still had his wits about him and would notice the difference; she gave him cream in a water vessel.

יָדָהּ לַיָּתֵד תִּשְׁלַחְנָה — *"She stretched her hand out to the tent-peg* (v. 26), and with her right hand she struck the fatigued Sisera. She struck him and cracked his skull, and the peg went through his temple and out the other side.

בֵּין רַגְלֶיהָ כָּרַע נָפַל שָׁכָב — *"Between her feet he bowed, fell, and lay* (v. 27), and there Sisera died.

"She looked out the window (v. 28), Sisera's mother, and sobbed; *Through the lattice* she peered, and asked: 'Why are they tarrying, the chariots, why are they not coming? Why is the sound of the chariots delayed?'

חַכְמוֹת שָׂרוֹתֶיהָ תַּעֲנֶינָּה — *"The wisest of her ladies answer her* (v. 29), and then she herself answers her own question: 'Why should I wonder at the delay? They are busy dividing the booty, each man with one or two women of Israel for his loot. My son has plundered a variety of colored garments for himself, embroidered alike on both sides, with colored needlework for the other soldiers.' So did Sisera's mother tell herself."

Of this Devorah said: "Your comfort is foolish. כֵּן יֹאבְדוּ כָל אוֹיְבֶיךָ ה' — *So shall perish all of Your enemies, God* (v. 31). Just as Sisera was doomed, so shall all of Your enemies meet their doom. But those that love God will be like the sun as it rises in its might."

After Barak's battle the land was at peace for 40 years.

HAFTORAH

Yisro

(Yeshayahu/Isaiah 6:1 — 7:6 and 9:5-6)

בִּשְׁנַת מוֹת הַמֶּלֶךְ עֻזִּיָהוּ — *In the year of the death of King Uzziahu* (6:1). The vision described in this chapter took place in the year that King Uzziahu contracted *tzaraas* (a disease resembling leprosy). Why is he called dead? Because one who has *tzaraas* is considered dead. We see in *Bereishis Rabbah* that four kinds of people are considered dead: a poor man, one who has *tzaraas*, a blind man, and a childless man.

Uzziahu was a king of Israel who also desired the priesthood, despite the fact that he was not a descendant of Aharon. This generally is true: when God gives a person wealth and honor he craves more. For this reason the author of *Menoras HaMaor* likens Israel to a grapevine. The more grapes there are on a vine, the lower it bends. So, too, should Israel be: the greater the honor heaped on one, the humbler he should be.

It is for this reason that we are commanded to bow down many times during the *Shemoneh Esreh* prayer. The first time we bow is at the beginning of the prayer, the second time at the end of the blessing *Magen Avraham*, the third time when we say *Modim anachnu lach*, and the fourth time at the conclusion of the blessing *Hatov shimcha*. More bowing than this is prohibited.

But the High Priest, because of his great importance, had to bow down at the beginning and conclusion of each blessing. And the king, because of his great stature, had to bow down lower at the beginning of *Shemoneh Esreh*, so that he would be humble.

But Uzziahu, not satisfied with the kingship, wanted the priesthood as well. God therefore afflicted him with *tzaraas*. We can learn from this that a person ought not take for himself a position which is not appropriate to him.

וָאֶרְאֶה — *I saw* (v. 1). "I, Yeshayahu, saw God seated on a high throne, His feet filling the Temple."

This is a difficult passage, since the Torah clearly states *(Shmos 33:20)*: *No man can see Me and live.* How could Yeshayahu have seen God and remained alive? The answer is that he did not see Him clearly; it was as if he saw Him through glass.

שְׂרָפִים עֹמְדִים מִמַּעַל לוֹ — *Seraphim stood above Him* (v. 2). Fiery angels stood above in heaven, to serve Him. Each angel had six wings: with two he covered his face so as not to see the Divine Presence; with two he covered his legs, so that his naked body should not be seen before God; and with two he flew.

The *Midrash Yelamdenu* writes that the words *his feet filled the Temple* refer to the eighty priests who accompanied Uzziahu in the *Beis HaMikdash* to burn his incense-offering, and *seraphim stood above him* hints at the fact that Uzziahu deserved to be burnt as were Korach and his followers. Only because God had said that no man would be like Korach was he saved from immolation, and instead he contracted *tzaraas*.

The *Midrash* states that Michael stands on God's right side, and is eighteen times 10,000 miles wide; Gavriel stands on His left side, with a width of eighteen times 10,000 miles. Thus they total thirty-six times 10,000 miles, or the numerical equivalent of the word לוֹ ("Him"), which equals 36. Gavriel can soar across the entire world in two bounds.

וְקָרָא זֶה אֶל זֶה וְאָמַר — *And one called to the other and said* (v. 3): The angels ask for each other's permission to begin their song, to ensure that no one begins before the other, for one who does so deserves to be burnt. For this reason we say, in our prayers: "*Kedushah* ('sanctity') they all answer in unison, as one." We learn from this that in the synagogue all should recite the *Kedushah* prayer in unison.

The *Gemara* says that three classes of angels say the Hymn of Praise daily. One group says *Kadosh* ("holy"), the second group *Kadosh, kadosh*, and the third group "Holy, holy, holy is God, Lord of Hosts." But Israel is more beloved by God, for while the angels say it only once a day, Israel says it each hour.

Some Sages say that the angels say the hymn just once in their lifetimes. In still another way is Israel favored — the angels do not say their hymn until Israel has said theirs.

Each angel says *Kadosh* three times: God is holy in heaven, holy on earth, and holy for eternity. He is the Lord of Hosts, and the whole world is full of His glory.

מְלֹא כָל הָאָרֶץ כְּבוֹדוֹ — *The whole world is full of His glory* (v. 3). The *Gemara* says, in Tractate *Kiddushin*: A man should not hold his head up in pride, for God's glory fills the entire world. A person should rather bow his head.

וַיָּנֻעוּ אַמּוֹת הַסִּפִּים — *The doorposts moved* (v. 4). The pillars of the Temple trembled at the sound of the angels' voices calling to one another. We should jump up slightly during recitation of *Kedushah*, remembering how the doorposts "jumped."

The *Beis HaMikdash* was filled with smoke, "and I, Yeshayahu, cried: 'Woe to me, I shall be destroyed and killed. I am a man of unclean lips, living among a people of unclean lips — that is, they are covered with sin. My eyes have seen the Lord, Master of Hosts, and I must die.'

"Then one of the fiery angels flew to me, holding a piece of coal which he had taken off the altar, with tongs." The fiery coal is here called רִצְפָּה, which suggests the words רָצוֹץ פֶּה — it *shatters the mouths* of those who speak ill of Israel.

וַיַּגַּע עַל פִּי — *"And he touched my mouth"* (v. 7) with the coal, and said: 'Through this your sin of speaking ill of Israel has been taken away, and your transgression is forgiven.' "

From this exchange we can infer that the power of a prophet is greater than that of an angel, for the coal touched the prophet's mouth without harming it, but the angel had to take it with tongs.

We can learn from this that a *rosh yeshivah* or head of a community should take care not to speak ill of Israel. Three spoke ill of Israel and were punished for it: Moshe, Yeshayahu, and Eliyahu.

The *Yalkut* writes that Menashe, grandson of Yeshayahu, killed him, saying: "I will bring you to judgment. Your Rebbe, Moshe, said that no man can see God and live, yet you claim that you saw Him and are still alive. Moshe said that God is near to all who call Him, but you say that one should *seek God when He is to be found* (*Yeshayahu* 55:6), indicating that one cannot find Him at all times."

"How can I answer you?" said Yeshayahu. "You will not listen to me, and your transgression will then be considered an intentional one. Better that I do not answer you, and your transgression will be considered unintentional."

Then Yeshayahu pronounced one of the Divine Names, and a cedar tree opened up in front of him. Yeshayahu entered and hid there, so Menashe ordered that the tree be sawed down. When the saw came to Yeshayahu's mouth he died. This was God's punishment because his mouth had spoken ill of Israel, by calling them *impure of lips.*

וְסָר עֲוֹנֶךָ — *Your sin will depart* (v. 7). The *Gemara* says, in Tractate

Shabbos, that Mar Ukva says: When a person prays on the eve of *Shabbos*, and says *Vayechulu*, two angels come, lay their hands upon his head, and say: "Your sin will depart, and your transgression will be forgiven."

Even Shoev writes, in his *derashah* on Shavuos: Why is it that his sins are forgiven when he says *Vayechulu*? The answer is that this prayer testifies to the fact that God created the world and rested on *Shabbos*. One who refuses to say *Vayechulu* refuses to testify to that. Of one who refuses to testify the Torah says, אִם לוֹא יַגִּיד וְנָשָׂא עֲוֹנוֹ — *If he will not tell, he will bear his sin (Vayikra 5:1)*. Therefore when a person does say *Vayechulu*, testifying to the fact that God created the world, the angels say, "Your sin will depart."

וָאֶשְׁמַע אֶת קוֹל ה' אֹמֵר אֶת מִי אֶשְׁלַח — *And I heard the voice of the Lord saying: "Whom shall I send* (v. 8) to rebuke Israel? I sent Amos, and the people called him a stutterer because he was slow of speech. 'God could have chosen anyone in the entire world,' they said, 'and He chose thick-tongued Amos.'"

וּמִי יֵלֶךְ לָנוּ — *"Who will go for us* (v. 8) on this mission?"
"Then I, Yeshayahu, said: 'I am ready, send me.'
"And God said to me: 'Go and tell Israel: I, God, tell you — you hear My words but do not understand, see My wonders but do not know Me. The hearts of this people have become fat and their ears dull; their eyes are closed. They are afraid lest they see with their eyes and hear with their ears, and their hearts will understand the words of the prophets, and they will make sense to them. Then they may repent and it will cure them.'"

וָאֹמַר עַד מָתַי — *"Then I said: 'Until when* (v. 11) will they harden their hearts and refuse to hear?'
"And God said: 'I know that they will not repent until terrible troubles come upon them and they are exiled. Their cities will be abandoned and unpopulated, their homes empty, their land a wasteland.'"

וְרִחַק ה' אֶת הָאָדָם — *And God will have removed men far away* (v. 12), and the land will be forsaken. וְעוֹד בָּהּ עֲשִׂירִיָה — *There will be within her one-tenth* (v. 13), that is, only a very small number shall remain, and this leftover I, God, shall once again make empty, until all that is left are those righteous men who repent whole-heartedly. Just as only the trunk of a terebinth or an oak remains after all of the leaves have fallen off, so the righteous will remain, the seed of the holy fathers Avraham, Yitzchak and Yaakov, and because of them I will not destroy them."

וַיְהִי בִּימֵי אָחָז בֶּן יוֹתָם בֶּן עֻזִּיָּהוּ מֶלֶךְ יְהוּדָה — *It was in the days of Achaz the son of Yosam the son of Uzziahu, king of Yehudah* (7:1). Retzin, king of Aram, and Pekach, son of Remaliahu, king of Israel, came to do battle against Yerushalayim, but they could not prevail because of Uzziahu's merit.

Why does the verse mention Achaz's righteous forbears? Because the angels said: 'Oh, woe, that such an evil man should be king!' Then God said: 'But he is a son of Yosam, son of Uzziahu, who were both pious.'

וַיֻּגַּד לְבֵית דָּוִד — *It was told to the house of David* (v. 2). It was told to Achaz, a descendant of David, that the king of Aram had allied himself with the king of Israel to come and fight them. Why does the verse not mention Achaz by name? Because he was a wicked man.

Achaz's heart swayed with fright, as trees in the forest sway in the wind. Achaz was terrified because he had fought each king separately without success. How much worse now that they were allied!

The *Midrash* writes: Why does the verse liken his fear to the swaying of trees in a forest, which do not grow fruit, rather than fruit-bearing trees?

This can be explained by means of a parable. The River Euphrates is asked: "Why do your waters not shout out loud like other waters, which roar and make themselves heard from afar?" Answers the river: "I have no need for shouting, for everyone knows who I am. Trees planted by my side grow fruits in thirty days, seedlings nurtured with my water grow in three days."

The River Tigris is asked: "Why do you shout so loud?" The Tigris answers: "I shout so that people will hear me. And even when I shout out loud no one hears me, for my water is not as good as the water of the others. Therefore I must shout to show that I, too, am somebody."

Similarly, one can ask fruit-bearing trees: "Why do we not hear you roar as the trees in the forest do when the wind blows?" Answer the fruit-bearing trees: "People know us through our fruits, and praise us for them." The trees of the forest, though, say: "We shout out loud, for otherwise we would not be recognized."

We learn from this that someone who boasts is worthless and, knowing that people think little of him, praises himself.

וַיֹּאמֶר ה' אֶל יְשַׁעְיָהוּ — *God told Yeshayahu* (v. 3): "Go to meet Achaz, you and those of Israel who returned to Me because of you, who are considered your children. Go to the end of the aqueduct of the upper pool, to the path of the field where the washers spread their clothing to dry. There you will find Achaz.

"Say to him: 'Be calm and still as wine resting upon its lees. Fear not, let your heart not weaken because of the tails of these two smoking pieces of wood, the people who fear the anger of Retzin and Pekach the son of Remaliahu.' "

יַעַן כִּי יָעַץ עָלֶיךָ אֲרָם רָעָה — *"Because Aram has counseled evil upon you* (v. 5), Ephraim and Pekach ben Remaliahu planned and said: 'We will go up onto the land of Yehudah, and rouse them up to war. We will then break them and crown a king over them, one who suits us.' That is what they say — but have no fear of them."

כִּי יֶלֶד יֻלַּד לָנוּ — *For a child is born to us* (9:5). Although Achaz is wicked, a child has been born to us — this is Chizkiyahu, the king who will rule in Achaz's place. He is righteous and will turn his shoulders to God's commandments.

God, who is called "wonderful Counselor, mighty God, eternal Father," will give Chizkiyahu the name of *Sar Shalom,* "Prince of Peace," for in his day there will be peace and truth.

HAFTORAH

Mishpatim

(Yirmeyahu/Jeremiah 34:8-22 — 33:25-26)

These are the words which Yirmeyahu had from God (הַדָּבָר אֲשֶׁר הָיָה אֶל יִרְמְיָהוּ מֵאֵת ה'; v. 8). It was after King Tzidkiyahu had made a covenant with the populace of Yerushalayim *to proclaim freedom* (לִקְרֹא ... דְּרוֹר; v. 8) — everyone would free his Jewish slave or maidservant after six years of servitude, so that no Jew would keep his brother in bondage.

And they listened (וַיִּשְׁמְעוּ; v. 10), all of these nobles and the whole populace, to the agreement to release their slaves from servitude. They listened, and sent them away, but then *they returned* (וַיָּשׁוּבוּ;

v. 11) and brought back the servants whom they had freed, once
again renewing their bondage.

And God's words came to Yirmeyahu (וַיְהִי דְבַר ה' אֶל יִרְמְיָהוּ; v.
12): "I made a covenant with your ancestors on the day that I took
them out of Egypt. I told them: *At the end of seven years* (מִקֵּץ שֶׁבַע
שָׁנִים; v. 14) each man must send out his brother, the Jew who has
been sold into bondage. He shall serve you for six years, and in the
seventh you must let him free.

"Your forefathers did not listen to Me or pay heed, but then you
returned and did what was right in My eyes, proclaiming freedom
for men. You made an agreement in the House which is called by
My Name. Now, suddenly, you have desecrated My Name, taking
those maidservants and bondmen whom you had set free and
enslaving them again."

"*Therefore* (לָכֵן; v. 17)," says God, "because you, Israel, have not
listened to Me and freed your slaves, your brothers, I will proclaim
your 'freedom' from Me. I will no longer be your Master, protecting
and saving you.

"You will be left open to the sword, to pestilence and hunger.
Your enemies will come upon you, and I will cast you into the hands
of all the kings of this earth. I will take those who break My
covenant, the nobles of Yerushalayim, and give them to their mortal
enemies. Their dead bodies will be carrion for the vultures and the
beasts of the earth.

"I will place Tzidkiyahu, King of Yehudah (Judah), and all of his
nobles, into their enemy's hands, into the hands of the army of the
king of Babylonia. They withdrew for a time, but now they shall
return. I shall bid them to come back to Yerushalayim, and they will
fight you, besiege your city, and send it up in flames. The cities of
Yehudah will be laid waste and barren."

Why did God punish them so severely? Because of their sin of not
freeing their slaves after six years of servitude. For this, as R'
Bechaye points out, is a remembrance of the time that God
miraculously freed the Jewish slaves from Egypt, to be His slaves, as
it says: "*For the Children of Israel are mine, as slaves* — כִּי לִי בְנֵי
יִשְׂרָאֵל עֲבָדִים. They are My slaves because I freed them from Egypt."

For this reason a servant should not serve his master for more
than six years. If the people refuse to free their slaves, the wonders
of the Exodus from Egypt may be forgotten.

Another reason for freeing the slaves after six years is that it is a remembrance of the fact that God created the world in six days and rested on the seventh. One who will not free his slaves denies, heaven forbid, God's creation of the world. For this reason God's anger was roused and He exiled His people from their land.

So said God: "*If not for the covenant which I made with night and day* (אִם לֹא בְרִיתִי יוֹמָם וָלָיְלָה; 33:25), and with heaven and earth, promising them that they would exist forever, I would humiliate the children of Yaakov and of My servant David (i.e., just as I will not destroy the creations, so I will not humiliate Israel); but instead, I will crown their kings and nobles."

The *Midrash Yelamdenu* writes that the words *If not for My covenant* (אִם לֹא בְרִיתִי) refer to the covenant of the circumcision (*bris*). The merit of circumcision enables Israel to survive in this world.

The *Yelamdenu* also writes that the commandments of *Shabbos* and circumcision once disputed between themselves. Said *Shabbos*: "I am the more important, for God rested on *Shabbos* after the Creation." Circumcision retorted: "I am the more important, as it says, *If not for the covenant with night and day* ... If not for circumcision God would not have created night and day, heaven and earth."

R' Yosei ben Shalom says that this can be likened to two important men standing one next to the other. No one can discern which is the more important of the two. But on their exit, everyone can finally decide who is the more exalted, for they see who steps back and gives way to whom.

Similarly, on *Shabbos* all creative work is forbidden, but if a circumcision is to take place it supersedes the *Shabbos*, and so it must be the greater of the two.

HAFTORAH
Terumah
(Melachim I/I Kings 5:26 — 6:13)

And God gave wisdom to Shlomo (Solomon) (וַה' נָתַן חָכְמָה לִשְׁלֹמֹה; 5:26). There was peace between Shlomo and Hiram, king of Tyre. They made a treaty between themselves, and because they were at peace, Hiram gave the wood with which to build the *Beis HaMikdash*. From this we see that good deeds result from peace between men.

The verse also shows us that a person must have great wisdom in order to be at peace with men. Because Shlomo was so wise, he was able to make peace with Hiram.

The Sages have said that when our people live peacefully together God forgives them their sins, even their idol worship. This is difficult to comprehend. Why should God forgive their idol worship, the most loathsome of transgressions, just because they live in peace?

Ollelos Ephraim gives an answer. If they are living peacefully, the Jews will speak to one another of their idol worship. Ultimately, they will come to understand that idol worship is meaningless, and they will begin to worship God. This is why God will forgive the sins of idol worshipers; if they live peacefully, they will soon abandon their sins. But if there is animosity between them, and they worship idols, one will not discuss it with the other, or listen to the other. Even if a wise man dwells with them, they will not listen to him, and they will remain sinners.

Peace is a great thing. Our Sages say: "Torah scholars increase peace in the world" (תַּלְמִידֵי חֲכָמִים מַרְבִּים שָׁלוֹם בָּעוֹלָם). Sages and the righteous try to make peace. They even meet with the wicked, praying with them and teaching them Torah, for every man has an obligation to rebuke and teach his fellows.

Of the wicked, however, it is written: *There is no peace, said God, for the wicked* (אֵין שָׁלוֹם אָמַר ה' לָרְשָׁעִים; *Yeshayahu* 48:22). The wicked do not try to bring peace by meeting with the righteous.

They are afraid that God will compare their deeds unfavorably and punish them.

Peace is the most important trait of all — avoiding conflict with men, forgiving them if they speak in anger.

The *Gemara* in Tractate *Rosh HaShanah* says that "one who 'overlooks' his natural tendencies will have his sins 'overlooked' " (כָּל הַמַעֲבִיר עַל מִדוֹתָיו מַעֲבִירִין עַל כָּל פְּשָׁעָיו). That is, one who forgives his fellow man for whatever hurt has been inflicted upon him will be forgiven.

The *Midrash* writes that Hiram was alive in the days of Yehudah. His name at the time was Chira, and he was involved in the righteous deeds which led to the birth of Peretz, forefather of David and his son Shlomo, who built the *Beis HaMikdash*. So too Hiram was found worthy of donating the wood for its construction.

King Shlomo raised a levy in all of Israel (וַיַּעַל הַמֶּלֶךְ שְׁלֹמֹה מַס מִכָּל יִשְׂרָאֵל; v. 27). This tax brought in such great revenue that they hired thirty thousand workers with it. Shlomo sent them to chop wood in the forest. Ten thousand went for a month, and then returned home, while another ten thousand went in their stead. Thus, each was in the woods for one month, and at home for two.

The *Gemara* says, in Tractate *Kesubos*, that when a scholar wants to leave his wife and go to learn Torah he is not allowed to go for longer than a month. If he wants to go for a longer time, he should ask her permission. Of course, it is praiseworthy indeed for a wife to allow her husband to go and learn; it is as if she herself had learned.

Shlomo had 70,000 porters (וַיְהִי לִשְׁלֹמֹה שִׁבְעִים אֶלֶף נֹשֵׂא סַבָּל; v. 29), and 80,000 stonecutters. Three hundred men supervised the work. The king commanded that gigantic stones be quarried to serve as the foundation for the *Beis HaMikdash*.

And it was in the 480th year (וַיְהִי בִשְׁמוֹנִים שָׁנָה וְאַרְבַּע מֵאוֹת שָׁנָה; 6:1) after Israel's Exodus from Egypt, in the fourth year and second month of Shlomo's reign, that he began to build a house of God.

And the house which King Shlomo built for God (וְהַבַּיִת אֲשֶׁר בָּנָה הַמֶּלֶךְ שְׁלֹמֹה לַה'; v. 2) was 60 cubits long, 20 cubits wide, and 30 cubits high. *And the porch before the temple of the house* (וְהָאוּלָם עַל פְּנֵי הֵיכַל הַבַּיִת; v. 3) was as long as the width of the house (i.e., 20 cubits). Its width on the eastern side was ten cubits.

And he made windows which were wide without and narrow within (וַיַּעַשׂ לַבַּיִת חַלּוֹנֵי שְׁקֻפִים אֲטֻמִים; v. 4). They were not like normal windows. Windows are generally built small on the exterior side of the wall, and large on the interior, in order to maximize the amount of light allowed inside. But in the *Beis HaMikdash* the windows were small from within and large from without, to show that the *Beis HaMikdash* did not need earthly light, for it itself illuminated the world.

And he built a side-structure against the wall of the house (וַיִּבֶן עַל קִיר הַבַּיִת יָצִיעַ; v. 5), and made it beautiful with beams. *And the house, while being built, was built of stone already prepared* (וְהַבַּיִת בְּהִבָּנֹתוֹ אֶבֶן שְׁלֵמָה מַסָּע נִבְנָה; v. 7). The *Pesikta* writes that the large stones cut themselves and climbed up the walls of the *Beis HaMikdash*.

R' Huna said, in the name of R' Ashi, that even the spirits and demons helped in the construction of the *Beis HaMikdash*.

R' Chanina ben Dosa saw his townspeople bringing gifts and contributions to Yerushalayim. He thought to himself: "I, too, should bring something to Yerushalayim some time."

He found a beautiful boulder, and he asked five passing men if they would bring it to Yerushalayim. "Yes," they answered, "for the sum of five gold pieces. But you must lay your hand upon it too, and then we will bring it to Yerushalayim."

R' Chanina put his finger upon it, and in an hour they were in Yerushalayim. He wanted to pay his helpers, but could find no trace of them. The Sages concluded that they were angels.

The *Gemara* says, in Tractate *Sotah*, that it was forbidden to use iron tools on the stones of the *Beis HaMikdash* once they were on the site, but when the stones were still in the mountains from where they were hewn, iron tools could be used. The sound of iron striking stone was not permitted within the *Beis HaMikdash*.

The worm known as *shamir* split all the stones. The builders indicated in black ink the places where they wanted the stones to be split, and then placed the *shamir* upon the stones, and it split them.

Midrash Shocher Tov writes that the *shamir* was brought by an eagle from *Gan Eden*. Shlomo HaMelech, who could converse with all the birds, asked the eagle to bring it for him.

The *Gemara* says, in Tractate *Gittin*, in *Perek Mi SheAchazo*: Shlomo HaMelech asked the wise men how they would be able to cut through the stones for the *Beis HaMikdash*. They answered: "With the *shamir* which Moshe used to carve the stones of the High Priest's breastplate." Shlomo asked them: "Where can I find such a thing?" They answered: "The demonic spirits will tell you."

Shlomo went to the spirits, and they referred him to Ashmedai (Asmodeus), king of the demons. Shlomo then sent Benayahu, son of Yehoyada, to find Ashmedai.

Benayahu went to the place where Ashmedai dwelt, and there on a hillside found a well marked with his seal. He dug a hole below, emptied out all of the water from the well, and sealed up the hole. Then he bored a hole at the top and filled the well with potent wine.

Ashmedai awoke and drank from the well, and the wine put him into a deep sleep. Benayahu then shackled him with a chain which had God's name written upon it, and brought the demon king to Shlomo.

Shlomo asked him where the *shamir* could be found, and he answered: "The guardian spirit (שַׂר) of the sea gave it to a certain bird for safekeeping." By means of a ruse, Benayahu was able to wrest the *shamir* from the bird, and finally got it.

God told Shlomo: "As long as you keep My Torah, I will keep the promise which I made to your father David, and I will live among you."

Such were the words of the prophet Achiyah HaShiloni, spoken in God's name. He told him this so that Shlomo would not think that everything was contingent upon the *Beis HaMikdash*. Rather, God's promise would be kept only if Shlomo HaMelech heeded the laws of the Torah.

HAFTORAH

Tetzaveh

(Yechezkel/Ezekiel 43:10-27)

You, son of man, tell the House of Israel of the house (אַתָּה בֶן אָדָם הַגֵּד אֶת בֵּית יִשְׂרָאֵל אֶת הַבָּיִת; v. 10).

God told Yechezkel: "Tell the House of Israel, now in exile, of the building of the *Beis HaMikdash* in the days of *Mashiach*, as you have seen it. *And they will be ashamed of their sins* (וְיִכָּלְמוּ מֵעֲוֹנוֹתֵיהֶם; ibid.), because they will hear how I will be gracious to them, and rebuild the *Beis HaMikdash*, and that I have not become disgusted with them because of their sins.

"And if they will be ashamed of all that they have done (וְאִם נִכְלְמוּ מִכֹּל אֲשֶׁר עָשׂוּ; v. 11), of all of their transgressions, *tell them and write before them the form of the house and its fashion,* the style of the rooms, its entrances and exits, the pattern of each and every room and all that is within it, so that they will know all of the details of its construction, so that they will know what to do when *Mashiach* comes to us. Because of their faith in his arrival they will merit rebuilding the *Beis HaMikdash.* He who does not believe will not be worthy of seeing its reconstruction, and will not be resurrected."

And the altar hearth shall be four cubits (וְהָהַרְאֵל אַרְבַּע אַמּוֹת; v. 15). This is its height, from the *sovev* which surrounded it, to the top.

From the hearth of the altar and above, four horns (וּמֵהָאֲרִיאֵל וּלְמַעְלָה הַקְּרָנוֹת אַרְבַּע; *ibid.*). There were four horns, one on each corner of the altar. Why is the altar called *Ariel* ("lion of God")? Because the heavenly flames on the altar took the form of a lion, king of the beasts.

The square top of the altar was twelve cubits in length and twelve in width, when measured from the center, so that we see that each side, from corner to corner, was twenty-four cubits. This was the portion of the woodpile, where the flames and the sacrifices were.

The top of the altar extended for an extra two cubits on each side. One cubit was occupied by the horns, and the other served as a path for the priests. Hence the verse says: *The Azarah was fourteen cubits long and fourteen cubits wide* (וְהָעֲזָרָה אַרְבַּע עֶשְׂרֵה אֹרֶךְ בְּאַרְבַּע עֶשְׂרֵה רֹחַב; v. 17), that is, the top of the altar, including the above, was — for each of its four quarters — fourteen by fourteen, giving a total of twenty-eight cubits for each side.

And the angel said to me (Yechezkel): *"Son of man, so said God, the Lord: These are the laws of the altar* (v. 18), to inaugurate it on the day that it will be built, so that it will be worthy of use, to bring the offerings upon it and sprinkle there the blood of the sacrifices. You will give to the priests, sons of the tribe of Levi, *who are of the descendants of Tzadok* (v. 19; they are called by Tzadok's name, because he served as the first High Priest in the *Beis HaMikdash* built by Shlomo), the priests who are close to Me, serving Me — *Give to them a young bull* (v. 19) as a sin-offering *(chatas).* Take of its blood, and put it on the four horns of the altar, and on the four sides of the top, and on its border, at its base below (the *yesod).*

With this you can purify the altar, cleansing it of all unholiness, so that it will be worthy of serving as an atonement from that time forward. *Take the bull which serves for the sin-offering* (v. 21) and burn it near the exit, outside the *Beis HaMikdash.*

"*On the second day* (v. 22) you shall sacrifice a he-goat, whole and umblemished, as a sin-offering. The priests shall cleanse the altar with the goat's blood, as they cleansed it with the blood of the bull the day before.

"*When you have finished cleansing it* (v. 23) sacrifice, in the court, a young ox and a ram, whole and unblemished, for each of seven days, as an offering."

The *Kohanim* were instructed to sprinkle salt on these burnt offerings (v. 24). And why were all sacrifices accompanied by salt? Because when God created the world none of the waters wanted to go down to earth: they all wanted to remain in heaven, closer to God. The Almighty thereupon assured them that in the earth below a distinctive privilege awaited them — for when in the course of the years the *Beis HaMikdash* would be built, no sacrifice would ever be offered without salt. And where does salt come from? It comes, of course, from the waters of the sea.

The *Kohanim* were thus commanded to cleanse the altar for seven days to purify it, and consecrate it with the blood of the sacrificial animals. At the end of seven days, the altar would be inaugurated and ready for daily use.

Accordingly, *from the eighth day onward* (v. 27) the *Kohanim* would bring the regular offerings and God promised to accept them willingly.

HAFTORAH
Ki Sisa
(Melachim I/I Kings 18:1-19)

וַיְהִי יָמִים רַבִּים וּדְבַר ה' הָיָה אֶל אֵלִיָּהוּ — *It was after many days, and the word of God came to Eliyahu* (Elijah) (18:1), in the third year of the famine, and said: "Go and show yourself to Achav (Ahab), and I (God) will bring rain to the earth, for many of the people have repented as a result of the famine."

God sometimes must strike Israel in order to bring them to repentance. Our Sages have said that as soon as Achashverosh gave his seal to Haman, empowering him to deal with the Jews as he saw fit, only then did the Jews repent. Forty-eight prophets rebuked Israel, but they did not repent; only the seal of Achashverosh brought them to repentance.

The *Midrash*, in *Vayikra Rabbah*, writes that when it goes badly for a person the days seem endless. Thus the verse says *many days* — although it was really only three years, it seemed like much more, because of the famine and troubles.

וַיֵּלֶךְ אֵלִיָּהוּ לְהֵרָאוֹת אֶל אַחְאָב — *Eliyahu went to show himself to Achav* (v. 2) while the famine in Shomron grew worse. וַיִּקְרָא אַחְאָב אֶל עוֹבַדְיָהוּ — *Achav called for Ovadiahu* (v. 3), a God-fearing man who was appointed over his household.

When Izevel (Jezebel) persecuted God's prophets, Ovadiahu gave sanctuary to one hundred prophets, hiding fifty in one cave and fifty in another, and supporting them with bread and water.

The *Gemara* says, in Tractate *Sanhedrin*, that Achav told Ovadiahu: "If you were truly pious, God would have blessed this household, as He blessed Lavan because of Yaakov, and Pharaoh because of Yosef." A heavenly voice rang out and said: "Ovadiahu is pious, but Achav's house merits no blessing, for Achav is wicked!"

R' Abba says that Ovadiahu was greater than Avraham when it came to charity and good deeds, for he risked his life by supporting the prophets. Had Izevel learned of his deed, she would have killed him.

Why did he hide them in two separate caves? R' Eliezer says that Ovadiahu learned this from Yaakov, who split his children and household into two camps, for if Esav would destroy one camp, at least the other would flee and be saved. Similarly, Ovadiahu felt that if Izevel would find one cave and kill the prophets, the others would have a chance to flee.

וַיֹּאמֶר אַחְאָב אֶל עֹבַדְיָהוּ — *Achav said to Ovadiahu* (v. 5): "We must go to the wells and rivers in the land and try to find grass for the horses and mules, so that we will not be left without animals." They divided the land between them, Achav going in one direction by himself, and Ovadiahu in another.

Eliyahu met Ovadiahu, who recognized him and fell on his face (v. 7). "Are you my master Eliyahu?" he said. "I am," Eliyahu replied. "Now, go and tell your master that Eliyahu is here."

"How have I sinned, that you are delivering me into the hands of my master, who will kill me?" asked Ovadiahu. "I swear by the eternal God, there is not one kingdom or nation to which my master did not send people in search of you, and all answered that you were not among them. He made all of the nations swear that you were not with them. And now you tell me that I should go to Achav and tell him that you are here! And what if, when I leave you, a wind comes from God and spirits you away? I will come and tell Achav that you are here, and he will find no trace of you!"

וְעַבְדְּךָ יָרֵא אֶת ה' מִנְּעוּרָי — *"Your servant has been God-fearing from youth* (v. 12). Please, therefore, have mercy upon me and do not let them kill me. You have undoubtedly heard what I did when Izevel persecuted the prophets, hiding one hundred of them, fifty in each of two caves, and supporting them with bread and water."

Pirkei deR' Eliezer, and so too the *Yalkut*, writes on this *Haftorah*: Ten kings ruled over the entire earth. The first is God, who rules both heaven and earth. The second was Nimrod, who ruled the entire earth. The third was Yosef, the fourth Shlomo, and the fifth Achav, as it says here that he had every nation take an oath that they did not know Eliyahu's whereabouts. The sixth king was Nebuchadnezzar, the seventh Coresh (Cyrus), the eighth Achashverosh. The ninth will be *Mashiach*, and the tenth will be, once again, God, Who will be recognized as King during the days of *Mashiach*, as it says, וְהָיָה ה' לְמֶלֶךְ עַל כָּל הָאָרֶץ — *God will be King in all the land* (Zechariah 14:9).

The *Gemara* asks, in Tractate *Nedarim*: How could Ovadiahu have boasted that he was God-fearing, when the verse states, יְהַלֶּלְךָ

Eliyahu's offering on Mount Carmel is accepted and consumed by a heavenly fire

זָר וְלֹא פִיךָ — *Let another praise you, not yourself (Mishlei* 27:2)? The answer is that in a place where people all know each other one should not praise himself, but in a strange place, where one is unknown, a person may praise himself in order to save himself. Ovadiahu therefore did this in order to save himself from Achav.

In light of this, it is difficult to understand the sorrow of R' Tarfon. Once, a man wanted to drown him because he had eaten something from his garden. Not recognizing who he was, he had placed him in a sack and was about to throw him in the water.

"Woe to you, R' Tarfon," R' Tarfon cried, "about to be drowned!"

When the owner heard that this was R' Tarfon he immediately freed him. R' Tarfon then grieved for the rest of his days, because he had derived profit from his Torah study in this world, since he had been freed because of his scholarship.

The explanation is that R' Tarfon was a wealthy man. He ought to have told the owner that he could redeem himself with his money, yet he saved himself by saying that he was the illustrious Rabbi Tarfon, the scholar. It was this that he regretted.

The *Tanchuma* and the *Yalkut* write of this *Haftorah:* The Sages say that Achav's servants all worshiped idols and yet were very lucky, and victorious in battle. This was because among all of Israel, no one spoke ill of another. Eliyahu had stood on top of Mount Carmel, and had announced in a mighty voice: "I am a prophet who has remained," and yet no one told King Achav.

In the days of King David, however, all of Israel served God, and even the young children learned Torah, but there were many among them who spoke ill of David to Shaul. Therefore Israel fell into the hands of neighboring nations, and their Torah study could not save them. We must be very careful not to speak ill of others, for much harm can come of it.

❀ ❀ ❀

Eliyahu assured Ovadiahu: "I swear by the eternal Lord of Hosts, before whom I have stood, that I will appear before Achav today."

וַיֵּלֶךְ עֹבַדְיָהוּ לִקְרַאת אַחְאָב — *Ovadiahu went to meet Achav, and told him* (v. 16) where Eliyahu was. And when Achav saw Eliyahu he said: "Is it you, the troubler of Israel?"

"I have not betrayed Israel," answered Eliyahu, "but you have, you and your father's household. You have abandoned God's commandments, and have worshiped idols. Now go and gather together all of Israel and bring them to Mt. Carmel, together with the priests of the idol Baal, four hundred and fifty of them, and the priests of the idol, the tree called Asherah, four hundred of them, who eat at Izevel's table. We will see who is right."

HAFTORAH
Vayakhel
(Melachim I/I Kings 7:40-50)

And Chirom made the basins (וַיַּעַשׂ חִירוֹם אֶת הַכִּירוֹת; v. 40). Chirom (Hiram) made the basins, and the copper shovels with which the ashes were put into the pots, and the bowls for the blood of the sacrifices. He made four hundred pomegranates, and ten bases, with ten lavers on them, also made of copper. He made a "sea" of copper, and twelve copper oxen underneath it. All the vessels which Chirom made for King Shlomo, for use in the house of God, were made of pure, clean copper.

The vessels were all cast in the thick earth of the Jordan plain; that is, molds were made of the hard earth, and within these the vessels were formed. They cast the molds between the cities of Succos and Tzarasan, because the earth there was very hard.

And Shlomo left all the vessels (v. 47). Shlomo ceased trying to calculate the weight of the vessels because there were so many of them. As a result, the weight of the copper was never ascertained.

Shlomo made all the vessels (v. 48) in the House of God. He made the golden altar, and the golden table upon which the *lechem hapanim* ("showbread") rested.

There were five *Menoros* ("candelabras") to the right of the *Menorah* made by Moshe (Moses) and five to the left of it. The *Midrash* asks: Why did Moshe make one *Menorah*, and Shlomo ten? Moshe was in the desert, and there was no need for harvests, because everyone ate the *man* ("manna"); thus, one *Menorah* was sufficient. But Shlomo lived in *Eretz Yisrael*, where it was important for the crops to flourish. He therefore built ten *Menoros*, and said: In the merit of the five candelabras standing on the right side, may God grant dew and rain in their proper time; in the merit of the five standing on the left side, may He keep away the harmful dew, which brings evil things to this world.

The ten *Menoros* symbolized the Ten Commandments. Each *Menorah* had seven branches, making a total of seventy, for the seventy nations. As long as all seventy branches burned, the nations had no authority over Israel; if the lights were extinguished, they gained power over them.

Shlomo first put the *lechem hapanim* on the table which Moshe had made in the desert, which was in their possession; similarly, he first had Moshe's candles lit, and then his own.

The twelve copper oxen standing underneath the "sea" symbolized the twelve constellations of the heavens.

HAFTORAH

Pekudei

(Melachim I/I Kings 7:51 — 8:21)

This passage is also read in the Diaspora as the Haftorah of the second day of Succos.

וַתִּשְׁלַם כָּל הַמְּלָאכָה אֲשֶׁר עָשָׂה הַמֶּלֶךְ שְׁלֹמֹה — *And all of the work which King Shlomo did was completed* (7:51), that is, the work which he did on God's house. Shlomo brought all that his father David had sanctified, silver, gold, and vessels, and put it in the treasure houses which had been built into the House of God, but he did not construct the Temple from these materials.

Some of our Sages say that Shlomo did not build the *Beis HaMikdash* out of these things because he knew that it would be destroyed, and the nations might say that this was because it was built of gold and silver which David had stolen from them.

Other Sages say that Shlomo said: "There were three years of famine in David's day. He had so much gold and silver, and yet he did not feed the poor with it." And that is why he did not want to use that gold and silver for the *Beis HaMikdash*.

We learn from this that it is better to give charity and feed the poor than to donate holy objects to the synagogue. There are many people who give beautiful things to the synagogue, but do not realize that it is more worthwhile to feed the hungry.

On the words, *the work was completed*, the *Midrash Pesikta Rabbasi* writes: God's work was not complete from the time of the Creation until the *Beis HaMikdash* was built.

The verse also teaches us that there was an abiding peace when the *Beis HaMikdash* was constructed (from the similarity of the words *shalom* — "peace," and *vatishlam* — "completed"). All of the workmen who labored on the *Beis HaMikdash* were energetic and healthy. There were no headaches and no deaths among them, and no working tools were damaged.

R' Eliezer says that this situation is not surprising. God did this for His glory, so that they would be able to build His Temple. Indeed, for the glory of Yaakov God did not kill any of the Egyptians who went to bury him. Many thousands of Egyptians went, and yet there was no illness or death among them, and all returned safely.

אָז וַיַּקְהֵל שְׁלֹמֹה — *Then Shlomo assembled* (8:1) the elders of Israel to bring God's ark. They all gathered together to Shlomo's side בְּיֶרַח הָאֵתָנִים — *in the month of the Esanim, that is the seventh month* (8:2), the month of Tishrei. Tishrei is called the month of Esanim ("strength") because it is mighty (אֵיתָן) with crops. Also, the mighty forefathers were born in the month of Tishrei. Finally, it is mighty in commandments and festivals. (It is called the seventh month, because months are counted from Nissan, and Tishrei comes out seventh.)

King Shlomo and all the assemblage stood before the ark. They slaughtered numberless sheep and oxen. Then the priests brought the ark to its place, under the cherubim which Shlomo had made, which stood on the ground and covered the ark and its poles with their wings.

וַיַּאֲרְכוּ הַבַּדִּים — *The poles were so long* (v. 8) that their tips could be seen, but they were not uncovered; that is, they projected from the curtain, resembling a woman's breasts, but they did not tear the curtain.

The poles remained there until today. The *Gemara* says, in Tractate *Yoma*, that when the *Beis HaMikdash* was destroyed the enemy did not take the ark and the poles. They sank into the earth, and were never found.

וַיְהִי בְּצֵאת הַכֹּהֲנִים מִן הַקֹּדֶשׁ — *And it was, when the priests came out of the holy area* (v. 10), from the Holy of Holies, a cloud filled the House of God. The Divine Presence rested within.

וְלֹא יָכְלוּ הַכֹּהֲנִים — *And the priests could not* (v. 11) stay and perform their tasks because of the cloud, which was like thick smoke.

אָז אָמַר שְׁלֹמֹה — *Then Shlomo said* (v. 12), ''I see today the Divine Presence is resting in the House which I have built, as God promised. I have built You a resting place, a place for You to stay eternally.''

From the time the *Beis HaMikdash* was constructed it became forbidden to offer a sacrifice on any other altar, and the Divine Presence rested only there.

וַיַּסֵּב הַמֶּלֶךְ אֶת פָּנָיו — *The king turned his face around* (v. 14) and blessed the populace, as they stood.

וַיֹּאמֶר בָּרוּךְ ה' אֱלֹהֵי יִשְׂרָאֵל — *And he said, ''Blessed be the Lord, King of Israel* (v. 15) who spoke to my father David, and promised to give him a son who would build the *Beis HaMikdash*. With His good

hand He has fulfilled that which He promised, as He said, מָן הַיּוֹם׳ —
Since the day (v. 16) that I took My people Israel out of Egypt, I did
not choose a city from among the territories of all the tribes in which
to build a house for Myself. But I chose David to rule over my
people Israel.'

וַיְהִי עִם לְבַב דָּוִד אָבִי — *''It was in the heart of David, my father* (v. 17)
to build a house for God, but God told my father, 'You have done
well in desiring to build a house for Me, but you will not build it;
your son will.'

וַיָּקֶם ה׳ אֶת דְּבָרוֹ — *''And God has fulfilled the words which He spoke*
(v. 20). I have taken my father's place, and have sat upon the throne
of Israel, as God promised, and have built the House of God. And I
have made a place for the ark, which contains the tablets of the
covenant which God made with our forefathers, when He took them
out of the land of Egypt.''

ארבע פרשיות

The Four
Special Torah Readings

Our Sages decreed that four special passages from the Torah be read in the synagogue at certain specified times: the portion concerning *Shekalim* (the coin contributed annually to the *Beis HaMikdash*); the portion of *Zachor*, which begins: *Remember that which Amalek did to you (Devarim 25:17)*; the portion of *Parah*, regarding the red cow; and the portion concerning the new month, *Parashas HaChodesh*, read on the *Shabbos* preceding the beginning of the month of Nissan.

HAFTORAH*
Shekalim
(Melachim I/I Kings 18:1-19)

וַיִּכְרֹת יְהוֹיָדָע אֶת הַבְּרִית — *Yehoyada made a covenant* (11:17). Yehoyada the *Kohen* made a treaty between King Yehoash and the people of Israel. This is what had happened: There was a king named Achazya, whose mother was Atalya. Achazya died, leaving several heirs. Atalya killed his sons, and usurped the throne.

Achazya's sister Yehosheva secretly concealed Yehoash, Achazya's only surviving son. Together with his nurse, he was hidden in the attic of the Holy of Holies. He remained there for six years, while Atalya ruled Israel.

*The *Maftir* reading of *Parashas Shekalim* is from *Sh'mos* 30:11-16; see pp. 429-431.

In the seventh year of her reign Yehoyada arranged that the people kill Atalya and crown Yehoash king. They brought the boy out of hiding and proclaimed him ruler. The people clapped their hands in joy and shouted, "Long live King Yehoash!"

When she heard the tumult Atalya came to the *Beis HaMikdash*. Upon seeing the new king standing, crown upon his head, surrounded by joyous people blowing trumpets, she tore her clothes in grief.

Yehoyada commanded that she be executed. She was immediately taken out of the *Beis HaMikdash* and killed. Yehoyada then made a treaty with Yehoash.

וַיָּבֹאוּ כָל עַם הָאָרֶץ — *All of the people of the land came* (v. 18) and destroyed the idols, and killed Matan, the priest of the false gods. Yehoyada and the people escorted the king from the *Beis HaMikdash* to the palace. They seated him on the royal throne, and everyone rejoiced that Yehoash was their king.

בֶּן שֶׁבַע שָׁנִים יְהוֹאָשׁ בְּמָלְכוֹ — *Yehoash was seven years old when he began to reign* (12:1). He ruled in Yerushalayim for forty years.

וַיַּעַשׂ יְהוֹאָשׁ הַיָּשָׁר בְּעֵינֵי ה' — *And Yehoash did what was right in God's eyes* (v. 3).

As long as Yehoyada was alive, he taught and guided him, but with Yehoyada's death the people and his nobles came and said: "For six years you were hidden in the Holy of Holies, the place where the High Priest himself dares to enter only once a year, on the Day of Atonement. Even he remains there only for one hour, and that, in great personal danger. Yet you were there for six years, and no harm came to you. You must be a god." And Yehoash allowed them to deify him and bow down to him.

Yehoash told the priests: "Use all of the silver which is brought to you for the *Beis HaMikdash* for the maintenance of the building." The silver he referred to [included] the two half-*shekels* which each person brought annually — one half-*shekel* as part of the redemption money of the census, which was used for the public sacrifices; and one half-*shekel* for maintenance and improvements on the Temple.

וַיִּקְרָא הַמֶּלֶךְ — *And the king called* (v. 8) to Yehoyada [in the twenty-third year of his reign] and said: "Why are the priests not maintaining the Temple building with the silver? Let them not take the money then!"

The priests did not want to take the money, nor did they want to be in charge of maintenance of the *Beis HaMikdash. So Yehoyada the priest took a chest* (v. 10), and bored a hole through it. Anyone who brought silver to the *Beis HaMikdash* placed it within the chest. When the chest was full the king's scribe came, together with the High Priest, and counted the silver. It was then given over to artisans, woodcutters, and stonemasons, for their work in the Temple.

וְלֹא יְחַשְּׁבוּ אֶת הָאֲנָשִׁים — *They made no reckoning with the men* (v. 16) who kept the money, for they dealt in good faith. We see from this that if men are honest we should not suspect them of embezzling charity funds.

כֶּסֶף אָשָׁם וְכֶסֶף חַטָּאוֹת — *Forfeit money and sin money* (v. 17). When a person set aside money to buy a guilt-offering *(asham)* or a sin-offering *(chatas)*, and some of that money was left over, it was not used to maintain the Temple. Instead, it was given to the *Kohanim* to be used to purchase sacrifices to be offered at times when the altar stood idle.

MAFTIR AND HAFTORAH
Zachor
(Maftir — Devarim 25:17-19)

⇜ Parashas Zachor follows Parashas Shekalim

Even Shoev makes this comment: *Parashas Zachor*, which concerns Amalek, follows *Parashas Shekalim*, to show that the *shekalim* which the people donated to the *Beis HaMikdash* canceled out the ten thousand silver coins which Haman, a descendant of Amalek, gave to Achashverosh for permission to destroy the Jews. God always sends the remedy before the blow.

⇜ Remembering Amalek

The verse tells us to remember what Amalek did to us: they lived at quite a distance from the people of Israel, with seven kingdoms separating the two. Yet they passed by them all in order to kill our forefathers. Despite the fact that they had witnessed the wonders which God had wrought, they strengthened themselves and fought against Israel, at a time when all others were terrified of them. For this reason we must verbally curse Amalek.

The *Midrash* asks: Why did Amalek not attack Israel before they went to Egypt, when they were weak and few in number? Some of our Sages answer that Amalek was afraid of Yaakov, whom Esav, even with four hundred men, could not harm; others say that it would have been humiliating to Amalek to attack such a small party; still others say that Amalek thought to himself: "If I destroy Israel now, before they go into Egypt, I will be forced to serve Egypt in their stead." For God had told Avraham that his children would serve the Egyptians, and Esav, Amalek's ancestor, was also one of Avraham's descendants.

Because Israel were weak in their loyalty to the Torah and observance of the *mitzvos*, Amalek had the power to harm them. At other times, there was a cloud around Israel, and no arrow could penetrate it. Moreover, the cloud threw out those of the people who had sinned, and they were killed by Amalek.

⇜ Remembering Haman

The circumstances were similar in the case of Haman, Amalek's descendant. Once again, the people behaved wrongly, eating at the king's feast. As a result, Haman gained ascendancy and wanted to kill them. Some say that they bowed down to the idols of Nevuchadnetzar, and that was what gave Haman power over them.

The verse used three words to describe Haman's plot: לְהַשְׁמִיד לַהֲרֹג וּלְאַבֵּד — to destroy; to kill; to decimate. "To destroy" means that he wanted to take them away from Torah and *mitzvos*; "to kill" means that he wanted to destroy their bodies; "to decimate" means he wanted to take away their money and belongings.

Because of this, we celebrate Purim in three ways: we read the *Megillah*, because Haman planned to take us away from Torah and *mitzvos*; we give our bodies strength and pleasure by eating and drinking, because he plotted against our bodies; and because he schemed to rob our money, we send money to the poor.

⇜ Fasting on Purim

Even Shoev asks: Why did our Sages make drinking wine and eating such a central part of Purim, commanding us even to get drunk, when on other festivals drinking does not play a major part? Further, how can they possibly have told us to get drunk, when so much harm is done by drunkenness, as we see in the case of Noach and of Lot?

⋖§ The First Feast

The answer is that the story of Achashverosh, from beginning to end, was connected with drinking. Achashverosh made four feasts. The first was made by both himself and Vashti, when in a drunken rage he ordered her execution. As a result Esther was crowned queen.

⋖§ The Second Feast

The second feast celebrated his taking Esther. As a result, when Bigsan and Teresh plotted to poison the king, speaking in a language which was unknown to all except for Mordechai, Mordechai told Esther, who warned the king. The men were executed, and Mordechai's deed was inscribed in the king's records. When Haman wanted to have Mordechai hanged, they read through the royal chronicles and found that Mordechai had saved the king from death. The king was very angry with Haman for wanting to hang a righteous man, and ordered that Haman be hanged. All this happened because of the second feast.

וַיִּבֶז בְּעֵינָיו — *But he disdained (Esther* 3:6). Haman did not want to kill Mordechai alone: he wanted to kill all of the Jews.

The *Midrash* says that God said: "I did not destroy the Jews in the desert after they worshiped the Golden Calf, and yet you, Haman, would destroy them?"

This can be compared to a bird who built a nest for himself by the seashore. One day a mighty wave engulfed and destroyed the nest, and in a rage, the bird vowed to dry up the sea. The bird took a tiny drop of water from the sea, then flew back and dropped a grain of sand into the waves. Another bird asked what it was doing, and the bird replied: "The sea destroyed my nest, so I am drying it out." Replied the other bird: "You yourself will be destroyed, and you will never do it."

Similarly, Haman planned to destroy the Jews, but God did not allow him to do so.

יֶשְׁנוֹ עַם אֶחָד — *There is one nation (Esther* 3:8). "This people," Haman told Achashverosh, "are distinctive in their beliefs, in their Torah, and in their holidays. Every seventh day is their *Shabbos,* and every thirty days the beginning of the new month. Besides, they celebrate Pesach, Shavuos, Rosh Hashanah, Yom Kippur, Sukkos, and Shemini Atzeres.''

"Wicked man," God answered, "you complain that Israel has too many holidays? I will give them still another holiday — Purim, the day that you will be hanged, and they will rejoice.''

✥ The Third Feast

The third feast which Achashverosh made was when he and Haman ate and drank together. The king gave Haman his signet, so that he could seal the decree to destroy the Jews. As soon as the Jews became aware of this, they repented. As a result of this repentance God saved them. This was all because of that feast.

וְצוּמוּ עָלַי וְאַל תּאֹכְלוּ וְאַל תִּשְׁתּוּ — *Fast for my sake, and do not eat and drink (Esther* 4:16). From this we see that Mordechai and Esther fasted on Pesach. For, as *Even Shoev* asks, why it is written that they should not eat and drink, if the verse has already said that they should fast? Obviously they would refrain from eating and drinking on a fast. The answer is that Esther was saying that they should fast *on Pesach*, and refrain from eating *matzah* and drinking wine for the Four Cups, despite the fact that one is normally obligated to do so on the first night of Pesach.

✥ The Fourth Feast

The fourth feast comprised the two festivities which Esther made, on consecutive days, for Achashverosh. As a result of those feasts Haman was hanged.

And that is why Purim is celebrated by feasting and drinking.

(Haftorah — Shmuel I/I Samuel 15:1-35)

Shmuel said to Shaul (Saul): "God sent me to crown you king, and it is only proper that you listen to God's words. You must take revenge on Amalek. כּה אָמַר ה' צְבָאוֹת — *So said the Lord of hosts* (15:2): 'I remember what Amalek did to Israel, on the way out of Egypt. And now, *go and strike Amalek* (v. 3). Have no pity on them. Destroy them all: men, women, and children alike, oxen and sheep, camels and donkeys.' ''

Why did God command that the animals, too, be destroyed?

Because the Amalekites were wizards, capable of changing their appearance into that of animals.

וַיִּשְׁמַע שָׁאוּל אֶת הָעָם — *Shaul assembled the people* (v. 4), and counted them by means of sheep. He told each to take one sheep from the king's flock. They then counted the sheep, because it is forbidden to take a head count of Israel. There were 200,000 foot soldiers and 10,000 men of the tribe of Yehudah (Judah).

Shaul came to Amalek's city, וַיָּרֶב בַּנָּחַל — *and fought in the valley* (v. 5). Our Sages say that this means that he learned from the example of the *eglah arufah*, the heifer which is killed in a valley. If a body is found and the murderer is unknown, a calf is sacrificed as an atonement. Shaul felt that if for one person a calf is offered to atone for the death, how much more important is the death of the many, many souls of Amalek. And if the adults had sinned, had the children? And if all the people had sinned, had the animals?

A heavenly voice then rang out, and said: "Do not be overly righteous." Do not be better than God asked you to be. Later, when Shaul killed out the entire priestly city of Nov, a heavenly voice rang out once again, and said: "Do not be overly wicked."

Shaul said to the Kenites (v. 6), the descendants of Yisro: "Leave Amalek lest I destroy you with them. You showed kindness to Israel when they left Egypt." Since Moshe, Aharon, and the elders had partaken of a meal with Yisro, it was as if all of Israel had enjoyed his generosity.

Shaul then struck Amalek (v. 7), smiting them all the way from Chavilah until the approach to Shur, near Egypt, He captured their king, Agag, alive, but the remainder of the people met death at his sword.

Shaul and the people had pity on Agag, and on the best of the sheep and other animals, and did not want to destroy them and all the valuable booty. All that was weak or unattractive, however, was destroyed.

וַיְהִי דְבַר ה' אֶל שְׁמוּאֵל לֵאמֹר — *The word of God came to Shmuel, saying* (v. 10): "I regret having crowned Shaul king. He has strayed from My service and has not obeyed My commands."

These words troubled Shmuel greatly, and all that night he cried to God.

In the morning, Shmuel rose early and hastened to meet Shaul. Told that he had gone to Carmel to offer sacrifices, and had then gone down to Gilgal, he met him there. Shaul blessed him, saying: "I have fulfilled God's commands."

"And what is that sound of sheep in my ears, and the oxen that I hear?" asked Shmuel.

"They are brought from Amalek. The people thought it a pity, and kept them to offer as sacrifices. All the others are destroyed."

"Wait a moment, and I will tell you what God told me last night," said Shmuel.

"Speak," answered Shaul.

"Perhaps you are humble in your own eyes, but you are still the leader of all of the tribes of Israel. God commanded that you destroy all of Amalek. Why have you not heeded God's words? You ran to your booty and did what was wicked in God's eyes."

"I have listened to God's words," protested Shaul. "I followed the path upon which God sent me. I captured Agag, king of Amalek, and destroyed his people. Our people only kept the sheep and oxen before they were proclaimed to be beyond bounds, to offer as sacrifices to God!"

"Does God, then, prefer sacrifices over obedience?" said Shmuel. "He much prefers that a man heed His commands, rather than bring Him the best of animals! Obeying Him is better than the fat of rams. Just as wizardry is sinful, so ignoring His words is equally sinful. Just as idolatry is evil, so rebelling against His commands is equally wicked. Because you have rejected God's words, God rejects you as king."

Then Shaul told Shmuel: *"I have sinned by not heeding God's words, and yours. It was because I was in fear of the people, and so I listened to them (v. 24)."*

Rashi writes that the words, כִּי יָרֵאתִי אֶת הָעָם (*because I was in fear of the people*) refer to Doeg the Edomite, who was considered equal in importance to the entire people.

"Forgive my sin and return with me to pray to God," asked Shaul.

"I will not return with you," replied Shmuel, "for you rejected God's words. He has rejected your kingship."

With this, as Shmuel turned around to leave, Shaul grasped a corner of his coat and it tore. Another possible interpretation is that Shmuel took hold of Shaul's coat and tore it, as a sign that another person who would one day tear Shaul's coat would be king after him. For this reason, when David later cut off the corner of Shaul's coat Shaul told him that he knew that he would be king.

"God has torn the kingdom from your hands," Shmuel said, "giving it to someone better than you. Even if you say you will repent, it will not change His decision. God will not take the kingship away from the person to whom He has now given it. נֵצַח יִשְׂרָאֵל לֹא יְשַׁקֵּר — *The Eternal One of Israel will not lie* (v. 29); the mighty God of Israel, unlike men, will have no regrets."

"I have sinned," said Shaul, "but honor me before the elders of my people and return with me, and I will bow down to God."

Then Shmuel returned with him, and Shaul prayed to God.

"Bring Agag, king of Amalek, to me," commanded Shmuel.

Agag was brought to him, joyfully seeking death, which was preferable to a life of captivity. Another explanation of this verse is that Agag was brought to him in fetters. He then said: "Indeed the bitterness of death is past."

Shmuel said: "Just as your sword made women mourn [for their children], so now shall your mother mourn, more so than any other woman." With this he hacked Agag into four pieces.

וַיֵּלֶךְ שְׁמוּאֵל הָרָמָתָה — *Shmuel went to Ramah* (v. 34), and Shaul returned to his home in Givas Shaul.

HAFTORAH*

Parah

(Yechezkel/Ezekiel 36:16-38)

וַיְהִי דְבַר ה' אֵלַי לֵאמֹר — *"The word of God came to me, saying* (36:16): 'You, man, see how Israel dwell in their land, in their evil deeds defiling it with the impurity of a menstruous woman.' "

Why is the impurity of Israel likened to that of a *niddah*? Just as a man waits for his wife to immerse herself and end their state of separation, so God waits anxiously and hopes for Israel to repent and be reunited with Him.

וָאֶשְׁפֹּךְ חֲמָתִי עֲלֵיהֶם — *"I poured My wrath upon them* (v. 18). I, God, have poured out My anger upon them, because of the blood which they spilled, they and their false gods. They have defiled their land, and so I will divide them amongst the nations.

*The *Maftir* reading of *Parashas Parah* is from chapter 19 of *Bamidbar*.

PARASHAS PARAH / פרשת פרה   [519]

[At this point in the Hebrew original, Yechezkel passes over to the prophetic perfect tense, predicting forthcoming events with such certainty that they are described in the past tense.]

וַיָּבוֹא אֶל הַגּוֹיִם — "They will come to the nations (v. 20), and My Name will be desecrated as a result. The nations will say: 'This is God's people, banished from His land!' I will then have pity on them, because of the glory of My Name.

"Therefore, tell the House of Israel that I will not redeem them because of their merit, but only to prevent My holy Name from desecration (v. 22). I will assemble them from all the lands.

"And if you ask: 'What is the benefit of God returning us to this land, when it cannot abide sin and will ultimately expel us again, since man inevitably sins?' I, God, therefore say: וְזָרַקְתִּי עֲלֵיכֶם מַיִם טְהוֹרִים — I will sprinkle pure water upon you (v. 25). I will give you new hearts and you will obey Me. I will tear the Evil Inclination out of you, וְאֶת רוּחִי אֶתֵּן בְּקִרְבְּכֶם — and I will put My spirit within you (v. 27). You will heed My commands and sin no more. Fear not, you will not be exiled again from your land; you will dwell there eternally, and I will save you from all your impurity.

"I will call upon the grain and make it abundant, and you shall know no famine (v. 29). There will be succulent fruits, and you will no longer suffer the humiliation of hunger among the nations. You will remember your evil deeds and wicked ways and conclude that God was just in exiling you."

Says God: לֹא לְמַעַנְכֶם אֲנִי עֹשֶׂה — "Not for your sake do I do this (v. 32), but only so all will recognize that I am God. Therefore, House of Israel, be ashamed of your sins."

כֹּה אָמַר ה' — Thus says God (v. 33): "On the day that I will cleanse you of your sins, I will rebuild your cities which had been destroyed, and everyone will marvel that cities which had been ruins will be rebuilt with the beauty of Eden."

וְיָדְעוּ הַגּוֹיִם — "And the nations will know (v. 36) that I rebuilt the desolate cities."

כֹּה אָמַר ה' — Thus says God (v. 37): "This request too shall I grant you: I will increase the population of Israel. They will be as numerous as the sheep which are brought to Yerushalayim as sacrifices on festivals. The ruined cities will be populated with masses of people, and they will know that I am God."

❀ ❀ ❀

Tanchuma writes, on the words *like the impurity of a menstruous woman* (v. 17): Why is their impurity likened to the impurity of a *niddah*, rather than the impurity of death? Because a *Kohen* may be in the same room as a *niddah*, but he may not be in the same room with a dead body. Had Israel been likened to a corpse, God could not have remained with them. Since their impurity is like that of the *niddah*, God's presence continues to dwell with them in the midst of their sorrow and distress, awaiting their repentance and purification.

The verse says וַיָּבוֹא אֶל הַגּוֹיִם — *He will come to the nations* (in the singular; v. 20), rather than "they will come," in the plural, to show that God Himself would accompany Israel among the nations, to be with them in their exile.

The *Gemara* says, in Tractate *Sukkah:* The Evil Inclination has seven names. God called it רָע ("bad"); David called it טָמֵא ("impure"); Shlomo called it שׂוֹנֵא ("enemy"), because it is man's veritable foe; Yeshayahu (Isaiah) called it מִכְשׁוֹל ("obstacle"), because it causes men to stumble; Yechezkel (Ezekiel) called it אֶבֶן ("stone"), because it stands in people's way, waiting for them to fall in sin; Yoel (Joel) called it צְפוֹנִי ("the hidden one"), because it conceals itself so that man will not be wary of it.

כַּצֹּאן אָדָם — *Like the flocks of man* (v. 37): *Tanchuma* writes that Israel is compared to sheep because although sheep often destroy foliage, their master does not punish them. Similarly, although Israel sins, God does not punish them harshly.

They are compared with men as well, for when they are pious they are rewarded as men, who have reason and understanding, deserving to be rewarded. But when they are evil they are only punished as sheep, which have no understanding.

HAFTORAH*
Hachodesh
(Yechezkel/Ezekiel 45:16 — 46:18)

כל הָעָם הָאָרֶץ — *All the people of the land* (45:16) shall bring this offering for the prince *(nasi)*, and the prince shall bring a sacrifice on festivals, on Rosh Chodesh and *Shabbos*, as an atonement for all of Israel.

כֹּה אָמַר ה׳ — *Thus says God* (v. 18): "On Rosh Chodesh Nissan the *Kohen* shall take an ox which has no blemish and purify the Temple with it."

וְלָקַח הַכֹּהֵן — *And the priest shall take* (v. 19) its blood and sprinkle it on the doorposts of the *Beis HaMikdash*, in the four corners of the courtyard, and on the doorposts of the inner court. This shall be done on the seventh day of the month as well.

This was done because sacrifices were first brought on the first day of Nissan, and it was possible that out of joy and excitement someone might stray into forbidden areas. Thus these sacrifices were needed as atonement.

The Pesach sacrifice was to be slaughtered on the fourteenth day of Nissan, and *matzos* were to be eaten for seven days (v. 21).

וְעָשָׂה הַנָּשִׂיא — *And the prince shall prepare* (v. 22), on that day, an ox for himself and for all of Israel. וְשִׁבְעַת יְמֵי הֶחָג — *And the seven days of the festival* (v. 23), on each day, he must bring a burnt-offering. He must bring seven oxen and seven rams on each of the seven days, and a goat as a sin-offering. He must bring one measure of meal for each ox, as an offering, and one measure for each ram, and a measure of oil for the meal.

בַּשְּׁבִיעִי — *In the seventh* [month] (v. 25), which is Tishrei, on the fifteenth day of the month, sacrifices must be brought, just as on Pesach — a sin-offering, a burnt-offering, meal and oil.

---

*The *Maftir* reading of *Parashas Hachodesh* is from *Sh'mos* 12:1-20; see pp. 350-351.

ה' אָמַר כֹּה — *Thus says God* (46:1): "The gate of the innermost court shall be locked all week, and opened on *Shabbos* and Rosh Chodesh.

הַנָּשִׂיא וּבָא — *And the prince shall come* (v. 2) through the outer gate and stand by the door. The *Kohanim* shall offer his sacrifices and he shall prostrate himself by the door and then leave. The gate must remain open until nightfall so that anyone who wishes to come and prostrate himself can do so."

This gate stood opposite the door of the Sanctuary, and the people were to prostrate themselves there on *Shabbos* and Rosh Chodesh. We learn from this that it is a very worthy thing to bow as one enters the synagogue, since the synagogue is likened to the *Beis HaMikdash*.

The offering which the prince brings on *Shabbos* (v. 4) is composed of six lambs and a ram, a *minchah*-offering of a measure of meal for the ram, and for the lambs whatever measure he could afford to bring; as well as oil for each measure of meal.

On Rosh Chodesh (v. 6) he must bring an ox, six lambs and a ram; a measure of meal for the ox and the ram, and for the lambs whatever he can afford to bring; and oil for each measure of meal.

הַנָּשִׂיא וּבְבוֹא — *And when the prince enters* (v. 8), the way in which he comes is the way in which he leaves. We can learn from this that we should not hasten out of the synagogue as if it is a burden to us.

On the other hand, when the people came for the festivals, they entered through one gate and left through the opposite gate, so that they would be seen on all sides of the Temple. The prince walked among them.

The *minchah* on the festivals was this: a measure of meal for each ox and for each ram, and for the sheep whatever measure the *nasi* could afford, and oil for each measure of meal.

הַנָּשִׂיא יַעֲשֶׂה וְכִי — *And if the prince shall make* (v. 12) a donation, they must open the [eastern] gate for him as though it were *Shabbos*. When he is finished he shall lock the gate.

שְׁנָתוֹ בֶּן וְכֶבֶשׂ — *A lamb, a yearling* (v. 13) shall be brought every morning, together with a *minchah* consisting of one-sixth of a measure of meal and one-third of a measure of oil, mixed together, as an acceptable offering for God.

ה' אָמַר כֹּה — *Thus says God* (v. 16): "When the prince gives a gift to any of his sons it shall remain his forever; if he gives a gift to one of his servants (v. 17), it shall be his until Jubilee year, when it reverts back to the prince."

The prince is forbidden to take any field of a Jew and give it to his children (v. 18), so that each man shall retain his own fields.

❧ ❧ ❧

This *Haftorah* is read so that when *Mashiach* comes the *nasi* will know how to conduct himself. It is known that *Mashiach* will come in the month of Nissan, and therefore we read this *Haftorah* on the *Shabbos* prior to Rosh Chodesh Nissan. If Rosh Chodesh Nissan falls on a *Shabbos*, we read the *Haftorah* of Rosh Chodesh instead.

מגלת אסתר

Megillas Esther

Megillas Esther

(Based on *Targum Sheni*)

◈ Ten Mighty Rulers

It was in the days of Achashverosh (Esther 1:1), ruler from India to Ethiopia, one hundred and twenty-seven lands. הוּא אֲחַשְׁוֵרוֹשׁ — *This is Achashverosh* (Ahasuerus), one of the ten kings who reigned, or who shall reign, over the entire world.

The first of these kings was the King of Kings (May His reign soon extend over us all!). Nimrod was second, Pharaoh, third. Shlomo (Solomon), king of Israel, was fourth, and the fifth was Nebuchadnezzar, king of Bavel (Babylon). The sixth was Achashverosh; the seventh, Alexander of Greece; the eighth, the emperor of Rome. The ninth will be the King *Mashiach*, and the tenth will once again be the King of Kings.

◈ The Prince of the Pursuit of Power

With the death of Nebuchadnezzar, king of Bavel, there was great internal strife, and the kingship seemed destined for oblivion. The people of Bavel simply did not know whom to crown as their king.

Nebuchadnezzar's son, Evil Merodach, hoped to assume the kingship, but the people did not want him and rebelled. They told him: "We admit that by right the kingship should be yours, but remember that God once punished your father by crazing him, sending him naked to run mindlessly through the forest for seven years, eating grass like a beast, his hair and nails grown long and wild. All thought him dead, but after seven years his sense returned.

"When he returned to his city, riding on a mighty lion, he found his son ruling in his stead. He killed his son immediately together with many of his servants.

"If you become king, perhaps your father will return once again, and seeing you ruling, will kill both you and us! Perhaps he will return, perhaps you have told us that he is dead merely to further your own ambitions for kingship!"

When Evil Merodach heard their words, he replied, "You have spoken correctly, but I can assure you that there is no need to fear.

He is most certainly dead, and that body which we buried was indeed that of my father."

"You are a good man," they replied, "and we believe you. Still, we are in terror of him. We have not seen the corpse, so how can we be certain that it was him? You are aware of the terror which the entire world felt at the mere sound of his voice. We do not know what to do!"

When Evil Merodach saw their determination, he ran to the cemetery and brought the body back to the city, dragging it in chains through the streets. Now everyone could see that it was indeed Nebuchadnezzar, and what had become of his mortal remains. Relieved that his son had complied with their request, they crowned him king.

⇜§ Achashverosh

הוּא אֲחַשְׁוֵרוֹשׁ — *He is Achashverosh* (1:1). He is Achashverosh, who sold the impoverished Jews (רָשׁ — "poor"); he is that same Achashverosh who darkened (שָׁחוֹר — "black") the Jews' faces with sorrow like a burnt pot; he is Achashverosh who gave orders to bring cedar wood from Lebanon and gold from Ophir, and never did [for Achashverosh is identified by some of the Sages with Coresh; and see *Ezra* chs. 3 and 4 on the building of the Second *Beis HaMikdash*]; he is *Achashverosh*, in whose times were fulfilled the words of the rebuke: *You shall have no assurance of your life* (*Devarim* 28:66).

The expression *he is* (הוּא) appears in reference to five wicked men, and five righteous men. The righteous men were: Avraham, Moshe, Aharon, Chizkiyahu and Ezra. The wicked men were: Nimrod, Esav, Dasan and Aviram, King Achaz, and Achashverosh.

He is Achashverosh, who never fulfilled what he had promised to do. As a result his kingdom was made smaller. First he ruled מֵהֹדוּ וְעַד כּוּשׁ, *from India to Ethiopia* (1:1), which includes virtually the entire world. Later, he ruled only שֶׁבַע וְעֶשְׂרִים וּמֵאָה מְדִינָה — *one hundred and twenty-seven provinces* (1:1).

He is Achashverosh, who murdered his wife Vashti because of his admirer Haman, and who murdered Haman because of his wife Esther.

⇜§ The Extent of his Empire

He is Achashverosh, who ruled from India to Ethiopia. This is difficult to understand, though, for Hodu and Cush are lands which are close to each other — what was the great accomplishment, then? The verse lets us know that just as he ruled powerfully over those two, so did he rule over 127 nations.

This same metaphor is expressed in King Shlomo's case. He ruled the whole world, and the verse tells us that he ruled "from Tifsach to Azah," although they were close to one another. Just as he ruled over those two places, so did he rule over the entire world.

There were four kings who ruled from one end of the earth to the other; two were Jews and two were not. Shlomo and Achav were the Jews, Nebuchadnezzar and Achashverosh were the other two. But ultimately Achashverosh's kingdom was lessened, until he ruled over 127 nations only.

He merited ruling over those 127 nations because of Esther, his future wife, granddaughter of Sarah, who lived for 127 years.

⊷§ The Greatness of Shlomo

בַּיָּמִים הָהֵם כְּשֶׁבֶת הַמֶּלֶךְ אֲחַשְׁוֵרוֹשׁ עַל כִּסֵּא מַלְכוּתוֹ אֲשֶׁר בְּשׁוּשַׁן הַבִּירָה —
In those days, when King Achashverosh sat on his throne of majesty in Shushan the capital (1:2). Our Sages say that the throne did not belong to Achashverosh or to his ancestors. It was actually the throne of Shlomo, built for him by Chiram (Hiram), king of Tyre.

This was Shlomo, beloved of God, chosen by Him even before his birth. God revealed many secrets to him, and granted him great wisdom, the wisdom to discern truth in judgment. Like his father before him, beauty and charm radiated from his face; the crown of majesty sat proudly upon his head.

He was crowned at the age of thirteen, and he was called Yedidyah, meaning "friend of God"; and Shlomo, because there was peace *(shalom)* during his reign. Ben was his name, for he built *(banah)* the Temple, and Itiel ("God is with me"), for God Himself attested to his superior wisdom. Yakeh, too, was his name, because he was the ruler of the world and all the nations feared him [Derivation of this interpretation: untraced].

The demons themselves fell into his hands, and fish and birds and beasts brought him tribute. When he made a banquet the beasts would come to the kitchen and offer themselves for slaughter.

He was very wealthy, possessor of much gold and silver. He revealed deep secrets, and his enemies became his friends; kings obeyed him and wanted to meet him. God raised him to greatness because of his father David. His name was renowned by all the kings, and his wisdom repeated by all the sages.

❧ The Marvelous Throne

This was Shlomo, who [owned] the marvelous throne. When Shlomo would sit in judgment upon his throne, crown on his head, he could delve into the hearts of the complainants and see by their faces who was guilty, who was innocent, and whose testimony was false. For this reason the verse says that Shlomo sat on *God's chair* — for God guarded the chair as if it were His own.

The throne itself was miraculously built. It had twelve golden lions upon it, and twelve golden eagles, the paw of a lion opposite the wing of an eagle. There were six stairs to climb upon, each with six golden lions and six golden eagles. They were made of elephant bones (i.e., ivory). The golden lions numbered 72 *(sic)*, with 72 eagles as well.

On the first step was a golden ox opposite a golden lion. On the second step lay a wolf of gold opposite a golden sheep. The third step had a panther facing a golden camel; the fourth a golden eagle facing a golden peacock. On the fifth step was a golden cat opposite a golden chicken, and on the sixth was a hawk facing a golden dove. All of this showed that in matters of justice the weak does not have to fear the strong.

All the animals were crafted with great skill and cunning. It worked this way. When Shlomo placed his right foot on the first stair, the ox extended him his foot, and he grasped it. When he placed his other foot on the first step, the lion extended his paw. Then the ox would display a scroll with the following verse inscribed upon it: *It is forbidden to take bribes;* and the lion would show a scroll with another verse: *Do not recognize anyone in judgment* — that is, do not recognize a person, even if he once did you a favor or if he is rich or important or pious or poor, by judging in his favor.

All the other animals did likewise, lifting Shlomo up with one foot and displaying their judicial maxims with the other.

❧ The King Enthroned

Shlomo would sit at the summit of the throne. There was a golden dove there, holding a hawk, for Israel is compared to a dove. On the very top of the throne was a *Menorah* (candelabrum), crafted with lights and branches and cups and flowers. Facing it were seven gold branches, bearing upon them the likenesses of the seven forefathers — Adam, Noach, Shem, Avraham, Yitzchak and Yaakov, with Iyov

(Job) in their midst. On the other side were seven gold branches bearing the likenesses of seven righteous men — Levi, Kehas, Amram, Moshe, Aharon, Eldad and Medad, and Chur; some say that Chaggai was among them.

On the tip of the *Menorah* was a golden pitcher full of the oil which was burned in the Temple. Underneath stood a large golden bowl, with a likeness of Eli the priest carved upon it. Two branches extended from it, bearing likenesses of his sons Chofni and Pinchas, and from these two other branches came out, bearing likenesses of Aharon's two sons, Nadav and Avihu.

There were two chairs there, one for the High Priest and one for his deputy. There were seventy chairs surrounding them, for the seventy members of the Sanhedrin, and there they sat in judgment before the king.

Near the approach to the throne there were two doves. Over the throne 24 golden branches were built, to shade the king. Wherever he turned, he was always protected by the shade.

When Shlomo reached the sixth step a golden eagle would seat him on the throne. The actual place where Shlomo sat was covered with silver leaf.

When other nobles and kings heard of Shlomo's throne they came and bowed down to him and said: "There is no king in the entire world who owns such a throne, no craftsman who could build such a marvel."

When Shlomo sat down a golden eagle, crafted with great skill and wisdom, held the crown over his head, without touching him, so that he should not be uncomfortable. The golden eagles and lions were made with great cunning, gathering around the king and providing shade for him. A golden dove would descend from the pillars and open the holy Ark, remove a tiny Torah scroll and place it into King Shlomo's hands, so that he could fulfill the admonition (cf. *Devarim* 17:18-20): the Torah shall be with him for all of his days, so that his reign, and the reign of his children, shall be long.

The High Priest and the Elders would come to greet the king. The judges and the Sanhedrin sat on his right and left sides to judge the people. When a person would testify falsely, the king would cause wheels to spin, oxen to low, lions to roar, and bears to pounce as if ready to tear something apart. Each of the animals of the throne would make his noise, as if he were truly alive. All this was done to terrify the perjurer, so that he would think to himself: "Why should I testify falsely, and lose such a world with my sin?"

When the animals opened their mouths to shout, a wonderful

fragrance, the fragrance of Eden, would pour out. It was a fragrance of spices, of all the wonderful smells which God created.

◁§ The Fate of the Throne

When Israel sinned Nebuchadnezzar came and laid waste to all of *Eretz Yisrael*, looting the holy city of Yerushalayim and burning the Temple (May God yet have mercy upon us!). Nebuchadnezzar then led the people into exile, taking the throne with him.

Nebuchadnezzar wanted to seat himself upon the throne, but he did not know how to ascend it. When he put his foot on the first step, the golden lion rose in order to help him climb up. But Nebuchadnezzar did not know what to do, and so the lion kicked him with his left foot, striking him on the right thigh and leaving him crippled for the rest of his life.

When Alexander the Great of Macedonia conquered Babylonia he took the throne with him and brought it to Egypt. He was pious and revered the throne as very holy, and refused to sit upon it. After his death Sheshak, king of Egypt, tried to sit on the throne, and the same fate befell him as had befallen Nebuchadnezzar before him. He was crippled for the rest of his life, and was called Pharaoh Necheh, Pharaoh the Lame.

Then Aniphonus, son of Antiochus, came and removed the throne from Egypt. He put it into a ship and brought it to his land. During the voyage one foot of the throne broke off, and he could not, in all of his lifetime, find a craftsman skilled enough to repair it. There was no king at this time who could have had such a throne built.

The throne found its way into the possession of Coresh of Persia, and because he allowed the Temple to be rebuilt he merited being able to sit upon the throne without harm.

בִּשְׁנַת שָׁלוֹשׁ לְמָלְכוֹ — *In the third year of his reign* (1:3). Achashverosh made a feast for all of his nobles and servants of Persia and Media, and all the governors of his provinces came to him.

In the third year of Nebuchadnezzar's reign the people of Israel wept and sighed, saying: "Woe to us since Nebuchadnezzar has prevailed over us, humiliating our land and destroying our nation, leading us into exile. Whatever injustice he could mete out, he did, chaining our elders in iron fetters, banishing our nobles, striking down our youth, and taking the smallest children into captivity. He has removed the crown of pride from our heads."

◆§ The King and the Birds

Before the destruction of the *Beis HaMikdash,* David rose to rule Israel, and his son Shlomo reigned after him. God placed Shlomo as ruler over the entire world: over the beasts of the field, the birds under heaven, and the reptiles of the sands; over the demons and shades. He understood all their languages. When he was merry he had the beasts and birds, the shades and demons, brought before him, to dance for him and for visiting kings, in order to prove his dominion over them. All came without need of persuasion, and none were coerced.

Once he asked the birds if all of them were there. The birds looked around to see if anyone was missing, and they discovered that the moor cock was not there. They told Shlomo, who in great wrath ordered that he be brought before him. He was brought to the king, and fell before him in terror.

He said to Shlomo: "I beg for mercy, my beloved lord, O king! It is a long while now that I eat my food in tears, and drink in trembling. I flew out into the world, seeking a place where you do not have dominion. Finally I came to a country whose capital city is called Kitor, whose land is covered with gold. Its trees are like the trees of Eden. A woman rules over this nation, and they worship the sun. If you wish I can assemble all the birds of prey, fly there, and destroy them."

King Shlomo demurred, but immediately called for his scribe, and dictated this letter: "From King Shlomo to the queen of the land of Kitor — peace to you and to your nobles. Be it known to you and to them that God, blessed is He, has made me ruler over all the peoples, the birds and beasts and demons and shades. I therefore wish you to bear my name as well. Send a tribute to me, as all the kings do. If you do so, you shall live in peace, but if you refuse, I shall send a great host to destroy you and your kingdom. Not soldiers alone, but wild birds and badgers and demons shall attack your kingdom and destroy it. Send me your answer with this bird, and peace to you."

◆§ The Queen of Sheba

They clipped the letter to the moor cock's wing and, together with an escort of many birds of prey, it flew to Kitor, to the Queen of Shva (Sheba). They arrived very early, right after sunrise. The queen arose to bow down as she normally did, but there were so many birds that the sun was obscured. Terrified, she rent her garments. The moor cock then flew down with his letter, and when she had read its uncompromising message she once again tore her clothing.

She immediately summoned her nobles and told them the contents of the letter, but they did not want to listen, and said that they did not recognize King Shlomo or his rule.

The queen did not rely on their opinion, and sent a ship laden with silver and gold, precious gems and fine wood. She chose 6,000 boys and girls of particular beauty, who had all been born on the same day, and dressed them all in identical clothing of silk and purple wool.

She sent a letter with the sailors, which said: "From the Queen of Kitor to my lord, King Shlomo, and all his nobles. Peace to you. Please accept my gift. I beg of you to appoint a time for me to come to you, for you know that it is a matter of seven years' journey. I hope to come and bow down to your rule in three years (sic)."

The Sages say that she knew, through stargazing, that the young children whom she had sent would die within a year. Shlomo too foresaw this, and sent them back to her with shrouds, with this message: "If you have sent these to me because of a lack of shrouds, here they are; now take them back. You may come to speak with me."

✌৽ Her Visit

At the end of three years she came. When Shlomo heard that she was approaching, he sent his courtier, Benayahu ben Yehoyada, a very handsome man. When she saw him she dismounted her horse and bowed low, for she thought that he was Shlomo. "I am not Shlomo," he assured her, "just one of his servants."

She returned to her nobles and said: "You have not yet seen the lion. If one of his servants looks like this, imagine what Shlomo himself looks like!" And Benayahu brought her to Shlomo.

When the king heard of her arrival he sat in a room made of glass. She bowed down before him, and he treated her courteously. Later, she said to him: "My beloved lord, I want to ask you three riddles. If you know the answers, I will know that you are truly wise; if not, you are just like other men." She asked him her questions, and he gave her the very answers which she had been thinking of.

The king gave her all that she desired. Then she bade him goodbye and returned with her retinue to her land.

✌৽ Nebuchadnezzar Defiles the Temple

When any of the kings of the world would hear the name of

Shlomo they would tremble, and all sent the best produce of their land to him.

Had Israel listened to the prophet Yirmeyahu, and repented, they would not have been exiled. Yirmeyahu prayed to God the entire time that he was in Yerushalayim, and he was able to hold Nebuchadnezzar at bay and keep him from destroying the city. But then he went to the land of Binyamin, and Nebuchadnezzar sent his general Nevuzaradan, who immediately breached the walls, and afterwards, together with Nebuchadnezzar, came to the *Beis HaMikdash*.

They could not enter it, because the gates had locked themselves. When Nebuchadnezzar saw that no one could open them, he wanted to break them down. He broke many axes upon them to no avail, for they would not open. Then a man by the name of Parnutos came and slaughtered an impure animal, sprinkling its blood on the *Beis HaMikdash* and defiling it. The doors then opened of their own accord. Nebuchadnezzar entered, and saw God's wonders before him.

One of the things he saw was blood on a rock, seething without rest. He asked the elders what it was, and they answered that it was the blood of sacrifices, but he soon realized that they were lying. Then he said: "If you reveal the secret, well and good; if not, I will tear your flesh with burning pincers."

Then they told him the truth — that among them had been the prophet Zechariah, who continually rebuked them. They did not listen to him, and finally stoned him on a *Shabbos* — which was the Day of Atonement was well — in the *Beis HaMikdash* itself. From that time on his blood would not rest.

"Why did you not wash the blood away?" asked Nebuchadnezzar.

"We have washed it away many times," they answered, "but it does not help. It comes right back. We have broken away the stones and replaced them with others, but nothing helps; the blood keeps returning."

◄§ Massacre

Then Nebuchadnezzar called his general Nevuzaradan and ordered him to still the blood. He took many thousands of priests and slaughtered them on top of the blood, but to no avail. He slaughtered the Sanhedrin and the elite of Israel, but still the blood would not rest. Then he slaughtered the young schoolchildren, but still the blood seethed. Finally he had pity, and said to the blood: "Zechariah, Zechariah, I have massacred the best of the Jews upon your blood. Be still now, or I will slaughter all of Israel on your account." And then, finally, the blood quieted down and sank into the earth.

Then Nevuzaradan thought to himself: "The Jews killed only one man, and God punished them so harshly. I have killed so many beautiful Jews — what will happen to me?" He fled, and ultimately became a righteous convert.

When the High Priest and the other *Kohanim* saw that the *Beis HaMikdash* and all within it was in flames, they threw themselves together with their harps into the fire.

When Nebuchadnezzar tried to enter the Holy of Holies, the doors locked themselves shut, until a heavenly voice rang out and said: "Open up your doors, Temple, and let the fire burn." Then they opened of their own volition. When that evil man entered and saw the glory of God, and the holy vessels of the Temple, which righteous kings used to use, they vanished before his eyes. The wicked man stormed out in a rage and killed, through our sins, many Jews. Many others were bound in chains and led, naked, bearing heavy burdens of sand, into painful servitude.

◄§ The Prophet Intercedes

The prophet Yirmeyahu accompanied them until he reached the graves of the Patriarchs. He fell upon their tombs and wept: "O merciful fathers, Avraham, Yitzchak, and Yaakov, rise up and see how they lead your children into exile, naked and barefoot, bent under heavy loads!"

Then he ran to the tombs of Sarah, Rivkah, Rachel and Leah. He wailed and said: "Arise, you mothers, and see how your children are being led naked into exile, and how bitter is their lot." Then he sped to the graves of Moshe, Aharon and Miriam, and said: "See how they are leading your flock into exile. You watched over them carefully; now see how the cruel wolves prey upon them and tear them apart, leading them naked and barefoot over the mountains and through the cities, laden with heavy burdens, while the wicked ones harass them without mercy."

Finally, he hastened once again to the forefathers, who asked him: "Why did you not pray that such a fate not befall them? Now you come to us to tell us the terrible news?"

And so the captives continued on their way until they reached a place called Beis Kuri. There Nebuchadnezzar commanded that their burdens be removed and they be given clothing. It was there that the prophet Yirmeyahu told Nebuchadnezzar: "You will go and boast in your idolatrous temple, and say that your might did this. But the truth is, and remember this well — what happened to those before you will happen to you, too."

Yirmeyahu went with the Jews, wailing and lamenting, until they reached a place called Yichud Medinta, where Nebuchadnezzar commanded that the chains be removed from the neck of King Tzidkiyahu, and new clothing be brought to him.

⇜ An Oriental Banquet

בְּהַרְאֹתוֹ אֶת עֹשֶׁר כְּבוֹד מַלְכוּתוֹ — *When he (Achashverosh) displayed the riches of his glorious kingdom* (1:4). Achashverosh displayed the utensils and vessels of the *Beis HaMikdash*. When the Jews saw these vessels they wanted to leave the feast. Achashverosh was told that the Jews were crying and lamenting when they saw the vessels; he responded that they were right, and ordered that they be seated in a separate place.

וּבִמְלוֹאת הַיָּמִים הָאֵלֶּה — *And when these days were fulfilled* (1:5), one hundred and eighty days, the king made a feast for all the people in the capital city of Shushan, from great to small. It was a seven-day feast in the court of the palace garden. This feast was followed by still another seven-day feast for the residents of Shushan alone.

חוּר כַּרְפַּס — *White hangings and fine cotton* (1:6). Linen, white as pearls, hung from one tree to the next, woven with threads of green, blue, and silk. A hanging of purple encircled it, bound all around with golden chains.

וְהַשְׁקוֹת — *And they gave them to drink* (1:7) in golden cups, with no two cups identical. Once one had drunk from a cup, it was used no more; each drink was served in a new cup. But when they displayed the vessels of the *Beis HaMikdash*, the other vessels seemed like copper in comparison. Each person drank as much as he wanted, and each was given wine the same age as he — wine in abundance, according to the king's bounty.

וְהַשְׁתִיָּה — *And the drinking* (1:8) was voluntary, so that no one would be harmed. It was customary at that time, when making a feast, that a person would be brought an enormous goblet of wine called the *piska*. Whoever was given this goblet by the butler was forced to drink the entire contents, though only Achashverosh was capable of such a feat. Whoever could not drink it was forced to give a huge sum of gold to the butler. In this way the butlers became very wealthy. But during this feast Achashverosh forewent this custom, and everyone drank whatever they wished, and no more.

◄§ The Queen is Summoned

גַּם וַשְׁתִּי הַמַּלְכָּה — *Queen Vashti, too* (1:9), made a feast for the women, in the palace. She served them black and red wines, and seated them in the king's palace, because she wanted to flaunt the king's wealth. "Where does the king sleep? Where does he eat?" they asked, and she showed them all that was to be seen, for women are very curious.

בַּיּוֹם הַשְּׁבִיעִי — *On the seventh day* (1:10) of the feast, when the king's heart was merry with wine, he spoke with Mehuman, Bizsa, Charvona, Bigsa, Avagsa, Zesar and Carcas, the seven chamberlains who were constantly with him. As they sat eating and drinking, the talk turned to women. The kings of the west said that the women of their lands were the most beautiful. The kings of the east said that their women were more attractive. Then the wine in Achashverosh began to speak, and he boasted that the women of Bavel were the most beautiful of all. "If you don't believe me," he said, "I will call for the queen."

"Yes, for we want to know the truth," the men replied, "but bring her in naked, so that we can truly see her beauty."

The king ordered that the queen be brought to him with the crown of majesty, to show the people her beauty. The king told his nobles, "Go to Queen Vashti and tell her to stand up from her throne, and undress herself totally. Let her put the golden crown upon her head, a golden bowl in her right arm, and a golden goblet in her left hand, and let her come before me and the 127 kings who are sitting with me, so that they will see that she is the most beautiful of all women."

וַתְּמָאֵן הַמַּלְכָּה וַשְׁתִּי — *Queen Vashti refused* (1:12) and haughtily told her servants: "I am Vashti, daughter of the kings of Bavel, descendant of Belshazzar. My father could outdrink a thousand men, and the wine would never cause him to say such foolish things."

King Achashverosh was told that the queen had defied him, and his fury burned within him.

◄§ Vashti's Downfall

וַיֹּאמֶר הַמֶּלֶךְ — *The king said* (1:13) to the wise men, who knew the temper of the times: "What shall be done to Queen Vashti, because of her disobedience?"

וַיֹּאמֶר מְמוּכָן — *Memuchan said* (1:16). This is Daniel. He was exiled to Bavel with the tribe of Yehudah, and through him great miracles and valorous deeds were performed. He was "prepared" *(muchan)* from heaven to be the instrument of Vashti's downfall, and so was called Memuchan.

As was customary, the king used to first consult with the least important of his advisers, and therefore he began with Memuchan. This adviser had a Persian wife of great importance, who wanted him to speak her language, and he sought a pretext to force her to speak his. Therefore he said: "Not only has Vashti behaved badly to the king, but to all of the nobles of all of the provinces of Achashverosh. When the words of the queen shall be known to all the other women, they will humiliate their husbands, for they will say, 'Are you, then, more important that Achashverosh, who commanded that the queen come before him and who was not obeyed?'

וְהַיּוֹם הַזֶּה — "*And on this day* (1:18) the princesses of Persia and Media will tell their husbands, when they hear what the queen did, and there will be much humiliation to be furious over."

אִם עַל הַמֶּלֶךְ טוֹב — *If it please the king* (1:19). When Memuchan suggested the decree he was afraid that the king would not follow his advice, and then Vashti would take revenge upon him. Therefore he saw to it that the following edict was immediately written in the laws of Persia and Media: "Since the queen refused to appear her position will be given to someone better than she. And this decree and action shall be heard in the entire kingdom, and all the women will respect their husbands, great and small."

This solution pleased the king, and he did as Memuchan had suggested.

וַיִּשְׁלַח סְפָרִים — *He sent letters* (1:22) to all the provinces of the kingdom, to each nation in its script, each people in its language, to let all know and understand the contents: that each man should be a ruler in his house, and women should speak the language of their husbands.

◈§ The King Relents

אַחַר הַדְּבָרִים הָאֵלֶּה — *After these things* (2:1), when the king's wrath had abated, he sent for his advisers and said: "Not only was I furious with Vashti, but now I am furious with you, too. When I was drunk you ought to have silenced my anger until I had come back to my senses, but you made me even more angry, and gave me the idea of killing her." When he had put them to death he remembered Vashti, and realized that she was innocent of any wrongdoing. This was all God's doing, for He wanted to destroy the descendants of Nebuchadnezzar.

The king's young servants said: "Let us search for a beautiful young maiden to be the king's wife. Let the king appoint men in all of his provinces to choose young and beautiful maidens, and let them be brought to the women's house in Shushan, under the care of the king's adviser Hegai, the custodian of the women. He will give them their cosmetics, and the girl who shall most please the king, shall be set up by the king in Vashti's place." And thus did the king do.

◈§ Mordechai and Esther

אִישׁ יְהוּדִי — *A Jewish man* (2:5) was in Shushan, the capital city. His name was Mordechai, and he was called *Yehudi* (the Jew) because he truly feared God. Targum translates the name Mordechai as meaning "pure spices." He was the son of Yair, son of Shim'i, son of Kish, from the tribe of Binyamin, who had been banished in the previous exile.

וַיְהִי אֹמֵן — *And he had raised* (2:7) Hadassah, that is, Esther. She was called Hadassah because the strong and fragrant smell of the *hadas*, myrtle, is not lost, even when it grows among thorns. So, too, did she retain her Jewishness when among the pagans. She was called Esther because her deeds were lovely and good. [The Talmud says that the pagans called her Estahar on account of her beauty, סַהַר ("the moon") being a common metaphor for the epitome of beauty.]

When the king's words were heard, and his decree was made known, many lovely young girls were assembled in the king's house, under the protection of Hegai, custodian of the women. When Mordechai heard of this he hid Esther away from the royal messengers, but the daughters of the Amalekites fussed and beautified themselves so that they should be taken.

The servants collected together all the young women, and saw that Esther was not among them. Long before they had remarked upon her goodness and beauty. They then told the king: "We have fatigued ourselves for no purpose, for the most beautiful girls have been hidden from us."

When the king heard this he decreed that anyone who had hidden his daughter and would not give her out would be hanged upon his own doorway. Then Mordechai saw what would come out of this, and that this was God's hand, and he took her out and led her to the palace. She was led to the other maidens.

וַתִּיטַב הַנַּעֲרָה בְעֵינָיו — *The young girl pleased* (2:9) Hegai, and he treated her kindly. He gave her cosmetics and all that she needed, as well as seven young girls of the palace; and he showed his preference for her and her maidens. Esther never revealed her nationality nor her descent, according to Mordechai's instructions.

וּבְכָל יוֹם וָיוֹם — *And every day* (2:11) Mordechai would go in front of the women's house to find out Esther's welfare, and what was happening to her, and what miracles would occur through her.

When the time came for Esther, daughter of Avichayil, uncle of Mordechai who had taken her in as a daughter, to come to the king, she asked for nothing to accompany her, taking only that which Hegai, the women's custodian, pressed upon her. Esther charmed all who saw her, and she was taken to the palace of King Achashverosh in the tenth month, that is Teves, in the seventh year of his reign.

⊷§ The King's Curiosity

וַיֶּאֱהַב הַמֶּלֶךְ אֶת אֶסְתֵּר — *The king loved Esther* (2:17) more than the other women, for she found grace and favor in his eyes. He placed the crown of majesty upon her head and made her queen in Vashti's stead. The king made a great feast for her.

He was exceedingly curious about Esther's origin, who her family was and what sort of people she stemmed from, and he tried to flatter the information out of her.

"Who are your people?" he asked her. "I would like to appoint them nobles."

"My dear king," she answered, "I do not know my people and my family. My father and mother died when I was very young, and I have not been able to find out who they were. Only Mordechai had mercy on me. If it were God's will that I know my family, I would certainly tell you."

Since Achashverosh could not find out who her relatives were, and thus could not lavish upon them the gifts which he wished to give, instead he freed the entire land of tribute for her sake, for he felt that her family must be somewhere in his land.

⇜§ A Dark Conspiracy

בַּיָּמִים הָהֵם — *In those days* (2:21), when Mordechai was sitting in the doorway of the palace, Bigsan and Teresh, two chamberlains of the king who were the guardians of his threshold, grew angry at their master, saying: "From the time that he has become king, we have no peace." They conspired to put snake venom into the goblet from which the king drank after waking from his sleep.

וַיִּוָּדַע הַדָּבָר — *And the matter became known* (2:22) to Mordechai through divine inspiration, and he told the queen, who told the king, in the name of Mordechai.

וַיְבֻקַּשׁ הַדָּבָר — *The matter was investigated* (2:23) and found to be true, so both were hanged on a gallows, and the incident was recorded in the king's book of chronicles.

⇜§ The Villain Rises to Power

אַחַר הַדְּבָרִים הָאֵלֶּה — *After these things* (3:1), King Achashverosh promoted Haman, son of Hamdasa the Agagite, over all the other nobles.

The words *after these things* shows us that our God, blessed be He, prepares the cure before the plague — Esther was appointed queen on account of her beauty, and Mordechai saved the king from death; and only then was Haman, who hated the Jews because he was descended from Amalek, raised to greatness.

וְכָל עַבְדֵי הַמֶּלֶךְ — *And all the king's servants* (3:2) who lived in the king's palace would bow and scrape to Haman, for the king had so ordered. But Mordechai refused to bow or kneel.

The king's servants said to Mordechai: "Why are you greater than we, that you refuse to bow to Haman, while we bow down?" Mordechai answered: "I will bow before our beloved Master, the Lord, Blessed is He, for He created the entire world with His might."

וַיַּרְא הָמָן — *When Haman saw* (3:5) that Mordechai would not bow nor kneel to him, he was filled with rage. It was contemptible to him to simply cast his hand at Mordechai alone. He had been told who Mordechai's people were, and he determined to destroy all of the Jews, Mordechai's people, throughout the whole empire of Achashverosh.

◆§ Haman Casts Lots

In the first month, that is Nissan, in the twelfth year of the king's reign, Haman cast lots to see when to destroy the Jews. Then a heavenly voice rang out and said: "Congregation of Israel, you have no reason to fear, if only you return in repentance! Then Haman will fall into your hands!"

Haman ordered Shamshai, the king's scribe, to cast lots for the day of the week. But this could not succeed, for on Sunday heaven and earth were created, on Monday the waters separated, on Tuesday the Garden of Eden came into being. On Wednesday, the sun, moon, seven stars, and twelve constellations were created; on Thursday the Leviathan and moor cock were created, prepared for the great feast of the future, when *Mashiach* comes. Adam and Chavah were created on Friday, and *Shabbos* is a testament between God and Israel. As a result, Haman despaired of the lottery of days, and began a lottery of months.

So reasoned Haman: "In Nissan I cannot prevail because of the merit of the Pesach sacrifice. Iyar, too, is not good for they have the merit of the *man* (manna), which began to fall in that month. In Sivan the Torah was given, and Tammuz, too, is eliminated, for in that month the walls of Yerushalayim were breached, and, having had one sorrow in that month, God will not put them through another. Av, too, is not good, for in that month the deaths in the desert ended, and the Divine Presence once again spoke to Moshe. In Elul Moshe ascended Mt. Sinai for the second set of Tablets. Tishrei is not good, for God forgives their sins then, and Cheshvan is out of the question because the great flood began in that month, and Noach and his children were saved, together with everything in the ark. Kislev is out, for they repaired the Temple then, and many miracles occurred in that month. Teves, too, is not good, for in that month the Jews already underwent much sorrow, for Nebuchadnezzar went up to Yerushalayim and besieged it. Shevat contains the New Year for Trees, and they bring the offering of the first fruits."

When he came to the twelfth month, the month of Adar, Haman said: "Now they will fall into my power as easily as a small fish does when eaten by a large fish" [for the zodiacal sign of Adar is the fish]. What Haman did not know was that the Jews were the children of Yosef, whose blessing had been that his children would increase like fish of the sea.

✎§ Persuading the King

Then Haman told the king: "There is among us a people — the Jews, spread among the nations in all of the provinces of your kingdom. They are haughty, and they go after all of the pleasures. In the winter month of Teves they bathe in warm water, in hot Tammuz they drink cold drinks. All their ways are different than the others.

אִם עַל הַמֶּלֶךְ טוֹב — *"If it please the king* (3:9), let him record that they are to be destroyed. I will give one hundred gulden for each Jew. When they left Egypt they numbered 600,000, which would total to 10,000 silver talents, and I will give that amount to the king's treasure houses. Let the king simply give me his signature so that I can write whatever I want concerning their fate."

God then said: "When Israel left Egypt they each gave half a shekel, which also totalled 10,000 talents of silver. You have no right to buy them, nor you, Achashverosh, to sell them."

וַיָּסַר הַמֶּלֶךְ — *The king removed* (3:10) his signet ring and gave it to Haman son of Hamdasa, enemy of the Jews. And the king said to Haman: "I give you the silver, and do what you will with the people." But God said: "You most certainly have not sold them!"

✎§ The Edict of Annihilation

וַיִּקָּרְאוּ סֹפְרֵי הַמֶּלֶךְ — *The scribes of the king were summoned* (3:12) on the thirteenth day of the month of Nissan, and all that Haman asked for was written down and sent to the king's nobles and to the governors of every province. It was sent to each nation in its writing, to each people in its language, signed with the king's name and inscribed with his seal.

Couriers swiftly ran everywhere with the news, and the letter was openly displayed in the city of Shushan. The king and Haman sat down to drink, while the city of Shushan wept and wailed.

וּמָרְדֳּכַי יָדַע — *And Mordechai knew* (4:1) through divine inspiration (*ruach hakodesh*) what was going to happen. God had sent three of His righteous servants — the prophets Chagai, Zechariah, and Malachi — to prophesy in the Chamber of Hewn Stone in the *Beis HaMikdash*, the seat of the Sanhedrin, that 72 towers would yet be built in Yerushalayim. This alluded to the 70 members of the Sanhedrin, together with its head, and the *nasi*. This prophecy in fact foretold the rebuilding of the *Beis HaMikdash* in the time of Ezra.

The evil Achashverosh sent for 127 scribes, from each of his 127 provinces each with book in hand, and they wrote down harsh decrees against the Jews. The first message was written in the name of the king, stamped with his seal, and was sent by couriers throughout the kingdom.

This is what it said: "Announce in my name, King Achashverosh, in all the land, each to his own language — peace to you. I want to announce to you that a man has come to us. He is not from our city, nor from our land, and he wishes to strengthen us so that we prevail over our enemies. He is Haman, son of Amalek, son of Reuel, son of Eliphaz. He bears a great heritage, is a great nobleman, rich in wealth. This man has asked a small thing of me in regard to the Jews. He has shown that they are not fair-dealing, and has offered me 100 gulden for each person. I have therefore sold these people to be killed and taken the money. In truth the idea pleases me greatly, and may you, too, eat and drink and be as merry as I."

✥ The Tzaddik Rallies his People

וַיִּקְרַע מָרְדְּכַי — *Mordechai tore* (4:1). After reading this letter Mordechai tore his garments, clothed himself in sackcloth and put ashes on his forehead. He ran through the city and cried bitterly, and said: "My beloved Lord, have mercy upon Your people, Israel. They have not made the decree on one half of us, nor on one quarter. They want to tear out the entire garden!"

When the Jews heard and saw this they grew terrified and did not know what was befalling them. They ran to Mordechai to find out what had happened. Many Jews gathered together, and Mordechai stood up and said: "Beloved brothers, people of Israel: have you not heard what Achashverosh and Haman have commanded and sealed? To destroy us from under the heavens, throughout the entire world! We have no king to rely on for succor, nor have we a prophet to beg for us and show us what to do. We have no land, no city to run to. We have only God: may He have pity upon us and help us. We are like sheep with no shepherd, a ship without a captain, orphans without a father, nursing infants with no mother."

Everyone started to cry. They took the holy Ark and carried it through the Jewish streets. They covered the Torah scroll with sackcloth and placed ashes upon it and they read the passage in *Parashas Vaeschanan* which begins: בַּצַּר לְךָ — *When you are in trouble* ... (*Devarim* 4:30). Then Mordechai stood up once again and exhorted the people to repent. As he spoke he cried, and tears ran down his cheeks. He cried: "Woe to you, O Israel, for this terrible decree," and once again ran, with bitter weeping, through the streets.

וַיָבֹא — *He came* (4:2) up to the king's gate, for the king had decreed that one could not enter that gate clothed in sackcloth. At this time a certain Jew came to an Amalekite and begged him to buy him, his wife, and his children, so that they would remain alive. The Amalekite answered: "We cannot buy the Jews, for we must kill them." That moment saw the fulfillment of the verse in the Torah which warned that *you shall sell yourselves to your enemies as servants and maids, and they will not buy* (Devarim 28:68).

Every day the Jews could see exactly how much time was left for them to live, thus fulfilling the dire words of the Torah: *And your life shall hang in doubt* (Devarim 28:66).

וּבְכָל מְדִינָה וּמְדִינָה — *And in each province* (4:3), in each place where the king's words reached, there was a great wailing among the Jews, with fasting and lamentation, and many lying in sackcloth and ashes.

◈§ Esther Rises to the Occasion

וַתָּבוֹאנָה נַעֲרוֹת אֶסְתֵּר — *Esther's maids came* (4:4) and told her, and she trembled. She sent clothing for Mordechai to put on in place of the sackcloth, but he refused them.

Then Esther called to Hasach, one of the king's chamberlains, and ordered him to go to Mordechai, to find out what was going on.

Hasach went out to Mordechai, into the street which stood before the king's gates, and Mordechai told him all that had happened, and of the money which Haman had promised the king in exchange for the Jews' lives.

וַיָבוֹא הֲתָךְ — *And Hasach came* (4:9) to Esther and told her Mordechai's words, and Esther sent her reply: לֵךְ כְּנוֹס — *"Go and assemble* (4:16) the Jews of Shushan. No one shall eat or drink for three days and nights. I and my maidservants shall do likewise. Then I shall go, unsummoned but willingly, to the king. Even if I (God forbid) lose this world for your sakes, I shall still have the World to Come."

◈§ Her Plea

וַיְהִי בַּיוֹם הַשְּׁלִישִׁי — *It was on the third day* (5:1) of their fasting that Esther stood up from her ashes and mourning, at first still stooping. She then dressed herself beautifully, in the fashion of a queen, in clothing of silk and fine gold from Ophir, with pearls and diamonds brought from Africa. She placed the crown upon her head and then prayed: "O great God of Avraham, Yitzchak, and Yaakov, God of Binyamin my father! Although I have no merit before You, I go for the sake of Your people Yisrael, lest they be doomed. For if they are destroyed, who shall say before You, three times a day, three times 'Holy'? Just as you helped Chananiah, Mishael and Azariah in the fiery furnace, and Daniel in the lions' den, help us also. Let me find favor in his eyes."

She said these words with tears in her eyes, and then continued: "I beg you, my God, hear my prayers. If it has been decreed upon us that the warning in the Torah is to be visited upon us — that we will be sold as slaves and no one will even want to buy us, and if it has been decreed that we die because of our sins, and thus we have fallen into the hands of Haman, wicked son of Amalek, then remember, Master of the World, how Avraham, our father, took hold of the neck of his son Yitzchak with his left hand, and with his right hand took the knife to slaughter him, just for his love for You. He fulfilled Your commands: heed our pleas!

"Open your windows, heaven, and let the merciful angels, too, pray for us. You, angels, cry with a mighty wail: 'Woe to the world if it be destroyed.' I have cried out to You — answer me, as You answer all those who are in anguish. You see our agony, and You are called 'Merciful and Forebearing' — have mercy upon us. You are called the One who 'bestows lovingkindness upon the thousands' — to the thousandth generation. You have been merciful to our forefathers. Is this, then, the vow which You swore to them? Just as You heard the agony of Yonah (Jonah) when he was in the fish, so hear us today.

"We are like a woman in the severest throes of childbirth. Help us out of our plight and remove it from us. I have fasted three fasts. What else can I do, Master of the World? More fasts I would fast, but I fast only three, so that You will recall the merit of Avraham, who walked for three days with Yitzchak in order to offer him for a sacrifice. You promised him that when his children were in trouble You would remember the merit of the *akedah*, the binding of his son. The three days also represent the *Kohanim*, Levites, and Israelites who accepted Your Torah, and said 'We will do and we will hear.' For their sake, save us from this sorrow.

"God, the Lord of Hosts," she continued, "remember the merit of Avraham, Yitzchak, and Yaakov; do not turn away from my pleas and do not refuse my request."

◈§ In the Throneroom

וַיְהִי כִרְאוֹת — *When the king saw Esther* (5:2) standing in the forecourt she charmed him, and he extended the golden scepter in his hand towards her. Esther approached and touched the tip of the scepter.

The king said to her: "What is it, Queen Esther, and what is your desire? It shall be given to you, even up to half my kingdom."

When Esther heard the king's offer of up to half his kingdom, out of great joy she mustered courage and answered, "If it pleases the king, let the king and Haman come to a feast which I have prepared."

The king commanded that Haman be called to the feast. At the wine feast, the king said to Esther, "What is your desire, and it will be given to you; what is your request, and it shall be done, up to half my kingdom?"

"My beloved master," she answered, "my request is this: if I have found favor in your eyes, then come to another feast of mine."

◈§ Haman is Vexed

וַיֵּצֵא הָמָן — *And Haman went out* (5:9) on that day, merry and joyous, but when he saw Mordechai sitting by the king's gate, refusing to stand up for him or bow down, he was filled with rage. He came quickly to his home, and called for his friends and his wife Zeresh. He told them of his great wealth and of the glory with which the king had honored him, and how the king had raised him up over all the other nobles and courtiers. Then he said, "Queen Esther, too, did not invite anyone to her feast, just the king and me. Tomorrow, again, the king and I are invited. But all of this means nothing to me when I see the Jew Mordechai sitting by the king's gate. I can have no joy in my heart."

וַתֹּאמֶר לוֹ זֶרֶשׁ — *Zeresh told him* (5:14), and all of his admirers: "You cannot incinerate him in fire, for his father Avraham, and also Chananiah, Mishael and Azariah, were saved from the fiery furnace, while those who threw them in were burned. You cannot kill him by sword, for his father Yitzchak was saved from the knife. Your cannot drown him, because Moshe Rabbeinu and all of Israel at the Red Sea were saved from drowning. You cannot throw him to the lions, because the prophet Daniel was saved from them. You cannot stone him, for King David killed the Philistine Goliath with a stone. There is no way to kill Mordechai, except by building a gallows fifty cubits high, for his ancestors have never been tried with this. Go to the king tomorrow morning and ask him to command you to hang Mordechai."

The suggestion pleased Haman, and he built the gallows — but it was built for himself!

✎§ The Slumberless Night

בַּלַּיְלָה הַהוּא — *That night* (6:1) the wails of the Children of Israel reached up to the blessed God, like the cries of little goats. The heavenly angels were disturbed, and stood in terror, and one said to the other: "For certain, the time for the world's destruction is at hand." They gathered together and went to God, and He asked them: "What is this cry of young goats that I hear?"

The Attribute of Mercy answered Him: "This is not the cry of sheep, it is the wail of the Children of Israel, who have been sold to their deaths through the wicked Haman."

God was at once filled with pity, and spoke compassionately of His people Israel, and ordered that the seal of their doom be broken. Then He commanded the angels in charge of confusion and disturbance to go and disturb the slumber of Achashverosh.

The king awoke very agitated, and told his scribe Shamshai to bring his book of chronicles, and see what had been the fate of the kings of Persia and Media, and what events had overcome his people throughout history.

When Shamshai came to the page which described how Mordechai had saved the king from the plot of Bigsan and Teresh, he tried to skip the pages, and did not want to read them. But by the will of God the pages would not be skipped over, and read themselves to the king.

וַיִּמָּצֵא כָתוּב — *It was found recorded* (6:2) how Mordechai had informed the king that his two chamberlains, Bigsan and Teresh, had plotted his assassination.

✎§ The Tables are Turned

The king said: "Who is out in the courtyard?" The young courtiers answered that it was Haman, who had come just then into the outer yard in order to ask the king's permission to hang Mordechai upon the gallows. The king ordered that Haman be admitted, וַיָּבוֹא הָמָן — *and Haman came in* (6:6).

"What honor should be done to a person whom the king wishes to honor?" asked the king.

"Whom would the king wish to honor, more than me?" thought Haman to himself.

Then Haman told the king: "The man whom the king wishes to honor should be brought royal garb, which the king has worn, and the horse which the king has ridden. The crown should be placed upon his head. The horse should be given to one of the king's nobles, who should dress the person and lead him on horseback through the streets of the city, crying before him: 'This shall be done to the person whom the king wishes to honor!' "

This suggestion pleased the king, and he decided to show Mordechai this honor. The king said to Haman: "Run to my treasure house and take all that you mentioned. Then go and dress the Jew Mordechai, and show him the honor which you described."

"My dear king," protested Haman, "there are many Jews called Mordechai. Which one shall I go to?"

"To that Mordechai who sits by my gate."

When Haman heard that the king meant Mordechai, his arch-enemy, he trembled, and his face grew dark. His mouth twisted, and his very organs quivered. His knees knocked together, and he said: "But mighty king, there are many gates. I do not know which gate you mean."

"I clearly told you that I meant the gate of my palace, near the entrance to the women's quarters."

"That Mordechai is my mortal enemy, and his forefathers were my ancestors' enemies. Therefore, my beloved lord, my king, I will give you ten thousand silver talents, but do not show him this honor."

"You shall give him the ten thousand talents," the king retorted, "and you must show him this honor."

"My dear king," Haman continued, "let my ten sons run before him, but do not show him this honor."

"You, your wife, and all of your children shall be made subservient to him," responded the king, "but this honor you must show him."

"But my beloved king," Haman protested, "you have sent letters to all of the lands, announcing that you wish to destroy his people. Now, if you do him such honor, it will seem that you want to rescind your decree. What will the people say? Since you cannot rescind the decree, you cannot show him this honor."

"If it comes to that, we shall rescind the decree," the king replied, "but the honor shall be done to him."

Then the king turned and shouted at Haman: "Go now, and do not delay. Do all which you spoke of to my faithful Mordechai, and do not omit anything!"

When Haman saw that his words were having no effect on the king, he went sadly to the king's treasure house and took out all which the king had commanded. Then he went into the stalls and took the best horse and all of its finery. He carried the garb of majesty on his shoulders, and led the horse by its golden bridle, to Mordechai.

⊷§ Mordechai and his Students

All of this was destined by God, and this was what the king had ordained. But when Mordechai saw the wicked man from afar, he told his students: "Whoever of you can flee should do so, for here comes the wicked Haman to kill me. Do not be killed for my sake."

"We shall all die together," answered his pupils.

"Then let us learn," said Mordechai, "and we will die in our studies and our prayers."

This was the 16th day of Nissan, and they studied how the grain offering of the *Omer* had been brought on that day, when the Temple still stood. Haman stood from afar and then asked the children what they were learning.

"When we were in our land," they answered, "we used to bring the *Omer* on this very day."

"What is the *Omer?*" Haman asked. "Was it made of silver or of gold?"

"Neither," answered the students. "It was nothing more than a small amount of barleymeal."

"Your meal has been of more help to you," said Haman, "than the ten thousand talents of silver which I offered to give to the king, and which he refused. You are beloved of your God, who helps you against your enemies."

⊷§ Haman Encounters Mordechai

Then Haman told Mordechai: "Stand up, beloved Mordechai, righteous child of Avraham, Yitzchak and Yaakov. Stand up and remove your sackcloth and ashes. Your prayers have helped more than the ten thousand silver talents which I offered the king, in order to spare me this humiliation. Praised be your God, who has planned this. Put on this royal garb which has been sent to you. You must ride this noble horse. See what great honor God has heaped upon you."

Mordechai thought that the wicked man was mocking him, for he never thought that he could act so gently, and he told Haman: "You, Haman, descendant of Amalek, let me eat my bitter bread and drink my bitter water in peace, and then do with me what you will."

"Come, beloved Mordechai," Haman repeated, "dress yourself at once, and ride this horse, and do not defy the king's words."

"How can I do this? I have been fasting now for three days and three nights," Mordechai answered. "I have been rolling in ashes, and am covered with dust. I must clean myself."

Then Haman ran swiftly to the king's warehouses and brought back sweet-smelling balsam, and anointed him. He served him food from Esther's feast, and then Mordechai rode the king's horse.

⇜§ Esther Witnesses the Miracle

Esther sent 27,000 chosen young men out of the palace, with golden goblets in their right hands and golden pitchers in their left, and they praised Mordechai and said: "So is done to the man whom the king wishes to honor." When the Jews saw what was happening to Mordechai, they said: "So shall be done to the man whom God wishes to honor."

When Esther saw Mordechai riding on the king's mount, dressed in the royal garb, crown upon his head, she praised God for His great help. She had previously seen him in torn garments, with ash upon his clothing, and now she saw him in his greatness.

She said: "Today the verse in *Psalms,* מֵאַשְׁפֹּת יָרִים אֶבְיוֹן — *from the dirt He lifts up the needy (Tehillim 113:7),* has been fulfilled."

Mordechai, too, praised God, and said: הָפַכְתָּ מִסְפְּדִי לְמָחוֹל לִי׳ — *You have turned my mourning into dancing (ibid. 30:12).* I praise You God, my redeemer, for You have not allowed my enemies to rejoice."

⇜§ Haman Returns to his Kinsmen

וַיָּשָׁב מָרְדֳּכַי — *Mordechai returned (6:12)* to the king's gate, while Haman, deeply distressed, returned to his home in a great depression, his head covered.

He had been humiliated by four menial tasks: he had been Mordechai's barber, having cut his hair; Mordechai's valet, having bathed him; Mordechai's driver, having led the horse; and a town crier, having cried out that this is what was done to the man whom the king wished to honor.

Haman came back to his house, and recounted all that had happened, and his wife and friends said: "If Mordechai is of Jewish descent, you should know that God performs miracles for them all the time. He performed miracles for Daniel when he was thrown into the lions' den, and enabled him to leave it unharmed. When

Chananiah, Mishael and Azariah were thrown into a furnace He helped them, and the people standing outside the furnace were incinerated. Therefore, we fear that you will not be able to harm him, and may even continue to fall before him."

⇜ The Fateful Banquet

While they were still speaking the king's servants came to bring Haman to the banquet which Esther had prepared. The king and Haman came to drink with Esther, and the king said to her at this wine feast on the second day: "What is your request, Queen Esther, and it shall be granted; and what is your desire? Up to half the kingdom will be given to you."

And Esther answered: "If I have found favor in your eyes, and if it pleases the king, let him give me my life as my request, and my people's lives as my desire; כִּי נִמְכַּרְנוּ — *for we have been sold* (7:4), I and my people, to be killed and destroyed. Had we simply been sold into slavery I would have held my peace, for the humiliation would not have warranted bothering the king."

Then the king told the interpreter to ask Esther who and where was the man who had set his heart to do this, and Esther answered: "The evil man, Haman, your enemy, who wanted to strike out against God's children, the Jews!" (The *Midrash* says that the name הָמָן can be seen as comprising the two Aramaic words הָא מָן, meaning, "[This is] he who [sought to kill God's children].")

Haman grew terrified before them, and the king, in a rage, left the feast and walked into the garden. Strong trees were felled in order to quell his anger, but to no avail. In the meantime, Haman stood before the queen to beg for his life, for he saw that he was about to feel the full measure of the king's wrath.

The king returned to the feast from the garden, while Haman had fallen upon the couch where the queen reclined.

"Will you seduce my queen in my own house?" roared the king, and Haman's face grew shamed.

⇜ Haman is Hanged

Charvonah, one of the king's retainers — this Charvonah is generally remembered unfavorably, but in one matter is remembered with kindness — was one of those involved in the plot to hang Mordechai, but when he saw that Haman's plot was not working out, he went to the king and said: "My master, the king, Haman wishes to destroy you and take away your kingdom. If you do not believe me, send someone to see the gallows which he has prepared for Mordechai, who has done such good for the king. It stands in the court of his house, fifty cubits high."

Then the king commanded that Haman be hanged upon it. Through Mordechai was fulfilled the verse which says that he whom God loves will see his enemies turn into friends.

Then the king told Mordechai: "Stand up, and take this wicked Haman, oppressor of the Jews, and hang him upon the gallows which he himself built. Do with him what you will."

Then Mordechai took Haman from the king's gate and told him: "You, wicked Haman, oppressor of the Jews, I will hang you upon the gallows which you built for yourself." They hanged Haman on his gallows, and God's wrath was stilled. With Mordechai was fulfilled the divine promise that the righteous will be rescued from anguish while the evil man comes in his place.

~§ A Further Request

בַּיּוֹם הַהוּא — *On that day* (8:1) king Achashverosh gave Haman's house into Queen Esther's hands. Mordechai came before the king, for Esther had told him that he was her relative. The king took the signet ring which he had taken back from Haman, and gave it to Mordechai, and Queen Esther appointed Mordechai over Haman's household.

Then Esther spoke to the king again, and fell before him, crying. She begged him to undo the evil which Haman the descendant of Agag had planned, and to foil his schemes against the Jews — *for how can I see the evil which will overtake my people? How can I watch as my people are doomed?*

The king told Queen Esther and Mordechai: "You yourself are guilty, for when I asked you at the feast about your ancestry, when I wanted to make your family nobility, you answered that your parents had died when you were young and unaware of it. Still, I give Haman's house to you. Haman has already been hanged, for he dared to strike against the Jews. And now write whatever you wish concerning the Jews, using the king's name, and seal it with the king's seal, for a letter written with the king's name and sealed with his seal cannot be revoked."

~§ The Second Prolcamation

וַיִּקָּרְאוּ סֹפְרֵי הַמֶּלֶךְ — *The king's scribes were called* (8:9) on the 23rd day of the third month, that is Sivan, and all that Mordechai the Jew requested was recorded. It was sent to all of the nobles and governors of 127 nations, each nation in its writing, each people in its language, and to the Jews in their language. It was written and sealed with the king's name, and it was sent out with couriers who rode horses and swift camels and young mules, that the king had given permission to the Jews of each city to assemble and destroy all of their oppressors, their wives and their children, and permission to keep their booty — on one day, on the 13th day of the twelfth month, that is, Adar.

פַּתְשֶׁגֶן הַכְּתָב — *The text of the letter* (8:13) was such, and was displayed to all of the people: "To all of the population of my kingdom, those dwelling on land and those in the sea, peace and prosperity. I today announce and write to you as follows. You know that God gave me dominion over many nations and people, on land and in the sea. He has made me king over all of them. You know well that I have not done harm to any of you. I have ruled over you with goodness and sincerity, and have let all those under my rule live in peace and friendship.

"Now I let you know that evil men approached me and insinuated themselves with me, until I entrusted them with the rule of the entire kingdom. I let them do as they saw fit, for I thought that they would deal truthfully and with goodness, but they were false and evil and tricked me, doing whatever they fancied.

"They had me write a letter which was wicked in the eyes of God and man. The desire of the evil men was that I should destroy many righteous men, men who never did any act of evil, and who were toally innocent of wrongdoing. These are Esther and Mordechai and their people. Esther is praised with all that is good, and Mordechai is outstanding in all manner of wisdom and nobility, and no one can find fault with either.

"When Haman told me to kill all the wicked Jews, I thought that he meant some other nation who were also called Jews, for he could not mean those Jews, who are called the children of Him Who created the heaven and the earth and all that is in the world, and Who performs miracles for them all the time, He Who is more awesome and greater and more mighty than all of the kings of the earth. How could I ever have thought of selling such a people?

"But the evil Haman urged me on, in order that the people should not respect me, for he schemed to take my kingdom away from me. Once I became aware of what was going on, I gave him his just deserts, and hanged him on his own gallows. Know, then, that He Who created heaven and earth has repaid him well, him and his evil comrades."

The king's message was delivered in great haste by couriers to all the corners of his kingdom, and was made known as well in Shushan the capital.

✑§ Shushan Exults

וּמָרְדְּכַי יָצָא — *Mordechai went out* (8:15) from the presence of the king wearing a white kingly garment of linen and a robe of purple wool, and a golden crown, and all the city of Shushan was merry and joyful.

The Jews had light and gladness, laughter and glory; and in each city where the king's words and his orders reached, there was rejoicing and laughter for the Jews, and many feasts and happy days. Many of the people around them converted, for the fear of the Jews had fallen upon them.

✑§ The Jews Defend Themselves

וּבִשְׁנֵים עָשָׂר חֹדֶשׁ — In the twelfth month (9:1), that is Adar, on the thirteenth day, as the king had commanded, the Jews assembled against their enemies, who had hoped to destroy them. Their plans were turned about, and it was the Jews who prevailed. The Jews assembled in their cities in all the provinces of King Achashverosh, to strengthen themselves against those who had planned to do evil to them. No one stood before them, for a fear of the Jews had fallen upon the land. All of the nobles of the provinces and those who followed the orders of the king upheld the Jews, for the fear of Mordechai was upon them. Mordechai was greatly honored in the king's house, and his name was known throughout the provinces.

The Jews struck at all of their enemies with their swords, and they did whatever they wished to their foes. In the capital city of Shushan the Jews killed five hundred men. Parshandasa, Dalfon, Aspasa, Porasa, Adaliah, Aridasa, Parmashta, Arisai, Aridai, and Vayzasa — the ten sons of Haman son of Hamdasa, the oppressor of the Jews — were killed. But the Jews did not put out a hand to plunder the spoils.

On that day the number of dead in Shushan came to the attention of the king. He called to Esther and told her: "See what the Jews have done in Shushan. I know well that in Shushan they have killed five hundred men. See what they have done in the other cities. If this is not sufficient for you, Esther, tell me your desire and it will be fulfilled."

"If it pleases the king," Esther said, "let tomorrow, too, be given to the Jews in Shushan, so that they can do what they did today. And let Haman's ten sons be hanged on the gallows."

The king commanded that this be done, and Haman and his ten sons were hanged on the gallows. Mordechai saw them hanging, and said: "You planned to do evil things to Israel, but God, Blessed is He, knows what man schemes. He repaid you well. You wanted to take us out from under God's wing, therefore you now have your children under your wing, on the gallows."

The Jews assembled on the fourteenth day of the month of Adar and killed three hundred men in Shushan, but no one put out a hand to take booty. The other Jews, of the provinces, fought for their lives and destroyed their enemies, and killed 75,000 men, but there too no one touched the spoils. That was on the thirteenth day of Adar, and they rested on the fourteenth day, making it a day of feasting and joy. The Jews repeat this every year, on the fourteenth day of Adar, just as on the day that they rested from their foes.

◄§ A Miracle to Remember

It was a month of turnabouts — their tears turned to joy, their mourning to happiness. Therefore we must make it merry and joyous, and every person should send gifts to his friend and give charity to those in need.

The Jews took it upon themselves to do what Mordechai had written, for Haman, son of Hamdasa, descendant of Agag, had schemed to destroy the Jews. But when Esther had approached the king she said: "Our Torah commands us to stamp out the descendants of Amalek. Haman knew this, and that is why he hatched his plot." But God turned his schemes upon his own head, and he and his sons were hanged. For this reason, these days are called "Purim" from the word *pur* — the lots which Haman cast.

Esther, daughter of Avichayil, and Mordechai the Jew, wrote to confirm the second letter of Purim. And they sent word to the Jews of the 127 provinces of King Achashverosh, with friendship and love, to celebrate the days of Purim in their rightful time, as Mordechai the Jew and Queen Esther had celebrated them. And Esther's words were fulfilled, and the episode of Purim, with its fasts and prayers, was written down.

King Achashverosh imposed a tribute on his lands and on the islands of the sea. All of his might and strength, and the honor and greatness of Mordechai, whom the king had honored, is written down in the chronicles of the kings of Persia and Media.

Mordechai was the second-in-command to King Achashverosh, a

chamberlain of the Sanhedrin and a noble over all the peoples of the kingdom. His words were respected from one end of the world to the other. This is the Mordechai who is likened to an aromatic spice, and to the star called Nogah (Jupiter), for it is brighter than all other stars. He is likened to a rose which blooms early. He was a teacher to the Jews and a friend to the Sanhedrin, bringing good to the people and speaking of peace to all of his children.

※　※　※

(The Torah reading on Purim morning is from Sh'mos 17:8-16. See pages 373-374.)